Wissenschaftliche Untersuchungen zum Neuen Testament

Begründet von Joachim Jeremias und Otto Michel
Herausgegeben von
Martin Hengel und Otfried Hofius

29

Paul and the Law

by

Heikki Räisänen

2nd Edition, revised and enlarged

J. C. B. Mohr (Paul Siebeck) Tübingen

CIP-Kurztitelaufnahme der Deutschen Bibliothek

Räisänen, Heikki:
Paul and the Law / by Heikki Räisänen. – (2. ed.) – Tübingen: Mohr, 1987.
  (Wissenschaftliche Untersuchungen zum Neuen Testament; 29)
  ISBN 3-16-145198-8
  ISSN 0512-1604

NE: GT

1st Edition 1983

© 1987 by J. C. B. Mohr (Paul Siebeck), P. O. Box 2040, D-7400 Tübingen.

Printed by Gulde-Druck GmbH in Tübingen; bound by Heinrich Koch KG in Tübingen.

Printed in Germany.

For Leena

Preface

Whatever faults the present work may have (and I know it has many), I wish to state in advance that *one* predictable objection to it is wrong: it is *not* based on a preconceived notion of what Paul's thought on the law may have been like. On the contrary, I long held a rather standard Lutheran view of the matter. In 1974, the reading of Hans-Joachim Schoeps's *Paulus* unexpectedly opened up a quite new angle of vision to me, exposing a whole set of problems I had been happily unaware of. The reader will see that I more often than not disagree with Schoeps's solutions, but the problems inherent in Paul's dealing with the law which his discussion of the topic pointed up have not given me rest ever since, the less so as most Christian replies to Schoeps are clearly beside the point. I soon came to discover that there are even more problems. I cannot, of course, preclude the possibility that some working hypotheses which developed relatively early during my research may have hardened too quickly in my mind and prevented me from giving due weight to eventual contrary evidence; that must be left for others to decide. But the solution was not there in advance.

Another major reading experience during my struggling with Paul was E.P. Sanders's magisterial *Paul and Palestinian Judaism*. Sanders argues cogently and with great expertise for a view of Palestinian Judaism rather different from that still prevalent in much New Testament scholarship. I had been groping in the same direction for quite some time without knowing too well just where I was or what the goal might be; the publication of Sanders's illuminating work was like a gift from heaven for my own quest.

Since then I have had the privilege of a fruitful correspondence with Professor Sanders in person. He read a draft of what is now chs. I–V in the present work, and I am very grateful for his critical comments and encouragement. Professor Sanders also made available to me his paper on Paul and the Law, presented to the SNTS meeting in Toronto in 1980, as well as the manuscript of the book *Paul, the Law and the Jewish People* which grew out of that paper. I regret that it was too late for me to take that latter manuscript into account as fully as I would have wished, although I have often referred to it in the footnotes. Above all, I was not able to give full consideration to Sanders's very suggestive account of the movement of Paul's thought, when Paul tried again and again new answers to the burning problem of the purpose of the law.

I am also indebted to others who have read one version or other of the manuscript and commented on it; my thanks go in particular to Thomas F. Best, Lars Aejmelaeus, Jarmo Kiilunen and Steve Motyer who also took the trouble to correct my English.

The research for this book has been carried out in three different places. It is my pleasant duty to thank the Finnish Academy and the Alexander von Humboldt Foundation for grants which enabled me to spend the year 1978 in Cambridge and a period of a year and a half in 1980—1982 in Tübingen. Some inconvenience arose from the fact that I used in Cambridge some German works also in English translations which were not available in Helsinki or in Tübingen later on. This has resulted in some technical inconsistencies which I hope the reader will forgive me; for instance it happens that I cite a work now according to the original (occasionally in my own translation), now according to the extant English translation.

As for the notes, the mere name of an author refers to a Biblical commentary. In all other cases a catchword from the title of the work in question is used along with the author's name; if the choice is not obvious, the catchword is mentioned in the bibliography. I have not been able to take account of works which appeared or became available after April 1982.

Last but not least, I wish to express my sincere thanks to my generous Tübingen host Professor Martin Hengel who also volunteered to include this study in the *WUNT*, though personally not too happy with some of its conclusions. My thanks are also due to the co-editor Professor Otfried Hofius, to the publisher and, once more, to the Alexander von Humboldt Foundation which contributed a substantial printing grant.

Helsinki, June 1982   H.R.

Contents

Abbreviations

The abbreviations used are those recommended in S. Schwertner, *International glossary of abbreviations for theology and related subjects* (Berlin-New York 1974). In addition, the following abbreviations occur:

AFG   K—W. Tröger (ed.), Altes Testament — Frühjudentum — Gnosis. Neue Studien zu "Gnosis und Bibel". Berlin 1980.

EWNT   Exegetisches Wörterbuch zum Neuen Testament (ed. H. Balz—G. Schneider)

FzB   Forschung zur Bibel

GCHP   God's Christ and His People. In honour of N.A. Dahl, 1977.

GTA   Göttinger Theologische Arbeiten

JCHT   Jesus Christus in Historie und Theologie. Festschrift Hans Conzelmann, Tübingen 1975.

JSNT   Journal for the Study of the New Testament

KuE   Kontinuität und Einheit. Festschrift F. Mussner, Freiburg-Basel-Wien 1981.

LCL   The Loeb Classical Library

NHC   The Nag Hammadi Codices

NHL   The Nag Hammadi Library in English (ed. J.M. Robinson), Leiden 1977.

NTK   Neues Testament und Kirche. Festschrift R. Schnackenburg, Freiburg 1974.

ÖTK   Ökumenischer Taschenkommentar

PFES   Publications of the Finnish Exegetical Society

PLT   S. Pedersen (ed.), Die Paulinische Literatur und Theologie. The Pauline Literature and Theology. Skandinavische Beiträge. Aarhus-Göttingen 1980.

PNTC   Pelican New Testament Commentaries

PSt   Pauline Studies (ed. D.A. Hagner — M.J. Harris). Essays presented to F.F. Bruce. Grand Rapids 1980.

RD   K.P. Donfried (ed.), The Romans Debate. Minneapolis 1977.

RelAnt   Religions in Antiquity. Essays in memory of E.R. Goodenough. SHR 14. Leiden 1968.

RF   Rechtfertigung. Festschrift E. Käsemann. Tübingen 1976.

RSRev   Religious Studies Review

SBL Diss Society of Biblical Literature Dissertation Series

SBL MS   Society of Biblical Literature Monograph Series

SNTU   Studien zum Neuen Testament und zu seiner Umwelt

StudBibl Studia Biblica 1978 III. Papers on Paul and Other New Testament Authors.

Sixth International Congress on Biblical Studies, Oxford 3–7 April 1978.
JSNT Supplement Series 3. Sheffield 1980.

SUTS   Suomalainen Uuden Testamentin Selitys

VIKJ   Veröffentlichungen aus dem Institut Kirche und Judentum bei der kirchlichen
            Hochschule, Berlin.

Preface to the second edition

I am pleased that the first edition of this book has caught the attention of colleagues and has thus contributed to the ongoing vivid debate about Paul's thought on the law. After having pondered the response, I do not feel that a revision is called for. Therefore, apart from correcting mistakes, I have made only a few minor changes in the text of the book. In this new preface, I wish to clarify some issues raised by my critics and also indicate some new emphases resulting from my own further wrestling with Paul.[1]

The problem of a synthesis

Everybody agrees that Paul was not a 'systematic' thinker. If, however, one goes further and claims that he was not a consistent thinker either, one will hit a nerve — not just in a devout religious congregation but in professedly critical exegetical scholarship. Not unexpectedly, some reactions to the present book testify to this situation.

The response also — again, not unexpectedly — brings to light the vast diversity of the exegetical guild.[2] Practically every judgment on the book can be confronted with an opposite one from a different review. While one reader

---

1 My thanks are due to Dr. Jarmo Kiilunen for a helpful critique of the first draft of this preface and to Ms. Virginia Johnson for improving my English.

2 As far as I know, the book has elicited two review articles and one extended treatment (of some aspects in it) in a book on Paul: A.J.M. Wedderburn, 'Paul and the Law', *SJTh* 38, 1985, 613–622. – J. Thurén, 'Paulus och Torah', in: S. Hidal et al. (ed.), *Judendom och kristendom under de första århundradena*, Oslo 1986, 165–92. – S. Kim, *The Origin of Paul's Gospel* (WUNT 2. Reihe 4, Tübingen ²1984), 345–58. Following reviews and shorter notes are known to me at present: J.-N. Aletti, *Bib.* 66, 1985, 428f. – Id., *RSR* 73, 1985, 288f. – G. Bouwman, *TTh* 24, 1984, 415. – F.F. Bruce, *HeyJ* 27, 1986, 77f. – A. von Dobbeler, *NT* 26, 1984, 374–76. – P. Fiedler, *ALW* 27, 1985, 349. – M.A. Getty, *CBQ* 47, 1985, 561–63. – R.B. Hays, *JAAR* 53, 1985, 513–15. – L. Houlden, *Theol.* 87, 1984, 384f. – H. Hübner, *ThLZ* 110, 1985, 894–96. – K.-J. Illman, *TAik* 89, 1984, 218–20 (in Swedish). – X. Jacques, *NRTh* 116, 1984, 759f. – L.E. Keck, *RSRev* 11, 1986, 291f. – H. Moxnes, *NTT* 87, 1986, 47–49. – P.-G. Müller, *BiKi* 4/1984. – A.S. Muñoz, *ATG* 47, 1984, 386f. – J. Oroz, *Augustinus* 30, 1985, No. 119–120. – J. Roloff, *BZ* 30, 1986, 137–40. – R. Trevijano, *Salm.* 33, 1986, 127–29. – S. Vollenweider, *KBRS* 21/1984. – F. Vouga, *ETR* 60, 1985, 139f. – N. Walter, *SNTU* 11, 1986, 245–49. – R.O. Zorn, *VR* 44, 1985, 36f. In this preface, a mere author's name refers to the reviews enumerated in this footnote.

finds its approach 'very unsatisfying',[3] another thinks that it 'presents as persuasive a picture as we are likely to get',[4] and so on.[5] Nevertheless, a closer
look reveals something like a pattern. There is at least a general agreement
that Paul's view of the law is a very complex and intricate matter which confronts the interpreter with a great many puzzles.[6] Therefore the occasional
allegation that the problems I see in Paul's theology are just problems in my
own mind[7] is extremely unfair. Even if everything else in this book turned
out to be in error, it would still demonstrate that a vast host of interpreters
has felt, and feels, that there *are* problems — logical and other — in Paul's
theology of the law. Few if any of what I have called contradictions in Paul's
view were discovered by me for the first time (although it was sometimes only
afterwards that I found out about my predecessors). What makes my book
different, I believe, is the cumulative effect, along with my refusal to accept
apologetic 'dialectical' explanations.

Thus it seems that a reasonable consensus can be reached about critical
details and points which seem to amount at least to 'apparent' contradictions
in Paul. Differences come to light when one tries to synthetize the individual
observations, which also entails deciding whether various tensions are apparent
or real. On this level, very diverse syntheses stand in opposition to each other.
Scholars quite often suggest that all previous syntheses are unconvincing —
and then bravely offer a brand new one.[8] It is here, in the craving after coher-

---

3 J.D.G.Dunn, 'Works of the Law and the Curse of the Law (Galatians 3.10–14)'
   NTS 31, 1985, 523; cf. E.J.Schnabel, *Law and Wisdom from Ben Sira to Paul*
   (*WUNT* 2. Reihe 16: Tübingen 1985), 270 f. n. 215: 'totally unconvincing'.
4 J.Neusner in a statement quoted on the back cover of the Fortress Press edition of
   this book (Philadelphia 1986); cf. Wedderburn 621; Illman 220.
5 The wholesale indictments come from 'conservative evangelical' circles (Kim, Schnabel,
   Zorn). The most unequivocally positive reviews include those by Wedderburn, Fiedler,
   Getty, Houlden, Illman, and Moxnes.
6 Cf. Walter 246: '... es ist klar, daß kein Paulusexeget die hier aufgezeigten Risse und
   Widersprüche ungestraft übergehen kann'. P. Stuhlmacher, 'Paul's Understanding of
   the Law in the Letter to the Romans', *SEÅ* 50, 1985, 102: 'It is ... very difficult for
   us to systematize the Pauline statements concerning the law ...'
7 Kim *Origin* 346 (even though he realizes himself that Paul's 'doctrine of the law' is a
   'most intricate problem' which is 'far from being transparent', p. 281).
8 Recently K.R.Snodgrass, 'Justification by Grace — to the Doers', *NTS* 32, 1986,
   72–93, proposes a new reading of Romans 2. He senses himself that his interpretation
   is 'somewhat adventurous in view of what is usually said on Romans 2'. 'However, the
   inadequacy of other explanations of Romans 2 and the *contradictions within Paul
   that result from those explanations are unacceptable.*' (86, my emphasis.) Note that
   those 'other' explanations means *all* previous ones. Even Snodgrass does not imagine
   he has solved all the problems, but 'tensions are loosened at several points'. I cannot
   discuss Snodgrass' proposal here. But I think his article demonstrates very clearly
   how great a price a scholar with a keen analytic eye must pay for the avoidance of
   contradictions in Paul. My colleague in Turku/Åbo, J. Thuren, actually develops in
   his lengthy discussion of my book an original systematic synthesis of his own.

ence, that religious convictions – often called 'theology' – naturally come into play, whether they are acknowledged or not. Leslie Houlden makes the point well in his review:

> Historical criticism of the Bible finds it hard to win its way. Many who have accepted it in principle have been reluctant to admit that any part of the Scripture might be either irrelevant to us or inconsistent with other parts. And some who have admitted inconsistency between one part and another (e.g. Paul and Acts) work hard to affirm consistency within a particular writer. And even those who admit development in Paul, for example, from one letter to another, often fight shy of seeing inconsistency between one part and another of the same letter. To admit such inconsistency comes close to admitting mental confusion in the apostle, the attribution to him of a less than first class intellect. *Is it donnish conceit to want the scriptural writers to be plainly of the dons' club, or a relic of older doctrines of inspiration?* (384, my emphasis).

While both suggestions have their merits, I would guess that the latter one is more to the point. As it has become increasingly difficult to regard Paul's ideas as literally 'inspired' or 'revealed', Christian sholars often stick to the second-best alternative of having in him at least a nearly-inspired, first-class thinker. This figure may, however, be a product of wishful thinking – or of partisan hermeneutics.

Hans Hübner's recent treatment of Romans 9 and 11 is a case in point. Having first stated that, as regards Israel, these chapters stand in an unresolvable, logical contradiction to each other, Hübner hastens to add that this is not due to any carelessness of thought. 'First class thinkers may let such dilemmas stand as they are not able to solve ...'[9] So whatever Paul says *must* be the result of first class thinking. If he is consistent, well and good. If he is not, even better. This confirms K.-J. Illman's astute observation (220): it is not just Paul who argues 'backwards'. The same seems true of Pauline scholarship: 'starting from the dogma that Paul is a penetrating and consistent thinker, one has tried to show how he is.'

It is indeed in the name of theology – *'Quo vadis, theologia?'* – that Hübner (896) calls me to task for playing off 'analysis against synthesis'. He is himself the author of an important book on Paul and the law, and it is fair to say that each of us recognizes the work of the other as a genuine alternative to one's own position. Hübner grants that many of my observations seem correct; 'very many' of my individual judgments are in fact shared by him. He feels, however, that my overall approach dissolves Paul's theology into 'meaningless fragments of thought', as an effort at a *synthesis* is lacking. He can only make this last assertion, however, by totally ignoring my reconstruction in the final chapter. Obviously, an historical-psychological account of the

---

9 H. Hübner, *Gottes Ich und Israel.* Zum Schriftgebrauch des Paulus in Römer 9–11 (FRLANT 136: Göttingen 1984), 122. Hübner applies here to Paul what F. Schupp has said of Augustine.

growth of Paul's thought does not satisfy his need for a synthesis (even though
Hübner himself speculates that the reaction of James to Galatians may have
caused Paul to change his mind[10]). But this is precisely the question: on *what*
kind of level *can* a plausible synthesis be given — on a theoretical theological
level or, say, on the level of practical strategy? It is a question of just *how*
complicated a theological synthesis can still make some sense. Hübner himself has to resort, e.g., to a very complicated interpretation of Gal 3.19f.
which 'has been repeatedly criticized'.[11] Moreover, he refuses, wisely enough,
even to attempt to bring Galatians and Romans into *one* synthesis regarding
the law, thus recognizing that there *are* limits to plausible systematization.
(I will comment on his development theory below.) It is therefore fully justified when Stephen Westerholm includes my work along with that of Hübner,
John Drane and E.P. Sanders in the *same* group of recent studies which do
not allow for logical consistency in Paul's thought.[12]

As for my lack of a conceptual synthesis of my own, I have seen enough
artificial syntheses to be convinced that I am not able to add still another one.
But it was important to me to sketch an historical-psychological overall view
(in however provisory a way) precisely to prevent the analysis from resulting
in a pile of meaningless fragments.

The problem of understanding

I agree, of course, that one should not *too hastily* jump to the conclusion
that Paul is inconsistent.[13] The question is simply: *when* is such a conclusion
no longer too hasty? More to the point, why should Paul be granted special
treatment, different from that given to everybody else?[14] Ought we to have
more patience with apparent inconsistencies in his writings than with those
possibly found in, say, Philo, Augustine, or Marx? When at one time I was
studying the idea of divine hardening in the Bible and in the Koran, it struck
me what different standards people could use in assessing their own tradition

---

10 H. Hübner, *Das Gesetz bei Paulus* (FRLANT 119: Göttingen 1980²), 53–58.

11 Schnabel, *Law* 272 n. 220, with references.

12 S. Westerholm, 'On Fulfilling the Whole Law (Gal 5:14)', *SEÅ* 51–52, 1986–87,
   228f., 237.

13 Cf. Dunn, 'Works' 523; Aletti, *Bib.* 428f.; Roloff 140.

14 Cf. Stuhlmacher, 'Understanding' 87f.: 'Moreover, the apostle ... also has a right not
   to be hastily evaluated by the criteria of the so-called "comparative history of religions" and the rational claims of that European liberality which stems from the Enlightenment. If we do otherwise, we pass by all too easily that which distinguishes
   Paul from the Pharisaism of his time and that which he himself, precisely as a result
   of his own perspective, gives us cause to consider theologically.' Does this mean that
   Paul's special significance is doomed to fade as soon as we measure him with the same
   rational standards as other mortals? Incidentally, critical remarks on Paul's consistency did not start with the Enlightenment. Cf. below p. 3–4 on Porphyry.

and an alien one. It sometimes seemed that what is called a contradiction in an alien tradition is called a paradox in one's own tradition. As I pointed out (below, p. 15), I am most of all concerned with *fair comparison*.

Quite properly, the demand is raised that scholars of Paul should try to *understand* him as profoundly as possible. This includes the demand to understand him *sympathetically*.[15] This is all right, as long as we do not make him the only hero of the drama. Paul's letters are part of an ongoing *process* of history in which *conflict and struggle* loom large. In this drama, *every* actor must in principle have the *same* right to sympathetic understanding. In practice, there are problems: we have only the arguments from the one party. Nevertheless, scholarship must be prepared to understand the silent side as fully and seriously as Paul. An interpreter of Paul must *also* reflect on how opponents and non-believers might have responded to his arguments.[16] Otherwise our exegesis becomes naive or even propagandistic.[17] *Fair comparison*, or fairness to the *others*, is one of the reasons why one should *not* try *excessively* hard to synthetize Paul's thought into a consistent whole.

Understanding, then, *is* the goal. But the ideal, as I see it, is not to understand just one text or one author. Rather, the ideal is to understand the *process* of which all the relevant texts and authors, as well as their opponents and co-actors, are a part.

I make no secret of the fact that, as a scholar, I prefer a *history-of-religions* perspective to a pronouncedly theological one. As the reader of my 'concluding thoughts' sees, however, this does not prevent me from indicating in the end what sort of theological paths might still be open to those who take fair comparison seriously. Obviously, then, I do have more than a merely historical

---

15 Walter, in an review which I much appreciate, detects in my work the danger of 'explaining' at the cost of 'understanding' (247). Therefore, I am glad to find that Getty (561) has received a somewhat different impression: 'The beauty of Räisänen's work is that he recognizes and respects this complexity without himself becoming too dense to understand.'

16 Secondarily, in view of hermeneutical *wirkungsgeschichtlich* considerations, one may also reflect on how a modern reader who does not share Paul's point of view in advance may respond. Both aspects are prominent in O. Kuss' discussion of Romans 9–11 in the third volume of *Der Römerbrief* (Regensburg 1978). I am happy to be able to refer to this candid work in which the author finds himself at a far greater mental distance from Paul than in his earlier production. Can one find a more eloquent testimony to the fact that one does not have to start with a 'negative' preunderstanding in order to arrive at a critical attitude to aspects of Paul's theology in the end?

17 Of course, one should not idealize the other party either. I hinted at the likelihood of rationalizations on the part of the Rabbis (below, p. 233 n. 23; cf. further the critical hints with regard to Hillel, p. 33, and Philo, p. 36); yet there may be a grain of truth in Kim's (348f. n. 15) demand that I should have taken that line further. Nor were Jewish traditions 'unanimous or consistent on the origins of sin'; cf. Wedderburn 617 with n. 9. See, however, the final paragraph below, p. 15.

interest in Paul.[18] But I fully agree with Francis Watson when, at the close of his own study, he asks whether Paul can

still be seen the bearer of a message with profound universal significance? Facing this question will mean that the permanent, normative value of Paul's theology will not simply be *assumed*, as is often the case at present. It must instead be *discussed* – and with genuine arguments, not with mere rhetorical appeals to the authority of the canon, the Reformers, or of an *a priori* Christology. Should Paul's thought still be a major source of inspiration for contemporary theological discussion? Or should it be rejected as a cul-de-sac, and should one seek inspiration elsewhere?[19]

Development and movement

As mentioned, Hübner joins those who cannot bring all of Paul's theology of the law into internal harmony. Paul's thought developed markedly between Galatians and Romans, he insists. To be sure, Hübner tries in the end to play down the difference between the two letters as interpreted by him (see below, p. 10 n. 66), as if nothing had in fact changed in what really matters to Paul. But, as a thoughtful lay reader observes, such a statement comes 'as a surprise, if not quite as a bolt from the blue' after Hübner's 'lengthy argument that Paul had changed his mind'.[20]

Despite some obvious shortcomings (cf. below, p. 7–10), the development theory seems to enjoy growing popularity. Nikolaus Walter, in his sensible review, expresses surprise at my rejecting it so categorically as I, too, emphasize the significance of Paul's experience in the Galatian conflict (248). I do indeed presuppose development in Paul's thought. But I 1) posit much of it

---

18 H. Weder mentions me along with E. P. Sanders and J. Jervell (!) as instances of a recent trend, 'Paulus bloß noch historisch wahrzunehmen'; 'Gesetz und Sünde', *NTS* 31, 1985, 357, 372 n. 1. For better or for worse, I do have critical interest in Paul's *Wirkungsgeschichte* as well. Contrary to Weder, Houlden (385) finds the perspective represented by the present book 'yet another sharpening of focus as we attempt to grasp Paul in his own setting. In so far as it helps to deflect us from seeing him in our (or Luther's) terms, it is wholly salutary. We are then in a better position to see exactly where his genius lay, and to identify more honestly such echoes as we may hear.'

19 F. Watson, *Paul, Judaism and the Gentiles.* A Sociological Approach (SNTS MS, Cambridge 1986), 180f. (his emphasis). In these remarks Watson thinks of Paul as interpreted by him: 'a Paul who devotes his energies to the creation and maintaining of sectarian groups hostile to all non-members, and especially to the Jewish community from which in fact they derived.' But even if one does not share this novel view of Paul's conscious intentions, Watson's comments remain relevant in view of other problems found in Paul's writings.

20 J. Hall, 'Paul, the Lawyer, on Law', *The Journal of Law and Religion* 3, 1985, 43. Hall makes several shrewd comments on Hübner's book (40–46), including the postulated three intentions in Gal. 3.19 (45). Cf. E. P. Sanders' (to my mind, correct) impression: 'Hübner ... thinks that Paul changed his mind about the law almost entirely ...' *Paul, the Law, and the Jewish People* (Philadelphia 1983), 96. Likewise Westerholm, 'On Fulfilling' 229.

in the tunnel period *before* the extant letters and 2) find neither Galatians nor Romans internally consistent. No doubt Paul developed new ideas between Galatians and Romans. But when he did that he did *not* at the same time reject all his previous ideas even when they contradicted the new ones. Nowhere is this clearer than in Romans 9–11. In his new book Hübner analyzes these chapters in a very shrewd manner (again the agreement on the *analytical* level between the two of us is striking). He finds in Romans 9 and Romans 11, respectively, *two* solutions to the problem of Israel's destiny which are incapable of conceptual harmonization (cf. above).[21] On the other hand, many features in Romans 9, above all the shocking identification of Israel with Ishmael, come quite close to Galatians 4.[22] Therefore, a development from Galatians to Romans explains nothing, as far as the problems of Romans 9–11 are concerned. If development of thought is posited as the solution to those problems, then the obvious conclusion would be that there was crucial development, not between Galatians and Romans, but between the dictation of Romans 9 and Romans 11, if not between Romans 11.10 and 11.11.

Nevertheless, the development model should be given more thought than I gave it. Perhaps *movement* would be a better term, though.[23] At some points, at least, one can follow a movement in the treatment of an issue from Galatians through Romans – a development that goes on within Romans! E. P. Sanders has given a persuasive account of Paul's view of the *purpose of the law* along such lines:

> The complexities of Paul's positions on the law, then, are partly to be explained as reflecting a development of thought which has a momentum toward more and more negative statements. Paul attempts to reverse the momentum in Romans 7, but other problems arise.[24]

I would assess the movement of thought in *Romans 9–11* as another process during which Paul wrestles with a problem, suggesting in subsequent passages different solutions (see below). What remains constant is the problem. The solutions can vary![25]

In this perspective, it comes as no surprise that one can detect different layers of the thought process in one and the same letter. Having worked recently on the *'Hellenists'* around Stephen, I have come to embrace the possibility

---

21 Hübner, *Gottes Ich* 122.
22 Israel's non-election as implied in Rom 9.6ff. amounts to a 'genauso diffamierende Ungeheuerlichkeit' as the allegory about Hagar and Sarah in Gal 4.21–31: Hübner, *Gottes Ich* 20.
23 I did refer to a 'process of thought', though (below, p. 201f.) Cf. Getty 563.
24 Sanders, *Law* 85. According to Sanders' persuative interpretation, the negative development finds its climax in Romans 6 where sin seems no longer to be an instrument of God, subject to God's control (73). This leads to a recoil in Romans 7 in which Paul, however, goes to another extreme (80).
25 For still another 'movement' cf. below p. 113 n. 101.

that some of Paul's more 'positive' statements on the law (e.g. those in Romans 2 or Romans 13) can be traced back to the congregation in Antioch and, ultimately, to the 'Hellenists'. Some of the tensions would then be differences between Paul's Antiochian heritage and his more recent ideas. In the polemical situation of Galatians, Paul puts forward his most negative statements on the law; in Romans when he looks back, among other things, to the Galatian conflict, many of the more balanced Antiochene ideas reappear.[26]

I have elaborated this hypothesis to some extent in my new book *The Torah and Christ*.[27] It now seems to me that in the present book I overemphasized to some extent the spontaneity of the rise of the law-free Gentile mission (cf. below, p. 255). It may, after all, not have been *just* a case of 'action preceding theology'; rather, the 'Hellenists' may have had a theological rationale for their action as well: a spiritualized view of the Torah, preformed in the Diaspora. They would have preferred, for theological reasons, a 'circumcision of the heart' to a circumcision in the 'flesh' (Rom 2,29; cf. Phil 3,3). They did not, however, present their giving up of certain commandments as a destructive critique of the law, but rather as a reinterpretation of its true meaning. If this is a correct reconstruction, there was in the beginning a *de facto* reduction of the law actually kept (at least in the context of the mission to Gentiles); simultaneously, the reinterpretation tended to obscure the radicalness of the step taken (although not in the eyes of outsiders as the persecution of the Hellenists shows).

From this perspective, the tricky question of how *conscious* Paul was of his actual reduction of the Torah (below, p. 24f.) should be reformulated. I have argued in *The Torah and Christ* that Paul persecuted the Hellenists precisely because they had given up the demand of circumcision and some other 'ritual' stipulations (above all, the *kosher* laws) in their work among non-Jews. Paul's conversion meant that he adopted their vision. He then had to make some *conscious* decisions about the law. He had to decide that Gentiles need not be circumcised and that *kosher* laws need not always be kept. I think, however (on the basis of an inference from his extant letters with their striking mixture of positive *and* negative statements on the law), that he did not regard this step as involving a negative critique of the law as a whole. He

---

26 Cf. the perceptive review of Hübner's book by J.M. Barclay in *JThS* 37, 1986, 183–87. He notes that Romans 'looks less like a deliberate retractation of earlier views than an attempt to clear up unresolved tensions in his thought (and, even then, without total success). This would still represent significant development, but it would require more careful definition.' (186)

27 'The "Hellenists" – a Bridge Between Jesus and Paul?', in: H. Räisänen, *The Torah and Christ*. Essays in German and English on the Problem of the Law in Early Christianity (*Publications of the Finnish Exegetical Society* 45: Helsinki 1986), 242–306. This book is available from the publisher: Neitsytpolku 1b, SF–00140 Helsinki.

had not consciously 'rejected the law'. What he is not or does not want to be wholly conscious of in his letters is the actual amount of tension between his (partly) radical practice and (partly) conservative talk about the law. If there was initially an implicit distinction between 'moral' and 'ritual' parts of the law, the distinction tends to get blurred in Romans, when most of Paul's sharp criticisms of the law are aimed at its 'moral' part (whereas in Galatians the battle is still mostly conducted in the 'ritual' field). I thus assume a development from a fairly clearly reflected distinction at the beginning towards a blurring of that distinction later on. The point that Paul's looseness of speech is essential for his theology remains unaffected. That very looseness is necessary to conceal the basic theological dilemma inherent in Paul's (and not just his) position (see below).[28]

I concede to Seyoon Kim that I should have indicated more clearly how Paul's *explicit references to his call or conversion experience* fit the notion that his critical view of the law developed later.[29] I have tried to fill that gap in a long article on 'Paul's Call Experience and His Later View of the Law', included in *The Torah and Christ*.[30] A more succinct version is forthcoming in *New Testament Studies*.[31] Both Galatians 1 and Philippians 3 indicate that the conflict over the law first concerned its 'ritual' part, i.e. circumcision and food laws. Some details which indicate the line of my argument are given below in a footnote that I have, by way of exception, thoroughly rewritten (p. 176, n. 75).

Exegesis and reconstruction

Some of those who insist that I should have tried harder to probe into the synthesis which supposedly underlies Paul's statements seem to think that

---

28 I think these considerations largely answer the questions raised by Westerholm, 'On Fulfilling'. He stresses that Paul creates a deliberate paradox in stating that the Christians 'fulfill' the law although they do not 'do' it (237). But he admits that Paul uses ambiguous language: using πληροῦν he can claim that the conduct of the Christians (alone) 'fully satisfies the "real" purport of the law in its entirety while allowing the *ambiguity* of the term to blunt the force of the objection that certain individual requirements ... had not been done': 'the verb πληροῦν has the advantage of positive connotations but not the liability of excessive specificity' (235, my italics). The last sentence could easily – contrary to Westerholm's intentions – be understood in a slightly ironical sense. In fact, it confirms my point: The ambiguity and lack of specificity is necessary for Paul, as he 'is bent on scoring a theological point' (Westerholm 233f. n. 16).

29 Kim, *Origin* 346, 349 raises a pertinent question but immediately loses himself in extravagant polemics.

30 *The Torah and Christ* 55–92. This essay includes a detailed interaction with Kim.

31 'Paul's Conversion and the Development of His View of the Law,' *NTS* 33, 1987, issue no. 3.

simply giving more space and time to 'sustained exegesis' would inevitably
have led to the discovery of a 'consistent thread' in Paul's thought.[32] I grant
that more sustained analyses of key passages might have been helpful in safe-
guarding my position,[33] although that did not seem to me to be the most
appropriate way to make a contribution.[34] More detailed analyses would have
added considerably to the length of the book without necessarily adding
much that is new. I have recently undertaken a lengthy sustained treatment of
Romans 9–11.[35] What emerged was not theoretical consistency, but rather a
Paul wrestling with a problem to which he tries, as it were, different solutions.

That a passage-by-passage analysis does not necessarily lead to the conclusion desired by my critics is confirmed by Francis Watson's recent book. He
proceeds by exegeting each letter and each relevant passage in turn. He does
discover a Paul whose arguments in individual passages are 'reasonably consistent internally'. However, 'it is *virtually impossible to relate them satisfac-
torily to one another*'.[36] Romans 9–11 is a case in point: '...the clear and
coherent argument of Rom. 11 is completely at variance with the equally
clear and coherent argument of Rom. 9, not to mention the rest of Romans.'[37]
Watson consequently sees 'the cohesiveness of Paul's statements about the
law not primarily at the theoretical level but at the level of practical strategy'.[38]

---

32 Kim, *Origin* 346f.; cf. Aletti, *Bib.* 1985, 428f.; *RSR* 1985, 289. When Dunn, 'Works'
   541f. n. 54 likewise blames me for an 'atomistic exegesis' of Gal 3.13 'which ignores
   the connection between vv. 13 and 14' (referring to pp. 59–61 and 249–51 in the
   present book), he ignores the fact that I do treat the said verses together in an
   earlier connection (see below, p. 19f.). Aletti, for his part, attributes to me the view
   that there is a contradiction between the Pauline ideas of judgment according to
   works and justification by faith (suggesting that a more patient contextual analysis
   would lead one to see that there is none). As a matter of fact, I have *not* assumed
   such a contradiction at all (see below, p. 184).
33 Perhaps it is fair to point out that other critics have failed to find that sort of fault in
   the book which is said to represent 'a penetrating and sustained scrutiny' (Wedderburn 621) or a 'careful, patient examination of various contexts' (Getty 561); cf.
   Hays 515; Oroz.
34 Initially, I did experiment with lengthy drafts on Romans 7 and Gal 2.14–21, e.g.,
   opting then, for better or for worse, for a different strategy.
35 'Römer 9–11. Analyse eines geistigen Ringens', forthcoming 1987 in *Aufstieg und
   Niedergang der römischen Welt* II 25,4. Cf. also H. Räisänen, 'Paul, God and Israel.
   Romans 9–11 in Recent Research', forthcoming 1988 in *The Social World of Formative Christianity and Judaism*. See further my sustained interpretation of another
   passage in Romans: 'Zum Verständnis von Röm 3.1–8', *SNTU* 10, 1985, 93–108 =
   The Torah and Christ 185–205.
36 Watson, *Paul* 170.
37 Watson, *Paul* 170.
38 Watson, *Paul* 22. However, Watson tends to convert Paul into a coolly calculating
   tactician, e.g., as he traces the contradiction between Romans 9 and Romans 11
   simply to different strategies to reach the same goal (172f.). Hall's picture of Paul as

Watson has carried out precisely the sort of project that one of my most perceptive critics would have liked me to do. I am thinking of Richard Hays, who found my final chapter the most interesting one[39] and was led to criticize my method of presentation:

> Räisänen has adopted a method which requires him to discuss exegetical problems piecemeal, apart from any clear construal of the pastoral/historical situation to which the various letters with their incommensurate utterances about the Law are addressed. Conspicuously absent is any serious engagement with J.C. Beker's view that the letters must be interpreted with a view to interplay between contingency (the situation) and coherence (Paul's gospel). Räisänen would probably agree with this in principle, but in practice his approach precludes it: he tends to treat Paul's statements about the Law as dogmatic propositions and to demonstrate their incompatibility at that level. Riskier but more illuminating would have been a sustained constructive exegetical exposition of this material in light of the proposed psychological-historical reconstruction of the final chapter.

Yes, I agree — most of all about the risk! As Hays correctly notes, I offered the final chapter 'very tentatively, with explicit cautions that the exegesis in the earlier part of the study should not be thought to depend on the validity of the conjectural reconstruction.' I still stand behind that view. When writing the book I had no such reconstruction at hand that would have seemed convincing enough to me to be made the basis of the whole presentation. The hypothesis that Paul's view of the law developed essentially in the course of his conflict with more conservative Christians, long ago suggested by William Wrede, is the one alternative that *remained after a process of elimination.* It was not my aim to construct a new hypothesis about the origin of Paul's view. That would have required a full analysis of the Apostolic Council and of the Antiochian incident[40] — especially the latter being an urgent desideratum but clearly a project distinct from mine. I simply wished to scrutinize hypotheses already in existence in the light of my analytic findings. I found that Wrede's explanation (which he had indicated very briefly) stood the test best. All I could do was to try to add some flesh unto its bones. A fuller account would have been a new task. Nevertheless, I found it necessary to draw up the sketch, however fragmentary, to indicate that there *is* a level on which Paul's statements cease to be meaningless fragments

---

a 'shrewd advocate' who used every strategy to win ('Paul' 38 etc.) also unwilfully borders on cynicism. My interpretation fares better on this score, I think, as I see Paul also wrestling with personal problems throughout. But Hall's interesting discussion from a juridical and rhetorical perspective amounts to still another demonstration of the implausibility of forcing Paul's statements into a theoretical synthesis.

39 Cf. also von Dobbeler 375.

40 Stuhlmacher, 'Understanding' 94 n. 14 agrees on the importance of the Antiochian incident for Paul and his thinking. See my discussion with James Dunn concerning some aspects of Paul's account of this incident: 'Galatians 2.16 and Paul's Break with Judaism', *NTS* 31, 1985, 543–553 = *The Torah and Christ* 168–184.

(Hübner) and fall into an intelligible pattern. It is understandable that some critics find the sketch 'in the absence of a direct possibility of verification in the texts fairly speculative'.[41] It is all the more gratifying to discover that quite a few readers find the reconstruction nevertheless to be on the right lines.[42] My recent article on the 'Hellenists' (see above, n. 27) may help to clarify my view of the earlier part of Paul's Christian career a bit. Furthermore, I hope that my still more recent work on Romans 9–11 (see above, n. 35) goes some way towards showing how psychological-historical considerations can, in my view, be brought to bear on sustained exegesis.

I can see the point in Hays' assertion that, in the bulk of the book, I tend to treat Paul's statements 'as dogmatic propositions and to demonstrate their incompatibility at that level.' He exaggerates quite a bit, though, for clearly I do take the differences between different letters into account.[43] If I discuss *these* differences in a 'piecemeal' way (Hays), it is because I do not regard them as the key to the kind of problems I am examining. But the importance of the respective *immediate* contexts is crucial for my interpretation of individual statements.[44] I would rather avoid so loaded a term as 'dogmatic' in this connection and call my approach, say, 'systematic' or 'topical'. Still, I felt myself that this approach is, in the final analysis, insufficient (below, p. 14). But I also pointed out the rationale behind it: to this day, most people use Paul's statements in just that way, as 'dogmatic propositions'! On the whole, students of Paul are no exception. It is Paul's *Wirkungsgeschichte* that calls for that sort of analysis, too — along with other approaches. Even Hays

41 Roloff 139; cf. Kim, *Origin* 346f. who even accuses me of 'free, subjective *Romanschreibung*'. However, Roloff 140 seriously distorts my argument in attributing to me the (indeed speculative!) thesis 'daß die Gesetzes- und Beschneidungsfrage ursprünglich auf dem Apostelkonzil keine (!) Rolle gespielt habe (257f).' Then what does Roloff understand under 'the liberal policy of the Antiochian congregation' which (as I wrote, p. 257) 'was accepted' in the meeting?

42 Wedderburn 620; Moxnes 48f.; Sanders, *Law* 51 n. 16; cf. also Getty 562; Walter 247. Walter has difficulties in relating my psychological explanation of Paul's 'liberation experience' (below, p. 236) to the historical one (below, p. 256–63). The psychological conjecture (which Wedderburn 619 finds 'plausible') was proposed as an explanation of 'Paul's *conversion* to Christ along with which went the acceptance of a more or less lax attitude to the Torah observance' (p. 236, the emphasis original), whereas the conflict with the Judaizers is supposed to account for the *later* development of Paul's view in a more radical direction. So I do not see the problem.

43 On the outlook of different letters see below, p. 68, 116f. (1 Corinthians); 67, 97 n. 22, 153, 188 (Romans); 79, 115f., 128–13ɔ (Galatians); 9 with n. 61, 189f. (the relationship between Galatians and Romans); 115 n. 108, 117 n. 111, 254 (1 Thessalonians).

44 Thus D. Zeller, *Der Brief an die Römer* (RNT: Regensburg 1985), 154 can make the following observation: '… die Nuancen in der Wertung des Gesetzes (sind) bei Paulus durch bestimmte Argumentationszusammenhänge gegeben … Die Methode, diese Kontexte zu differenzieren, wurde von U. Wilckens (modifiziert durch D. Zeller) und H. Räisänen vorangetrieben.'

comments that my work should be 'required reading for anyone inclined towards easy harmonization of Paul's thought.' If people do use Paul's statements as dogmatic propositions even on a sophisticated level (witness the role assigned in the Jewish-Christian dialogue to a statement like Romans 11.25!) and if they really cannot be used in that way, is it not about time that someone tells them?

The divided response to my book confirms that it is precisely the conclusions reached at the 'propositional' level that amount to a watershed. If a systematic analysis were of no intrinsic interest, why are my conclusions so strongly resisted in some circles? A letter-by-letter analysis easily becomes an apologetic means to avoid asking inconvenient questions.

Paul's theological problems

As for the distinction between contingency and coherence,[45] I would rather agree with E.P. Sanders that Paul 'held a limited number of basic convictions'.[46] It is not too clear to me what exactly Beker means by the coherent centre he detects in Paul's writings. But I take it to mean at least that in his gospel Paul has a *solution* which he applies to different problems in different contingent situations in contingent ways. My view is partially different: Paul's gospel itself also implies a grave *problem*. At the very core of his thought, Paul has 'conflicting convictions'.[47] To make this clear, a systematic (Hays: 'dogmatic') approach is required — to find out where the 'coherence' is to be found and where it is not.

---

45 J.C. Beker, *Paul the Apostle* (Philadelpia 1984[2]).
46 Sanders, *Law* 147. Critics often detect a difference between Sanders' position and mine: while Sanders acknowledges that Paul was, in the last analysis, coherent, I tend to render him 'completely incoherent' (thus Watson, *Paul* 18). This, I think, is an oversimplification. Of course I, too, am of the opinion that *some* things never changed in Paul's mind — for example the idea that God wanted to save all humans through the death and resurrection of Jesus Christ (cf. below, p. 23). Sanders correctly notes that we seem to disagree 'only about terminology'. He would call Paul a 'coherent' thinker, 'if each divergent statement comes from an identifiable central conviction' (148). If I hesitate to adopt this terminology, it is only because I then have difficulty in finding anybody who might qualify as an 'incoherent' thinker, in which case the statement that Paul is 'coherent' does not mean very much. It should also be noted that Sanders makes it easier for himself to paint a coherent Paul by relegating *Romans 2* to insignificance as a Jewish homily the ideas of which Paul does not really share and which can be treated in an appendix (cf. below, p. 107 n. 74). I tried to take seriously this chapter, too, as part of *Paul's* argument — with the result that I could not help seeing more inconsistency. I would now try to interpret Romans 2 in terms of Paul's Antiochene and 'Hellenist' legacy (*The Torah and Christ* 289f., 293).
47 Sanders, *Law* 198.

No wonder Paul was not able to solve his problem, for, given his and his contemporaries' views of divine revelation, it was hardly soluble. I described the problems thus: 'we find Paul struggling with the problem that a *divine* institution has been *abolished* through what God has done in Christ.' (Below p. 264f.). Wedderburn agrees that 'that will not work', and Peter Fiedler adds that to this day Paul's dilemma has not been worked through in our exegesis and theology.[48]

When writing the sentence in question I had the Torah in mind. But one should also reflect on Israel's *election* and God's *covenant* with the patriarchs and the people. Paul's theology implies that God's salvific acts of old are invalid or insufficient − which causes Paul to try insisting on continuity as well. His *de facto* break with the Biblical covenant has been persuasively articulated by E. P. Sanders[49] whose crucial argument I have repeatedly taken up in recent articles.[50] Paul asserts that no Jew can be saved as a Jew; even a Jew must convert and become 'a new creation'. Faith in Jesus involves quite a new step for a Jew: he has to accept that Jesus was the Messiah and that the final era has begun. He has to enter the new community, socially distinct from the synagogue. He has to undergo the new initiation rite of baptism and to be incorporated in the body of Christ. He has to give up Torah observance whenever it interferes with intercourse with Gentile Christians (Gal 2).

When Paul insists on the newness of the new aeon, he precludes true continuity with the old. On the other hand, when he tries to establish continuity, he thwarts his exclusive Christ-centred soteriology. That the place allotted to Abraham as a prototype of a believer actually undermines Paul's 'system' was, not surprisingly, seen long ago by liberals like Jülicher.[51] It was only after I had finished the present book that the contradiction dawned on me in connection with a lecture on 1 Clement.[52] Clement tells his readers that God has justified men through faith *from all eternity*. Clement has been blamed by modern theologians for letting God's action in Christ recede into the background. Indeed, the place of Christ in Clement's soteriology remains vague. As justification by faith was always the rule, what is Christ really needed for?

But this problem emerged at the very moment when Paul introduced Abraham as the prototype of the man justified by faith. If salvific faith was accessible to Abraham − or to David, as may be inferred from Romans

---

48 Cf. also Houlden's (385) description of Paul's 'massive dilemma'.

49 Sanders, *Law* 172, 176−78.

50 'Galatians 2.16 and Paul's Break with Judaism', *NTS* 31, 1985, 549f. = *The Torah and Christ* 181−84 (adding the point that is was *not* Paul who *introduced* the dilemma into Christian thought); 'Zum Verständnis von Röm 3,1−8' (see above n. 35) 106f. = *The Torah and Christ* 201f.

51 A. Jülicher, 'Der Brief an die Römer', *SNT* 2, 255.

52 H. Räisänen, ' "Werkgerechtigkeit" − eine "frühkatholische" Lehre? Überlegungen zum 1. Klemensbrief'. *StTh* 37, 1983, 79−99 = *The Torah and Christ* 307−33.

4.6–8 – why was the sending of Christ a necessity at all? One can hardly have both the soteriological continuity *and* the eschatological novelty at the same time.[53] Paul's attempt to usurp the all-important figure of Abraham adds to his insoluble problems.

In this book I may have overly stressed psychological factors (cf. below, p. 11f., 71). Therefore I now wish to call attention even more emphatically than I did (yet see p. 202, 262) to the fact that at the heart of Paul's theology lies a *theological problem* that can hardly be solved in terms of traditional Christian theology with its revelational claims. Paul's problems with the law are *not* the product of a muddled mind. They are the inevitable consequence of his bold *willingness to wrestle with the basic issues.* Other New Testament writers mostly passed in silence over them. For instance, Matthew offers 'fulfilment' of the law as a 'magic key' without making the practical implications clear (cf. below, p. 29f., 88 n. 226).

Paul and other NT writers

It is fair to emphasize this last aspect even more than I did in the first edition. I took some pains to compare Paul and his problems with the contributions of other early Christian writers (Ch. VII). I think this comparative chapter was necessary to gain a proper perspective and it is somewhat disappointing that few reviewers have cared to comment on it.[54] A still closer look at these other writers might, however, have brought to light more problems than I saw and thus greater justice might have been done to Paul.

---

53 Of course, 'normal' Jewish thought had to face analogous problems about God's constancy: the Torah had to be dated back – in one form or another – to the time of Abraham or even to Paradise.

54 Wedderburn, however, notes (619) that 'it is one of the strengths of the work as a whole that throughout it carefully compares Paul's view with those of his near-contemporaries, be they Christians or non-Christian Jews'. Von Dobbeler (376), on the other hand, finds the quest of 'analogies' to be 'unverfänglich und methodisch unklar (bezeichnenderweise wird nach Analogien, nicht nach Traditionen gefragt)'. 'So wird z.B. die frühjüdische Tendenz zur Reduzierung der Torahgebote auf das doppelte Liebesgebot oder die Beschränkung auf die ethischen Gebote in einigen Kreisen *nicht ernsthaft als gemeinsames Traditionsgut* paulinischen und frühjüdischen Denkens *in Rechnung gestellt.*' (My italics.) I confess that I see no methodological problem here. The tracing of analogies or traditions respectively are *two different questions* (both relevant), that is all. That Paul builds on originally Jewish traditions when reducing the law to the love command or to ethical commands is simply too obvious to demand further study in this connection; I was interested in the similar or dissimilar use of such traditions. In *The Torah and Christ* 254f., 288–95 I discuss the question of whether Paul received these sorts of ideas directly from Jewish tradition or rather through the mediation of the Jewish Christian 'Hellenists'.

Thus S. G. Wilson now argues that Luke's view of the law is inconsistent.[55] Some dissertations under preparation in Helsinki are about to introduce further differentiations. Kari Syreeni argues that Matthew had divergent basic convictions which he tried to reconcile by means of sweeping 'assimilations' (the notion of 'fulfilment' suggests that whatever Jesus teaches fulfils the law, which remains a valid authority).[56] Markku Kotila demonstrates divergent attitudes toward Moses and his law in the Fourth Gospel (the law functions as a witness to Jesus on one hand, while there is hard polemics against Moses in 1.17f., 6.32, 10.8 on the other), tracing them back to different layers in the Johannine tradition.[57] Insofar as Paul moves in still more severe contradictions than others (below, p. 228), it is mainly because he devotes more attention to the problems. He is trying to 'square the circle'.[58] Hard pressed between the claims of *sacred tradition* and the vision triggered by *new experiences* (which had already initiated the formation process of a new tradition) he tried to do justice to both. But the situation that forced him to try that was not created by him. It was not Paul who introduced an exclusive soteriology, based on Christology, into the new movement.

On the Jewish religion

I join the ranks of those who reject the traditional Christian understanding of the Jewish religion as anthropocentric legalism. One critic regards this decision as 'a product of sheer hybris', for I am (in his opinion) claiming that I know 'the Judaism of Paul's day better than Paul himself'.[59] But the question is *not* one of Paul's knowledge.[60] The question is whether Paul, writing in a

---

55 S. G. Wilson, *Luke and the Law* (SNTS MS 50: Cambridge 1983). A. J. M. Wedderburn, in his review of Wilson's book, calls attention to the similarity between Wilson's approach and mine: *SJTh* 38, 1985, 261.

56 K. Syreeni, *The Making of the Sermon on the Mount*. A Procedural Analysis of Matthew's Redactoral Activity. Part I: Methodology & Compositional Analysis (*AASF Diss. Hum.* 44: Helsinki 1987). See esp. p. 185–226.

57 M. Kotila, *Umstrittener Zeuge*. Studien zur Stellung des Gesetzes in der johanneischen Theologiegeschichte (forthcoming). My paragraphs on John (below, p. 195f., 217f.) would have to be rewritten in the light of Kotila's findings. That John's conception is 'the clearest within the New Testament' (below, p. 218) holds true as far as the *Evangelist* is concerned. In 1.17f., 6.32f., 10.8, however, we meet, according to Kotila's persuasive analysis, a later editor who was sharply critical of Moses and his law. The 'scribal apology' in 7.21–23 (below, p. 90) comes from the tradition of the Evangelist.

58 An expression used by N. Walter in his discussion of the problems of Romans 9–11: 'Zur Interpretation von Römer 9–11', *ZThK* 81, 1984, 177.

59 Kim, *Origin* 347f.

60 I have never attributed to Paul 'schlichte Unkenntnis des jüdischen Glaubens', as Weder, 'Gesetz' 359, 372 n. 7 alleges. Nor is it fair to assert that my whole book is essentially based on 'the traditional hypothesis of a misunderstanding' (thus Müller). That Paul misunderstood the nature of (Palestinian) Judaism is *not* part of my thesis.

conflict setting, does *justice* to the form of piety he has given up.[61] If he did, he might well be a unique person in the religious history of mankind. The concept of cognitive dissonance is pertinent here.[62] Of course I never intended to suggest that Paul *deliberately* distorted Judaism.[63]

Kim also complains that I display an 'overconfidence' which is 'not well advised' in Sanders' work on Judaism.[64] But the allegation that Sanders' work is based mostly on late documents is simply not true.[65] Nor do Jacob Neusner's somewhat harsh criticisms of Sanders' enterprise render it invalid. These criticisms are mainly concerned with Sanders' ambitious claim to have brought to light 'the pattern' of Rabbinic religion.[66] For my position as outlined in Ch. V, it is unimportant whether 'covenantal nomism' be the crucial pattern of all ancient Judaism or not; what is important is that this view of man's place in God's world *is there*. It is surely wiser to call it the 'common denominator' between different forms of Judaism, as Sanders does in a recent book.[67] In a recent article, Neusner himself summarizes the nature of Jewish piety in the first century with precisely the expression 'covenantal nomism', borrowed from Sanders, which he describes as follows:

---

61 That Paul may do justice to the way some (or even many) Jews may have practised their religion (cf. Walter 249: 'was im pharisäischen (und verwandten) Judentum faktisch weithin gelebt wurde') is, in the final analysis, irrelevant; see below p. 167f. with n. 40, 181f. with n. 102. Cf. *The Torah and Christ* 82f.

62 Cf. Hays 513. See also G. Theissen's interesting discussion of 'Dissonanzbewältigung' in 2 Corinthians 3: *Psychologische Aspekte paulinischer Theologie* (FRLANT 131: Göttingen 1983), 156–61.

63 Thus Kim, *Origin* 351, who asks me the meaningless question: 'What point would Paul have thought to score against the Jewish or Jewish Christian opponents by 'distorting' Judaism ...?' (italicized in the original). I regret that Roloff, likewise, attributes to me the view that Paul's statements on the law were 'subjektiv unwahrhaftig' (137).

64 Kim, *Origin* 347f. n. 14.

65 Half of Sanders' discussion of the Jewish material in *Paul and Palestinian Judaism* (London 1977) is devoted to the Dead Sea Scrolls, Apocrypha and Pseudepigrapha. Cf. Räisänen, *The Torah and Christ* 83. Kim 348f. finds my 'trust concerning the rabbis' testimonies about themselves' in sources much later than Paul 'strange', as I am prepared to be 'sceptical about Paul's testimonies'. But 'covenantal nomism' is not a phenomenon limited to late sources. Even if it were totally absent in the Mishna and Talmud, that would do no harm to my case, for it *is* found in early sources like the Old Testament, Ben Sira, the Qumran scrolls, Jubilees, and Pseudo-Philo (cf. below, p. 166f., 179f.). Its persistence in Jewish liturgy is a further point of extreme importance.

66 Kim 348f. n. 15 appeals to Neusner. It is pointed out below, p. 168 with n. 41, that Neusner finds the thesis of 'covenantal nomism' to be '*wholly sound*'. On the controversy between Neusner and Sanders about the religion of the rabbis, see now also Sanders' preface in the German translation of his great work: *Paulus und das palästinische Judentum* (Göttingen 1985), XI–XII.

67 *Jesus and Judaism* (London 1985), 336.

To state matters simply, the life of Israel in the first century found structure and meaning in the covenant between God and Israel as contained in the Torah revealed by God to Moses at Mount Sinai. The piety of Israel, defined by the Torah, in concrete ways served to carry out the requirements of the covenant. This holy life under the Torah has been properly called 'covenantal nomism', a phrase introduced by E.P. Sanders to state in two words the complete and encompassing holy way of life and world view of Israel in its land in the first century. Life under the Torah was so lived as to fulfill Israel's covenant with God, so one must state as the gist of Israel's piety in the first century (and not then alone).[68]

It is more than enough for me, if I can build on what Neusner and Sanders agree on.

If Paul suggested that Judaism is a religion of works and Christianity one of grace, the contrast seems unfair. To be sure, scholars like Sanders and Watson deny that Paul intended such a contrast at all. What he did intend, they say, was to contrast two ways of life with each other: one based on God's ancient covenant with Israel, the other on the plan he realized in Christ.[69] If this were correct, there would be no reason to speak of a distortion of Judaism. Instead, Paul could be criticized for not communicating his message very clearly. For it is very difficult to avoid the strong impression that Paul often speaks as if God's grace were limited to law-free Christianity.

Nowhere is this clearer than in Romans 4 with its talk of ἔργα, μισθός, ὁ ἐργαζόμενος and ὀφείλημα. Perhaps one should distinguish here more clearly than I – and others – have done between then 'target' of Paul's argument (he argues 'against privileged status') and the *way* he actually conducts his argument (alluding to a 'by works' soteriology on the part of the Jews and Judaizers). The latter aspect is too prominent to be totally excluded. In this regard my discussion (below, p. 171f.) is somewhat one-sidedly oriented to the 'target' of Paul's argument (but see the qualification on p. 176) and should be modified.[70]

---

68 *Major Trends in Formative Judaism III* (*Brown Judaic Studies* 99: Providence 1985), 31f.

69 Sanders, *Paul* 46f.; Watson, *Paul* 178f. and elsewhere. Watson strongly stresses the primarily sociological nature of the contrast.

70 This much I grant Hübner (895). On the whole, Chapter V was by far the most difficult one in the whole book to write. It is not the basis of the other chapters, either. In fact, it is of *less* significance for my understanding of Paul's 'theological difficulties' with the law than are chapters I–IV. These chapters deal with problems *immanent* in Paul's view. Chapter V tries to isolate a different kind of problem: a problematic presupposition in Paul's argument. Should I have erred regarding this problem, my overall argument would have to take only a slightly different shape: in that case Paul replaced, in his conversion, his normal Jewish 'by works' soteriology with a different view of salvation. This 'change of systems' then led him to think through the nature and purpose of the law. But he could not go through this process of thought without getting caught in inconsistencies, contradictions and problematic assertions (above all regarding the connection between law and sin). Thus what von Dobbeler (376) suggests

For a more detailed discussion of this part of my work, which includes a debate with Seyoon Kim, I refer to *The Torah and Christ*, p. 77–85.

On some recent studies

A number of recent studies stress the *continuity* between Paul and the Old Testament even regarding his view of the law. These include the following: C. T. Rhyne, *Faith Establishes the Law* (SBL Diss. 55: Chico 1981). – J. D. G. Dunn, 'The New Perspective on Paul', *BJRL* 65, 1983, 95–122. – J. D. G. Dunn, 'Works' (see above, n. 3). – R. Badenas, *Christ the End of the Law*. Romans 10.4 in Pauline Perspective (JSNT Suppl. Series 10: Sheffield 1985). – E. J. Schnabel, *Law and Wisdom* (see above, n. 3). – P. Stuhlmacher, 'Paul's Understanding' (see above, n. 6). Apart from Stuhlmacher, all these authors put forward some version of the old thesis that what Paul rejects is not the Torah itself but some Jewish misunderstanding of it. In my view, the objections put forward (below, pp. 42–50) to Cranfield's view apply in these cases as well.

Several authors adopt the thesis of Friedrich and others that νόμος πίστεως (Rom 3.27) means the Torah as seen from the viewpoint of faith.[71] There is nothing in these new discussions that would make me hesitate in my refutation of that interpretation (see below, p. 50–52).[72]

Rhyne argues that, in the light of Paul's usage of μὴ γένοιτο, Rom 3.31 points to chapter 4. 'We establish the Law' is interpreted in Rom 4 to mean that 'the law in its role as witness to righteousness by faith is established in the apostolic preaching of justification by faith'.[73] Even if this were the case[74], my point that Paul's answer does not meet the question asked in Rom 3.31 a (below, p. 70) remains unaffected. Even though I have taken 3.31 to refer to 3.21 b, rather than to Ch. 4, my interpretation of the meaning of

---

amounts to a discussible alternative (although I will insist on mine): 'Nicht die Kennzeichnung des Gesetzes als Heilsweg ist eine paulinische Verzerrung, sondern erst seine enge Verbindung zwischen Gesetz und Sünde.'

71 Rhyne, *Faith* 67–71; Schnabel, *Law* 285–290; Stuhlmacher, 'Understanding' 97f., 99f.

72 Schnabel insinuates that I used (in my *NTS* 1979 article) Cranfield's interpretation of ἐξεκλείσϑη in Rom 3.27 without mentioning that he interprets νόμος πίστεως in terms of the OT law (286 n. 291) and that I have (below, p. 50f. n. 34) misunderstood Wilckens 'who does *not* claim that νόμος does not mean "rule" or "order" in classical Greek' (289 n. 311). Both allegations are false. I did point out that Cranfield follows Friedrich in his interpretation of νόμος πίστεως: NTS 26, 1979–80, 103 n. 19, cf. 111f. (= *The Torah and Christ* 99 n. 1, 110f.). And Wilckens, *Römer 2*, 122 does make the claim denied by Schnabel: this is even clearer in Wilckens' page 89 to which I should also have referred. Cf. *The Torah and Christ* 121 with n. 3.

73 Rhyne, *Faith* 117f.

74 Hays (514) also regards it as a mistake to 'drive a major wedge between Rom 3:31 and 4:1'.

3.31 agrees almost word for word with that of Rhyne (below, p. 70). Rhyne shows no awareness of the fact that 'the question of the continuity between Judaism and Christianity' and the question of what sort of continuity Paul may assert there to be are two distinct issues.[75]

Despite his disagreement with my overall thesis, James Dunn comes fairly close to me in his interpretation of the central phrase 'the works of the law'. Having stressed (in the eyes of many, overstressed!) the significance of the problem of the inclusion of the Gentiles in the church as the background of Paul's statements on 'justification by faith' (below, p. 176f.), I am a little surprised at the criticism that I have 'still failed to grasp the full significance of the social function of the law'.[76] This surprise is not diminished by the fact that the same criticism is aimed at Sanders, who has presented a powerful argument (before Dunn who could already avail himself of it) precisely for the social function of the law.[77] The real difference between Dunn and me (and Sanders) is not the assessment of the social function of the law but the question of whether or not Paul criticized the *law as such and as a whole* or just the law as viewed from a limited perspective. As Dunn opts for the latter course[78], my criticisms of Cranfield's position (below, p. 42–50) apply to him as well.[79] His test case, the 'narrow and specific' understanding of the death of Christ according to Gal 3.13–14, does not carry conviction either.[80]

I dealt with Dunn's earlier article in a paper on 'Galatians 2.16 and Paul's Break with Judaism',[81] concluding that his emphasis on continuity corresponds to the picture that Paul (at least, in certain contexts) liked to paint of himself (*bona fide*, to be sure); we should not, however, overlook his (partial) *de facto dis*continuity with Judaism. What mattered most to an average Jew in Paul's environment was surely not what was said or thought of various aspects of the Torah, but the practical question *whether or not it was observed.* Paul thus combines practical (partial) discontinuity with ideological (partial) continuity; our interpretations should do justice to this complexity.

Badenas argues that τέλος means 'goal' in Romans 10.4. The price he has to pay is high: for instance, there is no contrast at all between Rom 10.5 and 10.6 (on the contrary, even 'Moses' speaks of righteousness by faith);[82] Gal

---

75 That is, he takes Paul's 'conservative' assertion at face value. Cf. Rhyne, *Faith* 1, 5, 121.
76 Dunn, 'Works' 534.
77 Cf. Sanders, *Law* 102 etc.
78 See, e.g., 'Works' 531f.
79 Cf. Wedderburn 618 n. 11.
80 The curse removed by Christ's death was, according to Dunn, 'the curse which had previously prevented that blessing (sc. of the Jewish covenant, HR) from reaching the Gentiles, the curse of a wrong understanding of the law'. Art.cit. 536.
81 *NTS* 31, 1985, 543–553 = *The Torah and Christ* 168–84.
82 Badenas, *Christ* 123–25.

3.12 does not elucidate the use of Lev 18.5 in Rom 10 at all;[83] $\tau\acute{\epsilon}\lambda o\varsigma$ means 'goal' even in 2 Cor 3.13.[84]

Stuhlmacher claims that 'what continues to count in Christ is the Decalogue and the corresponding deeds of love which are based on it.[85] It is a gift of God which shows to those who try to obey it that they are guilty. The Christians perceive the Decalogue anew; for them it becomes the 'Law of the Spirit of life in Christ Jesus' (Rom 8.2).[86] Stuhlmacher asks me to express my own opinion of the Decalogue 'more clearly and correctly'.[87] I think it is sufficient to put together my scattered references to the place of the Decalogue in Paul's thought to refute Stuhlmacher's thesis. According to 2 Cor 3.7 (cf 3.3), the killing letter which is characterized by *vanishing* glory is carved in 'stone'. This is difficult to interpret in a way other than that the Decalogue shares the destiny of the old covenant which is doomed to fade (below, p. 25, 45). In his concrete exhortation, Paul does *not* appeal to the Decalogue (or to any other code) in his argument against fornication (1 Cor 6.12ff) or even in that against idolatry (1 Cor 10.23ff) (below, p. 48f.). He does not refer the Christian to the Decalogue but encourages him to examine what God's will is (Romans 12.1f., Phil 1.10): thus, Christian ethics is not based on the Decalogue (below, p. 49, 77).[88] In fact, 'the reduction of the law to the love command also annihilates the meaning of the Decalogue as such' (below, p. 83). Stuhlmacher simply fuses the Decalogue with the love command. Romans 13.9, however, explicitly reduces the Decalogue to the one commandment of neighbourly love. Stuhlmacher's case would be more persuasive if he claimed that what counts in Christ is just the love command. Then, however, he would find himself in difficulty in his all-important effort to establish continuity between the old covenant and Paul. It is not enough for him that the Decalogue becomes the 'Law of the Spirit' (Rom 8.2) for Christians. This 'Law of the Spirit' also corresponds, 'from the perspective of Biblical theology', to the category of the eschatological 'Zion Torah', formulated by H. Gese.[89] But this category is a massive *tour de force* (cf. below, p. 239f.), as I have shown in detail in *The Torah and Christ*.[90] 'Biblical theology' must seek more realistic avenues.

December 1986

H. R.

---

83 Op. cit. 119.

84 Op. cit. 75. Badenas' philological survey is valuable, but he realizes himself that it is inconclusive, the final decision depending on the context (80).

85 Stuhlmacher, 'Paul's Understanding' 101.

86 Art. cit. 103.

87 Art. cit. 104.

88 Cf. the quotation from P. Bläser, below p. 49 n. 28.

89 Stuhlmacher, 'Paul's Understanding' 99f. n. 18.

90 Appendix, p. 337–65. Interestingly enough, my doubts about the 'Zion Torah' (as expressed in the present book) are shared by Schnabel, *Law* 288 with n. 307, although his overall view is diametrically opposed to mine.

Introduction

'One can hardly understand his theology, if one does not grasp his theology of the Torah', says G. Eichholz with respect to Paul.[1] This is probably true. And yet experience has shown that it is just that cardinal point that is particularly difficult to interpret, being indeed 'the most intricate doctrinal issue in his theology'.[2] Therefore, 'uncertainty remains concerning Paul's position vis-à-vis the Law, forcing interpreters to return to the question again and again in the hope that their new studies may shed some small light upon the texts by which their colleagues may see the problem in new perspective'.[3] It is with this purpose that the present study, too, has been written. Not that the perspective suggested is really new; it is rather an old one, which has been unduly neglected in recent times. And if the light offered be indeed small, I hope that it might still turn out to be — light.

Not seldom is it suggested that all the problems of the early Christians concerning the Torah were solved by Paul's clear, cogent and penetrating thinking. No one had before him reflected on the problems of the law with such clarity;[4] Paul's solution was indeed so convincing that there was at the end of the century no longer any need to return to the question of the law's role in salvation.[5] 'Paul's penetrating theological analysis' of the relationship between faith in Christ and the law of Moses 'had a decisive impact on the whole subsequent history of the church, and thereby on subsequent world history.'[6] Paul exposed with utter clarity the self-centred nature of Israel's attitude.[7] In Romans, he has treated the theme 'Law' dialectically with virtuosity and systematic power.[8] Paul is seen as 'the patron of Christian philosophy'[9] and 'the prince of thinkers'[10]; or as 'the truly perceptive intellectual

---

1 *Theologie* 178.
2 Schoeps, *Paul* 168.
3 McEleney, 'Conversion' 319 f.
4 Lohse, *Grundriss* 161; cf. id., *Israel* 22f.
5 Lohse, *Grundriss* 145; cf. Conzelmann, *Geschichte* 5; Fischer, *Tendenz* 85: 'Paul's theological significance' lies in the fact 'that he has overcome the law theologically'.
6 Dahl, *Studies* 19.
7 Goppelt, *Christentum* 312; cf. Verweijs, *Gesetz* 373.
8 Hübner, *Gesetz* 58; cf. Trocmé, 'Paul' 350.
9 Schweitzer, *Mystik* 366 (ET 377).
10 Moule, 'Interpreting Paul' 89 (speaking of the 'simple coherence' of Paul's 'basic convictions').

among the apostles and the NT writers' who 'really had a passion for clear theoretical thought'[11]. He 'will always remain the thinker and theologian par excellence of Christianity'[12]. He is even said to belong with 'the giants of the philosophy of religion'.[13] This catena of eulogies has been gathered from theologians representing quite different schools of thought.[14]

Not surprisingly, then, Paul carries to this day in Christian churches 'the undisputed classic's authority'.[15] Christian theology, it is said, will have to take his theology of the law as its starting-point and criterion.[16] But, in addition to that, Paul's theology is also seen as a model to be followed in debates between Christianity and Judaism and, by implication at least, between Christianity and any other religion.[17] The letter to the Romans points out the solution to the problem of Christianity and Judaism, which is fundamental for the church of all times: 'Christianity is the abolishing fulfilment of Judaism' ...[18] Jewish protests to Paul's exegesis are quickly dismissed, although the arbitrariness of that exegesis, by critical standards, is readily admitted.[19] Paul seems to have made his point in a very convincing way indeed.

All remarks on the logic of Paul's theology, in particular his theology of the law, have not, however, been of a panegyric nature. In antiquity, Porphyry commented that Paul displays the ignorant person's habit of constantly contradicting himself and that he is feverish in mind[20] and weak in his

---

11 Stendahl, *Paul* 52, cf. 71; cf. also Kuss, *Paulus* 277.

12 Cerfaux, *Christian* 353 f.

13 Gerhardsson, '1 Kor 13' 185. For Dahl, too, Paul belongs 'among the philosophers' and warrants 'a place in the history of Western thought' (op.cit. 2). Of late Paul has also come to be seen as a skilled rhetorician in the best Greek tradition; cf. Betz, 'Composition' and *Galatians*.

14 That modern scholarship 'still is under the spell of the myth of Paul the non-thinker' (Betz, *Galatians* xiv) I simply fail to see, at least as the European scene is concerned.

15 Gerhardsson, loc.cit.

16 Smend-Luz, *Gesetz* 144. Schulz, *Mitte*, defends vigorously the extreme thesis that Paul's doctrine of righteousness by faith is *the* normative 'canon within the canon'.

17 The implication is clearly spelled out by Schniewind, *Erneuerung* 61: ' ... our comparison of religions acquires its norms largely from the way the New Testament fights the double battle against nomism on one hand and the antinomistic gnosis on the other ... ' In this battle Paul proceeds 'by taking up the questions of the opponent, the Pharisee or the Gnostic, and answering to them with the testimony to Christ ... '

18 Goppelt, op.cit. 315. Cf. Althaus, *Wahrheit* § 16, esp. p. 136.

19 Käsemann states on Romans 10.5 ff.: 'In the eyes of the historical critic the violation of the literal sense of Scripture in the introduction to vv. 6 ff. is scarcely to be outdone.' Yet he can claim not only that this is 'valid on Paul's hermeneutical presuppositions', but also that 'no objection can be brought against this exegesis on Jewish grounds'. Romans 285.

20 An interesting parallel to this from a totally different perspective is supplied by the imaginative comment of the novelist Baring-Gould, *Study* 323 f.: when 'Paul's Hellenic

reasoning.[21] Of course, Porphyry was biased; nevertheless his critique did appeal to a Harnack,[22] and one wonders whether the Neo-Platonic philosopher would not, at this point, have won the approval of many Jewish Christians of Paul's day. A modern philosopher, too, may find Paul's theology 'utterly confused'.[23]

It is, however, unnecessary to turn to critics of Christianity to find out that something is amiss in Paul's theology of the law. It is symptomatic that the followers of the apostle have hardly ever been able to agree on what he really wanted to say. It may be understandable that Marcion reached quite different conclusions from those of his orthodox opponents,[24] or even that the way Paul's teaching is interpreted in Ephesians is quite unlike that of the Pastorals.[25] But what is one to make of the fact that still in our time, with all the historical-critical apparatus available, learned scholars like, for example, Cranfield and Käsemann can propose diametrically opposed views of Paul's intentions? Where Cranfield says that gospel and law are, for Paul, essentially one,[26] Käsemann maintains that they are quite non-dialectically mutually exclusive antitheses.[27] Moreover, each interpreter suggests that if you reject his way of seeing it, you are dangerously misusing Paul's theology![28] It is in fact striking that more than one interpreter can state that Paul's theology of the law is just a lot of nonsense, unless of course you opt for his particular

---

converts saw him floundering in dispute, they looked on with wonder and compassion as they did when he was in the throes of malarial fever', for 'his arguments were to the Greeks so marvellous and incomprehensible that they were disposed to regard them also with the superstitious respect that they paid to epilepsy'!

21 In Macarius Magnes, *Apocriticus* III, 30.34. See text and commentary in Harnack, *Kritik* 58–61, 64–67; cf. also Nestle, 'Haupteinwände' 66–69. To be sure, the identification of Macarius's source with Porphyry is not undisputed.

22 Harnack, op.cit. 133 f. comments: 'He reproduces the portrait of Paul ... partly more correctly than modern Protestant German critics who portray the Apostle one-sidedly according to some main passages in Galatians.'

23 Hedenius, *Helveteslären* 133 f.; cf. von Hartmann, *Christentum* 176.

24 Cf. Wiles, *Apostle* 50.

25 Cf. Lindemann, *Aufhebung* 171 ff. Lindemann (174) states: 'Evidently even immediately after Paul one was no longer able to grasp and to appropriate Paul's theologically differentiated teaching on the law ... ' Whether this is not a euphemism remains to be seen in the course of this study.

26 'Paul' 68; id., *Romans* 862.

27 *Romans* 282.

28 Cranfield suggests that behind more 'negative' interpretations of Paul's view of the law there is 'muddled thinking' ('Paul' 43), the effects of which 'will permeate the whole range of our thinking and doing' (44). According to Käsemann, on the other hand, certain 'positive' interpretations turn the gospel to a means of fulfilling the law and show that some statements of Paul are dangerously open to misunderstanding (op.cit. 218).

interpretation (different from most).[29]

We thus face a curious dilemma. On one hand, the clarity, profundity and cogency of Paul's theological thinking is universally praised. On the other hand, it does not seem possible to reach any unanimity whatsoever as to what his message really was.

As for Cranfield and Käsemann, both of them seem to play down some obvious tensions in Paul's thought.[30] Cranfield does this by way of manifest harmonizing, explaining away Paul's negative comments on the law. Käsemann's approach is more sophisticated. He presents a sort of redaction-critical thesis: Paul's conservative statements are Jewish-Christian traditional fragments, tacitly reinterpreted by the apostle; it is only the radical thoughts that should be taken seriously as Paul's own theology. The one-sidedness of each method is evident. Half of the material just cannot be explained away, neither the positive nor the negative statements.

There remains a refuge in the secure realm of dialectic and paradox.[31] We are constantly reminded of the delight the Semitic mind supposedly took in paradoxes.[32] One may wonder, why Paul's *Jewish*-Christian opponents were so unable to follow his Semitic paradoxes about the law; the suspicion creeps in that they might have felt Paul to be too much of a *Greek* for their liking! Anyway, it should be noted that Christian scholars hardly ever speak of dialectic and the like, when they interpret contradictions in, say, the Dead Sea Scrolls or in the Koran.[33] The talk of dialectic thus has an apologetic ring. Moreover, the notion of dialectic is so vague that it seems pointless to try to argue against it.[34] So I will rather try to establish an alternative perspective which makes more sense to me at least.

Excluding patent harmonization and the dialectical approach, a few alternative ways of dealing with the tensions in Paul's statements about the law remain.

---

29 See the views of Conzelmann and O'Neill (below, p. 5 f.). Bring, *Christus* 54 contends that Rom 10.5 is 'completely senseless'. if Paul really speaks in that verse of false self-made righteousness (as other interpreters universally believe!); similarly, Gal 3.10 is nonsense, if the apostle there speaks of works of the law (as everybody except Bring thinks). On Bring's own interpretation see below, p. 55 n. 57.

30 See below, p. 42 ff., 66.

31 Cf. Michels, *Paul* 1 and passim; Mussner, *Traktat* 223, 237 n. 41 (but cf. 231); Kim, *Origin* 281 ff. (leaning on Stuhlmacher, *Gerechtigkeit* 94 ff.); cf. also Stuhlmacher, *Evangelium* I, 97. For a critical comment see Gronemeyer, *Frage* 9f.

32 One of the more perceptive scholars to do this is Caird, *Age* 137 f. (with special reference to the problem of hardening, Rom 9.18, 10.21; yet in that case, too, the question is: is there not a real contradiction in Paul's views of divine hardening?).

33 Cf. Räisänen, *Hardening*, esp. 7–9, 13 f., 73, 97 f.

34 Cf. Michels, op.cit. 33: Paul's writing was 'full of paradoxes', for 'the truths which Paul conveyed were too big for human comprehension. To express these truths, he

1. The first alternative to be mentioned might be regarded as a sophisticated version of the dialectical approach. Interestingly enough, one of the harshest recent judgments on Paul's teaching on the law comes from one of the most
ardent admirers of Paul the theologian. According to Hans Conzelmann it is
clear that one does not understand Paul, if one stops at the *heilsgeschichtlich*
conceptions.[35] Taken literally (on the 'objectified' level), Paul's teaching on
the law leads to absurd conclusions.[36] Conzelmann, however, elevates himself
above the offence by denying in good existentialist fashion that these ideas
of Paul should be 'objectified'. They cannot be taken at face value.[37] Paul's
doctrine of the law is nothing but a theological interpretative device which
shows where man stands without the gospel. Conzelmann would have us
swallow even the following: 'The arguments are complicated, but it must be
asked whether their complexity is not appropriate. The gospel is not complicated, but my position is; it is therefore difficult to understand it in terms of
thought.'[38] Here a theological virtue is made out of historical necessity.
Obviously, what is complicated is not so much 'my' position in the light of
Paul's gospel, but rather *Paul's* position in a very particular social and historical situation.[39] If there really are such self-contradictions and other
problematic points at the very core of Paul's thinking as Conzelmann suggests
(not without reason), then ought not this to lead to a reassessment of the role
of Paul's theology in Christian thought, not least as regards Christianity's

---

had to speak in contraries.' Paul thus 'showed that God did not weigh things according to human standards'!

35 *Grundriss* 248. Unfortunately, the ET (*Outline* 225 ff.) does not manage to make
Conzelmann's intentions clear.

36 Ibid. 251.

37 Cf. the comment on the difference between the views of history in Gal 3–4 and Rom
5 respectively: 'Paulus kann sich diese Unausgeglichenheit leisten, weil es ihm nicht
auf die Vorstellung als solche ankommt.' Ibid. 248. Similarly Hübner, *Gesetz* 74,
commenting on the relation of Romans 5 to Rom 2.14. Cf. also Noack, 'Evangeliet'
141–144; Schmithals, *Anthropologie* 29 f. Interpretations resembling that of Conzelmann to a certain degree (without the particular existentialist ring) were put forward by Joest, *Gesetz* 165 ff., 176 ff., and Wendland, 'Gesetz' 47 ff. Joest admits
that, understood as a complex of intellectual statements, Paul's doctrine of justification would be 'a chaos of contradictory assertions without unity' (180), and Wendland speaks of contradictions in Paul's teaching on the law which cannot be surpassed
in their sharpness (49). Both interpreters struggle to find a theological way out of
such difficulties.

38 Ibid. 251. For some critical comments see Türcke, *Potential* 88.

39 Conzelmann's presentation reveals with rare clarity the two basic weaknesses of the
existentialist position: the refusal to distinguish between the exegetical and the theological tasks in the process of interpretation, and the reluctance to take into account
any psychological or sociological considerations. Cf. the remarks on Conzelmann's
revealing misuse of the first person pronoun by von der Osten-Sacken, 'Notwendigkeit' 249.

relation to other religious traditions?[40]

2. A few interpreters solve the tensions in Paul's letters violently by attributing large parts of Galatians and especially of Romans to later interpola-
tors. After the days of the Dutch conjectural criticism in the last century [41]
this approach was almost forgotten,[42] even though a single pericope (notably
2 Cor 6.14–7.1) is not seldom ascribed to an editor, not to speak of occasional short glosses (like Rom 7.25b). Recently, however, the interpolation
approach has been revived by J.C. O'Neill.

O'Neill starts from the conviction that Paul must have been a logical
thinker.[43] 'Paul uses arguments, and expects them to hold.'[44] By contrast, the
letter to the Romans as it stands is 'so obscure, so complicated, so disjointed,
that it is hard to see how Paul could have exerted such an influence on his
contemporaries' if the letter were a product of his.[45] Again, 'if Paul was "a
coherent, argumentative, pertinent writer" (Locke), Galatians as it now stands
cannot have been written by Paul, for, as Bruno Bauer demonstrated, Galatians is full of obscurities, contradictions, improbable remarks, and non
sequiturs ...'. [46] The conclusion: 'If the choice lies between supposing that
Paul was confused and contradictory and supposing that his text has been
commented upon and enlarged, I have no hesitation in choosing the
second.'[47]

It might be wiser to have some hesitation, though. It is not at all clear that
Paul's influence on his contemporaries should have been due, above all, to the
logic of his letters, rather than, say, to the spell of his person or to the massive effort of his missionary activity. And what exactly *was* Paul's influence on
his *contemporaries*? Did he not have greater success after his death, when his
thoughts were made palatable to the masses through, e.g., the Pastorals?
Consistency of thought is a dubious criterion of authenticity, and particularly
so in the case of a writer as impulsive as Paul.

But even if we must reject O'Neill's extreme conclusions, his contribution

---

40 Contrast the somewhat cavalier dismissal of H.J. Schoeps's approach by Conzelmann,
   Outline 180 f.
41 See esp. van Manen, *Unechtheit* 52, 66 ff., 76, 202 on inconsistent statements about
   the law in Romans, the composition of which van Manen attributes to various succes-
   sive redactors.
42 With the exception of Loisy in his latest works (e.g. *Origins* 255) and Pallis. Pallis
   found Romans as it stands to be 'one of the hardest (works) to follow in Greek
   literature' (*Romans* 9). To be sure, he did not ascribe the 'fairly simple' original form
   of the letter to Paul either.
43 *Romans* 150.
44 Ibid. 63.
45 Ibid. 16.
46 *Galatians* 8. O'Neill's confidence in Bruno Bauer's analysis remains perplexing to me.
47 Ibid. 86.

is helpful in that he has not shrunk from pointing out difficulties and contradictions in Romans and Galatians without hesitation, thus providing a healthy antidote to much uncritical praise of Paul's thought.

3. By far the most attractive device to do away with the difficulties caused by the tensions in Paul's thought are theories of development. On this view, Paul's doctrine of the law went through a development from the earlier letters (including Galatians) to Romans, which represents his mature view. After the early attempts of Sieffert and others,[48] development theories have been put forward by Dodd,[49] Buck and Taylor,[50] and, most recently, by Drane, Hübner, and Lüdemann.

---

48 Sieffert, 'Entwicklungslinie' found in Romans 'eine umfassendere und vertiefte, aber zugleich auch gemilderte' development of the doctrine of the freedom from the law (343), although he did not consider the difference to be very great. The Corinthian letters are supposed to be closer to Galatians than to Romans; Sieffert refers to 2 Cor 3.6 ff., 1 Cor 15.56 and 1 Cor 7.19 (!), the latter part of which goes unmentioned (350). Sieffert has to claim that Gal 5.14 represents a different view of the law than does Rom 13.8–10 (350 ff.) — a problematic interpretation shared now by Hübner. See below, p. 27 n. 72.

49 According to Dodd, Paul underwent in connection with the crisis reflected in 2 Cor a 'second conversion' whereby he was liberated, among other things, from his pride (*Studies* 80–82). 'The traces of fanaticism and intolerance disappear, almost if not quite completely, along with all that anxious insistence on his own dignity. The new temper shows itself in the way in which the controversies of Romans and Colossians are conducted, in a generous recognition of the natural virtues of mankind ... ' (81; as regards Romans, the reference is to 2.14 f. and 13.1–7). In Rom 2.14–15 we have 'evidence of the new valuation of "the world" which went along with Paul's revision of eschatology' (115). Paul's attitude to the law, too, became milder (123); passages like Rom 7.12, 14, Rom 8.3, and 2 Cor 3.14–18 indicate 'a less intransigent attitude in Paul's controversy with the legalists'. The 'new temper' is most clearly palpable in Philippians.

Dodd's scheme is open to serious criticisms. First, passages like Rom 1.18–32, 2.17–24 speak neither for the disappearance of intolerance nor for a new valuation of the 'world'. Secondly, Phil 3.2 hardly indicates a milder attitude in legal controversies. And thirdly, as Drane, Paul, has shown, it is in 1 Cor, a letter written *before* 'the second conversion', that Paul's attitude to the law is most positive (not to speak of 1 Thess where problems of the law are ignored). On Dodd see further Lowe, 'Examination', 138–140.

50 Buck and Taylor start from the development in Paul's eschatology, combining with this an analogous development in other segments of his thought. Their analysis is over-subtle. 2 Cor 3, e.g., is said to reflect Paul's 'recently developed eschatological possession of two natures', being 'nothing less than this doctrine in reverse'. 'For whereas in the eschatological doctrine it is the flesh that is destined to pass away, leaving only the living spirit, in the legal doctrine ... it is the spirit which has departed from the law, leaving only the letters carved on stone.' (*Saint Paul* 64). This ingenious interpretation presses the alleged parallelism between 'Christ gave up the form of God' (Phil 2) and 'Paul has given up his own righteousness' (Phil 3, p. 75 f.) in an extreme way. Cf. the review article by Furnish ('Development').

Drane constructs a line of dialectical development from the 'libertine' Galatians through the 'legalist' 1 Corinthians to the 'mature synthesis' of Romans.[51] To be able to do this, he has to accept the South Galatian hypothesis and an early date for Galatians.[52] Several reasons, however, speak in favour of the North Galatian hypothesis.[53] An early date for Galatians is especially puzzling in view of the striking similarities between this letter and Romans,[54] whereas no such relationship exists, e.g., between Galatians and 1 Thessalonians. There seems, in fact, to be no place at all for 1 Thess in the picture given by Drane.

If the South Galatian hypothesis is abandoned and Galatians is dated after the Apostolic Council, little basis is left for development theories, for which the *order* Galatians — 1 Corinthians (2 Cor) is of central importance. The order of Galatians and 1 Corinthians continues to be an open question; grounds can be given also for the view that Galatians is the later one of the two.[55]

A severe difficulty for development theories is posed by the short time space between Galatians and Romans. This applies in particular to Hübner's view, according to which Paul went through a remarkable theological development between the writing of these two letters.[56] In Galatians Paul, according to Hübner, maintains that the law has been abolished; in Romans, however, Christ is only seen as the end of the Jewish misunderstanding of the law and not of the law itself.[57] But the notion of a dramatic theological development within a very short period of time in the thinking of one already engaged in missionary work for some twenty years is strange enough.[58] In addition, there

---

51 Drane, *Paul*.
52 Even on the South Galatian hypothesis, however, the possibility remains that Gal may be later than 1 Cor. So, following Lightfoot, Robinson, *Redating* 55–57.
53 See Kümmel, *Introduction* 296 ff.; Vielhauer, *Geschichte* 104–108.
54 Cf. Borse, *Standort* 120–143.
55 Cf. Suhl, *Paulus* 343; Borse, op.cit. 58 ff.; Lüdemann, *Paulus* 114 ff.; Schade, *Christologie* 178 ff., 190; Wilckens, 'Entwicklung' 154.
56 Hübner, *Gesetz* 47. Without discussing the chronological question Hübner assumes that Gal did *not* come into existence 'shortly before Romans' (56), even though it must date from the period after the council (21 ff.). Yet the points of contact assembled by Borse (above, n. 54) show that the two letters must belong roughly to the same period. Borse assumes an interval of some three months; Suhl, op.cit. 343 f. about half a year. But even a year or two seems a short period of time for the alleged development to take place. Cf. Lüdemann, op.cit. 116 n. 139. Jervell, 'Der unbekannte Paulus' 45–47 proposes a theory not unlike that of Hübner; see now also Wilckens, 'Entwicklung'. In the second edition of his book Hübner (*Gesetz* 131 f.) by and large agrees with the view of Drane, failing to note that Drane dates Galatians in the early career of Paul.
57 Hübner, op.cit. 129.
58 Correctly Lowe, art.cit. 132 f. The situation would be even stranger, if Paul had

are already obvious tensions in Paul's thought on the law in Galatians,[59] and even more in Romans. Neither letter is internally consistent.[60] If this last point is correct, it constitutes a decisive objection to development theories.

To suggest that both Galatians and Romans are beset with internal tensions and contradictions is to anticipate my own conclusions. It is a claim that has to be substantiated in the course of the present study through analyses of the texts. I thus offer my own reading of Paul as an alternative to theories of development. To anticipate again, I think that the different outlook of different letters is sufficiently accounted for by the fact that Paul found himself in different situations. In face of different challenges this impulsive and flexible thinker often shifted his ground. In Galatians Paul makes a fierce attack; in Romans he has to be on the defensive.[61]

This is not at all to deny that Paul's thought underwent a development during his missionary activity. On the contrary, to anticipate once more, I am sure it did. But I do not detect any straightforward development from any one *extant* letter to another. Had we some writings of Paul from, say, the thirties, the situation might be different. Whatever major development there

---

spent some twenty years in meditation on the gospel before starting his mission, as Drane, op.cit. 180 n. 10, thinks!

59 Drane notes himself that already in Gal Paul's attitude to the law is 'strangely equivocal' (cp. 3.19 to 3.13, see below, p. 59); op.cit. 6.

60 In order to be able to maintain consistency in Gal, Hübner has to deny that Gal 5.14 refers to the Torah (see below, p. 27); similarly, he has to claim that Rom 5.20a refers to something different from Gal 3.19b (op.cit. 73 f.), to remove a major discrepancy from Romans. Buck and Taylor, op.cit. 16, likewise claim that 'the letters are internally consistent'.

61 Cf. Grafe, *Lehre* 27–32; Stendahl, *Paul* 48 (development theories are unnecessary, because Paul's writings are 'real, pastoral letters directed to specific situations'); Luz, Rev. Hübner 123. Even in Romans, Paul is hardly trying consciously 'to produce a "neutral" theology, taking account of the valid claims of both sides while avoiding the pitfalls that he had encountered in writing both Gal. and 1 Cor.'; so Drane, op.cit. 109 (cf. 124). In Romans Paul is speaking *pro domo*, in an apologetic way. For the ongoing intensive debate concerning the purpose of Romans see Kettunen, *Abfassungszweck*; Drane, 'Why'; and the articles in Donfried, *Debate*. The different purposes suggested need not be mutually exclusive; cf. the prudent evaluation in Williams, 'Righteousness' 245 ff. At any rate, an apologetic accent not least concerning Paul's view of the law is undeniable.

As a random example of a person's change of attitude when faced with a new kind of audience one may note Justin Martyr's 'sharp difference of attitude concerning philosophy' in his Dialogue and Apology respectively. 'Justin's theory of the Spermatikos Logos and his view of the great philosophers as Christians prior to Christ ... are nowhere in evidence in the Dialogue ... On the contrary, Justin in the Dialogue concedes nothing to philosophy!' Stylianopoulos, *Justin* 17. He concludes (195 n. 170) that Justin's true feelings about Greek philosophy appear in the Dialogue.

was in Paul's theology of the law, must, in my view, have taken place by the time of the writing of Galatians.[62]

There remains the possibility that 1 Thessalonians comes from the early forties, thus representing a different phase in Paul's thinking than the other letters. This is the thesis of Knox and Lüdemann.[63] It is impossible, in the framework of this study, to penetrate into the complicated problems of Pauline chronology.[64] Should Knox and Lüdemann turn out to be right,[65] then we could indeed construe a line of development from 1 Thess to the other letters. As 1 Thess, however, does not deal with the question of law at all, the chronological problem is not of major importance to the present study. Whatever the place of 1 Thess, Gal, the Corinthian letters and Rom belong closely together, not least chronologically.

Even though I must disagree with the development theories of Drane and Hübner, both scholars have undeniably put their finger on crucial points. They have found in Paul's thought various tensions which cry for a solution.[66]

4. Even if the (quite different) solutions proposed fail to carry conviction, scholars like Conzelmann, O'Neill, or Hübner have sharpened our eyes to see the problem posed by Paul's differing statements concerning the law. What, then, would make a suitable approach to the problem? I can see one way

---

62 So also J. Weiss, *Urchristentum* 151 (ET I, 206): 'It cannot be too much insisted upon that the real development of Paul both as a Christian and a theologian was completed in this period which is so obscure to us ... ' Cf. Feine, *Evangelium* 186.

63 Knox, *Chapters* 85; Lüdemann, *Paulus*; cf. also Schade, op.cit. 190 and elsewhere.

64 See the recent studies by Suhl, Jewett, and Lüdemann. For a brief comparison and evaluation cf. Wedderburn, 'Chronologies'.

65 Lüdemann's case is made rather attractive through his analysis of the differences in the eschatological outlook of 1 Thess and 1 Cor respectively (op.cit. 213 ff.). On the other hand, one hesitates in view of the many unusual interpretations (including the dating of the edict of Claudius in A.D. 41 and the placing of the Antiochian incident, Gal 2.11 ff., *before* the Apostolic Council, Gal 2.1 ff; as regards the latter I fail to be persuaded by the author's version of H.D. Betz' rhetorical interpretation of the letter) which this reconstruction seems to require.

66 Somewhat surprisingly, both scholars in the end play down their own findings. Having at first (over-)emphasized the difference between Gal and Rom, Hübner ends up by relativizing it (*Gesetz* 52 f., 58) — as if it made no real difference whether Christ did away with the law of Moses or only with its perverted interpretations. Drane (op.cit. 180 n. 10), again, finally speaks of 'a development of emphasis', telling us that 'when a theology worked out in the study (i.e., that of Galatians?!) is put to the test of practical performance, alterations to its expression, if not its essence, are almost inevitable'. What an understatement of Drane's actual findings and what a disappointing end to a stimulating study! Later on ('Diversity'15) Drane can speak of 'the different nuances' of Paul's thought, in reconciling which 'there is no problem at all'. All this harmonizing would seem to be contradicted by Drane's own contention that the development could *only* take place in *one* direction (from Gal to 1 and 2 Cor, never vice versa).

only: contradictions and tensions have to be *accepted* as *constant* features of Paul's theology of the law. They are not simply of an accidental or peripheral nature. The contradictions are undoubtedly historically and psychologically conditioned. Whether or not we, with the aid of the extant material, are able to trace the case history of Paul with any degree of probability (and we may not), the possibility that Paul's difficulties with the law are *in principle* explicable through psychological, sociological and historical factors, should not be thrust aside lightly. Emphasizing this entails a return to certain insights characteristic of the liberal theology at the turn of the century (not, of course, an uncritical acceptance of the whole of it as such). It seems that a certain open-mindedness characteristic of that current of thought was largely lost in the upsurge of dialectical theology. Up to that time it was open to anyone to be critical of the apostle's thoughts if thought necessary;[67] since then, criticisms appear only sporadically, or else they, too, are turned into praise (Conzelmann). Over against Conzelmann[68] and others, I find the following remarks by Wrede illuminating: Paul's reasoning has a very 'elastic' character. 'It is no great feat to unearth contradictions, even among his leading thoughts ...'[69] 'Tortured attempts to reconcile these opposites are in all such cases mischievous. It is also dangerous, however, to hold that Paul could not have meant a thing, because it leads to impossible consequences. The consequences may be "impossible", but did Paul perceive them? We may perhaps find instruction in the very fact that he did not.'[70]

This tradition of calling a spade a spade has survived here and there mostly in Anglo-Saxon literature on the subject. Early on in this century, Percy Gardner stated that 'Paul is seldom free from inconsistency'.[71] 'Paul was one of the last of mankind to be wholly self-consistent ...'[72] His statements 'are

---

67 There is no reason to turn to irony when speaking of this feature of liberal theology as Grässer, *Schweitzer* 159 does. Cf. M. Barth's wholesale indictment of critical assessments of Paul: '*Sachkritik* of the Bible is not one of the responsibilities of biblical scholarship, but is professional presumption.' 'St. Paul' 32.

68 See above, p. 5.

69 *Paulus* 48 (ET 77), with reference to, e.g., the relationship of Rom 2.14–16 to Rom 5.13. Cf. Weiss, *Urchristentum* 427 (Paul had, as regards the law, two contradictory lines of thought, both equally true and irrefutable to him, comprehensible as deposits of two different epochs of his life).

70 Op.cit. 49 (ET 77 f.).

71 Gardner, *Experience* 160, cf. 179.

72 Op.cit. 44. Gardner also remarks that 'on no subject are his inconsistencies so marked' as with respect to the law; op.cit. 46. Cf. Lowe, 'Examination': 'It is the easiest thing in the world to find verbal contradictions in Paul, and this means neither that he was unprincipled nor that he kept changing his mind. What did change with astonishing rapidity was his mood.' (140) Further factors were the 'change of external circumstances' and 'the perpetual tension within him between his Jewish heritage and his Christian experience, a tension never entirely resolved' (141). 'One of the grand

usually so steeped in emotion that they cannot easily be analysed in a dry light'.[73] Later on, James Parkes commented: 'Difficult as it is to penetrate into the contradictions of Pauline thought, it is better to do so than to attempt to make a logical and consistent whole of his teaching, if logic and consistency really lack.'[74] Consequently, scholars like Gardner and Parkes see Paul's real significance not in the field of theological thinking, but in his 'mysticism and his practical teaching'.[75]

To return to Wrede's opinion, it is indeed the thesis of the present work as well that the very tensions and 'impossibilities' of Paul's thought do, if not dialectically diluted, give us 'instruction', or at least indications, of what was going on in Paul's mind. Rather than gloss over contradictions, one should take them very seriously as pointers to Paul's *personal theological problems*, even if that means that his reasoning appears to take on a surprisingly sub-jective colouring.

So far we have been speaking of the question of the consistency or other-wise of Paul's thought on the law. A related and yet separate question is, how convincing Paul is in his main assertions. Of course, if the argument is inconsistent, the result cannot be wholly convincing in intellectual terms. Nevertheless, the possibility remains that the main points a preacher makes may be felt to be compelling, even if the arguments he uses to prove them are not. Thus, it is often said that certain central statements of Paul remain true, even though we cannot accept the way he 'proves' them from Scripture. On the other hand, even an internally consistent presentation fails to carry con-viction, if it is built on false premises.

---

things about Paul is that whenever he is one-sided, the corrective is always to be found in his own writings and as often as not on the same page.' Instead of producing a unified system of 'Paulinism', the apostle, fortunately, 'left the whole wonderful muddle unarranged and alive, and we are the richer for it'. Cf. further M. Grant, *Paul* 4 (Paul 'commits flagrant self-contradictions'; see also 34, 137).

73 Gardner, op.cit. 47. Cf. Deissmann, *Paul* 104 f.; Stacey, *View* 16 f.; Gaechter, *Petrus* 217. The Danish historian of religion Grønbech (*Paulus* 6 ff. and passim) found Paul's thinking extremely subjective. 'Paul is the most subjective and, therefore, the most dogmatic preacher in the world; what he has experienced that is the truth ... ' (6). 'One has to be Paul to understand the Pauline gospel ... ' (259).

74 Parkes, *Jesus* 140.

75 Parkes, op.cit. 128. F.C. Grant, 'Prolegomenon' xxxiii: Paul was not a theologian but 'a mystic' and 'a propagandist'; id., *Romans* 17: Paul was 'a man of intensely practical religious interests' rather than a 'theologian' or a 'thinker'. Cf. Stacey, op.cit. 241: 'He had a much greater mission, a mission for which he was ideally suited as he was not suited for the systematization of thought that is so often expected of him.' Andrews, *Teaching* 4: 'Perhaps he is not so much the deep thinker, the intel-lectual, as the fiery propagandist of his faith'; cf. id., 'Paul' 166. *Teaching* 24: 'That Paul has been pictured as the theologian par excellence is ... a gross injustice to Paul as well as to the theologians.'

We noted at the beginning that Paul is mostly thought to have made his point convincingly. Even his opponents, it is apparently thought, *ought* to have been persuaded by him. Over against these sentiments stand, of course, the opinions of Jewish scholars through the ages, including those who take a positive attitude to Paul the man. Thus, C.G. Montefiore states, from the view-point of a liberal Jew, that 'Paul's confused and often inconsistent reasoning ... is inclined to bore us'.[76] S. Sandmel (who does *not* consider Paul's theology of the law to be inconsistent) states in the course of a wholly benevolent evaluation that Paul has 'an undisciplined mind' and that he is 'we may say, a lyric poet', lacking philosophical acumen.[77]

But once again, it is quite unnecessary to turn to outsiders to hear some very critical voices. Thus, Paul Wernle stated that 'there was no single word in his theory (sc. of the law) that carried conviction with it'. It is 'an ingenious conjuring with ideas and nothing more', 'a very lame theory'.[78] James Parkes, for his part, far from attributing supreme dialectical skill to the author of Romans, writes as follows: 'The letter to the Romans comes as near being a theological treatise as anything which Paul wrote – and causes one to give thanks that he wrote no other, for the abiding genius of Paul lies in his mysticism and his practical teaching, not in systematic theology. His purpose is to establish the central position of the Cross and Atonement in relation to both Jewish and Gentile experience. The result is both artificial and unsatisfactory.'[79]

Hardly anyone within the Christian tradition, however, ever criticized Paul's reasoning – arguments and premises alike – as sharply as did Alfred Loisy. Commenting on Galatians, Loisy notes that Paul there repeats time and again his main principle in different variations.[80] Paul's logic, however, is 'capricious'[81] and his arguments consist of 'the most arbitrary interpretations and of fantasies' so that it is dubious whether we should speak of 'arguments' at all.[82] Galatians is the pleading of an enthusiast and a visionary, who is completely incapable of criticizing the flight of his thoughts.[83] Paul's assertion of the sin-engendering nature and purpose of the law (Gal 3.22–25) is incomplete and false, being indeed of 'infantile absurdity'. Paul 'invents the philosophy and psychology suitable to the needs of his thesis'.[84] Rom 6–8 displays a 'sincere and profound faith' and a 'high ideal of morality', but also a 'fan-

---

76 *Judaism* 138 f.
77 *Genius* 7.
78 *Anfänge* 216 (ET 299 f.).
79 *Jesus* 128; cf. Gardner, op.cit. 139 f. Contrast the praise of Romans by Hübner, above p. 1 n. 8.
80 *Galates* 41.
81 Op.cit. 140 (on Gal 2.18).
82 Op.cit. 41.
83 Op.cit. 36 f.
84 Op.cit. 159.

tastic argument, a massive and magical conception of sin, of the redemption
and of the Spirit, a system constructed in the air, which is too often celebrated for a psychological value of which it is in reality almost completely
void'.[85] It would have been easy for any Jewish teacher to refute Paul.[86]

Thus it seems that Paul's talk of the law is liable to widely differing, even
diametrically opposite, interpretations and evaluations. This being so, the
main task of the present study will be to *test Paul's reasoning* in this matter.
Attention is paid both to the *internal consistency* (or otherwise) of the reasoning and to the *validity of its premises*. Particular notice will be taken of
difficulties Paul seems to run into.[87] Tensions will not be resolved by way of
theological dialectic or theories of interpolation or development. They will
rather be seen as indications of a personal conflict which requires a historical
and psychological explanation (whether or not we will be able to provide
anything like it). The difficulties are analyzed in chapters I–V which constitute the main part of the study. Historical and psychological hypotheses
which could explain the difficulties to some degree are discussed in chapter
VIII. The analysis in chs. I–V does *not*, however, depend on the plausibility
of the solution developed in ch. VIII. It is in the nature of the matter that
any theory purporting to show how Paul got into the difficulties in which we
find him to be must needs be conjectural.

I am fully aware of a certain anachronistic touch in such an analysis of
Paul's theology from the point of view of common sense logic. This kind of
examination is bound to be 'somewhat microscopic'.[88] One may feel that it is
unduly pedantic to subject the thoughts of an ancient Jew, which proceeded
freely from one image and association to another, to such a rigid scrutiny. I
am the first to admit that this approach does not do full justice to Paul at all.
Nevertheless, I find it justified (and indeed necessary) as *one* approach among
others. It is a method that opens up *one* perspective, a perspective that is
neither the only one nor even the most important one. I feel that this approach

---

85 'Epîtres' 232. On p. 233 Loisy speaks of Paul's 'arbitrary and obscure gnosis'.

86 *Galates* 148 (on Gal 3.12). Lagrange, *Galates* 70 replied that it was not Paul's purpose
   to address a Jewish teacher, but rather Christians. This commonplace hardly removes
   the problem; while speaking to Christians, Paul undoubtedly believed that his reasoning *ought* to have made sense to Jews as well. To be sure, Moore, *Judaism* III 151,
   suggested that Paul 'can hardly have expected the argument (sc. that Judaism is not a
   way of salvation at all) to have effect with Jews'. 'He was, in fact, not writing to con-
   vince Jews but to keep his Gentile converts from being convinced by Jewish propa-
   gandists ... ' This cannot be correct, for the unbelief of Jews was so incomprehensible
   to Paul that he had to trace it back to divine hardening (Rom 9) or veiling of the
   Scripture (2 Cor 3), or to a ruse of the devil (2 Cor 4.4).

87 A preliminary survey of these appeared in my congress paper 'Difficulties'. A not
   quite dissimilar approach is taken in the same volume by Hickling, 'Centre' 199–
   203; cf. also Wedderburn, 'Adam' 424.

88 J. Weiss, op.cit. 427.

is badly needed as a corrective. It acquires its justification not least from the fact that, for better or for worse, *Paul has become a theological authority*. His statements, including those about the law, are in actual fact used as normative. His reasoning is appealed to even as a model for the position a Christian theologian should take in discussions between religions. Whether or not Paul can justly be called a theologian,[89] posterity has seen him as one and venerated him as such. If, therefore, an analysis of Paul's reasoning does less than justice to the apostle himself, it may at least render a service by placing Paulinism in perspective.

However, in order to anchor the analysis of Paul's thought as firmly as possible in his own time, special effort will be made to compare Paul's views to relevant Jewish and early Christian conceptions. I wish to explore which of the theological difficulties to be found are peculiar to Paul alone, and which he perhaps shares with other Christians or even Jews. It is of course the former class that will be of greatest interest to us. In this connection, too, many of the alleged parallels between the thought of Paul and that of his contemporaries will be discussed. Possible analogies to individual difficulties will be treated in the course of chapters I–V. In chapter VII, Paul's overall view of the law will be compared to other overall views within Early Christianity, with special respect to questions of internal coherence and validity of premises. This, I hope, will bring Paul's particular position into sharper focus.

Should Paul turn out to be a less consistent theologian than many have imagined, this need not a priori diminish his grandeur as a teacher in his own time and milieu. 'Whatever the faults of the Rabbis were, consistency was not one of them', says S. Schechter,[90] a writer hardly to be suspected of an anti-Rabbinic bias. If rigid standards are applied to the thought of Philo, it is possible to speak of its 'unscholarly nature'.[91] What matters most is a fair comparison.[92] To repeat, I do not think that Paul's stature is much affected by my analysis.[93] What *is* affected, if it is on the right track, is modern Paulinism — the theological cult of the apostle who may indeed have been at his best in areas other than speculative theology.

---

89 Drane, 'Diversity' is inclined to deny this.

90 *Aspects* 46, cf. 170.

91 Heinemann, *Bildung* 519 ff. Braun, *Wie man* ... 5, cf. 119, speaks of 'gross self-contradictions' in Philo; this may be all right, if only one is prepared to apply similar yardsticks to Paul.

92 It should be added that defective argumentation is not at all a phenomenon foreign to modern writers. Cf. Brandt's chapter on 'Defective Rhetoric' (*Rhetoric* 202 ff.) which begins as follows: 'Anyone who seriously considers modern argumentation rhetoric, in any genre whatsoever, must be astonished at its deficiencies. There are perhaps a dozen bad arguments ... for every one that might be regarded as reasonably persuasive.' (202).

93 Cf. the roughly analogous remarks of Andrews, *Teaching* 78.

I. The oscillating concept of law

1. General observations

Paul never defines the content of the term νόμος. He presupposes that the readers will know what he is talking about. On the face of it, the matter seems clear enough. Apart from a few cases, to be considered later on,[1] where Paul uses the word in a patently metaphorical sense, *nomos* seems to be identical with the OT *torah*, the Jewish 'law'.[2] In Hebrew, the word *torah* came to be used with different overlapping meanings, as can be seen from the saying, 'The *Torah* consists of the *Torah*, the Prophets and the Writings'.[3] This flexible usage, which as such constitutes no problem, is shared by Paul. He often connects the *nomos* with Moses (Rom 5.13 f., Gal 3.17, 1 Cor 9.8, 2 Cor 3.7 ff.), distinguishing it from the prophets (Rom 3.21). In Gal 4.21 the reference is to Genesis. At times, again, Paul cites prophets and psalms as words of the *nomos* (1 Cor 14.21, Rom 3.10–18). Thus the word *nomos* refers to the whole of Israel's sacred tradition,[4] with special emphasis on its Mosaic centre. Whether the unwritten *Torah*, the oral tradition of the fathers, is included in this usage, is not clear; at least, Paul never distinguishes between the written and the unwritten Torah.

Several times the fact is emphasized that *nomos* is the decisive *separating* factor between Jews and Gentiles. Possession of the *nomos* puts the Jews into a special class (Rom 2, 1 Cor 9.20 f., Gal 2.15).

In summary, *nomos* in Paul refers to the authoritative tradition of Israel, anchored in the revelation on Sinai, which separates the Jews from the rest of mankind.[5] The different occurrences can be compared to concentric circles: the radii can be different, but the Sinaitic centre remains the same. Paul never makes distinctions within the law — at least, no explicit distinctions.

To be sure, the notion was once popular that the meaning of *nomos*

---

1 Rom 3.27, 7.20–25, 8.2, Gal 6.2. See below, II 2 and II 7.

2 The discussion concerning the rendering of *torah* with *nomos* in the LXX need not be taken up here. Contrary to Dodd, *Bible* 25 ff. and Schoeps, *Paul* 29 it would seem that *nomos*, too, had a variety of shades of meaning, not being limited to 'law' in a legal sense. Cf. Werblowsky, 'Tora' 160 f.; Pasinya, *Notion*.

3 Tanh. Jethro 10; Gutbrod, νόμος 1047. On 'Torah' in Judaism see, e.g., Urbach, *Sages* 286 ff.

4 The word thus partly overlaps with ἡ γραφή (cf., e.g., Gal 4.21 and 4.30).

5 Cf. Bläser, *Gesetz* 34–38; van Dülmen, *Theologie* 130–134; Linton, 'Paulus' 177 f., and others. Differently Schlier, *Grundzüge* 79: Paul speaks of 'legalism in general'.

depends on whether Paul uses it with or without the article.[6] The extreme view was that ὁ νόμος denotes a different concept of law altogether than anarthrous νόμος.[7] Usually, however, one was content to infer from the absence of the article a special qualifying nuance: *nomos* still refers to the Mosaic law, but in the absence of the article it is viewed from a particular angle, emphasizing its 'legalistic' character.[8] But even in this milder form it is impossible to uphold the distinction. Paul can use *nomos* with and without the article even in the same verse, where no difference in meaning can be detected.[9] Since the investigations of E. Grafe, and, in particular, of P. Bläser[10], this distinction has justly been laid to rest.[11] Bläser showed convincingly that the use or omission of the article depends on 'a purely formal linguistic law'.[12]

One thus cannot find distinctions in Paul's use of *nomos* on linguistic grounds. But what about Paul's actual way of using the word? Even if he does not make any explicit distinctions, could he not have some *implicit* distinction in mind? Does not the way he talks about the 'law' reveal that *nomos*

---

6 The distinction is often traced back to Origen (so, e.g., Lietzmann on Rom 2.14). This view is refuted by Bläser, op.cit. 22 f.

7 Volkmar, *Römerbrief* 78 f. His conclusion is strange: anarthrous *nomos* refers either to 'a law' or to the Mosaic law; ὁ νόμος refers to 'the ethical obligation'. It was easy for Grafe, *Lehre*, 3 ff., to refute this by referring to Gal 3.13, 3.19, 1 Cor 9.8 f., Rom 2.18; in all these places ὁ νόμος is clearly the law of Moses. See further Bläser, op.cit. 2–4. Sanday-Headlam, too, in their commentary on Romans, occasionally interpret an anarthrous *nomos* as 'any system of law' (110, on 4.13), but such a distinction is not carried out systematically (it is mentioned neither in 2.14 nor in ch. 5). In Rom 10.4 the anarthrous *nomos* is said to denote 'law as a principle', not the Mosaic Law, but this is claimed because of 'the whole drift of the argument', not because of the lack of article (op.cit. 284).

8 Lightfoot, *Galatians* 118; Holsten, *Evangelium des Paulus* 158 f., 161, 179 f.; Gifford, *Romans* 41–48; Slaten, 'Use' 213–219; Stevens, *Theology* 160–162; Burton, *Galatians* 454 and passim. Cf. also Bandas, *Master-Idea* 92 f.

9 Thus Slaten, art.cit. 215, has to maintain that ἐν νόμῳ Rom 2.23a has a different nuance ('the legalistic nature of Jewish religion') than τοῦ νόμου Rom 2.23b (the legal code as such). And how could one distinguish between διὰ νόμου and ὁ νόμος ἔλεγεν in Rom 7.7?

10 Bläser, op.cit. 1–23.

11 See, however, Stamm, *Galatians* 482 and passim; Riedl, *Heil* 210 f. Riedl claims that in Rom 2 (other passages are not discussed by him) Paul uses the article when emphasizing the divine ethical norm contained in the law – an unintelligible specification in view of the anarthrous use of *nomos* in 2.12–13, 2.25, 2.27. Stamm goes even further. He assumes two concepts of law, distinguishing between which is said to be very important for the interpretation of the theology of Galatians. ὁ νόμος is the Mosaic law, mere *nomos* refers to all kinds of legalism. *Nomos*, then, in 3.18 would have a different meaning than 'the law' in 3.17 and 3.19! Similarly, 3.11 would speak of legalism in general, whereas in 3.12 ὁ νόμος is the Mosaic law!

12 Op.cit. 12.

does, after all, refer to different things in different passages? Scholars have indeed felt that it is rather difficult to let Paul's use of *nomos* always apply to the Mosaic Torah alone, and several distinctions have been proposed. A century ago, one interpreter set forth a very complicated definition of Paul's concept of *nomos*, the summary (!) of which comprised eight lines; the three main forms of nomos are the natural *Sittengesetz*, the mosaic Law, and the law of Christ.[13] Modern scholars have suggested distinctions between ritual and moral law,[14] haggadah and halakah,[15] God's will and Mosaic command,[16] the law as God's good requirement and the law as *Unheilsfaktor*,[17] the law and its legalistic misinterpretation,[18] the covenantal Torah and the law as seen by the Gentiles outside of the Sinai covenant,[19] etc. It is not always clear whether the interpreters think that Paul was conscious of some such distinction in his own thought. At any rate, the fact remains that Paul never alludes to any such thing. It would at least have been extremely difficult for his readers to find out what he was talking about, had he intended such distinctions. They would seem to be attempts of Paul's *interpreters* to create order in his theology of the law.

The following analysis starts from the observation that Paul at least argues *as if* the *nomos* were an undivided whole, firmly connected with Moses and Sinai. If, nevertheless, he makes statements about the *nomos* which are difficult to apply to the Mosaic law, we will have to ask whether Paul is conscious of this difficulty and, if not, *why* does the concept of *nomos* oscillate?

2. Gentiles under the law?

If *nomos* denotes the Mosaic law of Sinai, it by definition concerns the Jews, but not the Gentiles.[20] No wonder, then, that Paul often makes a clear

---

13 Fleischhauer, 'Lehre' 39; his summary can be summarized in the words 'die allum-fassende, feste Norm des sittlich-religiösen Handelns, wie sie in Form einer Forderung an den Menschen herantritt'.

14 See below, I 3.

15 J.A. Sanders, 'Torah and Paul' 133 underlines 'the binary nature of Torah', proposing a distinction between mythos and ethos, story and laws, haggadah and halakah (138). Paul, in his view, emphasized Torah as the story of God's works and 'de-emphasized those specific stipulations which seemed to present stumbling-blocks to carrying out the mandate' (138).

16 Bultmann, *Theology* 268; Vielhauer, 'Paulus' 55; Stuhlmacher, *Gerechtigkeit* 92 f., 96; cf. R.E. Howard, *Newness* 55 f.

17 Kertelge, 'Rechtfertigung' 205 f. (Does not Rom 7, however, describe how God's good requirement *becomes* an Unheilsfaktor, so that it is difficult to hold the two aspects apart?).

18 See below, II 1.

19 Gaston, 'Paul' 62 ff. This is surely the most artificial distinction of all.

20 Paul nowhere reveals an interest in the Noachian commandments, designed to make

distinction between the Jews 'under the law' and the Gentiles who are without the law (ἄνομοι, ἀνόμως) (Rom 2.12 ff., 1 Cor 9.20 f.; 1 Cor 7.17 ff.; Gal 2.14 f.). In such connections, *nomos* certainly cannot refer to anything but the Mosaic Torah.[21] In particular, the problems dealt with in Galatians are problems closely connected with the Torah: are the Galatian Gentile Christians to circumcise themselves and to take upon themselves the yoke of the Jewish law as a whole? In Gal 2.11–21 Paul makes clear that to comply with the Jewish food regulations is to cling to the 'works of law'. Paul, for his part, has 'torn down' (κατέλυσα, 2.18) the law even in (or: precisely in!) this respect; he is, in other words, 'through the law dead to the law'. Surely there could be no uncertainty whatsoever among the Galatian readers of the letter that it was the Jewish Torah with its food regulations that Paul was speaking of. It is just as clear that the same Torah is spoken of in 3.10–14, a passage in which Paul cites Deuteronomy to show the obligation of all who are 'of works of the law'. And in 3.17 the *nomos* is dated 430 years from Abraham.

Bearing this in mind, some statements of Paul in Gal 3 come as a surprise. He says in 3.13–14: Christ redeemed *us* from the curse of the law, in order that Abraham's blessing might in Christ come upon the *Gentiles*, in order that *we* would receive the promised Spirit. At the first glance it seems natural to think that 'we' in v. 13 refers to Paul and other *Jewish* Christians – it is only they that had been under the Torah before becoming Christians.[22] Several reasons, however, speak against this explanation.[23] In v. 14b the 'we' must in any case refer also to the Galatian Gentile Christians;[24] the mention of the Spirit ties with v. 2–5.[25] Now it would be strange, if the pronoun tacitly changed its reference in v. 14. There is no indication of any contrast between the 'us' of v. 13 and the 'Gentiles' of v. 14;[26] unlike 2.14ff. Paul does not deal with the difference between Jews and Gentiles at all in this passage.

---

the pious Gentile fulfil a minimum of the Torah; cf. Bruce, 'Paul' 270; against Edwards, *Christ* 242.

21 Despite Gaston, art.cit. 63; according to him 1 Cor 9.20–22 'must be interpreted in terms of four groups', of which 'those under the law' are the Gentiles!

22 So the commentaries of Lightfoot, Lietzmann, Burton, Duncan, Sieffert, Lagrange, Betz; Feine, *Evangelium* 200; Maurer, *Gesetzeslehre* 23; Hahn, 'Gesetzesverständnis' 55; Bligh, *Galatians* 264 f. Bligh also realizes that the context does not favour this explanation. He finds a way out with the ingenious hypothesis that ch. 3 was originally the continuation of Paul's speech in Antioch, which begins in 2.14 (cf. 235 f.).

23 See, above all, Schlier and Hübner's critique of Hahn (*Gesetz* 134 f.); further Bousset, Ridderbos, Oepke, Loisy, Guthrie, Stamm, Bonnard, Mussner, Becker; Holsten, *Evangelium des Paulus* 162 f.; J. Walter, *Gehalt* 81 ff.; Luz, *Geschichtsverständnis* 152; Klein, *Rekonstruktion* 206 f.; Howard, *Crisis* 59; Byrne, *Sons* 153 (with n. 69).

24 So also those mentioned in n. 22 (except for Bligh).

25 Luz, op.cit. 152 n. 70.

26 Against Lietzmann, Duncan.

And how could the redemption of the Jews from the curse of the law bring the blessing to the Gentiles?[27] The context does not speak of the removal of the wall between the two races;[28] Paul is explicating the liberty of the Galatians, which is connected with the crucifixion. V. 13 ties with the opening verse (v. 1) of the passage.

Strange as it may appear, the conclusion is hard to avoid that even the *Gentiles* were, in Paul's mind when dictating this passage, *under the curse of the law*. This is in tension with Paul's assumption in 1 Cor 9.21 or Rom 2.12, or even Gal 2.14. Still, our conclusion is reinforced by the next passages in Gal.

The alteration of the pronouns in 3.23 ff. shows that in that passage, too, the first person plural includes the Galatians. In v. 23–25 Paul speaks of 'us' being under the law, which is pictured as prison guard and tutor. From the point of view of the subject-matter one would again think that he has the Jewish Christians in mind.[29] In v. 26, however, which is firmly connected with γάρ with the previous verses,[30] Paul addresses the Galatians directly in second person. Having said, '*We* are no longer under the tutor', he goes on: '*For you* are all children of God.' This time, too, the tacit assumption is that even Gentiles had been tutored by the law[31] – notwithstanding the difficulty of spelling out in concrete terms the contents of such an assumption. How could namely the Galatians' pre-Christian past under the control of heathen idols (called 'elements of the world' in 4.3, 8 f.) in any way be conceived as a preparatory stage which was all right until the coming of Christ?

The same phenomenon occurs a third time in 4.5–6.[32] God sent his Son

---

27 Cf. Schlier, who concludes: 'Die Heiden müssen doch wohl selbst von diesem Fluche losgekauft sein, um den Segen empfangen zu können.' Differently Duncan: Jews were not able to mediate the blessing, until they were themselves redeemed from the curse; cf. Lagrange. D.W.B. Robinson, 'Distinction' 34 likewise states that the gospel came to the Gentiles 'by the mouth of liberated Jews' (in some tension to this he notes p. 39 that 'the Gentiles' standing is made to appear almost independent of that of the Jews'). The task of a mediator is not, however, touched upon in the text.

28 As even Robinson, art.cit. 39 admits, the sequence of thought of Eph 2.14–18 is lacking in this context; against Lightfoot.

29 Sieffert, Lagrange (despite the fact that γάρ 'makes of v. 26 the proof of the preceding verse'), Duncan ('primarily'), Betz; Byrne, op.cit. 164 f., 172 f. Robinson, art.cit. 35 assumes 'some unexpressed step in thought' – but why is the same step always left unexpressed throughout the chapter? Gaston, 'Paul' 63 claims that Paul is speaking of Gentiles alone!

30 Lagrange.

31 Most commentators think that Gentile Christians, too, are in view in v. 23–25; e.g. Bonnard, Schlier, Ridderbos, Mussner; van Dülmen, *Theologie* 46. More cautiously Oepke, Gyllenberg.

32 Bandstra, *Elements* 59 f. assumes that 4.3 and 4.5 (as well as 3.13) refer to Jewish Christians only, for the word 'heir' in 4.1–2. too, in his view, signifies Jewish Chris-

to redeem *those under the law,* in order that *we* would receive the status of children. Because *you* are children, *we*[33] have received the Spirit.

Still another cáse is 5.1. Christ has set *us* free; *be therefore* steadfast and do not allow yourselves to be bound again to the yoke of slavery.[34]

This accumulation of parallel cases[35] proves that we are not just faced with occasional careless phrasing.[36] Rather, we have to conclude that when Paul spoke of redemption from the curse of the law or of liberation from the power of the law, he did *not* always imply that the situation of the Gentiles was any different from that of the Jews.

Apparently without noticing it, Paul is thus tacitly operating with a double concept of 'law'. The context suggests that he is talking about the Sinaitic Torah, four hundred years later than Abraham, all the time. And yet the 'curse of the law' must, in view of the verses adduced, have a wider reference. One cannot avoid noticing 'a strange oscillation of the concept of law in Paul'[37] – an oscillation between the notion of a historical and particularist Torah and that of a general universal force. In view of Gal 3.23 ff. *nomos* cannot be understood simply as a 'historically limited phenomenon'. It is, rather, a 'qualifying concept'; ὑπὸ νόμον ἐφρουρούμεθα denotes 'the judgment passed from the view-point of Christ's coming on the pre-Christian existence of Jews and Gentiles'.[38] This 'qualifying' concept of law, besides being difficult in itself (see above), flatly contradicts the ideas set forth in 3.15–20, for in this passage the whole emphasis is placed on the fact that the

---

tians. In view of 3.29 (*you* are heirs), a verse referred to by Bandstra himself, I do not understand this argument. In 4.5–6 even Sieffert interprets the pronoun as including Gentile Christians.

33 Reading ἡμῶν with P[46] ℵ A B C D etc.

34 Robinson, art.cit. 34, sees even here an indication that the freedom of the believing Jew had consequences for the Gentiles.

35 To the verses cited Rom 7.4–6 can be added; rightly Howard, *Crisis* 59 f. There Paul proceeds by saying: *you* have died to the law; *you* belong now to another person (Christ), in order that *we* would bear fruit to God; for when *we* were in the flesh ... (in the rest of the passage the first person pronoun is used). Interestingly enough, the alteration of pronouns here takes place in reverse order in comparison with the passages in Gal – another proof that Paul does not have any 'mediating' role of 'us' in mind in Gal. It is, of course, difficult to know for sure, who the 'you' of Romans are, but surely they cannot be Jewish Christians only.

36 One might try to harmonize Paul's thoughts by saying that he thinks in 3.13 etc. of the Galatians as potential 'persons under the law', who have been set free from this yoke in advance by Christ, i.e., they have been liberated from the necessity to take the yoke of the law upon them. Yet v. 13b is clearly formulated from the point of view of those 'under the law', and 5.1 states: do not be *again* subjected to the yoke of slavery!

37 Luz, *Geschichtsverständnis* 153.

38 Op.cit. 155.

law arrived *late* on the scene. The chronological and the universal argument exclude each other.

Thus, while Paul is seemingly talking of the Mosaic law of Sinai, and even bases part of his argument on dating it in the time of Moses, the law nevertheless tacitly assumes much wider dimensions. Paul is simultaneously thinking of something that concerns all men, not just the Jews. The situation of Jew and Gentile melt together. The same thing in reverse order happens in 4.1–11. In this passage, the situation of the polytheist Galatians in their thraldom under quasi-gods before their conversion fuses together with the condition of the Jews under the law. *We* were enslaved under the elements of the world, says Paul (v. 3), thus including himself in the plight of his readers. Verse 4 then states that those *under the law* were redeemed and *'we'* became children. The Galatians had been slaves of the unreal gods (v. 8). Having become Christians, they now wish to *turn again* to those 'weak and beggarly elements', wanting *again* to be slaves to them (v. 9). The attempt to be subjugated to the *Jewish* law, represented in this connection by 'calendar piety'[39] (v. 10), is identical with a return to the previous thraldom (cf. 5.1, where the words 'again' and 'slavery' also occur).

If Paul previously assumed that somehow or other the Gentiles had been under the law, he now reversely suggests that the Jews are bound by the elements of the world. $\sigma\tauοιχεῖα$[40] most probably means cosmic astral powers[41]. The fact that Paul uses the word nowhere else as well as the fact that he can introduce it here without a word of explanation indicate that he got it from the Galatian scene (in Col 2 the term certainly goes back to the Colossian 'philosophy'). Paul intends to associate the Galatians' turning to the Torah with their pre-Christian pagan existence (which may have been characterized by subjugation to astral 'elements' of the world). Thus the Torah comes to look like a 'universally enslaving power'.[42]

It would be logical to conclude that Paul included the Torah in the 'elements' of the world.[43] It is doubtful, however, whether Paul would have pro-

---

39 Cf. Vielhauer, 'Gesetzesdienst' 552.
40 On the history of interpretation see Bandstra, *Elements* 5–30; for the use of the term outside the NT ibid. 31–46.
41 Dibelius, *Geisterwelt* 79–85; Lietzmann, Schlier, Bonnard, Oepke, Guthrie, Betz; Lohse, *Kolosserbrief* 146–149; Reicke, 'Law' 261 f.; Howard, *Crisis* 67, etc. The meaning 'what is characteristic of this world', proposed by Delling, '$\sigma\tauοιχεῖου$' 685 and Vielhauer, art.cit. 553 is too abstract. The argument that no clear evidence for $\sigma\tauοιχεῖα$ meaning astral powers is available from the period prior to the second or even the fourth century can, in view of the fragmentary nature of the extant evidence, hardly be conclusive.
42 Vielhauer, art.cit. 553.
43 Thus Reicke, art.cit. 259 and passim; Delling, art.cit. 684; Drane, *Paul* 38. While logical in one respect, this thesis would bring Paul into conflict with other statements

ceeded to this conclusion, however logical. In 3.19–20 he had suggested that the law had been given by the angels, therefore not by God himself; and yet in the very next verses he could argue that the law had a divine purpose.[44] It is quite common that Paul does not follow a line of argument to its logical conclusion. Moreover, if the logic of Gal 4.1 ff. were pressed, it would follow that the 'unreal gods' (which the elements are, according to verses 8–9) were destined by the one true God to have the positive rôle of ἐπίτροποι and οἰκονόμοι who watch over the minor heir until the time set by the father (v. 2). Something similar must be assumed, to be sure, if 3.23 ff. were to be taken literally (the heathen cult had been the Galatians' tutor until Christ!), but such cannot possibly be Paul's real view of heathen cults. Paul's point in Gal 4 is probably only the polemical one of suggesting that man's plight under the law is identical with his plight under the elements.

This point may seem plausible as long as it is kept in the abstract. If, however, one tries to give it a concrete form, one runs into the difficulty of having to accept the idols as 'tutors'. This state of affairs suggests that Paul did not always think through the logic of his arguments. Perhaps I may put it this way: *the solution is for Paul clearer than the problem*. The Christ event stands out as a liberating event of supreme importance, an event with universal implications, bringing freedom and peace to everyone willing to accept the message. At this point Paul is perfectly coherent. But when it comes to the description of *what men were liberated from*, the picture becomes more or less confused.[45] Thus we may see here already some evidence for E.P. Sanders's thesis (argued by him on other grounds) that Paul's 'description of the human plight varies, remaining constant only in the assertion of its universality'.[46]

3. Reduction of the Torah to the moral law?

Some interpreters assume that Paul made a conscious distinction between what might be called the cultic or ritual or ceremonial side of the Torah and its moral content.[47] Paul held that the cultic law was abolished in Christ,

---

of his, notably 3.15–20. The law can hardly be an episode in Jewish history, and simultaneously express that 'worauf die Existenz dieser Welt beruht und was auch das Sein des Menschen ausmacht' (thus the formulation of Delling, art.cit. 685).

44 On this, see below, IV 1.

45 Beker, *Paul* 49 n. correctly observes that 'the status of the Gentiles before Christ' remains unclear in Gal 3–4. 'The accent falls on the Christocentric confession of Gal. 3.26–29, which for Gentiles is the only reality that matters ... '

46 *Paul* 474.

47 It may be legitimate to use this somewhat anachronistic terminology for the sake of convenience. In terms of Jewish categories, one could speak of those 'commandments which govern relations between man and God' on one hand and those which 'govern

whereas the moral law remained in force.[48] On this view, the meaning of Gal 3.19 would be that what was given on Sinai by the angels was just the cultic law,[49] or parts of it, namely, the commandment of circumcision and the food regulations, which are in focus in Gal[50] – unless, with Hübner, one attributes the distinction to the Paul of Romans only.

In view of Rom 14.14,20, where Paul states that 'nothing is unclean in itself' and that 'everything is clean', Hübner, too, is inclined to assume that Paul had *consciously reflected* on the difference between the ritual and the moral aspects of the law and consciously rejected the ritual part.[51] It would thus be accidental that he never comes to speak of this distinction in his letters.

Despite Paul's sweeping assertions in Rom 14 (which are paralleled by 1 Cor 6.12, 10.23) several observations speak against such a distinction. For one thing, Rom 14 is not directly concerned with the Torah (nor are the passages in 1 Cor).[52] As will be shown below,[53] Paul did ignore the ritual Torah in his actual practice (when not pushed to act otherwise in a Jewish environment for strategic reasons); it is *not* clear, however, that this laxity witnesses to a reflected stance vis-a-vis the ritual law (as it is not clear either that Jesus' indubitable laxity in ritual matters stemmed from a reflected critical attitude to the cultic Torah[54]).

In Rom 9.4, the cult (λατρεία) is listed among the advantages given to Israel by God, and in the same breath with the 'promises' at that.[55] The 'glory' (δόξα) in the same verse undoubtedly includes, at least, the presence of

---

relations between man and man' on the other (E.P. Sanders, op.cit. 544). But this distinction does not quite match the evidence in Paul either; in the former class belongs also the prohibition of idolatry which is not, of course, rejected by Paul. It would be best to speak of such 'ritual' laws as 'created a social distinction between Jews and other races'; in practice this means circumcision, Sabbath, and food laws. See E.P. Sanders, *Law* 102. Unfortunately, the word 'ritual' may carry undesired negative overtones (cf. Neusner, *Idea* 1 f.); I wish to use it in a neutral sense.

48 C. Haufe, *Rechtfertigungslehre* 20 ff.; id., 'Stellung'; Ridderbos, *Paulus* 199. Holsten, *Zum Evangelium* 400 ff., assumed a self-explanatory distinction between the ethical and ritual stipulations. On this view, Paul would have excluded the ritual law from the Mosaic law altogether, possibly ascribing it to the πατρικαὶ παραδόσεις. Holsten later revoked this interpretation. His observation that Paul's polemic against the law, at the central places in Romans at least, is not directed to the ritual law, but rather to 'the law as God's absolute revelation' (401), was correct.

49 Thus Haufe, 'Stellung' (who thinks that the cultic law was fabricated by the angels); Bligh, *Galatians* 292, 296 f.

50 Thus Limbeck, *Ohnmacht* 93 f. and n. 28.

51 *Gesetz* 77–80; cf. also Luz, 'Gesetz' 108 f.

52 See below, p. 48.

53 See below, II 6.

54 See Braun, *Radikalismus* II, 7–14.

God's Shekinah in the cult.[56] Moreover, several of Paul's sharpest negative comments about the law have quite clearly the *moral* law in view. The indubitably moral injunction 'do not covet' led man into the power of sin (Rom 7.7–11, cf. Rom 7.5). The killing letter was found carved in stone tablets (2 Cor 3.6 f.) – a clear reference to the *Decalogue*; this is so despite the fact that according to Rom 13.9 the love command summarizes first of all the ethical precepts of the second tablet of the Decalogue! The law that brings about wrath (Rom 4.15) cannot be just – or even primarily – the ritual law; the same is true of the *nomos* apart from which righteousness has now become manifest (Rom 3.21). Had Paul really taught his converts that the 'ritual' law and that alone had been replaced[57], his task would indeed have been very much easier for instance when he set out to dictate Galatians. It would have been enough to refer to this definitive decision.[58] Paul's silence then appears symptomatic rather than accidental.

Thus, Paul can hardly have made any *conscious* distinction between the cultic and moral aspects of the Torah. Another thing is that *in actual fact* it is the cultic side of the law that stands in the forefront of Paul's discussion in Gal.[59] He there deals mainly with circumcision, food laws and calendar. It is actually quite commonly conceded that Paul does make an *unreflecting* or *unconscious* distinction (one speaks of an unconsciously-working principle of criticism) between ritual and moral law.[60] This state of things tends, however, to bring internal tension into modern interpretations of Paul: it is emphasized that he did not make the distinction and simultaneously also that he did.[61] Our survey starts from the observation that Paul at least does not make an *explicit* distinction. Should he nevertheless make the distinction implicitly, this would bring him into an implicit contradiction with his own notions. We will try to find out whether this is so.

Let us consider *Rom 2.12–16*. It is essential to realize that Paul is *in*

---

55 'Deutlicher könnte er nicht aussprechen, dass ihm die Thora eine durchaus einheitliche Grösse ist.' Werner, *Einfluss* 83. This is so whether or not Paul is using a traditional Hellenistic Jewish list in Rom 9.4 f. as is assumed by Byrne, *'Sons'* 83 f.

56 Michel.

57 Thus Ridderbos, op.cit. 199, cf. 83.

58 Correctly already Pfleiderer, *Paulinismus* 89; Stevens, *Theology* 166; Glock, *Gesetzesfrage* 142.

59 Cf. Bousset, *Galater* 50: in combating the law in Galatians, Paul has almost exclusively the ceremonial law in view. This is, according to Bousset, 'der ursprüngliche Sinn der Lehre des Paulus von der Rechtfertigung "nicht aus Gesetzes-Werken" '. Bousset, op.cit. 59, correctly notes that Paul does *not*, however make a 'grundsätzlich' distinction between ceremonial and moral law. He is followed by Guttmann, *Judentum* I 247 f.

60 Bultmann, *Theology* 261; cf. Conzelmann, *Outline* 223; Schrage, *Einzelgebote* 231; Grafe, *Lehre* 25.

61 Haufe, *Rechtfertigungslehre* 27 f., is correct in pointing this out.

principle talking of *the Torah throughout this passage.*[62] Possession or non-possession of the Torah divides mankind into two groups (v. 12). Still in v. 14a it is clearly the Torah that is spoken of: Gentiles, who do not possess the Torah, fulfil its requirements by nature. To assert that *nomos* changes its meaning after this — that Paul has a general moral law in mind in v. 14b[63] — is to spoil Paul's thought altogether.[64] The flow of thought requires that *nomos* carries the same meaning from beginning to end: the very law the Gentiles lack they actually 'are' for themselves, because they do what is required by this law.[65] Thus, it is possible to fulfil the Torah without actually possessing it.

The difficulty with this idea is, of course, that there were no Gentiles who fulfilled *all* commandments of the Torah, or even most of it. What Gentiles could fulfil was the ethical commandments.[66] Paul speaks of the 'law' in general, without hinting at any differentiation within it; still, in actual fact he seems to reduce it to a moral imperative.[67] This conclusion is reinforced when we turn to *Gal 5.14* and *Rom 13.8—10*.

In Gal 5.14 Paul states that 'the whole law (ὁ γὰρ πᾶς νόμος) is fulfilled (πεπλήρωται) in one word', namely in the command to love one's neighbour. This statement could be taken to mean that the Torah participates in the love command in all its individual commandments.[68] But then it is strange that

---

62 Against Riedl, *Heil* 198. He thinks that *nomos* means in Rom 2—3 'die göttliche Sittennorm, die sich für die Juden in ihrem mosaischen Gesetz und für die Heiden im sogenannten Naturgesetz kundgibt', for 'nur mit diesem weitgespannten Oberbegriff wird man allen neunzehn Stellen in Röm 2 sachlich gerecht (und ebenso den elf Stellen des dritten Kapitels)'. This interpretation makes nonsense of Paul's starting point (Rom 2.12) as well as of the ensuing statement that the Gentiles do *not* possess *nomos* (2.14).

63 Cf. Grafe, op.cit. 3; Bornkamm, *Ende* 101; Cambier, 'Jugement' 203.

64 Correctly Gutbrod, 'νόμος' 1062.

65 Correctly already Stevens, op.cit. 164; Bläser, op.cit. 20 f.; van Dülmen, *Theologie* 77: 'Diese den Heiden erkennbare Norm beurteilt Paulus so ausschliesslich vom mosaischen Gesetz her, dass man nicht von einem eigenen Gesetz der Heiden sprechen kann.'

66 There is no reason to take this to mean just occasional fulfilment of a few individual commandments, or the like; such watering down of the verse is disproved by 2.27. See the discussion below, III 3.

67 The statement by Käsemann, *Romans* 64, that 'the apostle does not restrict the Torah to the moral law ... and thereby dilute it' is correct, but only in so far as we are talking about Paul's *conscious* reasoning. That is, he did not *wish* to reduce the Torah to the moral law; what is implicit in his reasoning is another matter.

68 van Dülmen, op.cit. 60; cf. Ortkemper, *Leben* 179. Hübner, 'Das ganze Gesetz' 241 n. 13 is justified in pointing out a self-contradiction in van Dülmen's exegesis: on one hand she interprets the fulfilment of the law as keeping 'the whole law', on the other hand as keeping just the one commandment of loving one's neighbour. Thus, the following statement of van Dülmen, op.cit. 227, is extremely vague: 'Die Einzelgebote sind weder völlig beiseite gelassen, noch auch im einzelnen in ihrer ursprüngli-

Paul prohibits obedience to certain essential commandments of the Torah like circumcision and food regulations instead of viewing them, too, as interpretations of the love command.[69]

To be sure, in the parallel passage Rom 13.8–10 Paul seems to give just such an interpretation of the centrality of the love command: commandments like the prohibitions of adultery, murder, theft and coveting as well as 'any other commandment' (v. 9) are said to be 'summarized' (ἀνακεφαλαιοῦται) in the love command. But the striking thing here is precisely that Paul can in such a self-evident fashion *ignore* all 'ritual' commandments and indeed the whole question in which sense *they* may be said to be 'fulfilled' in the love command. Instead of making distinctions Paul seems simply to ignore the ritual part of the Torah as a non-entity.

It is, then, more natural to read Gal 5.14 and Rom 13.8–10[70] as speaking of a radical *reduction* of the law to the love command.[71] Where this one commandment is fulfilled, the Torah as a whole is fulfilled.[72]

---

chen Stellung geblieben, sondern sie sind in der Liebe in eins gefasst.'

69 Hübner, art.cit. 241.

70 Some interpreters construe Rom 13.8 as a statement about 'the other law', connecting τὸν ἕτερον with νόμον rather than with ἀγαπῶν; thus Gutbrod, art.cit. 1063, 1069 (who thinks of the 'law of Christ' without arguing the case, however); Marxsen, 'ἕτερος νόμος' 237; Merk, *Handeln* 165; Ulonska, *Paulus* 199 n. 146. According to Marxsen, the 'other law' refers to the law of Moses (as distinguished from the civil law of Rome, Rom 13.1–7). Thus in the end his interpretation leads to the same conclusion as the usual one. It is more natural, however, to connect τὸν ἕτερον with the participle ἀγαπῶν, especially as no *nomos* (from which the 'other law' could be distinguished) has been referred to in the preceding sentences (Cranfield). Marxsen (233) refers to the fact that the only unspecified objects of ἀγαπᾶν elsewhere in Paul are ἀλλήλους (1 Thess 4.9, Rom 13.8) and τὸν πλησίον (Gal 5.14, Rom 13.9); but this is a far too scanty sample to draw any conclusions. Note that Paul in Rom 2.1 speaks of κρίνειν τὸν ἕτερον, while the unspecified object elsewhere (Rom 14.13) is ἀλλήλους! Elsewhere in Paul ἀγαπᾶν is always used with an object. Cf. Ortkemper, *Leben* 128 n. 17; Michel, *Röm* 409 n. 5.

71 Thus, e.g., Maurer, *Gesetzeslehre* 30; Mussner; Furnish, *Love Command* 97. An implausible version of this interpretation is proposed by Feuillet, 'Loi' 797: when ἀνακεφαλαιοῦται (Rom 13.10) is interpreted in the light of Eph 1.10 and Barn 5.1, and πλήρωμα in the light of Col 2.9, 1.19, Eph 1.23, the sense turns out to be that love is 'the totality of the precepts of the law', which is more than the sum of its parts. 'Si la charité synthéthise tous les commandements, c'est en les dépassant.'

72 Hübner, art.cit. 243–248 and *Gesetz* 37–39 denies that Gal 5.14 refers to the Torah (as Rom 13.8–10 does). Instead, ὁ πᾶς νόμος is identical with the 'law' of Christ (Gal 6.2): 'Bear each other's burdens'. This interpretation, intended to remove an internal tension from Galatians (the discrepancy between 5.3 and 5.14) is not convincing, as it tries to drive a wedge between Gal 5.14 and Rom 13.8–10. Hübner (*Gesetz* 76) emphasizes the fact that the expression 'the *whole* law' is not repeated in Rom 13. But in enumerating commandments, which are comprised in the love command in Rom 13.9, Paul significantly adds: 'and if there is *any other* commandment'

It is only by tacitly reducing the Torah to a moral law that Paul can think of the Christians (as well as of some non-Christian Gentiles, Rom 2.14 f.) as fulfilling the Torah. This state of affairs is also revealed in Rom 8.4. If the 'just requirement *of the law*' is fulfilled in the life of Christians, *nomos* cannot really mean the Torah *in its totality*.

I find this very lack of explicitness significant. Paul conveys, after all, the *impression* of operating with one concept of law only, and I would assume that he is not conscious of his actual oscillation. Gardner seems to be right when he writes: 'The word "law"... he uses in many confused senses: sometimes of the Jewish ceremonial law, sometimes of the law of nature, sometimes of the voice of conscience; *but he does not realise this looseness of speech.*'[73]

But precisely such a 'looseness of speech' makes it more possible for Paul to impress his Christian readers on the emotional level. It is one thing to assert that we Christians (and we alone) fulfil the requirement of '*the law*'; it would be another thing (the connotations would be worlds apart) to note that Christians fulfil just the most important parts of the law (say, points *a* to *h*) while not fulfilling the rest (points *i* to *z*)! It is only by keeping his speech loose that Paul is able to assert that he 'upholds the law' (Rom 3.31).[74]

4. Analogies?

Are any analogies found to this looseness of speech, in particular to the implicit reduction of the law to its moral content, in early Christian or Jewish sources? We at first turn to the Christian sources.

a) Christian sources

It is not quite easy to compare the Gospels with Paul in terms of consistency. The Gospels, with the partial exception of the Fourth Gospel, do not set forth anything like connected arguments concerning theological themes. Statements about the attitude of a given Evangelist to the law are often second-hand inferences of the way he uses traditional materials. Where tensions occur, it is often difficult to determine whether this is a result of the gathering of differing traditions or whether the final editor's mind really is divided on a given point. The discussion must, therefore, remain inconclusive.

(καὶ εἴ τις ἑτέρα ἐντολή). This shows quite clearly that he has the idea of *totality* in mind in Romans as well; correctly Ortkemper, op.cit. 130 n. 32. Cf. E.P. Sanders, *Law* 96f.

73 Gardner, *Experience* 162 (emphasis added). Cf. M. Grant, *Paul* 49: it seems that Paul was 'shifting his ground to suit his argument'. E.P. Sanders, op.cit. 103: 'We cannot determine to what degree he was conscious of his own reduction of the law.' (See the whole discussion on pp. 96–105; note also the conclusion that Paul had unconsciously found 'a canon within the canon' p. 162.)

74 For a discussion of Rom 3.31 see below, II 5.

In *Mark*, the term νόμος does not occur at all. Mark does, however, speak of commandments (ἐντολαί 7.8 f., 10.5, 10.19, 12.28–31), and in this connection a difficulty at least remotely reminiscent of that found in Paul can be noticed. In Mk 10.18 f. Jesus points out that in order to inherit eternal life it is necessary to keep the commandments (τὰς ἐντολάς); the ensuing list of 'the commandments' includes moral commandments of the Decalogue only. Unfortunately, it is not quite clear how 12.28 ff. ought to be understood. The two commandments of love are singled out as the 'first' and 'second' commandment; in particular, love of God is said to be 'more' than 'holocausts and sacrifices' (v. 33). Are sacrifices rejected in this passage?[75] If so, Mark seems clear in his distinction between ritual and moral law (the former is rejected, the latter not). Yet 12.33 could also be understood as a distinction of value within an approved framework;[76] but then again – not least in view of 15.38 – this just mildly critical view of the cultic law could represent a traditional point of view and not quite that of Mark himself.

The greatest difficulty lies in the discussion of men's vs. God's commandments in ch. 7. There the tradition of the elders is condemned as implying a rejection of God's commandment (7.8 f.). And yet, in v. 15, interpreted in vv. 18–19 in a radical way, an essential part of *God's* commandments (mediated through the same Moses as the fourth commandment, cf. 7.10) is done away with. There is no problem in this, if we could ascribe to Mark ignorance of the fact that Jewish food laws were included in the Torah itself and were not just an invention of the tradition,[77] but can we really assume this? If yes, the problem is moved to another level; if not, then this gospel suggests that Jesus is 'the real fulfiller of the Israelitic-Jewish tradition' (ch. 12)[78] and simultaneously lets him tacitly abrogate central parts of it. It is not made clear what is meant by (God's) ἐντολαί.

Matthew offers the programmatic statement that Jesus did not come to annul (καταλῦσαι) the law, but to fulfil (πληρῶσαι) it (Mt 5.17). 5.18, a verse stemming from Matthew's tradition, states rigorously that not a single iota will disappear from the law. Whatever tensions may be caused by the nature of his traditions (individual commandments of the law are at least modified in Mt 5.21–48), Matthew clearly refrains from viewing the old law as annulled (Jesus is its final interpreter, to be sure). In view of this, a crucial question is, what is the attitude of the Matthaean Jesus to the ceremonial law? If he rejects it, then the talk of 'not annulling' cannot be taken at face value (however πληρῶσαι is interpreted) and Matthew is using a double concept of law, much as Paul is. Unfortunately, the situation is far from clear, and the answers of

---

75 Thus Pesch, *Mk* ad loc., following Berger, *Gesetzesauslegung* 197.
76 Cf. Nineham, *Mk* 327; Taylor.
77 See below, II 9.
78 H-W. Kuhn, 'Problem' 304.

different scholars to the question are different; we will have to return to that question in the next chapter.[79] 9.13 and 12.7 do not necessarily indicate that sacrifices are rejected in principle (although they certainly are subordinated to higher commandments). 24.20 hints at rigorous observance of the Sabbath in the community behind Matthew — but at which point in its history? 15.11, 17 would seem to show that food regulations were done away with by Jesus, but in the editorial comment v. 20 Matthew may indicate that the whole discussion has been concerned with the Pharisaic tradition about the washing of hands. At no point, then, does Matthew clearly state that the ceremonial law has been annulled. If his congregation did indeed observe the ceremonial Torah, 5.17 is not problematic; if, however, it did not (which is, of course, plausible if a large part of the congregation was Gentile) then we have here a tension comparable to that found in Paul.

It would seem that *Luke* does *not* reduce the Torah to the moral law. On the contrary, the law is for Luke 'the mark of distinction between Jews and non-Jews'. Its heart is circumcision, which is never spiritualized or reinterpreted.[80] Moreover, Luke does not even distinguish between the 'customs' (the tradition) and the law;[81] both are binding for the Jewish Christians. The Jewish Christians, including Paul, continue to observe the ritual law, which remains in force for those to whom it was designed; as for Gentiles, they are obliged to observe the minimum of ritual law set down in the Apostolic Decree. Stephen's harsh words about the Temple (Acts 7.48–50) are not developed to a critique of the sacrificial law; on the contrary, the accusations against Stephen speaking against the law are explicitly designated as false (6.13). In Luke, then, the concept of law is clear and does not oscillate.

Unlike Paul and others, the *Fourth Evangelist* does not say that the love commandment is the fulfilment of the law. It is offered as a new commandment given by Jesus. The idea of fulfilment is present in John only as far as the prophecying function of the law is concerned. Jesus transcends the law; it is not suggested that its commandments are fulfilled among Christians. John is thus free from the difficulties of Paul.

In *Hebrews* the law is viewed exclusively as cultic law. As such it is disparaged, retaining its value only insofar as it in a shadowy way points to Christ. The cultic law is scorned from a rational point of view: it is impossible that the blood of bulls and goats could take away sins (Heb 10.4). The moral side of the Torah is hardly touched upon.[82] The author deals with the law from a limited angle, but the coherence of his thought is irreproachable.

---

79 See below, II 9.

80 Jervell, *Luke* 137.

81 Jervell, op.cit. 136, 140.

82 It is not correct to say that the law is implicitly reduced to social law; thus Schulz, op.cit. 262. He refers to 2.2 f. and 12.25, inferring that the moral law has 'unein-

If the author of *Colossians* (whom I take to be someone other than Paul) is talking about the law in 2.8—15, which is not clear[83], then the notion of law oscillates in a way reminiscent of the authentic Paul. The concern of the author is with the ascetic stipulations typical of the syncretistic philosophy holding sway in Colossae (2.8, 20, 22). The addressees, uncircumcised Gentiles, had been made living by God, in that he, among other things, wiped off the 'document written by hands, which stood against us' through the death of Christ. Thus, the Gentiles had to be freed from that 'document'. *If* the law is meant, then we have here an exact analogy to Paul's argument in Gal 3 and 4.[84] Law takes on the general meaning 'legalism'.

In 1 Tim 1.4—10 the concept of 'law' oscillates as in Paul. The opponents of the writer call themselves νομοδιδάσκαλοι (v. 7), and they are concerned with 'myths and genealogies' (v. 4). They are thus pictured as (phoney) experts in Jewish law. Unlike those people who do not understand what they are talking about (v. 7), we know, the writer says, that the law (ὁ νόμος) is good, if it is used properly (νομίμως, v. 8). The sequel shows that the writer no longer has the Torah in mind, but rather a general moral law, or the law of the state,[85] for the law does not exist for the just man but only for the impious (a vice list follows, v. 9 ff.). *Nomos* is well on its way toward a broad 'moralistic' sense.

The letter of *James*, too, is reminiscent of Paul, as regards the use of *nomos*. In view of verses like 4.11—12 'nomos clearly means the "old" law'. Typically enough, however, the cultic stipulations the author 'simply passes over ... in silence'; 'when he speaks of *nomos*, even what he calls the "whole law", he simply ignores their existence'.[86] The ethical content of the OT law melts together with the new Christian ethical admonitions into one 'law',

---

geschränkte Heilsbedeutung gerade auch für das neue Gottesvolk'. Yet the Mosaic law functions in these verses, to which 10.28 can be added, only as a part within a conclusion *a minore ad maius*: if transgression of that law already incurred a severe punishment, how much more reason there is to take seriously that 'so great salvation proclaimed in the beginning by the Lord' (2.3)! Luz, 'Gesetz' 114 vigorously denies the law any role in the life of Christians according to Hebrews.

83 See below, VII 1.
84 Interestingly enough, even the pronouns alterate much as they do in Gal 3. *You* were made living, and God thus forgave *us* our trespasses (vl: you, K L P 6 323 326 al), wiping off the writing that was against *us*, the writer says. If the writer is writing from a Jewish Christian perspective (but is he? anyway, as 'Paul' he ought to!), then, exactly as in Gal 3—4, the plight of the Gentiles under angelic powers and that of the Jews under the law melt together. Yet this similarity turns out to be accidental, if E.P. Sanders is right in the suggestion that Col 2.13 is a conflation of Rom 6.11 and Rom 8.32 ('Dependence' 40 f.).
85 Cf. Dibelius; Houlden, *Past* 53, 58.
86 Seitz, 'James' 485.

the 'perfect law of liberty' (1.25). This assimilation is best revealed in 2.8–13, where, within the same thought, 'the royal law' (v. 8) and in particular 'the law of liberty', through which the readers are to be judged, suggests the new Christian norm whereas the "whole law" is seen as consisting characteristically of the Decalogue. At this point, then, at least, Paul and James come close together.

Later writers were able to avoid our problem altogether by explicitly making the very distinction within the law which Paul is so reluctant to spell out. Thus, the letter of Barnabas explicitly abandoned the ritual law, consciously reducing the law to its moral content, and Ptolemy, in his letter to Flora, worked out a clear-cut tripartite division within the Old Testament law. It is interesting, however, to conclude our survey by mentioning a thinker who was *almost*, but not quite, explicit in his distinction between moral and ceremonial law. For Justin, the moral law constitutes no problem. His problem is the ritual part of the law, and it is only this that is called *nomos* in his writings.[87] The ritual law was only given as temporal legislation for the Jews.[88] Yet, 'It is true that Justin does *not explicitly* isolate and designate a "ceremonial" Law, nor does he distinguish an "ethical" Law'; 'nevertheless, his concept of the division of the Law into various parts seems actually to determine his treatment of the Law' and 'constitutes one of the most decisive aspects of his understanding of the Law'.[89] Justin does not build his argument about the law on an oscillating use of the concept; he is reminiscent of Paul to a certain extent in not being explicit in his distinctions. Stylianopoulos' explanation of this lack of explicitness is interesting: 'Perhaps ... Justin's high regard for the authority of Scripture unconsciously prevented him from working out a bolder and more sharply defined breakdown of the unity of Scripture in the manner of Ptolemy. We find a similar case in Irenaeus and Tertullian both of whom are aware of a certain stratification and differentiation in Scripture, but do not proceed to an objective analysis of it ...' Not so Ptolemy, having 'few scruples about the authority of Scripture as a whole'. It is the Gnostic exegete who 'provides a kind of scientifically critical account of the diversity of the Mosaic Law, parts of which he rejects as unworthy of God and others as being the work of men'.[90] That Paul, too, had unconscious scruples about the authority of Scripture as a whole, which prevented him from making distinctions which the logic of his position would actually have required, seems a not unlikely conjecture.

---

87 Stylianopoulos, *Justin* 50 f., 59.

88 Cf. *Dial*. 21.1, 22.1 etc.; see the list of passages in Stylianopoulos, op.cit. 142.

89 Stylianopoulos, op.cit. 51 n. 19, 53; these statements tacitly correct the statement on p. 51 that Justin is 'the first Christian writer *explicitly* to distinguish different parts within the Law and the OT' (emphasis added).

90 Op.cit. 74 f.

Thus, Paul's problem reappears in the Deutero-Paulines as well as in the letter of James, possibly also in Mark and Matthew. Unclarity about the concept of the law is common to larger segments of early Christian thought. Lip service to the unity of God's word in Scripture is coupled with an actual rejection of parts of it — a rejection which is never directly admitted.

b) Jewish sources

In the Babylonian Talmud (Shab 31a) it is told that Hillel once summarized the law in the golden rule (in a negative form): 'What is hateful to you, do not do to your neighbour: that is the whole Torah, while the rest is commentary thereof; go and learn it.'[91] This famous dictum is hardly a real parallel to Gal 5.14, Rom 13.8–10.[92] The rest of the Torah is *not* branded as *unnecessary*; it is made to serve the love command as a commentary of it. This would seem to correspond to the notion, mentioned above[93], that 'the Torah participates in the love command in all its individual commandments'. The headache of Hillel would be to provide the proof that this is so; Paul's particular difficulty he does not share. We have here, furthermore, a typical *ad hoc*-statement, from which it would be utterly unwise to squeeze a general doctrine; the dictum is offered as proof of Hillel's celebrated gentleness, as an answer to the irreverent question of a Gentile (which *must* be answered briefly, if it is to be answered at all; and the moment of surprise contained in the answer is just what is appropriate in such a context).[94] Thus, we have an example of paraenetic and even missionary *concentration* of the Torah in a particular situation on its ethical content — concentration, not reduction. It is of course inconceivable that a Hillel would have rejected, or recommended to anybody a rejection, of the actual observance of the Torah in practice for the sake of the golden rule.[95] There is no watering down of the concept

---

91 The authenticity of the anecdote is denied by Neusner, *Traditions* I, 324.339 f. The story certainly reflects 'the Hillelite viewpoint, but we have no idea whatever which Hillelites' (324). Cf. n. 95.

92 Jeremias, 'Paulus' 89 f. thinks that Paul got the idea of summarizing the law in the love command from the school of Hillel, who in turn got this daring novelty from the Stoics (90).

93 Cf. above, p. 26.

94 Nissen, *Gott* 390 is correct in stating that Hillel's statement is more a *captatio benevolentiae* than a serious reply; cf. 396: 'Hillel wäre nicht Hillel, wenn er mit diesem Satz dem Heiden mehr als eine Brücke hätte bauen wollen, um ihn über sie zur Tora selbst zu bringen. This particular dictum belongs together with Hillel's answer to two other Gentiles: one wanted to become a proselyte because of his vanity, the other did not want to accept the oral law; Hillel turned neither away but introduced each pedagogically to start with learning the Torah. Nothing more is implied in the 'summing up' of the law in the Golden Rule, which is thus not intended as a 'summary' at all.

95 It is surely even less likely that later Hillelites using Hillel 'as a paragon of virtue' (Neusner, op.cit. 339) would have done so.

of the Torah here. But of course the fact of a concentration on the moral aspect commands attention; in *this* (partial) respect Paul comes close to Hillel.

Concentration on moral commandments and values in the law is all the more conspicuous in Hellenistic Jewish sources, notably in the Testaments of the Patriarchs, the Letter of Aristeas, Philo, Pseudo-Phocylides and the Sibylline Oracles. Klaus Berger has argued that there were among Hellenist Jews antinomian groups, who had actually reduced the Torah to a worship of the one true God plus certain social commands and virtues;[96] in their concept of law the ritual Torah played no part. Gal 5 and Rom 13 show that Paul stands wholly within that tradition.[97] If this were so, then Paul simply inherited his looseness of speech and his implicit reduction of the law from Hellenistic Judaism.

It is right that moral and 'social' commandments are vigorously emphasized in the said texts, which are either almost silent about ritual law (Test. Patr.) or give allegorical interpretations of it (Aristeas, Philo). And yet it is patently wrong to speak of *anti*nomian or anticeremonial traits in the piety of the people behind these writings. As for the Testaments, it is sufficient to refer to the critique of Berger's thesis by Hübner.[98] See, in particular, Test. Levi 9.7, 16.1; food laws are interpreted symbolically in Test. Asher 2.9–10, 4.5.[99]

That an emphasis on social values in the law does not exclude observation of the ritual stipulations and an appreciation of the cult, is perfectly clear from the Letter of Aristeas and the writings of Philo. Both writers contend that all precepts of the Torah serve its basic ethical intentions. The 'apology of the law' in the Letter of Aristeas (129–171) is summed up in the statements that the law prohibits injuring anybody (cf. Romans 13) and that everything has been laid down πρὸς δικαιοσύνην – so, too, the food regulations (167–169). The writer emphasizes the symbolical meaning that supposedly underlies every single stipulation, but does *not* conclude that, once the deeper meaning has been perceived, the external observance can be dropped. Observation of the ritual commandments is, on the contrary, important, not least because these commandments *separate* the Jews from perni-

---

96 *Gesetzesauslegung* 1, 38–55 and passim. The thesis is sharply dismissed by Nissen, op.cit. 229 n. 589.
97 Berger, op.cit. 51.
98 Hübner, 'Mark 7.1–23', 326–329.
99 Should Eissfeldt, *Einleitung* 858 f., 861 and others be right in the assumption that the Testaments are products of the Qumran community, this provenance would be enough to refute Berger's theory; one could hardly connect the idea of a relaxation of the Torah with Qumran. Yet this hypothesis is today rightly rejected; cf. Charlesworth, *Pseudepigrapha* 212.

cious company (esp. 139).[100] With the aid of allegorical method the writer manages to argue that all parts of the law, including the food laws, really serve to the attainment of justice. The method is, of course, as arbitrary as could be, but the resulting conception is coherent. There is no reduction of the law in content.

Philo is reminiscent of Rom 13.8—10 in that the Decalogue has the pride of place in his ethical thought as is clear from the fact that he feels no need to allegorize the Ten Commandments (see *Decal.*). With other parts of the Torah it is different. It is only by lavish allegorizing that Philo is able to squeeze a meaning from ritual stipulations. Yet he shrinks from the conclusion that the external rites could be left unobserved. His well-known critique of some Alexandrian 'allegorizers'[101] shows indisputably, where he draws the boundary line — as well as the fact that he himself is extremely close to stepping over the line (*Migr. Abr.* 89 ff.). Philo does not find any fault with the symbolic interpretation of the Torah by the allegorizers; this he fully shares with them. Yet when they draw practical conclusions and give up scrupulous observance of the law, Philo turns against them. The only reason, however, he is able to adduce to refute them, is a social (!) consideration: the allegorizers fail to appreciate the fact that they live within a community, overlooking all that the mass of men regard (!) and endangering their good repute (90). Circumcision, e.g., has a concealed symbolic meaning, 'but let us not on this account repeal the law laid down for circumcising'. Why not? Because keeping the external things helps to gain a clearer conception of the symbols — and, besides, 'we shall not incur the censure of the many and the charges they are sure to bring against us' (93)!

It is clear that in itself the ritual law is devoid of value for Philo. Ritual precepts can only be valued when interpreted symbolically. Yet there is an emotional bond between the exegete and practical observance of the Torah, which Philo cannot bring himself to break — largely because of social pressure, as the passage referred to reveals.[102] But in the end Philo makes it clear in no uncertain terms that the ritual side cannot be excluded from the law.[103] There

---

100 Cf. Tcherikover, 'Ideology' 79. Tcherikover makes a case for the assumption that the letter was intended for fellow Jews. The Torah alone could open the cultural world for Jews, and therefore the Jews ought to keep the practical prescriptions of the Torah with the utmost care and punctiliousness. Contrast Berger's talk of the reduction of the law in Aristeas 168; op.cit. 46.

101 See on these Wolfson, *Philo* I, 66—71.

102 Berger, op.cit. 173 states that for Philo and others 'war die Abschaffung der Ritual- und Reinheitsgesetze nur verhindert durch die Anwendung der allegorischen Methode, die mit der innewohnenden Inkonsequenz zur Erhaltung des Bestehenden beitrug'. This statement reverses the order of cause and consequence.

103 It is wrong to interpret the passage *Spec. leg.* III, 208—209 as a parallel to Mk 7.15, as Berger, op.cit. 465—467 does. Philo there develops the idea that 'Everything ...

is no reduction here either. In actual practice Philo shows a steadfast loyalty
to his tradition; as regards apostates he even gives expression to an over-
zealous sentiment (a hidden need to defend himself, one may psychologize).[104]

Thus both 'Aristeas' and Philo represent the notion that every single precept of the law in some way reflects an overriding ethical concern. The letter
of Aristeas calls this concern δικαιοσύνη; Philo tries to subsume the whole
Mosaic legislation under headings provided by the Decalogue. And yet the
discussion with the allegorizers shows how close Philo comes to the critical
line which was overstepped by the Christians when they gave up observing the
ritual law. The allegorizers, whoever they were, were predecessors of Paul
in this regard. One would wish to know more about them! But what little we
know through Philo at least does not suggest that they shared the oscillation
of the concept of law with Paul: they were quite consciously dropping major
parts of the law.[105]

One of Berger's witnesses is the didactic poem of Pseudo-Phocylides.[106]
At the end of the moral exhortations which make up the writing it is stated
(v. 228): ἁγνείη ψυχῆς οὐ σώματός εἰσι καθαρμοί.[107] 'Purifications are
for[108] the purity of the soul, not of the body.' Berger takes this line as a
parallel to Mark 7.15.[109]

---

that the unclean person touches must be unclean', for 'the unjust and impious man
is in the truest sense unclean'. Characteristically, Philo does not say that everything
is clean for a clean person; he contents himself with the statement that 'all the
doings of the good are laudable'. See for criticisms also Hübner, art.cit. 338; followed by van der Horst, 'Pseudo-Phocylides' 201.

104 In *Spec. leg.* I, 54–57, 316, Philo strongly supports the execution of apostates, even
without a court process, in the style of Phinehas (for the problems involved see
Heinemann, *Bildung* 223–225; Colson, *Philo* VII, 616–18). Cf. Philo's attitude to
death penalties in *Spec. leg.* II, 242–257. It should be noted, however, that apostasy
does not in this connection mean the neglect of Sabbath or food laws (the trespass
of the allegorizers), but participation in a pagan cult. This is where Philo drew the final
boundary line.

105 Should Vermes, 'Decalogue' be right in his contention that the *Minim*, whose claims
caused the Decalogue to be dropped from daily Jewish public prayer at about the end
of the first century, were Hellenistic Jews rather than Christians (cf. yBer 3c [1.5]
and parallel passages) then they, too, are to be mentioned in this connection. These
'heretics' are said to have claimed that the Decalogue alone was given to Moses on
Sinai.

106 Similarly Kasting, *Anfänge* 26 speaks (on the basis of Ps.-Phocylides and the Alexandrian allegorizers) of 'unhesitating negligence and critique' of the Mosaic law.

107 Bernays, *Abhandlungen* 247 n. 1 considered the verse, in view of its loose connection
with the context, a gloss. This theory, held 'unnecessary' by van der Horst, *Sentences* 258, would make a difference only if the supposed gloss was made by a
Christian and not by a Jew.

108 Reading ἁγνείη (dative) with van der Horst, op.cit. 200.

109 Berger, op.cit. 467.

Although some suspicion regarding the origin of the poem may remain,[110] it is safe enough to start from the assumption that it is a Jewish pseudepigraph,[111] all the more so as the writer seems to draw on a tradition used by Josephus and Philo as well.[112] As for the Torah, the poem is extremely selective. The material found in it is almost exclusively of a moral nature — almost but not quite. One or two ritual precepts are included, but they are susceptible of a (secondary) moral or aesthetic explanation, or have some point of contact with Graeco-Roman ideas.[113] This is the case with v. 147—148, an adaptation of Ex 22.31 (30) (cf. Lev 22.8, Ezek 44.31; a milder version in Lev 17.15). Interestingly enough, a 'humanistic' or 'aesthetic' motivation is given to the ritual precept: only beasts eat beasts.[114] These verses, as well as v. 139, converge with Graeco-Roman ideas. The command (v. 84—85) to leave the mother bird upon the nest when one takes her young is interpreted morally as a token of gentleness.[115] On the whole, 'it looks as if the author did his utmost to conceal his Jewishness'.[116]

What, then, is his attitude to the ritual law? The question is not easy to answer. It is connected with another unsolved problem: whom was the author writing to? One possible answer is that he is consciously making an effort to win the attention of Gentiles; this is why he leaves out all that is specifically Jewish, moving roughly within the framework of the Noachian commandments.[117] The surprising thing is, however, that not a word is said against idolatry, the Gentile sin par excellence in the eyes of any Jew. Another solution, too, has been offered: Pseudo-Phocylides is writing for fellow Jews and can therefore take a lot of things for granted.[118] It is extremely difficult

---

110 Dalbert, *Theologie* 9—11 leaves Pseudo-Phocylides out of his study of Hellenistic Jewish theology; cf. Hübner, art.cit. 338 n. 4.

111 Thus in a fundamental study that has not lost its relevance with time Bernays, op. cit. 192 ff.; recently van der Horst, *Sentences*; id., 'Pseudo-Phocylides' 188.

112 See Crouch, *Origin* 84 ff.

113 Bernays, op.cit. 227.

114 See Bernays, op.cit. 239—241.

115 Bernays, op.cit. 235. This precept is also found in the summaries of the Jewish law offered by Philo (*Hyp.*, in Eusebius, *Praep. evang.* VIII, 7, 9) and Josephus (*Ap.* II, 213); behind these authors a common tradition must have existed. See Crouch, op. cit. 86; van der Horst, 'Pseudo-Phocylides' 194. Rabbinic tradition (cf. DeutR 6.2) 'viewed this commandment ... as the least weighty of all commandments and coupled it with the weightiest of commandments, that one should honor father and mother'; Crouch, op.cit. 86.

116 van der Horst, *Sentences* 70. Verse 31 which warns of the eating of blood and sacrificing to idols is inauthentic both on internal and external (only one inferior manuscript contains it) grounds; see van der Horst, op.cit. 135. The interpolation is probably due to a Christian reader and its source is Acts 15. Flusser, 'Christenheit' 61 n. 3 considers the verse a Hellenistic Jewish interpolation.

117 Bernays, op.cit. 251 f.; Guttmann, *Judentum* I, 112; Crouch, op.cit. 98.

118 Cf. Hengel, *Judentum* 129 f., 307; see the discussion in van der Horst, op.cit. 71 f.,

to choose between these options.[119] As far as our problem is concerned, however, *either* of them could explain why so little is made of the ritual law. Either the author was silent about it because he wanted, before a pagan audience, to demonstrate the grandeur of the Jewish ethics while avoiding mention of what was the offence from the readers' point of view; or, he just did not have to mention the ceremonial Torah to his Jewish readers, whose sense of identity he perhaps tried to strengthen by pointing out that what was valued by the Gentile environment was already found in their own Torah. Either way, the prominence of general moral teaching in the poem could be accounted for without the hypothesis that the author had abandoned the ritual law.

Even apart from these considerations, v. 228 is in itself a rather tenuous basis for far-reaching conclusions; 'the text and meaning of this verse are rather uncertain'.[120] Should the reading τοῦ σώματος be original instead of οὐ, we would have a clear reference to purifications of the body that are not abandoned. But even reading οὐ, does not the verse take the existence of cleansing rites for granted? It would seem to be intended to point out the real *meaning* of the external rites, a meaning that is spiritual and internalized. On this reading, the line is in perfect harmony with Philo and with the letter of Aristeas, where a spiritual interpretation is given to food laws and sacrifices (170) and attention is called to the state of mind of one making a sacrifice. Compare Aristeas 234: 'Honouring God is done not with gifts or sacrifices, but with purity of soul ...'[121] Just as this statement does not mean that Pseudo-Aristeas rejects gifts and sacrifices, one cannot safely conclude that rites of purity are rejected by Pseudo-Phocylides. There is no solid support for Berger's thesis in Pseudo-Phocylides. There is, to be sure, a heavy *concentration* on the moral side of the law, which is helpful for understanding Paul, but *no* demonstrable *reduction* of it to a moral law.

Berger further appeals to the Jewish portions in the Sibylline oracles. Following Friedländer[122] he claims that III Sib means by 'law' only 'pure worship of God, philanthropy and noble manners'.[123] His most important proof is III 246. This verse is the conclusion of a panegyric description of 'the race of the most righteous men' (219), in particular of the Jews' δικαιοσύνη and ἀρετή (234). In v. 246 these social virtues are summed up in the words πληροῦντες μεγαλοῖο θεοῦ φάτιν ἔννομον ὕμνον, which Berger takes to mean:

---

76. This solution is connected with an overall view of Hellenistic Jewish literature as directed to the Jews themselves; cf. also Hengel, 'Anonymität' 306.

119 After a careful weighing of the alternatives van der Horst, op.cit. 70 ff. prefers to leave the question open.

120 van der Horst, op.cit. 258.

121 van der Horst, op.cit. 259.

122 Friedländer, *Geschichte* 48 f.

123 Berger, op.cit. 41.

the law is *completely* fulfilled, when righteousness has been reached in this way. This is a highly doubtful interpretation of the line. What purpose would it have served to dwell on the particularist aspects of the Jewish way in this piece of eloquent missionary propaganda? The particularism has been consciously concealed in the poem, for the 'Sibyl' tries to find points of contact in the Gentiles' own thought. It is the author's aim to convert his readers to observe the Noachian commandments, not the whole Torah; the perfect and final conversion of the nations is expected to take place in the Reign of God only.[124] When dealing with this kind of literature, conclusions from silence can be very misleading.

There are, in fact, several indications in the poem of the continuing relevance of ritual precepts for the writer. In v. 272 the 'customs' ($\tau\dot{\alpha}$ $\check{\epsilon}\vartheta\iota\mu\alpha$), with which the neighbours in the Dispersion take offence, are referred to in a quite positive fashion. Self-evidently, this does not mean the social virtues, but things like the Sabbath. The attitude to the Temple is positive throughout, as is clear from numerous verses (266, 281, 575, 686, 688, 717, 733–34). The animal sacrifices in the Temple are spoken of in an affirmative fashion in 575–79. 592 mentions daily ablutions in the same breath with moral virtues (cf. 591–595 as a whole). The ritual aspect of the law is, to be sure, held to a minimum in the poem, but no antinomian attitude can be detected.[125] We move in the same world with the writings dealt with above.

Nevertheless, a broadening of the notion of the law comparable to that found in Paul is visible in III 600: Gentiles have (through homosexuality) 'transgressed the holy law of the immortal God'. But we hear nothing of Gentiles *fulfilling* that law, except in the eschatological Reign of God.[126] Thus, III Sib, like the other writings discussed, comes close to Paul in its concentration on the moral law and, at the same time, is clearly different from Paul in that the ritual Torah is not discarded either.

According to some interpreters, *IV Sib* (unlike III Sib) rejects the Temple, the sacrificial cult and the ceremonial law altogether.[127] This is inferred from IV 8.27–30. Yet in these verses only temples with images are criticized, that is, pagan shrines. At the first glance IV 29–30 goes further, criticizing all animal sacrifices (which will cease in the eschatological future). But in view of

---

124 Cf. Nikiprowetzky, *Sibylle* 170 ff.
125 Nikiprowetzky, op.cit. 78 n. 1.
126 Cf. v. 719, 757–759. One would like to know, which law they will then fulfil, the whole old Torah or the moral law? If it is the latter, then one has to concede that the concept oscillates here much as it does in Paul. But the temple of Jerusalem will remain the centre of universal cult (v. 772 ff.) so that most probably the nations are thought to convert to the actual Torah.
127 Friedländer, op.cit. 52 f.; similarly Simon, *Stephen* 87 f. Friedländer's view is connected with his improbable thesis of the Essene character of the Sibyllines; on this, see Nikiprowetzky, op.cit. 229 ff.; Noack, 'Essenes'.

the context, the most natural interpretation seems to be that even these verses are directed against pagan temples only.[128] The fourth book of Sibyl was written about 80 AD. At this time nobody had any reason to attack the Jerusalem Temple, which had lain in ruins for a decade! And elsewhere in the same book (130–136) the eruption of Vesuvius is explained as a punishment for the destruction of the temple of Jerusalem. One could hardly wish for a clearer proof of the affirmative attitude of the author to the latter.[129]

We have thus found concentration on the moral side of the Torah, but not its reduction to that side only, in Hellenistic Jewish literature. But what about the Jewish missionary practice in the Dispersion? This practice aimed more at winning over 'God-fearing' sympathisers than full proselytes, a procedure which was rationalised by the theory of the Noachian commandments designed — unlike the Torah — for the whole of mankind.[130] In Paulinist jargon, one might detect here an 'unconsciously-working principle of criticism'[131], emphasizing the moral side of the law at the cost of the ritual side; the Jews were only more explicit in their reflection on these matters.

It is sometimes claimed that Hellenistic Jews did not necessarily require even circumcision from proselytes. To be sure, IV Sib 165 cannot bear the burden of proof.[132] McEleney, however, adduces evidence for the thesis that the requirement of circumcision was not *always* strictly observed, if special circumstances made it appear undesirable.[133] He concludes: 'Jews of the Hellenistic world seem much more ready to accept someone who refused circumcision as a convert to Judaism and as a brother Jew, *provided that in all things else he kept the ordinances and customs.* Even Palestinian Jews speak of those opposed to only this precept.'[134] It is clear that we cannot

---

128 Schürer, *Geschichte* IV, 580; Noack, art.cit. 97 f.
129 Nikiprowetzky, op.cit. 233 f.
130 See on these e.g. Guttmann, op.cit. 98–114; Crouch, op.cit. 91 ff.
131 Cf. above, p. 25.
132 Berger (who mistakenly gives the reference as 'III Sib 164') thinks that this verse presupposes that only a baptismal bath was required of converted Gentiles; similarly Billerbeck, *Kommentar* I, 106 n. 1; Schmithals, *Römerbrief* 73 f; Scharlemann, *Stephen* 114. Yet there is no warrant for the suggestion that the reference is to the proselyte baptism; we probably have a simple allusion to the language of Isa 1.16 (thus Kurfess, *Weissagungen* ad loc.; cf. Nikiprowetzky, op.cit. 243–248). Billerbeck and Berger mistakenly appeal to Schürer, *Geschichte* IV, 173. To be sure, Schürer uses misleading language, speaking of proselyte baptism (p. 184, 580). Yet he makes clear that he is *not* thereby thinking of proselytes proper: 'Also selbst da, wo eine *volle* Aufnahme in die Gemeinschaft Israels *nicht* stattgefunden hat, ist wenigstens das Wasserbad gefordert worden' (184). Schürer thinks that the Gentiles of IV Sib 165 are 'God-fearers'.
133 Cf. the story of Izates in Josephus, *Ant.* XX, 38 ff.; Philo, *Quaest. in Ex.* II, 2; Pes 96a; Hull 4b; Ned 3.11; Yeb 46a. See McEleney, 'Conversion' 328–333, but also the critique by Nolland, 'Proselytes'.
134 Art.cit. 332. McEleney points out that first-century Judaism was apparently 'much

speak of reduction or rejection of the ritual law here. Circumcision is the *only* ordinance that can, under special circumstances like a danger of life, be unobserved, provided everything else is kept![135]

Thus the difference between Palestinian and Dispersion missionary practice is not that the Hellenistic Jews accepted proselytes with mitigated conditions; they did not. The difference is that they welcomed 'God-fearers', who did not make a full conversion, whereas in Palestine a convert who did not accept the whole Torah remained a Gentile, hardly or not at all distinguished from other non-Jews in Jewish judgment.[136]

Paradoxically, the Hellenistic Jewish practice both diminished and enhanced the significance of the ritual law. It diminished it in that the Noachian commandments were admitted to be sufficient for Gentiles. But observance of these commandments did not bring with it membership in Israel. Thus, at the same time, it became clear that circumcision and ritual law were *very* essential — they constituted the difference between a God-fearer and a proselyte. In taking this difference seriously the theology of Jewish mission was logical, avoiding blurring the contours of the Torah. In reading Hellenistic Jewish propaganda literature one must take its concrete setting into account. The Gentile addressees were, of course, not expected to make a conversion in a private vacuum. They were expected to join the gathering in the Synagogue. And in a synagogue they would see what the Jewish way of life *in its totality* looked like.[137] Characteristically enough, many God-fearers were not content with the moral law alone, but strove to observe the Sabbath and the food regulations as well, and often the next generation would proceed to take the decisive step and become full proselytes (see esp. Juvenal, *Sat.* 14, 96–106).[138]

In comparison with this literature, Paul looks both similar and dissimilar to it. But where Hellenistic Jews clung to the whole Torah with a new accentuation, Paul's solution amounted to 'the whole Torah and yet not the whole Torah'. In our survey we have not found real parallels to Paul's oscillating use of the concept of law.

---

more open on this question' than is usually thought, (332 f.) but this has nothing to do with a reduction of the ritual law, as circumcision *alone* was involved.

135 This very reason, the danger of life, underlay the advice of Ananias that Izates should not be circumcised. For the correct interpretation of this story which is often wrongly made to serve the thesis of laxity concerning the Torah in Hellenistic Judaism, see Bamberger, *Proselytism* 49; Kasting, op.cit. 25; Siegert, 'Gottesfürchtige' 129.

136 K.G. Kuhn, 'προσήλυτος' 734; Kuhn-Stegemann, 'Proselyten' 1267; cf. Siegert, art. cit. 125 f. The existence of 'God-fearers' as a class is doubted by Kraabel, 'Disappearance'.

137 See Guttmann, op.cit. 96.

138 See Schürer, op.cit. III, 172–175.

II. Is the law still in force?

1. The abolition of the law

Paul makes several harsh and biting comments about the law, emphasizing the Christians' freedom from it. There is no unanimity, however, about how such statements should be interpreted. Does Paul really mean that the Torah has been superseded, or is he speaking of something else? One of the recent interpreters who deny emphatically that Paul regarded the law as abolished is Cranfield.[1] According to him, it is not the law itself that is criticized and rejected by Paul, but rather the (alleged) Jewish misunderstanding and misuse of the Torah, which was perverted by Jewish teaching to a legalistic code requiring meritorious deeds. It is not astonishing that Cranfield's view is shared by many conservative scholars. But there are also surprisingly close points of contact between his interpretation and that of much less conservative exegetes, including Bultmann.[2] Recently Hübner has argued that, whereas Paul in Galatians argues that the law has been superseded, in Romans he holds that the law is in force; it is only the perverted and misunderstood law that is done away with. God's Torah has been reinforced as the 'law of faith' (Rom 3.27) and as the 'law of Spirit' (Rom 8.2).[3] It will be convenient to postpone the discussion of Hübner's view to the next section and begin with an examination of Cranfield's interpretation.

Cranfield asks us in particular to bear in mind that the 'Greek language of

---

1 'Paul', esp. 53 ff.; id., *Romans* 851 ff. Cf. Moule, 'Obligation'; Ellis, *Use* 27; Siegwalt, *Loi* 199 ff.; Bring, 'Paul' 25 ff.; Dequeker, 'Dialog' 14; Stegemann, 'Jude' 134 f.; Thyen, 'Exegese' 151; von der Osten-Sacken (see below, II 2). A somewhat similar view was already set forth by A. Zahn, *Gesetz*, esp. 15 ff.

2 Bultmann, *Theology* 341 states ambiguously that Christ is the end of the law insofar as the law 'claimed to be the way to salvation or was understood by man as the means of establishing "his own righteousness" '. The first part of the sentence attributes the fault to the law itself, the latter part to man alone. Schlier, *Grundzüge* 92 ff., would seem to side with the latter alternative. Käsemann is more explicit: he speaks of a perversion of the law's original intention (*Romans* 198; cf. 89) through men in that the law came to be understood as a demand for achievement. He adds, however, that the law was eventually *'irreparably'* perverted (216), giving thus a reason why the divine law, the intention of which was to bring grace, was nevertheless radically done away with by Paul. One wonders a little, though, at the demonic power thus ascribed to man's interpretation of the law!

3 Hübner, *Gesetz* 118–129.

Paul's day possessed no word-group corresponding to our "legalism", "legalist" and "legalistic" '. We should, therefore, always 'be ready to reckon with the possibility that Pauline statements, which at first sight seem to disparage the law, were really directed not against the law itself but against that misunderstanding and misuse of it for which we now have a convenient terminology'.[4] It turns out that this is, for Cranfield, always the case, when Paul appears to be critical of the law.

In Gal 3.15–20 Paul makes five points which are hard to reconcile with Cranfield's view. 1) The law arrived late on the scene: on Sinai, 430 years after the promise. 2) The law had a negative purpose: it was given 'for transgressions.' 3) It was to be a temporary arrangement, valid (but really valid!) until the 'seed' comes. 4) It was given by angels. 5) It was received (or given, see below) by a mediator, and this somehow or other shows its distance from God who is one.

Cranfield's attempt to get rid of these difficulties is an eloquent bit of special pleading. In the mention of the angels he sees only 'a certain superiority of the promise ... over the law', and in the statement about the mediator 'a certain depreciatory flavour'.[5] The statement that the law was added has a purely chronological content without any critical theological note.[6] As for the negative purpose of the law, that was not its only purpose. Finally, commenting on the ἄχρις-clause which refers to the temporary nature of the law, Cranfield, appealing to Calvin, states that there is 'a tendency in this passage to regard the law somewhat narrowly'. This is so because Paul was disputing with false teachers and refuting their 'excessive exaltation of the law'. *Nomos* means here the 'bare law' (*nuda lex*, Calvin), understood 'in a narrow sense'. It 'is not the law in the fullness and wholeness of its true character, but the law as seen apart from Christ'.[7]

One wonders whether Paul's vocabulary really lacked words to express clearly such a meaning if he intended it. Of course he had no technical term corresponding to Calvin's *nuda lex* or our 'legalism' at his disposal; yet a Paul might have been able to form a few sentences through which to indicate that he wished to make such an important distinction between the law and its false interpretation.

Be that as it may, the weakness of Cranfield's view becomes evident as soon as one tries to give it a concrete form. Where did the 'bare law' actually

---

4 *Romans* 853; cf. 'Paul' 55.
5 'Paul' 61 f.; *Romans* 858. Still further in diluting Paul's message goes the systematic theologian Bring, *Christus* 82 f. He interprets the mention of the angels in the light of Acts 7.53 as appreciative and constructs a special interpretation of v. 20 (see below, p. 130 n. 16).
6 'Paul' 61; *Romans* 857 f.
7 'Paul' 62 f.; *Romans* 859.

come from? As Paul says in v. 19 that the *nomos* was given by angels, and as
the word can hardly tacitly change its meaning in the middle of the sentence,
Cranfield's explanation must imply that the 'law as seen apart from Christ'
was given by the angels. Did the angels, then, add the possibility (or necessity?)
of a legalistic perversion to the law given at Sinai 430 years after the promise?
What could that mean? And if we somehow manage to imagine that this is
what happened at Sinai, according to Gal 3.19, then when was 'the law in the
fullness of its true character' given? Furthermore, why were temporary limits
set to the 'bare law', and by whom? Was the 'bare law', after all, intended by
God for a certain period — even though legalism is emphatically said to be a
perversion caused by men? One sees that Calvin's and Cranfield's interpretation has no chance of survival except in the abstract. The same is true of *any*
interpretation that lets Paul only reject a misunderstanding but not the
Torah: Gal 3.15—20 constitutes an insuperable difficulty for all such attempts.
The perversion is a deed of *men*, not of angels; but Gal 3.19 explains the
inferior character of the *nomos* by hinting at its angelic origin. Whatever Paul
may have meant elsewhere, in this particular passage he certainly makes a
case against the Torah itself.[8] The law is seen as a temporary addition to
God's real plan.

In 3.24, the law is compared to a παιδαγωγός — no flattering image.[9] V. 25
states that after the faith has come we are no longer under the παιδαγωγός.
4.5 says that Christ redeemed those under the law, in order that they would
receive sonship; according to 3.26 'sonship' is the new situation where the
παιδαγωγός is no longer needed. For sonship to be available, men had to be
redeemed from under the *nomos*. That this cannot mean 'bare law' should be
clear from the statement that Christ himself became 'under the law'. Would
Paul have said that Christ was subjected to the 'bare law', the 'law as seen
apart from Christ'? Cranfield ignores all these statements in his article.

The allegory in Gal 4.21—31 is also to be mentioned here. While the application that Hagar is equivalent to the 'present Jerusalem' may be compatible
with the idea that Jewish misunderstanding alone is under attack, her identification with 'mount *Sinai*' (v. 24 f.) is not. It is the Mosaic law itself that
enslaves those under it.

In *2 Cor 3* Paul speaks of the law as 'letter' which 'kills', as opposed to the
life-giving Spirit. This, according to Cranfield, again means the legalism of the
Jews[10] or — as Cranfield notes on the same phrase in Rom 7.6 — the letter of

---

8 This has to be said also against Vielhauer, 'Gesetzesdienst' 553, according to whom
   Paul does not speak of the law 'as such' in Gal, but only as a 'principle of achievement'; in a similar vein Harrington, *People* 50.
9 On the image see Oepke and Betz.
10 'Paul' 57; *Romans* 854.

the law 'bereft of the Spirit'.[11] Rom 7.6b cannot oppose the law itself to the Spirit, 'for only a few verses later (7.14) Paul says that the law is "spiritual" .[12]

In 2 Cor 3 the interpretation that γράμμα means Jewish legalism rather than the Torah is impossible, however. Paul speaks of the activity of *Moses* (not Pharisaic teachers) and makes a deprecatory reference to the *tablets of stone* — the very core of God's law in as original a form as possible. *Here* is the killing letter to be found![13] V. 7 reinforces the point: the ministry of Moses was a ministry of death, being in the service of that which was 'carved in *letters* on stones'. The association of this reference to the Decalogue with the talk of the 'letter' in the previous verse is unmistakable. There is no allusion at all to a later misinterpretation or misuse of the stone tablets. That this evaluation of the law stands indeed in an irreconcilable contradiction to Rom 7.14 ('we know that the law is spiritual') is another matter and must not obscure the clear message of 2 Cor 3.6–7, amply confirmed by the context there.[14] When interpreting the participle 'fading away' (τὸ καταργούμενον v. 11, to reappear in v. 13) Cranfield does his utmost to remove any thought of the passing away of the law or of the old covenant: the reference is merely to 'the ministry of Moses at the giving of the law'.[15] But how could one thus isolate the ministry of Moses from the larger context of the old covenant? How could the 'ministry' of Moses *per se* be called 'the ministry of condemnation' (v. 9)? Paul is indeed speaking of the ministry of Moses — but not as an isolated event, but as a symbol of the old covenant.[16] It is just as clear that the ingenious piece of exegesis in v. 13 does not merely speak of the face of Moses; this, too, is offered as a symbol of the old system of the law, which was 'fading away'.[17]

Both in Gal 3 and in 2 Cor 3 Paul speaks quite clearly of the inferior,

---

11 'Paul' 56.

12 'Paul' 56. Once more Cranfield's interpretation comes close to that of scholars of a quite different school of thought. γράμμα is understood as a reference to Jewish misinterpretation of the law also by Bultmann and Barrett, ad loc., and by Käsemann, *Versuche* I, 222; Schrage, *Einzelgebote* 76 f.; Dugandzic, 'Ja' 113. Correctly Kremer, 'Buchstabe' 225 f.

13 The 'killing' probably refers to the condemning function of the law; 'the ministry of condemnation' v. 9 is identical with the 'ministry of death' v. 7.

14 In the framework of a development theory (see above, p. 7)   Sieffert, 'Entwicklungslinie' 348 noted that Paul speaks in 2 Cor 3 in a way 'definitely different' from that in Romans.

15 'Paul' 58; *Romans* 855.

16 The word καταργούμενον in v. 11 is correctly interpreted by Barrett: the reference is to 'the law as a transient phenomenon belonging to a past age'. Cf. Fung, 'Justification' 260 n. 37: 'Since ministry is based on covenant, the two stand or fall together.'

17 It is improbable that Paul would think that Moses covered his face just 'from reverential motives', because the end of the radiance, as well as its beginning, was 'too sacred for human gaze'; thus Hickling, 'Sequence' 390 f.

transient and temporary character of the law given at Sinai. There is no hint whatsoever in these passages of a secondary legalistic misinterpretation. Instead, one may ask whether the talk of the law as 'letter' in 2 Cor 3 does not imply the idea of an *original* 'legalism' inherent in the law. In this case, 'legalism' certainly cannot be interpreted as human self-righteousness; it would merely denote slavery to precepts and ordinances (cf. Gal 4.25) without taking into account the attitude of the man under law. This understanding would fit together with the emphasis on freedom both in Gal 4–5 and 2 Cor 3.17; in the latter case ἐλευθερία is introduced rather abruptly into the discussion. Freedom, at least in Gal, is not pictured as freedom from self-centredness, boasting and the like, but from slavery under the law and/or the elements of the world. These considerations will concern us later on (see below, p. 233f.).

Rom 7.1–6 is just as clear. The Christians have become dead to the law through the (mortified) body of Christ (v. 4); they have been 'destroyed' as regards the law, liberated from its bondage (v. 6). The 'old situation' of the 'letter' has been replaced by the 'new situation of the Spirit' (v. 6). Once more Cranfield takes *nomos* 'in a limited sense'. The Christians have been freed from 'the law's condemnation and also all legalistic misunderstanding and misuse of the law'.[18] This statement is unclear in that it introduces two limitations of the law which do not easily fit together; the power to condemn is something inherent in the law, having nothing to do with men's perversion of it. A 'limitation' of the concept of law which would cover such quite different aspects would have been unintelligible to Paul's readers, to say the least.[19] As for the 'misunderstanding' aspect, it is hard to understand why a method as drastic as the *death* both of Christ and of the Christians would have been necessary to get rid of a mere misunderstanding about the law. A new revelation about its true meaning would have sufficed. Nothing in 7.1–6 suggests that men's perversion of the law is being spoken of. On the contrary, Paul is speaking of something that is *absolutely binding* except in quite particular circumstances. Paul is *struggling* to find a valid reason for the Christian's freedom from the *nomos*. It seems that he has no clear argument conveniently at hand; on the contrary, he has to take refuge in a rather tortured allegory, the application of which is lost in internal contradictions.[20] Clearly, much more is at stake than a human misunderstanding of what the law was about.

---

18 'Paul' 56.

19 In his commentary on Romans (853) Cranfield in fact mentions only the 'condemnation' aspect at this point; yet he mentions Rom 7.6b again on p. 854, this time in connection with the misuse theory. Meyer, 'End' 73 likewise maintains that, according to Rom 7.1–6, the law is not annulled, but 'the power of the law to condemn is broken'.

20 On this, see below, p. 61 f.

The limitation of the meaning of *nomos* to the condemning power of the law in this passage seems arbitrary, too. The allegory does not suggest that some partial aspect of *nomos* is being spoken of. The impression is, on the contrary, of something 'totalitarian'. The *nomos* is the master of man as long as he lives; death is needed to change the (total) situation. With death follows the change of master (or of 'husband', in the language of the allegory). Who could have taken this to mean that man is no longer bound to *one* aspect of the law, whereas the bond connecting him with other sides of it still holds? To be sure, Paul does think that condemnation and curse are among the unpleasant features of the law, and it is an essential part of the Christian's freedom that he has been liberated from them (Gal 3.13, Rom 8.1). But precisely this is characteristic of his thinking, that he is not content with a revision of the law, but proclaims freedom from the law as a whole. Or so he writes in the passages we have dealt with so far. Finally, it should be noted that Rom 7.6 takes up central elements from both Gal 3 (the notion of bondage under the prison-guard, κατειχόμεθα) and from 2 Cor 3 (the contrast between letter and Spirit), so that it would be highly unnatural to interpret this verse in a different way altogether. A new emphasis is on the aspect of 'newness': God has done something 'new', and therefore one ought not to cling to what is old.

The idea of liberation from the law is alluded to briefly in *Rom 6.14*. The Christians are 'not under law, but under grace'. This means for Cranfield that they 'have been freed from its condemnation and curse' and 'from the vain quest for righteousness by works of the law'. Neither idea is suggested by the context. There the question is raised whether it is a consequence of the freedom from the nomos that 'we' should *sin* (v. 15). It is indeed the false inference that to be under the dominion of grace (the opposite of nomos in v. 14) means to remain in sin that is the starting-point of Paul's discussion in Rom 6 (v. 1). The assumption, then, must be that the Christians are free from the *ordinances* of the law. The abstract assertion that they are free from the condemnation that the law proclaims over sinners, while observing its actual commandments, could hardly have given rise to objections or mocking questions about bad life among the Christians (v. 1, 15).

We turn to passages which are not treated at all by Cranfield. In *Gal 2.18* Paul says explicitly that he has (along with Peter and others) 'torn down' the law or at least parts of it. The context shows that the reference is (at least primarily) to the food regulations which Paul as well as Peter had once given up (but which Peter and Barnabas had, under external pressure, taken seriously again).[21] To observe such ordinances is, for Paul, an ἔργον νόμου (v. 16).

---

21 It is debated whether Gal 2.15–21 in general and 2.18 in particular is meant as a

Before the episode in Antioch both Paul and Peter had lived ἐθνικῶς not ἰουδαϊκῶς (v. 14). Paul has, by dying to the law, changed a life for the law to a life for *God* (v. 19). The attitude taken to the law is thus wholly negative, and there is in the context nothing to suggest a limited sense for *nomos*. Whatever διὰ νόμου in v. 19 may mean, the idea can hardly be that by discovering the true meaning of one aspect in the law, Paul become dead to another!

The sweeping statements about a Christian's freedom, which to be sure must not be misused and which can be voluntarily limited for the weaker brother's sake, but which on principle is quite unlimited, also witness to the fact that Paul felt free from the Torah. Thus, he can say with respect to foods that 'nothing is unclean in itself' (Rom 14.14) or that 'everything is clean' (Rom 14.20). Admittedly, what is spoken of in Rom 14 is not the Torah, but an ascetic piety which may or may not have been connected with some sectarian Jewish currents of the time.[22] Nevertheless, a statement so sweeping in its implications would be very surprising in the mouth of one who considered the Torah as valid as ever. The point is reinforced in 1 Cor 10.23, where Paul treats the question of meat offered to idols. This time, too, the question of the law is not in focus; nevertheless, it is clear that the eating of εἰδωλόθυτα, an abomination for any 'normal' pious Jew, was an *adiaphoron* for Paul. It is striking that he does not resort to the first commandment.[23] The tie between him and the Torah had been much relaxed indeed.

This is true not only of the ritual side of the Torah. The Corinthian slogan 'all things are lawful', cited twice by Paul (10.23 and 6.12), is used in 6.12 in connection with a moral issue (fornication). The Corinthians seem to have appealed to this slogan in favour of sexual licence, and Paul does nothing to refute the principle as such! He knows that fornication is incompatible with the life in Christ, but *he has no code to which he could appeal to persuade*

---

report of Paul's reply to Peter in Antioch, or whether he has at this point moved to deal with the Galatian situation alone. In the latter case one could not draw from this verse conclusions about the background of the Antiochian conflict. This is the view of Kümmel, 'Individualgeschichte' 161 f. It is clear that Paul has not just Peter in view in 2.15 ff.; that is, he is also thinking of the situation in Galatia. But the point is that he still has the Antiochian episode, *too*, before his eyes. It is precisely because he sees an analogy between the two situations that he takes up the old conflict in the new situation. Cf. Burton, Schlier, Oepke, Ridderbos, Mussner (135, 178); Ridderbos is falsely listed by Kümmel as representing the narrower view.

22 Cf. Lietzmann. Some interpreters think that the talk of selecting 'days' (v. 5) may reflect the process of the Sabbath giving way to Sunday (Dodd); yet fasting days or some other special days may be meant (Lietzmann). Michel thinks nevertheless that 'Paul is consciously opposing Israel's understanding of the law', allocating the contrast of clean and unclean to the old aeon (*Röm* 432).

23 Cf. E. P. Sanders, *Law* 95.

the Corinthians about this, so that all he can do is to show how the slogan is correctly interpreted.[24] Everything is lawful, to be sure, but everything is not 'useful'.

One may ask, where the Corinthians got their slogan from. It is not impossible that it represents an element of Paul's own teaching in Corinth, from which the Corinthians had later made inferences not intended by Paul.[25] *If* this is so, if Paul had indeed said to the Corinthians that everything was lawful, such a statement must originally have belonged to the context of an evaluation of the Jewish law;[26] otherwise its libertinism is simply unintelligible. But even if the slogan does not go back to Paul himself, it is striking that Paul does not feel called to refute it. The slogan represents a sentiment shared by him! All he can do is to argue for a different application of the libertinist principle.

It would seem, then, that in his actual teaching Paul ignored the Torah — the ritual and moral side alike. That much of his ethics actually conformed to the standards laid down in the Torah is another matter. Paul is not at all without concrete standards, he is no moral anarchist. In the actual contents of his ethics he is clearly a Jew.[27] But he does not derive his moral exhortations formally from the Torah — despite occasional references to the Bible.[28] This is also clear from such passages as Rom 12.1–2, Phil 1.10 and Phil 4.8. The two first-mentioned passages admonish the Christians to *examine* (δοκιμάζειν) *what* God's will is, what is 'good and well-pleasing and perfect'. There is no code to tell this in all concrete situations;[29] cf. also Rom 14.22 f.[30] Phil 4.8 again summarizes the ideals of a Christian life in terms of popular moral philosophy (no doubt mediated through the Hellenistic Synagogue).[31]

---

24 Cf. Burton, *Gal* 453.

25 Cf. Lütgert, *Freiheitspredigt* 37 f.; Lietzmann (as a question); Drane, *Paul* 67 f. ('presumably'); Holtz, 'Frage' 387.

26 Holtz, ibid.

27 Sanders, op.cit. 94–96.

28 See Bläser, *Gesetz* 229, and below. Bläser (229 f.) notes: 'And how often would Paul have had an opportunity to refer to the commandments of the Decalogue! That he does not do so indicates that even the Decalogue as such does not lay obligations upon the Christian.'

29 In Rom 2.18 Paul says that the Jew 'examines' what is important (δοκιμάζεις τὰ διαφέροντα, cf. Phil 1.10!) as well, but he adds: 'being instructed through the law' (κατηχούμενος ἐκ τοῦ νόμου). Instead of the law, the Christian's δοκιμάζειν is guided by the 'renewal of his mind' (Rom 12.2), his growing in ἐπίγνωσις and αἴσθησις (Phil 1.9). The lack of 'law' language in these contexts would seem symptomatic. Cf. Maurer, *Gesetzeslehre* 89; Therrien, *Discernement* 179.

30 Rom 14 provides a concrete example of what δοκιμάζειν could be in practice. The use of the word in 14.22 shows that Paul recognizes the possibility of divergent opinions in some matters at least as a consequence of the δοκιμάζειν. Cf. Therrien, op.cit. 148–154.

31 Schrage, Einzelgebote 170 f. would take λογίζεσθε in Phil 4.8 in a critical sense:

In summary, Paul's writings abound in statements which justify the claim that a radical critique of the Torah is the 'unmistakable characteristic' of his theology.[32] That this is not the whole story we will see shortly. For the moment the point is that this radical line of thought cannot be explained away. Paul did assert that the Torah had been superseded in Christ.

It will be noted that the classical statement about Christ as the *telos* of the law has not even been mentioned so far. This is because the interpretation of that very verse is particularly disputed. But no matter whether Paul in that particular place is speaking of the end or of the goal of the law, the existence of the notion of Christ as the 'end' or termination of the law must be regarded as an established fact. Before turning to an exegesis of Rom 10.4, however, we will discuss a recent attempt to show that in Romans, at least, Paul does not reject the law.

2. Is the 'law of faith' the Torah?

Peter von der Osten-Sacken and Hans Hübner have, independently of each other, argued on the basis of Rom 3.27 and 8.2 that Paul did not, after all, regard the Torah as abolished. Hübner makes, it will be remembered, a distinction between Galatians and Romans in this regard.[33] According to these scholars, the expressions 'law of faith' (Rom 3.27) and 'the law of the Spirit of life' (Rom 8.2) are not metaphorical ways of speaking of the new order of things or the like, as most interpreters have thought, but refer to the Torah.[34] When the Torah is, in faith in Christ, rightly interpreted, it is seen to be a 'law of faith' and a 'law of Spirit'. These are proper designations of the Torah

---

Christians have to contemplate what men regard as good and right, but they have to measure this by the critical standards provided by apostolic teaching and example (cf. v. 9). But it is surely artificial to take v. 9 as a limitation or corrective of the virtue list of v. 8 (as if the Philippians were to ponder all customary virtues but to realize only those of them that they have learnt from the apostle or seen come true in him – a method which would in fact render the pondering superfluous). It is more natural to take the verses together: the Philippians should keep in mind the virtues in question and put them into practice, for it is along the same lines they have been taught by the apostle in word and deed; cf. Gnilka ad loc. I cannot find evidence for the use of λογίζεσθαι in the sense of 'ponder critically' in Paul.

32 Käsemann, *Romans* on 7.1–6.

33 See above, p. 8.

34 Wilckens, *Römer* II 89, 122 claims that there is in classical or Hellenistic Greek no evidence for νόμος meaning 'rule' or 'order'. This is wrong. To mention only cases where νόμος is used with a genitive: νόμος or νόμοι πολέμου designates the kind of conduct usually shown in a war: Josephus, *Bell.* II, 90; VI, 239.346.353; *Ant.* I, 315; XV, 157; Polybios II, 58, 10 etc. Sometimes πολέμου νόμῳ means simply 'in a war', e.g. Appianus, *Basil.* I, 2. To walk νόμῳ πομπῆς means 'in a procession' (Polyaenus, Strategem. V, 5, 2); νόμῳ φιλίας again 'in a friendly way' (id. VII, 11, 6). A man and a woman can have intercourse κατ' ἔρωτος νόμον (Antonius Diogenes in Photios,

'insofar as one responds to it in faith'.[35] The 'law of faith' designates 'the right attitude to God's will ... as it finds its expression in the Torah'.[36]

There is a growing tendency among scholars to take *nomos* in the passages in question 'literally' as a reference to the Torah,[37] even if Osten-Sacken and Hübner have gone farther than others in their conclusions. I have discussed this interpretation in detail elsewhere[38] and believe that a short resumé will suffice here.

The main fault with the 'literal' interpretation is that it fails to take the linguistic structure of the verses in question seriously. Both in 3.27 and 8.2 the *nomos* has a very active role. 3.27 states that boasting was excluded (once and for all, aorist ἐξεκλείσθη)[39] *through* the νόμος πίστεως. The *nomos* is thus the *instrument*, by which boasting (namely, the boasting of the Jew of his distinction with respect to the Gentile) was excluded. This is hardly a way to describe the role of the Torah in the Christ event.[40] von der Osten-Sacken and Hübner have recourse to circumlocutions that do not correspond to the syntax of the text. They interpret it as a statement of what has happened to the *Torah* through *faith* (the true understanding of the Torah in faith has

---

Bibl. 109a 25 f.). ὁ νόμος τῆς ἱστορίας (Josephus, *Bell.* I, 11) or τῆς γραφῆς (*Bell.* V, 20) refers to the rules of historiography, οἱ ἀλληγορίας νόμοι (Philo, *Somn.* I, 102) to those of allegorical exegesis. οἱ σωφροσύνης νόμοι are the rules of modesty (Philo, *Spec. leg.* IV, 96) and οἱ νόμοι τῆς οἰκονομικῆς ἀρετῆς the rules of good economy (*Spec. leg.* II, 187). Perhaps the most striking case of all occurs in Josephus, *Ant.* I, 230. Abraham there tells Isaac that he is to leave this life νόμῳ θυσίας, 'through the rites of sacrifice', rather than by the common road (τὸν κοινόν ... τρόπον). νόμος is here almost equivalent to τρόπος. The list is by no means exhaustive. See now Räisänen, 'Sprachliches'.

When Wilckens adds in a footnote (*Römer* II 122 n. 491) that 'vor allem aber fehlen Belege für die Vorstellung verschiedener, gar einander entgegengesetzter "Ordnungen" bzw. "Normen", die jeweils als νόμος c.gen. bezeichnet würden', he is obviously requiring too much. Such an argument would hit Wilckens's own interpretation as well (where are the precedents for juxtaposing two νόμοι with genitive referring to two aspects of the same law?!). Nevertheless, in the last mentioned example from the Antiquities Josephus *could* have used νόμος (in the sense of 'way') twice.

35 von der Osten-Sacken, *Römer* 8, 245.
36 Hübner, *Gesetz* 119 f.; cf. id., 'Proprium' 465 f.
37 For 3.27 Friedrich, 'Gesetz'; Cranfield; for 8.2 Fuchs, *Freiheit* 85; for both verses Lohse, 'νόμος'; Hahn, 'Gesetzesverständnis 38, 41, 47–49; Wilckens; more references in Räisänen, 'Gesetz'. Cf. now also Stuhlmacher, *Versöhnung* 112, 160; Byrne, *Sons* 92 n. 47; Gaston, 'Paul' 65; Meyer, 'End' 73; also Berger, 'Abraham' 64 f.
38 Räisänen, 'Gesetz'.
39 Cf. Sanday-Headlam: 'an instance of the "summarizing" force of the aorist; "is shut out once for all", "by one decisive act". St. Paul has his eye rather upon the decisiveness of the act than upon its continued result.' Wilckens's suggestion that the unmentioned predicate of v. 27 might be supplied from v. 28 (δικαιοῦται) rather than from v. 27 (ἐξεκλείσθη) is implausible.
40 Wilckens's interpretation that the 'Torah of faith' is the Torah insofar as it is 'related to faith' faces the same difficulty.

given the law its proper place).[41] Paul, however, speaks of what has happened
to *boasting* through the '*law*' of faith. *Nomos* must be metaphorical; the new
'order of faith' is being referred to. It is hard to avoid seeing a polemical
nuance in the choice of words: the 'law of works' (3.27), that is the order of
the Torah, has been replaced by another 'law', which is actually the opposite
of the old one.[42]

In 8.2 the sentence runs: the *nomos* of the Spirit of life in Christ has
liberated thee from the *nomos* of sin and death. The first nomos is thus the
subject of man's liberation. Paul is not saying that the man who understands
the law in the right way will experience the Torah as the law of Spirit.[43] The
subject of the event in question is the nomos, not the understanding man![44]
Paul is speaking of the 'order' of the Spirit. There is no reason to abandon the
until recently almost universally accepted view that in these two passages Paul
is playing with words and using *nomos* — *this* time consciously, to be sure! —
in different senses. That he is conscious of what he is doing is clear from the
fact that the word *nomos* is each time furnished with a qualifying genitive.
As for 8.2, this word-play starts in 7.21—25, a passage where *nomos* is used in
three or four different senses![45] In both cases the choice of the word nomos
seems to be polemical; the positive *nomos* stands in contrast to the 'law of
works' (3.28) or to the 'law of sin and death' (8.2). It is these negative expressions alone that denote the Torah or at least the state of affairs closely
associated with the reign of the Torah[46], and not the positive ones! Rom
3.27 f. and 8.2 support the conclusion that Paul often speaks of the actual
abolition of the Torah.

---

41 von der Osten-Sacken, op.cit. 245; Hübner, op.cit. 119.

42 Cf. Käsemann, op.cit. 103, 215; Gyllenberg, *Rechtfertigung* 20.

43 Against Hübner, op.cit. 125 f. Wilckens, too, distorts the syntax of the sentence
when he writes: 'Thus the sentence 8.2 describes(!) the annulment of all condemna-
tion that took place in Christ (v. 1) as *a turn in the law itself* (his italics) from its
condemning function to the function that annuls this condemnation.' von der Osten-
Sacken, 'Befreiung' 350 emphasizes that we have 'to cling without compromise to
Paul's wording', but does not do so in his own paraphrase of Rom 8.2: 'Durch den
Geist Gottes ... wird das Gesetz ... aus einem Medium der Sünde und des Todes zur
Weisung der Gerechtigkeit und des Lebens.' (355). The syntactical position of νόμος
also warns against equating the law of the Spirit with 'the new morality' or with an
'inner law' (thus Michels, *Paul* 31, 49).

44 This mistake is especially clear in Fuchs, op.cit. 85, 87. In his short reply to me
Hübner (*Gesetz* 136 f.) evades the real issue by positing 'a .fundamental *theological*
dissent' between us. For me, the issue at stake is a strictly *syntactical* one.

45 See Räisänen, art.cit. 113 f. In this passage *nomos* is always used with a genitive
except in v. 23a where it has the attributive ἕτερος and in v. 21 where the unusual
meaning 'rule' is made plain in a clause which explicates the nature of the *nomos*
(v. 21bc).

46 In 3.28 the meaning may be 'the order of justification by works' rather than simply

3. The 'end of the law'

The meaning of τέλος in Rom 10.4 is, now as before, disputed. Is Christ the 'end' of the law (in the sense of termination)[47], or is he its 'goal'?[48] According to a popular interpretation Paul had both aspects simultaneously in his mind.[49] Given Paul's loose use of νόμος (Ch. I), it is hard to exclude categorically a comparable looseness in the use of another term.[50]

The decision is made difficult by the fact that there are indications in the context pointing in both directions. The 'goal' interpretation ties with 9.30– 33, esp. v. 31: Ἰσραὴλ δὲ διώκων νόμον δικαιοσύνης εἰς νόμον οὐκ ἔφθασεν. One would have expected Paul to write that Israel was striving at 'the righteousness of the law',but did not attain 'righteousness'. Instead, the text as we have it[51] reads: Israel, striving at the 'law of righteousness', did not 'arrive at the law'. In view of these striking reversals of the genitive relationship it is difficult not to think of the realisation or otherwise of the true

---

'the Torah that requires works', but this distinction is academic. The expression in 8.2 takes up the phrase 'the *nomos* of sin' from 7.23c. In 7.23c the reference is not to the Torah, but to the 'rule' (*nomos*) described in v. 21. But the rule of not being able to do what one wants to do applies to man under the Torah. In 8.2 these two νόμοι seem to melt together (this time unconsciously, it would seem), for in 8.3 which is meant as a logical sequel to v. 2 ὁ νόμος clearly denotes the Torah.

47 E.g. Lipsius, Lietzmann, Lagrange, Michel, Murray, Best, Käsemann, Jervell, Nikolai-nen; Luz, *Geschichtsverständnis* 139 ff.; Stuhlmacher, *Gerechtigkeit* 93; Jüngel, *Paulus* 52 f.; Delling, τέλος 57; Zeller, *Juden* 193; van der Minde, *Schrift* 107 n. 2; Dugandzic, *'Ja'* 65–71. – Paul is sometimes wrongly quoted as saying that 'Christ is the end of the law *for every believer*' with the implication that the law is still in force for the non-believers; cf. Nygren; Longenecker, *Paul* 152 f. What Paul actually says, however, is that Christ is the τέλος of the law *to the effect* that the possibility of *righteousness* is open to every believer.

48 E. g. Cranfield, 'Paul' 40; *Romans* 516–520; Bläser, *Gesetz* 177; Bring, *Christus* 49; Ellis, *Use* 119; M. Barth, 'Stellung' 516f.; Baulès, *Evangile* 231; Flückiger, 'Chri-stus'; Démann, 'Moses' 256; Howard, 'Christ'; von der Osten-Sacken, op.cit. 255f.; J.A. Sanders, 'Torah' 382f.; Fuller, *Gospel* 84f.; Worgul, 'Romans 9–11' 101; W.S. Campbell, 'Christ'; Meyer 'End'.

49 Fleischhauer, 'Gesetzeslehre' 64; Wiles, 'Conception' 144; Ladd, 'Paul' 58; Furnish, *Theology* 161; Drane, *Paul* 133; Bandstra, *Elements* 101 ff; Feuillet, 'Loi' 794 (who thinks that this is the most common interpretation); cf. Byrne, *'Sons'* 172 f. n. 136; Harrington, *People* 62. This interpretation actually comes close to the option 'goal'.

50 Differing from the first edition, I grant this point to Wedderburn, *SJTh* 38, 1985, 615.

51 It is possible, of course, that Paul was careless in dictating this passage, or that the secretary failed to catch the intended meaning (cf. Lietzmann); yet it would be pre-carious to divert from the extant wording. The two surprising expressions cohere and support each other. The attempts to take *nomos* in a metaphorical sense (like 3.27 or 7.21), meaning 'norm', 'position' and the like (Grafe, *Lehre* 10; Sanday-Headlam; Murray) are unconvincing.

purpose of the Torah. There is no critique of the law here. Instead, Israel is blamed for not 'arriving' where it, on the basis of the law, *ought* to have arrived.[52] Israel did not strive after righteousness in faith (v. 32), since it failed to believe in Christ (v. 33).[53] Had Israel understood what the law really was about, it would have realized that the law points to Christ and drives men to believe in him. It would be a fair summary of this passage to say that Christ is the goal of the law. The same point is made later on in 11.7: except for the elect remnant, Israel 'failed to obtain what it sought'. Paul presupposes that the salvation *in Christ* is what Israel has been seeking and what it ought to have obtained *because of* the attention paid by it to the *law*.

The τέλος statement Rom 10.4 does not, however, follow immediately after 9.33. There is a break after that verse; in 10.1 a new passage is clearly opened with the address 'brethren'.[54] In *this* passage, which constitutes the *immediate* context of v. 4, Paul uses polemical language about the law.[55] There is a polemical contrast between the 'righteousness from the law' about which Moses has written (v. 5) and 'the righteousness from faith' which speaks of Christ (v. 6). In view of this, bearing in mind that v. 5 is connected with an explanatory γάρ to the previous verse, the nomos in v. 4 must be associated with the righteousness from the law disqualified in v. 5. It must then belong together with the 'own' righteousness which the Jews try to establish (v. 3). With regard to such a law Christ can only be its end!

Supporters of the 'goal' interpretation must deny that a contrast is intended between v. 5 and v. 6,[56] which has resulted in some quite eccentric exposi-

---

52 It is not said that this was because the law had been perverted to 'a summons to achievement' (thus Käsemann, *Romans* 277).

53 Cf. van Dülmen, *Theologie* 177 f. For the exegesis of v. 32–33 see below, p. 174 f.

54 Flückiger, art.cit. 154 detects in διώκειν the image of a race and concludes that only 'goal' is compatible with this. In the new passage beginning with ἀδελφοί in 10.1 Paul does not, however, use pictorial language at all. Flückiger (154 f.) claims that supporters of the 'end' interpretation are bound to break the logical connection of v. 4 with the preceding context even though γάρ denotes a connection backwards. But this is not true; it is only that this connection does not reach as far back as 9.30–33. The γάρ, on the 'end' interpretation, connects v. 4 with vv. 1–3.

55 Cf. Michel, Jervell, H.W. Schmidt, Nikolainen; Delling, art. cit. 57.

56 Flückiger, art.cit. 155 claims that a contrast would require μὲν-δέ instead of mere δέ; cf. Fuller, *Gospel* 67; but in 9.30–31, too, μέν is lacking and δέ alone indicates the contrast between the Gentiles and Israel. On the other hand, γὰρ-δέ *need* not indicate a contrast (cf. 10.10) so that the syntax remains inconclusive. Flückiger also comments that it is not Paul's habit to look for contradictions in Scripture and to cite the OT in order to show that it is invalid; cf. Fuller, op.cit. 70. But this is not what Paul is doing on the 'contrast' interpretation either; rather, he wants to show positively that 'righteousness from faith' is found in the OT already. Against the contrast are also Bläser, op.cit. 175 ff.; Howard, art.cit. 335 f. Note, however, that even Cranfield, *Romans* 520, considers it plain that a contrast is intended; for his peculiar interpretation of it see the following note.

tions of v. 5.[57] All such attempts are made futile through Gal 3.10–12. In this passage Paul cites Lev 18.5, the same verse as in Rom 10.5, to make precisely the same point: 'law' and 'faith' are principles that are *opposed* to each other. 'The law is not from faith, but he who does them will live by them' (Gal 3.12).[58]

An argument used to support the 'goal' interpretation has been that the prediction of the 'righteousness from faith' in Rom 10.6–8 is actually taken from the *law* itself (Deut 30). Such a hermeneutical procedure is only possible, it is argued, on the assumption that Christ is the fulfilment of the Torah; verses 5 ff. thus speak for the interpretation of τέλος as 'fulfilment' rather than 'end'.[59] Yet one should bear in mind that e.g. the author of Hebrews, too, builds his whole argument on the Old Testament. In this sense the Old Testament is valid for him, and Christ is its goal. And yet the author views the old covenant as superseded, being even more explicit than Paul in this respect.[60] And even the anti-Jewish letter of Barnabas regards the Old Testament as a supreme authority.[61] The use of the law as a gold-mine of proof-texts and arguments does not, therefore, prove that the person using it cannot also regard it as superseded in some fundamental sense.

The argument, again, that had Paul thought that the law had come to an end, he ought to have insisted that the Jews and Jewish Christians give up

---

57 Bring, *Christus* 54 understands 'the righteousness from the law' in 10.5 as the righteousness, 'von der das Gesetz in seinem tiefsten Sinne spricht'; ὁ ποιήσας ἄνθρωπος is the man who does not look for righteousness of works, but pursues it 'on the path of faith'. 'Doing' means believing! In 'Paul', 49 f., Bring develops his system further: Deut 30.11 f., quoted by Paul in Rom 10.6–8, speaks (in the original context) of the commandment (ἐντολή) of the law. Even though Paul leaves this unmentioned, Bring infers that the commandment of the law which deals with righteousness 'has now become incarnate in Christ'; thus, 'one could say that Christ *is* the commandment, in its fulfilled and revealed form'. 'Christ is himself the law of God and the command of God'; 'he is the commandment (ἐντολή) which brought righteousness to one who kept it (ὁ ποιήσας)'!

For Cranfield, 'Paul' 49, the ἄνθρωπος of v. 5 is Christ! Christ fulfilled the law 'by doing perfectly that which is required and has thereby earned eternal life not just for Himself but also for all those who will believe in him'. Cf. id., *Romans* 521 f. The contrast between v. 5 and v. 6 is thus one between the righteous status of Christ and that of men (and thus no real contrast). Cf. also Bandstra, op.cit. 104.

58 To be sure, Bring, *Christus* 55–62 would interpret 'doing' as believing here as well; but see the use of ποιεῖν in Gal 5.3 – the clearest possible commentary on 3.10.

59 von der Osten-Sacken, op.cit. 255; Cranfield, *Romans* 519; Williams, 'Righteousness' 284. Williams paraphrases Rom 10.4: 'with respect to the attaining of righteousness Christ is the end of the Law' (but in no other sense); cf. Longenecker, op.cit. 144 f. But εἰς δικαιοσύνην denotes the *consequence* of the τέλος νόμου statement as a whole; linguistically it can hardly be interpreted as a qualification of νόμου.

60 See below, p. 208.

61 See below, p. 220 f.

the law in the first place, is inconclusive.[62] Paul, along with others, did 'tear down' the law (Gal 2.18), and he at least insists that Jewish Christians should not put any crucial emphasis on their observance (or non-observance!) of the law.

Finally, it should be noted that 2 Cor 3.13 supports strongly the meaning 'end'. Of course, Paul is there not speaking explicitly about the law, but about the fading glory of Moses' face. Yet this glory is closely associated with the 'letter' and the 'ministry of death'. The glory on Moses' face when receiving the tablets stands for the vanishing grandeur of all that, and its *telos* definitely means its end.[63]

In summary, I believe that Paul *could* have written that Christ is the goal of the law. Some such statement would have been quite appropriate after 9.30—33; such a formula would also neatly summarize Paul's concern in Rom 3.21 or Gal 4.21. It is important to him that Christ and the righteousness through faith can be found already in Scripture. Yet Rom 10.4, in view of the immediate context of this verse, does not fit into *this* line of thought. In this verse Paul is concerned about the contrast between law and faith. In his theology differing lines of thought can be found even in adjacent passages (or in one and the same passage).

4. Why was the law abolished?

How and why was the law abolished? Paul suggests several answers to this question.

1. He points out that the law was given just for a *limited period of time*. Gal 3.19 makes it clear that the law was to be in force 'till the offspring should come to whom the promise had been made', i.e. until the coming of Christ. The provisional character of the law is underlined even more by the other statements about it in the same verse (to be discussed later on[64]), namely, its purely negative purpose of bringing about transgressions and its merely angelic origin. The God-willed temporal limitation of the law is also assumed in verses 23—25. 'We' were confined under the law 'before faith

---

62 Against Flückiger, art.cit. 156. He adds that Gentiles had never been under the law, so that to speak of an 'end' of the law for them would have had no meaning. But, apart from the fact that Paul's language at times suggests that even Gentiles had not been free from the law (see above, ch. I), the 'end of the law' does have great significance precisely for Gentiles in Paul's thought: it makes their inclusion in the people of God possible.

63 τέλος is even here interpreted as 'goal' by Bring, *Christus* 48; id., 'Paul' 34 f.; Bandstra, op.cit. 82; Hering; but even Cranfield, 'Paul' 59 n. 3 admits that this 'is really not feasible'. Curiously, Siegwalt (*Loi* 117) who accepts the meaning 'termination' for τέλος in Rom 10.4 would take the word in the sense of 'goal' in 2 Cor 3.13.

64 See below, p. 128 ff., 140 ff.

came' (v. 23). The law was our custodian 'until Christ came' (εἰς χριστόν)[65] (v. 24); 'now that faith has come we are no longer under a custodian' (v. 25).

A similar point is made in 2 Cor 3. The old Mosaic order, symbolized by the tablets of stone, on which the letter of the law was carved, as well as by the ministry of Moses, is characterized as something 'fading away' (v. 11), as opposed to the new covenant, which is 'permanent'. The old order is like- wise designated as 'fading away' in v. 13, where Paul sets forth 'one of the most unusual exegetical arguments ever contrived'[66], when he suggests that the reason for Moses' putting a veil over his face (Ex 34.33, 35) was his will to prevent the Israelites from seeing that the splendour on his face faded away. The splendour on Moses' face here stands for the relatively small glory of the Mosaic order. The logical conclusion from Paul's ingenious exposition would no doubt be that Moses deceived his people, leading them to ascribe to the law an eternal and glorious character.[67] This conclusion was not, however, intended by Paul, as v. 14 shows:[68] the Jews' stubborn clinging to the law is a consequence of hardening (explained in 4.4 as diabolic blind- ing[69]) rather than of any act of Moses. The point of the passage is that right from the beginning the Sinaitic order finds itself in a process of 'fading away', making room for something better.

2. Secondly, Paul suggests in Gal 2.19 that the abolition of the law was, somehow or other, *due to the law itself.* 'I through the law died to the law, that I might live to God.' The precise meaning of διὰ νόμου is far from clear; Paul gives no clue as to the meaning of this 'abbreviation'[70]. Three explana- tions have been suggested. The first one, according to which Paul is hinting at his alleged bitter experiences under the law[71] can be safely dismissed.[72] Others point out that the law itself, for Paul, pointed to Christ, whether in pronouncing the death sentence over the sinner[73] or in confining everybody

---

65 The phrase is to be taken in a temporal sense as is acknowledged by almost all modern interpreters.

66 Buck-Taylor, *Saint Paul* 63. Cf. Strachan, ad loc. Hooker, 'Use' 296–305 offers some interesting comments on Paul's logical troubles in the passage in question. The strained character of Paul's exegetical argument makes the theory attractive that he is reinterpreting a midrash of his opponents (Schulz, 'Decke' 26 ff.; Georgi, *Gegner* 265 ff.); yet one wonders why Paul should have resorted to so indirect a comment. Against the assumption of a midrash e.g. Collange, *Enigmes* 68.

67 Buck-Taylor, op.cit. 63; Vos, *Untersuchungen* 139.

68 Cf. Bläser, *Gesetz* 209.

69 It is therefore questionable whether God is thought of by Paul as the subject of the hardening in 3.14; thus Windisch ad loc. In the light of Rom 9 this is, of course, possible.

70 Cf. Betz ad loc.

71 Duncan; R.E. Howard, *Newness* 83.

72 Cf. below, VIII 1.

73 Lietzmann.

under sin[74]. Still others speculate that it was the law that caused Christ to die
(3.13) and, as a consequence, his followers to be crucified 'with Christ'
(2.19b).[75] It is difficult, however, to find in Paul the idea that the law *caused*
the death of Christ; that the death of Christ caused the curse pronounced by
the law to be removed is surely something different. Perhaps the general
and somewhat vague idea that, by pointing to Christ as the redeemer, the law
pointed beyond itself and thus paved the way for the Christian's liberation
from it, is a sufficient explanation.[76] Whatever may have been the precise
intention of Paul, the emphasis in his statement lies certainly on the idea that
his freedom from the law (his 'tearing' it down, v. 18!) was *not an arbitrary
decision of his*. It was something necessitated by the law itself.[77]

It may be admissible to detect a similar point in Rom 7.1 ff. The expression γινώσκουσιν γὰρ νόμον λαλῶ no doubt refers to the Jewish law.[78]
To 'know' the law probably has the overtones of having some understanding
of its true meaning: Paul says that he is speaking to those 'who *understand*
what the law is all about'.[79] Those who can get the real meaning of the law
can realize that the law itself points to the abolition of the bond that ties
man to it (according to Rom 7.1 ff. this much can be inferred from a principle inherent in the legal practice; see below, p. 61).

Another important point is that the Christian's freedom from the law is
equivalent to *death*. Paul has died to the law. This idea seems to be a specifically Pauline variation of the common Christian notion that, in baptism, the
Christian shares in the destiny of Christ and, being crucified with him, dies to
sin. This idea is taken up and developed by Paul in Rom 6.2–11. As we will
see in a later chapter, sin and law are closely connected in their functions in
the mind of Paul; it is perhaps no wonder then that he comes to speak of a
death to the law as well in the life of a Christian. In Rom 6 Paul suggests that
death makes it possible for a bond such as that tying man to *sin* to be broken
(Rom 6.7). In Rom 7 he goes further, arguing that it is death alone that can
break such a bond as unites man with the *law*. The same idea may be implicit
in Gal 2.19 as well. To be sure, Paul is here thinking of the death of the Christian to the law, whereas in Rom 7.4 the most important thing is the death of
Christ; by sharing in this, however, Christians are dead to the law (7.4, 6).

---

74 Betz.

75 Oepke, Schlier; Bläser, op.cit. 225 f.; van Dülmen, *Theologie* 26; Tannehill, *Dying*
   58 f.; Bultmann, *Exegetica* 397; Weder, *Kreuz* 176 f.; Thüsing, *Per Christum* 87.

76 Cf. Gyllenberg, who assumes intentional ambiguity behind the abbreviation.

77 The importance of this for Paul is emphasized by Linton, 'Paulus' 183 f.; cf. Dahl,
   Studies 175.

78 Thus most modern commentators, e.g. Lietzmann, Leenhardt, Michel, Kuss, Cranfield, Barrett; Schmithals, *Römerbrief* 87. Differently Käsemann.

79 Thus Michel; cf. also Cranfield.

This importance ascribed to death as a condition of freedom from the law would seem to stand in some tension at least with the idea that the law was *designed* to hold its sway for a limited period of time only. The argument from death presupposes that the law reigns further in the world; it is only when certain legal requirements are met that certain persons can escape from under its sway.

3. We have already anticipated Paul's third answer. It is not only the Christian that has to 'die'. It is in fact the death of *Christ* that has liberated and, obviously, was needed to liberate men from under the law. This is stated as a thesis in Gal 3.13 (cf. 4.4 f.) and the point is developed with the aid of an analogy from marriage law in Rom 7.1–6.

In Gal 3.13 Paul uses dramatic language. Christ redeemed us from the curse pronounced by the law by becoming 'a curse', i.e. accursed, for us. This is clear from the manner of his execution for Scripture (Deut 21.23) says, 'Cursed be every one who hangs on a tree'. In agreement with other interpreters of his time[80] Paul applies this statement to crucifixion.

By taking upon himself the curse deservedly impending on us, Christ has redeemed us from this curse. This much is clear, granting the premise. It is not clear, however, that the thesis about the abolition of the law follows logically from the notion of a vicarious curse. If the requirement of the law is met, why should it follow that the law is to be rejected after that? There is hardly any reason to doubt that Paul's Jewish Christian opponents shared the notion of Christ's death ὑπὲρ ἡμῶν; yet they did not draw the conclusion that the law had come to an end. Paul's statement in 3.13 would seem to be a specific application of this general Christian soteriology: the death on behalf of us is interpreted as bearing the curse on behalf of us.[81]

Paul at any rate concludes that, because of the death of Christ, the law is for the Christian a thing of the past. It cannot require anything of him any more. This is clear from the context of Gal 3.13 where those 'under curse' (v. 10) are identical with those who 'rely on works of the law'. The same conclusion is drawn, e.g., in Gal 5.1: 'For freedom Christ has set us free'. The idea of 3.13 stands, however, in tension with 3.19. If the law was just a temporary arrangement from the outset (3.19), is it not strange that an act as dramatic as the death of Christ was needed to liberate men from it?[82] It is

---

80 4 Q pNah 3–4 I 6–8; Temple Scroll 64, 6–13; Justin, *Dial.* 32.1, 89.2, 90.1, 94.5. Cf. H-W. Kuhn, 'Jesus' 33 f.

81 Cf. Mussner.

82 Cf. Drane, Paul 6; sharply von Hartmann, *Christentum* 222: 'Das zur Aufhebung bestimmte Gesetz ist ganz ausser stande, den göttlichen Entschliessungen einen Zwang aufzuerlegen und die Äusserungen der göttlichen Barmherzigkeit an formelle Bedingungen zu knüpfen, bloss um dem Gesetze formell genug zu tun.' The contradiction would be quite intolerable, had Paul only had the curse of a *misunderstood* law (legalism) in mind (thus Burton ad loc.).

often said that since men had transgressed the law, the death of Christ was
rendered necessary because of God's justice and holiness. 'The law is a holy
divine order, an expression of God's will, and God the Righteous One does
not simply disregard his holy order. The order had to be satisfied ...'[83] The
notion of a law with such impositions even on God stands in an irreconcilable
contrast with Gal 3.19–25 or with 2 Cor 3. If that is what Paul meant then it
is he, not his Jewish contemporaries, who makes God 'serve the law' or makes
the law an absolute entity between God and man (a sin commonly ascribed
to non-Christian Jews by Christian interpreters[84]).

It is doubtful, however, whether Paul really had in mind a Law that must
be satisfied at all costs. The origin of Gal 3.13 probably lies in reflections of
an apologetic nature concerning the manner of Jesus' death which was bound
to present a grave difficulty to any law-abiding Jew like the Pharisee Paul.
How could one who died as 'cursed' (by God, as the original text, shortened
by Paul in his quotation, says!) be God's chosen Christ? Whether or not the
idea of Christ's vicarious death as a whole arose from reflections on the problem posed by the crucifixion,[85] need not be decided here. For Paul, the idea
of Christ's vicarious death on behalf of us was already a fixed part of the
gospel (cf. Rom 3.24 ff., 5.6 ff., 8.3, 8.32; 2 Cor 5.21; Gal 2.20, etc.). But
the particular interpretation of this idea in Gal 3.13 would seem to owe its
origin to Paul's reflections on the cross. If so, Paul was concerned with the
scandal of the manner of Jesus' death rather than with the nature of the law.
In any case the emphasis would seem to lie in the other passages on God's
free initiative (cf. esp. 2 Cor 5.18–21). God's action was needed because of
the plight of mankind[86] rather than dictated by the nature of the law. Thus
Rom 3.24 f. portrays the offering of Christ as God's response to the fact that
'all had sinned' (v. 23). In Rom 8.3 God's work is seen as an *improvement* on
the efforts of the law: what the law was unable to do, God himself brought
about — the idea can here hardly be that the law was unable to satisfy itself!
I cannot find in the other passages the idea of a law which *had* to be satisfied. If that is correct, then it is precarious to read such an idea into Gal 3.13
where it is not *required* by the context either.

---

83 Thus Bläser, op.cit. 218; cf. Bring. Oepke goes as far as to state that God himself
   must 'tragically let the law rage further until it is satisfied'. In this way 'God creates
   for himself the possibility (!) of getting rid of the law notwithstanding his holiness'!
   Would this not be casuistry at its worst?
84 See below, p. 164.
85 Cf. e.g. Dinkler, *Signum* 37; Schrage, 'Verständnis' 51 ff.; Williams, *Death*.
86 That even this idea is a secondary conclusion resulting from the interpretation of the
   Christ-event as redemptive is another matter. What Christ's death redeemed men *from*
   need not always be identical, and the meaning may not have been for others so sweeping as it appears in Paul. Yet we will see that even for Paul the idea of a hopeless
   plight of mankind is a secondary theoretical abstraction rather than a primary conviction; see below, pp. 107 ff.

The idea of Christ bearing vicariously the *curse* pronounced over mankind by the law was, then, the solution of one particular problem (the manner of Christ's death) and of nothing else.[87]

It is, for example, rather absurd to ask to whom the 'ransom' was paid.[88] Speculations about a law so mighty that God has only one way to satisfy its requirement may constitute a logical consequence of Paul's statement within a certain framework of thought, but it can hardly be a consequence intended by Paul himself. If this is so, the contradiction between the first and last answer to the question of our heading is somewhat mitigated.

In Rom 7.1–6 Paul develops the notion of the death of Christ as the rationale for the Christians' freedom from the law. The argument used is curious.[89] Paul starts from the idea that a law is binding for a human being as long as he or she lives.[90] One would expect the conclusion to be: when a man dies, he is free from the law; Paul actually states this much in v. 4a.[91] Verses 2–3, however, introduce a picture that confuses more than clarifies the issue. Logically, a picture would be needed in which the one who dies corresponds to the Christian who, according to Paul, has 'died' (with Christ) to the law. In Paul's analogy, however, it is not the wife who dies, but the first husband, and he must correspond to the *law*. Christ is then introduced as the new husband, as τῷ ἑτέρῳ in 4b (referring to ἀνδρὶ ἑτέρῳ in 3b) shows.[92] The analogy is simply confusing: it suits neither the opening state-

---

87 Byrne's assertion ('Sons' 154 f.) that according to Gal 2.19, Rom 7.1–6 and Rom 6.4–7 *we*, too, 'have paid the penalty, hanging upon the cross with Christ ... , and this is why we are now free from the curse of the Law' is hazardous in the extreme; according to him, 'we are able to die and so allow the Law to satisfy the claim it has upon us'.

88 Bläser, op.cit. 218 thinks it was paid to the law.

89 On Rom 7.1–6 see Gale, *Analogy* 189–198.

90 Against Hommel, '7. Kapitel' 93, who thinks of the law as the subject of ζῇ in v. 1. Besides being a very unnatural usage this would spoil the correspondence between 6.7 ff. and 7.1 ff.

91 The argument corresponds formally to the Rabbinic rule 'as soon as a man has died he is free from the Torah and from the commandments' (Shab 30a); cf. Schoeps, *Paul* 171 and Billerbeck III 232 for further evidence. It seems, however, that Paul does *not* take advantage of this Rabbinic principle. If Paul had proceeded from 7.1 right away to the conclusion in v. 4, then the thesis might be plausible that he was simply drawing his own personal conclusions from general Rabbinic premises. The fact, however, that he resorts to the example set forth in v. 2–3 shows that he is looking for analogies in the law and does *not* have a clear-cut 'ready-made' argument at his disposal. Anyway, no Rabbi would have accepted the assertion of a metaphorical death as a sufficient condition for the rule mentioned to be in force.

92 The talk of 'bearing fruit' in verses 4b–5 is an agricultural metaphor which has nothing to do with the marriage picture (against Dodd, ad loc.; Hommel, art.cit. 91, 94); correctly Gale, op.cit., 196–198.

ment (v. 1) nor the conclusion (v. 4).[93] It is no valid argument against this common sense observation that 'it would at least be strange if Paul had proved the idea of the Christians' freedom from the law, which was so important to him, with such a false picture'.[94] The fact remains that Paul did resort to just such a 'false picture', or to a halting comparison.[95] This appears to be symptomatic. Apparently, Paul had *no* convenient and persuasive arguments at hand, by which he could have without pains demonstrated that freedom from the law is the obvious consequence of Christ's death and the Christian's death with him. He also had to resort to an equally halting analogy (of a will, which would logically have required the death of God!) in Gal 3.15 ff.[96] Paul was at pains to find *some* argument at least for his radical conclusion!

5. The fulfilment of the law

We have thus far found in Paul clear statements to the effect that the law has indeed been superseded in Christ. Yet is would be one-sided to conclude that Paul is a 'consistent antinomist'[97] who rejects the law altogether[98]. To be able to hold fast to such a picture one has to ignore or to explain away Pauline statements which have quite a different ring.[99] Such statements

---

93 Correctly Lietzmann, Dodd, T.W. Manson ad loc. Kümmel, *Römer* 7, 38 denies the weakness of the analogy by appealing to the associative character of oriental logic; cf. further Lagrange, Käsemann and Cranfield ad loc. Käsemann, *Romans* 187 states that 'the only point of comparison is that death dissolves obligations valid throughout life'. This is wrong, for the idea of the wife married (γένηται, γενομένη) to the new husband (ἀνδρὶ ἑτέρῳ twice in v. 3) reappears in the application in v. 4 (εἰς τὸ γενέσθαι ὑμᾶς ἑτέρῳ). As far as the main thrust of Paul's thought is concerned, it is of course true that 'belonging to Christ does not presuppose the end of obligation to the law; it establishes it' (Käsemann), but in Rom 7.1–4 Paul nevertheless *attempts* to argue the other way round, looking for arguments for his position in the law itself (as he does also in Gal 3.15 ff., 4.21 ff., Rom 10.5 ff.)

Cranfield, followed by Wilckens, underlines that it is not a question of a parable at all; ὥστε (instead of οὕτως) is not a word of comparison. But the καί in v. 6 shows anyway that Paul does think of an analogy between the example set forth in vv. 2–3 and the situation of the Christians.

Gifford, Sanday-Headlam and Derrett, *Law* 461 ff. try to rescue Paul's argument by developing complicated constructions which (they think) allow for the comparison to be carried out consistently. It is difficult to find more eloquent proof for the failure of Paul's picture.

94 Kümmel, op.cit. 40 f.

95 The weakness of the comparison did not escape the eye of Chrysostomus (*Homil. in Rom.* XII, 2; PG 60, 497); cf. Wiles, *Apostle* 18.

96 See below, p. 129; cf. Gale, op.cit. 41–46.

97 Pfleiderer, *Paulinismus* 308.

98 Cf. Wernle, *Anfänge* 210 ff.; Bousset, *Gal* 59; Grafe, *Lehre* 20 ff.; Glock, *Gesetzesfrage* 146 ff.; Kühl, 'Stellung' 137 ff.; Prat, *Theology* 232; J. Knox, *Ethic* 103; Marshall, *Challenge* 228, 230; Schubert, 'Oekumene' 15; Gronemeyer, *Frage*, passim.

include Gal 5.14, 1 Cor 7.19, Rom 3.31, 8.4, and 13.8−10. Cranfield's overall thesis, which we had to reject, is not, after all, completely pulled out of thin air. *Along with the radical statements* Paul offers a series of 'conservative' ones, and on these the thesis that, for Paul, 'gospel and law are essentially one'[100] might be based. M. Barth has gone even farther, calling Paul 'an enthusiastic (!) teacher and advocate of the law'.[101] How are the 'conservative' statements to be understood?

In Gal 5.13 Paul turns from the discussion of the law to a warning about the misuse of Christian freedom. Instead of 'biting and devouring' each other, the Galatian Christians ought to serve each other in love. In view of the hard polemic against the law in the previous sections it is surprising to find Paul now emphasizing the necessity of love by way of a reference to that very *law*.[102] He is now speaking of love rather than of law. He is not defining the essence of the law with the aid of the concept of love. Rather, he is telling his readers what *love* is all about, and he does this by taking for granted that love can be defined, as it were, in terms of the *law*. He could have made his appeal for mutual love without any reference whatsoever to the law. But obviously it is a great 'plus' if something can be said to be in accordance with the law. To be sure, a critical note is not lacking here, either. It is emphasized that the *whole* law is fulfilled in *one* single commandment; there is a polemical correspondence between Gal 5.3 and 5.14.[103] Whoever accepts the Torah, must fulfil it *in its totality;* as for Christians, the same law *in its totality* is fulfilled in the love command.[104] Similarly, the somewhat enigmatic verse

---

99 Thus Sandmel, who denies contradictions in Paul's theology of the law (*Genius* 25, 57) and attributes to the apostle a 'virtual abrogation' of the law (32, 40 ff., 60), simply ignores Rom 8.4, 13.8−10, Gal 5.14. Sandmel also claims, contrary to the evidence, that Paul 'wanted Jews on their becoming Christians to leave their Jewish ways behind them' (112). Paul only attacks 'Jewish ways' when they are being imposed on *Gentiles*.

100 'Paul' 68; *Romans* 862.

101 'Stellung' 517.

102 Cf. J. Walter, *Gehalt* 192 ff.; Hübner, 'Das ganze Gesetz' 240; Betz. Sieffert, 'Entwicklungslinie' 351 plays down the reference: 'es ist da nur die Rücksicht auf das gehässige Partheitreiben unter jenen Leuten, welches den Apostel veranlasst, im Vorbeigehen hier noch dem Gesetz eine gewisse positive Beziehung zum Christenleben zu geben'; but precisely the fact that Paul *can* do so, and even in passing, is most revealing. The law comes *self-evidently* to his mind in such a connection.

103 The critical aspect is underlined by Eckert, *Verkündigung* 134 f.; in fact the 'other gospel' which takes the law literally is 'durch die Gesetzesinterpretation des Paulus noch einmal zurückgewiesen'; cf. Walter, op.cit. 193; Kühl, art.cit. 138; Becker ad loc.

104 Betz, *Galatians* 275 ascribes to Paul a careful intentional distinction between the 'doing' and the 'fulfilling' of the Torah; 'the "doing" of the Jewish Torah is not required of Christians, but the "fulfilling" is'. ποιεῖν is indeed used in Gal 3.10, 12,

23b both affirms and devalues the law: the law is affirmed in that it would be a bad thing if the Christians' behaviour were such that the law could indeed object to it; it is devalued in that a purely negative role of an (irrelevant) accusator is assigned to it. But it is interesting that Paul can still appeal to the law when he is advocating something else. And it is probably very satisfying to him that the 'one' word which is sufficient is found in the law itself (Lev 19.18).

It is hard to avoid the impression that there remains a 'kernel law' which still makes a claim on the Christians, despite all the categorical denials in chs. 3—4.

When we turn to Rom 13.8—10, where the law is similarly summed up in the love command, we find no polemic against the law. It is not necessary to regard this passage as a mere excursus.[105] It can be seen as a summary which corresponds to the opening statement of the larger section in 12. 1—2.[106] But such a connection does not exclude possible associations with the sequel. The passage in question seems indeed also to prepare the discussion in 14.1—15.13. Note the verbal similarities: one has to walk κατὰ ἀγάπην (14.15); we, the strong, are obliged (ὀφείλομεν) to bear the burdens of the weak (15.1, cf. Gal 6.2); one has to please one's neighbour (ὁ πλήσιον) 15.2.[107] The love command, set forth in 13.8—10, serves as a basis on which Paul can build in the sequel when he tries to clear up the quarrels within the community. It is love that is in focus in 13.8—10, rather than law. This time, at least, the reference to the law is used simply as an argument to emphasize the significance of love.[108] Thus, the law is viewed favourably in a curiously

---

5.3, whereas πληροῦν occurs in Gal 5.14, Rom 13.8 and 8.4 (and πλήρωμα in Rom 13.10). But while, from the linguistic point of view, Paul could have used πληροῦν in Gal 5.3 (cf. the reading of 436 pc sy^h Epiphanius), he could not have used ποιεῖν in Gal 5.14 anyway, for there the idea of 'summarizing' is also present, leaving the option free between πληροῦν and, say, ἀνακεφαλαιοῦν (thus the reading of 365 pc). In Gal 3.10, 12 the use of ποιεῖν is dictated by the OT quotations, and the usage in 5.3 may well be a reflection of this passage. Furthermore, Rom 2 renders an intentional terminological distinction dubious. The 'doing' ascribed to the Gentiles in 2.14 f. can hardly refer to 'individual laws' that 'have to be done' (thus Betz about Gal 3.10, 12, 5.3). The Gentiles Paul had in mind could not 'do' the law (or its ἔργον) in any other sense than the Christians 'fulfilled' it, i.e. by living according to its central principle(s). The meaning 'to fulfil through concrete acts' is attested for πληροῦν e.g. in III Sib 246 (see above p. 38), 1 Macc 2.55 (πληροῦν τὸν λόγον), Pol 3.3 (πληροῦν ἐντολήν); more evidence in Bauer, *Wörterbuch* s.v. 3.

105 Cf. Michel.
106 Käsemann.
107 Cf. Schmithals, *Römerbrief* 185.
108 von der Osten-Sacken, op.cit. 258, constructs a rather fantastic christological theory on the basis of Rom 13.8 ff.; 15.1 ff.; Gal 2.20; Rom 8.37: Jesus Christ has fulfilled the law precisely as ὁ ἀγαπήσας μέ/ἡμᾶς; analogously, the law of Christ Gal 6.2 is the

self-evident way. Far from feeling any need to justify the law in this connection, Paul can use the law as a supporting argument for something else, and this time surely without any polemical overtones.[109]

It has been noticed that Paul seems here simply to have forgotten what he wrote in ch. 7 or in 10.4.[110] Is this an occasional lapse into a Jewish mode of thought which Paul had on principle overcome?[111] Or is the lack of any polemic against the law to be accounted for on the hypothesis that Paul makes parenetical use of a piece of Jewish-Christian tradition which he himself does not understand literally?[112] These theories are rendered implausible by Rom 8.4.

Soon after the statement that the Christians have died to law and left behind them the old situation of the 'letter' (Rom 7.1–6), Paul says that God sent Christ 'in order that the just requirement (δικαίωμα)[113] of the law might be fulfilled[114] among us' (8.4). Paul thus 'describes the Christian

---

law that is fulfilled by him who loved me (259); like Hübner (cf. above, p. 27) von der Osten-Sacken identifies the *nomos* of Gal 5.14 with this law. There is not the remotest indication of anything like this in Rom 13 – Paul does not even speak of ὁ ἀγαπήσας but of ὁ ἀγαπῶν.

109 The nature of love as πλήρωμα νόμου is paraphrased in v. 10a: love does not harm the neighbour. J. Walter, op.cit: 193, observes correctly that, according to this passage, 'man damit, dass man liebt, dem Gesetz genugtue'.

110 Lietzmann. He finds this typical of Paul's 'unschematic' way of speaking, for Paul is not really speaking of the Torah.

111 Cf. Marshall, op.cit. 231; Simon, *Israel* 98; Knox, *Ethic* 103; Feine, *Evangelium* 73; also Gronemeyer, *Frage* 135 n. 1 (as an alternative interpretation; his main hypothesis is that πλήρωμα means the end of the law and not its fulfilment in Rom 13.10!). Klausner, *Jesus* 557 speaks of Paul's unconscious 'Verwurzelung im pharisäischen Judentum' (which *he* views, of course, favourably).

112 Käsemann. Cf. also Betz, *Gal* 275.

113 'δικαίωμα τοῦ νόμου means the legal claim as in 1.32, and correspondingly πληροῦν means the keeping of a norm': Käsemann, *Romans* 217 f.; cf. Kuss; Schrenk, δίκη 225 (for the Greek usage see ibid. 223 f.); van de Sandt, 'Research'. This seems a more natural reading than that proposed by Keck, 'Law' 51–53; he takes δικαίωμα τοῦ νόμου to mean 'the right intent of the law – life', which the Spirit accomplishes in us (53). It is right that 'the passive πληρωθῇ must be taken seriously' (52). I think the passive emphasizes that the Christian fulfilment of the law takes place charismatically, as 'fruit of the Spirit' (Gal 5); it is something accomplished by the Spirit, not by man himself. ἐν ἡμῖν means 'among us'; cf. van de Sandt, 'Explanation' 377. δικαίωμα is given a curious interpretation by Benoit, *Exégèse* 30 f., who understands it as 'verdict'; 8.4 speaks of 'le verdict', which is 'réalisé (= πληρωθῇ!) dans les chrétiens dans toute sa plenitude'. See against this Lyonnet, 'Nouveau Testament' 583 f. Lyonnet himself thinks (585) that Paul uses the singular δικαίωμα because all the precepts of the law melt for him into a single one, that of love; cf. van de Sandt, 'Research' 268 f. Yet a closer counterpart to the expression is found in Rom 1.32, in the light of which the meaning must be 'that which the law lays down as right'; cf. Sanday-Headlam.

114 The content of πληροῦν should not be diluted. Gerhardsson, 'Ethos' 57 f. interprets

fulfilment of the law as a fruit of the saving act, which goes even beyond 13.8–10[115] and reminds us of the Jewish-Christian view in Matt 5.17 ff.[116] Käsemann goes on to remark that it would be very strange if Paul were really speaking of a legal claim (which is what δικαίωμα means) of the law on the Christians after what he has said in 7.1–6. 'But if he is taking over an existing formulation, he can apply it to the doing of the will of God of which he speaks also in 13.8 ff.'[117] That is: Paul is citing a tradition, in which *nomos* really denotes the law, but he is tacitly twisting its meaning, so that *for him nomos* means God's will independently of the law. The procedure appears 'dangerous', because Paul's interpreters have believed that he spoke indeed of the law.

Käsemann thus shares the methodology of Cranfield: to maintain that Paul's theology of the law is consistent it must be assumed that *nomos* means something other than the law in the 'difficult' passages. It is just that his premises are opposite to those of Cranfield's. But Paul's favourable statements about the law cannot be explained away so easily.[118]

In his 'redaction-critical' interpretation Käsemann is correct in that Paul follows a fixed tradition at least in Gal 5.14 and Rom 13.8–10. On the other hand, it is not altogether clear that the fulfilment clause in 8.4 is received from tradition.[119] The notion of Christians fulfilling the law may be traditional, but the formulation is not. There is no break in the flow of thought. The norm of the law is fulfilled among 'us'; 'we' are then defined as those who walk according to the Spirit not flesh. This statement, again, builds a bridge to the following discussion of existence according to the flesh or according to the Spirit – a passage with a characteristically Pauline emphasis. Thus, even if Paul were using tradition in the fulfilment clause – an assertion that can hardly be proved – that tradition serves his argument beautifully; there can be no talk of an unassimilated fragment.

---

it in the light of Gal 5.22 f. as saying that 'the Spirit can never do anything that is bad in God's eyes' or that 'the law – rightly understood – can never have anything to object to what the Spirit effects'; cf. already Grafe, op.cit. 23; Nygren, ad loc. This is too negative. See below, p. 113 ff.

115 '12.8–10' (both in the original and in the translation) is a mistake (it is also corrected in the next quotation). I have also added 'even' to Bromiley's translation to preserve a nuance of the original.

116 Käsemann, *Romans* 217.

117 Op.cit. 218.

118 Käsemann is rightly criticized by Wilckens, *Römer* II, 129 n. 526.

119 Osten-Sacken, op.cit. 145 thinks that the traditional fragment is limited to the clause ὁ ϑεὸς τὸν ἑαυτοῦ υἱὸν πέμψας plus the conjunction ἵνα. Paulsen, *Überlieferung* 43 f., 63 regards similarly 'the teleological expansion of the sending formula with ἵνα' as pre-Pauline, but Paul makes use of an existing 'functional scheme' in order to explicate his own theology (64). Keck, art.cit. 44 regards the purpose clause as Paul's own, though he may have followed a traditional pattern.

Rom 8.4 brings to an end the argument about the nature of the law which started in 7.7 with the question, 'is the law perhaps sin?' Apart from the playful metaphorical language in 7.21–25, 8.2, the nature of which is indicated through genitives or other clear indications,[120] *nomos* denotes the Torah throughout the section. It has quite clearly this meaning in 8.3, that is, in the beginning of the very sentence that ends with the statement about the fulfilment of the δικαίωμα τοῦ νόμου. Paul cannot have intended *nomos* to change its meaning abruptly in such a connection. Moreover, when contrasting the φρόνημα of the flesh with the φρόνημα of the Spirit in the sequel, Paul says about the former: the mind of the flesh is enmity against God, for it is not obedient to God's *nomos* (8.7). Here, too, *nomos* must mean the law.[121] The next verse then states that those in flesh cannot please God. Obedience to God's law, then, is shown to be identical with pleasing God, which again is possible only to those living in the Spirit. Taken together, verses 8.4 and 8.7 very much suggest that the law 'remains the norm of the Christian's existence'.[122] Christians fulfil what the law justly requires from them; it is desirable and necessary to live up to the standard set up by the law.

It is true, of course, that the Christians did not fulfil the precepts of the Torah. The concept of *nomos* thus tacitly changes its meaning in 8.4, meaning the law as interpreted by Paul the Christian. But the point is that Paul's language does not reveal that shift.[123] 8.4 is intended as the climax of his 'apology of the law' (or rather 'apology of his theology of the law'!). The idea suggested in the mind of readers is that what was impossible to do under the dominion of the Torah is now done by the Christians who walk according to the Spirit. Paul suggests that his teaching stands in unbroken continuity with the Torah.

A statement like Rom 8.4 cannot possibly be regarded as an occasional slip of thought. It is the concluding statement of an argument concerning precisely the nature of the *law*. In other words, it was important for Paul to stress his 'conservatism', at least before the Roman audience.

A surprising statement from 1 Cor must be mentioned here, too. There is an interesting parallelism between Gal 5.6, 6.15 and 1 Cor 7.19. In all these instances, it is stated in the opening clause that neither circumcision nor

---

120 See above, p. 52 with n. 45.
121 To be sure, Käsemann understands even this *nomos* as 'God's will' as distinct from the law (219).
122 von der Osten-Sacken, op.cit. 244. He even asserts that, for Paul, 'the salvation consists now as before in the fulfilment of the law' (232). Cf. Hoheisel, *Judentum* 198: 'Für die Gläubigen gewinnen die Gesetzeswerke erneut heilsentscheidende Bedeutung.'
123 Cf. above, p. 28.

uncircumcision matter anything. That which matters is according to Gal 5.6 'faith active in love' and, correspondingly, according to Gal 6.15, 'the new creation'. The new existence in faith has annulled the old distinction between Jew and non-Jew. In 1 Cor 7.19, however, the latter part of the comparison is characteristically different: circumcision is nothing, and uncircumcision is nothing, but only the *keeping of God's commandments*. The observation that this statement sounds very much Jewish and very little specifically Christian[124] is quite correct. It should not be harmonized with the Galatians statements;[125] it differs markedly from them in content.[126] It is no accident that this 'conservative' version is found just in 1 Corinthians. As Drane has shown,[127] the general outlook of this letter is almost 'legalistic' as compared with Galatians. Paul's problems in Corinth were caused by pneumatics rather than legalists, and in 1 Cor he takes a more affirmative attitude to the law as a whole. It is hard to reconcile this totally favourable reference to the 'commandments', whose relevance is simply taken for granted, with the devaluation of the ἐντολή (however 'holy', 'just', or 'good') in Rom 7.7 ff., where it is only able to cause death, or even with the reduction of the many commandments to the one command of love in Rom 13.9. The tension should be allowed to stand.[128]

Paul also, at least occasionally (and just in his Corinthian correspondence) appeals to the Torah to prove individual assertions. Thus, in discussing the problem of financial support of the missionaries through the congregations, he appeals to 'the law of Moses' (1 Cor 9.9). This gives Paul the opportunity to underline that he is not speaking κατὰ ἄνθρωπον (v. 8). Indeed, what the 'law says', what is 'written in the law of Moses', is — self-evidently — the word of God ('is *God* concerned about oxen?', v. 9). The law, reinterpreted to be sure, can thus be used not only as a collection of Christological proof-texts, but also as a *norm for behaviour*.[129] Another instance is — if authentic[130] — the appeal to the law in 1 Cor 14.34 in order to silence the women in the congregation.[131] So far from being content with merely repeating the

---

124 Gyllenberg.

125 Thus van Dülmen, *Theologie* 230 n. 97; Furnish, *Theology* 201; id., *Love Command* 97.

126 Correctly Drane, 'Tradition' 170 f.; id., *Paul* 65.

127 'Tradition' 170 ff.; *Paul* 62 ff.

128 The consonance of the conservative formulation with the general outlook of 1 Cor dissuades one from simply ascribing 1 Cor 7.19b to a tradition cited by Paul, although it does less than justice to his own thought (thus Gayer, *Stellung* 173 ff.). Symptomatically, Gayer would likewise (with Käsemann, see above p. 66) devalue Rom 13.8 ff. and Gal 5.13 f. as mere pieces of tradition (op.cit. 175 n. 205).

129 Cf. also the citation from Ex 16.18 in 2 Cor 8.15, used to encourage the Corinthians to participate in the collection; and that from Deut 32.35 in Rom 12.19.

130 See the commentaries.

131 In 1 Cor 14.21 a quotation from 'the law' (actually Isa 28.11 f.) is adduced to expli-

love command, Paul appeals to the law (whatever passage he may have in mind[132]) to support a particular demand. The continued relevance of the law is thus taken for granted, even if the number of these cases is rather limited.[133]

Thus we find two conflicting lines of thought in Paul's theology of the law. Paul asserts both the abolition of the law and also its permanently normative character. Throughout he refrains from making any distinctions within the law. Subsequent theologians from Justin to Cranfield and Käsemann have proposed a legion of different distinctions to resolve the tension in Paul's thought. It would, however, have been a sheer impossibility for the original readers of the letters to notice such distinctions, and it is inconceivable that Paul should *never* have given the remotest hint of them, had he had some such distinction in mind.

Paul asserts his 'orthodoxy' with respect to the law in *Rom 3.31*. He had established in the previous passage that the system based on the Torah had been superseded: 'God's law has been manifested apart from the law' (3.21). The order (*nomos*) of faith had replaced the system of works (3.27—28). The question 'do we therefore cancel the law by faith?' (3.31a) is, in the light of these statements, quite understandable. Paul, however, replies emphatically (using the μὴ γένοιτο formula): not at all! On the contrary, we establish the law (νόμον ἱστάνομεν). The law is not invalidated by my teaching, says Paul.[134]

The statement is vague enough, and it is scarcely possible to make out the precise sense with any certainty.[135] Some scholars interpret v. 31 in the light of 3.19—20: the law is established, in that it is allowed to stop everybody's mouth.[136] This is not impossible, but there is no positive indication in this direction in the immediate context. Others think that the reference is only to the argument about Abraham in 4.1 ff.:[137] Paul says that he will establish the position of the law in a proper way in what follows. Yet in ch. 4 there is no statement to the effect that the law itself asserts that justification is by

---

cate the real value of glossolalia.

132 Commentators think of Gen 3.16; e.g. Bläser, *Gesetz* 36; Lietzmann.

133 Klausner, *Jesus* 557 exaggerates not a little when he states that Paul, 'despite the annulment of the Torah laws', appeals to verses of the Torah 'almost on every important religious issue'; contrast Bläser, *Gesetz* 229. It is correct, however, that *when* Paul does so (not almost always but now and then), this is 'an internal contradiction' (557). Paul was blamed for this inconsistency already by Porphyry (above, p. 3 n. 21).

134 The common opinion that the pair of words καταργεῖν/ἱστάναι corresponds to Rabbinic terminology used of legal interpretation (*battel/qayyem*) (e.g. Michel, Käsemann, Cranfield) is rendered dubious by Hübner, *Gesetz* 121 f.

135 For the options see Hübner, op.cit. 122 f.

136 Nygren; Jervell, *Gud* 78; Bornkamm, *Geschichte* 111; cf. also Dugandzic, *'Ja'* 175.

137 Lipsius, Jülicher, Sanday-Headlam, Lagrange; Friedrich, 'Gesetz' 416; Osten-Sacken, op.cit. 247 ff.; Williams, 'Righteousness' 280.

faith (unlike e.g. Gal 4.21). On the contrary, *nomos* is used in 4.13, 15 with exclusively negative overtones. Besides, the phrase τί οὖν ἐροῦμεν in 4.1 suggests a new passage so that 3.31 must belong with what precedes it.[138]

Perhaps the most natural solution is to take v. 31 as a reference to the predictive function of the law as indicated in 3.21b: the righteousness through faith had been 'witnessed by the law and the prophets'.[139] We 'establish its permanent significance by demonstrating that the law itself preaches the faith'.[140] Paul's message corresponds to the deeper intentions of the law, as is clear from Gal 4.21 ff. or Rom 10.5 ff.;[141] also the phrase τὰ λόγια τοῦ θεοῦ in 3.2 may refer to the predictive function of the law.[142] It is difficult, however, to exclude categorically still another interpretation, namely, that Paul is thinking of the fulfilment of the law in the life of Christians (cf. 8.4, 13.8—10).[143] The verse could well be understood as an answer to accusations reflected in 3.8 or 6.1, 15. There is no hint at these accusations in the immediate context, however. Perhaps the two last-mentioned interpretations do not exclude each other. Paul had accusations to face both on the ethical and on the 'dogmatic' front.

In actual fact Paul's answer does not meet the question. Paul had, as passages like Gal 2.15—21 show, actually torn down (κατέλυσα v. 18) important parts of the law and he held that Christians were free from the law. Indeed, with respect to Gal 2.18, written by Paul 'a few months before', Gifford found it 'inconceivable that St. Paul, after this, should say "we estab-

---

138 Schlier; Zeller, *Juden* 99.
139 Cf. Lietzmann, Michel, H.W. Schmidt, Dodd; also Hübner, op.cit. 123 f. (with the misleading addition that the law does not want to be the law of works, but the law of faith, see above p. 50 f.). Hübner also constructs a quite artificial associative connection between different sentences with ἵστημι (it occurs also in Rom 10.3), asserting that this verb is especially appropriate to give expression to God's activity (as e.g. in Gen 6.18 LXX); Rom 10.3 describes 'Gottes Aktivität usurpierendes Verhalten'! On ἵστημι see below, n. 146.
140 Lietzmann.
141 Luz, *Geschichtsverständnis* 171 f. objects that 'wieso nach 3, 27 ff. die Frage aufkäme, ob denn das Alte Testament beseitigt werde, wäre unverständlich', particularly so after 3.10—18. But the point is just that Paul's answer does not really match the question. Hearing the question in 3.31a the reader must think of the Torah; but Paul actually evades the critical question by gliding tacitly into another concept of *nomos*.
    Moxnes, *Theology* 225 f. is correct in pointing out that Paul speaks in v. 31b of the Torah in a different sense from that in 31a (the law as interpreted in the light of faith in Christ). But I do not think that Paul is consciously trying to interpret and correct the traditional concept of *nomos* presupposed in v. 31a (cf. 227 f.); he has a vague and flexible concept of *nomos*, and this very flexibility suits his argument (see above, p. 28).
142 Cf. Doeve, 'Notes', esp. 121 f.
143 Thus Best; cf. Nikolainen, Schlier; van Dülmen, *Theologie* 88.

lish the law" '.[144] And Dodd states in view of the preceding context: 'The natural conclusion from all this *is* that "by this faith we cancel the law". Paul hesitates to draw the conclusion. It would have made things clearer if he had boldly done so, for in the sense which "Law" has borne in most of this discussion it is confusing and misleading to say that we uphold the law.'[145]

It would seem that the very lack of 'boldness' which Paul at times reveals is typical of him and his situation. Paul is thoroughly radical in his missionary practice and in many of his theological conclusions. Yet, on the other hand, he has a need to pass for a loyal Jew, faithful to the Torah. This can hardly be just missionary strategy, although it would, of course, have been convenient for Paul to keep up some relations with the stricter Jewish Christians, too. It is difficult not to detect a deeply felt personal urge as well, a 'nostalgic' longing for a harmony with his own past. Or perhaps this is too mild a way of putting it. Paul may be actually engaged in an attack rather than in defense, so that the message is: it is I, not you, that bring the real meaning of the law to bear.[146] Whatever the reasons, the puzzling brevity of Paul's statement serves to conceal, to some extent at least, the radical nature of his actual position.

Paul's language, though, could only have deceived those who were already convinced. Any 'normal' Jew would have disagreed with his assertion in 3.31, and that for good reasons. If we are not to resort to a semantic trick, *abandoning circumcision and food laws can only be deemed as an annulment of the Torah.* Of course, Paul had not abandoned *everything* that the law stood for. Christian expositors of Paul sometimes seem to assume that as long as some aspect of the law remains important to Paul, he cannot be charged with annulling it. But, for a Jew, to be *selective* about the Torah meant to disobey it, indeed to reject it. 200 years before Paul's time the pious had preferred a martyr's death to eating pork and thus 'tearing down the paternal law' (τὸν

---

144 Romans 46; Gifford concluded that the anarthrous *nomos* must mean something else than the Jewish law.

145 Dodd lessens the weight of his observation by suggesting that Paul knew what he was doing. He knew that *nomos* meant Torah and that the Torah had, besides the meaning 'the code of commands', also the wider meaning of 'the total revelation of God in the OT'; the confusion arose, as 'his Greek readers ... could not be expected to bear in mind that "Law" meant Torah, and that Torah had a wider sense'. It seems to me that the source of confusion lies deeper in Paul's own mind.

146 It is intriguing to note that in the few cases in which ἰστάναι is used in connection with the law or the like with a man as subject in the LXX, it is a question of *returning* the law to its proper place: Josiah carried out his reform ἵνα στήσῃ τοὺς λόγους τοῦ νόμου (4 Regn 23.24, 2 Chr 35.19), and Mattathias was to be followed by πᾶς ὁ ζηλῶν τῷ νόμῳ καὶ ἰστῶν τὴν διαθήκην (1 Macc 2.27). The oft-cited statement in 4 Macc 5.25 (Michel, Wilckens etc.) is less illuminating, for in this verse καθεστάναι τὸν νόμον refers to the legislation as God's act.

πάτριον νόμον καταλῦσαι, 4 Macc 5.33). Because the law is divine, transgression of it in 'small' cases (as eating pork would appear to an outsider) is just as serious as a 'great' transgression, 'for in both cases one confronts the law with equal wantonness' (4 Macc 5.16–21). In Paul's time, too, the desire to remove the separating fence that the Torah set up between Israel and the nations was the principal motive for apostasy (see Josephus, *Ant.* IV, 145–147).[147] That kind of attitude is opposed in a Tannaitic midrash: 'Whoever says, I will take upon me the whole Torah except for this one word, of him it is true: "For he has despised the word of the Lord." ' (Sifre Num 112 to 15.31). Cranfield admits that, 'for Paul, the literal fulfilment of the ceremonial ordinances is no longer obligatory', but goes on: 'But the ritual regulations remain *valid* as witness to Christ, and they are *established* as we allow them to point us to Him ...'[148] But clearly that is just another way of saying that the regulations are *in*valid and *not* being established!

Paul's suggestion that his teaching 'establishes' the law is thus both internally inconsistent and externally problematic. It stands in tension with the 'abolition' statements. The premises of the conservative assertion, on the other hand, could not be acceptable from the Jewish point of view.

For Paul, the law rightly interpreted was full of testimonies to the Christian way. One only had to be able to interpret it in the Spirit, unlike the Jews, on whose eyes a veil lies when Scripture is read (2 Cor 3.15). As everyone except for the extreme conservatives admits, Paul's actual reinterpretations of the Old Testament are rather ingenious; no one will today seriously suggest that we should follow Paul in his exegesis.

In Gal 4.21 ff. he maintains that Hagar means the mount Sinai and the old covenant, of which slavery is characteristic.[149] In Rom 10.5 ff. he forces Deuteronomy to bear witness to the righteousness of faith and against the testimony of Moses[150] in a way that the systematic theologian Bring (who concludes that we must have misunderstood Paul's message) can only regard

---

147 See below, p. 133. One of the rare Christian scholars to admit that Paul was an 'apostate' who had 'renounced' Judaism is F.C. Grant, 'Prolegomenon' xvii, xix. Cf. J. Maier, 'Faktoren' 250: Paul 'represents something like a rebellion against Judaism'; Riddle,'Jewishness' 244: 'Always regarding himself as a faithful and loyal Jew, his definitions of values were so different from those of his contemporaries that, notwithstanding his own position within Judaism, he was, from any point of view other than his own, at best a poor Jew and at worst a renegade.' The opposite is maintained by M. Barth: 'St. Paul – a Good Jew'.

148 'Paul' 67.

149 The judgment of Nietsche, who called Paul's use of the Hagar story an 'unheard-of philological farce in regard to the Old Testament', is quoted by Schoeps, *Paul* 235, and by Betz.

150 Cf. Vielhauer, 'Paulus' 50: 'One has to establish without apologetical ameliorations that the apostle consciously perverts the sense of a scriptural word into its opposite'; Bornkamm, *Geschichte* 109 f. with n. 83.

as completely absurd.[151] Speaking of Abraham as a prototype of those 'who are men of faith' in Gal 3 Paul in the course of his polemic against those insisting on circumcision simply fails to mention that Abraham, too, was circumcised. In Rom 4 he at last mentions this fact, having found – in addition to the chronological argument in Rom 4.10 – the ingenious explanation that the patriarch got circumcision as a sign, a 'seal of the righteousness by faith'. Paul found in the sacred texts what he was looking for, and often interpreted them against their original intention. In this Paul is, of course, no exception in his time, even though one could debate whether Paul is arbitrary in the same way as the rabbis, Philo, and the Church Fathers are,[152] or whether his lack of disciplined method displays unique arbitrariness.[153] Occasional attempts to defend Paul's use of the OT against Jewish critics[154] are, however, futile.

6. Paul's practice

The opinions of scholars about Paul's practical attitude to the Torah in his daily life differ widely. At one end of the scale there is the view that Paul ignored the Torah and even demanded that Jewish Christians give up its observance.[155] At the other end is the notion that Paul lived as a practising Jew and forbade Jewish Christians to abandon it![156] Both views are disproved by Gal 2.11 ff. This passage makes it clear that, far from forbidding anybody to ignore the food laws at least, Paul disapproved of the Jewish Christians' *return* to observance of them, after they had given them up.[157] On the other hand, the passage does not suggest that Paul required Jewish Christians to ignore the (ritual) Torah; the point is that *if* they do, it is dishonest to return to the old practice and even to compel Gentiles to 'judaize'.

But even if Paul did not compel anybody to this or that way of life, the

---

151 *Christus* 54; cf. above, p. 4 n. 29. It is interesting to note in passing what a conservative scholar like Ellis (*Use* 71) has to say on Paul's interpretation of the singular σπέρμα in Gal 3.16: if Paul really infers a single person from the grammatical singular, his argument is 'baseless caprice' and 'outrabbis the rabbis'. The usual view of Paul's handling of σπέρμα (rejected by Ellis 71–73) 'puts the apostle in the rôle of a charlatan fooling his audience with a bit of chicanery'.
152 Thus Sandmel, *Genius* 25 f. On Philo cf. Heinemann, *Bildung* 522.
153 Thus Vielhauer, art.cit. 51. F.C. Grant, art.cit. xxxiii comments that 'Paul was a very poor exegete of the Hebrew scriptures'.
154 Käsemann, op.cit. 285; see above, p. 2.
155 Sandmel, op.cit. 112.
156 Schweitzer, *Mystik* 193, building on the theory of a 'status quo' -idea in Paul's thought.
157 Schweitzer, op.cit. 199 has to assume that Paul came with his demand of table fellowship into conflict with his own theory of status quo, which made his hopeless battle even more difficult.

question of his personal attitude and practice remains. It is widely held that, even though the Torah may have been an *adiaphoron* for Paul, he nevertheless remained loyal to it in his own practice.[158] The strongest support for this view is supplied by Acts. Now the evidence of Acts is undoubtedly of different value in different cases. The mention of Paul's vow (Acts 18.18) would seem to the Luke's 'pious addition'.[159] The account of Paul's compliance with James' strategy Acts 21.24 ff. appears to be based on reliable tradition; here, however, we surely have an *adiaphoron*, and Paul's attitude corresponds to the principle stated in 1 Cor 9.20.[160] This case thus tells us nothing of Paul's daily practice.

There remains the mention of the circumcision of Timothy (Acts 16.3). [161] In this case the interpreter must opt between sacrificing either the reliability of Luke's sources or Paul's theological consistency. If Paul had indeed circumcised Timothy, he had in advance undermined his argument with respect to the Galatian controversy; Gal 5.11 might be taken as a reference to that occurrence.[162] To give credence to Acts on this point entails finding in Paul's practice a flexibility, which — however much Paul may have justified it theologically — in the eyes of a detached observer borders on dishonesty.[163] And yet this state of affairs cannot be used as a historical argument against Luke's account.[164] We have in any case other evidence for the enormous flexibility Paul allowed *himself* while taking offence when others tried to apply the same method. A case in point is his attitude to Peter's behaviour in the Antiochian affair. It is a correct observation that in Antioch Peter actually followed the 'all things to all men' canon, which Paul advocates in 1 Cor 9;[165] the

---

158 Thus Davies, *Paul* 70, 73 f.; Parkes, *Jesus* 118–120; Schoeps, *Paul* 199; Wrede, *Paulus* 45; Jervell, 'Paul' 303; idem, 'Paulus' 37. Cf. also Harnack, *Acts* 236.

159 See Haenchen.

160 Haenchen; Schmithals, *Paulus* 93 ff. Strobel, 'Aposteldekret' 94 ff. speaks of Paul's 'unheard-of change of position' expressed in Acts 21 as compared with Gal; at the end of his mission Paul puts the unity of the church above the norm of the truth of the Gospel (94). The flexibility shown by Paul in Acts 21 is, however, already present in 1 Cor 9 – a writing roughly contemporaneous with Galatians.

161 Others read from Gal 2.3 that Paul had even the Gentile Christian Titus circumcised; e.g. J. Weiss, *1 Kor* 244; D.W.B. Robinson, 'Circumcision'; Stoike, *Law* 204 ff.; Gunther, *Opponents* 82. Had Paul done this, then the letter to the Galatians would have been a futile and indeed absurd enterprise.

162 Cf. Burton, Oepke, Schlier on Gal 5.11.

163 Parkes, loc.cit., actually speaks of dishonesty on Paul's part; Schweitzer of an 'incredibly yielding' apostle. Haenchen comments: 'Der Gedanke, dass man die Beschneidung an sich vollziehen lässt, um Schwierigkeiten der Mission zu vermeiden (Gal 5.11 wird er von fern gestreift), wäre für ihn Lüge und Blasphemie Gottes in einem gewesen.' That may be wishful thinking, however.

164 Cf. Gardner, *Experience* 45; Wrede, *Paulus* 45.

165 Cf. on this Chadwick, 'All Things'.

Corinthian non-eaters found themselves in a situation very similar to that of Peter in Antioch.[166] Being all things to all men Paul might have been able to do surprising things which defy our logic as they defied the logic of his contemporaries. If Paul did *not* circumcise Timothy it is very difficult to account for the rise of such a tradition in the first place.[167] Thus I am inclined to accept Luke's information on this point. But the circumcision of Timothy, a decision facilitated by the fact that he was the son of a Jewish mother, does *not* prove the thesis of Paul's overall loyalty to the Torah in his practice. It was a question of missionary strategy rather than conviction.[168] Luke is surely correct in his suggestion that the act took place in order to avoid trouble with Jews.

Turning to Paul's letters, the advice μὴ ἐπισπάσθω given to the Jewish Christian in 1 Cor 7.18 has been cited as an indication that, in Paul's view, every Jewish Christian was to remain a practising Jew with respect to the ceremonial law.[169] Yet it is surely an illegitimate generalization to take μὴ ἐπισπάσθω to mean 'do not cease to observe the Torah'. The advice is given in connection with Paul's reply to the Corinthian pneumatics (in particular, with respect to their view of man and woman); περιτομή and ἀκροβυστία express only 'the irrelevance of any particular earthly position in which a Christian might find himself'.[170]

Numerous indications in the letters prove in fact that Paul, when among Gentiles, did not scrupulously observe the Torah. Paul's famous principle to be τοῖς ἀνόμοις ὡς ἄνομος (1 Cor 9.21) already implies this.[171] A variation of the same principle occurs in 1 Cor 10.33: πάντα πᾶσιν ἀρέσκω. Among the Galatians Paul had lived 'like you' (Gal 4.12).[172] Gal 2.11 ff. shows that even

---

166 Thus Drane, *Paul* 67–69; Richardson, 'Inconsistency'; cf. Gaechter, *Petrus* 246 f. M. Smith, 'Persecution' 263, 268, returns the accusation of hypocrisy (made by Paul about Peter) to Paul himself with respect to 1 Cor. 9.19 ff.

167 Cf. Schmithals, op.cit. 95.

168 Other possible motives are with good ground rejected by Haenchen (who, to be sure, discounts the tactical motive as well). J. Weiss (loc.cit.) who believes that Paul had even Titus circumcised, states that these were individual cases and rejects the thesis of Paul's loyalty to the Torah. Cf. also M. Smith, 'Persecution' 267.

169 Jervell (see n. 158).

170 Bartchy, *Mallon Chresai* 164; cf. 137 ff. on the meaning of 1 Cor 7.18 in the context.

171 Correctly e.g. Héring ad loc;· Riddle, 'Jewishness' 241. Paul states in unmistakable terms that he *changes* his behaviour according to his environment: for Jews he is something other than for those without the law. To what else *could* this possibly refer than to Paul's attitude to the 'ritual' Torah? It cannot refer to his ethical conduct, nor can Paul's temporary subjection to the law mean the law as a 'way to salvation'. 1 Cor 9.20 f. is absolutely incompatible with the theory of an observant Paul.

172 That this verse really refers to Paul's freedom from the Law is shown by Merk, 'Beginn' 86–90, refuting the views of Oepke, A. Schulz, and in particular Güttgemanns, *Apostel* 170 ff. See also Betz.

under pressure Paul in a mixed community refused to comply with the food laws, when this would have threatened the position and freedom of the Gentiles. In Gal 2.18 the reference to the once and for all rejection of the (ritual) law is offered precisely as a motivation for (liberal) *practice*; v. 17a is probably intended to state that the new life-style of (Peter and) Paul has put them into the position of 'Gentile sinners' (cf. v. 15) from the point of view of the Torah.[173] In Rom 14 and 1 Cor 10 the question is not directly one of the law;[174] nevertheless, Paul could hardly have made such sweeping statements about the cleanness of *everything* or about eating any kind of meat available, had he in his personal life been keen on observing the kosher laws.[175] In the light of Gal 4.10 one can only doubt that Paul observed the Sabbath in Galatia.[176] Last but not least, the sarcastic comment 'in obscene language'[177] on circumcision in Gal 5.12 (cf. Phil 3.2) reveals in a flash to what degree Paul had become alienated from a piety centred around the Torah. To use four-letter-words about a sacred tradition, as Paul does in Phil 3.8[178], shows

---

173 Thus Tannehill, *Dying* 56. Pancaro, *Law* 30—44 shows that the word ἁμαρτωλός was used especially to denote behaviour not corresponding to the norm laid down by the law. Whereas ἁμαρτωλός takes up the same word in v. 15, ἁμαρτία in 17b has a different meaning. Paul admits that he has become a 'sinner' in a relative (Torah-oriented) sense (v. 17a), but denies that this makes Christ a servant of 'sin' in a pregnant sense. This means that those who, according to the norms laid down in the law, are 'sinners' nevertheless do not necessarily live in sin. That is, the law does not provide reliable criteria of sin.

　　　Implausible is the interpretation of v. 17a as an imaginary statement, made as a reply to an allegation comparable to that stated in Rom 6.1 (Lietzmann). See against the hypothetical explanation Tannehill, op.cit. 55; Lambrecht, 'Line of Thought' 490 (what Paul rejects is the conclusion, not the premise).

　　　Many interpreters would take ἁμαρτωλοί in v. 17a in an absolute sense (different from that in v. 15): within the new order based on faith and grace it has become clear that we have no merits, but are just poor sinners (cf. Rom 5.8). Cf. Schlier, Oepke; Lambrecht, art.cit. 490 f. Whereas 'we' are sinners because of 'post-conversional acts' according to the interpretation adopted above, we are, on this view, sinners because of 'pre-conversional acts' (see for the terminology Lambrecht, art.cit. 485). The difficulty with the latter view is that it does not explain why the Jewish Christians were 'found' (εὑρέθημεν) 'sinners' in Jewish eyes after becoming believers in Christ (cf. Tannehill, op.cit. 56). Still another explanation is proposed by Bultmann (*Exegetica* 395 ff.) who equates 'being found sinners' with 'being under the law' (397). This is very strained. Bultmann overlooks the connection of v. 17 with v. 15 where Gentiles are singled out as sinners; the word καί in v. 17a serves to juxtapose Paul and Peter to Gentiles. Cf. Feld, 'Christus' 125 n. 2. Feld's attempt to interpret v. 17 as 'a timid objection by Peter' (art.cit. 125) is, however, quite arbitrary; cf. Mussner, *Gal* 187 n. 90.

174 See above, p. 48 with n. 22.

175 Cf. above, p. 48 f.

176 Thus Noack, 'Evangeliet' 137.

177 Betz, *Gal* 270 n. 164.

178 Güttgemanns, *Studia* 95.

that one has really become an outsider with respect to that tradition.

Of course, Paul did not transgress the Torah ostensibly when he was among Jews, nor did his way of life contradict the moral commandments of the Torah. As regards morality, Paul was definitely not an antinomian.[179] His ethics converged with that of the law, even though Rom 12.1−2 shows that when Paul gives an independent account of the basis of Christian ethics, he does it without any reference to the law − the Decalogue included; he is content with speaking of a transformation of the mind and 'rational' (!) testing (δοκιμάζειν) to find out what is God's will in each case (cf. Phil 1.10).[180] Rather than being an outspoken antinomian, Paul, in his practice, was *selective* about the law. He regarded it as an *adiaphoron*, and he *treated* it as such, too. In Jewish eyes such an attitude amounted, of course, to a rejection of the law.[181] The evidence is definitely against the view that Paul scrupulously observed the whole Torah throughout his life.

7. The 'law of Christ'

Several scholars think that freedom from the Mosaic law implies that Paul *replaced* it with another law, viz. the new law of Christ, the Torah of the Messiah. The expression, of course, occurs in Gal 6.2; 1 Cor 9.20−21 is another cornerstone of this interpretation.

It is held by some that this law of Christ is identical with the Mosaic law, as far as its content is concerned. The law has not been changed; what has

---

179 A comparison with truly antinomian movements like that of Sabbatai Zwi (Schoeps, op.cit. 173) is therefore beside the point. Davies, 'Schweitzer', developing this comparison, is rather meagre *re* law. See below, part III. For the same reason, Gager's attempt to apply sociological rules of thumb to Paul's teaching on the law (*Kingdom* 35 f., using K. Burridge's scheme 'old rules − no rules − new rules') is not very illuminating (although the book as a whole is important). The 'no rules' is not at all attested in Paul; things were different with some members of the community in Corinth.

180 The talk of λογική λατρεία implies perhaps a critical attitude to the sacrificial cult (Rom 9.4 notwithstanding) and thus to an important side of the Torah; cf. Käsemann.

181 Rordorf, *Sonntag* 137 correctly points out that the Jewish fear that Paul might seduce Jews to abandon the law was not so ill-founded. Even if Paul was outwardly a Jew and did not unnecessarily shock his kinsmen by violating the law, 'so liess er sie wahrscheinlich doch früher oder später fühlen, dass er sie, sobald sie einmal Christen geworden waren, als "schwache Brüder" ansah, wenn sie dann immer noch an ihren überlieferten Gebräuchen festhielten (Röm. 14−15; 1 Kor 8, 7 ff.). Das wird nicht ohne Folgen geblieben sein. Viele Judenchristen werden seinem Beispiel gefolgt sein und sich vollkommen den Heidenchristen assimiliert haben, besonders, wenn sie in einer heidenchristlichen Gemeinde in der Minderheit waren ... Wenn er auch nicht direkt einen Einfluss auf sie ausübte, ... so ging doch sein heimliches Werben dahin, sie zu "Starken" zu machen, wenigstens soweit sie in seinen Gemeinden lebten.' Cf. Richardson, 'Inconsistency' 354, 361 (the accusations made against Paul in Acts 21 are probably not untrue); E.P. Sanders, *Law* 177f. For the opposite view cf. Gaston, 'Paul' 55.

changed with the Christ event is man's possibility of fulfilling the law (in
Spirit). This is the view of Andrea van Dülmen.[182] She argues, however, in a
totally aprioristic way: otherwise Paul would undermine the continuity of
salvation history, which he could not possibly do.[183] Recently, a somewhat
similar view has been put forward by some interpreters who identify the 'law
of faith' (Rom 3.27) and the 'law of Spirit' (Rom 8.2) with the Torah: the
'law of Christ' of Gal 6.2, too, is the renewed Torah.[184] If the arguments
advanced earlier to refute this interpretation of Rom 3.27 and 8.2 are sound,
we can safely dismiss this corollary of it.[185]

Another interpretation is that what is substituted for the Mosaic law as the
'law of Christ' is a code of authoritative 'words of the Lord', *verba Christi*.
The main representative of this view is C.H. Dodd.[186]

Dodd starts from the fact that in 1 Corinthians Paul a few times explicitly
refers to commands of the Lord. One such command, the precept that the
proclaimer is to live by the gospel, occurs shortly before the key passage
1 Cor 9.20–21, where Paul says that he is ἔννομος χριστοῦ. In 7.10, again,
Paul notes that the Lord himself 'commands' that a woman shall not be separated from her husband (cf. also the reference to the lack of a command of the
Lord with respect to the virgins, 7.25). These statements supply for Dodd the
key of interpretation for 1 Cor 9.20 f. and Gal 6.2. The law of Christ, to
which Paul is bound, is 'a code of precepts' derived from the tradition of the
sayings of the Lord. Even where Paul's letters contain (possible) reminiscences
of the gospel tradition, but Paul fails to say that he is citing precepts of the
Lord (as in Rom 14), we have, according to Dodd, evidence for the law of
Christ as defined by him.

This theory is beset with serious difficulties. In the first place, the argument about words of the Lord which are *not* marked as such, cuts both ways.
Could not the very fact that for instance the love command in Rom 13.8–10
(or Gal 5.14) is *not* cited as a saying of the Lord, be significant?[187] It is
disputed whether the phrase 'I know and am convinced in Lord Jesus' which

---

182 Theologie 67 f.; cf. Hoheisel, *Judentum* 199; Roloff, *Testament* 163.
183 Cf. op.cit. 220 f.
184 Lohse, 'νόμος' 283 f.; Hahn, 'Gesetzesverständnis' 49 n. 63; Wilckens, 'Entwicklung'
    175. It should be noted that Friedrich, who was the first to argue at length that
    νόμος πίστεως Rom 3.27 means the Torah, *refuted* such an understanding of Gal 6.2
    and 1 Cor 9.20 f.: 'Gesetz' 405–409.
185 See above, II 2.
186 Dodd, 'Ennomos'; see further Davies, *Paul* 142 ff.; Gerhardsson, *Memory* 310, 319;
    Stuhlmacher, *Gerechtigkeit* 96 n. 1; Feuillet, 'Loi de Dieu' 46 ff. Davies, op.cit.
    143 f. offers the curious suggestion that Paul participated in the development that led
    to the formation of Q.
187 Romans 12–13 abounds in reminiscences of the Gospel tradition which are not
    marked as such.

in Rom 14.14 introduces the statement that nothing is unclean in itself, reminiscent of Mk 7.15, is intended by Paul as a quotation formula.[188] If it were, then it would be strange that Paul did not have recourse to this most effective means of refuting his opponents anywhere when arguing about the law. What better weapon could he have had, say, in the Galatian conflict than a word from the Lord himself to settle the issue? In Galatians, as it stands, the idea of a νόμος τοῦ χριστοῦ is introduced almost as an afterthought when Paul is no longer discussing the problem of the Torah at all. It would be curious indeed that he has been silent of a new authoritative law in his extended treatment of the old Torah in ch. 3–4.[189] In ch. 3 Paul is at pains to produce an explanation for the replacement of the Mosaic Torah, and he has to take recourse to the unfortunate comparison with a will,[190] as well as to the unique suggestion that the law was only the work of angels. How very much easier Paul's task would have been, if he could have appealed to the code of Christ's precepts which has superseded the old code! Now we only hear of the law giving way to 'faith' (3.25) after having fulfilled its historical task. Add to this that after the very strong emphasis on the fruit of the Spirit which is expected almost automatically, as it were, of the Christian in ch. 5[191], the notion of a law-code of Christ would come as a bolt from the blue. In the total outlook of 1 Corinthians such a code would make better sense.

If the law of Christ refers to Christ's words, to what command does the statement 'bear each other's burdens' (Gal 6.2) refer? To this question Dodd can give no plausible answer; the suggestion that the reference is either to the Pharisees binding heavy burdens (Mt 23.4) or to the church order (Mt 18. 15–20), is artificial.[192] It is more natural to take the bearing of burdens as a reference to the previous verse, in which Paul exhorts his readers to admonish transgressing brethren ἐν πνεύματι πραΰτητος.[193] It is a question of 'spirit',

---

188 See below, VIII 4.
189 Analogously, Betz ad loc. argues that 'if the concept of the "law of Christ" were fundamental to Paul's theology, Paul would have introduced it at the beginning of the letter and the concept would play a prominent role in his letters'. O'Neill, *Galatians* 70 finds it improbable that Paul actually could have spoken to the Galatians of a *law* of Christ; his solution, as might be expected, is to attribute 5.13–6.10 to an interpolator.
190 See below, p. 129.
191 See below, p. 114 f.
192 Dodd, art.cit. 108 f. A curious interpretation is put forward by Strelan, 'Burden-bearing'. He would take τὰ βάρη Gal 6.2 in a financial sense; Paul would be alluding to the saying Mt 10.10 par (276). The arguments used are weak, in particular the assertion that the context of the verse abounds in commercial terminology (270 f.). In this word list are found, i.a., παράπτωμα, ἀναπληροῦν, δοκιμάζειν, ἔργον, λόγος and καιρός!
193 By 'burdens' are meant the sins alluded to in v. 1: Burton, Schlier, Mussner. van

of an *attitude* — of showing that love which is the fulfilment of the (Mosaic) law according to 5.14. *Nomos* is being used in a loose sense, almost metaphorically, much as it is used in Rom 3.27 or 8.2.[194] To fulfil the *nomos* of Christ is simply to live the way a life in Christ is to be lived.[195]

If it is difficult to identify the particular command of the Lord to which Paul, on Dodd's interpretation, refers in Gal 6.2, it becomes even more difficult when we turn to 1 Cor 14.37. Paul there concludes a long treatment of spiritual gifts by stating that what he writes to the Corinthians is commandment of the Lord (ἃ γράφω ὑμῖν ... κυρίου ἐστιν ἐντολή). Apart from the fact that it would be difficult to find any extant word of Christ which would fit the context, the reference does not seem to be to any single statement at all; rather, *everything* Paul has written in this connection is characterized as κυρίου ἐντολή.[196] If this is so, it is hard to reconcile with the notion of a dominical code. Dodd has recourse to the assumption that ἐντολή is a copyist's addition. The original reading, preserved in D F G Origen, was κυρίου ἐστίν, meaning: 'All that I here write to you is dominical', i.e., Paul's teaching 'has upon it the stamp of Christ'.[197] But this looks suspiciously like an expedient required by the overall theory. The paraphrase of Héring is plausible: 'The orders given by the Apostle should be considered as orders from the Lord — not as referring to "logia" handed down, but because the Lord has guided him by His spirit.' Paul thus refers to his *own* apostolic authority.[198]

Stempvoort, 'Gal. 6.2' 362 f. would interpret τὰ βάρη in the light of 6.3 as 'arrogance' (cf. 1 Thess 2.7, 2 Cor 10.10).

194 Thus Oepke, Mussner; Schlink, 'Gesetz' 327; Bammel, 'νόμος' 128: the expression is 'coined in an almost playful manner'; it is 'used only with regard to the legalism of the Galatians' (126). Nevertheless, Paul may be exploiting an existing formula which he reinterprets. Hengel, 'Jesus' 191f. conjectures that Paul got the expression from the group around Stephen; cf. Stuhlmacher, *Versöhnung* 82, 154f.; Stoike, *Law* 239ff. thinks that Paul borrowed it from his opponents; cf. Betz. The latter alternative is more plausible. Stuhlmacher further speculates that the *nomos* of Christ, called by him 'the Torah of Christ', is the 'eschatologically transformed' Torah established by Jesus through his obedient expiatory death which fulfilled the Mosaic law and freed it from the power of sin which had usurped it; all this constitutes a fulfilment of Jer 31 (op.cit. 158f.). None of this can be read out of the use of the phrase in Gal 6.2 (much less of the ἔννομος χριστοῦ in 1 Cor 9.21). On Stuhlmacher's construction of a 'Zion Torah' in general see below, p. 239f.

195 Cf. Bläser, *Gesetz* 234–242; Luz, 'Gesetz' 107 f.

196 See, e.g., Sjöberg, 'Bud' 169 n. 3.

197 Dodd, art.cit. 105 n. 1. ἐντολή is regarded as an addition also by J. Weiss (who regards it as pedantic but nevertheless correct) and Barrett; Robertson-Plummer consider this possible. Even if the shorter reading were correct, it would not support Dodd's interpretation of the law of Christ; it would, at any rate, be striking that Paul's teaching can have 'upon it the stamp of Christ' when *no* words of Christ are available!

198 Cf. Sjöberg, art.cit. 171.

If this is a correct interpretation — if Paul occasionally uses 'the Lord's commandment' in such a loose sense, this can be seen as a further piece of evidence for the thesis that the 'law' of Christ is not literally a law either.

In the second crucial passage 1 Cor 9.20–21 ἄνομος first quite clearly means Gentiles as opposed to the Jews (v. 21a). But then the word tacitly takes on another meaning. It occurs to Paul, says Dodd, 'that the expression *nomos* might very well be gravely misunderstood by readers to whom the equivalence of *nomos* and Torah was by no means familiar. He must guard his statement carefully against such misunderstanding ... he is not ἄνομος in the sense of leading an unregulated and irresponsible life.'[199] Paul, therefore, adds θεοῦ to *anomos*: he is not independent of what is God's will. On the contrary, he is ἔννομος χριστοῦ. The expressions are coined ad hoc. From the juxtaposition of ἄνομος θεοῦ and ἔννομος χριστοῦ nothing more can be inferred than that Paul is *bound* by God's will which, again, has something to do with Christ. It is quite plausible to understand this to mean that Paul is in all his doings dependent on Christ and obedient to him[200]; there is nothing to suggest a concrete code of precepts.

This interpretation is reinforced by 1 Cor. 7.19.[201] In this verse Paul states that neither circumcision nor uncircumcision matters, but the keeping of *God's* commandments alone (ἐντολαὶ θεοῦ). If Paul had such a notion of the law of Christ as Dodd suggests, one wonders why he did not speak of the commandments of *Lord Jesus* in this connection. Anyway, he has mentioned a commandment of the Lord shortly before (7.10), and will mention the lack of one in another matter shortly (7.25). In the light of this, the expression ἔννομος χριστοῦ (instead of, say, ἔννομος θεοῦ) in 9.21 appears accidental. Had the rhythm of the sentence not demanded a change of the genitive noun, he might as well have mentioned God rather than Christ. It would have made no difference.

In 9.14 and 7.10, where Paul appeals to the commandments of the Lord Jesus, it is a question of individual problems, not of the general principles of Christian existence. We have to do with what might be called beginnings of church order.[202] Questions of divorce and finance are concrete matters with

---

199 Dodd, art.cit. 97.
200 J. Weiss, Kümmel, Conzelmann, Grosheide.
201 Cf. above, p. 68.
202 Cf. Weiss, *Urchristentum* 118, 431; Bultmann, *Theology* 188; Schürmann, 'Gesetz' 283. This distinction is disputed by Schrage, *Einzelgebote* 245 f. He emphasizes that sayings of the Lord were always authoritative for Paul; Paul seems, however, to have had a rather limited collection of them at his disposal (242). This is possible. Note that Schrage, too, (100 n. 116) disagrees with Dodd's understanding of the 'law of Christ'; that sayings of the Lord did have indisputable authority for Paul is another matter!

a legal dimension in a way that the command to love one's neighbour —
which Paul does *not* cite as dominical — is not.

The conclusion is that the talk of the 'law of Christ' refers simply to the
way of life characteristic of the church of Christ. To be sure, Paul did not
shrink from giving clear commands to instruct his congregations, as is clear
from both the Corinthian and the Thessalonian correspondence.[203] These
instructions are not, however, based on a code of dominical words. It might
have made Paul's task in explicating the function of the law easier, if he were
to argue from a new Torah of the Messiah which has superseded the old one;
if such an argument was known to him, we must conclude that he chose to
ignore it.

8. Conclusion

Paul's practical attitude to the Torah is characterized by unmistakable
laxity, even though he displays amazing adjustability in trying to avoid obsta-
cles to his mission. His theoretical answer to the question whether or not the
law is still in force, contains a strong tension. The law, 'letter' by nature, is
a thing of the past. Christians are no longer under it; they have died to it.
Christ is the end, that is the termination, of the law.

And yet Paul can exhort his readers to Christian love by emphasizing that
love is the fulfilment of that very law. He can also motivate various moral or
otherwise practical instructions by appealing to words of the law. Now as
before the law is justified in putting a claim on man, even on the Christian.
The special thing with the Christians is that they alone fulfil that just requirement. Paul underlines that, far from annulling the law, he actually establishes
it. He is thus quite reluctant to admit how far he has actually gone in his
rejection of the law.

Paul thus wants to have his cake and eat it. Depending on the situation,
he asserts, as it were, now the καταλῦσαι now the πληρῶσαι of Mt 5.17.
It is not advisable to concentrate on just one or the other of these contradictory lines of thought, as is done by many scholars. The tension cannot be
resolved by way of development theories, either, for it is still there in
Romans. Various distinctions within the law with the intention of telling in
what sense the law is in force and in what sense not are modern expedients,

---

203 See below, p. 115 ff. Paul's statement that he has given the Thessalonians orders διὰ
τοῦ κυρίου 'Ιησοῦ (1 Thess 4.2) can hardly be taken to mean that his instructions
were based on *verba Christi*. The phrase is difficult to explain; a 'mystical' meaning
'through the activity of Christ in whom we are' (Best, with reference to Thüsing, *Per
Christum* 165 ff.) makes sense, particularly in the light of Rom 15.30, where Paul
asks the readers to help him in his prayers διὰ τοῦ κυρίου 'Ιησοῦ Χριστοῦ καὶ διὰ
τῆς ἀγάπης τοῦ πνεύματος. Thüsing, op.cit. 171 compares 2 Cor 5.20 and Rom 15.18:
the exalted Lord himself speaks through Paul. Also Wilckens, 'Jesusüberlieferung'
315 stresses that Paul has the exalted Lord rather than the historical Jesus in view.

attempts to be over-precise where no precision is possible. They cannot be consistently carried through either. This is also true of the popular explanation that the law is annulled as a way to salvation while remaining in force as the expression of God's moral will.[204] This explanation runs counter to 2 Cor 3.6 f., where the Decalogue is in no uncertain terms branded as killing 'letter' in a negative sense and the temporary character of the glory of the Mosaic legislation is stressed. The reduction of the law to the love command also annihilates the meaning of the Decalogue as such. And what actual content could the law as a valid ethical norm have, if the Christians are in each case called to *judge* or to *examine* (δοκιμάζειν) what God's will is? While surely doing justice to some passages in Paul, the distinction in question is no more successful than others as an overall statement of Paul's view.

Furthermore, this idea is hard to reconcile with the other, often proposed by the *same* scholars[205], that the law was never intended to be a way of salvation at all! If it was not a way of salvation, then how can it come to an end in that capacity?[206] With more justification one could say that Paul regards the law as being abolished as norm or standard (*both* as a way to salvation *and* as an expression of God's will) while remaining in force as prediction, promise and 'paraclesis' (Rom 15.4), that is, as γραφή,[207] but even this distinction cannot be carried through consistently, for, as we have seen, as often as not Paul *does* view the law as a valid norm.

I suggest that Paul's theology of the law can only be understood if the tensions and self-contradictions in it are taken seriously. The tensions are to be acknowledged; they should be accepted as clues to Paul's internal problems. We will return to these considerations later on.

9. Analogies?

It is hardly surprising that the closest equivalent to the Pauline tension between an abolished and yet valid law should occur in *Ephesians*. The author states very clearly that 'the law of the commandments in precepts' (ὁ νόμος τῶν ἐντολῶν ἐν δόγμασιν) has been destroyed by the death of Christ, so that the separating wall between Jews and Gentiles has been torn down (2.14 f.).[208]

---

204 Thus, among others, Maurer, *Gesetzeslehre* 53; Bultmann, *Theology* 268 f.; Conzelmann, *Outline* 224; Percy, *Probleme* 356 f.; Wilckens, *Rechtfertigung* 109; Schrage, *Einzelgebote* 232; Hoheisel, *Judentum* 182; cf. Mussner, *Traktat* 235. Correctly Bläser, *Gesetz* 229.

205 E.g. by Bultmann, op.cit. 263, 267, and Maurer, op.cit. 88.

206 This discrepancy is correctly pointed out by Bläser, op.cit. 206.

207 Cf. D'Angelo, *Moses* 194.

208 Possibly the words τὸν νόμον τῶν ἐντολῶν ἐν δόγμασιν are the author's comment on his source which may have spoken of the separating wall only; thus Fischer, *Tendenz* 132 f.; Lindemann, *Aufhebung* 171.

Yet in the *Haustafel* at the end of the writing (6.2 f.) children are exhorted to honour their parents with the motivation that this command of the Decalogue is 'the first commandment (ἐντολή!) with a promise'. The validity of the Mosaic ἐντολαί is thus simply taken for granted. This is a typically 'Pauline' self-contradiction. And yet, like Paul, the author does *not* systematically consider the Decalogue or the Torah as the basis of his ethics; like Paul, he advises his readers to 'examine' (δοκιμάζοντες) what is pleasing to the Lord (5.10).

The author of *Hebrews* is quite emphatic about the abrogation of the old (cultic) law. Like Paul, he still appreciates the law with respect to its predictive function; this can, without further ado, be coupled with a negation of its other aspects. But the author, unlike Paul, never cites the law as an ethical norm. His conception is thus clearer and more consistent than Paul's.[209]

The Gospels are difficult to evaluate from this point of view, since so many important questions about the law are not treated explicitly. Thus *Mark* does not tell us, whether the law was, in his view, abrogated by Christ. In the gospel an implicit distinction seems to be made between ritual stipulations and God's ethical will.[210] Like Paul, Mark never points out that this actually means breaking God's written law in two. God's will as expressed in the Decalogue (10.17 ff.), the two commandments of love (12.28 ff.) or in the demand of inward purity (7.15 ff.) are valid further on, even though the OT commandments are occasionally intensified by Jesus (10.2 ff., cf. 10.21). By contrast, it remains unclear what the evangelist's attitude to the ceremonial law is. It is not clear whether he rejects animal sacrifices in 12.33; at any rate, these are located on a lower level than the 'greatest' commandments.

Various ordinances concerning purity are, in any case, clearly repudiated by Mark (ch. 7). He comments in a derogatory way on ablutions (7.3 f.), lets Jesus clearly show that they are unnecessary (7.6–13) and finally declare that nothing that enters man from without can defile him (7.15). Mark's understanding of the saying – whatever its original purport – is clear from 7.18–20: Jesus declared *all foods clean*.

As regards the actual contents of the OT law, Mark 7.15 ff. runs counter to certain sections of that law, notably the food regulations of Lev 11.[211] Understandably, interpreters often conclude that, for Mark, the Torah is abrogated by Jesus.[212] Conspicuously, however, Mark never frames either his

---

209 Hebrews also regards the law as a shadowy typos of the new covenant; the relatively favourable evaluation of the law is shared by Colossians (2.17).

210 Cf. Werner, *Einfluss* 80; Schulz, *Mitte* 216.

211 This is denied by Banks, *Jesus* 144 f. who claims (arbitrarily) that Mark thinks of 'foods involved in idol-worship'.

212 Thus Hasler, *Gesetz* 26; Hübner, *Tradition* 223, cf. 226; Hummel, *Auseinanderset-*

editorial comments on Jewish customs or Jesus' critical remarks as a critique of the *Torah*.[213] In 7.5 Jesus is criticized by the Pharisees merely on the score of neglecting the post-Biblical tradition of the elders. The evangelist never suggests, in the course of ch. 7, that anything other than just this tradition is put under fire.[214] His readers, who seem to have had rather vague notions of Judaism, must have gained this impression from the book.[215] To what extent Mark himself was aware of the actual conflict between ch. 7 and Leviticus is difficult to assess.[216] Apparently he did not reflect on the contents of the Torah; somehow he seems to presuppose that God's old revelation *must* have been based on the same principle of 'inwardness' as Jesus'

zung 53 f.; Luz, 'Gesetz' 117. Schulz, *Botschaft* 86 f. thinks that the purity laws of both the OT itself and of the later tradition are, from Mark's point of view, absurd.

213 Mark's traditions contain elements which suggest some amount of indifference to the law; e.g. his touching the leper (1.41) or, indirectly, his dining with sinners and publicans. Mark, however, reveals no consciousness of a tension with the law.

214 On the 'thematic unity' of 7.1–23 in the editor's mind see Lambrecht, 'Jesus' 25. – The conflict stories in chs. 2–3 likewise stress the antagonism between Jesus, the teacher κατ' ἐξουσίαν (1.22, 27) and the scribes who had replaced God's will with their own precepts; cf. 2.6, 2.16, 2.24, 3.1, 3.6. Not even the story 2.23 ff. gives the impression that the Torah is being transgressed (contra Hasler, *Gesetz* 18 f.). The Pharisees define what they consider unlawful (2.24), but Jesus is able to show that the authority of Scripture is on his side (2.25 f.). 2.27 draws the conclusion as to the intention of the law and 2.28 shows who is the authorized interpreter. The force of 2.21 f. is not clear. In themselves the words suggest a rejection of Jewish customs; yet in v. 20 the custom of fasting (declined as regards the time of Jesus) is affirmed as regards the time of the church. Mark is no systematic thinker; often he is content to juxtapose different materials. Probably 2.21 f. also suggested to him the freedom from Pharisaic ordinances. On the conflict between Jesus and the Pharisees/Scribes in Mark see further 3.22 ff., 8.11 f., 8.15, 11.27 f., 12.9, 12, 12.38 ff., and the Passion Narrative.

215 Readers who needed an explanation of the custom of washing hands were surely not able to distinguish between Torah and halakah.

216 Hübner, op.cit. 225 puts cautiously forward the question, whether Mark realized that what was abrogated in 7.15 was actually contained in the OT itself. This question presupposes that the Evangelist was a Gentile Christian – a view that has gained considerable ground in recent years. Indeed, 7.3–4 looks like 'derision of the non-Jew' (Schweizer; cf. Niederwimmer, 'Johannes Markus' 184). The editor looks at Judaism from without also in 7.13b and 7.19. But then he could also have been a Hellenistic Jew, alienated from Judaism to a similar degree as Paul was; indeed 7.19 parallels the sarcasm of Gal 5.12 or Phil 3.2. In any case Mark must have been a Christian, most probably a teacher of a congregation, for quite some time before he undertook to compose the gospel. It is difficult to imagine that such a person could have been quite ignorant of the conflicts over the Torah, notably the food laws, between Paul and the 'Judaizers' some twenty years earlier. Could he have been totally ignorant of the 'Apostolic Decree' which is, of course, also hit by 7.19? So the most likely solution is simply that Mark failed to reflect on the Torah; critique of the Torah and critique of traditions of the elders simply fuse together.

proclamation of God's will.[217] For in other sections in his gospel Mark places great emphasis on the *continuity* between genuine Jewish faith and the teaching of Jesus.

One such passage is 12.28–34. Answering a Jewish scribe's question about the 'greatest' commandment Jesus isolates a 'first' and a 'second' commandment. Significantly, the scribe concurs and even complements Jesus' answer with a 'critical' remark: loving God and one's neighbour is much more important than all the sacrifices. Mark then makes the point that the remark is 'intelligent'; the man is not far away from the reign of God. It is important for Mark that he can show 'that a representative of the present Jewish tradition, indeed a representative of the main opponents in the Gospel of Mark, bears witness that Jesus stands on the fundament of the rightly understood Biblical-Jewish tradition' and represent Jesus as the real fulfiller of that tradition.[218] The pericope in question impressively closes a series of debates between Jesus and the Jewish authorities, implying that the tradition is on Jesus' side.

In all this, Mark shares to some extent the anomaly of Rom 3.31. On the one hand he suggests that Jesus brings the intentions of the old religion to completion; on the other hand he ignores the material conflict between some sayings of Jesus and the actual contents of the Torah. The difference is that in Mark we have a clash between two implicit suggestions, whereas in Paul two explicit claims stand in mutual contradiction.

Matthew differs from Paul in that he programmatically denies the abrogation of the Torah through Christ (5.17). He is clearly somewhat more conservative than Mark in his handling of the relevant texts.[219] Some traditions preserved by Matthew emphasize the absolute validity and immutability of the law in the present age (5.18) or even the binding nature of the Pharisaic traditions (23.2 f.).

On the other hand, Matthew views the law in the light of a consciously critical principle: the law is to be interpreted in the light of its kernel, the dual commandment of love, on which 'all the law and the prophets hang'

---

217 Thus Werner, op.cit. 81.

218 H-W. Kuhn, 'Problem' 304, followed by Pesch. Cf. also Nineham.

219 ' ... where Matthew can rework his sources so that passages critical of the law are mitigated and domesticated he does so'. 'If possible, he preserves or restores the authority of the Torah'. Hübner, *Tradition* 196, 197. Apart from ch. 15, discussed below, cf. Matthew's edition of his traditions in 11.13 and 22.40. Where the Q-saying (Lk 16.16) spoke of the law and the prophets being there 'until John', Matthew's wording (11.13) rules out any idea of the termination of the validity of the law; cf. Barth, *Gesetzesverständnis* 59 f. On 22.40 see Manson, *Sayings* 227; id., *Teaching* 304 n. 2.

It is certainly wrong to speak of Matthew as a 'radical antinomian', as Walker, *Heilsgeschichte* 135 does.

(22.40). God wants mercy rather than sacrifices (9.13, 12.7); the law and the prophets can be summarized in the Golden Rule (7.12). Through the antitheses of the Sermon on the Mount (5.21–48)[220] certain commandments of the Torah are radicalized and internalized.[221] At least the prohibition of oath and the rebuttal of the *ius talionis*, however, run counter to statements of the OT Torah itself.[222] Whether Matthew understood these antitheses in this way is another matter. As the new commandments amount to radicalizations which make the law more difficult to keep, *Matthew* can well have understood them as a new *interpretation* of the old law rather than as its modification.[223] Matthew's intention is evident in 5.17, a probably wholly editorial verse[224]: Jesus did not come to abrogate (καταλῦσαι) the law (and the prophets), but to fulfil (πληρῶσαι) them. The programmatic saying is strangely ambiguous in content.[225] The general idea would seem to be:

---

220 For a bibliography see Strecker, 'Antithesen' 36 n. 1.
221 The first and second antithesis are undisputedly only internalized and radicalized interpretations of the old law; the same is probably true of the sixth one. Cf. Meier, *Law* 135 ff.; Broer, *Freiheit* 85–91. The third antithesis (the statement on divorce) is difficult to assess; the meaning depends on the interpretation of the notorious παρεκτός-clause. This antithesis is understood as a revocation of the old commandment by Meier, op.cit. 140 ff.; differently Sigal, *Halakhah* 104 ff.; Dietzfelbinger, 'Antithesen' 9 and apparently Hübner, op.cit. 61 ff.; cf. also Broer, op.cit. 95–101.
222 Cf. Meier, op.cit. 150 ff.; but see Broer, op.cit. 91–94. Sigal, op.cit. 93 f. thinks that Matt 5.34 refers to personal vows and oaths but not to the judicial oath (Ex 22.10).
223 Cf. Davies, *Setting* 99–102 who also points out that in his redaction of Mk 1.27 Matthew *omits* the Markan expression διδαχὴ καινή (Mt 7.28, the end of the Sermon on the Mount!); Luz, 'Gesetz' 82; Przybylski, *Righteousness* 81 (he, however, proposes that Matthew portrays Jesus as 'making a fence around the Torah' in 5.21–48, which is quite unlikely; Matthew displays no such concern for the old law, see below n. 232); cf. Burchard, 'Versuch' 422–424.
   By contrast, others emphasize that the antitheses in question represent decisive modifications of the OT commandments; cf. Strecker, *Weg* 147; Hummel, op.cit. 71 ff.; Hübner, op.cit. 84 f.; Montefiore, *Gospels* II 488, 513; Meier, op.cit. 157 ff.; Sand, *Gesetz* 53. This may be true as regards the actual content of the commandments. It is a different question, however, whether *Matthew* admitted or perceived this. Cf. Barth, op.cit. 148; Strecker, 'Antithesen' 55, 69 n. 104.
   The issue is, to be sure, further complicated through the possibility that the antithetical form of the antitheses is due to Matthew himself; thus Suggs, 'Antitheses'; Broer, op.cit. 102 ff. Yet Matthew need not have understood under that which had been 'said to the men of old' the Torah itself (thus Broer); he may well have had the scribal interpretive tradition in mind (thus Burchard, art.cit. 423 f.; Suggs, art.cit. 441). And after all a case can be made for the possibility that Matthew got the antithetical formula from his tradition; thus e.g. Strecker, art.cit. 45.
224 Thus Strecker, *Weg* 144; Hummel, op.cit. 66. Others try to isolate a traditional kernel; thus, e.g., Hübner, op.cit. 33 f.; Meier, op.cit. 82 ff. (who assumes an extremely hypothetical original form οὐκ ἦλθον καταλῦσαι τὸν νόμον ἀλλὰ ποιεῖν); cf. also Luz, 'Erfüllung' 403 f.
225 What is fulfilled by Jesus, and how? The use of καταλῦσαι suggests the command-

Jesus has realized the true intentions of the 'law and the prophets', but it
seems impossible to pinpoint the precise meaning of πληρῶσαι.[226]

The main difficulty is posed by the phrase οὐκ ἦλθον καταλῦσαι. Is Matthew, too, caught in the dilemma of Rom 3.31? The answer to this question
depends on how one sees the attitude of Matthew to the ritual law. Unfortunately it is not clear whether or not Matthew thought the ritual law to have
been abrogated by Jesus.[227]

Matt 9.13 and 12.7 show at least that sacrifices are subordinated to higher
values. Ch. 12 does not suggest a strict observance of the Sabbath, but 24.20
does.[228] What relevance circumcision may have had in Matthew's community we do not learn.[229]

The crucial passage is in ch. 15 (Matthew's reinterpretation of Mk 7).
Verses 11 and 17 suggest an abrogation of food laws. On the other hand,
however, Matthew omits the Markan generalization 'he declared all foods

---

ments of the law, whereas πληροῦν makes one think of the theme of fulfilment of
prophecies, dominant throughout the gospel. For the problems connected with
πληρῶσαι see Trilling, *Israel* 147 ff.; Meier, op.cit. 73 ff.; Luz, art.cit. 413 ff.

226 Trilling shows that each antithesis 'fulfils' the old commandment in a different sense
and concludes: 'Mit dem Begriff des πληρῶσαι ist dem Evangelisten tatsächlich ein
Zauberschlüssel an die Hand gegeben, der allen Problemen um das Gesetz die Türe für
ein konservatives und zugleich fortschrittliches Verständnis öffnet.' Op.cit. 188;
cf. also Luz, art.cit. 416. It thus seems that the evangelist can only hold all his traditions (plus the view expressed in the editorial comments) together by resorting to a
sufficiently vague key concept that is able to suggest a wide variety of associations.
One is reminded of Paul's handling of the term *nomos*; cf. ch. I.

227 He did according to Strecker, *Weg* 30 ff., 135; Schulz, *Mitte* 180 f.; Broer, *Freiheit*
114–122; cf. Simonsen, 'Auffassung' 53–58. He did not according to Barth, op.cit.
83 ff.; Hummel, op.cit. 48; Davies, *Setting* 104; Fenton, *Mt* 251 f.; Luz, art.cit. 425;
id., 'Gesetz' 83 f.

228 Barth, op.cit. 85 and Hübner, op.cit. 127 regard Mt 24.20 as an insertion by Matthew
himself. As the verse is hard to harmonize with ch. 12, it is difficult to understand
it as a Matthaean addition, however. Barth, op.cit. 86 wants to understand the decline of a flight on a sabbath as a practical expedient with regard to the hostile Jews;
yet he himself notes that a flight on a sabbath was at the time of Matthew no longer
regarded as sin. It is much more natural to view the remark as a piece of tradition;
thus, e.g., Schweizer, ad loc.; Strecker, *Weg* 32.

229 Circumcision is conspicuously ignored in the mission commandment 28.16–20;
cf. Meier, op.cit. 28 f.; Luz, 'Erfüllung' 428 ff. Yet the early history of Christianity
shows that even Jewish Christians (Peter!) could accept Gentiles into the congregation without circumcision without thereby on principle taking a critical attitude to
the ceremonial law. It may be that circumcision was no problem in Matthew's community: the Jewish members were circumcised anyway, and the rite was not imposed
on Gentiles. Cf. the reflections of Luz, art.cit. 430; id., 'Gesetz' 80, 86; he asks
whether the community of Matthew had only recently opted for a mission among
Gentiles, so that the consequences for the understanding of the law had not yet been
thought through. Similarly S. Brown, 'Community' 217 f.

clean' (Mk 7.19).[230] Moreover, he concludes the section with the editorial comment that eating with *unwashed hands* does not make a person unclean (v. 20). This suggests that, in *Matthew's* mind, the topic of the discussion is the 'tradition of the elders' (v. 2) alone. This conclusion is reinforced by the Matthaean insertion of verses 12—14 which point out that just the Pharisees (with their traditions) were hurt by what Jesus said; even more importantly, Jesus remarks that the custom criticized is to be uprooted, because it is a 'plantation' not planted by God. Such features render the assumption of a critique of the ceremonial parts of the Torah on Matthew's part unlikely. The conclusion is, then, that (as was the case with the antitheses of 5.21 ff.) Matthew understands his 'radical' traditions in a milder sense.[231] On the other hand, the traditions of Matthew also include extremely conservative sayings like 5.18 f. or 23.2 f.; of these, too, the evangelist must have taken a moderate view.[232]

If something like the above reflections correctly represents Matthew's stance, then his point of view is reasonably clear; certainly much clearer than Paul's. However, the fact that careful scholars can produce widely differing interpretations of Matthew's view[233] commends caution at this point. If Matthew's statements are read on just one synchronic level and the interpreter refrains from an extensive reading between the lines, then Matthew's book certainly displays a rather strong tension and a good deal of vagueness with regard to the law.[234] His redactional operations (5.17!) do not help to

---

230 Matthew also replaces Mark's generalizing οὐδέν with the expression οὐ τὸ εἰσερ-χόμενον.

231 Hübner, op.cit. 179 f. interprets, instead, Matthew's treatment of the section on the basis of the Rabbinic distinction between primary and secondary uncleanness; Matthew's Jesus abrogates the notion of secondary uncleanness, stating that foods which have become unclean through cultically unclean *hands* (but not being prohibited in Lev 11) are actually clean. I find it difficult to discover such a subtlety in Matthew's text.

232 Mt 5.18 must be read in the larger Matthaean context; cf. Hübner, op.cit. 34, 197. See, however, Simonsen, art.cit. 51—53, 65: Matthew wishes indeed to emphasize that in the present aeon the law remains valid; the tension that thus results should not be explained away from Matthew's view of the law. Meier, op.cit. 29 f., 43 f., and passim proposes an artificial solution of the tension between the conservative and the moderate statements: the sayings about the validity of the law are meant to apply to the period before Jesus' death and resurrection alone, in analogy with the particularist mission directions in 10.5 f. A comparison of 11.25 ff. with 28.16 ff. shows that Matthew makes no distinction between the teaching of the earthly Jesus and that of the risen Jesus; cf. Bornkamm, 'Risen' 208; Hübner, op.cit. 198 f. Meier has indeed to resort to the explanation that the vanishing of heaven and earth in 5.18 means 'the apocalyptic event of the death-resurrection of Jesus' (op.cit. 65)! It is patently wrong to conclude that the scribal tradition still has authority for Matthew (23.2 f., 23.23); thus Hummel, op.cit. 47; correctly Simonsen, art.cit. 47 f.

233 Simonsen's instructive study makes this abundantly clear.

234 Cf. the conclusion of Simonsen, art.cit. 67.

remove the tension between his conservative (5.18!) and radical (15.11!) traditions. It remains unclear, in what sense Christ 'fulfils' the law and how it can be claimed that it is not 'annulled'. This unclarity Matthew shares with Paul.

John, too, is a man of the fulfilment line. Christ is the fulfilment of the Scriptures pointing to him. This fulfilment, however, means that the law has been emptied from meaning; it has completed its task. John offers no statements about the law's continuing validity. The final revelation consists of the words of Jesus. Characteristically, the love commandment is not given as a summary of the old law, but as a new commandment of Jesus. John thus connects continuity with the law and freedom from it in an impressive way.

There may be some tension, however, between John's apologetic reasoning in 7.21–23 to prove that Jesus' transgressing the Sabbath was not against the intention of the law[235] and the blunt statement in 5.18 that Jesus 'abolished' the Sabbath – if that is what ἔλυεν means.[236] It is emphasized in ch. 5 that Jesus sets himself over the Sabbath on the ground that he is continuing his Father's work of creation; such a sovereign act is hardly in need of a scribal apology like that set forth in 7.21–23. But the point of the latter section is in fact to show that the Jews' arguments against Jesus are weak.[237]

John is free to take a relatively positive attitude to the law, since he stresses exclusively its *predictive* function.[238] Like John the Baptist, the law, too, witnesses to Jesus. This is its only purpose after the revelation of Jesus has taken place.[239] Some of John's OT testimonies well match those of Paul in arbitrariness (see e.g. 8.17).[240]

John does *not* speak of Jesus as the fulfilment of the law (but merely as the fulfilment of the Scriptures).[241] From the point of view of the Christians, the law is definitely a thing of the past. We hear nothing about the permanence of the law in the vein of Mt 5.18, Lk 16.17. Only the words of Jesus have an imperishable value, first of all the new commandment of (fraternal) love. The love command is *not* set in the framework of the law, as it is in

---

235 The law itself requires men to break the Sabbath ordinances in certain cases (circumcision on the eighth day), and a *qal-wa-homer* conclusion shows that to heal the whole man must be more important than the Sabbath.

236 Thus Schnackenburg; Pancaro, *Law* 160; Ljungman, *Gesetz* 71.

237 Cf. Becker.

238 Pancaro, op.cit. 525.

239 Cf. Pancaro, op.cit. 525 f.

240 The argument in Jn 8.17 is artificial to such a degree that Bultmann ad loc. and *Theology* 28 regards it as a parody of the Jewish appeal to the law. Yet John must have understood the argument as juridically valid, given the perspective of faith; cf. Pancaro, op.cit. 277.

241 Pancaro, op.cit. 543.

Mark, Matthew and Paul; it is not set forth as the greatest commandment in the law or even as its fulfilment.[242]

If my reading of *Luke* (following Jervell) is correct, Luke does not think of an abrogation of the law at all; it continues to be valid for Jewish Christians, whereas Gentile Christians are to observe only the minimum law laid down in the Apostolic Decree. Luke's work is indeed almost free from the problems we are concerned with at present. 'The life of the primitive church at Jerusalem as depicted in the early chapters of Acts is determined by universal adherence to the law ...'[243] Likewise, the charges against Stephen (Acts 6.14) are said to be false. Paul is described as a pious, Torah-abiding Pharisee (Acts 16.3, 21.20 ff.). In the Gospel, Luke 'avoids any criticism of the law or parts of it by Jesus'[244], getting therefore here and there into some tension with his sources.[245] Unlike Mark and Matthew, Luke gives 'no summary of the law in the one central commandment of love' in his version of Jesus' discussion with the lawyer (Lk 10.25 ff.)[246] The discussion is on inheriting eternal life, not on the greatest commandment, and the right answer is given by the lawyer rather than by Jesus, which further underlines the continuity between the old religion and Jesus' message. Likewise, in the discussions over the Sabbath there is 'no conflict with the law'. Luke 'is concerned to show that Jesus acted in complete accordance with the law, and that the Jewish leaders were not able to raise any objections' (see Lk 13.17a, 14.6).[247] Treating divorce, Luke 'avoids the obvious renunciation of Moses' in Mark's pericope.[248] Mk 10.2 ff. is omitted, and the critical saying Lk 16.18 is embedded into a context which emphasizes the permanence of the law (16.17!).[249]

The critical section Mk 7 is lacking in Luke. As this is part of Luke's 'great omission', we cannot be sure whether he knew the story; Lk 11.37 ff.

---

242 Cf. Pancaro, op.cit. 444 f.; Luz, 'Gesetz' 124.

243 Jervell, *Luke* 138.

244 Jervell, op.cit. 138.

245 Parts of the OT law are actually revoked in 6.27 ff. (*ius talionis*) and 16.18 (prohibition of divorce). The OT passages in question are not quoted, however, and the juxtaposition of 16.18 with 16.17 makes one think that Luke did not admit the contradiction between the OT commandment and the new injunction. See Hübner, *Tradition* 207; cf. also Montefiore, *Gospels* II 508. Lk 10.8 also stands in tension with Luke's tendency in Acts; it is therefore natural to ascribe this verse to Luke's source (Q?) rather than to the Evangelist himself. Cf. Räisänen, 'Jesus' 83, 95 n. 52.

246 Jervell, op.cit. 139.

247 Op.cit. 140.

248 Op.cit. 139.

249 In the light of 16.17 one cannot but give 16.16 a non-radical meaning on the editorial level. According to Jervell, op.cit. 150 n. 35 it means, for Luke, 'that only since John is the kingdom preached'. Cf. Hübner, *Tradition* 207. Differently e.g. Caird: the old order is over. Caird must, however, take v. 17 as 'an ironical attack on the pedantic conservatism of the Scribes' (so also Manson, *Sayings* 135) which cannot be correct.

may suggest that he did.[250] Elsewhere, at least, Luke asserts that the 'customs from the fathers' are in harmony with the law (Acts 6.14, 21.21, 28.17; cf. 10.14 ff., 11.3, 8). From this point of view, the disagreement between Jesus and his Pharisaic host over washing oneself (Lk 11.38 ff.) seems somewhat inconsistent[251]; anyway, the final comment of the section ταῦτα δὲ ἔδει ποιῆσαι καὶ ἐκεῖνα μὴ παρεῖναι (Lk 11.42c Q) betrays no criticism of the traditions of the elders. The statement that 'everything will be clean for you', if you use what is 'inside' the cup for almsgiving (Lk 11.41), sounds rather liberal, but Luke's own interpretation of it is difficult to determine.[252]

While the Lukan Jesus' solidarity with the law is hardly in dispute, many scholars find an abrogation of the law in the new 'history-of-salvation' situation described in Acts. In Luke's view, it is thought, the law was replaced by the Apostolic Decree (Acts 15.21 ff.)[253] One can indeed refer to Peter's vision (Acts 10.11–16) which finds its climax in the statement that Peter is not to regard as unclean what God has cleansed (v. 15). But does this mean that *foods,* too, have been cleansed, and not just Gentile *people*? Luke's own interpretation is clear from Acts 10.28, 15.9: it is a question of cleansing a man, the Gentile Cornelius (who stands for other believing Gentiles, too).[254] That all foods are *not* clean is clear enough from the Decree itself![255]

The notion of the law as an epoch is nevertheless correct – with one important modification. The law is replaced by the Apostolic Decree as regards *Gentile* Christians. For *Jewish* Christians (who may not have been obsolete in Luke's day[256]) the law remains fully in force. Even after the apostolic council both Paul (Acts 16.3, 25.8, 28.17) and all other Jewish Christians (21. 17–26) meticulously observe the law. As for the freedom of the Gentile Christians, Luke is at pains to show that the decision was made because of God's clear guidance (Acts 15.7–14) and in accordance with the words of the prophets (Acts 15.15–17). God himself had shown that it is not necessary for Gentile Christians to observe more than the minimum law (the Decree).[257] Luke thus does not at all share Paul's problems.

Turning to *Jewish* texts of the time we can find little that could be regarded as in any sense analogous to Paul's problems – for the simple reason that

---

250 Cf. Hübner, op.cit. 182 ff.; Jervell, op.cit. 139.

251 Cf. Hübner, op.cit. 188.

252 Jervell, op.cit. 140 ascribes the talk of almsgiving to Luke's redaction, but this is uncertain; on the discussion see e.g. Hübner, op.cit. 187.

253 Conzelmann, *Mitte* 148.

254 Cf. Haenchen; Jervell, op.cit. 149 n. 24; differently Hübner, op.cit. 189 ff.: food laws are abrogated in Acts 10–11.

255 Correctly Haenchen. It is another matter that the *original* point of the story of Peter's vision may have been that all *foods* are declared clean; cf. Conzelmann, *Apg* 61. We are concerned with *Luke's* view on the matter.

256 Cf. Jervell, 'Minority'.

257 Jervell contends that in Acts 15 'Luke labors to prove that the salvation of the

it is very hard to find anything resembling an abrogation of the law in Jewish sources. Secularized renegades are of no interest in this connection. There was, *pace* Berger, probably no antinomian stream in Hellenistic Judaism.[258] Unfortunately, we are not sufficiently informed of the Alexandrian allegorizers mildly rebuked by Philo (*Migr. Abr.* 89—93), who ascribed (like Philo) symbolic meaning to the ritual precepts, and (unlike Philo) had therefore given up their practical observance. In view of the mildness of Philo's criticism of them it is impossible to see in them militant Jewish precursors of Paul who demanded the abrogation of the law;[259] it is probably more to the point to see in them rather harmless (from the Jewish community's point of view) contemplative individualists.[260]

As for Philo, it may be noted in this connection that he is inconsistent in ascribing to the *literal* sense of the laws some profound wisdom also in his allegorical writings.[261] This is especially marked in his polemic against mocking outsiders in *Conf. Ling.* 2 ff. In such a connection Philo can approvingly refer to an apologetic interpretation of the literal sense (14), although he in general often uses objections to the literal sense to justify his allegorization. Evidently he does not want to concede anything to decided opponents of the Bible.[262]

Had Philo carried through consistently his allegorical theory, he ought to have given up the literal sense of the passages interpreted allegorically altogether. He displays a 'both — and' -attitude, especially when the question of the authority of the Bible is explicitly involved. Not least from the psychological point of view, the situation Philo found himself in recalls that of Paul. But there is altogether very little light on this particular problem to be gained from Jewish sources. Paul's problem is that of a radical Jewish-*Christian* in search of a balance between his past and present experience.

As regards other NT writers, Paul would seem to share the vagueness of his 'fulfilment' assertions with Matthew and perhaps with Mark. The tension between explicit radical statements and explicit conservative ones is, interestingly enough, found outside of Paul's letters only in the Deuteropauline Ephesians.

Gentiles occurs in complete accordance with the law' (Luke 143); 'it is not lawful to impose upon Gentiles more than Moses himself demanded' (144). Acts 15.21 does not, however, give the impression that Moses is invoked as a witness of the validity of the decree. The decree is not understood as an OT precept but as an expression of consideration for Jews or Jewish Christians who are present everywhere; correctly Luz, 'Gesetz' 155 n. 206.

258 See above, I 4 b.

259 Cf. Friedländer, *Bewegungen* 285, 353 f. Wolfson, *Philo* I 68 points out that all Philo felt he needed to 'make them turn aside from the error of their way' was to point out the implications of their attitude.

260 Wolfson, op.cit. 69.

261 Heinemann, *Bildung* 514 f., cf. 468.

262 Heinemann, op.cit. 573 n. 2.

III. Can the law be fulfilled?

1. Fulfilling the whole law is impossible

In Gal 3.6 ff. Paul sets forth the contrast between 'those of faith' and 'those of works of the law' (v. 7, 9; v. 10). Those who are 'of faith' are blessed along with Abraham (v. 9). Not so 'those who are of works of the law' (v. 10):[1] they are all under a curse. This is proved from Deut 27.26 (LXX): it is written that everybody who does not cling to all (precepts) written in the book of the law to fulfill them is accursed. The majority of interpreters assume that Paul is thinking here of the impossibility of fulfilling the Torah, although he does not say this in so many words.[2] All those who stick to the law are accursed, because they all transgress it. No doubt this interpretation is correct.[3]

To be sure, it is held by others that the idea of unfulfillability is absent from Paul's argument. The fault with the law is not that it cannot be fulfilled, but rather that it drives man to *do* things.[4] The function of v. 10 is, according to this view, only to show 'that what is important in the sphere of the law is doing'[5]; the stress is placed on the word ποιῆσαι.[6] 'The conclusive proof that the law does not bring righteousness is found in verses 11 and 12.'[7]

This interpretation is on the right track — as far as verses 11—12 are concerned. As an exposition of v. 10, however, it is untenable.[8] Had Paul wished

---

1 V. 10 shows that v. 9 is meant as exclusive; the γάρ of v. 10 indicates that v. 9 implies that the people of 'works' do not get the blessing. Cf. Mussner.

2 Thus, e.g., Lipsius, Sieffert, Bousset, Lietzmann, Loisy, Oepke, Becker, Neil; Zehnpfund, 'Gesetz' 398 f.; Schlatter, *Glaube* 332; Grundmann, 'Gesetz' 57; Buber, *Zwei Glaubensweisen* 53 f.; Berger, 'Abraham' 51; van Dülmen, *Theologie* 32; Hübner, *Gesetz* 19 f.; Luz, *Geschichtsverständnis* 149; id., 'Gesetz' 94 f.; Schoeps, *Paul* 176 f.; Wilckens, *Rechtfertigung* 92; Stendahl, *Paul* 80; Vos, *Untersuchungen* 89; Hoheisel, *Judentum* 187; Byrne, 'Sons' 151 and n. 56.

3 The curse probably is the curse with which the law threatens its transgressor; as everybody is a transgressor, all men of 'works' *are* under it (and not merely exposed to it); see on this Mussner.

4 Thus, e.g., Schlier; Maurer, *Gesetzeslehre* 22; Kertelge, *Rechtfertigung* 209; van der Minde, *Schrift* 131.

5 Maurer, ibid.

6 Schlier.

7 Maurer, ibid.

8 Cf. Luz, op.cit. 149 n. 56: in itself, v. 10 is quite clear; it is only in the light of v. 12 that anybody can come to an interpretation like that of Schlier.

merely to emphasize the falsity of the principle of 'doing', the best method
would have been to omit v. 10 altogether; the idea would then have been
clear enough from verses 11–12. To read this idea into v. 10, however, one
actually ought to cancel the negative particle οὐκ! Gal 5.3 confirms the unfulfillability interpretation.[9] Paul there stresses that one who is circumcised is
obliged to fulfil (ποιῆσαι, as in 3.10) the *whole* law.[10] Obviously this should
be enough to discourage the Galatians from being circumcised and searching
for justification in the law (v. 4). The implication thus is that it can be taken
for granted that nobody is able to fulfil the Torah in its totality. Taken together, 3.10 and 5.3 seem to reveal 'an enormously rigorous attitude',[11] from
the Jewish point of view even an 'overstrained definition' of the obedience to
the law required of man[12]: total obedience alone is sufficient, but total
obedience is impossible.

Rom 1.18–3.20 confirms the view that Paul hints at the idea that everybody is a transgressor in Gal 3.10.[13] It is Paul's explicit concern in this pas-

---

9 Correctly Schoeps, op.cit. 177.
10 Gal 5.3 definitely refutes Bring's peculiar interpretation of 3.10 (*Christus* 44, 56 ff.).
   For Bring, Gal 3.10 as usually interpreted is an absurdity. He thinks that ποιεῖν τὸν
   νόμον is identical with fulfilling the law in Christ (Christus 44); ποιεῖν thus refers to
   something quite distinct from the ἔργα. Cf. also Lull, *Spirit* 124 ff. 5.3, with ποιεῖν,
   would be incomprehensible on this view.
11 Hübner, 'Das ganze Gesetz' 244.
12 Moore, *Judaism* III, 150. Yet from the fact that a Jew did not see the law in this light
   one should not jump to the conclusion that Paul could not either; thus Howard, *Crisis*
   53.
13 Cf. Mussner; Luz, 'Gesetz' 95. E.P. Sanders, *Paul* 483 emphasizes that what is wrong
   with the law is that 'it does not rest on faith', which is the purport of v. 11–12.
   In *Law* 20ff. he develops an interesting argument against the unfulfillability interpretation. Paul uses in Gal 3.10–13 those proof-texts he can find in the LXX to support the view that Gentiles are justified by faith. Having seized on the Abraham passages
   where 'blessing' is mentioned he is concerned to find a text where *nomos* is connected
   with 'curse'; the *only* such passage in the LXX is Deut 27.26! Paul simply *has* to quote
   that verse, and Sanders proposes 'that the thrust of Gal. 3.10 is borne by the words
   nomos and 'cursed', not by the word 'all', which happens to appear' (21). 3.10–13
   as a whole is 'subsidiary to 3.8' (22). I would agree with Sanders' methodological
   principle that Paul's own words are more important than the wordings of his quotations; they are 'the clue to what he took the proof-texts to mean' (22). Nevertheless,
   Deut 27.26 would be a surprisingly poorly chosen proof-text had Paul only wished to
   show that 'those who accept the law are cursed' (Sanders, op.cit. 22); the text would
   seem to say precisely the opposite. Of course Paul is quite capable of turning verses of
   the OT into their opposites. Yet it would seem that Sanders does not take Gal 5.3
   seriously enough when he reduces it to 'a kind of threat' with the aid of which Paul
   can discourage the Galatians from being circumcised: 'if you start it *must* all be kept'
   (op.cit. 27). I would put the decisive emphasis on Rom 1.18–3.20. In this passage Paul
   surely argues that no one has lived according to the law and that no flesh can therefore
   be justified by works of the law (Rom 3.20). I would apply to Gal 3.10 Sanders' own
   insight into the operating of Paul's thought: in this verse Paul does assume that the law

sage to demonstrate that *all* have sinned (3.20) and that *all* are under sin (3.9). Gal 6.13, too, is to be mentioned in this connection. In this verse Paul states that his Judaizing opponents do not even themselves fulfil the law. One should not search for subtle indications of the opponents' doctrine in this verse.[14] It is quite simply a piece of polemic along the lines later set forth in Rom 2.17 ff. Paul wants 'here, as so often, to caricature the opponent in his typically Jewish incapability of fulfilling the law, instead of giving an objective description'.[15]

The interpretation we rejected for Gal 3.10 is, however, quite appropriate as an interpretation of the next two verses. Formally, verse 11 is introduced as if it were proof for v. 10.[16] From the point of view of its content it looks more like a new argument, parallel to v. 10. Verse 10 suggests an empirical fact; verse 11 refers to a fundamental principle which is valid independently of such facts. The two arguments stand in tension.[17] Two different explanations of the curse of the law are juxtaposed to each other. This leads to the problem that the failure to keep the law makes one guilty (cf. Rom 2.1 ff.) while being simultaneously from the view-point of righteousness in Christ a *necessary* failure.[18] We will see in the course of the discussion that it is the idea of verse 11 that is of more fundamental importance in Paul's thought.[19] But whatever the reasons for the existence of the two differing arguments side by side,[20] for the moment it is important to underline that Paul offers the 'empirical' argument that those under the law do not actually keep it totally.

---

cannot be fulfilled, but he came to this view 'backwards'; see below, p. 108 f.

14 It is futile to speculate, on the basis of this verse, about opponents who were allegedly lax about parts of the law, while insisting on circumcision; thus, e.g. Lütgert, *Gesetz* 101 f.; Munck, *Paulus* 82, 84; M. Smith, 'Persecution' 264; Schmithals, *Gnostics* 33; Suhl, *Paulus* 16, 25 (suggesting political view-points); Kertelge, op.cit. 197–200; M. Barth, 'St. Paul' 19 f.; cf. Gunther, *Opponents* 83. Correctly Betz.

15 Eckert, *Verkündigung* 34 f., cf. 41 f.; similarly Mussner. Somewhat differently Howard, op.cit. 15 f.

16 Thus Bousset.

17 Luz, *Geschichtsverständnis* 150: 'Nachdem er vorher also vom faktischen Nichthalten des Gesetzes gesprochen hat, tritt nun gleichsam ein neues Argument neben das erste, obschon es jenes faktisch aufhebt: Weil nämlich ein anderes Rechtfertigungsprinzip ... in der Gegenwart wirksam ist, ist Rechtfertigung aus dem Gesetz ausgeschlossen.'

18 Luz, op.cit. 151.

19 Luz arrives at the conclusion that verse 11 f. 'markiert wohl gleichsam den Standort, von dem aus das empirische Urteil V. 10 gefällt werden kann.' Somewhat similarly Tyson, 'Works' 428.

20 I cannot find in the passage any indications that Paul was consciously trying to resolve a contradiction between two Scriptural verses; thus (with differences in details) Schoeps, *Paul* 177 f.; Dahl, *Studies* 161 ff.; Drane, *Paul* 30; Hübner, *Gesetz* 43. The idea that Paul apparently wants to convey is that the verses quoted *support* each other. Cf. Betz, *Gal* 138 n. 8.

2. All are under sin

In Rom 1.18–3.20 Paul argues that nobody can be justified by 'works of law' (3.20). The reason is that all, Jews as well as Gentiles, are 'under sin' (3.9).[21] Every mouth has thus been stopped by the law (3.19) – even that of the Jew boasting about the Torah. The section as a whole should indeed be understood as addressed to the Jews, even though it is found in the letter to the Roman Christians.[22]

When Paul states in 3.9 that all, Jew and Greek alike, are under sin, he says that he has set forth this charge before (προητιασάμεθα). He must, then, think that this has taken place in the section 1.18–2.29. Finally, in 3.10–20 Paul clinches with words of Scripture the argument which he has already demonstrated with empirical proof.

Paul proceeds by beginning with the charge against the Gentile world (1.18–32).[23] He then goes on to demonstrate the sinfulness of the Jews

---

21 It will be seen that I agree with E.P. Sanders, *Paul* 474 f. as against Bultmann, *Theology* 227 in the thesis that Rom 1–3 does *not* make out the *fundament* of Paul's soteriology; Paul actually started with the solution and moved backwards to define the problem. But in Rom 1–3 Paul certainly *argues as if* 1.18–3.20 were such a basis. This is not, of course, denied by Sanders either, who emphasizes the *secondary* nature of Paul's argument in Rom 1–3. It is therefore no valid argument against his position simply to point out that in Rom 1–5 'the human need for redemption precedes the divine initiative in Christ' as Beker does (*Paul* 242). See further below, n. 80. Cerfaux, *Christian* 141 and Klein, *Rekonstruktion* 146 (the section is 'propaedeutic') concur, among others, with Bultmann.

22 It is often assumed that Rom 1.18 ff. reflects Paul's missionary proclamation; cf. Bussmann, *Themen* 109 ff.; Dodd, Michel. It is beyond the scope of the present work to enter into a discussion of this. I would suspect that at best certain themes used by Paul in such connections appear in ch. 1. The tone and content of ch. 2 is hardly suitable for a sermon preached to Jews and it is irrelevant in missionary preaching to Gentiles. But probably ch. 2 reflects trains of thought habitual with Paul by the time of writing Romans. Jeremias, *Abba* 271 is surely justified in calling the section a *dialogus cum Iudaeis*; cf. Synofzik, *Aussagen* 88. It is a fascinating hypothesis that Paul is in the letter to the Romans, as it were, preparing the apology he wishes to deliver in Jerusalem (although this cannot be the *only* reason for writing Romans); cf. Bornkamm, *Geschichte* 120 ff.; Jervell, 'Letter' and above, p. 9 n. 61.

By contrast, it seems wrong-headed to assume that 2.17 ff. is addressed to the Jewish *Christians* in Rome (in view of their former life), and 1.18 ff. correspondingly to the Gentile Christians; thus Ulonska, *Paulus* 157, 163 f.; cf. Viard, *Romains* 53 ff.

23 Some scholars question this general opinion and claim that Paul is in 1.18–2.8 speaking of man in general; attention is called to the term ἄνθρωπος (1.18), the word διό which suggests an inference from the preceding section in 2.1, and to an allusion to the Golden Calf – a sin of the Jews, to be sure – in 1.23 f. (Ps 106.20). See Jervell, *Imago* 316–319; Hahn, 'Gesetzesverständnis' 31; Schmithals, *Römerbrief* 13 f.; Berger, *Exegese* 25 f. According to Dabelstein, *Beurteilung* 68 ff., 1.18–32 speaks of the 'impious' and 2.1–16 of the 'righteous' without regard to an ethnic division. It is doubtful, however, whether Ps 106.20 is cited with the intention of bringing the

(2.1–29). The sinfulness of the Gentiles is depicted with colours supplied by traditional Jewish polemics. That the Jew is no better off is first asserted in general ('you do the same things' 2.1–3) and later on described in some detail (2.17–24).

The actual character of Paul's empirical argument is, however, rather surprising. One might have expected him to proceed, say, along the following lines:

> 'Even if one claims to be blameless according to the Law (as Paul himself did), one is in fact guilty, because sin has such a grip on men and women that it is impossible for them to worship God and obey his commands *from pure motives.* ... We should probably all agree that it is well-nigh impossible to analyse one's own motives accurately. Is love ever genuinely altruistic? Can anyone avoid for very long thoughts about one's own well-being, happiness, security, reputation? Certainly the emphasis on reward in the Jewish religious system made it difficult to love God for his own sake.'24

I would certainly agree that our motives are always impure. But I cannot admit that this is what *Paul* is saying in the passage at hand! We instinctively tend to think that he must have said something like that, in other words, we interpret him in the light of later Christian insight. But the point is that Paul does not at all develop his argument by showing that even the best fall short here and there,[25] even less that at least the motives are impure when the deeds are good. On the contrary, Paul first brands the Gentile world wholesale as a *massa perditionis* – they are lumped together as idolaters and homosexuals, of which the vice list in v. 29–31 is characteristic. Turning to the Jews, he brings forward a number of very harsh charges, which are intended to demonstrate that the Jew, too, is a 'transgressor of the law'. 2.1–3 insinuates that the Jew is guilty of all those glaring pagan sins listed just before.[26] In verses 21–24 Paul is quite explicit: the Jew is charged with stealing, adultery and sacrilege so that he dishonours God by his transgression of the law and gives the Gentiles reason for mocking God. There is absolutely no talk of motives and the like; gross sins are put under fire.

Calf into the reader's mind; after all, Paul omits the crucial words μόσχου ἐσθοντος χόρτον, no doubt because it was too specific for his argumentation (Käsemann, *Romans* 45). Rom 3.9 presupposes that Paul has made a charge against the Greek as well as against the Jew earlier in the letter, and this can only refer to ch. 1. Jervell and Hahn have to take 2.14–16 as such a charge; see on that below, p. 105 f.

24 Hooker, *Pieces* 37. To be sure, she adds that 'Paul is surely being unfair to Judaism'.

25 It is Justin, not Paul, who tried to go that way: 'And no one ever did *all* exactly (not even you will dare deny this), but some have kept the commands more, and some less, than others.' *Dial.* 95.1.

26 Paul must here have the vice list of 1.28–31 in mind (rather than idolatry and homosexuality). It is quite arbitrary to suggest that the Jew does the 'same' as the Gentile by establishing his own righteousness and boasting. Thus Bornkamm, *Studien* 96; correctly Kuss, 'Nomos' 217.

Logically Paul's argument proves no more than that circumcision is of no avail to a Jew who is guilty of serious transgressions of the law, and that a true Jew is one who behaves like one (whether circumcised or not). The syllogism suggested in v. 9 (Jews and Greeks are all under sin) would only follow, if the description given of Jews and Gentiles were empirically and globally true – that is, on the impossible condition that Gentiles and Jews were, *without exception*, guilty of the vices described. It looks almost as if Paul were half conscious of the limited nature of his argument: in 3.3 he starts his next argument from the fact that *some* (τινές) have been unfaithful. And this is exactly what the preceding argument should have led to! But to jump from this to the assertion that *'every* human being is a liar' (3.4), let alone to the final consequence in 3.9, is a blatant non sequitur.[27] The picture is rounded off by the in itself trivial observation that Paul's concluding argument, the appeal to Scripture (3.10–18), badly twists the original meaning of the Biblical sayings. Paul makes use of a catena of citations[28] which originally described the nature of the impious (as opposed to the pious). That this should demonstrate that *all* are 'under sin' is another *petitio principii.*[29]

---

27 Cf. Dodd, *Romans* 44.

28 Paul probably used an existing catena (cf. the shorter version in Justin, *Dial.* 27.3); see van der Minde, *Schrift* 54–58; Keck, 'Function'. Keck (152 f.) argues that the catena 'is not an appendage but the theological starting-point for Paul's reflection'; Paul had it in mind 'when he began his exposition of the human situation'. A comparison with CD 5.13–17 (art.cit. 148 f.) suggests an original apocalyptic collection, an 'indictment against sinners' proving that the holy remnant was living in the last times, when corruption had reached its climax. Hanson's interpretation (*Studies* 13 ff.) that the catena speaks of the vindication of the Messiah is far-fetched.

29 Rom 3.9 might suggest that sin is viewed as something more than doing sinful acts, i.e. as a demonic power; thus e.g. Dibelius, *Geisterwelt* 122 f.; van Dülmen, *Theologie* 158–168; Hübner, *Gesetz* 63; Schottroff, 'Schreckenherrschaft' 497 ff.; cf. Rom 5–7. But throughout the section in question the condition of men is seen as 'a matter of their own deliberate and informed choice and action'. The citations in 3.10–18 'show, not that man is under demonic power, but that men do wicked and sinful things': Kaye, *Thought Structure* 40.

It should be noted, too, that in 3.23 the idea of 'being under sin' (3.9) is taken up and expressed through the verb ἥμαρτον; thus the standard distinction between ἁμαρτία ('sin as power') and ἁμαρτάνειν ('sinful acts'), made e.g. by Schottroff, art. cit. 498, appears doubtful.

Synofzik, *Aussagen* 89 also admits that in Rom 1.18–3.19 Paul 'operates with a concept of sin that consists in transgressing the law known to man'; the concept is thus based on the traditional Jewish understanding of sin. For Synofzik's understanding of Rom 3.20 see below, p. 106 n. 73. Kaye argues carefully that throughout Romans, including chapters 5–7, 'the same basic concept of sin makes sense, namely the sense of sinful action, or the guilt consequent upon such action' (137). He rejects, with good reason, the idea that sin is thought of as a power. The 'more personal and dynamic looking expressions regarding "sin" ' in ch. 5 'are due to the influence

The exegetical literature abounds in attempts to justify Paul's allegations. We can here leave aside the description of the Gentiles and concentrate our attention on the desolate picture of the Jews in Rom 2. To support Paul's accusations reference has been made to Yohanan ben Zakkai's lament of moral depravation.[30] But the problem remains: it is not Paul's point that some Jews sometimes do such things; he pretends to be speaking of things that are characteristic of 'Judaism *as a whole* and of *every* individual Jew without exception in view of the coming judgment'. Yet it would be, in historical terms, 'very bold indeed to claim that Paul gives ... an accurate, just and complete picture of contemporary Judaism, and no one will say that the gross sins of the heathens ... were simply typical of the Jew of that time'.[31] In fact, Paul himself gives in Rom 10.2 a quite different characterization of the Jews who have genuine zeal for God's cause.

Since Paul's description leaves, from the historical point of view, much to be desired, interpreters prefer to emphasize the prophetic or even 'apocalyptic' truth of his diagnosis. Paul draws no caricature, but rather a 'prophetic apocalypse' which has 'the totality of all actions of the Jew and of all Jews in view'![32] The apocalyptic way of seeing presents 'what may be empirically an exception (!) as representative of the community'.[33] 'In the disobedience of the individual the impossibility of the whole attitude and teaching comes to light'.[34] Paul tries 'to peer through the concrete surface at the roots and at the bottom from where the murky things he is speaking of rise up ... again and again. The gross offences of individuals show what all are capable of'.[35] If this is so, then what should one infer from, say, 1 Cor 5.1 about the 'attitude and teaching' of the Christians? Paul has double standards when evaluating Jewish and Christian transgressions respectively.[36]

No wonder, then, that some interpreters have found it necessary to play

---

of the style, the literary context' (44). Note that 'trespass' and 'sin' occur as parallels in 5.20. The same is true of chapter 7 (46) and even of chapter 6, where the language is 'metaphorical, rather than realistic', as is shown i.e. by a 'certain untidiness about the parallels' in 6.16–20: 'In verses 16 and 17 sin is contrasted with obedience, in verses 18 and 20 with righteousness, and only in verse 22 with God.' Op.cit. 54.

30 Billerbeck, *Kommentar* III 105–107 with reference to T. Sot 14.1 ff.
31 Kuss; cf. Wilckens.
32 Schlier, 'Juden' 272; followed by Eichholz, *Theologie* 98.
33 Käsemann, *Romans* 69 (who admits that 'in general the life of Pharisees was strict and not infrequently even attracted Gentiles').
34 Michel. Schlatter, *Gerechtigkeit* 107 emphasizes that Paul has communities, rather than individuals, in view. 'Nicht das erwägt er, wie weit sich einzelne gegen die sie verderbende Macht ihrer Gemeinschaft (!) schützen können, sondern wie weit das Vermögen der Gemeinschaft reiche.' If this be so, then the logical conclusion is that the community needs faith in Christ, but the pious individual does not.
35 Kuss. Cf. id., *Paulus* 389, 399 f.
36 Correctly W.L. Knox, *Jerusalem* 123 n. 57: 'The weakness of his position lay in the fact that it did not allow for similar failures among Christians.'

down the vehemence of Paul's charges against the Jews. Barrett admits frankly that 'Paul's argument is lost if he is compelled to rely on comparatively unusual events, and it is simply not true that the average Jewish missionary acted in this way' (as described in Rom 2.21–24). He tries to find a way out of the problem by taking the charges in a figurative sense, but the result is ingenious rather than persuasive.[37] This applies to other similar attempts as well.[38]

Sandmel notes that Paul's account is 'grotesque and vicious'.[39] 'A Jewish reader must ... conclude ... that Paul lacks for those who disagree with him that love which he described in 1 Cor. 13.'[40] A Christian reader should agree! Far from being a 'sober and absolutely realistic judgment of the"world" ',[41] Paul's argument is here simply a piece of propagandist denigration.[42] It is somewhat embarrassing to note that it is given pride of place in Paul's argument in Rom 1–3.[43]

3. Non-Christians fulfilling the law

Verses 2.14–15 and 2.26–27 constitute a special difficulty for Paul's main thesis in the section Rom 1.18–3.20, namely that all are under sin and

---

37 Paul's point, according to Barrett, is simply that the Jewish nation is inwardly guilty. 'When theft, adultery, and sacrilege are strictly and radically understood, there is no man who is not guilty of all three.' Barrett refers to the antitheses of Mt 5.21–48 and to some prophetical texts: the 'theft' means that Israel has usurped the glory that belongs to God (Mal 3.8 f.); 'Israel as the bride of God can hardly escape the charge of adultery' (Hos 1–3, Jer 3.8); the sacrilege consists in that the Jew raises himself to a judge of his neighbour (2.1), thus appropriating the glory due to God! In a similar vein already Kirk, *Romans* 44.

38 Goppelt, *Christologie* 137 ff.: it is with reference to Jesus' radical interpretation of the law that Paul says: you steal and commit adultery, 'denn du umgehst das Gesetz ... selbst in vielfältiger Weise' (142 f.); Goppelt's allegorical interpretation of the sacrilege (145 f.) is particularly incredible. Cf. also Cranfield; Roloff, *Testament* 158, 165.

39 Sandmel, *Genius* 29. Cf. M. Grant, *Paul* 145.

40 Sandmel, op.cit. 30; cf. Montefiore, *Judaism* 203 f.

41 Mussner, *Gal* 193.

42 One of the very few Christian exegetes to admit this is von der Osten-Sacken, 'Verständnis' 564; cf. Luz, 'Gesetz' 97 f. and for the denigration of Gentiles in 1.18–32 Kasting, *Anfänge* 30 n. 19. Osten-Sacken, art.cit. 565 observes that Rom 1–2 entails 'eine erschreckende Ähnlichkeit mit den Prozessen im wörtlichen Sinne, die ablaufen, wenn politische Regimes einander ablösen und über die Vorgänger Gericht halten'. Wrede, *Paulus* 23 commented that Paul might well have had recourse to violent action against his opponents even as a Christian, had he had the necessary power; Osten-Sacken, 'Paulus' 60 f. agrees. Even sharper von Hartmann, *Christentum* 171 n.

43 My understanding of Rom 1.18–2.29 (first outlined in 'Difficulties' 308 f.) is shared by E.P. Sanders, *Law* 124f. He states that 'Paul's case for universal sinfulness, as it is stated in Rom. 1.18–2.29, is not convincing: it is internally inconsistent and it rests on gross exaggeration ...'.

that there is no one doing what is good. In these verses he indicates that there *are*, after all, Gentiles who fulfil the law. No such concession is made to the Jews in this connection. It is certainly symptomatic that these favourable mentions of Gentiles occur just in a passage devoted to polemic against the *Jews*, and not for instance in the course of the hard attack against Gentiles in 1.18—32.

There is no need here to enter into a discussion of the tradition history behind 2.14 f.[44] Paul's overall intention in ch. 2 is to expose the Jew as a transgressor of the law of which he is so proud. From 2.9 onwards Paul makes a clear distinction between Jew and Gentile. The distinction is based on the possession or otherwise of the Torah. Yet neither group has privileges before the righteous God — that is, the Jew is no better off (cf. 3.9a). Those who have sinned ἀνόμως will perish ἀνόμως; those who have sinned ἐν νόμῳ will be judged διὰ νόμου (v. 12). For hearers of the law, i.e. the Jews *per se*, are not righteous, but the 'doers' of the law will be 'rightwised' (οἱ ποιηταὶ νόμου δικαιωθήσονται, v. 13).

Verse 14 is intended to shed light on this last statement: ὅταν γὰρ ἔθνη τὰ μὴ νόμον ἔχοντα φύσει τὰ τοῦ νόμου ποιοῦσιν, οὗτοι νόμον μὴ ἔχοντες ἑαυτοῖς εἰσιν νόμος. 'When Gentiles who do not have the law, do by nature what the law requires, they — although they do not have the law — are a law for themselves.' V. 15 specifies this by speaking of the 'work' (ἔργον) of the law[45] which is written in the hearts of the Gentiles,[46] and of their conscience and of thoughts which either accuse or defend them on the day of judgment.

At this point Paul inserts the harsh polemic against the Jew (v. 17—24). Then he takes up afresh the case of the good Gentile in order to stress the condemnation of the Jew even more effectively. 'Therefore, if one who is uncircumcised keeps the righteous requirements of the law (ἐὰν οὖν ἡ ἀκροβυστία τὰ δικαιώματα τοῦ νόμου φυλάσσῃ), is not his uncircumcision counted to him as circumcision? Thus the one who is by nature uncircum-

---

44 See Bornkamm, *Studien* 101 ff.

45 One should· not infer from this phrase that, by using it, Paul denies that the *law* is 'written' in the hearts of men; cf. Bornkamm, op.cit. 106 as against Nygren and Michel.

46 To conclude with the Reformers that ἔργον τοῦ νόμου in 2.15 corresponds to the negatively qualified 'works of the law', denoting 'that Jewish and human attitude to the *nomos*, by which according to Rom 3.20 no flesh will be rightwised' (Lackmann, *Geheimnis* 215 f.), is inadmissible systematization. 2.15 hints, on the contrary, at the possibility that the pagans in question may stand at the judgment; 2.27, ignored by Lackmann, is a decidedly favourable reference to the Gentiles. Highly artificial also is the interpretation of Reicke, 'Syneidesis' 160: the 'work of the law' denotes the negative task of the law in awakening consciousness of guilt in man (Rom 3.20, 7.7) as preparation for righteousness of faith. It is natural to take v. 15a as parallel to 14b, and surely the Gentiles cannot 'themselves' awaken the sense of guilt in themselves! Nor can the 'work of the law' refer to faith (thus Flückiger, art.cit. 35).

cised (ἡ ἐκ φύσεως ἀκροβυστία) but fulfils the law (τὸν νόμον τελοῦσα) will *condemn you* who are a transgressor of the law (v. 26—27). For a true Jew is the one who is a Jew inwardly, and true circumcision takes place in the Spirit, not in the letter (v. 28—29).[47]

2.14—15, 26—27 stand in flat contradiction to the main thesis of the section. Understandably there is no lack of attempts to reconcile these obstinate statements with Paul's main concern; many theories have been developed to deny that they speak of Gentiles really fulfilling the requirements of the law. None of these is, plausible, however.

1. Some interpreters emphasize the 'casual' nature of the occurrences referred to in these verses: Paul is saying no more than that some precepts of the law are occasionally fulfilled by some Gentiles.[48] But while the wording of v. 14 may remain open to such an interpretation, it clearly fails to do justice to v. 26—27. The expression τὸν νόμον τελοῦσα (v. 27) refers unequivocally to the *totality* of the law.[49] As for verses 14—15, the phrase ἔθνη τὰ μὴ νόμον ἔχοντα is analogous to ἔθνη τὰ μὴ διώκοντα δικαιοσύνην (9.30); Paul has an unspecified number of Gentiles in mind — whether many or few he does not indicate.[50] Moreover, there is in the expression τὰ τοῦ νόμου nothing to suggest a limitation of the number of the precepts fulfilled. As a comparison with corresponding nominalizations shows, it means in general 'that which belongs to the scope of the law'; the quantity of the commandments fulfilled is not limited.[51]

In addition, the 'casual' interpretation does not match the polemical function of the verses. Gentiles fulfilling just a few requirements of the law could hardly condemn the Jew (as v. 27 states), for undoubtedly he has fulfilled a few things as well![52] And as regards the thesis of the section, even a couple of righteous Gentiles would be fatal to it. Yet no stress on the (allegedly) exceptional character of the Gentiles' fulfilling the law is visible in the text.

2. Another suggestion is that Paul is speaking only hypothetically of a case which cannot occur in reality at all.[53] It is hard to see, however, what

---

47 For the traditions behind 2.28 f. see Schweizer, 'Jude' 115 f., 120 ff.

48 Nygren; cf. Maurer, *Gesetzeslehre* 38 f.

49 Of course Paul does not mean that *all* Gentiles do 'the things of the law'; thus Walker, 'Heiden' 304. Walker's conclusion (305) borders on the absurd: since law and sin belong together in Paul's theology, τὰ τοῦ νόμου ποιεῖν must mean sinning!

50 Cf. Feine, *Evangelium* 115.

51 Feine, op.cit. 116. Feine carries through a comparison with τὰ τῆς σαρκός and τὰ τοῦ πνεύματος Rom 8.5, τὰ τῆς εἰρήνης Rom 14.19, τὰ τοῦ ἀνθρώπου 1 Cor 2.11, τὰ τοῦ πνεύματος θεοῦ 1 Cor 2.14, τὰ τοῦ κυρίου and τὰ τοῦ κόσμου 1 Cor 7.32—34.

52 Correctly Flückiger, 'Werke' 27—29.

53 Grafe, *Lehre* 25 f. (Paul puts himself hypothetically in the position of his opponents!); van Dülmen, *Theologie* 77, 82; Vos, *Untersuchungen* 110; R.E. Howard, *Newness* 92; cf. also Lietzmann.

point there would have been in taking up such a fictitious matter at all. Above all, such an imaginary Gentile would be of no use for Paul's polemic against the Jew. How could a non-existent Gentile 'condemn' him?[54]

3. A few scholars think that the verses are to be understood in the light of Rom 8.4. That is, Paul is speaking of Gentile *Christians*.[55] This view is often supported by the argument that Paul alludes in v. 15 to Jer 38.33 LXX – to the prediction of the new covenant which belongs to the Christians.[56]

But from 2.9 onwards Paul systematically juxtaposes Jew and *Greek* (explicitly twice in v. 9–10). In this context it is very difficult to take ἔϑνη in any other sense than 'non-Jew' in general.[57] Furthermore, it is inconceivable that Paul could say that Gentile Christians fulfil the law by *nature, φύσει*,[58] for the Christians' fulfilment of the law is the fruit of the *Spirit* (Rom 8.4, cf. Gal 5.22 f.). And how could he say that Gentile Christians are without the law in the sense that it is unknown to them?[59] But supposing he could, then what does it mean that Gentile Christians *are* a (the) law for themselves?[60] One would have supposed them to be ἔννομοι χριστοῦ (cf.

---

54 Käsemann, *Perspektiven* 242 objects that an uncircumcised pagan cannot fulfil the whole Torah, and therefore he must be a fiction. But Paul's concept of the 'law' is extremely flexible (see ch. I); in fact he has only the moral content of the Torah in view here. If this objection were decisive, Paul would not be able to argue elsewhere that the Christians fulfil the law either.

55 T. Zahn; Feine, op.cit. 122–126; Mundle, 'Auslegung'; K. Barth, *Dogmatik* I, 2, 332; Souček, 'Exegese' 101 ff.; M. Barth, 'Stellung' 521 n. 62; König, 'Gentiles'; Cranfield, Viard. For 2.26–27 also Bultmann, *Theology* 261 n.; for 2.27 Schlier. For a history of this interpretation see Riedl, *Heil* 222 (Riedl himself is critical of it); for criticisms also Kuss, 'Heiden' 78 f.

56 See, e.g., Mundle, art.cit. 251; Souček, art.cit. 102 f.; K. Barth, loc.cit.; M. Barth, art.cit. 521 n. 62; Viard, *Romans* 79.

57 Correctly Bornkamm, op.cit. 109.

58 Correctly Kuhr, 'Römer 2₁₄ f.' 255 ff. This difficulty is conceded and extensively reflected upon by Souček, art.cit. 106 ff. He ends up by (following Flückiger, 'Werke' 32 f.) taking φύσει in the sense of 'artgemäss', so that it is in Rom 2.14 'Bezeichnung der vom Geiste Gottes geprägten "Art" des Glaubenden' (109). Cf. also Feine, op.cit. 117. It is, however, very difficult to understand why Paul should hit on an expression that was so highly open to misunderstanding, when he could simply have written πνεύματι (cf. 2.29, on which see below, n. 64). The definition 'artgemäss' is far too abstract; Paul elsewhere never refers to the new existence in Christ with φύσις. Cranfield connects φύσει with what precedes, making Paul speak of Gentile Christians who 'by nature do not have the law' (cf. ἡ ἐκ φύσεως ἀκροβυστία 2.27; φύσει Ἰουδαῖοι. Gal 2.15; τέκνα φύσει ὀργῆς Eph 2.3); so also König, art.cit. 58. This would indeed resolve the just mentioned difficulty. Even Cranfield's interpretation, however, fails to do justice to the phrase ἑαυτοῖς εἰσιν νόμος; see n. 60.

59 Cf. Lackmann, art.cit. 214 f.; Kuhr, art.cit. 252; Bornkamm, op.cit. 109.

60 Cranfield takes refuge to circumlocutions like 'they now *know* it (the law)', or '(they) have the *desire* to obey it'. This is, however, something other than ἑαυτοῖς εἰσιν νόμος.

1 Cor 9.21) or something like that. Surely Rom 2.14 f. speaks of something else than 8.4 (which verse, incidentally, does not have specifically Gentile Christians in view).[61]

Moreover, it is unlikely that v. 15 is intended as an allusion to Jer 38 (31), even though the wording may owe something to that passage.[62] There is no talk at all of a new covenant in this connection, in contrast to 2 Cor 3.6 ff. (even though a reference to Jeremiah is dubious even there[63]); when Paul speaks of the new covenant, he does not fail to stress the role of the Spirit in it (2 Cor 3.6).[64]

4. Some scholars think of a special theological qualification of the ἔϑνη, be it the Christians (Jewish and Gentile) as God's eschatological people,[65] or Jews and Gentiles from a 'typological' point of view[66], or the 'eschatological' Jew,[67] or Jews and Gentiles actually already under the influence of Christ and the Spirit.[68] The simple, clearly ethnic distinction between Jew and Greek in v. 9—10 would seem sufficient to preclude such speculations, and the word ἀκροβυστία certainly excludes any Jewish element.

We thus have to accept that Paul is really speaking of Gentiles who fulfil the law outside the Christian community. It is also wrong to play down these statements by claiming that their point is that the Gentiles, too, can be justly judged (since they are not actually without a knowledge of God's will either).[69] Surely this idea need not be excluded from v. 14—16 as a second-

---

61 Souček, art.cit. 104, also refers to the verb λογίζεσϑαι in 2.26, which is said to be 'fast ein technischer Terminus der paulinischen Rechtfertigungslehre'. But if Paul were speaking of the justification of the Gentile Christians in 2.26, he would actually claim that fulfilment of the law, or producing the fruit of the Spirit, is counted by God as righteousness — instead of faith!

62 Correctly Kuhr, art.cit. 259 f.; Kuss; Bornkamm, op.cit. 107; Köster, φύσις 268 n. 231; Hahn, 'Gesetzesverständnis' 32 f. does assume a direct allusion to Jer 38 (31) but does not share the Gentile Christian theory.

63 See below, VIII 3.

64 In 2.29, however, Paul seems at last to have the Christian in mind, as is indicated by the reference to the Spirit — not just Gentile Christians (thus Käsemann) but Christians at large (cf. Phil 3.3 'for we (including Paul!) are the true circumcision, we that worship God *in the Spirit*'). To be sure, the train of thought would be clearer and the contrast more effective, if this verse, too, were intended as a reference to mere Gentiles (thus Nygren; E.P. Sanders, *Law* 127 who takes πνεῦμα in the sense of 'heart'). That Paul can 'glide' in his reasoning from Gentiles to Christians is another indication that Gentiles have no 'self value' in the argument; their importance lies only in the possibility of charging the Jew.

65 Flückiger, art.cit. 24 f.

66 H.W. Schmidt.

67 Käsemann, op.cit. 74.

68 Bläser, op.cit. 195 f.

69 Thus Bornkamm, op.cit. 98 f., 110; Kuhr, art.cit. 254; Jüngel, *Paulus* 26—28; Kümmel, *Bild* 185; Walker, art.cit. 304, 308; Käsemann; Synofzik, *Vergeltungsaussagen*

ary theme (there is a reference to the judgment in v. 15 f., although it is not said that the Gentiles will not stand it). But in v. 26–27 there is no reference whatsoever to a judgment over the Gentiles; these are mentioned in an altogether favourable tone.

It is important to observe that the Gentiles are merely a means to an end for Paul's argument in ch. 2.[70] There is no interest in them as Gentiles. Paul is only interested in proving the Jew guilty. For this purpose, and for it alone, law-fulfilling Gentiles appear rather abruptly, and disappear again. They are used as convenient weapons to hit the Jew with. Hereby Paul, surely without noticing it, creates a contradiction with both 1.18–32 and 3.9. *When Paul is not reflecting on the situation of the Gentiles, it is quite natural for him to think that they can fulfil the law.* (When he turns to reflection, the picture is quite different, as 1.18–32, but also 3.9 shows.)

If Gentiles can fulfil the law, then logically that ought to be possible for the Jews as well, although Paul (reflecting on the Jews) does not say so in this passage. In another connection (Phil 3.6) he says, however, that he himself was 'blameless' ($\check{\alpha}\mu\epsilon\mu\pi\tau\sigma$) 'according to the righteousness of the law'.[71] Even in retrospect Paul omits to suggest that he might have transgressed the law in his Pharisaic life; quite on the contrary. From the new Christian point of view that life according to the law is, of course, given a negative qualification as righteousness 'of the law', but the actual fulfilment is not called into question. The conclusion suggests itself: *when Paul is not reflecting on the situation of the Jews from a certain theological angle he does not presuppose that it is impossible to fulfil the law.*[72]

The theological thesis in Rom 1.18–3.20 is that all are under sin and that, therefore, no one can fulfil the law.[73] Inadvertently, however, Paul admits

---

81 f.; Keck, art.cit. 153. According to van Dülmen, *Theologie* 78, the point of vv. 14–16 is that 'Heiden und Juden versagen in gleicher Weise'! Correctly Vos, op.cit. 109 f. with n. 11.

70 Cf. Pohlenz, 'Paulus' 75; Beker, *Paul* 80.

71 There is no irony in Phil 3.5 f.; correctly Gnilka, ad loc.

72 Correctly Drane, *Paul* 29: 'As a Pharisee, it was quite likely that he could have imagined a situation in which he was capable of keeping the law ... ' Drane continues (152 n. 36): 'In more optimistic moments even as a Christian, Paul could say as much: cf. Philippians 3.4 ff.' I would only substitute some such expression as that given above in the text for 'more optimistic moments'.

73 Synofzik, Aussagen 88 claims that the message of Rom 3.20 is that the works of law man has *accomplished* cannot make him righteous before God (being an expression of man's basic sin, the desire to 'be something' before God). He denies the connection of v. 20 with what precedes and interprets the verse in the light of (a Bultmannian interpretation of) 3.21–30 – despite the $\delta\iota\acute{o}\tau\iota$ (v. 20a) that clearly shows that v. 20 is the consequence of the preceding section (this difficulty is seen but not removed by Synofzik, op.cit. 89). On the Bultmannian understanding of the basis of Paul's critique of the 'works of the law' see below, V 2.

even within that very section that, on another level of his consciousness at least, he does not share this idea. Paul's mind is divided.

The implications of these inadvertent admissions are highly significant. As for Rom 2, O'Neill's comment is to the point: the whole assumption of Rom 2 'is that Jews and Gentiles can keep the Law, and can act in a manner to deserve God's praise by obeying the commandments'. On the basis of 2.1–16 'the best way to help Gentiles to be righteous would be to preach to them the Law.'[74] Paul Feine made the point even sharper: 'If Paul made the statement 2.14–16 about unconverted Gentiles (Feine denied this), then he was wrong with his preaching about the crucified Son of God. Humanity did not need him. For it had indeed in its moral disposition, in its natural equipment a possession it only had to cultivate in order to fulfil God's will. It was able to do φύσει, by nature, that which according to the teaching of the Apostle only becomes possible for the Christian through the power of God's Spirit ... '[75]

Feine declares, understandably enough, that such thoughts seem to be for Paul as foreign as possible. That is for him the decisive reason for taking refuge in the 'Gentile Christian' interpretation of the verses we have been dealing with.[76] But as this interpretation is not feasible, as we indeed have to take the 'Gentile' interpretation at full value, the conclusion is inevitable that there is a formidable tension in Paul's thought at this point.

We have detected a double weakness in Paul's argument in Rom 1.18–3.20. The empirical argument does not correspond to empirical facts, but amounts to denigration pure and simple. On the other hand, Paul inadvertently admits that some people are not under sin in the sense he has argued; this destroys his theological conclusion. These observations indicate that *there is something strained and artificial in Paul's theory that nobody can fulfil (or has fulfilled) the law.* I do not mean artificial from *our* point of view; it is easy enough for us, with all the introspective Christian insights from Augustine onwards at our disposal,[77] to agree that no man comes close

---

74 *Romans* 48. Cf. already van Manen, *Unechtheit* 52; W.L. Knox, *Jerusalem* 351 n. 10. O'Neill draws the rash conclusion that Rom 2 is not by Paul (cf. van Manen). See further Bremer, *Understanding* 198; Pregeant, 'Grace' 76. E.P. Sanders, *Law* 123–135 argues that the section is a Synagogue sermon, altered by Paul 'in only insubstantial ways' (123). He notes that 'the treatment of the law in chapter 2 cannot be harmonized with any of the diverse things which Paul says about the law elsewhere' (122). Because what is said about the law in this chapter 'cannot be fitted into a category otherwise known from Paul's letters' (132), Sanders resorted to dealing with Romans 2 in an appendix. I fear that this procedure results in a picture of Paul's treatment of the law, which, for all the trenchant analyses presented by Sanders, still looks a bit too coherent.

75 Op.cit. 123. Cf. also König, art.cit. 54, 58 f.

76 Feine later revoked this interpretation without presenting new arguments: *Theologie* 190.

77 That Paul lacked the 'introspective conscience' which was only introduced into Chris-

to moral perfection. But the theory is artificial in terms of *Paul's* own heart-felt convictions. As Dodd puts it, 'For the purpose of his general argument he takes the extreme view that no one ... does or can obey the law; but in concrete cases he allows that in some measure at least the good pagan (and of course the good Jew, as he implies in ii. 28) can do the right thing.'[78] The explanation must be that Paul is *pushed to develop his argument into a preordained direction.* It can only be the firmness of a preconceived conviction that has prevented Paul from seeing the weakness of his reasoning. He simply *had* to come to the conclusion that the law cannot be fulfilled.

The reason for this compulsion is clearly enough stated in Gal 2.21: the law *must* not be a viable way to God, for in that case the death of Christ was not necessary. Christ would have died in vain! The argument that no one can fulfil the law is a device to serve the assertion that the death of Christ was a salvific act that was absolutely necessary for all mankind (including the Jews).[79] Paul argued, as E.P. Sanders has emphasized, *'backwards'.* He tried, as it were, to define man's disease by analyzing the medicine which he knew to be wholesome and indispensable. 'Paul actually came to the view that all men are under the lordship of sin as a reflex of his soteriology: Christ came to provide a new lordship for those who participate in his death and resurrection.'[80]

---

tian thought by Augustine, was pointed out by Stendahl, *Paul* 78 ff.

78 Romans 37. I would delete the words 'in some measure at least'. Cf. also Stendahl, op.cit. 81.

79 Thus already Wernle, *Anfänge* 164 f.; cf. Kuss, 'Nomos' 217. Wernle wrote: 'Weil Jesus allein der Erlöser ... ist, darum muss die Menschheit ausser Christus so ganz verdorben und verloren sein, dass ihr jeder andere Rettungsweg abgeschnitten ist ... Nicht eine vorausgehende Erkenntnis der Grösse der Sünde und der Ohnmacht des Menschen ist die Wurzel dieser Theorie, sondern der Glaube an Christus hat die pessimistischen Postulate als Voraussetzungen erfordert ... Paulus entwarf ein Gemälde der Geschichte der Menschheit so trostlos grausam und dunkel, wie noch nie ein frommer Mensch es ausgedacht hatte, damit wir um so herzlicher für das wunderbare Licht danken könnten ... Diese Uebertreibung des Wahren im Dienst der Apologetik ist um so verhängnisvoller geworden als die Kirche nun mit diesem Pessimismus gute "Geschäfte" zu machen begann.'

80 Sanders, *Paul* 499. The point that in Paul's reasoning the solution preceded the problem is not at all an 'absurdity', as Caird asserts in his review of Sanders. Caird refers to the fact that Paul is (in Rom 1.18–32) probably following the line of thought set forth in Sap 13–14 (whether or not he knew the book, I would add); Paul then shows that the Jews participate in the sin of the pagans – which is no novel allegation, as it had been pronounced already by John the Baptist. The point for me is, however, that Paul *does not succeed* in showing the sinfulness of the Jews in any empirically or logically convincing way. Whatever John the Baptist may have thought, Paul (when thinking spontaneously and not aprioristically as here) did *not* assume that the Jews were a *massa perditionis* from the moral point of view. On the contrary, they were aiming at righteousness (Rom 9.31) and displaying zeal for God (Rom 10.2).

If this is so, Rom 1.18–3.20 helps us to solve the problem that was seen to consist in the juxtaposition of two independent arguments concerning the curse of the law in Gal 3.10–12.[81] It is the latter argument (verses 11–12) that expresses the core of Paul's soteriological theory. That law and faith exclude each other as opposed principles is his aprioristic starting-point, in analogy to the statement in Gal 2.21. Just as in Rom 1.18–3.20, Paul tries to support the preconceived theological thesis with an 'empirical' argument which is not really suited to support it. In the light of Rom 2.14–16, 26–27 and Phil 3.6 we may surmise that the 'rigorous' presupposition that the law must be fulfilled 100 per cent (Gal 3.10) is artificial in the same sense as the contention that nobody fulfils the law in Rom 1.18–3.20. No 'normal' Jew would have subscribed to such an 'overstrained definition'[82] of the claim of the law; there are indications that at bottom Paul agreed with them. When he was not arguing a soteriological thesis, Paul apparently did not subscribe to his rigorous definition. And precisely because in his 'normal' state he did *not* think that a 100 per cent fulfilment of the law was necessary for one to speak of fulfilment at all, it was natural for him to think that pagan and Jew were indeed able to fulfil it. It is the theological theory that has occasioned a radicalization of the law's claim in retrospect.[83]

4. Non-Christians cannot do good at all

It is hardly necessary to argue once more that the famous passage *Rom 7.14–25* is not intended by Paul as a description of the Christian.[84] It can by now be taken for granted that he is speaking of man's existence under the law; whether the description contains any autobiographical elements or not need not be considered here (see VIII 1). The 'I' of the passage does not do good (v. 19); he does the evil he hates and did not want to do (v. 15, 19).

---

81 See above. p. 96.

82 Moore, *Judaism* III 150; cf. above, p. 95.

83 Kuss, art.cit. 217, discussing Rom 2, points out that Paul radicalizes the claim of the law 'nachträglich', the reason being that 'indem Paulus seinen Standpunkt bei Jesus Christus einnimmt, ohne den es Rettung, Heil für ihn schlechthin nicht mehr geben kann, ist er gezwungen, die Nutzlosigkeit des Gesetzesweges zu behaupten'.

84 See above all Kümmel, *Römer* 7. For the 'Christian' interpretation see Nygren, Cranfield; Dunn, 'Rom. 7, 14–25'; D.H. Campbell, 'Identity'; Wenham, 'Life'. To uphold this interpretation Dunn (263) has to assert that even in Rom 8.4–11 'Paul does not contrast believer with unbeliever; rather, he confronts the believer with both sides of the paradox, both sides of his nature as believer'. For a critique see Gundry, 'Frustration' 236–238, 243 n. 32. In this article Gundry presents a powerful argument from a *conservative* perspective *against* the 'Christian' interpretation of Rom 7.14–25. His own explanation, however (Paul speaks of his pre-conversion sexual difficulties), fails to carry conviction. Feuillet, 'Loi de Dieu' 35 ff. thinks that the passage speaks of all men, including the Christians (in view of the 'law of Christ'!).

Taken literally, these repeated statements convey a completely wretched picture of the 'ego'. He is not able to do any good at all. He is completely incapable of realizing his good intentions. It is not said that *something* is always amiss even in the best actions; the idea is that of a *total* failure.[85] Interpreters mostly wonder at the allegedly too favourable picture of the unredeemed man's will and 'mind' in this passage.[86] Yet it would seem that its peculiarity consists in that it paints a more *negative* picture of that man's *actions* than might be expected. The general tone reminds one of the polemic caricatures in Rom 1.18–32, 2.17–24 with the difference that the charges in chs. 1–2 are very concrete, whereas the description in ch. 7 is abstract; in addition, nothing is said about the non-Christians' will to good in chs. 1–2. It goes without saying that the favourable flashes in Rom 2.14–15, 26–27 stand in an irreconcilable tension with ch. 7.

The intention of Rom 7 is comparable to that of Rom 1–3 or Gal 3: it is a sustained argument about the significance of the law. The question of the nature of the law is raised in 7.7. The conclusion is that the law is 'good' (v. 16), but without power to help man (8.3). The section starts as an 'apology for the law', but in his attempt to show that the law, far from being 'sin', is actually 'good' – the man under law has to concede this (v. 16) – Paul glides back to a criticism of the law. The description of man's moral conflict in v. 14–25 thus serves two purposes with respect to the law: it is intended to show both the goodness of the law and its weakness. Man under law cannot resist the might of the indwelling sin (v. 17).

In 7.14–25 Paul is taking up the notion, well-known in Greek tradition, of a moral conflict in man: man does what is wrong, even though he knows what is right.[87] This experiential wisdom is to some extent paralleled by the confessions of sin found at Qumran,[88] and Rabbinic speculations about the power of the evil inclination over man come rather close to it, too.[89] As Paul had taken up Jewish Wisdom traditions in his polemic against Gentiles in 1.18–32, he now draws on Hellenistic traditions which serve his apology for the law.

Paul is reflecting on the significance of the law for the man under it. That he presupposes in such a connection that no one can fulfil the law, should

---

85 Cf. Bultmann, *Exegetica* 199; Gundry, art.cit. 238.
86 Cf. Kümmel, op.cit. 135 f.; Käsemann, *Romans* 207. For Cranfield (Romans) and Feuillet (art.cit.) the difference between this passage and Rom 1.18–32, 6.17–20, is an indication that Paul is not describing the existence of unredeemed man in it.
87 See Hommel, '7. Kapitel', who traces the tradition back to Euripides' criticism of the pedagogical optimism of Socrates.
88 Cf. H. Braun, 'Römer 7, 7–25'.
89 Cf. Schoeps, *Paul* 185 f. (but the assertion that 'Paul's doctrine of sin was not unusual but indeed typical of his time', op.cit. 187, goes definitely too far).

come as no surprise after our previous discussion in this chapter. Once more Paul takes an empirically observable phenomenon and jumps from it to a radical theological conclusion (actually a *non sequitur*). In Rom 1–2 the observation was that 'many people live in grave sins', the conclusion: 'all are under sin'. In Rom 7 Paul infers from the well-known discrepancy between intentions and actions that no one (under the law) does any good at all. So the law is incapable of helping man to a life according to God's will, *q.e.d.*[90]

The above interpretation presupposes that Rom 7.14–25 speaks indeed of a moral conflict and man's moral impotence. This is denied by a number of scholars, notably Bultmann and his followers, who propose a 'transsubjective' interpretation. 'Good', 'evil' and 'doing' are taken in a very special sense. Man wills 'life', but 'effects' something else, namely 'death' – not so much by his inability to fulfil the law, but above all because he *attempts* to fulfil the law and thus to establish his own righteousness.[91] Moreover, the passage is taken to reflect the effects of man's 'desire' ($\epsilon\pi\iota\vartheta\nu\mu\acute{\iota}\alpha$), which was mentioned in 7.7–8, and this $\epsilon\pi\iota\vartheta\nu\mu\acute{\iota}\alpha$ is interpreted primarily as a 'nomistic' desire[92] – man's will to fulfil the law which leads to his elevating himself and boasting.

I cannot but concur with Paul Althaus in the judgment that this interpretation is 'completely artificial'. It 'has to reinterpret all essential concepts of Rom 7 in a blunt contradiction to the context and to Paul's usage elsewhere. This holds true of "good" and 'evil", the meaning of which cannot be different from that in 2.9, and of $\vartheta\acute{\epsilon}\lambda\epsilon\iota\nu$ ... It is likewise an act of violence to understand $\pi o\iota e\tilde{\iota}\nu$ and $\pi\rho\acute{\alpha}\sigma\sigma\epsilon\iota\nu$ in 15b like $\kappa\alpha\tau\epsilon\rho\gamma\acute{\alpha}\zeta\epsilon\sigma\vartheta\alpha\iota$ as "bringing in", as one should on the contrary interpret $\kappa\alpha\tau\epsilon\rho\gamma\acute{\alpha}\zeta\epsilon\sigma\vartheta\alpha\iota$, which can in itself have different meanings in Paul (cf. 2.9 with 7.13), at this place in accordance with ... $\pi o\iota e\tilde{\iota}\nu$ and $\pi\rho\acute{\alpha}\sigma\sigma\epsilon\iota\nu$ in the sense of "doing" as in 2.9. The same is true of the concept $\epsilon\pi\iota\vartheta\nu\mu\acute{\iota}\alpha$ ... In the text of Rom 7.7 ff. it is unequivocally a question of the desire which leads to transgression of the law.'[93] I have dealt

---

90 I first suggested this interpretation of Rom 7 in 'Difficulties' 310f. For a convincing analysis of the passage along not dissimilar lines see now E.P. Sanders, *Law* 73–81, 124. He correctly points out that 'the human plight, without Christ, is so hopeless in this section that one wonders what happened to the doctrine that the creation was good' (75). Sanders suggests that part of the passion of Rom 7 'is generated by the depth of Paul's dilemma' (80), his desire to exonerate God who gave a law which is on the side of sin, death and the flesh.

91 Bultmann, *Exegetica* 198 ff.; id. *Theology* 247 f. Cf., e.g., Bornkamm, *Ende* 62 f.; Braun, art.cit. 3; Käsemann, op.cit. 200 f., 203 f.; Sand, *Fleisch* 191; Furnish, *Theology* 141 f.; Schlier ad loc.; Schmithals, *Anthropologie* 47 ff.; Jewett, *Terms* 147.

92 The term comes from Bornkamm, op.cit. 55.

93 Althaus, *Paulus* 47–49. In his reply Bultmann, *Glauben* II 45, only reiterates his view; while pointing out some weaknesses in Althaus' overall position, he does nothing to weaken the force of Althaus' objections to his exegesis. For criticisms of the Bultmannian interpretation see further Gutbrod, *Anthropologie* 45 f.; Kuss, *Römerbrief* I 470; Schrage, *Einzelgebote* 195 f.; also Niederwimmer, *Freiheit* 129 n. 130

with Bultmann's and his followers' understanding of ἐπιθυμία elsewhere[94] and think that I may simply refer the reader to that discussion instead of repeating it here.[95] Besides its general artificiality (caused by the need to harmonize a difficult passage with the interpreter's overall view of sin in Paul's theology — sin understood as hybris and pious boasting), it is a deficiency of the Bultmannian interpretation that it makes a lesson in anthropology out of a passage explicitly intended by Paul as a discussion about the *law*.[96]

It is interesting to see both Bultmann and especially Käsemann attack the natural 'moral conflict' interpretation of Rom 7.14–25 because of its theological implications.[97] Käsemann will have nothing to do with a Paul so understood. 'If he were simply bewailing our lack of will-power, he would have to be resisted in the name of mankind, even though the lamentable aspect cannot be overlooked.' In such a hopeless theology 'not even the level of Qumran is reached'. '*The ethical conflict as such ... does not demonstrate the "sold under sin,"*' as precisely Qumran is able to show ... It does not show us what sin is as resistance to the right of the Creator. This is reflected on a lower level only to the extent that a person is never finished with himself. If the apostle were to rest content with this truism of experience he would be working with *inadequate means* and would be presenting a *weak theology*, or, more accurately, *no theology* at all, but a psychology oriented to the ethical problem.'[98]

So what? If the transsubjective interpretation is artificial, we are left with the quite correct observation that 7.14–25 does not prove the thesis 'I am sold under sin' it was designed to prove — just as Rom 1.18–32, 2.17–24 fails to demonstrate that 'all are under sin'. However, before harsh value judgments are passed on Paul's theology (or 'psychology') along the lines suggested by Käsemann it should be remembered that the passage is not really

----

despite his general sympathy with Bultmann's position. Even Käsemann, op.cit. 202 refutes Bultmann's interpretation of κατεργάζομαι; it is not clear to me how he nevertheless manages to concur with Bultmann's overall view.

94 Räisänen, 'Gebrauch'; the article is devoted to a critique of the views of Bultmann, Bornkamm, Käsemann, Mauser (*Gottesbild* 155 ff.), and Lyonnet ('Tu ne ... pas'). The 'nomistic' interpretation of ἐπιθυμία in Rom 7.7 f. now also appears in Hübner, ἐπιθυμία 70 f.

95 Outside of Rom 7, ἐπιθυμία (when used in a negative sense) always carries moral overtones in Paul's writings: Rom 1.24, 6.12, 13.14, Gal 5.16, 5.24, 1 Thess 4.5. In Rom 7.7–8 ἐπιθυμία is paralleled by τὰ παθήματα τῶν ἁμαρτιῶν in 7.5.

96 Cf. Räisänen, art.cit. 87.

97 Bultmann, *Exegetica* 201 called it a 'cheap insight'.

98 *Romans* 201 f. (emphasis added). Käsemann is quite correct in his observation that Rom 7 (on the 'moral conflict' interpretation) with its 'global statements' conceals the 'differentiated reality' and above all contradicts Rom 2.12 ff. 26 f. (p. 201). But this is no reason to have recourse to an unnatural interpretation of ch. 7.

meant to be an anthropological lecture.[99] It is concerned with the law, and it is hardly safe to base any other Pauline 'doctrines' on it. Again, the pattern appears to be that the thesis is clear in advance, and Paul snatches up more or less suitable arguments to support it wherever he meets them.

The treatment of the law ends up with the statement that the Christians are able to fulfil what it requires (8.4). Then Christian and non-Christian existence are once more contrasted in 8.5–11. The picture of the non-Christian is even darker than in the previous passage. There is nothing that would correspond to his 'delight in the law of God as far as his inward man is concerned' (7.22); there is no 'mind' ($\nu o \tilde{v} \varsigma$) as an antipode to the flesh in Rom 8 as there is in ch. 7. Thus the comparison in ch. 8 is absolutely black-and-white. The 'fleshly' non-Christians display a fleshly mind ($\tau \grave{o} \ \varphi \rho \acute{o} \nu \eta \mu a \ \tau \tilde{\eta} \varsigma$ $\sigma a \rho \kappa \acute{o} \varsigma$ v. 6, $\tau \grave{a} \ \tau \tilde{\eta} \varsigma \ \sigma a \rho \kappa \grave{o} \varsigma \ \varphi \rho o \nu o \tilde{v} \sigma \iota \nu$ v. 5), which is enmity to God (v. 7) and neither will nor can be subjected to God's law (v. 7).[100] Therefore, men living 'in the flesh' are unable to please God (v. 8). The passage reminds one of Rom 1.18–32 and 2.17–24, but the introduction of the concept of $\sigma \acute{a} \rho \xi$ adds a new tone. One is inclined to speak of a demonization of non-Christian existence.[101]

5. Christians fulfil the law

Paul assumes within the framework of his theological theory first that the law cannot be fulfilled apart from the union with Christ and, secondly, that the Christians fulfil what is required by the law (Gal 5.14 ff., Rom 13.8–10, Rom 8.4, cf. Rom 2.29).[102] Throughout this discussion the law is under-

---

99 Correctly Kümmel, op.cit. 135, 137; Stendahl, *Paul* 92 f.; as against e.g. Althaus, Dunn, and Schmithals.

100 This phrase makes the assumption quite unlikely that Paul is thinking primarily of the self-righteous who misuse the law; thus Schweizer, $\sigma \acute{a} \rho \xi$ 133 n. 274.

101 Stacey, *View* 162–164 put forward a tempting thesis, apparently ignored in subsequent scholarship: as regards $\sigma \acute{a} \rho \xi$ in Paul's theology, Rom 8 represents the end result of a theological development, an extreme statement that is not suited to be the point of departure when one sets forth Paul's conception of the 'flesh'. This view runs parallel to our observations about the artificiality of some of Paul's most 'radical' statements about unredeemed man. Stacey does not assume that we could trace a development in the notion of $\sigma \acute{a} \rho \xi$, say, from Gal to Rom; rather, both letters show signs of *various* phases of that development. I disagree, however, with Stacey's explanation of the rationale of the development, which he would find in Paul's 'intensity of feeling' (165), 'desperation' (163), 'the anguish of his unique personal struggle with sin' (173). Stacey has to assume that Rom 7 is a description of Paul the Christian (178 f.). His basic observation, however, is sound: there is a development in the use of $\sigma \acute{a} \rho \xi$ which leads to exaggerated statements about the flesh as quasi personified in Gal 5 and Rom 8 (165).

102 1 Cor. 13, too, should be read as an account of what the Spirit effects (or, in the special case of the Corinthians, *should* effect) in the Christian community. It is wrong to

stood in the sense of the moral content of the Torah; we need not be concerned with the oscillation of the concept in this connection, for the non-fulfilment of the Torah by the Jews is 'demonstrated' by Paul in purely moral terms, too. The trouble with this argument is, however, that its first part could only be supported with denigration and caricature, as we have seen. Not only that; the second part that the Christians really — albeit charismatically, with the aid of the Spirit — fulfil the law is equally problematic.[103]

It is essential for Paul's argument that he can confront Jewish transgression of the law with Christian fulfilment of it. Man under law is incapable of coping with the law (Rom 7.14–25, 8.5–8); not so the Christians (8.4, 8.9–11). Rom 6.14a states with joyous assurance that sin will not reign over Christians who have died to it (6.7);[104] v. 14b tells that this is so because they are not under law, but under grace, thus implying that those under the law are slaves of sin. Gal 5.18 likewise suggests that 'works of the flesh' as described in v. 19–21 are the product of an existence under the law.[105] In freedom from the law the fruit of the Spirit is grown (v. 22–23); the purport

assert that 'the description of ἀγάπη in these verses goes far beyond a description of human existence', so that the passage 'describes what man is not' (J.T. Sanders, *Ethics* 53, following K. Barth). Sanders presses Paul's words, reading too many modern introspective insights into the phrases 'does not seek its own' (v. 5a) and 'all' (v. 7). V. 5a is paralleled in 1 Cor 10.24 within the framework of very concrete exhortation; in 1 Cor 10.33 Paul states without the slightest hesitation that he for one does not seek his own advantage! Phil 2.20 f. says the same thing about Timothy. As for v. 7, Paul applies the πάντα στέγει to himself and Barnabas in 1 Cor 9.12. 1 Cor 13 is thus simply intended as a description of what the normal Christian should be and usually is. In a more prosaic and exhortatory form Paul says as much in Phil 4.8 (J. Weiss on 1 Cor 13). All in all, Paul is following traditional models (cf. Test. Patr.) in 1 Cor 13 (see Conzelmann, ad loc.). Interestingly enough, Conzelmann can judge that the passage stands out as Christian only because of the context!

103 It is quite wrong to weaken the content of Rom 8.4 the way Cranfield, 'Paul' 66 does: the establishment of the law 'is as yet imperfect (for even those who have received the Spirit fall very short of full obedience)'; cf. id., *Romans* ad loc.: Christians fulfil the law 'in the sense that they have a real faith in God', 'in the sense that their lives are definitely turned in the direction of obedience'. Cf. also Nygren. This is simply an attempt to make Paul's extravagant statement tolerable to the sensitivities of a modern Christian. Best observes that 'Paul does not say that "we are now able to fulfil the actual commandments of the Law" ' and thinks that the point is that the requirement of the law 'has been met because sin has been condemned' (that is, in the death of Christ). Cf. also Dugandzic, 'Ja' 174 f.; Beker, *Paul* 107, 186, 243. This interpretation fails because of the ἐν ἡμῖν. Correctly e.g. Lietzmann; Ladd, 'Paul' 66; Bruce, 'Paul' 275.

104 οὐ κυριεύσει is a real future, expressing 'dogmatic assurance' (Lietzmann); cf. Kuss; Mauerhofer, *Kampf* 94.

105 Cf. Loisy, *Galates* 190; Cerfaux, *Christian* 461 f. One may note here that when Schmithals, *Gnostics* 46 ff. argues that Paul's opponents were libertinist Gnostics rather than Judaizers and that Paul is attacking their way of life in Gal 5.13 ff., he ignores verses 5.18 and 23. These verses do in fact indicate a conflict with 'Judaizers'.

of v. 23b is probably to suggest that the law has nothing to object to a life producing fruit of the Spirit. This remark thus gives in a slightly ironic form expression to the thought which is then positively stated in Rom 8.4.[106] It is the Christians and they alone who really fulfil what the law requires.

Gal 5.16 implies that it is possible for a Christian to walk in the Spirit so that he does not 'fulfil the desire of the flesh'. This is indeed the normal situation of the Christian.[107] Galatians conveys an extremely 'optimistic' picture of the spiritual life of the Christian community. It almost seems that the 'Christians live on a new level of existence, and so their actions will automatically follow from this new kind of existence'.[108] And yet Paul, in the same letter, has to hint at internal strifes among the Galatian Christians in

---

106 Cf. Lietzmann; van Dülmen, *Theologie* 63.
107 Gal 5.17 refers, however, to the threat posed even for the Christian by the tempting power of the flesh. It is difficult to make out the precise meaning of the sentence. The point can hardly be that man is but the battle-field of two opposed forces, an empty vessel as it were, to be filled either by the flesh or by the Spirit (thus, e.g., van Dülmen, op.cit. 61 f.). The context is one of exhortation – *walk* in the Spirit (v. 16)! It seems best to take v. 17bc as a parenthesis and ἵνα in 17d in a final sense: the flesh desires against the Spirit, trying to effect that you will not carry out what you intend; cf. Althaus, *Paulus* 116 f. The flesh thus tries to destroy the work of the Spirit. The Christian, however, is called to resist this desire of the flesh. He can do it, too. Cf. Oepke: 'Far from declaring this situation somehow normal, the apostle wants rather to urge his readers to overcome it through a complete devotion to the Spirit ... ' Mauerhofer, *Kampf* 195: 'The battle of faith is a reality, but victory or defeat are put into the hands of the believers!' 5.16b denotes a fact rather than an irreal wish: if the Galatians let themselves be guided by the Spirit, they *will not* 'fulfil the desire of the flesh'.
108 Drane, *Paul* 53. Similarly, Betz, 'Spirit' 159 speaks of Paul's 'almost naive confidence in the Spirit' in Gal. Schneidermayer, 'Galatians' 138 refers to the theoretical side of the dilemma: ' ... somehow miraculously it would seem that we will know without question what constitutes right action once we achieve the Spirit. To say the least, Paul outlines a complicated miracle!' That Paul did not in fact believe in this miracle – that he thus must have had special reasons for his extravagant 'confidence' in Galatians – is borne out by 1 Thess (and 1–2 Cor). 1 Thess shows that in a situation where no Judaizing danger was to be feared, Paul did not rely on the guidance of the Spirit alone. He expects of his converts a decent life according to normal Jewish standards, with ἀγάπη and φιλαδελφία as the overarching moral concepts (1 Thess 1.3, 2.8, 3.6, 3.12, 4.9–10, 5.8, 5.13). 4.1 f. shows that Paul did not shrink from giving clear precepts about how one has to (δεῖ!) walk in order to please God and attain sanctification (3.13). Concretely, one has to avoid fornication, impurity, greed, and exploitation. Whoever rejects these ethical requirements, rejects God, the giver of the Spirit (4.8). Far from representing an *ama et quod vis fac* -ethics, Paul gives concrete orders (even more so in 1 Corinthians; cf. Drane, op.cit. 61 ff.). In 1 Cor 4.17 Paul refers to the ethical instruction (his 'ways') he gives 'everywhere, in every congregation'. Schrage, *Einzelgebote* is correct in stressing that concrete precepts are by no means foreign to Paul's ethic, as against Bläser, *Gesetz* 234 ff.

drastic language ('bite' and 'devour' in 5.15!); in 6.1 he clearly indicates that transgressions are possible or indeed to be expected in the community.[109]

It is above all the story of the Corinthian congregation that makes Paul's optimistic assertions appear in a dubious light. In 1 Cor 5.1–5 Paul has to hint at a gross sexual transgression 'such as is not found even among pagans (!)'.

Far from being led by the Spirit to grieve about such mischief, the Corinthian pneumatics are 'puffed up' for it (v. 2). Already in his previous (lost) letter Paul had had to advise the congregation to exclude such members as were fornicators, greedy, exploiters or idolaters, mockers or drunkards (5.9–13)! Some Corinthians had found union with prostitutes compatible with the life in Christ (6.12–20), and Paul has to argue the case at length when pointing out that this is not so. 6.1–11 reveals that the Corinthian Christians had internal strifes which were taken to the court. 'You wrong and rob, and even brethren!' (v. 8) Add to this the 'schisms' in the celebration of the Lord's meal, when 'one is starving and the other is drunk'. Still in 2 Cor 12.20–21 Paul expresses his fear that he may find among the Corinthians precisely those vices that he had in Gal listed as 'works of the flesh': ἔρις, ζῆλος, θυμοί, ἐριθεῖαι ...

1 Cor 3.3 shows that Paul had discerned this theological problem, without being able to solve it, however. He says that, as there is ζῆλος and ἔρις among the Corinthians, then they must in fact be σαρκικοί . Paul has not been able to speak to them as πνευματικοῖς (v. 1)![110] This concession to reality flatly contradicts the black-and-white distinction between those in the flesh and those in the Spirit made in Rom 8.5 ff. Embarrassingly enough, it is precisely the excessive reliance on the guidance of the Spirit that had misled the enthusiastic Corinthians in their behaviour. But despite his branding the Corinthians as fleshly, Paul a little later states that God's Spirit dwells in them (3.16). When confronted with concrete real-life problems, his distinction between life in the flesh and life in the Spirit gets blurred. He has to admit, reluctantly to be sure, that what he calls in another context works of the flesh can also be produced in the Christian community. They are an anomaly

---

109 Perhaps one should not attach too much importance to Gal 5.15, for Paul probably attributes the 'biting' and 'devouring' to the intrusion of the nomistic heresy. But it is improbable that the latter should be made responsible for the case envisaged in 6.1.

110 J. Weiss, ad loc., speaks of the juxtaposition of the ideal and reality, typical of primitive Christianity as a whole. Bultmann, 2 Kor 240 (on 12.20) notes that the vice list shows that 'the Corinthians are no pneumatics (in the Pauline sense), cf. 1 Cor 3.1–3'; precisely that is the problem! It may be that Paul is in 1 Cor 3.1 taking up the Corinthians' own proud terminology (they looked on themselves as 'pneumatics' on the basis of their charismatic experiences) and that he 'quite deliberately re-defines the concept ... in terms of day-to-day conduct' (Thiselton, 'Eschatology' 523). This, however, does not remove the problem; the contradiction between this passage and Rom 8 remains.

to be sure, but they *are* there nevertheless.[111] The caricatures of Paul's moral teaching reflected in Rom 3.8, 6.1, 6.15 may well have been fed on some knowledge of what went on in a place like Corinth.[112]

We have seen that Paul once more ignores empirical facts in the course of his polemic against the law-abiding Jews. In Romans he implicitly draws up a contrast between the Jews who transgress the law and the Christians who fulfil it (and this in a letter written from Corinth!). In Gal 5 this contrast is made explicitly. In his attack against the Judaizing tendencies in Galatia Paul tries to show that bad life is not at all a consequence of the law-free gospel. Quite on the contrary: works of the flesh come into being under the law, whereas life in Christ produces fruit of the Spirit. But when Paul tries to demonstrate the superiority of the gospel over the law in this way, his argument goes hopelessly astray. He compares Christian life at its best (if not an ideal picture of it) with Jewish life at its worst (if not a pure caricature).[113] Paul thus uses different standards for Christians and Jews respectively.

It might be possible to abstract some such synthesis of Paul's view of Christian life as follows: The Christian walks according to the Spirit. Nevertheless, the flesh which fights with the Spirit (Gal 5.17) is a constant threat

---

111 Admittedly, the moral condition of the Corinthian congregation is an exception among Paul's congregations. About the Thessalonians Paul, on the whole, gives a rather favourable testimony (cf. 1 Thess 1.7 f.) Some interpreters find that he is aware of a few (not very serious) moral defects in the life of the congregation; for this reason he wrote 1 Thess 4.3–12 (Best, Friedrich). Differently Wernle, *Christ* 28 (referring to 3.13 and 5.23): 'for the short period of time still left before the parousia they can and should live without sin'. Wernle (29 f.) admits the occurrence of disorder in the congregation, but states: 'As their faith still has its shortcomings (3.10), thus some things are in ethical regard, too, imperfect in the congregation; yet through mutual admonition and support everything will turn out well.' Cf. Windisch, *Taufe* 107 ff.; Schade, *Christologie* 136. Windisch (116 ff.) further observes that the Philippian congregation remained for almost ten years an almost ideal community.

112 This ancient polemic is still perpetuated by Klausner, *Jesus* 547; cf. M. Grant, *Paul* 101. Klausner speaks of 'die Ausbreitung der Unmoral im jungen Christentum infolge der Entwertung der Thoragesetze und des Eindringens grosser heidnischer Massen'. He makes the methodological mistake of reading Paul's paraenetical exhortations as literal descriptions of the condition of the congregation addressed; thus he infers from Rom 13.10–14 and Eph 4.24–32 that drunkenness and stealing were common among the Christians. Nevertheless, 1 Cor 5–6 and 2 Cor 12.20 f. are serious indicators of what could happen in a congregation which, by and large, lacked the moral basis provided by Judaism. Wernle, op.cit. 35 ff. infers that no ethical μετάνοια preceded the conversion of the pagan Corinthians, who were probably simply overwhelmed by Paul's enthusiasm (36).

113 Cf. Jülicher, *Römer* 274: 'Die Gegenfrage, ob denn Christus und das Evangelium die volle Gerechtigkeit gebracht haben, lässt sein Glaube gar nicht zu, da nimmt er naiv und kühn das Ideal für die Wirklichkeit, während er dem Juden Gleiches versagt.' Cf. Loisy, *Galates* 190; Ruether, *Faith* 104, 241 f.; W.L. Knox, *Jerusalem* 117 n. 25, 142, 347.

even to the Christian. A Christian who yields to the flesh and ceases to walk in the Spirit, no longer bears fruit of the Spirit; the just requirement of the law is no more fulfilled in him. This is the situation of the Corinthians. The Spirit still dwells in them, but if they do not change the direction of their life, they risk finally falling back to the fleshly existence. But even this 'systematization' (which Paul did not carry out in so many words) would destroy the basis of Paul's polemic against the Jews. He would be left with the assertion: you do not fulfil the law; we do fulfil it, except when we do not!

That Paul was subjectively sincere in all this there is not the least reason to doubt. He was not conscious of any personal sin in his own life.[114] His ideal picture of the Christian existence was based on his own genuine experience. He was living in the new aeon, participating proleptically in resurrection life. Conversion and baptism had signified a new creation for him.[115] He had also observed real transformation of life in other Christians around him.[116] The notion of the shortness of time, the eschatological fervour, made it seem a real possibility that the congregations might be able to live a sinless life for the short time still left before the parousia.[117] Granting all this, one can nevertheless hardly overlook the 'doctrinaire' character of Paul's conviction. 'Paul does not want to see the problem of sin in Christian life; therefore it does not exist.'[118]

6. Summary

Paul's theological theory pushes him in his thinking about the law into a direction in which he would apparently not go spontaneously. His point of departure is the conviction that the law *must not* be fulfilled outside of the Christian community, for otherwise Christ would have died in vain. Among Christians, on the other hand, the law *must* be fulfilled; otherwise Christ would be as weak as the law was (Rom 8.3). That the law is neither fulfilled by Jews nor Gentiles Paul 'proves' by way of denigrating generalizations. Another device is to radicalize the claim of the law ad absurdum: only 100 per cent fulfilment of the law will hold (Gal 3.10).

Paul's spontaneous view is revealed in Rom 2.14 f., 2.26 f., Phil 3.4–6. God's will in the law can be fulfilled even by non-Christian Gentiles. When Paul speaks of the fulfilment of the law by Christians, he does not presuppose

---

114 See Stendahl, *Paul* 90 f.; Althaus, *Paulus* 71 f. The one sin Paul shows awareness of is a thing of the past: his persecution of God's *ekklesia* (1 Cor 15.9).

115 Wernle, op.cit. 5–25, 103 f. Recently, Mauerhofer has stressed that *'posse non peccare'* is a real possibility for Paul; see *Kampf* 104 f., 207 etc.

116 Cf. Windisch, op.cit. 147, 153.

117 Wernle, op.cit. 42 ff., 50, 56, 60, 72.

118 Wernle, op.cit. 104.

any radicalized standards (unlike the Sermon on the Mount).[119] The Christian fulfilment of the law corresponds to such normal Hellenistic moral ideals as were filtered through the Diaspora Synagogue (Phil 4.8). But even these were in fact not always reached in the Christian congregations.

7. Analogies?

a) Christian sources

During the first Christian generations Paul is the only writer to imply that it is impossible to fulfil the law and to use this as an argument about the law. In the gospels it is taken for granted that the commandments can be kept. In *Mk* 10.17−20 Jesus refers the man who asks how he can inherit eternal life to the commandments of the Decalogue. When the man says that he has observed 'all these' from his youth, Jesus does not object.[120] Instead, he adds one more commandment. Mk 12.28−34 also presupposes that the commandments can be fulfilled. The particular ethical claims put by Jesus on his followers (see 8.34−10.45) also presuppose fulfillability. They are supposed to be able to follow the sharpest requirements of an ascetic ethic and 'it is not thought that the infusion of a new divine principle would be a necessary precondition for this'; metanoia will be enough.[121]

Nothing suggests unfulfillability of the commandments, which are simply radicalized by Jesus' interpretation of them, in *Matthew*. *Luke* portrays both the Christians and their pious Jewish predecessors like the parents of the Baptist as wholly fulfilling the law. Zacharias and Elisabeth were 'righteous before God', 'walking blameless in *all* precepts and commandments (ἐντολαῖς καὶ δικαιώμασιν) of the Lord' (Lk 1.6), and the piety of the Christian community in Jerusalem is painted in the same colours.[122]

In the *Pastorals*, the law is intended for the ungodly only; the pious do not even need it (1 Tim 1.7−10). There is no talk of unfulfillability.[123] Of other New Testament writers *James* can be singled out in this connection. Jas 2.10 f., joining Jewish discussions (cf. below), offers a thought that, on the face of it, looks parallel to Gal 3.10: if one transgresses one commandment, he is guilty of transgressing the whole law. The intention of James is, however, purely paraenetic.[124] He will prevent his readers from transgressing

---

119 Against Grundmann, 'Gesetz' 57.
120 Cf. Werner, *Einfluss* 95; Schulz, *Botschaft* 93. It is simply impossible to squeeze from Mk 10.19 the message that if the man honestly tries to keep the commandments, 'he will be brought to recognize his bankruptcy'; thus Cranfield, *Mk* ad loc.
121 Werner, op.cit. 125.
122 To be sure, Peter's statement in Acts 15.10 f. brings some internal tension into this picture; see below, p. 215 f.
123 Cf. Holtzmann, *Theologie* II, 296.
124 Walker, 'Aus Werken' 161 ff. exaggerates not a little when speaking of the 'nomistic radicalism' or 'sharp nomism' of 2.10 f.

the 'one' commandment that seemed to be in danger among them − they are
not to rank the rich man before the poor in the congregation. James develops
no argument concerning the law from the obvious fact that we all 'transgress
in many ways' (3.2). The lesson is simply the practical one that one should
not too eagerly attempt to become a teacher.

The letter of *Barnabas* occasionally notes 'the impracticability of the OT
requirements': as the Sabbath is to be celebrated with a pure heart, it cannot
be rightly celebrated in the old aeon (15.6 f.). But the conclusion is entirely
different from Paul's: where Paul infers that a new order of salvation is necessary, 'Barnabas' is content with predicting 'the practicability in the new
aeon'.[125]

Paul is thus unique in his (seeming) rigorism about the unfulfillability of
the law. As regards the polemic against the Jews' actual transgression of the
law he is not alone, however. That the Jewish opponents of the writer do not
fulfil the law is asserted both by Luke in the speech of Stephen (Acts 7.51−
53) and by John (7.19).[126] And Justin 'never loses the opportunity of pointing up the sinfulness and evil inclination of the Jews'.[127] In this, as we shall
see, the Christian polemic against Jews was no different from standard Jewish
polemic against pagans. Within the NT, however, it is Paul alone who builds
an argument about the insufficiency of the law on this allegation. Justin can
be regarded as a partial parallel at least: it is against the vividly painted background of the Jews' total wickedness 'that the Apologist constantly rehearses
the purpose of the legislation of the Law as enacted because of the hardness of
heart of the Jews'.[128]

b) Jewish sources

Any Jew would have agreed with the statement that a perfect obedience to
the law is impossible. Everybody else, however, would have disagreed with
Paul's implication that a hundred per cent fulfilment of the law was a necessity. 'Paul's definition of righteousness as perfect conformity to the law of
God would never have been conceded by a Jewish opponent, to whom it
would have been equivalent to admitting that God had mocked man by offering to him salvation on terms they both knew to be impossible ...'[129] 'There
is no hint in Rabbinic literature of a view such as that of Paul in Gal 3.10 ... ,

---

125 See Windisch, *Barn* 394.
126 This is the natural reading of Jn 7.19. Pancaro, *Law* 137 suggests a particularly Johan-
     nine interpretation: doing the law is identical with the recognition of Jesus; 'the Jews
     do not keep the law, because they fail to grasp its true meaning and purpose'.
127 Stylianopoulos, *Justin* 143 f., with reference to *Dial.* 12.2, 20.4, 27.4, 55.3 etc.
128 Ibid.
129 Moore, *Judaism* I, 495.

that one must achieve legal perfection ... Human perfection was not considered realistically achievable by the Rabbis, nor was it required.'[130]

There are Rabbinic statements to the effect that to leave one commandment unfulfilled is tantamount to transgressing the whole law.[131] 'Anyone who lends on interest transgresses every prohibition in the Torah and finds no one to plead in his favour.' (ExR 31.14) Such statements, however, are made with a clearly paraenetic intention; they encourage people to keep all commandments.[132] Often the 'thesis' of the value of any one commandment is developed in the opposite direction, with an equally paraenetic intention: to fulfil one commandment is tantamount to fulfilling the whole law. The statement just quoted from Exodus Rabbah has indeed the sequel: 'An Israelite who lends money to his neighbour without taking interest is regarded as if he had *fulfilled all the commandments* ... ' (a similar sequence is also found in 31.13). Such statements have nothing to do with soteriology.[133]

Still, there are traces of a wrestling with the problem of fulfillability even in rabbinic Judaism (cf. Sanh 81a, Makk 24a); 'only there was no intention of a reductio ad absurdum of the law by the law, rather "the works of the law" as a basis for the conduct of life as a whole was regarded as the will of God.'[134]

The legal rigorism of the *Qumran* community is well-known. The radically interpreted Torah had to be observed scrupulously. The Rule of Community stipulates excommunication for transgressing one single word of the Torah (1 QS 8.8, 8.16 ff.; cf. 1 QS 1.13 f.).[135] The clearly ecclesiological nature of this rigorous procedure should not be overlooked, though.[136]

On the other hand, the hymnic confessions of sin reveal a profound sense of human sinfulness and insufficiency. But 'the frequent statements to the effect that man is worthless and incapable of doing good are always said *in the context of comparing man and God*'.[137] It is remarkable that 'these profound views of human sinfulness *do not touch soteriology*'.[138] Nor do they touch, of course, the status of the Torah in any way. Thus the theology of Qumran does not constitute a real parallel to Paul's assumption in Gal

---

130 E.P. Sanders, *Paul* 137. Cf. Sanders's remarks in *Law* 24.
131 This rabbinic speculation is reflected in the letter of James; see above, p. 119 f.
132 Cf. Dibelius, *Jak* on 2.10.
133 See the discussion in Sanders, *Paul* 134–138.
134 Schoeps, *Paul* 177; cf. already Löwy, 'Lehre' (1903), 420 ff.
135 Cf. Hübner, *Tradition* 109.
136 Cf. E.P. Sanders, *Paul* 286: 'It is noteworthy that of the list of offences for which a permanent expulsion is prescribed, all but one – blasphemy – are offences against the community.'
137 E.P. Sanders, op.cit. 289.
138 Op.cit. 283. The same is true of the statement 'all sons of men are unrighteous (ἄδικοι), and all their works are unrighteous' in 3 Ezra 4.37. It is offered as a general experiential wisdom in the context of a eulogy of God's ἀλήθεια (see v. 34–40).

3.10. It would seem that the 'profound and pessimistic view of human ability'[139] in Qumran was reached empirically, in part at least through introspection,[140] whereas the sinfulness of man is, for Paul, part of his tortuous theory. Both Qumran and Paul dwell on other people's (the outsiders') sinfulness, but Paul leaves it at that. It is the people of Qumran alone who confess their *own* sinfulness before God! It is a correct observation that Luther's insight, reached via introspection, of man's radical corruption is more reminiscent of Qumran than of Paul![141]

A special problem is posed by IV Ezra. It is often thought that this work shares Paul's pessimism about the possibility of fulfilling the law.[142] There are indeed statements about a universal sinfulness in the book. 'We are all full of ungodliness' (4.38). (As in Qumran, but unlike Paul, the writer here includes himself among the 'ungodly'.) There is 'none of the earth-born who has not dealt wickedly' (8.35); the seer asks that God have compassion on those without good works (8.31–36). Those who sin perish – but the law abides in its glory (9.36 f.).

It is important to observe the literary structure of the book, however. As Brandenburger and Harnisch have shown, the theology of the writer is not found in the mouth of 'Ezra', but rather in the statements of the angel who *corrects* Ezra's views time and again.[143] Thus the angel passes a more favou-

---

139 E.P. Sanders, op.cit. 284.
140 Garnet, *Salvation* 36 ff. traces in the hymns probably to be attributed to the founder of the community 'an increasing awareness of his own sin, leading to a realization of universal sinfulness and the fact that God alone can bring man's justification' (36); this view 'was forged on the anvil of the crises of his pilgrimage' (37).
141 Luz, *Geschichtsverständnis* 162 n. 102. Cf. also the humble confession of one's own sinfulness in Ps.-Philo, LAB 49.5, 62.9. Ps.-Philo goes further than Paul in the direction of introspection in clearly emphasizing that 'I' intention mauvaise est déjà condamnable' (Perrot, 'Introduction' 45); see LAB 12.7, 25.9–13, and Perrot, 'Commentaire' 154.
142 See, e.g., Davies, *Paul* 11, 13; Dodd, *Studies* 118 f.; Buber, *Zwei Glaubensweisen* 148 ff.; cf. also Schottroff, 'Schreckensherrschaft' 506 f.; Luz, 'Gesetz' 56 f., 100. Recently, Maier, 'Faktoren' 250 has suggested that the dialogues in the first part of IV Ezra might be earlier than AD 70 'und etwa der Zeit und dem Milieu angehören, in dem der Apostel Paulus seine religiösen Grundanschauungen erhalten hat, also in der syrisch-kleinasiatischen Diaspora'. Here the danger of a circular argument is imminent; we may explain Paul by IV Ezra and vice versa.
143 Mundle, 'Problem' 236; Brandenburger, *Adam* 30 f.; Harnisch, *Verhängnis* 60 ff.; E.P. Sanders, *Paul* 410 ff. The opposite view is held by Thompson, *Theodicy*: 'the author has the angelic figure both as a spokesman for a point of view which he considers to be unrealistic and as a mediating figure to absorb some of the sharpness of Ezra's complaints against God' (355); cf. 217: 'Uriel represents an orthodoxy which is too optimistic about Israel and quite unrealistic about human nature.' But which ancient writer would have put an *angel* in such a role?! One can concur with Thompson, however, that 'Ezra' hardly represents any one concrete party (Harnisch) or

rable judgment on Ezra than the seer himself does, referring to his rectitude and chastity (6.32, cf. 7.77, 8.48 f.). When Ezra asks the lamenting question: who has not sinned or transgressed God's covenant, the angel answers by expressing his joy 'over the few that shall be saved' (7.60). Those who perish have transgressed wilfully; they are without excuse (7.72).[144] But the blessed ones who will be saved have actually fulfilled the law. They 'painfully served the Most High, and were in jeopardy every hour, that they might observe the Law of the lawgiver perfectly' (7.89); 'they have striven much and painfully to overcome the innate evil thought that it might not lead them astray from life unto death' (7.92).

It is beyond question for the author that God's will can be fulfilled.[145] He attacks and refutes the thesis that sin is unavoidable.[146] There are some that will be saved. In its pessimism IV Ezra diverges clearly from mainstream Judaism: it is held that fulfilment of the law is difficult, painful, and rare. It is not clear whether one has to fulfil the law absolutely or 'almost perfectly'[147] to be saved. At any rate, the pessimism of the book has little to do with that ascribed to Paul. The message of IV Ezra is unseparably tied with the destruction of Jerusalem. The catastrophe of AD 70 has triggered off the reflections of the author and led his thought in the direction of radicalized nomism. 'Ezra' can find no other explanation for the fate of the holy city than that the elected people must be full of sin in the eyes of God. In retrospect he concludes that 'normal' observance of the law (in which Israel is certainly not worse than 'Babylon'!) has not been enough. Paul lived in a different situation. But there is a parallel feature between him and IV Ezra in that each writer — in a different way — proceeds 'backwards' in his theology and ends up proclaiming (all but) universal sinfulness.

IV Ezra remained an individual exception among Jewish literature. In 2 Baruch the legalism has been toned down,[148] and it is possible that already the concluding chapters of IV Ezra itself are designed to mitigate the rigorism displayed in the bulk of the book.[149]

While there are no real parallels to Paul's contention that the law cannot be fulfilled (outside the dominion of Christ), he is certainly not alone in his

---

'Seinsverständnis' (Brandenburger). 'We see, rather, various propositions being put to the angel and confirmed or denied.' Sanders, op.cit. 412.

144 See Harnisch, op.cit. 146–165.

145 Harnisch, op.cit. 152.

146 Harnisch, op.cit. 161 (with respect to 7.71 f.); cf. Mundle, art.cit. 243–249.

147 Cf. Sanders' formulation: 'perfect (or nearly perfect) obedience', op.cit. 416.

148 Cf. Sanders, op.cit. 427; idem, 'Covenant' 20 f.

149 Thus Sanders, *Paul* 416 ff., as against Breech, 'Fragments' and Harnisch. Should Breech and Harnisch be right, then IV Ezra could come even less in question as a parallel to Paul.

denigration of the opponent in Rom 1—2. This is rather an almost universal characteristic of religious polemic. It is well-known that Paul follows in Rom 1 closely the traditional attacks of Jewish literature against pagan cult (esp. Sap 13—15).[150] Instances of a wholesale demonization of the other side can be collected, e.g., from the Testaments of the Patriarchs (Test. Levi 14.4 ff., 16.1—2) and from Qumran (CD 4.12 ff.), but also from Philo. Goodenough's judgment on Philo's criticisms of idolatry could apply mutatis mutandis to Paul in Rom 1 as well: 'To accuse Philo of deliberate misrepresentation of paganism is perhaps unfair, but the only alternative is to ascribe to him such Jewish loyalty as blinded his eyes and mind to what must have been plain facts before him.'[151] A fairer judgment on the pagans is found, e.g., in IV Ezra 3.36 — a statement reminiscent of Rom 2.14 f.: 'Individual men of note indeed thou mayst find to have kept thy precepts; but nations thou shalt not find!' The idealization of one's own 'side' is, of course, implied in such denigration. To Paul's beautiful picture of the Christians fulfilling the law and producing the fruit of the Spirit one may compare III Sib 218—247 (esp. 234—247) — a passage describing the δικαιοσύνη and ἀρετή of the Jews — or the assertion of Philo that a proselyte immediately becomes temperate, continent etc. in *Virt.* 180 ff.[152]

c) Deuteronomy

In a much quoted essay Martin Noth undertook to show that there is a profound theological similarity between Paul's statement in Gal 3.10 and Deuteronomy (from which the citation Gal 3.10 is taken — Deut 27.26). [153] Starting from the obvious question, 'whether Paul has not wrongly appealed to the passages he quotes from Deuteronomy in support of his judgment on the law in general',[154] Noth reaches the conclusion that this is not so. Paul's assertion is justified from the point of view of Deut itself:

'On the basis of this law there is only one possibility for man of having his own independent activity: that is transgression, defection, followed by curse and judgment. And so, indeed, "all those who rely on the works of the law are under a curse".'[155]

Paul, however, suggests that fulfilling the law is impossible, whereas the idea in Deut, as interpreted by Noth, is that Israel has collectively transgressed the covenant law and this is why the curse contained in it has become

---

150 For references see Synofzik, *Aussagen* 91 f.
151 *Introduction* 84 f.
152 See Borgen, 'Observations' 98. Philo, *Virt.* 182 closely parallels the virtue list in Gal 5.22 f.
153 *Studien* 155—171 (ET *Laws* 118—131). Noth is followed, among others, by Eichholz, *Theologie* 247; Vos, *Untersuchungen* 89 n. 12; Edwards, *Christ* 206—209, 227 f.
154 Op.cit. 156 (ET 119).
155 Op.cit. 171 (ET 131).

a reality which in the day of the author had already appeared, whereas the blessing is for him already something unreal.[156] To say this is to say no more than that *transgressing* the law brings about curse.

Noth concedes that the OT apparently opens out from the law the perspectives, ' "blessing *and* curse", i.e. *either* blessing *or* curse, according as the individual or the group fulfils or does not fulfil the requirements of the law'.[157] Noth refers to the clear statements Deut 11.26–28, 30.19 which after this simply disappear from the discussion.[158] He calls, however, attention to 'the external inequality' in Deut 28.1–68. There, the effects of the curse are depicted in much fuller detail than those of the blessing, which shows 'that the emphasis ... lies quite one-sidedly upon the section of curses'; the same is true of the parallel passages in the law of Hammurabi and in oriental treaties.[159] The lawgiver is interested in transgressors rather than in those who observe the law.

Noth goes on to emphasize that it is natural that a law has to be obeyed. 'Whoever keeps the law does no more than his duty and can make no claim to a reward.' The blessing contained in Deut 28 'was already present before the law, for it rests on a previously given divine promise'.[160] This is certainly true, but it does *not* follow from it that in Deut 28 the blessing would be 'a purely formal counterpart to the curse'.[161]

Noth in fact blends together two quite distinct questions: 1) could the law be, according to Deut, a real source of blessing for Israel? 2) is the blessing seen in Deut as a reward which man could justly claim for having fulfilled the law? Noth seems to assume that an affirmative answer to the latter question is a necessary presupposition for answering the first question positively. As the blessing is not a reward, no blessing is possible. But this is a *non sequitur.*

In the light of the profane parallels it is striking how *much* Deut, after all, speaks of the blessing. It *promises* much more than a normal law does for its fulfiller (whether or not as 'reward' in the sense of merit). Noth himself mentions five verses, in which the fulfilling of an individual provision is, as he puts it, 'occasionally ... motivated by the divine blessing which is being kept in view'.[162] Noth is inclined to regard such motivations as an actual (occasional) inconsistency within Deut. He has, however, overlooked some twenty places where the blessing connected with fulfilment of the law is spoken of, even

---

156 Op.cit. 168 (ET 128 f.).
157 Op.cit. 156 (ET 119).
158 Noth only mentions them in the concluding passage stating that it is just a question of a 'formal association of the words of blessing and curse' (171, ET 131).
159 Op.cit. 157 ff. (quotation from p. 160; ET, 122).
160 Op.cit. 165 (ET 126).
161 Ibid.
162 Op.cit. 166 n. 27 (ET 126 n. 28): Deut 14.29, 15.10, 15.18, 23.21, 24.19.

though the word *berakah* is not used![163] It is therefore wrong to claim that blessing appears as a purely formal counterpart to curse. It appears that blessing through promise and blessing through fulfilling the law by no means exclude each other in Deut; the law is seen as a divine promise.[164]

Besides emphasizing that the curse must have appeared to the author(s) of Deut in the seventh century an actual reality, Noth claims that, according to 2 Kings 22, no one at the time Deut was found doubted that the curse was in operation. The message of Hulda the prophetess 'does not consider the possibility that the curse might be changed into blessing by any future fulfilment of the law'. 'There is no human possibility of changing the position.'[165] Surely not, but what about a divine possibility – repentance and grace? The prophecy of Hulda is no doubt *ex eventu*[166] – as is the section about the curse in Deut 28.25–69![167] Noth thinks that the Deuteronomic history excludes the possibility of repentance.[168] This thesis can hardly be upheld. Both Deut and the Deuteronomic history are to be seen as works of paraenesis[169], and in this framework the talk of curse and blessing can easily be integrated. Lev 26, too – a chapter to which Noth appeals in this very connection – assumes that the punishments by Yahweh are time and again also meant as correction of the people (v. 21, 23, 27).

One more observation. Noth describes the position of Deut in words reminiscent of Gal 3.10: 'Transgression of the law – *even though it be only one particular* – implies a forsaking of covenant-loyalty, and consequently covenant-breaking and defection, and for all defections the curse attached to the law comes into operation, executed by Yahweh himself.'[170] How significant the transgression of 'only one particular' was, is explained by Noth in a note: 'The trespass of an individual against a provision of the law must be visited with his expulsion from the community (cf. Deut. 13.6, etc.).'[171] But Deut 13.6 is an example unfortunately chosen. The 'one' provision of Deut 13 is enticement to apostasy – it is a question of transgressing the first

---

163 Cf. Deut 5.33, 6.3, 6.18, 6.24 f., 7.9, 7.12 f., 8.1, 10.13, 11.8 f., 11.13–15, 11.21, 11.22 ff., 12.1, 12.28, 15.4 f., 16.20, 19.8 f., 22.7, 28.9. 7.13 explicitly mentions 'blessing'.
164 Koch, Review 831 f. Cf. von Rad, *Theology* I, 230; Clements, *People* 58 ff.; Lohfink, *Siegeslied* 158 ff.
165 Noth, op.cit. 169 (ET 129).
166 Dietrich, *Prophetie* 13 f., 55 ff.
167 von Rad, op.cit. 221 with n. 77.
168 Cf. Noth, op.cit. 109.
169 On Deuteronomy as paraenesis see von Rad, op.cit. 225 f., 231; on the Deuteronomic history as a preaching of repentance von Rad, op.cit. I 346; Wolff, 'Kerygma'; Kellermann, *Messias* 81 ff.
170 Noth, op.cit. 167 f. (ET 128).
171 Op.cit. 167 n. 35 (ET 128 n. 36).

commandment by following foreign gods! The requirement 'remove the evil from thy midst' (13.4 etc.) appears indeed almost always in the connection of gross transgressions;[172] 'the integrity of the community' is at stake.[173] Not all transgressions of the law are visited with expulsion.[174] And last but not least we should note that *Paul* himself applies the same excommunication formula in a Christian congregation in 1 Cor 5.13![175]

Noth has thus failed to show that Paul is justified in appealing to Deut 27.26.[176] According to Deut and the Deuteronomists, the curse had indeed befallen the people that had forsaken Yahweh and sacrificed to other gods. Transgression of the law had brought the curse with it, but the blessing, too, remained a real possibility.[177]

---

172 17.7 apostasy, 17.12 rejection of a priestly judicial decision, designed as impudence (the priest has a divine authority, cf. von Rad, *Deut* ad loc.); 18.20 a prophet's speaking in the name of other gods, or falsely speaking in the name of Yahweh; 19.13 murder, 19.19 false witness, 22.21–24 fornication and adultery, 21.21 obstinacy leading to licentiousness and drunkenness; 24.7 stealing and maltreatment of a slave.

173 Rose, *Ausschliesslichkeitsanspruch* 38 f.; see 33 ff. on the formula in question.

174 For instance, there is no talk of capital punishment in chs. 14 and 16.

175 Lohfink, op.cit. 158 points out that blessing and curse in the covenantal pattern do not mean the legalism condemned by Paul and refers to the fact that 'auch bei Paulus kann der Christ, der aus dem Glauben lebte, durch Nichtbeachtung des Gotteswillens das Gericht über sich zusammenziehen und sich aus dem Raum der Gnade ausschliessen'.

176 Reventlow, *Heiligkeitsgesetz* 143 observes that 'der dogmatische Zweck ist für Noth offensichtlich der Mittelpunkt und eigentliche Anlass seiner Ausführungen'.

177 Noth, op.cit. 171 (ET 131) is correct in stating that Deut does not contain the view 'that there were positive and negative performances of the law, and that these attitudes could be reckoned up against one another as from a neutral centre point and add up to a store of good or evil works.' This, however, is a different question altogether! For the ideological background of the emphasis on the material 'blessing' in Deut see von Rad, *Theology* I 299 (Yahweh victoriously takes the place of Baal as the bestower of every blessing of the arable land).

IV. The origin and purpose of the law

1. The origin

Paul states in Gal 3.19 that the law was given 'through angels'. Does this assertion amount to a denial of its divine origin? Albert Schweitzer indeed proposed the thesis that Paul systematically presupposed that the law was given by evil spiritual powers, the rulers of the old aeon. Obedience to the law was, therefore, obedience to these evil rulers.[1]

Whatever Paul may have thought when dictating Galatians – we will return to that question – his other letters render Schweitzer's view impossible. Outside Galatians Paul always refers to the law as given by *God*. The law is called *God's* law in Rom 7.22[2] and 8.7.[3] 'Law' and 'God' belong together in Rom 2.17; that this is not merely a Jewish view foreign to Paul is clear from 2.23: the Jews' transgressions of the law cause *God's* name to be dishonoured. In 1 Cor 9.8 f. what 'the law says' or what is written 'in the law of Moses' is tantamount to *God's* concern. In Rom 9.4 the νομοθεσία is mentioned favourably among the advantages given to Israel (even before the 'promises'!), and it is perfectly possible that 'the words of God' (3.2) refers (also?) to the law and not (merely?) to the promises.[4] And even the statement that the Christians constitute the true 'circumcision' (Phil 3.3, cf. Rom 2.28 f., 4.11) implies a high appreciation and indeed the divine origin of that rite. In view of all this it is clear that the high qualities attributed to the law in Rom 7.12, 14 are connected with its divine origin. The law is 'holy' and 'spiritual', the commandment 'holy', 'good' and 'just' precisely because it stems from God.[5]

In the light of Paul's other statements the assertions about the law in Gal 3.15–20 seem strange.[6] Emphasizing the absolute priority of the promise over the law, Paul states that the law 'came' only 430 years after the promise

---

1 Schweitzer, *Mystik* 71 ff.

2 Also in Rom 7.25b, the authenticity of which is disputed.

3 Schweitzer never refers to Rom 8.7 at all.

4 Cf. above, p. 70.

5 Schweitzer regards these statements as part of Paul's tactics: approaching an unknown congregation with an apologetic purpose, Paul tries to write about the qualities of the law as tactfully and favourably as possible. He manages indeed to talk in the manner of the 'worst Judaizers' – without actually speaking of the origin of the law at all! Op.cit. 198, 209.

6 This, however, is no reason to remove the passage as a later addition: thus O'Neill, *Galatians* 51 f. For Steck, *Galaterbrief* 75, this passage was one of the (many) reasons to declare Galatians as a whole inauthentic.

given to Abraham. It is curious that he chooses to use the participle γεγονώς when speaking of the law: he gives the impression that the law had come on the scene independently, on its own initiative, unlike the covenant-will based on promise which was 'confirmed by God' (v. 17). The expression 'sounds almost contemptuous'.[7] Interestingly enough, a correspondingly 'active' expression turns up again in Rom 5.20 (the law 'came between', παρεισῆλθεν, cf. Gal 2.4). Gal 3.17 serves to create a distance between God and the law.

An impression of distance is likewise produced by the statement that the law was 'added' (προσετέθη).[8] The preceding context suggests an invalid addition not willed by the testator; οὐδείς in v. 15 makes one think of some-one other than the testator himself − of an outsider.[9] The illustration used seems to be an anomaly in terms of normal juridical practice; it is already affected by the application. When setting forth his 'human' analogy, Paul is already thinking of the angels as giving 'extra stipulations'; note the connec-tion between ἐπιδιατάσσεται (v. 15) and διαταγείς (v. 19).[10]

The illustration fits neither Greek nor Roman legal practice. Bammel argues for a connection with the Jewish *mattanah* institute, within which there is no emphasis on the death of a testator, nor can such a will be changed.[11] This theory requires that οὐδείς in v. 15 refers to the testator himself.[12] Yet Paul's thought is in vv. 15–17 guided by the fact that the law *was* added (this is explicitly stated in v. 19) which contradicts the principles of *matta-nah*.[13] Thus the observation that the comparison limps[14] remains valid.

---

7 Oepke.

8 προσετέθη cannot here mean merely 'was given' (thus Gyllenberg). The prefix πρόσ-must be given full weight (cf. Bauer, *Wörterbuch* s.v.; van Dülmen, *Theologie* 43 n. 90); it is comparable to ἐπί in ἐπιδιατάσσεται (v. 15). The whole reasoning from v. 15 on aims at proving that *additions* are invalid.

9 Lietzmann, Oepke.

10 Cf. Lietzmann. Note further the correspondence between οὐδείς ἀθετεῖ (v. 15) and ὁ νόμος οὐκ ἀκυροῖ; J. Walter, *Gehalt* 87.

11 Bammel, 'Diatheke'.

12 Thus Bammel, art.cit. 316, followed by Schlier and Mussner; cf. Byrne, 'Sons' 158 n. 85. If that were Paul's intention, he would in fact be saying that God has indeed made additions to his will (προσετέθη and διαταγείς in v. 19!) but these are legally invalid and cannot, therefore, affect the promise! Linguistically, too, it is natural to take οὐδείς in the sense of 'no one else' as in Phil 2.20 and elsewhere (Oepke). More-over, in v. 20 Paul unmistakably drives a wedge between God and the law by suggest-ing that the law could not have been given by him who is 'One' (see below). Not surprisingly Bammel has to deny this. He assumes in v. 20 a reference to the 'one' seed in v. 16b and takes the meaning of v. 20 to be that 'der νόμος ist nicht auf Christus bezüglich' (art.cit. 317 n. 2).

13 Moreover, one may ask whether Paul would have expected the Galatians to under-stand niceties of Jewish legal practice (cf. Betz).

14 Lietzmann. That Paul moves rather loosely from one related picture to another, with-

Formally, the question who is the logical subject in the clause διαταγείς δι' ἀγγέλων (v. 19) is left open. As Paul uses διά rather than ὑπό, it might be possible after all to think of God.[15] Yet both the preceding context (discussed above) and the succeeding verse 20 discourage this interpretation. V. 20 is regarded as a crux interpretum, but mainly because interpreters are not willing to swallow Paul's message.[16] In itself, the message is clear enough. God, being One, needs no mediator between himself and mankind. A mediator was needed, because God was *not* involved. A mediator was necessary, because both parties involved consisted of many persons; unlike God, neither party was 'one'.[17] The idea sounds certainly strange;[18] it may be rendered a bit more intelligible through the recent suggestion that μεσίτης refers to the angelic mediator of the heavenly party rather than to Moses.[19] In any case,

---

out connecting them in a logical way, becomes clear in v. 18: the question is now no longer whether the νόμος is a legitimate part of God's 'will' and thus of the heritage; instead, Paul asks whether or not the heritage is gained *on the basis of* the *nomos*. That the answer to this latter question must be 'No' is in fact Paul's theological starting-point; v. 15–17 are a secondary 'empirical' illustration of an aprioristic theological thesis (as are Gal 3.10 and Rom 1.18–2.29, see above, III 1–2) and it comes as no surprise that the logic of such an illustration is not watertight.

15 The passive form does not decide the question (against Mussner, *Gal* 247 n. 17); not *every* Semitic passive implies a reference to God! Josephus, *Ant.* XV, 136 formulates carefully: the laws came δι' ἀγγέλων παρὰ τοῦ θεοῦ.

16 Thus Bring, *Christus* 86 explains that ἑνός (v. 20) refers (unlike the following εἶς in v. 20b!) to the recipients of the law rather than to God. A mediator would not have been needed, had Israel alone been the recipient of the law; the law was, however, given both to Israel and to the Gentiles (!). Bring totally overlooks the emphatic contrast between v. 20a and 20b. No wonder he also regards the reference to the angels as favourable to the law (see above, p. 43 n. 5). For criticisms see also Mussner, *Gal* 250 n. 30.

Artificial also is the explanation of Mauser, 'Galater iii. 20' 269 f.: while v. 20b refers to God's unchanging will to save man, v. 20a underlines that Moses is a 'mediator of cleavage' (a particularist note).

Guthrie thinks Paul is speaking of 'a contract which depended on the good faith of both parts concerned' in v. 20a; similarly Bläser, *Gesetz* 55.

Percy, *Probleme* 358 (referring to Bauer, s.v. μεσίτης, and Lagrange): the meaning is that 'das Gesetz nicht ein unbedingter Ausdruck des Willens Gottes in bezug auf das Heil der Menschen sei, indem es die tatsächliche Beschaffenheit der Menschen berücksichtigt'. Callan, 'Midrash' 567 suggests that 'Moses is divided between the interests of Israel and those of God'. None of these interpretations can explain the relationship between v. 20a and v. 20b naturally.

17 Correctly, i.a., Lietzmann, Schlier, Mussner; Dibelius, *Geisterwelt* 25 f.; Hübner, *Gesetz* 28. I fail to understand the objection of Betz that 'it is not at all necessary to identify this plurality (of which the mediator is the representative, HR) as the angels in 3.19d, or as the people in the Sinai tradition'; that 'anything that stands in contrast to the oneness of God is inferior' remains far too abstract.

18 Cf. Loisy, *Gal* 156; Neil: a 'curious afterthought'.

19 Vanhoye, 'Médiateur': the μεσίτης of v. 19–20 refers to the mediator of the angelic

Paul appears for the moment to regard the angels as the originators of the law, thus denying its immediately divine origin.[20]

Schweitzer and others wish to establish a connection between these angelic law-givers and the 'elements of the world' mentioned in 4.3, 9.[21] Paul, however, never points up such a connection. It is actually the law itself (rather than its givers) that functions in the role of ἐπίτροποι and οἰκονόμοι (4.2), to which the 'elements of the world' are compared in 4.3 – much as it functions in the analogous role of παιδαγωγός or jailer in 3.23 f.[22] Clearly the expression 'under the elements of the world' corresponds to 'under the law' in 4.4 f. The στοιχεῖα-νόμος is also firmly under God's control – its rule is at the outset limited to last only until the προθεσμία τοῦ πατρός – which could hardly be true of inimical angels.

Recently Hübner has argued, without mentioning the στοιχεῖα in this connection, that the angels of Gal 3.19 f. were, for Paul, 'demonic beings' with evil intentions.[23] It has to be borne in mind, however, that Paul is 'simply adapting a common interpretation of the Sinai events' (cf. Acts 7.38 and Heb 2.2, where angels – undoubtedly *good* ones – are said to have participated in the giving of the law). 'Had Paul intended to use a common view in so radically a different way, he would certainly have been compelled to make his point more clearly.'[24]

Moreover, there are in the context of Gal 3.19–20 itself strong indications that Paul could not ascribe a demonic origin to the law. As Hübner concedes,

party; that Moses was the mediator of Israel is presupposed but not mentioned. It was a common Jewish notion that an angel spoke to Moses on Sinai (Acts 7.38; in Jubilees he is called 'the angel of presence', whereas Philo, *Somn.* I, 142 and Test. Dan 6.2 actually call him a μεσίτης; Vanhoye, art.cit. 410). But even if the μεσίτης be Moses (cf. Philo, *Vit.Mos.* II, 166; Ass. Mos. 1.14, 3.12) the suggestion is far-fetched that ἐν χειρὶ μεσίτου may refer to *beyad Moshe* (MT! the LXX reads ἐπὶ τῶν χειρῶν) in Ex 34.29; thus Callan, art.cit. 561 f. Nothing in Gal 3.19 f. suggests that Paul had the episode with the Golden Calf in particular in mind when dictating this passage.

20 Thus Loisy, op.cit. 157; Klein, *Rekonstruktion* 209 f.; Drane, *Paul* 34; Hübner, *Gesetz* 27 f.; Hickling, 'Centre' 201, etc. For some evidence for the Jewish view that mediation as such is inferior to direct dealing see Callan, art.cit. 555–559.

21 E.g. Schweitzer, op.cit. 71 f.; Loisy, op.cit. 164; Reicke, 'Law' 261 ff.; Percy, op.cit. 164 ff.; Caird, *Principalities* 47–49; Gronemeyer, *Frage* 66; Limbeck, Ohnmacht 94 f. n. 29. Cf. also Gunther, *Opponents* 59, 172 f. Against the identification Dibelius, op.cit. 28 n. 2, 85 n. 1, 187; Leivestad, *Christ* 104 f.

22 It is therefore wrong to appeal to the personal metaphor οἰκονόμοι and ἐπίτροποι in v. 2 to support the personal character of the στοιχεῖα in v. 3; thus, e.g., Percy, op.cit. 165 f. Gal 4.2 is a comparison intended to cast light on the rôle of the law, not a description of the στοιχεῖα. One might just as well claim on the basis of 3.23 f., 4.2 f. that Paul regards the law as personal. That the στοιχεῖα *are* in fact of a personal nature only becomes clear from v. 8 f.

23 Op.cit. 28 f.

24 Westerholm, Review 196.

'even in Gal., what the law commands is thought of as the holy will of God', 'transgressions of the law are thought of as sin', and 'the curse of God is over those who transgress it'. The criticism is valid that 'the dialectic involved when such a law is held to come from demons is almost unbearable'.[25]

There are even more features that point to the direction that Paul did not, at bottom, intend to exclude God altogether from the act of law-giving.[26] The temporal limit set to the law at the outset ('until the promised seed comes') clearly indicates *God's* plans in regard with the law, including a pre-ordained subordination to the 'promise'.[27] Furthermore, it is difficult not to see in the next passive form ἐδόθη in v. 21b a reference to God as the law-giver, for in this verse Paul speculates about the (unreal) possibility that a law capable of 'making alive' was 'given'; if the giving of the law had nothing to do with God, such a possibility was certainly excluded from the outset. Now Paul is at pains to produce an explanation why the law has been abolished. If it was just an invention of the angels, no further arguments would have been needed! These considerations also apply to the question raised by Paul in v. 21a: was the law then against God's promises? If the law was an addition on the angels' part to a 'will' to which nothing can be added, one would expect an affirmative answer. Instead, Paul answers with an emphatic 'No'. Finally, in v. 22 he shows how the law is to be integrated into God's overarching plan. The giving of the law is connected with the 'including' of everything 'under sin' by 'Scripture'. Thus the law, at the deepest level, serves in all its negativity God's good purposes.

All this does *not* mean that the natural literal understanding of 3.19–20, according to which the law was given by the angels alone, should be rejected. On the contrary, we are apparently once more faced with an internal contradiction in Paul. Once more we find him in the course of a polemical discussion suggesting something radical about the law; and this time, too, there is something 'unnatural' – from Paul's *own* point of view – in the radical suggestion. We have seen that Paul could seize on various traditions and reinterpret them for his own use (see above on Rom 1.18–3.20 and Rom 7.14–25).[28] In Gal 3.19 f. he has taken up the Jewish tradition about the presence of angels on

---

25 Westerholm, loc.cit. (with reference to Hübner, op.cit. 33, 40).

26 This is reflected in Oepke's cautious conclusion: 'Bei der Gesetzgebung schalteten die Engel relativ selbständig; nicht ohne Gott, aber auch nicht in seinem Auftrage, eher unter seiner einstweiligen Duldung.'

27 Hübner, op.cit. 29 sees this difficulty, admitting that the temporal clause refers 'undoubtedly' to *God's* intention. He tries to evade the problem by assuming a 'cumulation of perspectives' in the text: we have to reckon with 'different intentions' that are mentioned 'abruptly side by side'. On Hübner's very complicated view of these different intentions see below, p. 153 f.

28 See above, III 2, 4.

Sinai.[29] The radical application seems to be an *ad hoc*-adaptation of that tradition. In the light of the context and the fact that Paul never returns to this suggestion of the origin of the law it looks as if he were simply toying with an idea which, however, seemed rather too daring even to him – at least later on.[30] But while the 'radicalizations' in Rom 1–3 and 7 seem scholastic and theoretical, the statement in Gal 3.19 f. would seem to be steeped in emotion. Paul dictates his letter in anger. He has 'overreacted'.[31] One can agree with Cranfield's statement that 'it would be extremely unwise to take what Paul says in Galatians as one's starting-point in trying to understand Paul's teaching on the law'.[32] But it is no wiser to explain the Galatians statements away (as Cranfield does). We are left with the intriguing question, How is this *sic et non* at all possible? How is it possible that Paul came to express *such* starkly negative statements about the law, however heated the battle with the Judaizers? Is it precisely in Gal 3 that we meet Paul's deepest feelings about the law – feelings he mostly succeeds in repressing? I am inclined to conjecture that this is so. The verses in question seem to express a latent resentment towards the law of which Paul was normally not conscious. Be that as it may, the strong impression remains that Paul's mind was divided with regard to the law.

2. Analogies regarding the origin of the law?

a) Jewish sources

It is clear at the outset that close parallels to Paul's problems with the origin of the law are not to expected within the pale of Judaism.[33] The belief

---

29 Deut 33.2 LXX; Josephus, *Ant.* XV, 136; Jub 1.29; Test. Dan 6.2; Philo, *Somn.* I, 141 ff.; Acts 7.38, 53; Heb 2.2; Apoc. Mos. 1; PesiqR 21; for more Rabbinic texts see Billerbeck III 554–556. For a discussion of these texts see Callan, art.cit. 550–554.

30 Leivestad, op.cit. 105 correctly points out: 'If the idea that the angels were responsible for the law had played an important part in Paul's thought, his anti-judaistic polemic would have assumed a very different form. As it is, Gal. 3.19 only offers an argument by the way; it is a casual idea which tends to accentuate the depreciation of the law, but no further theological consequences are drawn from it.'

31 Drane, 'Tradition' 169; cf. idem, *Paul* 31. Similarly Schoeps, *Paul* 183.

32 Cranfield, 'Paul' 62; id., *Romans* 858. By contrast, Sandmel, *Genius* 55 and elsewhere regards Gal 3.19 f. as the fundamental pillar of Paul's theology of the law.

33 Excepting renegades, of course. A singular account of the views of a (typical?) Jewish renegade about the law is given by Josephus, *Ant.* IV, 145–147, in a speech of the sinner Zambrias. Zambrias ascribes the whole legislation to Moses, who is viewed as an impostor; Moses has duped the simple-minded Hebrews. His orders are those of a tyrant in that he has robbed them of the possibility of free decision. A Jew of whom Zambrias is the typical example wished to make his own decisions and follow the ideas of the majority of men rather than to live in seclusion in a minority position. For a discussion of the passage see van Unnik, 'Account' 254 ff. It goes

in the divine origin remains unshakable. Occasionally, however, it has been thought that some traces can be detected of the idea that *parts* of the law were secondary additions to the divine legislation from Sinai. Even this would not be a very close parallel to Paul, since Paul attributes in Gal 3.19 f. the very Sinaitic law *in its totality* to the angels, not just some part of it. Nevertheless, Paul's view could be a bit more understandable as a radicalization of already existing Jewish criticisms of the law. But are there really traces of such criticisms?

The OT does not come into question. The assertion that Paul's reasoning in Gal 3.19 f. is 'a rejection of Pharisaism based on the development of tradition within the OT itself'[34] is simply false. It is equally incorrect to regard a passage in the Damascus document (CD 3.14 f.) as a reflection of a tradition (later found in Christian writings) according to which the cult laws were given because of the Jews' hardness of heart.[35] Nor can Philo's (alleged)

---

without saying that such a 'fully-fledged, frontal attack on the Mosaic Law' (van Unnik, art.cit. 258) is quite different from Paul's position. Void of any divine purpose or content, the Torah is here seen merely as 'an instrument of Moses' tyranny'. 'Here the voice is heard from a man 'that says that the law is not from Heaven' (Sanh 10.1) (van Unnik, ibid.). For a discussion of apostates and their views and motives in Philo see Wolfson, *Philo* I, 73–76.

Cf. also Ps.-Philo, LAB 25.13, where there is a reference to people who wanted to 'scrutinize the book of the Law to find out whether God had really written what it contained, or whether Moses had imposed his own teaching on it'; and 16.1 (Korah objects to the 'intolerable law' of the garments).

34 Thus Gese, *Theologie* 83. He asserts: 'Already the Deuteronomic tradition distinguished the revelation of the Decalogue as an immediate revelation from the revelation of the "details" of the law, indirectly mediated through Moses (Deut 5; cf. Ex 20.18–21); this corresponds to the angelic mediation to Moses in Gal 3.19 f. (cf. Acts 7.53, Heb 2.2) ... ' But even those precepts that were given 'indirectly' came to Moses directly from *God* (Deut 5.31) and were just as obliging as the Decalogue (Deut 5.32 f.); there is no indication of any kind of inferiority. The 'angelic mediation' in Gal 3 is something quite different, the function of the angels being quite different from that in Acts 7.53, Heb 2.2; *no distinction* is made within the law. According to R.M. Grant, *Letter* 52 f. Paul may have thought that Deuteronomy (δεύτερος νόμος!) contained a 'second' law between Deut 5.22 and Deut 32 – that is, an 'addition' given to multiply transgressions (Rom 5.20)! 'In the earlier additions in Deuteronomy we read of sacrifices, food laws and festivals; but all of these had been superseded and abrogated.' These only? Paul speaks of the law without distinctions.

35 Thus Berger, *Gesetzesauslegung* I 16, 19; id., 'Hartherzigkeit' 46. The text says only that God revealed to the remnant 'the hidden things in which all Israel had gone astray', including 'His holy Sabbaths and His glorious feasts'. There is not the least criticism of the Sabbath *law*. The Sabbaths are 'holy' and the feasts 'glorious', and these commandments of God are in the context set side by side with 'the testimonies of God's righteousness', 'the ways of his truth' and 'the desires of His will which a man must do in order to live' (translation of Vermes, with some modifications).

appreciation of the law of nature as the primary principle be considered a parallel to Paul's radical suggestions about the Mosaic law.[36]

One passage remains to be considered. The geographical work of Strabo includes a description of Moses and his followers (XVI, 2, 34–45). In this excursus it is told that Moses was an Egyptian priest who opposed idols and pleaded for a sublime (Stoic) pantheism. Along with several wise men he left Egypt and founded in Jerusalem the cult centre of a new religion. After Moses, however, the Jewish religion fell into decay. In Strabo's words, 'superstitious men were appointed to priesthood, and then tyrannical people; and from superstition arose abstinence from foods, from which it is their custom to abstain even to-day, and circumcisions and excisions and other observances of the kind' (37). Then follows an account of the 'bands of robbers' (the Hasmonean rulers are meant). Circumcision, food laws and the like are thus ascribed to post-Mosaic superstitious priests.

It has been customary to think that Strabo copied this passage from Posidonius.[37] This seems doubtful, however;[38] it would be strange had the (according to Josephus) anti-Jewish philosopher given so favourable an account of the original religion of the Jews.[39] More important for our topic is to find out whether Strabo's account goes back to some Hellenistic *Jewish* source (whether or not mediated by Posidonius), as some scholars have

---

'All Israel' had gone astray for not celebrating the sabbaths and feasts correctly, i.e. because of their wrong calendar (cf. CD 6.18 f., Jub 6.34). Cf. Klinzing, *Umdeutung* 15–17.

36 Sandmel, *Genius* 47 ff. sees a common feature in Philo and Paul in that 'to neither of them was the law of Moses the primary principle'. He does not overlook the differences either (53 ff.) and he correctly abstains from setting up Philo as Paul's 'background'. Curiously enough, Sandmel ascribes the thought expressed in Gal 3.19 f. to the pre-Christian Paul.

The notion of the primacy of the law of nature over the Mosaic law in Philo's thought is vigorously refuted by Nikiprowetzky, *Commentaire* 117 ff.; it is cautiously reaffirmed by Myre, 'Loi' 173–181. Philo makes a threefold distinction as regards the sources of various parts of the Mosaic law. Some laws (notably but not only the ten commandments which are seen as general principles which summarize the particular laws) were delivered directly by God. Others were uttered by God as answers to questions. Finally, many laws were 'spoken by Moses in his own person, when possessed by God and carried away out of himself' (*Vit. Mos.* II, 188). In these cases Moses functions as the interpreter (ἑρμηνεύς) of God's sacred utterances (*Decal.* 175). It should be emphasized, however, that even the laws of this category are perfectly in accordance with the divine will, as they were delivered under the guidance of God's Spirit. Cf. Myre, 'Caractéristiques' 37–58; Fallon, 'Law' 47–51.

37 Norden, 'Jahve' 292 ff.; Reinhardt, *Poseidonios* 6 ff. Jacoby, *Fragmente* II A, A 87, F 70 places the text among the fragments from Posidonius.

38 Aly, *Strabon* 191–210; for a convenient summary see Gager, *Moses* 44–47. See also Lebram, 'Idealstaat' 234 ff.

39 See especially Aly, op.cit. 198 f. etc.

assumed.[40] Nock asked the question, 'May it be that the excursus reproduces the creation of a Jew familiar with the ideas of Posidonius, a Jew whose Hellenization was not, like Philo's, controlled by an overpowering loyalty to Scripture? Such a Jew might have resented legalism on the one hand and Hasmonaean militancy on the other.'[41] Others have tried to construct a closer picture of this Jew by combining the information from Strabo with the ideas of the Hellenistic aristocracy in Jerusalem (1 Macc 1.11) and the reference of Philo (*Migr. Abr.* 89 ff.) to the Alexandrian allegorizers.[42] The boldest conclusion is that of R.M. Grant: In Gal 3.15—20 'Paul seems to be using a historical theory not unlike that apparently found among Hellenistic Jewish allegorists. These theorists ... believed that after Moses' time the law was corrupted; circumcision and dietary laws were added.'[43]

Support for the existence of a Jewish source for Strabo's account might be seen in the surprisingly favourable picture given of Moses and his followers, 'not a few intelligent men'.[44] All extant pagan accounts of the Exodus (except for that of Celsus) tell that the Jews were driven away from Egypt, whereas in this one an intellectual elite goes away voluntarily. Yet this feature can hardly be regarded as sufficient evidence for the theory of a Jewish source.[45]

There are indeed strong reasons against the theory. The description of the Exodus is totally different from the biblical account. Furthermore, which Jew would have regarded Moses as an Egyptian priest (Μωσῆς τις τῶν Αἰγυπτίων ἱερέων)?[46] It is striking, moreover, that the narrator jumps from

---

40 Schürer, *Geschichte* III 156; Nock, 'Posidonius' 8; Hengel, *Judentum* 469–472; 550 f. (he combines both hypotheses: Strabo used Posidonius who had used a Jewish source); Gager, op.cit. 47; Lebram, art.cit. 243 f.

41 Art.cit. 8; Nock's position oscillates, however (in the preceding passage he considers it quite possible that Posidonius himself is the author).

42 Gager; he also appeals (with Nock) to Artapanos' ascription of the Egyptian idolatry to the initiative of Moses. In a vaguer form cf. Bickermann, *Gott* 131; Betz, *Gal* 167.

43 Op.cit. 49. Grant goes on by claiming that Paul merely places the corruption earlier: 'it was Moses himself who made the additions'. This, however, is a distortion of Paul's idea. It was not Moses who made 'additions', but the angels; furthermore, they did not add anything *to* the law, but gave the whole law as an addition to God's promise. Betz, op.cit. 167 speculates that the 'formulation ... that the Torah "was given in addition" may come from a pre-Pauline tradition, where it expressed the view that the introduction of *the Torah* was due to a later state of depravation in the Jewish religion' (my italics). But such a formulation goes considerably beyond the view expressed in the Strabo fragment!

44 Cf. Nock, loc.cit.

45 If Strabo (or a pagan informant) had a favourable view of Moses, perhaps on the basis of his general views about religions, it was consistent to think that those following the noble founder of the religion shared his ideas.

46 Cf. Norden, art.cit. 294; Stern, *Authors* 266. The method of Artapanos (cf. above,

Moses straight to the Hasmons. The next person to be mentioned after Moses is Alexander Jannaios, and the reader gets the impression that the Hasmonean rulers were those 'followers' (οἱ δὲ διαδεξάμενοι) under whom the religion was corrupted 'after some time' (χρονοὺς μέν τινας). And it would be very strange had a Jewish source mentioned along with circumcision and dietary laws also the ἐκτομαί, which means either castration or (more probably) the circumcision of females – both equally foreign to Judaism. Finally, it is artificial to connect the philosophy of Strabo's fragment with what .little we know about the ideas of the Alexandrian allegorizers. For them the contrast between the original legislation and later additions would not necessarily have been 'welcome'.[47] The problems of these people with the law had already been solved by the allegorical method, the use of which implies that the texts to be so interpreted were God-given.[48]

Thus it appears hazardous to build on the theory of a Jewish source behind Strabo; 'it seems best to look for a pagan philosophical source, whatever that may be'.[49] Perhaps Strabo had no 'sources' at all, but combined his own knowledge with 'prevailing philosophical ideas on the emergence and development of religions'.[50]

At best, one may speculate that Strabo (or his source) has partly misinterpreted the ideas of some heterodox Jewish informant(s). Even if this were the case it would not get us anywhere close to Paul, for whom the issue is not a distinction between Mosaic and post-Mosaic commandments.

Paul thus appears to have no Jewish predecessors as regards the ideas contained in Gal 3.15–20. The notion of the angels as the originators of the law is peculiar to him; the tension between this idea and his 'normal' conception of the Torah as God's law is a private and personal problem of his.

b) Christian sources

In Mk 10.2–9 the Marcan Jesus confronts a stipulation of Moses, written

---

n. 42) is no real parallel; to make an Egyptian of a Jewish leader and to make 'Jews' of Egyptians are two quite different things (for a Jew).

47 Against Grant, op.cit. 38.

48 Wolfson, *Philo* I 85 correctly notes that the allegorists shared the belief in the divine origin and the perfection of the law. See on the allegorizers the remarks above, p. 93. Cf. already Löwy, 'Lehre' (1903), 328: 'Man kann kühn behaupten, dass selbst der eingefleischteste und in der religiösen Praxis sich am freiesten gehabende alexandrinische Allegorist sich dem System Paulus' gegenüber ebenso schroff ablehnend verhalten haben würde, wie irgend ein strenger palästinischer Pharisäer. Ist es doch ohne Zweifel ganz etwas anderes, zu sagen, der Wortsinn der mosaischen Gesetze sei nur ein Gefäss für geheime, aber hohe Wahrheiten, oder aber mit Paulus, dass das Gesetz nur um der Uebertretungen willen dazwischengekommen sei.'

49 Stern, loc.cit.; Aly, op.cit. 207 underlines the influence of Hecataeus.

50 Stern, loc.cit. The theory of a process of degeneration of religions had been set forth, before Posidonius, by Theophrast; in the last analysis, the theory can be traced back to Plato.

merely for the hardness of heart of the Jews (v. 4 f.), with the divine order established 'from the beginning of creation' (v. 6 f.). Divine and human acts are being opposed to each other: 'what God has joined together, man shall not separate' (v. 9). The passage reminds us of Gal 3.15—20 in that Jesus refers back to what was before Moses — to God's original purpose in the creation. The original order remains the valid one.[51] The words are not, however, directed against Moses, but against the Jews who are viewed at an almost 'Johannine' distance: what did Moses ordain for *you*? Because of *your* hardness of heart he wrote for *you* ... We would seem to be dealing with a Gentile Christian point of view, for which the Torah is no longer a live problem.

In other passages, however, Moses appears in Mark, too, as the spokesman of God. In Mk 7.8—13 'the commandment of God', 'the word of God' and 'Moses said' are used as interchangeable expressions; the fourth commandment of the Decalogue is quoted as a saying of *Moses*.

A contrast between God and men also occurs in Mk 7.7 f. The mistake of the Pharisees consists in their rejection of God's commandment because of human doctrine, human commandments, traditions of men. In chapter 7, too, Moses appears, but this time he is appealed to as a witness *against* the Pharisees (7.10). The role of Moses, and consequently the role of the law, remains unclarified in Mark. Mark does not reflect on the relation between God's will and the Mosaic law.[52] We get no clear picture of the origin and intention of the law.

At most we can say that Mark's Jesus faintly adumbrates the idea that some particulars in the Mosaic law are human modifications of God's will. Paul, on the other hand, makes no distinctions within the law. And in any case, the idea of angels as originators of the law is quite foreign to Mark.[53]

Similarly, Stephen's words in *Acts* 7.48—50 can be construed (on the pre-Lucan level) as criticisms of the Temple and the Temple cult as alien to God's original law. But if this is so, the trouble with the temple is that it is *not* included in the *Mosaic* legislation — *not* prescribed by the *angel* speaking to Moses on mount Sinai (7.38, 44) who only gave orders about the 'tent of witness'. There is no contact with Paul's idea here. Moreover, Luke personally does not seem to be at all critical of the Jerusalem temple[54] (cf. the role of the temple in Lk 1—2).

---

51 The logic is reversed, i.a., in Hebrews, where it is the *new* order of the new covenant that cancels the old one.

52 Cf. Hübner, op.cit. 225.

53 Cf. Werner, op.cit. 85.

54 Cf. von Campenhausen, *Bibel* 51 n. 93. Recently Stanton has persuasively argued that, in the Lucan perspective, even Acts 7.44—50 is not an attack on the temple. For *Luke* the charge against Stephen was false and Stephen's speech must be understood in this light as well as in the light of Luke's overall attitude to the temple. See Stanton, 'Stephen' 347 ff.

There is no devaluation of the law in Heb 2.2. The mention of angels as law-givers cannot here be interpreted as 'debasing the law'[55]; it serves to put the even greater significance of the Gospel into relief. The angels function as mediators of the law in the good Jewish sense.

In the letter of *Barnabas* we find the closest counterpart to Gal 3 in early Christian literature. To be sure, the writer does not reject the law at all. The law of the OT belongs to the Christians who understand it in the right way. The Jews have misunderstood the law in interpreting the ritual precepts literally. In particular, 'Barnabas' attributes the literal understanding of circumcision to an evil angel (9.4)! The similarity to Paul is more verbal than real even in this case. Correspondingly, the apologist *Aristides* viewed the ritual law as a service rendered (through ignorance) to angels, not to God (ch. 14 in the Syriac text).

Interestingly enough, however, even 'Barnabas' is inconsistent in his attribution of the (misunderstanding of parts of) the law to an angel. If circumcision is at first asserted to be a perversion of God's original command, it is soon after regarded as irrelevant to man's relationship with God (9.6), and then the circumcision of Abraham and his men is acknowledged as a fact, to which a prophetic numerical value is ascribed (9.8). But it is clear that 'the real position of the author' is revealed in 9.4; the other explanations are due to purely exegetical difficulties.[56] The decisive difference between Paul and 'Barnabas' is that the question of law is not an existential one to the latter.

Marcion resembles the Paul of Gal 3.19 f. in that he ascribes the whole law without distinctions and indeed the whole OT to someone other than the God of the NT, namely, to the creator god. Nevertheless, Marcion left in his 'expurgated' text of the NT several Pauline statements which one would expect him to have removed to begin with, above all the statements that the law is good, holy, just, and even spiritual (Rom 7.12, 14) as well as the 'most striking concession of all'[57] that 'I serve God's law with my mind' Rom 7.25. Marcion even retained 1 Cor 9.8 f. where a statement of the law is opposed to what is merely human (κατὰ ἄνϑρωπον). He also preserved the summarizing of the law in the love commandment (Gal 5.14, Rom 13.9 f., Lk 10.25 ff.).[58] Apparently, 'the creator God has some elements of righteous-

---

55 Against Simon, *Stephen* 47; Callan, 'Midrash' 553.
56 Cf. Klevinghaus, *Stellung* 22 f. In comparison with Paul these discrepancies are not very conspicuous. In Paul, too, we find along with the negative evaluation of circumcision the notion of its irrelevance (Gal 5.6, 6.15, 1 Cor 7.19) and the positive assessment of Abraham's circumcision (Rom 4).
57 Harnack, *Marcion* 108.
58 In Marcion's version of the Lucan pericope it is Jesus himself who cites the law in a favourable sense; cf. Harnack, op.cit. 110 f. Marcion also preserved, i.a., Rom 2.12 f., 14a, 2.20, 2.25, 7.7 (the law is not sin), 8.4, 1 Cor 9.8 f.

ness in his character and this is reflected in his book'.[59] Moreover, despite his rejection of the OT Marcion regarded the book as a throughout reliable document and as a unitary whole without any interpolations or falsifications (contrast his treatment of the NT documents!).[60]

A lucid solution to the problem of the law was proposed by the Valentinian Gnostic *Ptolemy* who, in his letter to Flora, undertakes to make clear distinctions within the law. The contents of the law indicate that different parts have a different origin. The better parts go back to the demiurge (none of the law can be from the perfect God), whereas other parts are human additions by Moses and the elders. All this is very different from Paul's global assertion in Gal 3.

A comparable approach is found in the Jewish Christian *Kerygmata Petrou*, where a number of 'false pericopes' are assumed in the OT law, including 'the sacrifices, the kingship, female prophecy and the like' (Hom 3.52). The original will of God had been forgotten after the death of Moses due to false instruction etc.; thus mistakes crept in when the law was written down after the time of Moses (Hom 1.18, Rec 1.15, Hom 3.47, 2.38). This theory, too, differs from Paul's assertion in Gal 3 — most of the law is ascribed to God.

Thus it appears that nobody took up Paul's suggestion about the origin of the law in Gal 3.19 f. before the Gnostics who equated these angels with the demiurges[61] and rejected the notion that the law stemmed from the good God. Therefore no one else got caught in the particular difficulties of Paul's *sic et non* either. The problem of the origin of the law is a problem peculiar to Paul.

3. The negative purpose

In several places Paul establishes a close connection between the law and sin. Thus he states in Gal 3.19 that the law was added $\tau\hat{\omega}\nu$ $\pi\alpha\rho\alpha\beta\acute{\alpha}\sigma\epsilon\omega\nu$ $\chi\acute{\alpha}\rho\iota\nu$. The phrase is ambiguous. In any case it can hardly be taken in the good Jewish sense of 'preventing transgressions'.[62] In a comparable statement in Rom 5.20 Paul says that the law came 'in order that the transgression be magnified' ($\H{\iota}\nu\alpha$ $\pi\lambda\epsilon o\nu\acute{\alpha}\sigma\eta$ $\tau\grave{o}$ $\pi\alpha\rho\acute{\alpha}\pi\tau\omega\mu\alpha$); according to Rom 3.20 'knowledge of sin' is brought about by the law. Law and sin are also connected in

---

59 Blackman, *Marcion* 114.

60 Harnack, op.cit. 67, 86.

61 According to Hippolytus, Cerinthus taught that the law and the prophets were given by angels; the law-giver was one of those angels who had created the world (Epiph., *Panarion* 28, 1, 3). For more Gnostic evidence see the references in Schlier on Gal 3.19.

62 Against W.L. Knox, *Gentiles* 108 f.; Bring, 'Paul' 34; Gyllenberg ad loc.; Lull, *Spirit* 125.

Rom 7.5, 7.7–11, 7.23, 6.14, 4.15, 5.13, and 1 Cor 15.56. But what exactly is this connection?

Several explanations of Gal 3.19, Rom 3.20 and Rom 5.20 have been proposed. Most commentators seek to find a common explanation for all these verses, even though some are inclined to distinguish between them. There are three main alternatives which, to be sure, do not completely exclude each other and can be combined in various ways.

A. The *revelatory* or *cognitive* interpretation: in the light of the law man learns what is sin. Or, more pointedly: man realizes, in the light of the law, that he is a sinner.[63]

B. The *'definition'* interpretation: the law defines sin as 'transgression'. The intervention of the law makes sin a conscious and wilful activity; it makes man guilty.[64]

C. The *causative* interpretation: the law brings about sinning. Some interpreters take this to refer to legalism and hybris (C_1).[65] Others think of transgressions as bad deeds (C_2).[66]

The clearest clues to help one to choose between these options are found in Rom 7. Verse 5 clearly suggests the causative alternative 'C_2'.[67] Through the law, 'sinful desires' were brought about in the persons 'in flesh' (τὰ παθήματα τῶν ἁμαρτιῶν τὰ διὰ τοῦ νόμου). The plural 'passions' suggests concrete sinful acts, rather than a legalistic attitude. The references to 'fruit-bringing' (cf. 6.21) and 'members' (cf. 6.19) show that Paul here gives a brief summary of the slavery to sin he had described in ch. 6, as does the verb δουλεύειν in 7.6. In ch. 6, however, sinning is spoken of in unmistakably moral terms. To be enslaved to sin is to surrender one's 'members' to the service of impurity and lawlessness. *A-nomia* is attacked, not zeal for the *nomos!* Paul thus insinuates that the law engenders immorality, however blasphemous this allegation may sound in Jewish ears. An explanation is supplied in the next passage (7.7–13).

According to 7.7 ff. it is only through the command of the law that man

---

63 Duncan on Gal 3.19; Ladd, 'Paul' 64; Cranfield, 'Paul' 45 f.; id., *Romans* 846 f.; cf. Bring, art.cit. 25.; Wilckens, *Römer* 1, 177. Wilckens, 'Entwicklung' 171 emphasizes that the law was given to condemn transgressions.

64 Lietzmann, Oepke (on Gal 3.19); Whiteley, *Theology* 80 f.; Cranfield, 'Paul' 46; id., Romans 847; Kümmel, *Römer* 7, 50 f.; for Rom 5.20 Sanday-Headlam, Dodd, Barrett, Nikolainen; for Rom 3.20 and Gal 3.19 Luz, *Geschichtsverständnis* 187; id., 'Gesetz' 100.

65 Cf. Bultmann, *Theology* 264 f. (both legalism and transgressions); Käsemann, *Romans* 89 f. (on 3.20); for Rom 5.20 Jüngel, 'Gesetz' 68 n. 88; cf. also Cranfield, 'Paul' 47; id., *Romans* 847.

66 Sieffert on Gal 3.19; Bläser, *Gesetz* 136; van Dülmen, *Theologie* 42; for Gal 3.19 alone Hübner, 'Das ganze Gesetz' 248; id., *Gesetz* 27; for Rom 5.20 and 7.8 Dodd ad loc.; for Rom 7.7 ff. Luz, op.cit. 188.

67 This is played down by Wilckens, 'Entwicklung' 171.

comes to know sin concretely. Desire is only awakened after the law prohibits it. The prohibition makes the desire active. We have here something like
the psychological theory of the forbidden fruit, to which Augustine referred.[68] Using the law as a base for its actions, sin induced man to break the
commandment against desire (of the Decalogue), working in him 'all kinds of
desire'. The phrase πᾶσαν ἐπιϑυμίαν can hardly be taken as a reference to
man's self-centred attitude or the like;[69] like the plural 'passions' in v. 5
it refers to the rich variety of sinful desires. Interpretation 'C$_1$' is thus excluded. The alternative 'B' cannot come into question either.[70] Paul underlines in v. 8 that sin was 'dead' before law entered the stage. Sin was powerless or latent[71]; only the law made it 'alive' (v. 9). So active an expression
must refer to something other than mere definitions. The same is true of the
mention of sin's 'deceit' in v. 11. Interpretation 'A' need not be totally excluded; the revelatory aspect could be there as a secondary aspect. The main
point, however, is that the law *causes* (unwillingly, to be sure) men to sin.

According to Rom 7.8 sin thus was powerless and inactive ('dead') before
the introduction of the law. One may ask whether this is compatible with
7.14. In this verse, man under law is characterized as 'sold under sin'. V. 23
similarly envisages him as imprisoned in the 'law of sin'. If v. 7.14b states the
consequences of the events described in verses 7–11,[72] there is no internal
problem in this. Sin's misuse of the law has led to man's being a helpless
victim of sin. Many interpreters, however, think that 7.14 gives the *reason*
why the process described in verses 7–13 could take place: it is *because* of
man's carnal (σάρκινος) nature that the law, being spiritual, was not able to
produce the right effects in him.[73] Should this be the correct interpretation
then Paul is involved in a glaring self-contradiction: on one hand he states
that the intervention of the law is necessary to induce man to sin; on the
other hand man is already 'sold under sin' when he encounters the commandment of the law.

Various features in the text indicate that Paul did in fact intend to state
the reason for the process 7.7–11 in 7.14. It is clear that verse 13 is intended
to give an explanation for 7–11. Sin, not the law, is the ultimate cause of

---

68 Correctly Dodd ad loc.; Lietzmann ad loc.; Kümmel, op.cit. 45.

69 Against Bornkamm, *Ende* 55; see Räisänen, 'Gebrauch' 90 f.

70 Against Kümmel, op.cit. 50 f.; Hübner, *Gesetz* 68; Schrage, *Einzelgebote* 65 (they
    refer to Rom 5.13); see Brandenburger, *Adam* 209–211. Brandenburger (211) notes
    that 'the sin of men before Moses '(to whom Rom 5.12–14 refers) 'is absolutely
    living, active and personal – the ἁμαρτία νεκρά, on the contrary, is not'.

71 Käsemann, op.cit. 194.

72 Thus Bornkamm, op.cit. 53; Brandenburger, op.cit. 217; Luz, op.cit. 163; Käsemann,
    op.cit. 199.

73 Thus Kümmel, op.cit. 10, 58, 89 f.; Bläser, op.cit. 118; van Dülmen, op.cit. 112 f.;
    Hommel, '7. Kapitel' 102.

man's fall. In itself, v. 14 would be quite appropriate to describe man's plight under law as a consequence of 7–11; its contents correspond to 7.5.[74] Yet what is the force of γάρ in v. 14? It is not unnatural to take it as indicating an explanation of what was set forth before.[75] This understanding seems to be reinforced by 8.3. There the reason for the inability of the law to effect what it ought to have effected is said to have consisted in its 'being weak through the flesh'. σάρξ must here refer to man's fleshly nature, as is clear from the sequel (God sent his son in the 'likeness' of this same sinful σάρξ); it is the encounter with carnal man that rendered the law feeble. That 7.14 describes the necessary conditions for the process described in 7–11 to take place thus seems a plausible hypothesis. It is thus at least possible that Paul gives a contradictory account of the relation of law to sin.

It is probably the same idea − that the law brings about sin − that is hinted at in 1 Cor 15.56: it is the law that gives sin its power.[76] In 1 Cor 15 this idea is introduced very abruptly; it has no connection with the main thrust of the section.[77] The assumption of a gloss, however, makes the verse even more difficult to understand.[78] Like a flash, 1 Cor 15.56 shows how closely Paul had come to associate the law with sin and death: at times he just could not help spelling out this connection, although it was of no relevance for his present purpose.

In Rom 5.20 the role of the law is described in perplexingly active terms: the law 'came in between' (cf. the equally active word γεγονώς in Gal 3.17). This characterisation contains a negative nuance. The purpose and consequence of the intervention of the law is expressed with the clause ἵνα πλεονάσῃ τὸ παράπτωμα. It is surprising how many interpreters take this phrase in a

---

74 Cf. Luz, op.cit. 159 n. 86, 161.

75 To the phrase οἴδαμεν γὰρ ὅτι (7.14) compare οἶδα γὰρ ὅτι 7.18 and οἴδαμεν γὰρ ὅτι 8.22. In 7.18 and 8.22 the phrase introduces a statement that explains or specifies what was said before.

76 Cf. Bauer, *Wörterbuch*, s.v. δύναμις 7.

77 Sandelin, *Auseinandersetzung* 71 f. would infer from v. 56b that Paul is engaged in a polemic against nomistic Wisdom traditions of Alexandrian origin. But if Paul had to face a nomistic front in Corinth, so indirect a comment would be an unintelligibly mild reply (cf. Gal!). As Drane, *Paul*, has shown, Paul himself moves quite a bit in a nomistic direction in 1 Cor as compared with Gal. 15.56 could be directed against any Jewish or Jewish Christian position. On the other hand, Paul may in 15.45 quite possibly take up similar Adam traditions as those found in Philo, but it does not follow from this that he is attacking *sophia* traditions in this chapter.

78 V. 56 is considered a gloss by J. Weiss and Lietzmann; cf. also Noack, 'Evangeliet' 133. Weiss is inclined to ascribe the addition to Paul himself (made later on). But why should Paul make such insertions? 1 Cor 1.14, 16 shows that he was not concerned to check and revise what he had dictated. In Romans Paul several times inserts a comment on the law, which he explains only later on (e.g. 4.15, 7.5; cf. the phrase διὰ νόμου in Gal 2.19 which is never explained).

cognitive sense[79]: man comes to know more painfully that he is a sinner. Such a 'subjective' explanation of the increase of sin is contradicted by the context. Parallel to the increase of sin Paul speaks of the superabundant increase of *grace*. The latter cannot possibly refer to an individual's subjective experience! Both sin and grace are in 5.20 f. metaphorically[80] spoken of as powers which reign over two different realms or aeons. 5.20 refers to an 'objective' increase of sin: an increase of transgressions.[81] Paul does not have in mind individuals, but the whole world.[82]

There is a difference between the roughly parallel statements Rom 5.20 and 7.7–11. According to ch. 7, it is only the law with its commandments that *brings about* actual sinning. According to 5.20, however, transgressions and sin are concrete realities already *before* the intervention of the law; the law just *increases* the number and significance of the transgressions. Once more, Paul's thoughts about law and sin stand in tension with each other.[83]

In Gal 3.19 the context does not provide us with sufficient clues to make out the meaning of the phrase $\tau\tilde{\omega}\nu \pi\alpha\rho\alpha\beta\acute{\alpha}\sigma\epsilon\omega\nu \chi\acute{\alpha}\rho\iota\nu$. As the talk of the law being added, however, parallels the idea of its intervention in Rom 5.20, and as the law is spoken of in rather negative terms in both passages – even more so in Gal 3 – it seems natural to take Gal 3.19 in the radical

---

79 Dodd, Michel, Nikolainen; cf. also Hübner, *Gesetz* 73 f.

80 See above, p. 99 n. 29.

81 Many interpreters, to be sure, think rather of an increase of legalism and self-right-eousness in this connection: thus Käsemann, ad loc.; Brandenburger, op.cit. 252 f.; Stuhlmacher, *Versöhnung* 112. For Jüngel, art.cit. 68 n. 88 this understanding is even 'self-evident'. Yet it should be noted that the confrontation of this increasing $\pi\alpha\rho\acute{\alpha}\pi\tau\omega\mu\alpha$ and the increasing grace immediately leads Paul to formulate the suggestion (to be emphatically dismissed) that Christians may wish to 'remain in sin' to let the grace grow great. The $\pi\alpha\rho\acute{\alpha}\pi\tau\omega\mu\alpha$ of 5.20 thus denotes that sin to which the Christians have died in baptism (6.2 ff.). Its nature is made clear in 6.12 ff.: it expresses itself as $\dot{\alpha}\delta\iota\kappa\acute{\iota}\alpha$ (v. 12), $\dot{\alpha}\kappa\alpha\vartheta\alpha\rho\sigma\acute{\iota}\alpha$ and $\dot{\alpha}\nuo\mu\acute{\iota}\alpha$ (v. 19); cf. above. It should be clear that Paul speaks of sin as immorality, not as legalistic zeal.

These observations also refute the assumption that Paul's statements about the close connection between law and sin should be traced back to his own experience (as his persecution of the Christians out of nomistic zeal turned out to be opposition to God, i.e. sin); thus Kim, *Origin* 280 f.; cf. Luz, 'Gesetz' 100, 110; Jeremias, *Schlüssel* 23 f. Paul never indicates anything like that. In another connection (commenting on Rom 7, op.cit. 53) Kim proposes indeed the quite different suggestion that Paul's view of the law as 'a spur to sin' has something to do with 'the very human experience that prohibition tends to awaken desire to do what is forbidden', of which Paul could not be unaware. But one can hardly have it both ways! This last mentioned suggestion is the more likely one.

82 Correctly Kühl, ad loc.; van Dülmen, op.cit. 98 n. 86. Feuillet, 'Loi ancienne' 803 dilutes the meaning of Rom 5.20: far from having willed the transgressions in question, God has merely foreseen and permitted them! H.W. Schmidt quite arbitrarily interprets 5.20 as a reference to the crucifixion.

83 Cf. Brandenburger, op.cit. 214 f.

causative sense: the law was added to bring about, or to increase, transgressions.[84]

On the other hand, the statement 'through the law ἐπίγνωσις ἁμαρτίας (is brought about)' in Rom 3.20 seems to have a different point. To be sure, it is not impossible, in the light of γινώσκειν τὴν ἁμαρτίαν in 7.7, to take ἐπίγνωσις ἁμαρτίας in the sense of practical 'learning', i.e. sinning.[85] The sense would then be that through the law man learns to sin. Yet the immediate context (3.9–20a) would seem to point to another direction: the law (here practically equivalent with 'Scripture') stops every mouth by showing that all (including the Jews) have sinned. The alternative 'A' is plausible here,[86] although 'C' cannot be excluded. The choice between these two options does not affect my argument.

A special problem is posed by Rom 5.13. In v. 12 Paul has stated that sin and death came into the world as a consequence of Adam's fall. He has also indicated (however precisely one interprets ἐφ' ᾧ) that all men have sinned. In v. 13 he consequently admits that even before the law sin was in the world. Yet, when there is no law, 'sin is not counted' (ἁμαρτία δε οὐκ ἐλλογεῖται). The coming of the law thus makes a difference; it is only now that sin is 'counted'.

It is clear that ἐλλογεῖν is a term which has here to do with heavenly book-keeping. On the surface, the meaning would seem to be clear: even though men sinned in the period between Adam and Moses, their deeds were not registered in the heavenly book – probably because there was no code which they had formally transgressed.[87] But what can such a statement really mean? According to 2.12–16 those who have sinned 'without the law' (ἀνόμως) will perish without the law (v. 12) in the last judgment (v. 16).

Moreover, the people of the interim period certainly did not avoid death, the corollary of sin (5.12; according to 6.23, death is the 'wages' of sin), as Paul himself says in 5.14.[88] Whether or not their deeds were written into a book, the people of that period, according to the OT, were punished extremely severely for their sins (the Flood!).[89] Whether these sins were 'counted' or

---

84 Gal 3.22 also points in this direction. Yet it has to be admitted that the image of παιδαγωγός (3.24) suggests rather the notion of preventing transgressions (cf. above n. 62). The train of thought in Gal 3.19 ff. is not unequivocal.

85 Thus Bläser, op.cit. 138 f.; van Dülmen, op.cit. 84.

86 Correctly Kümmel, op.cit. 48; Hahn, 'Gesetzesverständnis' 35 f.

87 Paul states in v. 14 that between Adam and Moses people were not guilty of a transgression similar to that of Adam. This may mean that Adam's case was analogous to that of those under the law: for him, there was a clear divine commandment to obey or disobey. Cf. Brandenburger, op.cit. 191 f.

88 The contradiction between verses 13 and 14 is correctly pointed out by Türcke, *Potential* 90 n. 79.

89 Cf. Kuss, *Römerbrief* 233.

not in some technical sense would seem to be a matter of no consequence whatsoever. The explanation that the people of the interim period were punished immediately, whereas other people are only punished on the day of judgment[90] is artificial. If the law is given merely an informative function[91], the use of ἐλλογεῖν becomes very strange. If Paul's statement can be filled with any concrete sense at all, it would seem to refer to a technical trifle. Until the law sin had been punished because it was sin; since the law, the very same punishments are imposed because of 'transgression'. This, of course, does not fit the case of Adam, which was one of transgression (παράβασις)[92],

---

90 Thus Käsemann, ad loc.; cf. O'Neill; Jüngel, art.cit. 54–57. Käsemann takes the sense to be that before Moses evil deeds immediately incurred evil consequences as is described in 1.24 ff. But Paul hardly thought that the pagans condemned in 1.24 ff. were freed from the eschatological judgment (cf. 2.16)! – A strange interpretation is put forward by Danker, 'Romans V. 12'. He thinks that the notorious ἐφ' ᾧ in v. 12 refers in anticipation to νόμος (v. 13), the sense being: 'And so death passed on to all men, on the legal basis in terms of which all (including the Gentiles) sinned. This must be maintained, for until the law (of Moses) sin was in the world, and one must admit that sin cannot be charged up in the absence of law.' (431) On this reading, the relative pronoun of v. 12 has as its implied correlate the νόμος of v. 13 which, however, is there used in a different sense (the Mosaic law) than in the 'implicit' case (a legal basis)! And even apart from this curiosity Paul would have expressed himself unintelligibly in a matter he was quite capable of putting in clear words (2.12–16).

91 Luz, op.cit. 199 f. interprets v. 13: 'What was lacking was thus merely a law that could have unmasked death as the punishment for sin.' Cf. Maurer, *Gesetzeslehre* 41 f. Kaye, *Thought Structure* 105 speculates that perhaps 'the contrast between the time before the law, and that afterwards, is not absolute, but only relative. The law would thus have the effect of clarifying the situation of sinners. It would provide a clear form for the demand of God which was there already on men, and which they did not heed. This would place such men in the same position as had been argued for the Gentiles ... ' If the law is given just an interpretive or clarifying role, the 'not counting' is emptied of all concrete significance.

   Brandenburger, op.cit. 201 ff. argues that, having set forth in 4.15 the principle that without law there is no transgression, Paul now has to show how this claim harmonizes with the well-known biblical fact that men between Adam and Moses sinned and died. In the meantime there was no νόμος, so that sin as παράβασις νόμου could not be there. Brandenburger puts the emphasis on v. 14 and renders ἀλλά with 'despite that': in the interim period sin was not registered as 'transgression' in the heavenly books; despite that, sinners were at that time, too, subjected to the reign of death. – This may indeed be the best interpretation of the verse, although the reference to 4.15 may be circular (that verse is in itself ambiguous and becomes clearer if it is interpreted in the light of 5.13, see below, p. 148!). But in the end it only makes it all the clearer that the statement ἁμαρτία οὐκ ἐλλογεῖται is a mere verbal expedient without any real significance. Paul tries to show that, as regards man and sin, the coming of the law makes a difference; what he actually shows is that there is none.

92 Unless the purpose of v. 14 is to put Adam in the category of those who sinned against a 'legal' commandment, see n. 87.

nor does it harmonize with the synonymous use of παράπτωμα and ἁμαρτία in 5.20.

It remains to be added that verses 5.13 f. contradict Rom 7.8. According to 7.7 f. sin was 'dead' before the coming of the law. 5.13 f. – more naturally – assumes that sin was a mighty power ever since Adam.[93]

One has to admit that 5.13 is an artificial expedient which disturbs the argument of chapter 5.[94] It is an infelicitous attempt to introduce secondarily the problems of the law into a train of thought with which they originally had nothing to do and into which they do not logically fit.[95] In different contexts Paul gives two different and incompatible reasons for the power of sin in the world: on one hand, this is due to Adam's fall (ch. 5), on the other, to the law (ch. 7). The former idea is traditional, the latter peculiarly Pauline. It seems that Paul was not totally unconscious of the tension between these explanations, since he tries, by way of two incidental remarks, to integrate the contribution of the law into the argument about Adam as well. In 5.13 he does this by ascribing to the law the quality to define sin as transgression (a statement probably prepared by 4.15). In 5.20, again, he attributes to the law a sin-increasing role. In this case he is not involved in such logical difficulties as with v. 13. The law does not bring about sin; it just increases it, or accelerates a process already in motion. The trouble is simply how 5.20 harmonizes with empirical reality. As sin is alive and well long before the introduction of the law, even the theory of the forbidden fruit is not very relevant here (it suits 7.7–11 better).

In Rom 4.15 Paul, who is concerned to deny that the law has anything to do with the promise, states that the law brings about wrath. That is, the law causes man to be subjected to God's judgment. This claim is apparently explained in the next statement: 'but where there is no law, there is no transgression either'. It would be possible to understand this in the sense of the causative alternative 'C', in the light of 7.7: transgressions are only brought

---

93 Against Kümmel, op.cit. 50 f. who finds 5.13 and 7.8 identical in content; see above, p. 142 n. 70. Brandenburger, op.cit. 205–214 shows that the two statements cannot be harmonized with each other. His assertion that there is not, however, a genuine contradiction between them (213 f.) is hardly convincing. Cf. Wedderburn, 'Adam' 424.

94 F.C. Grant, 'Romans' 35; Bultmann, *Theology* 252: 'completely unintelligible'; even sharper Loisy, *Remarques* 20. Later on, Loisy (*Origins* 255) commented on Rom 5.12–14 that 'in this statement there are some enormous absurdities which neither philosophers nor historians need spend time in discussing'. In this late period Loisy had accepted the theory (set forth by J. Turmel) that Paul's letters were full of interpolations, and he further commented on the passage. Rom 5.12–21: 'If anyone choose to believe that this wholly abstract, scholastic and false conception of the Law was imagined and professed by a man who had long lived in obedience to the Law, we shall not pause to argue with him.'

95 Cf. Strecker, *Eschaton* 249.

about when there is a law to forbid them and thus to lead man to tempta-
tion.[96] Another possibility is to connect 4.15 with 5.13: although there is
sin in the world since Adam's days, 'transgressions' in a technical sense are
not there until there is a law which can be transgressed. I am inclined to
accept this interpretation, but the choice is not important. As I see it, both
'B' and 'C' are represented.in Romans, so that 4.15, whichever way it is interpreted, does not add anything novel to the picture.[97]

In sum, Paul seems to understand the relation between the law and sin in
different ways in different passages. He possibly has the cognitive aspect —
the law reveals man as sinner — in mind in Rom 3.20. In Rom 5.13 (and
possibly in 4.15) the law is seen as a formal standard which qualifies transgressions of it as different from other ways of sinning. The most remarkable,
however, is the causative aspect: the law brings about sin (Rom 7.5, 7—11,
Gal 3.19, 1 Cor 15.56) or increases it (Rom 5.20). Paul thus gives a variegated
picture of the 'law of sin'. There is no development, say, from Galatians to
Romans in this matter,[98] for all the different aspects are there, side by side,
in Romans.

There are no particular problems connected with the cognitive aspect. This
side of the matter is, however, the one least emphasized by Paul. The 'definition' aspect is full of logical problems to which reference has been made
above. It remains to consider the inherent problems of the characteristically
Pauline view that the law engenders sin (or increases it — the two ideas stand
in tension with each other, as we have seen).

Paul's bold statements about the negative effects of the law have often
been regarded as insights of genius.[99] One may be inclined to question this
in the light of the self-contradictions involved in the notion. Yet the most
aggravating problems arise when one moves from immanent logic to ask questions about Paul's premises.

In Rom 7.7 f. Paul sets forth an empirical claim: the commandments of
the law awaken in man the desire to transgress them. The law thus promotes
sin. That this really should have been the case empirically in the Judaism of
Paul's day few would dare to claim. The standard Jewish reaction to such a
claim is indeed quite justified.[100] But one should go further and ask: 'Why is

---

96 Thus Michel; Hahn, art.cit. 41.

97 It might also be possible to take 4.15 in still another sense in the light of 6.14: where
   there is *no longer* a law, there no transgressions come about; when one is not under
   law, sin reigns no more over one.

98 Against Hübner, *Gesetz* 73 f., and Drane, *Paul* 34 f. Both have to deny a causative
   sense in Rom 5.20. But it is the statement of Gal 3.19 that is ambiguous — its sense
   can only be established as causative with the aid of the parallels in Romans!

99 See, e.g., Beck, 'Gesetz' 129; Bandas, *Master-Idea* 110 ('marvellous insight into
   human nature').

100 Klausner, Jesus 467 speaks of strange 'Phantasterei'.

it *only* the commandment of the *law* that incites to transgression?' Why does not, say, the apostolic paraenesis — or paraclesis, if you like — lead to the same result?[101] Paul, too, imposes clear prohibitions on his readers. In Rom 6.19, e.g., he forbids them to put their members into the service of impurity. Why does this prohibition not awaken the desire to impurity? Or, when Paul in Rom 13.13 warns the Roman Christians of revelling and drunkenness, why does this prohibition not incite them to desire these things, if the prohibition of the Decalogue 'Thou shalt not desire' does have such an effect?

One sees that Paul simply has different standards for Jews and Christians respectively. He ascribes to commandments of the law qualities which he would never ascribe to his own apostolic commandments (and nevertheless, now and then, resorts to appeal to the commandments of the law in his Christian exhortation, notably in 1 Cor 7.19).

We have seen above that in passages like Rom 1.18–32, 2.17–24, or 7.14–25 Paul takes up some everyday experience and radically generalizes it to make it serve his particular aim.[102] In view of this one may hazard the conjecture that the negative view of the effects of the law as set forth in 7.7–11 and elsewhere is due to an analogous *generalization of an everyday experience* which has, in retrospect, been charged with a vigorous theological emphasis. Paul had observed the general fact that prohibitions sometimes incite people to transgress them — that the forbidden fruit is sweet. In a Jewish milieu, such prohibitions were, of course, prohibitions imposed by the Torah. In his search — whether conscious or unconscious — for grounds for his not uncritical attitude to the Torah, Paul made a tremendous generalization: the prohibitions of the law *always* incite to transgressions, and this is indeed the real *purpose* of the law as well.

What was observed in connection with the problem of the fulfillability of the law is reinforced here: first there was the aprioristic theological thesis (Christ has superseded the law). Afterwards, Paul tried to undergird his thesis with various arguments. Several arguments take as their point of departure some empirical observation. The observations are, however, interpreted very one-sidedly and artificially. Christian interpreters of Paul have been astonishingly blind to the artificial character of Paul's allegations about the sin-engendering nature of the law. The sharp comment of Loisy that Paul 'invents the

---

101 For the designation parachesis see Schlink, 'Gesetz' 326 f. Following K. Barth, Schlink (331) comments on the paraclesis: 'Von der Paraklese gilt nicht, was vom Gesetz im Unterschied zum Evangelium gilt: die Sünde wird dadurch nicht gross gemacht ... sie richtet und tötet nicht ... gilt auch nicht, dass sie ohnmächtig ist, nicht zustande bringt, was sie fordert'. That is precisely how Paul sees the situation (although his paraclesis in Corinth may have seemed rather impotent to others!) — and such a characteristic clearly reveals Paul's begging of the question.

102 See above, III 2, 4.

philosophy and psychology that suit the needs of his thesis'[103] is not so wide
off the mark. Paul *had* to show that the effects of the law are negative, and
only negative, and he carried through his thesis with violence.[104]

To round off this chapter, mention should be made of the fact that Paul
often portrays man under law as hopelessly entangled in the power of sin.
Sin is his lord (Rom 6.14), under which he is sold (7.14); the 'law of sin and
death' reigns in his members (7.23). If what I have said before is on the right
track, it follows that this picture represents a radicalization in retrospect,
triggered off by Paul's Christological conviction. He does not consistently
hold that man apart from Christ is a helpless victim of sin, and this very
inconsistency betrays the secondary character of the radicalism. It is to be
doubted, whether Paul really thought of sin as a quasi-personal power at all;
the language that may seem to suggest this in Rom 6.12−21 and elsewhere is
well capable of a metaphorical interpretation.[105] Paul had inherited the idea
that sin and death belong intrinsically together (Rom 5.12−14, 17, 21).
Having established a close connection between sin and the law as well, he
quite naturally takes the next step and connects the law with death, too.
The commandment of the law brings death to man (Rom 7.8). Consequently,
'the law of sin' (Rom 7.23) is also called 'the law of sin and death' (Rom
8.2). The letter of the law 'kills' (2 Cor 3.6). The ministry of Moses was a
ministry of death and of condemnation (2 Cor 3.7, 9).

4. A positive purpose?

Did God have any direct positive intention when giving the law? Was the
law originally designed to give life to the person who fulfilled it, or was it
not? On this question, too, different answers are given by Paul's interpreters.

1. Most interpreters think that the law never had, according to Paul, any
salvific purpose. The purpose of the law was the negative one to bring about
sin.[106] This interpretation is often coupled with a particular overall view of
Paul's message: the way of 'works' is in itself false and would never lead to
life, even if man were able to fulfil the law in its totality. In the final analysis,
however, the negative purpose of the law is embedded in God's overarching
salvific plan: in leading man to death the law lets 'God appear as God'[107] and

---

103 Loisy, *Galates* 159 (on Gal 3.22−25).
104 Schoeps, *Paul* 173−175 is correct in stressing that 'the retrospective way of thought
    is the real axis of his argument' (175), even though one has to disagree with Schoeps
    as to what Paul's axiom was (see below, VIII 2).
105 See above, p. 99 n. 29.
106 Cf. Maurer, Gesetzeslehre 88 (but see below, n. 117); Bultmann, *Theology* 263,
    267; Bläser, *Gesetz* 134 ff.; Conzelmann, *Outline* 226 f.; etc.
107 Bultmann, op.cit. 267.

thus makes all and sundry totally dependant upon God's grace in Christ.[108]

This understanding of the purpose of the law has a good basis in Gal 3.21. Paul states that the law is not 'against (God's) promises', since it does not at all vie with them. The promises are a direct expression of God's salvific will. Abstractly considered, the law could have mediated righteousness, i.e. salvation and life, 'had a law been given that is able to produce life' (v. 21b). This, however, would have rendered the promises unnecessary. The case is set forth as imaginary and unreal. As no life-giving law has in fact been given, righteousness by the law has been excluded at the outset. The same principle is stated in 3.17−18: the law and the promises exclude each other as means of salvation. That no life-giving law has been given is, according to v. 22, part of God's good purpose: Scripture has shut everything under sin in order that the promise would be effective for the believers. It is only indirectly that the law serves God's purpose. That the law was, according to 3.19, designed to be in force for only a limited period of time, also shows that it could only have an indirect purpose in God's plan.[109]

2 Cor 3 is also to be mentioned in this connection. There the contrast between the old and new covenant is described as the contrast between the *'killing'* letter and the *life-producing* (ζωοποιεῖ) Spirit (v. 6). The law thus has nothing to do with life; quite the contrary.[110] The ministry of Moses was a ministry of death (v. 7). In the light of the phrase 'the ministry of condemnation' (v. 9) this probably means that the law 'kills' by proclaiming the death sentence to every transgressor of it − that is, over everybody.[111]

2. Other interpreters, however, have seized on other passages in Paul. Thus Cullmann writes on the basis of Rom 1−3: 'All divine salvific efforts, his revelation in the works of creation and his revelation in the law could in prin-

---

108 The law is seen in an extremely negative light by Aulén, *Christus* 67 f. Building on Gal 3.13 and 1 Cor 15.56 in particular, Aulén emphasizes that the law is one of the destructive hostile powers, for 'the way of legal righteousness which the Law ... demands can never lead to salvation and life'. The ambiguity of the law is comparable to the ambiguity of the devil (!) and of death in the theology of the old church, where they are hostile powers on one hand and executants of God's judgment on the other. Such an interpretation requires, however, that ἡ κατάρα τοῦ νόμου in Gal 3.13 is construed as an epexegetical genitive (the law *is* the curse; thus also Gulin, *Freude* 160; Gronemeyer, *Frage* 6 and passim; Weder, *Kreuz* 187). It would seem clear from 3.10 that Paul speaks of the curse pronounced *by* the law. Caird, *Principalities* 43, 45, 51 also speaks of the law as 'demonic'; Nygren, *Römerbrief* 205 ff. also reckons the empirical law among the 'powers of destruction'; so, too, S. Hanson, *Unity* 61 f., 71 f.
109 This is emphasized by Linton, 'Paulus' 137. By delegating the legislation to the angels (Gal 3.19), 'God himself has given the law a lower dignity'.
110 It was argued above, p. 45, that 2 Cor 3.6 refers to the Mosaic law itself (the tablets of stone!) and not to a misunderstanding of it.
111 Cf. Windisch, ad loc.

ciple already have led men to salvation, had Gentiles and Jews responded to
them with faith. As this was not the case, the decisive salvific act had to take
place in Christ ... '[112] Rom 3.23 f. seems indeed to indicate that the law was
intended as a way to life; it is only because of its practical, empirical ineffec-
tiveness that God decided to provide a new way to salvation. '*First* all men
sinned ... *then* God provided the free gift as an alternative means of salvation.
This would imply that the free gift would not have been needed had men not
sinned in the first place, and consequently that it was at least theoretically
possible to obey the law and thus be justified.'[113]

A comparable intention can be found in Rom 7.10. It was found, says
Paul, that the commandment which was to be 'unto life' ($\dot{\eta}$ ἐντολὴ ἡ εἰς ζωήν)
for the Ego, effected in fact his death. The law thus had been given 'unto
life', even though, because of the deceit of sin, things did not work out that
way in the practice. The preposition εἰς must be given its full final force [114]:
the law contained the promise of life[115]; it was to lead unto life.[116] It was,
after all, good, holy and spiritual (7.12, 14). It is quite correct to say that
'grace revealed itself originally in the law'.[117] The law had a positive task,
which it was, however, unable to carry out. It was weak 'because of the flesh'
(8.3); i.e., man, being carnal, was not able to obey the spiritual (7.14) law.[118]

There are thus two lines of thought in Paul. According to one, the possibility that the law could lead unto life is excluded already in principle.
According to the other, that possibility is shown to be irrelevant merely on
empirical grounds. Either God did not want the law to be a way to salvation,
or the actual law did not suit that purpose and another means had to be provided. Clearly these two lines contradict each other.[119]

Rom 7 stands in contradiction not only to Gal 3, but also to 2 Cor 3.

---

112 Cullmann, *Heil* 243. Cf. Wilckens, *Rechtfertigung* 81–84.
113 E.P. Sanders, 'Question' 105.
114 Against Bläser, op.cit. 196 f.
115 Lietzmann, Michel.
116 Kühl, cf. Wilckens.
117 Käsemann, *Romans* 198. It is incorrect, however, to go on by saying that 'this was
    perverted when the law was misunderstood as a demand for achievement'; cf. the
    critical remarks of Türcke, *Potential* 87. I have argued above in ch. II against the
    notion that Paul had a Jewish misunderstanding of the law in mind. The misunder-
    standing theory is also represented by Maurer, op.cit. 53, 87 f. – in blunt contradic-
    tion to his exposition earlier on p. 26. A somewhat similar oscillation is found in
    Nygren on Rom 7.10.
118 Cf. van Dülmen, *Theologie* 112 ff.; 138 ff.
119 This is seen by Joest, *Gesetz* 165; cf. already Ritschl, *Lehre* II 254; Holtzmann,
    Theologie II 37. E.P. Sanders, art.cit. 108 also observes two different answers, of
    which the 'grundsätzlich' one (Gal 3.21 etc.) 'is truer to the whole thrust of Paul's
    thought'.

According to 2 Cor 3 the law 'kills'; according to Rom 7 it is just too weak to prevent man's death. One might say that the former passage presents it as poison, the latter merely as an ineffective medicine. Paul, who is on the whole defensive and apologetic about his attitude to the law in Romans, has in this letter shifted his ground in comparison with 2 Corinthians.[120]

In addition to the internal contradictions, the texts in question are fraught with problems of theodicy. As regards the line of thought present in Rom 1–3 and 7.10 one may ask, why God gave men so weak a law in the first place. If this line is consistently thought through, Christ will be seen as God's second attempt to save mankind after his first device turned out to be unsuccessful. This consequence is indeed one of the reasons why some interpreters refuse to find in Rom 7.10 the idea that the law was given 'unto life'. [121] Yet this idea cannot be suppressed.[122]

With respect to the second line of thought (that expressed most clearly in Gal 3.21) the question is relevant, why God *did not want* to give a law that would have been able to lead man unto life, even though a promise of this life is expressed in this law (Lev 18.5, cited in Gal 3.12 and Rom 10.5). If the law's only direct purpose was to provoke sin (Gal 3.19), one is entitled to ask, with Hübner, whether this does not sound rather cynical.[123] 'God ... brings men into the ... damnable and immoral situation of sinning only in order to prove his divinity in his goodness and unsurpassable grace'![124] This problem was perceived already by the Church fathers.[125]

Hübner attempts to remove the cynicism from the picture painted by Paul by distinguishing between three different intentions operative at the giving of the law: the intention of the angels who gave the law, that of God who permitted it, and the immanent intention of the law.[126] This complicated speculation does not carry conviction,[127] and serves all the more to show how

---

120 This is no reason to assume a theological development of Paul between the writing of the two letters. The contrast between the letter and the Spirit is still there in Rom 7.6. When Paul nevertheless asserts in 7.14 that the law is πνευματικός by nature, he gets involved in one more blatant self-contradiction.

121 Cf. Bläser, op.cit. 197 n. 61.

122 Conzelmann, op.cit. 226 points out that Paul's reasoning (on the 'objectified' level) amounts at this point to 'a senseless theory'. 'What kind of God is it who makes known his will and cannot carry it out?' On Conzelmann's attempt to gloss over such difficulties in Paul's thought see above (Introduction), p. 5 f.

123 Hübner, *Gesetz* 27. Cf. also Türcke, *Potential* 87 f.

124 Hübner, ibid.

125 See the comment of Origen on Rom 5.20 below, p. 156.

126 Hübner, op.cit. 27 ff.; id., 'Proprium' 462 f.

127 Abstractly considered, it is certainly possible to distinguish between the intention of the angels giving the law and God who permitted it. It is however extremely difficult to make sense of the third intention assumed by Hübner: 'the immanent intention of the law'; cf. Luz's review, p. 122. If this intention was neither that of God (this

hopeless it is to defend Paul against theological criticisms regarding the idea
of God implicit in some of his statements about the law. The logical conclusions from Gal 3.21 (conclusions which Paul certainly did *not* perceive) are
theologically dubious. The idea that the law was so designed as not to be able
to lead unto life is, as Parkes puts it, 'both offensive and ridiculous to any
Jewish saint and scholar, and it is a pity that we do not more readily admit
that it is equally offensive to all Christian conceptions of God'.[128]

To avoid misunderstanding, let me emphasize that I am not suggesting that
Paul's picture of God *is* cynical. My point is this: *if* we draw certain logical
implications from some of Paul's statements about the law, then strange conclusions will result. Paul did not see these conclusions and would, of course,
have rejected them emphatically.

This state of affairs would seem to indicate that in this case, too, Paul got
involved in intellectual difficulties, because he started from an aprioristic
(Christological) conviction. Instead of considering the intention of the law in
its own right he deduced his statements about it straight from his Christological insights. That is why he ended up by putting forward artificial and
conflicting theories about the law.

5. Analogies regarding the purpose of the law?

a) Christian sources

The author of *Hebrews* makes it clear in no uncertain terms that the old
law, which has been abrogated (7.12), was 'weak' and 'useless' (7.18), not
being able to make anything perfect (7.19). Correspondingly, the old covenant was growing old and was not blameless (8.13, 8.7). Had it been blameless,
then no new covenant would have been needed in the first place (8.7, cf.
Gal 3.21!). The law was merely a shadow of the good things to come (10.1).
It is indeed 'impossible' — in principle — that 'the blood of oxen and deer
could remove sins' (10.4).

The writer is very clear in his rejection of the old law as being weak in
nature. Consistently enough, it is the *law* itself that is σάρκινος in this writing
(7.16). There are in the letter only slight traces of the rival view of the empiri-

---

difference is important on p. 40 f., whereas the intentions fuse together in Hübner's
interpretation of Rom 7.10, p. 64) nor that of the angels, then where on earth did it
come from? (Moses does not come-into question!) But even the distinction between
the intention of God and that of the angels breaks down in view of the temporal
clause in 3.19. Hübner must indeed resort to the explanation that Paul has not expressed himself quite clearly in that verse (29). As he understands Gal 3.19, 'because
of the transgressions' (v. 19b) refers to the intention of the angels, but the ἄχρις-
clause (v. 19c) to that of God; the intention of the angels is hinted at in v. 19b,
although the angels are only mentioned in v. 19d, *after* the statement about *God's*
intention! Cf. Westerholm's review (195 f.).

128 Parkes, *Jesus* 129.

cal disobedience of the members of the old people of God.[129] On the whole Hebrews is much more consistent than Paul on this point, underlining the weakness of the law. Consequently, however, the accusation of an implicit cynicism in the conception of God can with even better reason be directed to this address.

What was God's purpose in his giving the law through angels (2.2), with all the majestic glory described in the Sinai story (12.18 ff.)? Why did God give a weak, useless and 'fleshly' (!) law, which was bound to induce men to 'dead works'? Why was the old covenant in itself 'blameful'? The idea that the law was also a pale shadow of the coming salvation is hardly sufficient to remove the suspicion of implicit cynicism from the portrait of God in Hebrews. Of course the author did not mean it that way, any more than Paul did, but that is what results as soon as the question τί οὖν ὁ νόμος (almost by-passed by the author) is seriously raised.

In *Luke* 10.25–28 we meet a positive reversal of Paul's negative idea. Yet in Peter's speech (Acts 15.10 f., cf. also James's statement in v. 19) the law is said to be a 'yoke' that 'neither our fathers nor we have been able to bear'. How can God-given 'living words' (Acts 7.38) be such a burden? A related difficulty is that these words, from which not a single iota will disappear (Luke 16.17) come to be seen, from the Gentile point of view, as 'a preliminary stage and an early form of God's will'.[130] Apparently Luke did not reflect very much on the purpose or nature of the law. This is, however, a rather mild tension when compared with the Pauline views.

Other writers avoid Paul's dilemma — mainly because the question is never raised! Of later writers, *Marcion* and *Ptolemy* escape Paul's theological difficulty at the cost of running into another: the attribution of the OT law to an inferior god. Ptolemy also reckons with human additions.

Justin comes close to Marcion: the law 'belongs to the old dispensation, it was intended for the Jews, and it was completely abolished by Christ'. 'The only important difference is that for Justin the Mosaic Law was given by the same God and Father of all.'[131]

To be able to maintain this against the Marcionites, Justin had to find a divine purpose for the ritual law. He is indeed the first Christian writer who attempts in a systematic way to define the role and purpose of the law. That purpose was a strictly historical one. The (ritual) law as a whole was given 'on the account of the sinfulness of the Jews'; 'particular precepts were also

---

129 Cf. 3.16 ff., 4.6, and Luz, 'Bund' 330 n. 42. Luz (329) rightly refutes the view of Michel (*Hebr* on 8.7) that only men are 'blamed' by the author and not the covenant itself.

130 Luz, 'Gesetz' 133.

131 Stylianopoulos, *Justin* 89.

ordained for particular reasons'.[132] Unlike other precepts, that of circumcision had the punitive purpose 'to identify the Jews in order to facilitate their just punishment by the Romans'! (16.2)[133] For other precepts more positive explanations are found. Thus, the sacrifices 'were instituted in order to restrain the Jews from idolatry', 'the sabbath was commanded so that the Jews would nurture remembrance of God', as was the abstinence from certain foods (19.6–20.1).[134] Behind Justin's efforts to present the law as a remedial and a beneficent discipline, given 'as a kind of divine "accommodation" suitable to the evil propensity of the Jews' (19.6, 67.10) lies 'defence both of the perfection of God and the meaningfulness of the Law'.[135] 'Contends Justin: if his interpretation of the Law as temporal legislation for the Jews is not accepted, then unthinkable inferences about God would follow, that is, either that one is not dealing with the same God in the pre-Law period' or that God is inconsistent.[136]

Justin thus consciously tries to evade the problem of theodicy. While his explanation is logical as a whole, its individual parts are infelicitous. The explanation given to circumcision is ridiculous, and 'Ezekiel's complaints against the *breaking* of the rule of the sabbath, God's Law, are now cited as the *reason* for the giving of the sabbath in the first place!' (ch. 21)[137]

To some extent, then, Paul shares his difficulties with the purpose of the law with subsequent Christian writers; yet the tension between a positive and a negative intention is peculiar to him alone.

Nowhere in the NT do we find a parallel to Paul's radical association of the law with sin. The gospel of John lets Jesus say to the 'Jews' confronted with him that they are slaves of sin, but this assertion (John 8.34) is not connected with the law. The sin of the Jews is, instead, traced back to the devil (8.44). Later on, we find the Church Fathers carefully reinterpreting Paul's radical statements in order to take the sting from them. Thus, Origen considered the idea that any increase of sin could be attributed to the coming of the Mosaic law simply impossible; that would be to fall into the heresy of Marcion! [138] Indeed, only Marcion and some Gnostics took up Paul's ideas in this regard.[139]

---

132 Op.cit. 147.
133 Op.cit. 136.
134 Op.cit. 147 f.
135 Op.cit. 159.
136 Stylianopoulos, op.cit. 157.
137 Op.cit. 150.
138 *Comm. in Rom.* V. 6 (PG 14,1032B); cf. Wiles, *Apostle* 52.
139 The Testimonium Veritatis of Nag Hammadi states that the law of the god of the Jews effects ἐπιθυμία and πάθος (NHC IX, 30, 2–18; NHL 407), for the injunction to propagate (Gen 1.28) calls forth sexual lust; 48, 4–8 (NHL 412) refers to the

b) Jewish sources

For details of Paul's negative ideas about the law verbal points of comparison can be found here and there in Jewish literature. Understandably, the context and scope of such statements differ greatly from those of the Pauline statements. Thus one may compare to Paul's assertion that the letter of the law kills the statement of R. Banna'ah in Sifre Deut: 'If you do the words of the Torah for their own sake they are life to you ... But if you do not do the words of Torah for their own sake they kill you.'[140] The law may thus bring about death — but only to one who obeys it for the wrong motives. If Paul sometimes regards the law as poison, the Rabbis regard it as a medicine which can be wrongly applied. The law likewise brings death to those who do not fulfil it[141] or to the peoples who did not accept it when it was given.[142]

More important is a striking parallelism between what Paul says about the Torah and what other Jewish teachers said about the *evil inclination*. The evil *yeser* is identified in Rabbinical literature with Satan and the angel of death (Baba Bathra 16a). As the angel of death the *yeser* 'accustoms (or entices) man to sin and kills him' (ExR 30.11). 'The Yezer of man assaults him every day, endeavouring to kill him ... ' (Sukk 52b). 'The Evil Yezer persuades man (to sin) in this world, and bears witness against him in the future world' (Sukk 52b).[143]

IV Ezra also ascribes to the evil inclination (called there *cor malignum*)

---

intention of that malicious god to increase and bring about sin. The Pauline idea is thus reinterpreted and placed into a quite different dualistic-ascetic framework. See Koschorke, 'Paulus' 181–183. More in a genuinely Pauline vein is a section in the Gospel of Philip (NHC II, 73, 27–74, 12; NHL 144) where a quite unusual exposition of the Paradise story is given: the tree of knowledge, which is identical with the law, effected death for Adam; cf. Koschorke, art.cit. 194–196.

140 Sifre Deut 306 (on 32.2); cited by E.P. Sanders, *Paul* 121.

141 This point is made in a rather pessimistic tone in ARN 2: seeing the Golden Calf, Moses wanted to turn back in order not to have to oblige the people to 'heavy precepts' und thus to 'doom them to death'. Cf. PesiqR 21.16 (107a). Both texts are cited by Löwy, 'Lehre' (1903), 535. To be sure, in the first instance Rabbinic exegesis is concerned to find a reason for Moses' breaking the tablets; in the second an explanation had to be found for Jer 20.7 'Thou hast enticed me and I was enticed'. Because of these circumstances it is only with due caution that we may see in these (late!) texts parallels to Paul's view that the law introduces a situation where sinning is a more serious matter than it was before (as, by the way, the Gospel does according to the Epistle to the Hebrews!); cf. Callan, 'Midrash' 563 f.

142 ExR 5.9; cf. Billerbeck III 238.

143 Citations from Schechter, *Aspects* 244 f. Caird, *Principalities* 41 f. has noted that in its capacity as a 'tempter' (Rom 7.7 f.) the law in Paul duplicates a function elsewhere attributed to Satan. He goes, however, too far in seeing such functions also in the role of the law as 'the great accuser' (Rom 2.12, 3.19) or as the 'executioner of the law' (2 Cor 3.6 f.).

things which Paul attributes to the law.[144] 'For a grain of evil seed was sown in the heart of Adam from the beginning, and how much fruit of ungodliness has it produced unto this time, and shall yet produce.' (4.30, cf. Rom 5.20). The blessed must fight hard to overcome the evil inclination, lest it lead them astray from life to death (7.92).

To ascribe the sad effects of the evil inclination to the law instead is a striking Pauline *tour de force*.

c) The Old Testament

Can Paul's idea of the sin-engendering and sin-promoting effects of the law, or the notion of a close connection between the law and sin be paralleled in the OT?[145]

To trace Rom 5.20 back to Dan 9.24 is certainly incorrect.[146] A more likely candidate would seem to be Ezekiel's bold assertion (Ezek 20.25 f.) that Yahweh had given Israel 'statutes that were not good and ordinances by which they could not have life', defiling them through their very gifts in making them offer by fire all their first-born, that he might horrify them. This puzzling statement is regarded by many exegetes as a kind of anticipation of Paul's critical statements. According to Zimmerli, the law here 'becomes a means through which God himself causes Israel's sin to be magnified. What is said here concerning a single commandment occurs later in Paul in an even deeper perspective in the light of Jesus Christ as a statement about the law as a whole.'[147] Peter Stuhlmacher, concerned to discover in the OT traces of the idea that the Torah revealed on Sinai carries in itself 'signs of historical provisionality and of such a deficiency that it is in need of change'[148], sees in Ezek 20.25 f. a reference to 'the horrifyingly provisional nature' of the law of Sinai.[149]

The assumed analogy is, at best, of a very limited nature. Ezekiel speaks of

---

144 For the evil inclination in IV Ezra see Harnisch, *Verhängnis* 165–175; Thompson, *Theodicy* 332–339.

145 It may be of some interest to note that G. Murray, *Oresteia* 20 ff., thought that Paul had been anticipated by Aeschylos in his dealing with the problem of blood vengeance: as sin must, according to the law of the vengeance, receive its punishment, the law thus introduces a whole chain of bloody deeds, which can only be broken by a wise deity who understands the motives of events. Of course, this problem is beyond the horizon of Paul, for whom the law is something different. Murray is followed by Wells, *Jesus* 298. But see also Oepke on Gal 3.13!

146 Gottlob Klein, *Studien* 78 asserted that Rom 5.20 is a paraphrase of Dan 9.24. In that verse, however, there is no talk of the law at all (correctly Schoeps, *Paul* 174).

147 Zimmerli, *Law* 82; cf. id., *Ezechiel* 449; von Rad, *Theology* II, 402 n. 19; Blank, 'Warum' 90 f.; de Vaux, *Studies* 72; Meyer, 'End' 77 n. 23.

148 See below, VIII 3. Quotation: *Versöhnung* 142.

149 Stuhlmacher, *Versöhnung* 143.

one commandment (or a few commandments) that was not good and that was imposed on Israel as a *punishment* for continuous transgression of the law. Paul never suggests anything like this. When he attributes a negative purpose to the law, then this is the *original* purpose of the *whole* law.[150]

However, the analogy breaks down altogether, if the common interpretation of Ezek 20.25 f. is correct. The verses are usually taken as a reference to the custom of sacrificing the first-born child in the cult of Moloch,[151] a custom at least occasionally taken up in Israel. To justify such a procedure, one might conceivably have appealed to some passages in the Torah, above all to Ex 22.29.[152] Ezekiel would then actually be criticizing a disastrous *mis*interpretation or *mis*use of the law.[153] The reference to God would only imply that he did not prevent this misuse. If so, no connection can be established between this statement and Rom 5.20 etc.

Zimmerli objects to this standard interpretation that the practice of child-

---

150 Cf. Buber, *Zwei Glaubensweisen* 88–90.
151 This explanation is questioned by Gese, 'Ezechiel'. He rejects the connection of the verse with child sacrifices altogether. V. 26 refers, according to him, to the normal sacrifice of first-born animals. The statutes concerning these constitute a 'second revelation'. Gese correctly points out some difficulties involved in the current interpretation. He also shows that *he 'ebir* was not a technical term the use of which was limited to the cult of Moloch; the verbal connection between Ezek 20.26 and Ex 13.12 (an ordinance concerning the offering of first-born animals within the legitimate cult of Yahweh) is indeed striking. Nevertheless, *he 'ebir* is also used in 16.21 with clear reference to the sacrifice of children, and if this verse is authentic (Gese does not tell us) that would seem to decide the issue (cf. on the authenticity below, n. 156). But even if it were a later addition, Gese's view is not without difficulties. He says that the 'second revelation corresponds to man's "natural religion" '; the piety of Israel is thereby defiled by the spirit of Canaanite religion. Man believes that he can give God something. But if this is what Ezek 20.25 f. is all about, then why are the sacrifices of the *first-born* singled out in the first place? (Gese gives two explanations, which may not be mutually compatible; discussing these would lead us too far away.) Moreover, even though Gese praises Zimmerli for having avoided the misinterpretation theory, he himself comes in the end out with something very much like a misinterpretation or misuse theory. It is at least a bit difficult to reconcile the defilement of Israel's religion through influences from the surrounding world with Yahweh's active initiative. It is important for Gese's overall view about the 'dynamic' character of the law and his theory of a 'Zion Torah' (see below p. 239 f.) that Ezek 20.25 f. refers to an actual statute of God and not to a mere misunderstanding; it is all the more regrettable that his presentation is so vague at this crucial point.
   Garscha, *Studien* 119 f. also denies a connection with the sacrifice of children. He suggests that the reference is to precepts that could not be observed in certain circumstances as in the exile. This is hardly convincing.
152 'The first-born of your sons you shall give to me.' Unlike the parallel passages in Exodus, no mention is made here of a 'redeeming' procedure that would exempt the sons from their fate.
153 So, e.g., Eichrodt and Wevers, ad loc.; de Vaux, op.cit. 72.

sacrifice *is* actually in keeping with the letter of Ex 22.29 so that strictly speaking there is no misinterpretation. He notes that Ezekiel is not able to push the literal interpretation of the Exodus passage lightly aside. Ezek 20.25 f. represents the sentiment of a generation for which the secure possibility of self-righteousness is shaken, a generation that has the courage to find God's punishment, mysteriously enough, in the commandment itself.[154]

It would seem, however, that Zimmerli tries to make the passage yield too 'profound' a message. In other passages in Ezekiel, the sacrifice of children is mentioned in plain words as a sin of Israel, without any indication that a mysterious statute of God was being carried out (16.20 f.).[155] There is no sense of a divine mystery in these verses; the tone is one of outright condemnation.[156]

Whatever the intended message of Ezek 20.25 f., the passage does not look like a theological program.[157] Theoretically, it could have been used to provide a starting point for a reform program which wished to purge the Torah of additions, as the Jewish Christians of the Pseudoclementines were to do much later.[158] As Justin (*Dial.* 21.1) shows, some Christians seized on these verses.[159] But Ezekiel does not show signs of such a concern. The verses in question do not seem to carry the weight placed upon them by some inter-

---

154 Zimmerli ad loc.

155 Ezek 16.20 f.: 'And you took your sons and your daughters, whom you had borne to me, and these you sacriciced to them to be devoured. Were your harlotries so small a matter that you slaughtered my children and delivered them up as an offering by fire to them?' There is a similar accusation in 20.31, but this should probably be discarded — with Zimmerli, ad loc. — as a later addition; it is attributed to Ezekiel by de Vaux, op.cit. 72.

156 To be sure, 16.20 f. is also regarded as an addition by Zimmerli (and others). But added by whom? Zimmerli notes, at any rate, that there is no compelling reason to deny that Ezekiel himself played a part, when verses 16.16—20 were inserted (op. cit. 363). At the very least the verses show that the radical idea of 20.25 f. (supposing there was one) was *not* taken up, not even by those circles who provided in 16. 16—21 a 'first exposition' which still largely retains the intention of the original proclamation (thus Zimmerli himself!). This observation contradicts Zimmerli's idea that Ezek 20.25 f. as he understands it betrays the sentiment of a whole generation.

157 It is not used by Ezekiel as a starting-point for the expectation of a better law. Chs. 40—48 which, according to Stuhlmacher (op.cit. 143) go beyond the Sinai Torah, are not connected with it in any obvious way. Gese, to be sure, points out that no sacrifices of the first-born are mentioned in chs. 44 f. and suggests that this is not so by chance.

158 See below, p. 226 f.

159 Justin says that the sabbath was imposed on the Jews because of their sins — a singularly ridiculous interpretation in that Ezekiel presents the 'not good' ordinances as a punishment for Israel's transgressing the sabbath!

preters. They look strangely isolated.[160] There seems to be no better way of explaining them than the standard misinterpretation theory. They hardly constitute a parallel to Paul's radical statements in any sense at all.

With special emphasis on Ezek 20.25, Gerhard von Rad suggests that even the proclamation of the prophets as a whole can be construed as a kind of analogy to Paul's critical theology of the law.[161] 'Never again was there in Israel a more incisive or menacing "preaching of the law" than the prophets'.[162] The analogy is, however, limited to the 'revelatory' function of the prophetic preaching on one hand and that of the law (Rom 3.20) on the other. [163] *This* (relatively uncharacteristic!) aspect of Paul's teaching of the law can indeed be supported by the OT. But in attributing to the law a negative, sin-provoking and sin-engendering function Paul goes his own way, parting company with the prophets.[164]

---

160 Lust, 'Traditie' 134 ff. regards v. 26a.b as a later gloss. One would be tempted to agree, were it not for the fact that it is even more difficult to make sense of them as an insertion of a later editor.
161 Theology II, 395 ff.
162 Op.cit. 402.
163 Cf. Hübner, 'Thema' 269.
164 Lohfink, *Siegeslied* 168–172; Hübner, art.cit. 270.

V. The antithesis between works of law and faith in Christ

1. The antithesis

In a number of key texts in Galatians and Romans Paul suggests that the law is a rival principle of salvation. To be sure, he never sets out to give a sustained account of the Jewish religion, and a great many of his comments on the law are made with regard to Christian 'Judaizers'. Nevertheless, Paul's comments at least imply the notion of the Torah as the Jewish gateway to salvation or righteousness, which occupies in the old system the very place that belongs to Christ in the new order of things. As God's act in Christ is the only true basis of righteousness, the rival way of the law is, of course, a dead end.

Thus, Paul states in Gal 5.4 that whoever tries to be justified 'in the law' (ἐν νόμῳ) is 'destroyed' away from *Christ* or fallen away from *grace*. As regards salvation, one has to choose between Christ and grace on the one hand and the law on the other. Gal 2.21 also makes it clear that righteousness can be attained only in Christ: were it available through the law (διὰ νόμου) then Christ would in fact have died in vain, and God's grace would be null and void. The state of rivalry between two different orders of salvation is here portrayed in the clearest possible terms. The Christian is 'under grace' and not 'under the law' (Rom 6.14).

Paul often sets forth the contrast by opposing 'the works of the law' to 'faith'. This antithesis is stated programmatically in Gal 2.16: ' ... a man is not justified by works of the law but through faith in Jesus Christ[1]; thus we, too, have believed in Christ in order to be justified by faith in Christ and not by works of the law, for by works of the law no flesh is justified'.[2] This

---

1 That Paul actually sets up this contrast is denied by Howard, 'Christ' 331–337; cf. id., 'On the Faith'; Gaston, 'Paul'. Rightly perceiving that Rabbinic Judaism did not teach 'merits as gained through works' as the basis of salvation, Howard is concerned to show that Paul did not attribute such a view to them either. He thereby construes πίστις χριστοῦ (Gal 2.16 and elsewhere) as a subjective genitive; thus also Howard, 'Faith'; id., *Crisis* 57 f., 95 n. 191; M. Barth, 'Stellung' 514; Bremer, *Understanding* 75 ff.; Williams, 'Righteousness' 272–275. It is unnatural, however, to break the parallel between πίστις χριστοῦ and εἰς χριστὸν Ἰησοῦν ἐπιστεύσαμεν in Gal 2.16. On the expression see now Hultgren, 'Pistis', esp. 253 ff.

2 If 2.16d is meant as a Bible quotation (so e.g. Betz) as is probable, since the clause

strongly suggests that Paul (and other Jewish Christians) have indeed replaced an old soteriological system by a new one, works of the law by faith in Christ.[3] In Paul's view, Peter and others have actually returned to the old system by their 'Judaizing' in Antioch.

In Gal 3.2–5 'the preaching of faith' (ἀκοὴ πίστεως)[4] is opposed to the 'works of the law' (v. 2, 5). Paul reminds the Galatians of their gift of the Spirit and asks the rhetorical question, whether their charismatic experiences resulted from doing works of the law or from accepting the preaching of faith. It is the latter alone that can lead to a bestowal of the gift of the Spirit. The law is incapable of effecting that.

In Gal 3.6 Paul states that Abraham gained righteousness because he had faith in God. In the next verses he speaks of 'those of faith' as blessed (v. 7–9). By contrast, those who are 'of works of the law' are cursed (v. 10). Furthermore, 'law' and 'faith' are contrasted sharply in v. 11: it is clear that no one can be justified by the law, for the simple reason that according to the Bible the righteous man will have life *by faith*.[5] Paul thus assumes a priori that faith and law exclude each other. In the next verse (v. 12) he indeed gives a categorical 'definition': 'the law is not of faith'. The law has nothing to do with faith, because it requires that its commandments be 'done' if man wants to receive 'life'. The law is also the opposite of God's promise (v. 18, 21–22). Similar contrasts reappear in Romans (Rom 3.27–28, 4.2–5, 4.14, 10.5–6); cf. also the contrast between the righteousness of faith and one's 'own' righteousness in Phil 3.6, 9 (cf. Rom 10.3).

Paul thus makes a sharp distinction between two sets of concepts. On the one side stand the law and the works (of the law); on the other side Christ, grace, the Spirit, faith and promise. In fact, Paul's argument for the thesis

---

would otherwise be tautologous, Paul has added the decisive words ἐξ ἔργων νόμου to the OT text. The same thing happens in Rom 3.20! Cf. e.g. Vielhauer, 'Paulus' 49; Dahl, *Studies* 105 f.; Hays, 'Psalm 143' 113. We see how self-evident the contrast must have seemed to Paul's mind.

3 Cf. the expression ζητοῦντες δικαιωθῆναι which suggests an effort to find righteousness.

4 On the expression see Schlier; Lull, *Spirit* 55 f.

5 It does not make much difference, whether ἐκ πίστεως is connected with 'righteous' or 'to live'. The latter alternative is the natural one; see the recent treatment of the question by Cavallin, 'Righteous'. In any case, ἐκ πίστεως is connected with the predicate verb in Gal 3.22; when Paul does connect the phrase with the subject (Rom 10.6), he does so in an unambiguous way (ἡ δὲ ἐκ πίστεως δικαιοσύνη). If we postulate a being called 'the one righteous by faith' (ὁ δίκαιος ἐκ πίστεως) who will 'live', then what would constitute the opposite? Who does not gain life? A phrase like ὁ δίκαιος (ὁ) ἐξ ἔργων οὐ ζήσεται does not make much sense, for such a righteous person does not exist at all for Paul; there can hardly be a question whether he will gain life or not. Cf. Ellis, *Use* 118; Hanson, *Studies* 40 ff. (although Hanson's explanation that ὁ δίκαιος refers to the Messiah is fanciful).

that Christ, not the law, is the basis of salvation, consists almost exclusively of a repetition of this basic contrast in numerous variations.[6]

2. The meaning of the antithesis

Interpreting this central antithesis set forth by Paul, Christian exegetes have (from the late 19th century on) developed a desolate picture of 'late Judaism'[7]. It is held that the Jewish religion, against which Paul reacted, was characterised by a formal, mechanical and anthropocentric piety, an arrogant counting of one's merits, etc. It is said to be 'Paul's glory to have argued against a decadent Judaism to ensure the victory of a profound belief in the power of God'.[8] For the Jew of Paul's day, the law was 'an arrogantly and arbitrarily chosen target of human ambition', 'a system of human achievement'.[9] 'The requirements of the law had become dead ceremonies' so that 'the fulfilment of the commandments does not, in the final analysis, serve the holiness of God, but is accomplished for the sake of man ... When the pious man fulfils the commandments, God cannot find any fault with him any more and must declare him righteous at the last judgment. It is therefore in man's power to acquire salvation through pious life.'[10] Indeed, in the framework of this 'purely formal obedience' and 'hopelessly perverted' religiosity[11] God is made to obey the dead law which, thereby, takes on the character of a demon![12]

To this day, Christian exegetical literature abounds in such comments on the Judaism of Paul's day. It is, to be sure, commonly acknowledged that the law originally belonged to the framework of God's covenant with Israel.[13] According to a popular theory, set forth by Martin Noth but going back to Wellhausen, the law was after the Exile to an ever greater degree detached from this framework; the law became, it is held, an independent and absolute entity which stood between God and man blocking man's way to God and throwing him upon his own deeds.[14] Bultmann's description of the Jewish

---

6 This was emphatically noted by Loisy, *Galates* 41, 134 f., 141 f. etc.

7 The term has come to involve a negative valuation and should be replaced by '*early Judaism*' (Frühjudentum).

8 Cerfaux, *Christian* 391.

9 Moule, 'Obligation' 393, 397.

10 Maurer, *Gesetzeslehre* 11.

11 Niederwimmer, *Freiheit* 123, cf. 125 n. 125. Cf. R.E. Howard, *Newness* 56.

12 Niederwimmer, op.cit. 131.

13 For the understanding of the Torah in the OT see, e.g., von Rad, *Theology* II, 388 ff.; Schmid, 'Gesetz'; Gross, 'Tora'; Smend, 'Gesetz'; Myers, *Grace*; Liedke-Petersen, 'Torah'; Illman, 'Tora'.

14 Wellhausen, Geschichte 302 ff., esp. 304; Noth, *Studien* 99 ff., esp. 126; Würthwein, 'Gesetz' 1514 f.; Bornkamm, *Geschichte* 90.

 Some scholars attribute the distortion of religion to the Jews of the Dispersion;

way (which can be traced back to Bousset and F. Weber)[15] has been particularly influential. He understands Jewish Torah piety as an individual expression of the innate human desire to show off (*Geltungsbedürfnis*), which drives man to accomplish works, whether beneficial or absurd.[16] The Jew tried to earn God's acceptance. The attempt to become righteous by obeying the law is an expression of man's need to *boast*. The pious man does not need grace![17]

Jewish scholars have, of course, energetically objected to such caricatures of the Jewish religion.[18] For decades, their protests went on deaf ears. Recently, however, there have been many signs of a change in the situation. It is more and more realized how distorted the standard picture is. Noth's account of the development of the religion of Israel has not gone unchallenged in OT study.[19] As for post-Biblical Judaism, a devastating critique of its

---

thus Schoeps, *Paul* 27–32, 213 ff. He speaks of a legalistic 'Septuagintal piety' and tries to show, following Dodd and Bertram, that the covenant and the law have been separated from each other by the Septuagint translators in a way that betrays their legalistic piety. This attempt fails to carry conviction.

With respect to Dodd's contention (*Bible* 34) that the rendering of *torah* with νόμος shows that 'the Biblical revelation was conceived as a hard legalistic way' (accepted by Schoeps, op.cit. 29; cf. also Wallis, 'Torah' 330 f.) see the remarks by Werblowsky, 'Tora' 160 f. The meaning of the Greek word νόμος was not limited to a 'paragraph law' either; cf. Pasinya, *Notion* 32–54, 139 f., 201–205.

Bertram has treated the question in several articles (see Bibliography). He deals with two books of the LXX only; on such a basis any generalizations should be suspect. In addition, all his decisive illustrations come from the translation of Proverbs. It is precarious to draw any conclusions even about the relation of the piety of the translator(s) of this one book to classical OT thought, as the relation of the Hebrew book of Proverbs to the mainstream of OT thought is in itself problematic. The theological differences detected by Bertram between the translation and the original are often very subtle and dubious. For some criticisms see Gerleman, 'Religion' (Schoeps refers to this article without mentioning that its attitude to Bertram's work is not uncritical); Wevers, 'Septuaginta-Forschungen' 183; Barr, *Semantics* 251 n. 1, 252.

15 F. Weber, *Theologie*, esp. 277 ff.; Bousset-Gressmann, *Religion* 119 ff., 378 ff.; see also Billerbeck, *Kommentar* IV/1 3 ff. For the history see Moore, 'Writers' 228– 254; E.P. Sanders, *Paul* 33–59, 233 ff.; Hoheisel, *Judentum* 7 ff.

16 Bultmann, *Glauben* II 38 f. etc. He puts forward a tasteless and ill-advised comparison of legalistic piety with a child incapable of useful achievements who therefore attempts to distinguish itself through silliness or even naughtiness, and with the 'modern mania for records' as an attempt to show off through achievements which are in themselves absurd (39).

17 Op.cit. 41.

18 On the nature of the Jewish obedience to the Torah see e.g. Schechter, *Aspects* 18 etc.; Büchler, *Studies* 1–118; Heinemann, *Loi*; Werblowsky, 'Tora'; Jackson, 'Legalism'; Ehrlich, 'Tora'; Flusser, 'Erlebnis'.

19 Cf. Kraus, *Aufsätze* 179 ff., esp. 187; Zimmerli, *Offenbarung* 249 ff.; Lohfink, *Siegeslied* 151 ff.; Limbeck, *Ordnung*; Hoheisel, op.cit. 48 ff.; Smend, 'Gesetz' 34 ff. On Ps. 119 see now also Wallis, 'Torah' 325–329.

theological denigration was presented, on the Christian side, sixty years ago by G.F. Moore.[20] Moore also laid the foundations for a fair appraisal of Rabbinic Judaism as a 'revealed religion'.[21] For a long time, however, his monumental work had little influence on Christian exegesis.[22] In recent times, dissatisfaction with the current denigration of Judaism has been voiced to an ever growing degree.[23] With the publication of the pertinent studies by Meinrad Limbeck[24] and especially by E.P. Sanders[25] the discussion has been carried a long step forward.

Limbeck has directed his attention to the understanding of the Torah in the Qumran texts and related (non-Rabbinic) literature including, above all, 1 Enoch, Jubilees, Pseudo-Philo and IV Ezra. He emphasizes the understanding of the Torah as the order of *creation*.[26] The law witnessed to God's benevolent initiative toward man's salvation.[27] Observance of the God-given order was understood, even in Qumran, 'only as a response, but not as an achievement'.[28] 'Precisely the effort not to lose God's undeserved benevolence through negligence and wilfulness in one's own life had brought it about that *also* the letter of the law came to have a decisive significance for Israel.'[29] But the point was not 'that man could in the end stand before God through his own power, but that man should prepare himself for that salvation which

---

20 Moore, 'Writers'.

21 Moore, *Judaism*. On 'legalism' see ibid. I, 117.

22 To be sure, lip service is often paid to Moore's work. It is frequently referred to, but it is used as a collection of examples which are actually interpreted in the light of the very different works of Bousset and Billerbeck. See E.P. Sanders, op.cit. 33 ff.

23 Cf. already Loisy, *Galates* 133 and passim; Parkes, *Jesus*; id., *Judaism*; id., *Foundations*; Odeberg, *Pharisaism* 16 ff.; Sjöberg, *Gott*, esp. 154–169, 184–190, 261–264; F.C. Grant, *Judaism* 19 f., 23 f. etc.: id., 'Prolegomenon' xvii–xix. Recently J. Maier, 'Gesetz' 77–79, 175 f. etc.; id., 'Überlieferungen' 60; Ch. Klein, *Theologie*; Ruether, *Faith* 62; Hruby, 'Gesetz' 49 ff.; Howard, 'Christ' 331 ff.; id., *Crisis* 75; Maher, 'Yoke'; Lührmann, *Glaube* 39 ff.; Nickelsburg, Review of Klein; Mussner, *Traktat* 37–45; Gaston, 'Paul', esp. 51; Luz, 'Gesetz' 45 ff.; Stemberger, *Judentum* 126 f., 138 f., 159 f. Longenecker, *Paul* 66 ff. pleads for a distinction between 'acting legalism' and 'reacting nomism', thus admitting that *some* currents in Judaism (notably the Qumran sect) were non-legalist; somewhat similarly J.A. Sanders, 'Torah and Christ' 385; cf. also Jaubert, *Alliance* 128 f., 138.

24 *Ordnung*; the main results are reproduced in a popularized form in Limbeck, *Ohnmacht* 16–60. Limbeck's insights are taken up and developed in a context of comparative religion by Hoheisel, *Judentum*. See also Fiedler, *Jesus* 51 ff., esp. 60–63, 73–75, 86–95; Zenger, 'Weisheit'.

25 *Paul*. Sanders, op.cit. 233 notes that his understanding of Judaism differs from that of Longenecker (see note 22) in that he regards the notion of 'acting legalism' as a Christian fiction altogether.

26 *Ordnung* 63 ff.; *Ohnmacht* 16 ff. Cf. J. Maier, art.cit. 70 f.

27 See, e.g., *Ordnung* 79–84; *Ohnmacht* 28–34.

28 *Ordnung* 173 (with n. 218).

29 *Ordnung* 193.

God wanted to grant him'.[30] Observance of the 'ritual' commandments witnessed to the aspiration to realize communion with God by respecting the God-given commandments about circumcision, sabbath and ritual purity. Far from being tokens of legalism, these requirements expressed only 'the forms, by the aid of which the individual affirmed his calling by God and sought to take seriously and to preserve the membership of the community offered by God'.[31] One can speak here of 'the effort, carried to an extreme, to appropriate consistently a divine offer of grace'.[32] The law was *not* 'an end in itself'.[33]

.E.P. Sanders devotes most of his attention to the Tannaitic literature, but he also studies the Dead Sea Scrolls and several apocryphal and pseudepigraphical writings (Ben Sira, 1 Enoch, Jubilees, Psalms of Solomon, IV Ezra).[34] He finds in these writings a common soteriological pattern which he calls 'covenantal nomism'. This can be briefly defined as 'the view that one's place in God's plan is established on the basis of the covenant and that the covenant requires as the proper response of man his obedience to its commandments, while providing means of atonement for transgression'.[35] The centrality of the covenant means, in fact, that the law was not understood as a means of salvation at all. We will, however, postpone a discussion of this important point to the next section. Here it is sufficient to take note of Sanders's explicit intention 'to destroy the Weberian view which has proved so persistent in New Testament scholarship'.[36] That is, he argues that the 'view that Rabbinic religion was a religion of legalistic work-righteousness in which a man was saved by fulfilling more commandments than he committed transgressions' is 'completely wrong': 'it proceeds from theological presuppositions and is supported by systematically misunderstanding and misconstruing passages in Rabbinic literature'.[37] On the contrary, Judaism 'kept grace and works in the right perspective, did not trivialize the commandments of God and was not especially marked by hypocrisy'.[38] One may have to allow for

---

30 Op.cit. 194.
31 *Ohnmacht* 44 f. Cf. J. Maier, art.cit. 69 f. etc. on the 'sacramental' function of the (holistically understood) Torah.
32 Hoheisel, op.cit. 173.
33 Thus the title of a chapter in Limbeck, *Ohnmacht* 40–52.
34 Tannaitic literature: op.cit. 33–238; The Dead Sea Scrolls: op.cit. 239–328; Apocrypha and Pseudepigrapha: op.cit. 329–428.
35 Op.cit. 75. For a fuller summary see 180 f. and 422.
36 Op.cit. 234.
37 Op.cit. 233.
38 Op.cit. 427. That Matt 23 represents a polemic caricature of the Pharisees is nowadays generally recognized; see, e.g., Kümmel, 'Weherufe'. It is less often realized that the Pharisee in Luke 18 represents a 'characteristic caricature' rather than a characteristic product of the Jewish religion; so Montefiore, *Gospels* II 556; correctly Schottroff, 'Erzählung' 448 ff.

more actual distortions of the religious ideals of Judaism among its adherents than Sanders does;[39] this, however, is irrelevant to his main thesis. As he rightly points out, 'the frequent Christian charge against Judaism ... is not that some individual Jews misunderstood, misapplied and abused their religion, but that *Judaism necessarily tends* towards petty legalism, self-serving and self-deceiving casuistry, and a mixture of arrogance and lack of confidence in God'. But, says Sanders, 'the surviving Jewish literature is as free of these characteristics as any I have ever read'.[40]

Whereas Sanders has been criticized by other experts in Rabbinics for imposing the pattern of Paul's religious expression on Tannaitic sources, even the harshest critic has admitted that the thesis of 'covenantal nomism' is a 'wholly sound' and 'self-evident' proposition and in this regard the work is 'a complete success'.[41] That is: regardless of how other aspects of Sanders' work will stand the test, with respect to the topics relevant to Paul's treatment of the law he has made his point.

When, therefore, the Jewish religion of Paul's day is allowed to speak for itself, the notion of it as perverted anthropocentric legalism turns out to be a vicious caricature. The question is, then, whether it is Paul himself or merely his latter-day interpreters who should be blamed for this distortion of Judaism. Does Paul suggest that behind the Jews' zeal for the law (Rom 10.2) lurks the arrogant and boastful desire to show off, or is this just a misinterpretation of his intention?

This question can be put in another way: is Paul's critical attitude to the Torah rooted in *anthropology* or in *Christology*? In the former case the trouble with the law is that in his attempt to fulfil it, man goes astray in the

---

39 Jewish scholars are indeed more willing than Sanders to admit actual distortions of the religious ideals; cf. Montefiore, op.cit. 34 f., 153 ff.; Schechter, op.cit. 169; Werblowsky, 'Tora' 159.

    Interestingly enough, however, both John the Baptist before Paul (Mt 3.7 ff. par) and Justin Martyr after him (Dial 44.1–2, 25.1, 102.6, 141.2–3 and, in particular, 140.1–2) regard as a typical fault of the Jews their *exaggerated* trust on the covenant and the sonship of Abraham – as does Paul himself in Rom 2! It seems that *this* kind of distortion of the religious ideal was the more characteristic one. 'If anything, Judaism erred on the side of over-emphasizing the free grace of God, his infinite loving-kindness (if this be error!) and in consequence made forgiveness much too simple and too easy to obtain.' F.C. Grant, *Judaism* 64.

40 Sanders, op.cit. 427. This point remains unaffected, when Sanders is criticized (in itself perhaps rightly) for disregarding the difference between religious writings and lived religion. Thus Murphy-O'Connor, Review 123; Horbury, 'Paul' 116 f.

41 Neusner, 'Judaisms' 177, 180; id., 'Use' 47, 50 (where 'complete' is omitted). Cf. the roughly analogous evaluations in the reviews by Dahl (155, 157), Saldarini (299), Brooke (248) and King; cf. also Hartman, 'Bundesideologie' 105. As for the criticisms put forward by Neusner and others, see Sanders's important reply 'Puzzling out', esp. 70 ff.

direction of boasting and arrogance. The most prominent advocate of this interpretation is, of course, Bultmann.[42] In the latter case the fault with the law is that the unbelieving Jews prefer it to Christ, putting the Torah in the place that God has reserved for Christ.[43]

Bultmann emphasizes that the will to obtain salvation by obeying the law is sin (as an expression of man's boasting). Such a desire to show off is a characteristic of human nature in general; Jewish legalism stands in Paul's writing for something universally typical of natural man. Reading Bultmann, one gets the impression that zeal for the law is really more damaging than transgression. Bultmann's key texts are Rom 3.27, 4.2 ff., 7.7 ff., 10.2–3 and Phil 3.4 ff.

Strikingly enough, passages from Galatians are absent from this list! No wonder, for in this letter, where Paul mounts his most vehement attack on the way of the law there is absolutely no polemic against man's boasting and the like. Paul does not criticize the Galatians for giving room for boasting, but simply for turning away from Christ (while contemplating circumcision).[44] The decisive statement appears in 2.21: if salvation comes by law, then Christ died in vain![45] The issue is: either the law or Christ, not: either boasting or faith. The theme 'boasting' only occurs in Galatians in 6.4, 13, 14. The analysis of these verses shows that the (Bultmannian) idea that 'renunciation of glorying before God belongs inseparably to the self-understanding of one who believes in Christ' is missing in Galatians.[46] Gal 6.4 'is remarkable because it condemns neither works nor boasting.'[47]

It is noteworthy that the statements against the law are situated in a context where the freedom of Paul's non-Jewish converts from the law, especially its 'ritual' precepts, is at stake (2.14–21; 3.8). In 3.8 Paul even stresses that, according to Scripture, God justifies the *Gentiles* by faith.

---

42 See especially Bultmann, *Theology* 259 ff. (cf. 281 f., 340 ff.); id., *Glauben* II, 32 ff.; id., *'Romans 7'*. Cf., however, already Kühl, 'Stellung' 121, 136, 145 f. Gulin, *Freude* 160 states bluntly that, in religious terms, 'the law was sin'. A popularized version with a psychoanalytical accent is found in Scroggs, *Paul*.

43 Cf. Mundle, *Glaubensbegriff* 109–111; van Dülmen, *Theologie* 174 ff., 251 ff.; Wilckens, *Rechtfertigung* 94, 99 f., 102, 108 f.; Limbeck, *Ohnmacht* 90; Lührmann, *Galater* 44 f.; Hoheisel, *Judentum* 195 f., 206; Räisänen, 'Legalism' 66–72. Sanders's position in his book was slightly ambiguous (cf. Räisänen, art.cit. 72), but in a subsequent work he has modified it (*Law* 59 n. 77) and represents now an unambiguously christological view. Against Bultmann's interpretation of 'boasting' also Luck, 'Jakobusbrief' 169 f.

44 Sanders, *Paul* 482 ff.; cf. Howard, *Crisis* 75 f.

45 Gal 2.21 is hardly discussed at all by Bultmann in his *Theology*.

46 Hübner, *Gesetz* 91. Hübner, to be sure, thinks that in Galatians Paul does *not yet* offer the view he is going to set forth in Romans.

47 Tyson, 'Works' 429.

Again, there is no indication of the Bultmannian type of criticism of the law in Rom 2.1–3.20. In this passage the Jews are charged for transgressing the law rather than for trying to keep it.[48]

To make Rom 7.7 ff. to speak for his view, Bultmann has to make two untenable assumptions.[49] First, he interprets the crucial term ἐπιϑυμία in 7.7 f. in a rather curious way as a perverted desire to *fulfil* the requirements of the law, whereas the only natural understanding is to take ἐπιϑυμία here as elsewhere as the desire to do what is forbidden.[50] Secondly, he denies that 7.15 ff. describes an empirically observable moral conflict within man, resorting to an artificial 'transsubjective' interpretation.[51] On a more natural reading, Rom 7 speaks against Bultmann's view.

It is, moreover, notable that in Rom 8.7 f. the enmity of the man in the 'flesh' against God is described in terms that are far from suggesting a Bultmannian understanding of the law: it is an expression of the 'mind of the flesh' that man refuses to be '*subjected* under God's law', thus being unable to '*please* God'. There is thus nothing wrong in trying to please God by obeying his law; quite the contrary.

It is doubtful whether Rom 3.27 speaks of 'boasting' as the general human attitude outside the dominion of Christ. In this connection, boasting must surely be connected with the boasting of the *possession of the law*, mentioned in 2.17, 23.[52] In itself, the Jew's boasting of the law is not to blame. In a parallel statement (Rom 2.17) Paul also speaks of boasting of God, which is all right (cf. 1 Cor 1.31). It is transgression of the law that is condemned. But since the Jew, according to Rom 2, actually transgresses the law, he has no more reason to boast over its possession.

'Boasting' has in Rom 3.27 above all to do with the special status of the Jews, not with man's innate pride. All men are sinners, including the Jews (3.20, 22, 23). God has given, in the death of Christ, all men a chance of being saved apart from the law (3.21–26); thus the way to salvation is open to Gentiles as well. The aorist form of the predicate verb in 3.27 (ἐξεκλείσϑη) is to be noted. 'Boasting' has been excluded by an once-and-for-all act of God. The exclusion is thus an objective event. But then 'boasting', too, must refer to something more concrete than man's general attitude – such an attitude was hardly shut out once and for all through the 'principle' (νόμος) of

48 See above, III 2; cf. against Bultmann also Roloff, *Testament* 157.
49 Note that Bultmann introduces the idea of one's 'own' righteousness into the message of *this* section from Rom 10.2 and Phil 3.
50 See Räisänen, 'Gebrauch', and above, p. 111 f.
51 See above, p. 111 f.
52 Cf. Wilckens, op.cit. 94; Sánchez-Bosch, *Gloriarse* 137 f., 145 ff. Justin (*Dial*.102.6), too, connects the charge that the Jews are 'puffed up with pride' with their boasting of their *race*, their reliance on being descendants of Abraham, and their *transgression* of the law.

faith.[53] The reference must rather be to the special status of the Jews which caused them to boast over the law. Because of the new situation created by God there is no point in being proud of the law and clinging to a system that prevents intercourse with Gentiles (cf. Gal 2.15 f.). The point of Rom 3.27–30 is, as v. 29 f. emphatically states, *the inclusion of Gentiles in the people of God*.[54] Having stated that a man is justified 'without works of the law', Paul goes on by asking in 3.29 the rhetorical question: 'Or does God belong to the Jews alone? Does he not belong to the Gentiles, too? Surely he does ... ' Thus works of the law are something that *separates* the Jew from the Gentile, and *not* (against Bultmann) something characteristic of man in general.[55]

In Rom 4.2, καύχημα refers to an 'objective' ground for boasting (cf. Gal 6.4), rather than to an attitude. Had Abraham really been justified by works, then he would have had a reason to boast about the law. But as this was not the case, as already v. 2b indicates,[56] there was nothing to boast about; the point is the same as in 3.27. The Jew is no better off than the Greek. Paul does *not* say that, had Abraham tried to be justified by works, then his attitude would have been that of one who boasts. The argument is that one could well boast of the law, *if* one could in fact be justified by it. Since this is (for Paul, by definition!) not the case, no boasting!

The verses that would seem to best lend themselves to a Bultmannian interpretation are Rom 4.4–5. They apparently refer to the attitude of one who tries to earn salvation by his own merits, expecting to receive his 'reward' (μισθός) according to them. Yet Paul does *not* say that the real fault with the one who 'works' would be that he *boasts* of his accomplishments. He does not attack the notion of a reward either. The Christian, too, expects a reward, if only by grace. It is questionable whether one should seek in these verses more than Paul's usual axiom of the place of the law as a way to salvation in Judaism: within the framework of the law one is saved according to works done. Paul's real point in the passage is the surprising chance given by God to the μὴ ἐργαζόμενος: no works of the law are required of the Gentile![57]

In the context there are indeed clear hints to the fact that it is the problem

---

53 See Räisänen, 'Gesetz' and above, II 2.
54 Cf. Sanders, op.cit. 489 f.; Schmithals, *Römerbrief* 15.
55 If human hybris were meant, this would be something *common* to Jew and Gentile.
56 Sanday-Headlam and Lietzmann interpret v. 2b: Abraham did have something to boast of, yet only before men, not before God. With respect to the γάρ in the next verse, however, it seems better to take 2b as a rebuttal of 2a: Abraham was *not* justified before God by works; thus Barrett, Käsemann, Jervell.
57 I cannot find in the context any hints to the effect that the talk of God's justifying the ungodly (ἀσεβής) in 4.5 alludes to Paul's Damascus experience (thus Kim, *Origin* 287 f.; cf. also Hengel, *Geschichtsschreibung* 73). The 'ungodly' is here one who is *not* able to produce the 'works' in question; it is not suggested that he is a zealous legalist. On Rom 4.4 see esp. Sanders, *Law* 35.

of the relation between Jews and Gentiles that stands behind this whole discussion. Having made the statement about the one who 'works' and the one who does not, Paul confirms his assertion with a proof from Scripture: the man to whom God 'counts righteousness without works' is blessed (v. 6–8, quoting Ps. 31.1 f.). The next step in the argument is noteworthy. Far from explicating the allegedly meritorious character of the works or the boasting of him who works, Paul introduces instead the question whether the blessed man of his quotations is *circumcised* or not (v. 9). *This* is the real issue.

The formulation of the question is surprising. Paul asks whether the blessedness pertains to the circumcised alone[58] or *also* (ἢ καί!) to the uncircumcised. This is paralleled by v. 11–12: Abraham became 'the father of circumcision' not *only* to the circumcised but *also* to those who have faith in their state of uncircumcision. Paul is not developing an argument against the Jews here at all; he is, instead, arguing for the inclusion of the Gentiles. The same emphasis is manifest in 4.16. This verse makes clear what Paul was aiming at throughout the passage: salvation is by faith and the promise is by grace, in order that it would benefit *all* the seed of Abraham and not *only* the one ἐκ τοῦ νόμου. Throughout the passage Paul, surprisingly perhaps, presupposes that the promises do belong to the circumcised; he only wants to show that they do not pertain to them *alone*.[59] The new order of things is based on faith, in order that it would be based on grace – that is, in order that Gentiles, too, could be included in the people of God. Instead of setting forth a purely dogmatic thesis about justification, Paul is arguing all the time for the inclusion of the Gentiles.[60] When he in this connection inserts a negative comment on the law, he does *not* say: the law brings about boasting! He says: the law brings about *wrath* (4.15), for without law there is no transgression, and transgressing the law incurs the threat of punishment.

Far too much weight has often been placed upon the sentence 'in order that no flesh may boast before God' (1 Cor 1.29).[61] This clause was not formulated by Paul to express a general soteriological principle to the effect that 'boasting' is the root of the evil as regards man's relation to God. The verse has instead a very concrete relationship to the Corinthian schism. What the rejection of human wisdom in 1.26–31 really is all about becomes

---

58 The reading τὴν περιτομὴν μόνον ἢ καί (D), though secondary, correctly stresses the point.
59 The point is missed by Käsemann when he states that Paul is speaking of Christians in general in a careless way. Correctly Jervell. For a recent treatment of the expressions see Mussner, 'Samen'.
60 Cf. Sanders, *Paul* 489 f.; id., *Law* ms 32–36; van Dülmen, op.cit. 174 n. 50; Schmithals, op.cit. 16.
61 E.g. Bultmann, καυχάομαι 649; Käsemann on Rom 3.27; cf. Fung, 'Justification' 249.

perfectly clear in 3.18–4.7: the Corinthians must not boast of some human teachers (like Apollos) to the exclusion of others (read: Paul! 3.21–23, 4.6–7). 3.21 corresponds to 1.29: let no one boast of men (i.e., of Apollos)!

Clearly the activities of Apollos in Corinth had caused tensions and difficulties which Paul discreetly tries to clear away. He avoids anything that might be interpreted as a break with Apollos and his supporters; nevertheless, the talk of building of worthless stuff in ch. 3 is a clear reference to the work of Apollos.[62] Thus, the warning of boasting has a paraenetic or communal rather than soteriological function; this is also true of Rom 11.17 f. The warning of boasting is not offered as a theme of missionary preaching, but as an attempt to solve concrete problems concerning communal life in the church.[63]

Moreover, one has to bear in mind that Paul himself does not boast only

---

62 On the reflection of the tension between Paul and Apollos in 1 Cor 3–4 see Haenchen, *Apg* 532 f.; R.M. Grant, 'Wisdom' 55; Pearson, *Terminology* 18; Ollrog, *Paulus* 215–219; Horsley, 'Wisdom' 237, cf. 231 f. Horsley, however, overemphasizes the role played by *sophia* in Corinth, making it a soteriological factor. Obviously, Paul's trouble was caused by the effects of Apollos' preaching in Corinth, quite possibly contrary to the intentions of Apollos himself (cf. Ollrog, op.cit. 217 f.).

For a rather plausible attempt to explain 1 Cor 1–4 (esp. 2.6–16) on the basis of Alexandrian thought (akin to that of Philo), represented by Apollos, see Pearson, op.cit. 27 ff. Apollos was σοφός and imparted σοφία to his hearers, he was also good at 'words'. He had caused some Corinthians to feel superior to others and boast (καυχᾶσθαι) of the divine (allegorical?) mysteries revealed to them by Apollos (pneumatic revelations to pneumatics). Paul's position is weakened in that he lacks 'wisdom of words' (1.17). *This* is why Paul inserts in 1.18 ff. a discussion of σοφία (and δύναμις) vs. μωρία. He is not here concerned with general soteriological truth; rather, he has a paraenetical and apologetic aim. It is not some 'wise' Greeks outside the congregation who are his targets (*pace* 1.26), it is the 'wise' *within* the congregation. This is clear from 3.18 (εἴ τις δοκεῖ σοφὸς εἶναι ἐν ὑμῖν ἐν τῷ αἰῶνι τούτῳ) and 3.21 (let no one boast of men). 1 Cor 2 makes up Paul's apology because of his lesser *sophia*. At first (2.1–4) he states that it was not his purpose in the first place to display wisdom, but rather give an ἀπόδειξις πνεύματος, display God's power (there is tension between this train of thought and Paul's critique of σημεῖα in ch. 1; cf. the talk of the signs of an apostle in 2 Cor 12 and Rom 15). In 2.6 ff. Paul shifts his ground: he, too, teaches wisdom – but not to anybody! (This argument, again, stands in tension to the critique of wisdom in ch. 1.) In 3.1 ff. Paul, in the course of his apology *pro domo*, moves into attack: he *could* not speak 'wisdom', because the Corinthians would not have borne it. In 3.4 ff. he tries to play down Apollos' influence, and still in 4.15 Apollos may be meant when Paul, slightly derogatorily, speaks of a παιδαγωγός. Nevertheless, 16.12 shows that Paul does not oppose Apollos himself. It is just that he finds himself in a delicate situation: enthusiastic followers of Apollos have caused disturbance in the congregation, and as far as human capacities are concerned, Paul feels inferior to his rival. For a somewhat different reconstruction, which does not contradict the conclusion that communal rather than theological problems are here Paul's main concern, see Dahl, *Studies* 40 ff.

63 Cf. Sánchez-Bosch, op.cit. 133.

when he is 'forced' to do so (2 Cor 11–12). He also has right and acceptable objects of boasting (like a congregation, 2 Cor 1.12–14, or even his own way of life, 2 Cor 1.12, 14!). There is nothing wrong with boasting, when it happens 'in the Lord' (1 Cor 1.31). All in all, 'boasting' cannot be construed as the true Pauline antithesis to faith in Christ.

The Jews' establishment of their own righteousness (Rom 10.3) is, in the light of the context, identical with their *rejection of Christ*. God has made Christ the only true way to salvation, but Israel stubbornly insists on an anti-quated (or simply wrong?) system, that of the law. There is no talk of *relying* on one's own merits, still less of boasting of one's works. The Jews just do not *understand* (ἀγνοοῦντες, v. 2) that a new age has begun, or that in the light of the Christ-event the old system has shown itself as false.[64]

Undoubtedly Rom 9.32a is also to be understood from this point of view. Paul there explains why Israel has not 'attained at the law' (v. 31), i.e. under-stood what the law is all about and thus received the blessing promised in it, although she has been pursuing the 'law of righteousness'.[65] Why? Because she pursued it[66] 'not on the basis of faith but as on the basis of works'. At first glance one might be tempted to interpret this pursuit of the law ἐκ πίστεως as an attitude of humble trust toward the old law, expected of Israel through the ages;[67] instead, Israel had, on this interpretation, sought to come to terms with God's law 'on the basis of their works, their deserving, cherish-ing the illusion[68] that they could so fulfil its demands as to put God under an obligation to themselves'[69] – an 'illusory quest' resulting in 'imprisonment in one's own self-centredness'.[70] Verse 32a is, however, immediately followed and explained by 32b–33 which shows that the main reason for the Jews' unbelief is a Christological one: *Christ* is the 'stumbling-stone'[71] over which they stumble. The theme of 'believing' recurs in the quotation v. 33 (ὁ πιστεύων ἐπ᾿ αὐτῷ οὐ καταισχυνθήσεται). Clearly ἐκ πίστεως should be taken in v. 32 in the normal *Christological* sense of the expression: here as elsewhere it denotes faith *in Christ*. 'The question here is why the Jews stand outside the Messianic salvation; the question whether and why the Jews in the

---

64 Cf. van Dülmen, op.cit. 177 f.
65 See above, II 3.
66 The verb is correctly supplied by Cranfield, *Romans* 508 f.
67 The point is elaborated by Cranfield, op.cit. 510.
68 The ὡς is correctly interpreted by Cranfield as 'underlining the illusory character' of Israel's quest; similarly Sanday-Headlam, Lietzmann; Bläser, *Gesetz* 176; Käse-mann, *Romans* 278.
69 Cranfield; cf. Michel; Fuller, *Gospel* 84.
70 Cranfield; cf. Käsemann, Schlier.
71 Meyer, 'End' 64 offers the startling proposal that the rock placed by God in Zion is the Torah. Does he also hold (cf. 68) that Rom 10.11 refers to the law, or that the 'Lord' in 10.12–13 is not Christ?

time *before Christ* have not attained righteousness is *not* being discussed here.'[72]

In v. 32a Paul simply states his basic axiom: 'faith' (in Christ) and 'works' are contrary principles of salvation. When the OT is read as a testimony to Christ, one is setting himself on the path of faith. If, on the other hand, one rejects the OT testimony to Christ (along with the apostolic preaching about him), one rejects also the salvation offered in Christ and thus, by definition, clings to the system of 'works' (of the law). The character of the works or man's attitude to them is not reflected on. This interpretation of 9.32 and 10.3 is reinforced by the fact that these statements are embedded in a larger context where Paul is concerned with the Jews' (for him) inexplicable stubbornness in refusing to accept Christ.

The classic statement about Christ as the end of the law in 10.4 is actually not offered by Paul as a thesis, but as a *ground* (γάρ) for the implicit assumption that Israel ought to give up her 'own' righteousness. That is, the 'own righteousness' is implicitly defined, as it were, as the opposite of faith in Christ. Note further that the 'speech' of the 'righteousness of faith' in 10.5 ff. is interpreted by Paul through explicitly Christological explanations (the τοῦτ' ἔστιν-clauses in verses 6–7).

In accordance with this, Paul further emphasizes in 10.4: Christ's putting an end to the law as the gateway to salvation means that righteousness is available to *everyone* who believes. Paul is here concerned with the relation between Israel and Gentiles. The problem of Israel was taken up in the beginning of ch. 9, and in 9.24 ff. the Gentile Christians entered the picture (cf. in particular 9.24 καλέσω τόν οὐ λαόν μου λαόν μου; 9.30 'Gentiles not striving after righteousness have acquired righteousness'.) One should further note the talk of 'everyone who believes' in 10.11, of the lack of any distinction between Jew and Greek in 10.12, and the statement that Christ is 'the Lord of all', in whose name 'all ... will be saved' (10.12–13). Once again, the inclusion of Gentiles into the people of God is the real point Paul wants to make.[73]

According to Bultmann, Paul condemns in Phil. 3.4 ff. 'his earlier zeal for

---

72 Bläser, op.cit. 176; cf. Wilckens; Buber, *Zwei Glaubensweisen* 50. Cf. the talk of the 'coming of the faith' in Gal 3.23, 25 ('faith' is possible only after the coming of Christ!) as well as the use of ἡ πίστις in Gal 1.23. Israel's rejection of the law and her rejection of Christ are therefore not 'two rejections' (thus Fuller, *Gospel* 84) but one! Cf. also Zeller, *Juden* 190 f.

73 The context does not indicate that Paul is speaking of 'the tragedy of Israel in the light of his conversion experience' (thus Kim, *Origin* 4). For a contextual analysis of Rom 9.30–10.13 see now E.P. Sanders, *Law* 36–42. He concludes that 'their own righteousness' means 'that righteousness which the Jews alone are privileged to obtain'; it 'is not characterized as being self-righteousness, but rather as being the righteousness which is limited to followers of the law' (38).

the law and his fulfillment of it'.[74] But this cannot be the case. Paul does not
condemn his previous blamelessness. He is, on the contrary, rather proud of
it (v. 4a)! Only, he brands it as blamelessness 'according to the law' and as his
'own righteousness, coming from the law', which is nothing in comparison
with the union with Christ. From the new view-point 'in Christ' all previous
values can be branded as 'flesh'. This is analogous to the juxtaposition of the
vanishing glory of Moses and his ministry with the permanent glory of the
ministry of Christ in 2 Cor 3.[75]

In summary: for Paul, the Jews err in imagining that they can be saved by
keeping the law rather than by believing in Christ. The root of evil lies in a
Christological failure, not in an anthropological one. It may be too much to
exclude all overtones of the idea of anthropocentric legalism e.g. in Rom 4.4.
Paul may have seen some tendency toward smugness and self-righteousness
in the Jewish way. But if so, this was a by-product, not the underlying error.

It is striking how often the polemics against law as the way to salvation are
found in a context where the question of the *inclusion of the Gentiles* is the
most important problem (Gal 2–3, Rom 3–4, Rom 9–10). It is above all in
this connection that Paul underscores that faith in Christ is the only 'pre-

---

74 'Romans' 149.
75 Cf. Sanders, *Paul* 550f.; id., *Law* 44f. Stuhlmacher, *Versöhnung* 182f. claims that Paul
came upon his view of the justification of the impious as an immediate consequence
of his call experience: in his zeal for the Torah Paul had opposed God's decision to
effect reconciliation without the Torah. He takes Phil. 3.4–11 as an account of Paul's
call interpreted as an event where an impious one is justified without works of the
law. Now Paul is not *describing* his call experience in Phil 3.4–11. Rather, he *alludes*
briefly to its decisive significance and then gives a short description of his Christian
existence which grew out of it. Verse 9 – the statement on Paul's 'own righteousness'
– stands out in its context, both syntactically and terminologically. In it, Paul moves
from 'participationist' to 'juridical' language in interpreting his conversion. Strecker
(*Eschaton* 237) infers that Paul did *not* originally interpret his call in the language of
the 'doctrine' of justification. This conclusion is reinforced by Gal 1.10–17, where
'justification' vocabulary is conspicuously lacking. According to Gal 1.16, Paul's
vision resulted in an awareness of the missionary task among Gentiles. This indicates
that the crucial issue on which he changed his mind was the main obstacle to efficient
Gentile mission: *circumcision* and what went with it. The context (Gal 1.10–14,
2.1–10) also points in the same direction. Paul comes to mention his call precisely
because he has been accused, in Galatia, of wishing to 'please men' in not demanding
the circumcision of Gentile converts (1.10). The gospel he received (1.11f.) was a
'gospel of uncircumcision (2.7) which he successfully defended in the Jerusalem meeting
(Gal 2.1–10). Phil 3.2–8 complements the picture: one could only become an apostle
to Gentiles if one gave up the Jewish covenantal privileges: pride of one's Jewish origin,
one's zeal for the law, the demand of circumcision (and the *kosher* laws which went
along with it). For a fuller discussion of Gal 1.12ff and Phil 3.4ff, see H. Räisänen,
The Torah and Christ (PFES 45, Helsinki 1986), 63–73; id., 'Paul's Conversion and
the Development of his View of the Law', *NTS* 33, 1987.

requisite' for man's salvation. Even for the Gentiles, who cannot produce the works required by the law, the way to salvation has been opened by God: faith in Christ is enough.

In the light of the above discussion it is easy to decide what Paul means by 'works of the law' (Gal 2.15 f., 3.2–5, 3.10–12 etc.). The reference is not to 'self-chosen' works accomplished with the purpose of acquiring a reason for boasting.[76] The 'works of law' are simply the works demanded by the Torah.[77] They are the works which, if demanded of the Gentiles, would actually exclude them from the union with Christ.[78]

3. The notion of the law as the Jewish gateway to salvation

We have rejected the notion that, for Paul, Jewish Torah-piety was an expression of human pride, or that he thought of the Jewish religion as dead formalism. It was not for *that* reason that Paul attacked the law. He attacked it, however, as the Jewish gateway to righteousness. Observance of the law need not necessarily lead to boasting (rather, it leads — according to Paul —

---

76 Fuller, *Gospel* 96 f. and 'Paul' 36 pleads for such a meaning referring to II Bar 48.38 'and walked every man in his own works'. Yet 2 Bar is speaking of *evil* works, not of one's 'own righteousness'; cf. 48.40, IV Ezra 3.8. A curious interpretation of 'works of the law' is proposed by M. Barth, 'Stellung' 509 f.: 'Solche Werke verrichten jene Menschen, welche eine minimale Anzahl von Vorschriften ... auslesen.'

77 Thus, e.g., Mundle, *Glaubensbegriff* 100; Duncan, *Galatians* 65; Lührmann, *Galater* 43 f. Specifications are unnecessary, so e.g. that of Barrett: 'works done in obedience to the law and regarded as, in themselves, a means of justification' (*Romans* 70). In the thought of Paul, of course, the phrase, in the last analysis, takes on this nuance, as he postulates that the 'works of law' constitute a rival way to righteousness.

78 This is argued in a short but perceptive article by Tyson ('Works'). He summarizes some of his findings concerning the phrase ἔργα νόμου in Galatians: '(1) "Works of law" refers specifically to a life dedicated to nomistic service; it is not to be confused with human deeds of a possibly meritorious quality. (2) Nomistic service is primarily associated with circumcision and food laws.' (431) These 'served as signs of exclusivism and separation'. 'In the death (sc. of Jesus), God has opened the door to Gentiles and Jews and consequently must say no to nomistic service as a condition of existence.' (431) The expression 'nomistic service' is a rendering of 'Dienst des Gesetzes', the phrase coined by Lohmeyer, *Probleme* 66 f. The English designation is better, as it can be understood as meaning 'nomistic service *to God*'. Lohmeyer, op. cit. 66, thought of service rendered *to the law*, which is wrong. – For the focusing on circumcision and laws of purity in this connection see Mundle, op.cit. 103; Lull, *Spirit* 29 f., 55; and already Wernle, *Christ* 84.

In Rom 9.11 f., 11.6 Paul uses the formula 'not by works' in a new context, where it is no longer a question of the law or of justification, but of election. The problem is no longer the inclusion of Gentiles, but the hardening of Israel. These statements (where the notion of human boasting plays no part) fall outside the scope of the present discussion. See Räisänen, 'Römer 9–11', *ANRW* II, 25,4 (1987).

to an occupation with the killing letter, 2 Cor 3.6, Rom 7.6), but the law had nevertheless a *soteriological* function (or so Paul implies). *Paul* ascribes saving value to the works of the law within the Jewish system (which some Jewish Christians, as he understood it, attempted to introduce into Christian congregations). He attributes to the law in the old system a place analogous to that taken by Christ in the new order of things. One has to choose between God's grace in Christ and the Torah. Only one of the two can be the true way to eschatological salvation. To opt for grace means automatically to opt against the law.

Paul suggests that non-Christian Jews (and wayward Christians) agreed with him on the goal of religion, which was righteousness, but disagreed on the means of attaining it: the 'non-believing' Jews tried to achieve righteousness by works, whereas Paul had realized that it could only be received by grace through faith.[79]

Precisely this, however, is the problem: *Did* the Jews really look for 'righteousness' (in anything like the Pauline sense of the word) in the Torah? Here the answer must be a clear 'No'. In the words of Werblowsky: ' ... one thing seems to me fairly sure: It is not "righteousness" that the Jews look for in the Torah ... One went to the Torah, because one wanted to live his life as a member of an elect community under God, in thankful acceptance of the guidance shown by him.'[80] Sanders agrees: 'Being righteous is not the goal of a religious quest; it is the behaviour proper to one who has accepted the covenant offered at Sinai and the commandments which followed the acceptance of God's kingship.'[81]

Actually, the law should not be called (from the Jewish point of view) a 'way of salvation' at all — at least not if by such an expression is meant something comparable to the place taken by Christ in the Christian tradition. Salvation was understood as *God's* act. He had elected himself a people and made a covenant with them. Salvation, i.e. a share in the age to come, was based on God's faithfulness in his covenant. When giving the covenant God had also given his people the stipulations connected with the covenant — the Torah, the guidance. The Torah was to be observed by a pious Jew out of gratitude and obedience to its Giver. In the jargon of NT scholarship one might say that the law had the status of the *'imperative'* which was *based on the 'indicative' of God's prevenient gracious acting.*[82] Observance of the law

---

79 *Pace* E.P. Sanders, *Paul* 551; see below, p. 187 f.
80 Werblowsky, 'Tora' 159; cf. Lapide, 'Rabbi' 42 ff.; Flusser, 'Erlebnis' 24 f.
81 Sanders, op.cit. 205.
82 I am using this terminology in the same way as Schulz does (*Mitte* 188, 218 and elsewhere: indicative = 'die Zusage des Heils'). This usage seems to be slightly different from that of Bultmann who first introduced the terms to the theological discussion (*Exegetica* 37 ff.).

was a holistic thing; the point was not a hundred per cent perfection, but the will to carry the 'yoke of the commandments' and thus to remain within the framework of the covenant. If one transgressed a commandment, the path of repentance (*teshubah*), totally glossed over by Paul in his polemics, was always open to him.[83] Repentance is indeed 'the crucial criterion in the soteriological system of the Tannaim'.[84] Salvation could not be gained by gathering 'merits'; it remained a gift of God. Thus grace and law belong closely *together*.[85]

This total view of post-Biblical Jewish soteriology is called 'covenantal nomism' by E.P. Sanders.[86] By obeying the law, man showed his willingness to *stay* within the covenant established by God, but he did not '*get in*' by fulfilling the legal requirements. 'Righteousness' is, in Judaism, 'a term which implies the *maintenance of status among the group of the elect*', whereas it is a 'transfer term' (to be righteous meaning 'to be saved by Christ') in Paul.[87] As a pupil of Sanders puts it, 'being righteous is a necessary but not sufficient ground for salvation'.[88]

There may be an overemphasis on *covenantal* categories in Sanders' work. Many Jews paid attention to God's prevenient activity without resorting to covenant language, e.g. by paying attention to how the divine order of creation is reflected in human affairs (e.g. Jub, 1 Enoch).[89] For my present purpose the point is simply that the theme of *gratuity* with regard to salvation is conspicuously present in Judaism.

In addition to the Tannaitic texts, Sanders finds the same pattern everywhere in the Apocrypha, Pseudepigrapha and the Dead Sea Scrolls[90] as well (with one exception, to be mentioned shortly). Quite consistently 'election and ultimately salvation are considered to be by God's mercy rather than human achievement'.[91] From the consistency with which covenantal nomism

---

83 Cf. on this especially Montefiore, *Judaism* 75 f.
84 Przybylski, *Righteousness* 51; cf. ibid. 76.
85 See esp. Werblowsky, art.cit.; Hruby, 'Gesetz' 49 ff.
86 For a definition see above, p. 167.
87 Sanders, op.cit. 544.
88 Przybylski, op.cit. 51, 52. Cf. also Sloyan, *Christ* 93: for the rabbis of the Tannaitic period the law 'was not the means of salvation'; Gaston, 'Paul' 51.
89 Cf. Limbeck, *Ordnung*.
90 For the 'soteriology' of Qumran cf. Garnet, *Salvation* (esp. 36, 56, 115 ff.). His conclusion: 'Salvation is a work of God and manifests his power, love and justice.' (115) Obedience is 'a *sine qua non* for salvation', but it 'was deemed to be the product of a work of God in the human heart' (116 f.). Cf. Garnet, 'Light' 19 but see also the qualifications introduced on pp. 20 ff. Garnet's attempt (art.cit. 22 f.) to refute Sanders's evaluation of Judaism on the basis of a peculiar interpretation of Gal 2.15 ff. is not convincing at all. It is fanciful to take Gal 2.18 as a reference to Paul's 'destroying Christianity' which he is now building up again (28 f.).
91 Sanders, ibid. 422.

is maintained in the extant texts from Ben Sira to late in the second century
AD Sanders concludes that covenantal nomism must have been pervasive in
Palestine before AD 70.[92]

The one exception is, for Sanders, IV Ezra. In this writing the framework
of the covenant has collapsed and one really has to earn one's salvation by
perfect obedience to the law.[93] IV Ezra can, however, hardly come in question as a representative of the Judaism known by Paul. It is so profoundly
marked by the crisis caused by the fall of Jerusalem that 'it may be doubted
if its viewpoint could have been held at all had it not been for the difficult
situation of Israel after the war'.[94] In any case, the pessimism of the dialogues
of IV Ezra was corrected by 2 Baruch, if not already by the author of the
concluding vision of IV Ezra itself.[95] Indeed one may ask whether Sanders
has not overemphasized the significance of perfection for IV Ezra. The radicalized view of the obedience required of man would seem to be a device that
is intended to serve the author's theodicy and that alone: contrary to all
appearance God *has* remained faithful to his covenant; it is themselves men

---

92 Op.cit. 426. A writing not mentioned by Sanders which might have rendered added
force to his argument is the work of Pseudo-Philo, dated before 70 AD by the editors
of the most recent critical edition (Perrot, 'Introduction' 42 f.; Bogaert, ibid. 74;
Dietzfelbinger, *Pseudo-Philo* 95 f. sticks to a date between 73 and 132 AD) and quite
possibly of a Palestinian provenance (Perrot, op.cit. 65; Dietzfelbinger, op.cit. 96).
The writing shows signs of Pharisaic influence (Perrot, op.cit. 32; Dietzfelbinger, op.
cit. 91). According to Perrot (p. 31), the book 'nous livre les idées et les thèmes
les plus vulgarisés du Judaïsme courant du Ier siecle du notre ère'. Pseudo-Philo is
concerned to tell 'the history of the Covenant'. The term 'covenant' is indeed the
key-word of the book, much more so than 'law' which also occurs often enough
(Perrot, op.cit. 44). In the terminology of Sanders, Pseudo-Philo must be called a
prominent representative of covenantal nomism. His is 'a religion of the heart', resembling in many ways that of Deuteronomy ; there is no trace of a 'formalistic or
legalistic mentality' (Perrot, ibid. 44). Perrot's interpretation is that Pseudo-Philo
does *not yet* represent the legalism that is *later* to be found in Rabbinic literature.
'Dans toute l'oeuvre on sent vibrer l'âme d'un auteur-prédicateur qui exhorte et con-
sole, avertit sans indulgence le pécheur, mais se confie éperdument dans la miséri-
corde de Dieu (15, 7).' (Perrot, op.cit. 44) He is 'the apostle of an internalized religion' (op.cit. 45). In summary, 'C'etait un homme possédé par la religion de l'Alliance, une religion véçue intérieurement, dans la ligne des Prophètes. Voilà qui réha-
bilite singulièrement les scribes du Ier siècle, que aucuns voudraient confiner dans
l'exposition minutieuse des règles halakhiques!' (Op.cit. 64). For covenant and law in
Pseudo-Philo see, e.g., LAB 9.7–8, 11.1–3, 13.10, 21.10, 23.2, 10; 30.7. For a full
list of the covenant passages see index, s.v. Alliance. (Tome II, 307).

93 Op.cit. 409 ff.

94 Op.cit. 427.

95 So Sanders, op.cit. 416 ff., wishing to modify the results of Harnisch, *Verhängnis*
and Breech, 'Fragments'. Should Sanders, however, be incorrect in his analysis of
IV Ezra, the result would then be that there are no exceptions to covenantal nomism
in the extant literature.

have to blame for what has happened.[96] God is reliable and will carry out his salvific plan in the future.

It thus seems that, as far as Palestinian Judaism is concerned, Paul either (implicitly, at least) gives an inaccurate picture, or else bases his view on insufficient and uncharacteristic evidence. Supposing that (contrary to Acts) Paul spent his youth in the Dispersion[97], Montefiore and Schoeps have suggested that he does after all give a correct picture of Judaism as *known to him*, i.e., the religion of the Dispersion, which these scholars take to have been by far inferior to Palestinian Judaism.[98] For various reasons it is very difficult to uphold this view.[99] Sanders has briefly analyzed Philo's writings and Joseph and Asenath from the point of view of covenantal nomism. He concludes that even in these Alexandrian documents this pattern of religion dominates.[100] Thus even the extant texts from the Jewish Diaspora hardly support the picture given by Paul.[101] Of course, we know very little of Jewish piety in Asia minor in Paul's time. The possibility cannot therefore be ruled out that there could have been elements in Paul's earlier experience with Judaism which would justify his account of it in terms of his personal history. In that case, Paul's view would be understandable as a generalization

---

96 Cf. Limbeck, *Ordnung* 101.

97 On the question of Paul's background see below, p. 234.

98 Montefiore, *Judaism* 81 f., 92 ff.; Schoeps, *Paul* 27–32, 213 ff.

99 Thus Montefiore came to posit a close connection between 'Hellenistic' and 'Apocalyptic' Judaism and ended up by citing (beside Paul himself) IV Ezra as a characteristic representative of Diaspora Judaism.

On Schoeps see above, n. 14. Werblowsky, 'Paulus' 139, states bluntly but not without justification: 'To portray Paul as a typical "Dispersion Jew" is sheer nonsense.' It is, furthermore, to-day hardly necessary any more to point out that it is impossible to draw a clear-cut cultural boundary-line between Palestinian and Hellenistic Judaism; cf. Hengel, *Judentum*.

100 'Covenant'. For the apocrypha in general cf. the summary of Marcus, *Law* 113: ' ... the scrupulous fulfilment of the requirements of the ceremonial law was not considered sufficient in itself to form the sum of the religious duties of the people'.

101 Sandelin has argued that the Alexandrian wisdom tradition represented by Philo and especially by Wisdom of Solomon is of a 'strictly nomistic' nature in that 'it emphasizes that man has to fulfil the commands of the Jewish law in order to be saved'; the law is 'a power to righteousness before God' ('Vishetstradition' 152; cf. *Auseinandersetzung* 84 f.). His main proof is Sap 9.18 ('through Wisdom they have been saved'). This verse, however, most probably speaks of being rescued from worldly dangers (correctly Bussmann, *Themen* 188), as is often the case when σῴζειν is used in Sap (cf. 16.7, 18.5, 7). Moreover, 9.13–18 is part of the prayer of Solomon in which the king asks for wisdom to reign over his people; this is not a soteriological context. No doubt Sap is a 'nomistic' book, but its nomism is patently of a *covenantal* kind. This is shown most clearly by chs. 10 ff. In these chapters God's *acts* (the acts of 'Wisdom') in the history of Israel (especially in connection with the Exodus and subsequent events) are emphatically spoken of; cf. also Hartman, 'Bundesideologie' 104. Salvation comes from *God*: see, e.g., 11.23 ff., 12.2, 12.19 ff.

of a certain individual experience.[102] This state of affairs is not, however, very probable.

But what about the Christian 'Judaizers' of Paul's generation? In the Lucan account of the Apostolic Council the teaching of 'some' is summarized in the words: 'Unless you are circumcised ... you cannot be saved.' (Acts 15.1). Along with this statement, we hear of the demand of some Christian Pharisees (v. 5): 'They must be circumcised, and they must be ordered to obey the law of Moses.' Was it in view of these Christians, or of those called in Gal. 2.4 'false brethren'[103], that Paul (correctly) formulated his antithesis between the law and Christ as rival soteriological entities?

Even supposing that Luke's account of the doctrines set forth some half a century earlier in Antioch is accurate (which is not self-evident)[104], Acts 15.1 is far too brief a summary to give us much information about the real views of the 'Judaizers'. Did they regard all those Gentile Christians who did not accept circumcision as damned? Or did they just hold that, in order to be integrated with the people of the covenant, the Gentiles would have to comply with the covenantal regulations, although they could be *saved* (in the eschatological judgment) even outside the pale of the covenant proper? Taken by itself, Acts 15.5 could be understood in the latter sense.[105] The Jews had no generally accepted doctrine of the fate of righteous Gentiles.[106] As long

---

(note the mention of the 'covenants' and 'promises' in v. 21), 15.1 ff.; in a this-worldly sense also 16.7 ff. In the first part of the book: 3.9, 4.15. In this covenantal context must statements like 6.18c ('keeping the commandments warrants incorruptibility') – an injunction, moreover, given in an exhortation for regents, i.e. in a purely paraenetic context – or 8.17c (in communion with wisdom there is immortality) be understood: it is a question of the 'imperative' based on the 'indicative'. 'Solomon' states indeed: 'But I perceived that I would not possess wisdom, unless God gave her to me' (8.21). On the covenant theme in Sap see further Ziener, *Begriffssprache* 78–97; Jaubert, *Alliance* 350 ff., esp. 370 ff.

102 That is, no further generalizations regarding, for instance, Christianity's relation to Judaism could be based on it. 'Judaism' is in itself a vast complex of religious phenomena which have thus far been insufficiently distinguished; cf. Neusner, ' "Judaism" after Moore'. For the present thesis it is enough, if it can be shown that large currents of 'Judaism' put an emphasis on gratuity rather than merits in man's relation to God.

103 It seems probable that we are allowed to connect these people at least ideologically with the right wing party in the Council; cf. Betz, *Gal* 90.

104 Loisy, *Galates* 26 f. thinks that either Acts 15.1 is not to be taken literally (thus idem, *Actes* 568) or, more probably, Luke has exaggerated the Judaizing thesis in Pauline spirit.

105 Neil ad loc. interprets v. 5 in a weaker sense than v. 1: v. 5 indicates a question of admission 'to full fellowship with Jewish Christians' rather than of salvation). He makes, however, a distinction between the Pharisees of v. 5 and 'the bigots of v. 1'. Others take v. 5 as an elaboration of v. 1; thus e.g. Conzelmann ad loc.

106 See Moore, *Judaism* I, 325; M. Guttmann, *Judentum* 168 ff.; Helfgott, *Doctrine* 140 f. In later times at least the idea became dominant that Gentiles need *not* become Jews to receive a share in the eschatological salvation (see Guttmann). The main-

as these did not become proselytes, no effort was made to impose the Jewish law upon them. It is difficult, though not impossible, to assume that Jewish Christians would have represented a stricter view on this point. But even if they did, they need not have ascribed saving value to the *law*; they may merely have pointed out that one cannot be saved outside of God's *covenant*.

It is impossible to enter here into a detailed discussion of who Paul's opponents e.g. in Galatia and/or in the Apostolic Council really were.[107] The most natural view seems now as before to be that they were Jewish Christians with a rather normal Jewish identity.[108] It is they who represent the continuity between the mother religion and the new community. Indeed they represented an 'entirely understandable' Jewish Christian position.[109]

One has full grounds to assume that the earliest Christians (all of them) understood themselves to be the people of the covenant. Now the sign of the covenant was, of old, circumcision. Again, the condition of staying in the covenant was compliance with the Torah as the covenantal law. If the Christians constituted the true Israel, it must have seemed natural to many to think that Gentiles joining God's people would do so in the way ordered by God – the ecstatic experiences of Peter and others with non-circumcised Gentiles (Acts 10.44 ff., 11.15 ff., 15.8 f.) notwithstanding. Why should glossolalia, after all, cancel the word of God as revealed in Scripture? Such misgivings with regard to the practical course taken by the new community in its attitude to Gentiles represent serious conservatism and need not imply any kind of 'merit theology'. What was at stake was probably not so much the question of the fate of the Gentiles as the responsibility and conscience of the 'Judaizers' themselves. 'What *right* do we have to let this happen, ignoring the clear words in God's law?', they must have asked. 'Theirs was an entirely reasonable position, and its great strength was almost certainly the support which reading the Bible would give it.'[110] At the very least it is easy to

stream of the Talmud opts for this lenient view. 'Indeed, one might almost be tempted to assert that, according to Rabbinic teaching, it was easier for a righteous Gentile to be saved than for a Jew.' Petuchowski, *Heirs* 142.

107 For recent surveys see Mussner, *Gal* 11–29; Gunther, *Opponents*; Betz, *Gal* 5–9.

108 Cf. Betz, op.cit. 7; Lüdemann, 'Antipaulinismus'; Lull, *Spirit* 10 f., 30 ff. On the thesis of Munck, *Paulus* 79–126, adopted by M. Barth, 'St. Paul' 19 f., that the Judaizing movement was a purely Gentile Christian development see the reviews by Davies, Bultmann and Smith; cf. further Mussner, op.cit. 17.

Mussner, 'Wiedergutmachung' makes much of the observation that Paul's opponents were fellow Christians rather than non-Christian Jews, trying to make this point fertile for a Jewish-Christian dialogue. This, however, does not remove any problems connected with the battle in Galatians, for the opponents seem to have attacked Paul precisely because of their *Jewish* identity (i.e., because of their covenantal nomism).

109 Sanders, *Law* 20. Cf. Andrews, *Teaching* 38: 'The Judaisers had logic on their side.'

110 Sanders, op.cit. 18.

understand that it was possible and indeed obvious to attack Paul at precisely those points his opponents seem to have done *without* subscribing to 'legalist' soteriology based on works, or anything like that. All one needed was the standard Jewish attitude to God's revelation in Scripture. If you like, it was a question of 'Biblicism' rather than of 'legalism'.[111]

Let us approach the problem posed by Paul's implied picture of Jewish soteriology from another point of view. It may be objected to the above discussion that, all told, however much the mercy and initiative of God may have been stressed, the law remained after all in Judaism the only way – even if the way ordained by God – to salvation.[112] It is admittedly extremely difficult to define what constitutes a 'means of salvation' and what does not; when the law is a 'way' to salvation and when it is merely a 'guidance'; or to define when the law functions only as an 'imperative' based on an 'indicative' and when it has a more independant status; or to distinguish between hard 'legalism' and 'covenantal nomism'. Nice distinctions are bound to remain academic. Fortunately they are, in the last analysis, unnecessary. The important thing is simply to use the *same* kind of standards when reading the NT, in particular Paul.

Paul, too, speaks of right behaviour as *necessary* for salvation. The judgment will still be according to *deeds* (2 Cor 5.10, cf. Rom 2.1–16). This is no self-contradiction on his part. As E.P. Sanders puts it, 'It is not at all inconsistent that he expects correct behaviour on the part of those who are in Christ, nor that he thinks that transgressions on the part of Christians will be punished. This is in accord with the general Jewish view that election and salvation are by God's grace, while reward and punishment correspond to deeds. There is no conflict between God's mercy and his justice, and in fact on this point Paul is a perfect example of the view which is characteristic of first century Judaism . . .'[113]

---

111 No doubt political factors (the worsening of relations between Jews and Gentiles in Palestine and the 'terror of the Zealots') also played a part – but hardly a decisive part. Their significance seems to be over-estimated by Dix, *Jew* 30 ff.; Reicke, 'Hintergrund'; Suhl, *Paulus* 15 ff., 72. οἱ ἐκ περιτομῆς in Gal 2.12 can hardly refer to non-Christian Jews, as this theory requires. For a sound assessment of the role of political factors in the formation of the theology of the 'Judaizers' see Becker, *Galater* 3 f., 23 f., 65, 81. See also Ellis, *Prophecy* 116 f.; Lüdemann, *Paulus* 101 n. 97.
112 Cf. Byrne, 'Sons' 230 f.
113 Sanders, *Law* 105f. Cf. Donfried, 'Justification' 102: ' ... the gospel is the means of salvation – but only if one holds fast to its power, only if one is obedient to its claim ... When one does not hold fast, when one is not obedient, then one has believed in vain (1 Cor 15₂) ... Paul affirms that the man who has received the gospel of God's gracious mercy by faith and who has been justified through it, will receive the final gift of salvation at the last judgment. This is purely an act of God's grace which

According to Paul, salvation has to be 'worked out' with fear and trembling (Phil 2.12). God is severe toward those who fall away from his kindness (Rom 11.20–22). In 1 Cor 6.9 Paul threatens the licentious and quarreling Corinthians by reminding them of the exclusion of the unrighteous (ἄδικοι) from God's reign. The implication is that the Corinthians risk their salvation if they continue their bad behaviour (cf. Gal 5.21b). Gal 6.7, the reminder of the correspondence between sowing and reaping, likewise implies that 'God can and will reject disobedient Christians'.[114] 1 Cor 10.1–13 strongly warns against an understanding of baptism as an automatic guarantee of salvation. [115] This passage is remarkable in that in it Paul himself establishes an exact soteriological analogy between the 'fathers' in the wilderness and the Christians.[116]

---

the believer will receive if he remains obedient to the gift of God and His Spirit. For the man who has been justified, but who then makes a mockery of God's gift by his gross abuse and disobedience, such a one will not receive the gift of salvation at the last judgment ... Thus the final criterion at the last judgment is, for Paul, not how, many good works man has performed ... but whether man has held fast and remained obedient to his new life in Christ.'

See also Fiedler, *Jesus* 84: ' ... auch für Paulus ein aus dem Empfang des Heils im Glauben gefolgertes Tun "eine conditio sine qua non" ist, im Heil zu bleiben'; Fiedler also refers to Jesus, 'dessen das Heilsangebot realisierendem Umkehrruf der Forderungscharakter nicht gut abgesprochen werden kann'.

114 Donfried, op.cit. 107. Synofzik, *Gerichtsaussagen* 73 interprets Gal 6.7 f. differently. But the verses are addressed to *Christians* in order to be taken seriously: falling back from the sphere of the Spirit into that of the flesh will have disastrous consequences. Synofzik's correct observation that in 1 Cor 10.1–10 Paul does not ascribe to baptism (i.e., to the reception of the Spirit!) a 'character indelebilis' (op.cit. 56) can be made to bear on the interpretation of other passages as well.

115 Cf. J. Weiss ad loc.; Roetzel, *Judgement* 172.

116 Stuhlmacher, *Versöhnung* 163 claims that the final justification is promised to the believers even in the case that their acts prove a failure before God; cf. id., *Gerechtigkeit* 230 f. Stuhlmacher refers to Rom 8.31 ff. and 1 Cor 3.11–15. The latter passage is, however, concerned with the ἔργον of a missionary (Apollos), not with the moral life of believers; correctly Donfried, art.cit. 106. In Rom 8.33 f. Paul asks the rhetorical question, Who could accuse or condemn God's elect as Christ has died for them? In this context Paul is not, however, concerned with the question of Christian moral conduct. He wishes to show that the earthly *sufferings* of Christians are of a transient character and that the future glory by far excels the present troubles. No inimical powers, be they cosmic or mundane, can really threaten a Christian's existence. This is the point of vv. 35–39 which take up vv. 17 f. Sins are *not* listed among the factors which might, but actually cannot, separate Christians from God's love in Christ. In fact, vv. 31–39 constitute the conclusion of the treatment of life in Spirit, begun in 8.1 ff.; in the course of this treatment Paul presupposes that Christians will not live 'according to the flesh'. Yet elsewhere he expresses the view that an unrepentant Christian sinner ought to be excluded from the community (cf. 1 Cor 5.1 ff., 2 Cor 12.21; 1 Cor 5.5 is a difficult verse, but hardly a sufficient ground for the view that Christ's intercession will save all baptized). A rejection of the central gospel message likewise brings with it a final separation from Christ (Gal 5.4, cf. 1 Cor

Bearing this in mind, it would be possible to claim that Paul actually teaches salvation (or at least reward) by works![117] If we (reasonably enough) refrain from such a claim, it might be wise not to apply it to Paul's Jewish contemporaries either.[118] There is a difference of emphasis, to be sure, as the 'doing' is more in focus in Jewish texts; it is not clear that the pattern itself is much different.[119]

In this light it also becomes easy to understand why the author of the letter of James, true to the Jewish vision, just *had* to misunderstand Paul's teaching. If the proper context of 'works' was that of the 'imperative' based

---

15.2b). Yet is has to be added that only heinous sins, which are not repented of, will effect condemnation; other transgressions may be punished at the judgment, but final damnation is another matter. See Sanders, op.cit. 110–112 and below, n. 119.

117 Synofzik, *Gerichtsaussagen* 152 actually criticizes Donfried (see above, n. 113) on the dogmatic ground that his position 'does not avoid the danger of a synergistic understanding of salvation' and that 'the final salvation is here explicitly made to depend on man's acts in faith'; obviously, it is impossible to teach a 100 per cent *sola gratia* doctrine except in theory.

118 Byrne, op.cit. 230 writes on Judaism in the course of his critique of Sanders: 'Whatever be the fundamental case in *theory* – that is, that the covenant and God's mercy overarch the whole pattern of progress to salvation – if works are a condition of remaining "in" the covenant community and if exclusion from that community means loss of salvation, then in *practice* – that is, from the point of view of one on the road from election to salvation – works *are* a means of gaining salvation.' (B's italics.) But if 'Christ' is substituted for 'covenant', this observation (whatever its worth) is applicable to Paul as well (cf. the previous note). By this logic, the doctrine of double predestination is the only way to prevent 'works' from being a means of gaining salvation. It is wrong to confront Jewish 'practice' with Christian 'theory'. Nickelsburg, Rev. Klein 166 f. correctly points out that 'the concept that one's eternal destiny will correspond to one's deeds on earth is so prevalent in the New Testament as to be a commonplace', occurring in the Pauline letters as well. This 'indicates that judgment on the basis of works cannot be used as evidence that *Jewish* religion was legalistic'.

119 Admittedly, the passages mentioned are open to a somewhat 'milder' interpretation. Sanders concludes his discussion as follows: 'It thus appears that, while Christians can revert to the non-Christian state and share the fate of unbelievers, there is no deed which necessarily leads to the condemnation of a believer, although Paul appears to waver with regard to food offered to idols.' But he also points out that 'the difficulty in determining precisely what, if anything, will permanently exclude and condemn a member of the group does not make Paul's letters atypical'. We can say that 'in both rabbinic literature and Paul's letters, remaining in the in-group is conditional on behavior. In neither case, however, does an act of disobedience bring automatic expulsion. Thus when the rabbis discuss atonement it turns out that every sin can be atoned for. Only willful and unrepentant transgression brings condemnation, since that indicates rejection of God. In the end, it comes down to intention: those who intend to deny the God who gave the commandments have no share in his promises. It is not significantly otherwise with Paul ...' (op.cit. 111f.).

on the 'indicative', and if Paul attacked the works, then from the classical Biblical and Jewish point of view this attack had to seem ill-founded.

In the last analysis, Paul's *sola gratia sine operibus* is not an abstract theological thesis at all. As we have seen, Paul, at heart (when expressing himself spontaneously), does not subscribe to the assumption of universal guilt which can only be removed through the death of Christ (see Rom 2.14–16).[120] He does develop a theological theory to that effect, to be sure, but when the theological control relaxes, his thought proceeds along other paths. The background for Paul's *sola gratia* is the practical problem of the *inclusion of Gentiles* in the people of God. Where this problem is absent (as in 1 Thess), there is no polemic against works of the law either.[121]

The conclusion, then, is hard to avoid that Paul tears apart, not without violence, what belonged together in 'genuine' Judaism. It is he who drives a wedge between law and grace, limiting 'grace' to the Christ event. He pays no attention to the central place of God's free pardon to the penitent and the role thus accorded to repentance in Judaism.[122] *It should not have been possible to do away with the 'law as the way to salvation' for the simple reason that the law never was that way.*

Here my assessment of Paul's position differs from that of E.P. Sanders, if I understand him correctly. What Sanders regards as an *incorrect* formulation of the issue, seems to me a quite *correct* statement: 'Paul agreed on the *goal*, righteousness, but saw that it should be received by grace through faith, not achieved by works.'[123] Sanders expressly admits that this formulation is *Paul's own*; nevertheless he thinks that it 'actually misstates the fundamental point of disagreement' (between Judaism and Paul).

I think that is correct as regards the disagreement between Paul and *real* (characteristic) Judaism (covenantal nomism); but the kind of Judaism that emerges from *Paul's* writings has a somewhat different face. The disagreement between Paul and that (at least partly) distorted or uncharacteristic Judaism is another matter.

Sanders is led to the conclusion that Paul explicitly rejects covenantal nomism. 'Paul in fact *explicitly* denies that the Jewish covenant can be effective for salvation, thus *consciously* denying the basis of Judaism.' 'It is not first of all against the *means* of being properly religious which are appropriate to Judaism that Paul polemicizes ("by works of law"), but against the prior

---

120 See above, p. 107 f.
121 Cf. already Wernle, *Christ* 83 ff.: the doctrine of justification only serves the Gentile mission. Stendahl, *Paul* 26 f., 84 f., 130 f. etc. The point has been forcefully made by E.P. Sanders.
122 Moule, 'Obligation' 398 ff. may succeed in refuting Knox's theory of the lack of 'repentance' in the life of Christians in Paul's theology (see Knox, *Chapters* 141 ff.). In Paul's portrayal of Judaism this gap remains.
123 Sanders, op.cit. 551.

fundamentals of Judaism: the election, the covenant and the law; and it is
because these are wrong that the means appropriate to "righteousness according to the law" (Torah observance and repentance) are held to be wrong or
are not mentioned. In short, this is what Paul finds wrong in Judaism: it is not
Christianity.'[124] Thus far Sanders.

Something like this would probably be the logical outcome of much that
Paul says about the law. But certainly such convictions are *not* 'explicitly'
stated or 'consciously' held by Paul! He makes emphatically explicit statements of a quite different sort.

Here as elsewhere we will have to distinguish between what Paul actually
says and what the *logical* conclusions (which Paul may not even remotely
perceive) might have been.[125] Paul strongly affirms both the election, the
covenant and the giving of the law (Rom 9.4 f.). God has *not* revoked the
election of Israel (Rom 9.6, 11.1 f., 11.29). Perhaps contrary to the inner
logic of his position, Paul explicitly *acknowledges* (in Romans, at least) *the
covenant* as a gracious act of God in his conscious reasoning. He pays, we
might say, lip service to covenantal nomism. He wants his own position to be
understood in far less radical terms than Sanders's reading of it suggests (and
also in far less radical terms than what it actually amounts to!). As so often,
his theology has a Janus face. He points in one (covenantal) direction and
goes in another (without, I think, realizing where he actually is). We may
agree with Sanders that 'Paul was not trying accurately to represent Judaism
on its own terms, nor need we suppose that he was ignorant on essential
points'.[126] But I cannot avoid the strong impression that Paul actually does
give his readers a distorted picture of Judaism. He comes to misrepresent
Judaism by suggesting that, within it, salvation is by works and the Torah
plays a role analogous to that of Christ in Paulinism.

We will try to take a closer look at the reasons for Paul's misrepresentation
in a later chapter.[127] Here we shall briefly consider three individual points

---

124 Op.cit. 551 f. I have added the emphasis on 'explicitly' and 'consciously' (in Sanders,
    the whole sentence is italicised). Sanders has reformulated his statement in *Law* 47
    as follows: 'What is wrong with the law, and thus with Judaism, is that it does not
    provide for God's ultimate purpose, that of saving the entire world through faith
    in Christ, and without the privilege accorded to Jews through the promises, the
    covenants, and the law.' It is not quite clear to me whether this is just 'a more precise
    and more understandable way' of putting the matter, as Sanders says, or whether
    Paul's 'charge' is here actually understood in a milder way. On p. 160, anyway,
    Sanders again states that Paul was 'denying the efficacy of the election', thus striking
    at 'something which is crucial to Judaism'.
125 Compare the discussion of Paul's idea of the intention of the law (above, p. 154). In
    that case, too, Paul's statements would logically lead to conclusions certainly not
    intended by him.
126 Op.cit. 551.
127 See below, VIII 7.

which are connected with the mistaken notion of the law as the *basis* of salvation in Judaism.

1. Paul asks whether the Galatians received the Spirit 'by works of the law, or by hearing with faith' (Gal 3.2 ff.). This is a question-begging alternative. One could just as well have asked, whether the Galatians received the Spirit 'by obedience to the apostolic paraenesis, or by hearing with faith'. Obviously, the reason for their experiencing great things had not been their love of their neighbours or avoidance of fornication, so why bother about such things? One would never come to the idea that observance of the law ought to be the *source* of spiritual gifts, as long as the law is properly viewed as the imperative resulting from the indicative of God's covenant.

In addition, this argument is beset with empirical problems. It seems that, in Paul's view, spiritual gifts were still a reality in Galatia, the new nomistic trend notwithstanding.[128] Charismatic experiences were not unknown to the more conservative community in Jerusalem either (Acts 2!), nor were prophecy, miracles etc. unknown in Judaism, although they were not appreciated as highly as they were among Christians.[129] Paul has simply concocted an *ad hoc* argument, based on the aprioristic view that faith and the Spirit belong together, whereas the law and the Spirit do not.

2. In the same connection Paul sets up Abraham as a *typos* of those who are 'of faith' (Gal 3.7). The example of Abraham demonstrates that 'Scripture' saw in advance that οἱ ἐκ πίστεως will receive the blessing along with Abraham, unlike those ἐξ ἔργων νόμου. Gen 15.6 is cited as proof: Abraham ἐπίστευσεν τῷ θεῷ. Paul again begs the question by tacitly identifying Abraham's 'faith' with faith *in Christ*, rather than taking it in the sense of trust in God.[130] Apparently Paul was forced to take up the case of Abraham, to

---

128 The present participles ἐπιχορηγῶν and ἐνεργῶν indicate that God has not revoked his gifts; Mussner, Betz; Lull, *Spirit* 38, 50 n. 82.

129 For the connection between law and Spirit in Qumran see Jaubert, *Alliance* 238 ff.; in Rabbinic Judaism: Davies, *Paul* 209 ff.; A. Guttmann, 'Miracles' 384 ff., 405 f. Guttmann argues that the valuation of miracles and the *bat qol* declined in the period after AD 70, because the Christians put so much emphasis on such things. Comparing the NT and the Talmud may thus produce an optical illusion with respect to pneumatology. Cf. the references to Essene prophecy in Jos. *Bell*. II, 159; I, 78–80; *Ant*. XIII, 311–313; see O. Betz, *Offenbarung* 99 ff.; Hengel, *Judentum* 439. The threads are completely confused, should the assumption be correct that ecstatic experiences were not foreign to Paul the Pharisee either; thus Dodd, *Studies* 69 f.; Hengel, op.cit. 376. This, however, is purely conjectural.

130 That Paul sees Abraham totally from the view-point of faith in Christ, identifying in an unreflective way the Septuagintal πίστις with his own 'faith', is well perceived by Mundle, *Glaubensbegriff* 96 ff. On faith as trust cf. the use of Hab 2.4 in Makk 3.16 (Makk 23b) as a reduction of the 613 commands. The point of the homily is that 'the moral law ... may be compressed into the principle of seeking God (Amos), or of faith in God (Habakkuk)'; Schechter, *Aspects* 140. There is no tension here between

whom his opponents probably referred as their 'father'. In Galatians Paul manages to evade the fact that Abraham, too, was circumcised — a fact that might have proved embarrassing for Paul's cause in that letter.

By the time of writing Romans he has found an explanation: the circumcision of Abraham was a 'seal of righteousness by faith' (Rom 4.11). But why, then, was it prohibited for the Galatians to accept this very seal? Or, conversely, why was Abraham after his circumcision not obliged to fulfil the whole law (Gal 5.3)?

3. Paul discredits the law by pointing out its weakness: its inability to supply the power needed for its observance. The argument of Rom 7.7—8.4 is based on this allegation. But why *ought* the law to have been the *source* of moral power in the first place? Why the law and not its giver? This difference was perceived in Judaism, for 'even the Torah is not an all-powerful remedy in itself without the aid of heaven, which gives the Torah its real efficiency'. 'The Torah by itself is ... not sufficient to defeat the Evil Yezer. The conquest comes in the end from God.'[131] In IV Ezra it is vigorously stressed that man's weakness is due to the evil inclination (and thus, indirectly, to God!) rather than to the law: 'Yet thou didst not take away from them the evil heart, that thy Law might bring forth fruit[132] in them. For the first Adam, burdened with the evil heart, transgressed and was overcome; and likewise also all who were born of him. Thus the infirmity became inveterate; the Law indeed was in the heart of the people, but (in conjunction) with the evil germ; so what was good departed and the evil remained.' (3.20—22; cf. 3.26, 7.48).

As for the Christians, neither the apostolic paraenesis nor the commandments of Jesus himself were regarded by them as *giving* power to the Christians to live up to their ideals; the source of power lay elsewhere. It would have occurred to no one to blame the paraenesis or the verba Christi for ethical shortcomings. Paul is only able to make his charge, because he ascribes to the law an independent soteriological status which it probably never had in genuine Jewish thought. The question should have been: 'Why did *God* not give men before the coming of Christ power to fulfil the law, which can now (so Paul's theory) be fulfilled charismatically by the Christians?[133] It would have been natural to locate the source of man's plight in man himself, rather than in the law. No wonder that according to, e.g., Jer 31 only the human

---

'faith' and the legal commandments. Howard, *Crisis* 63 thinks that 'it must have been clear to all that faith was the very warp and woof of the law', inferring that Paul could not set them up as opposites. 'Paul would have been laughed off the scene even to have suggested a contrary notion.' Unfortunately, this seems to be wishful thinking.

131 Schechter, op.cit. 278.

132 Cf. the talk of the fruit of the Spirit in Gal 5!

133 Montefiore, *Judaism* 72 notes that, from the Jewish point of view, 'to throw the blame for human sin upon the Law ... would be like throwing the blame upon God!'

heart is expected to be transformed by God (so also Ezek 11 and 36), while nothing is expected either to be achieved by the law or happen to it during this process.[134]

4. Law and salvation in the rest of the New Testament

According to some interpreters, Jesus takes in *Mark 10.17–27*[135] a critical attitude to the law as the way to salvation[136] or 'disqualifies the path of accomplishments'[137]. In this case Mark would more or less represent the view-point (often falsely ascribed to Paul, as we have seen) that the Jewish religion consists of 'legalism'. Let us consider this claim.

A man asks Jesus what he has to do in order to inherit eternal life (v. 17). The assumption thus is that *doing* certain things leads to (eschatological) life — a reversal of Paul's contention, to be sure. It has to be emphasized that in his reply (v. 18–19, 21) Jesus does *not* decline the question as inappropriate.[138] He refers the man to the Decalogue (v. 19).[139] When the man asserts that he has observed the commandments in question from his youth (v. 20), Jesus does not object; he does not set forth any criticisms or reservations with regard to this claim. On the contrary, the gesture mentioned in v. 21 (ἠγάπησεν αὐτόν) shows that he accepts the answer.[140] Jesus, according to this passage, sees nothing wrong in the typical Jewish question 'what shall I do?'.[141] 'Works' are not criticised.[142] What man *does* is important to

---

134 See below, p. 241 f.

135 For a literary analysis of the passage see Reploh, *Markus* 191 ff.; Kuhn, *Sammlungen* 146 ff., 170 ff.

136 F.G. Lang, 'Sola gratia'.

137 Harnisch, 'Berufung' 174. Harnisch shares the traditional interpretation of Judaism as legalism and he finds in v. 21b an antithesis 'zu jenem Denken jüdischer Provenienz, der den Erwerb der ζωή αἰώνιος menschlicher Tat anheimstellt'.

138 Against Lohmeyer, *Markus* 210 and Harnisch, art.cit. 170 etc. According to Egger, *Nachfolge* 127, the answer of Jesus invalidates 'die im ἵνα-Satz (sc. v. 17b) zugrundeliegende Auffassung vom Tun um zu erben'. But the use of καί instead of ἵνα is a weak argument for the assertion. For stylistic reasons alone one could hardly expect ἵνα in the reply of Jesus in v. 21. Cf. 132: verses 21 and 29–31 replace 'die Frage nach dem "Tun, um ewiges Leben zu erben"' with a 'Verheissung für den, der tut'. Cf. 135 f. This is an oversubtle distinction. 'Doing' is a prerequisite of 'inheriting' anyhow, whatever the precise nuance.

139 The rejection of the attribute 'good' may suggest that far from setting forth a doctrine of his own, Jesus only teaches what God has revealed long ago through Moses; cf. Pesch ad loc.

140 Cf. Zimmerli, *Offenbarung* 318. Harnisch ignores the accepting gesture altogether.

141 Correctly Werner, *Einfluss* 91. Speculations to the effect that the question itself shows that the man in question is unhappy with the law or with its common interpretations (Branscomb, Grundmann, Nineham) fail to take seriously the Jewish parallel Ber 28b bar (Rabbi Elieser; Billerbeck I, 808). Nor is it suggested in the text that the man wanted to 'accomplish' something special (thus Schweizer; correctly Haen-

Jesus: his family consists of those who *do* God's will (Mk 3.35). The fault with the man in question is indeed that *he has not done enough!* 'Jesus refers in view of the man's alleged comprehensive law observance to *one* shortcoming', namely, the lack of almsgiving.[143] The demand of God's law is radicalized in v. 21, but the framework of law is not abandoned.[144]

This is not to say that salvation is, according to our passage, 'by works'; it is a question of *teshubah*, of obedience to the radically interpreted will of God. On the other hand, if one chooses to call the common Jewish view 'salvation by works' or 'a doctrine of reward' or the like, then this terminology should be applied to our passage, too. Contrary to Gal 3.21, it is assumed in the passage that the way of the law does lead unto life.[145] Mark assumes a soteriological continuity between the OT and the new situation.[146] Verses 26–27 are certainly not meant to cancel the relevance of the commandments;[147] it is to be borne in mind that the whole of Paul's decisive soteriological vocabulary is conspicuously lacking in Mark[148] and an individual statement is not, therefore, to be too quickly interpreted in a Pauline sense. Most probably verses (24)26–27 are designed to explain 'the failure of the gospel to come home to some to whom it was preached'[149] (cf. Mk 4.11 f., Rom 9.6 ff. etc.)[150].

---

chen, *Weg* 352).

142 Against Braun, *Radikalismus* II, 75 n. 1.

143 Pesch; cf. Montefiore. This view is found already in the Gospel acc. to the Hebrews, Fragm. 11.

144 Verse 21 does not stand in contrast to the Torah-centred question in v. 19; against Taylor, Nineham; Kuhn, 'Problem' 147 n. 11. There is no denying that Jesus lays down a demand for the rich man as a condition for entering the reign of God. It is doubtful to distinguish between the giving up of possessions and the call to follow Jesus, as does e.g. Harnisch, art.cit. 174: 'Die Forderung des Besitzverzichts ist ... nicht im Sinne einer ... Vorbedingung gemeint, die erst zur Nachfolge instand setzt. Sie stellt vielmehr nur die Konsequenz vor Augen, die der Nachfolger Jesu natürlicherweise (!) auf sich nimmt ... ' Cf. also Zimmerli, op.cit. 323. Such a distinction is purely theoretical. Not surprisingly, the Evangelist at least is led to think of the reward for those who give up everything (10.28–31).

145 Werner, op.cit. 93.

146 Thus no critique of the law is derived from Jesus' death on the cross. One might rather say that the saving value of that death consists 'im Loskauf von der Schuld, die man sich durch Verfehlungen gegen das Gesetz aufladet' (Werner, op.cit. 92); yet Mark refrains from any reflections on the law *qua* law.

147 Verses 26–27 are sometimes taken as representing Pauline soteriology: cf. Schweizer; Harnisch, art.cit.; F.G. Lang, art.cit. 335; Egger, op.cit. 206, 220.

148 See Werner, op.cit.

149 Best, *Following* 112.

150 I have argued that 'predestinarian' statements in the NT (and elsewhere!) are best understood as reactions to the negative social experience of the community in question (*Hardening*, esp. 79–98).

In any case, the insertion (by Mark![151]) of v. 28—31 shows that the evangelist did not at all think that salvation is something totally independent of man's activity; this is not his reading of the preceding verses 26—27. The decision to leave everything and follow Jesus is an act which brings a wonderful *reward* with it (v. 30) to *everybody* who has done so (v. 29). The spirit of Mk 10.17—31 is thoroughly Jewish throughout. If you stress God's prevenient grace in this passage, you should interpret Jewish texts in the same way; if you read Jewish texts as teaching a doctrine of works, you should not shrink from seeing the same thing here! Unlike Paul, the Markan account does not tear apart the following of Jesus and obedience to the law; only, to follow Jesus demands more than usual obedience. The passage is, however, in full consonance with that train of thought in Paul which comes to expression in Rom 2. But as regards Paul's theological theory, set forth by him in other passages, it is not wrong to say with S. Schulz that from its point of view the Gospel of Mark is 'a book of law'.[152] It *is* wrong, however, to go on by claiming that in the centre of Mark's 'doctrine of justification' (!) stands 'the pious man of accomplishment'.[153]

In *Matthew*, the law plays a much more important part than in Mark. Matthew plays down critical Markan statements, preserves ultra-conservative traditional statements about the law (5.18!) and portrays Jesus as the authoritative interpreter of the law. 'Better righteousness' than that of the scribes and Pharisees is programmatically demanded of the disciples of Jesus — as a *condition* for entering the reign of God (5.20)! All this is well-known and needs no elaboration here. It is interesting to consider Schulz's evaluation of Matthew's view of the law. He correctly notes that the antithesis of faith and works, so typical of Paul, is unknown to Matthew.[154] Faith is, on the contrary, 'obedient moral action and, unlike Paul's view, in no way contrary to the work of the law, but rather itself a work of the pious man'. The gulf between Matthew and Paul 'cannot be bridged'.[155] 'The legal-ethical thinking is in no way made dubious as the way to salvation'.[156] Matthew does not speak of Christ 'as the end of the law as the way to salvation and as a media-

---

151 Also Egger, op.cit. 192 presupposes that v. 29—31 were inserted by Mark.
152 Schulz, *Mitte* 219.
153 Ibid. According to Werner, op.cit. 93, Mark stands on the side of those 'deren Bekämpfung der ganze Galaterbrief gewidmet ist'. This goes too far, since Mark would undoubtedly have included circumcision along with the washing of vessels among the obscure Jewish rites. What can be said is that if the argument of this section is sound, neither Paul's opponents in Galatia nor the Markan Jesus presuppose that the law is the basis of salvation.
154 Schulz, op.cit. 186. For a comparison of Matthew with Paul see also Hummel, op.cit. 69 f.
155 Op.cit. 187.
156 Op.cit. 188.

tor', but rather 'against Paul of the validity of the law down to every iota and dot which is necessary for salvation'.[157] Matthew presents Christianity as a 'law religion'. He does know 'indicative material', but this indicative never succeeds in making the imperative of the law problematic as a way to salvation.[158]

Schulz's sharp critique of Matthew is beneficial in that it reveals with relentless clarity the logical consequences of the standard view that the law was the way to salvation in Judaism. If the Jew is held to be saved by law not grace, then the same is true of the Christian according to Matthew (along with most other NT writers)! If Jewish piety reflects a religion of works, then so does Matthew's. Schulz is quite correct in insisting on the necessity to apply similar standards on both sides. He is wrong, however, as I see it, in taking Paul's soteriology (understood in the Bultmannian way) as the yardstick. If we prefer Sanders' interpretation of Judaism as covenantal nomism, it is quite natural to read Matthew in the same way.[159] Both the Jewish teachers and Matthew called men to repentance and return to God and his will. Obedience and works are necessary; they can even be spoken of as a precondition of salvation (as Matthew does in 5.20); but this does not necessarily constitute 'legalism' in a bad sense.[160]

Luke follows Paul in Acts 15.1 in that this verse seems to portray the law as the way to salvation for the Jews.[161] He, however, understands the situa-

---

157 Op.cit. 183; thus also Bornkamm, 'Risen' 228.

158 Op.cit. 188.

159 Matthew inserts Jesus' commands into a book of *history* which tells of God's acting through Jesus. Jesus is portrayed as the One, whose helpful and salutary presence is time and again experienced in the congregation (cf. 1.23, 8.23 ff., 14.28 ff., 28.20, etc.). See also Przybylski, *Righteousness* 106f. (although his clearcut distinction between 'righteousness' and 'will of God' pp. 107ff. is untenable; the 'righteousness' terminology is not applied merely to 'properly religious Jews' – op.cit. 114).

160 This is well perceived by Luz, 'Gesetz' 85 who emphasizes that Matthew's theology is 'a theology of the law but not a theology of righteousness by works'. 'Matthäus kennt kein automatisches Heil ohne menschliche Gerechtigkeit. *Aber es gilt für ihn, was für das gesamte Judentum gilt:* Menschliches Handeln ist nicht gleichzusetzen mit menschlicher Leistung, aufgrund derer der Mensch bei Gott auf Gerechtigkeit pochen darf.' (My italics.) If the standard Jewish views are branded as legalism, then Matthew is a legalist, too; it is better to avoid this characterization in both cases.

161 On the historical background of Acts 15.1 see above, p. 182.

tion differently from Paul. Thus Luke lets Paul say in his speech in the Pisidian Antioch that, in Christ, every believer is justified ἀπὸ (!) πάντων ὧν οὐκ ἠδυνήθητε ἐν νόμῳ Μωϋσέως δικαιωθῆναι (Acts 13.38). The way of law and the way of faith are not opposites. Instead, faith comes in as a complement to obedience to the law, making good the lack of perfection as regards the latter.[162] There is no need to take this as an indication of 'meritorious' thinking.[163] Acts 13.38 can quite well be understood as man's humble confession of his insufficiency.

There is a similar emphasis in Acts 15.10 f. The Jewish Christians have not been able to bear the yoke of the law, but they believe that they will be saved 'through the grace of the Lord Jesus' in the same way as the Gentiles. As for Gentiles, faith replaces the way of law; as for born Jews, it seems to complete it. The genuinely Pauline contrast is altogether lacking.[164] No wonder then that Paul's position is reversed in the discussion about inheriting eternal life: τοῦτο ποίει καὶ ζήσῃ (Lk 10.28), says Jesus! Once again it turns out that it is *Paul* who is the odd man out.

Unlike Paul Luke 'does not separate *pneuma* and *nomos*, charismatic life and observance of the law' either.[165] Thus he avoids one more anomaly into which Paul has run. Even Stephen is both 'adherent to the law' and 'a charismatic-ecstatic prophet', and Paul is the charismatic Pharisee! In summary, 'the *combination* of *nomos* and *pneuma* is all-important'.[166]

As for *John*, we can, by and large, follow the account of his theology of the law by S. Pancaro. The closest equivalence to the Pauline 'works of law' is in John the 'work(s) of God' (Jn 6.28 f.). John, however, sees *faith* as such a work of God (i.e., a work expected by God), cf. also 7.17. 'Paul would avoid such language ... John draws a line of continuity where Paul draws an opposition.'[167] John 'seems to be trying to present faith as that which absorbs and surpasses the works of the Law, rather than as something radically distinct and even opposed to the "works of the Law". For Jn the Law should lead to Jesus, the "works of the Law" to faith in Jesus!'[168] 'What is attacked and condemned by Jn is a false understanding of the Law which would oppose the Law and Jesus, observance of the Law and faith in Jesus.'[169] The Jews

---

162 Harnack, *Acts* 285 f.; Vielhauer, 'Paulinism' 42. The terminology used suggests that Luke attempts to portray Paul as the 'theologian of justification' (Lindemann, *Paulus* 59.)
163 Against Schulz, op.cit. 112, 150.
164 Cf. also Löning, *Saulustradition* 168 f.
165 Jervell, 'Paul' 301 f.
166 Jervell, ibid.
167 Pancaro, *Law* 527.
168 Op.cit. 392 f. Cf. von Wahlde, 'Faith'.
169 Op.cit. 527.

err in clinging to the law as the sole revelation of God and his will and, therefore, refusing to accept Jesus.[170]

In Jn 1.17 'grace and truth' that came through Christ are juxtaposed to the 'law' given through Moses. In itself the verse is inconclusive: it is difficult to decide whether the parallelism between law on one hand and grace and truth on the other should be regarded as synthetic[171] or antithetical[172]. In the light of the gospel as a whole it becomes clear that the former interpretation is too positive as regards Moses and the law, whereas the opposite view is too negative. The Son's revelation of the Father simply by far surpasses that of Moses and thus outdates it.[173]

The Pauline contrast is lacking in *Hebrews* as well. In 10.38 f. as well as in the great treatise on faith in ch. 11 πίστις is understood as trust in God and obedience to him. Unlike Paul, the author refrains from a Christological interpretation of the πίστις of the OT examples. He also ignores the doctrine of justification by faith.[174] Hab 2.4 receives a characteristically different interpretation from that of Paul (Heb 10.38 f.), and the phrase ἡ κατὰ πίστιν δικαιοσύνη occurs in connection with Noah, denoting trust in and obedience to the divine oracle (11.7).

The law is *not* spoken of as a way of salvation which was abolished in Christ[175] nor is there any polemic against works of the law in the Pauline sense (the 'dead works' are of cultic nature, whether heathen, 6.1, or Jewish, 9.14). There is nothing surprising in this, for if ever there were documents that may justly be called 'legalist', then Hebrews with its emphatic denial of the possibility of repentance after baptism (10.26, 29) is one.

James's famous controversy with Paul's *sola fide* (2.14–26) has nothing to do with the problem of the Torah. Unlike Paul, James does not have to wrestle with the problem of the inclusion of the Gentiles. James surely fights a misunderstood Pauline thesis – whether the misunderstanding is due to him or to some ultra-Paulinist opponents.[176]

---

170 Pancaro, op.cit. 528. Pancaro thinks John is at variance with Paul in this. If, however, my analysis is correct, Paul and John move on common ground. It is only in developing his theology of the law in a more polemical direction that Paul gets into his particular dilemmas.

171 Thus e.g. R.E. Brown (John names 'the two occasions of God's demonstration of the covenant love'; *John* I, 35); cf. also Sloyan, *Christ* 117 f.

172 Thus Grässer, 'Polemik' 78 f.; Dassmann, *Stachel* 37.

173 On Jn 1.17 see esp. Pancaro, op.cit. 534 ff.; Haacker, *Stiftung* 30 ff.; Panimolle, *Dono*. It should be noted, however, that Richter, *Studien* 149 ff. has presented powerful arguments for regarding 1.14–18 as a secondary addition to the gospel.

174 Loisy, 'Épitres attribuées' 311.

175 Correctly Percy, *Probleme* 288.

176 I think it is correct to say that James fights here a 'Paul become a formula'; thus Eichholz, *Glaube* 37 f. Walker, 'Aus Werken' 191 f. is certainly wrong in denying any reference to Paul or 'Paulinism'.

According to Schulz, theology is for James 'in principle legal piety, righteousness of works and a doctrine of merits'.[177] Such a view is possible only as long as one clings to the view of Judaism as man-centred legalism. When this distorted view is given up, it is easy to realize that James simply had to misunderstand the Pauline formula about justification by faith alone.

For all his emphasis on 'works', James's 'imperative' is certainly grounded in the 'indicative'[178] — in good Jewish fashion. To apply the formula of Sanders, works belong for James in the context of 'staying in' — not perhaps in the covenant, which is not mentioned in James, but in the proper relationship to God within the congregation. Works will show whether faith stands the test (cf. 1.3, 12), as is clear from the example of Abraham (2.24). This is close enough to the actual position of Paul as regards the eschatological salvation, the differences in terminology and in the nature of the arguments notwithstanding.[179] That James had to enter this dispute with Paul is another proof that various things, even central ones, in Paul's letters were not without reason felt to be 'difficult to understand' (2 Pet 3.16); indeed, misunderstandings were unavoidable.[180]

The author of *Ephesians* speaks in the language of Paul's 'doctrine' of justification in 2.8 f., but the point of that doctrine has disappeared: the question of the Torah is no longer a live issue.[181] The readers have been saved 'by grace' and 'through faith' — 'not by works so that no one may boast'. The works declined are not, however, works of the *law*, but man's own accomplishments in general.[182] Ephesians represents indeed to some degree the idea often ascribed to Paul: man is not saved 'by works' 'in order that no one would boast' (2.9). Salvation is God's gift, it is not 'from you' (2.8). The heathen past of the readers is, however, depicted in 2.1 ff. in dark colours (cf. 4.17 ff.). It is not suggested that they were not saved by works even though they had done a lot of good works; the idea is rather that they had none, but have nevertheless been saved by God's grace. The boasting declined in v. 9 is not that of a Jew proud of his fulfilling the Torah, but rather the pride

---

177 Schulz, op.cit. 286; similarly Lindemann, *Paulus* 248 ff.; Walker, art.cit.

178 Cf. Eichholz, op.cit. 38 ff. There is a notable difference between this letter and Hebrews with its intransigent negation of a second repentance. James explicitly presupposes the possibility of repentance in Christian life: 5.15 f., 5.19 f. God is πολύσπλαγχνος and οἰκτίρμων!

179 To be sure, Paul and James could hardly have understood each other. 'Paul could surely never have tolerated James's explicit assertion that justification is *not by faith alone* ... However much one may modify the superficial contrast, a basic lack of sympathy must remain.' Laws, *James* 133.

180 Burchard, art.cit. 43 f. n. 77, admitting that James is not Paul, justly asks whether he is any more 'un-Pauline' than are, e.g., the Pastorals or Luke. I think not.

181 Vielhauer, *Geschichte* 214; cf. Gnilka, Comm 129 f.

182 Against Schlier; correctly Gnilka, op.cit. 130; Luz, 'Rechtfertigung' 374 f.

of *Gentile* Christians over against Jewish Christians.[183] The line of Rom 11.13 ff. is prolonged here, probably in a concrete situation where Gentile Christianity is getting impatient over Jewish Christians who still hold to their status quo (cf. 1 Cor 7.17).[184] Otherwise the question of Torah is no longer a live problem. There is no attack on Jewish legalism or the like. We hear nothing of the law as a way to salvation.

In the Pastoral letters, too, we find formulas about salvation by grace rather than by works that sound almost Pauline. God saved us and called us with a holy calling 'not according to our works, but according to his own plan and grace' (2 Tim 1.9). God saved us 'not by works done in righteousness which we had done but according to his mercy' (Tit 3.5). There is no longer any trace visible of the problem of the inclusion of the Gentiles. The 'works' are no longer 'works of the law' in the sense of the Mosaic demands, but good, indeed 'righteous' works in general. 'Not according to works' means here simply putting the indicative before the imperative; requiring 'good works' of the Christians is indeed a standard theme in the Pastorals. [185] Actually Tit 3.3 shows that the 'we' of 3.8 did not have 'works done in righteousness' at all in their heathen past, which is described with the aid of a vice list. We find in the Pastorals no longer any polemic against Jewish soteriology; Jews as opponents are for the author already a thing in the past (unlike the Gnosticizing Jewish Christians he is warning his readers of). On the contrary, there is a strong Jewish flavour in the author's insistence on good works as a necessity in Christian life. 'Getting in' is due to God's grace; in the context of 'staying in' the deeds are of great importance.

Our survey shows, then, that *Paul is alone* in early Christianity in setting up a contrast between the Torah with its demands on one hand and God's grace or man's faith in Christ on the other.

---

183 Fischer, *Tendenz* 79 f.
184 See Fischer, op.cit. 79 ff.
185 1 Tim 2.10, 6.18; 2 Tim 3.17; Tit 2.14, 3.1, 3.8, 3.14.

VI. Conclusions

1. The concept of 'law' (never defined) oscillates. In contexts where *nomos* clearly denotes the Torah Paul can simultaneously presuppose that Gentiles, too, have been subject to it. The contours of the *nomos* are blurred; the liberating Christ-event is much clearer than the description of the plight men were liberated from.

Paul never makes an explicit distinction between different ('moral' as against 'ritual') parts of the law, and several passages in his letters run counter to such a distinction. Nevertheless he more than once tacitly reduces the Torah to a moral law, apparently without realizing the looseness of his speech. This vagueness is shared by some other NT writers. (Ch. I).

2. Paul states in unambiguous terms that the law has been abolished. In his actual teaching he ignores it, the ritual and moral side alike.

The reasons given for the abolition of the law stand in some tension to each other: on the one hand the law was designed to hold its sway for a limited period of time at the outset, whereas death (that of Christ as well as of the Christians) is required for its dominion to be terminated on the other. In developing the latter thought Paul resorts to a confused analogy.

The abolition notwithstanding, Paul also makes positive statements which imply that the law is still valid. The claim it justly puts on men is fulfilled by Christians. Now and then Paul appeals to OT commands. Above all, he asserts that he does not cancel the law with his teaching; on the contrary, it is he who really establishes it. Apart from the tension with the abolition statements, this conservative assertion hardly manages to refute the Jewish claim that selectivity about the Torah actually means its rejection. By way of an arbitrary exegesis Paul tries to show that the law itself is on his side.

Paul did not live among Gentiles as a practising Jew. He treated the Torah as an *adiaphoron.* He did not replace it with a new 'law of the Messiah' either.

Paul apparently shares the vagueness of his 'fulfilment' assertions at least with Matthew. The tension between radical and conservative statements is paralleled in Ephesians. (Ch. II).

3. Paul implies that no one is able to fulfil the law. Gentiles and Jews are without exception under sin. This assertion is demonstrated by exaggerating blanket accusations. Nevertheless, some Gentiles actually do what the law requires. The Christians are able to fulfil, and do fulfil, the requirements of the law. In setting up this contrast between Christians and Jews, Paul comes to compare Christian life at its best with Jewish life at its worst. No other NT writer shares the notion of the unfulfillability of the law. (Ch. III).

4. While generally holding fast to the divine origin of the law, Paul once in a heated debate also suggests that it was only given by angels and is thus inferior.

The purpose of the law was a negative one: it was to increase and even bring about sin. This explanation of the origin of sin in the world of men clashes with the usual one, also given by Paul, that the dominion of sin is to be traced back to Adam's fall. Paul fails to explain why a commandment of the law necessarily incites to sin while a commandment of an apostle does not.

At some places Paul also presupposes that the law had a positive purpose as well: it was designed to lead men to life. This explanation runs counter to Paul's assertions of an exclusively negative purpose for the law. Apart from this contradiction, each of the two explanations is also problematic in itself. While the positive explanation tends to downgrade the law to God's un-successful first attempt to save humanity, the negative one logically leads to a somewhat cynical picture of God's strategy. To some extent Paul shares his difficulties in determining the purpose of the law with other Christian writers, but the tension between a positive and a negative intention is peculiar to him. No one else shares Paul's radical association of the law with sin. (Ch. IV).

5. Paul implies that the law is a rival principle of salvation, occupying in the Jewish system a place analogous to that of Christ in the new order of things. He constructs a sharp contrast between the law and the 'works of the law' on the one hand and Christ, grace, Spirit, faith and promise on the other. No other NT writer sees such a contrast between law and grace or faith. Apparently Paul misconstrues Jewish 'soteriology', ignoring the pattern of gratuity on which it was based as well as the role accorded to man's repent-ance. (Ch. V).

Paul's actual attitude to the Torah thus amounts to its abrogation. He ignores the ritual side (except as an element in missionary strategy among Jews), for which the fathers had died as martyrs. His ethics, by and large, corresponds to standard Jewish ethics; it is not, however, based on the Torah in principle. Paul selectively singles out the love command and obliges the Christian to 'examine' in new situations what the will of God is (Rom 12.2). If a Jew chooses to call Paul a renegade, he can hardly be blamed for this.

On the other hand, Paul has by no means broken all bonds that tie him to his Jewish heritage. No doubt he always considered himself a Jew, and one of the rather few true Jews at that. Now and then he makes use of the Torah as if it were still as valid as ever. It is symptomatic that he never makes any explicit distinctions within the law. His readers will receive the impression that God's revealed will is unitary; Scripture cannot be split up in diffe-rent parts, each of various value. Like other Christian writers down to the latter half of the second century, Paul never admits that he has actually rejected large parts of God's word. It is only the Gnostic Ptolemy who can afford to be explicit and outspoken in this regard. Paul is inclined to conceal his radicalism from others — and probably from himself as well.

Paul has a need to maintain that his view of the Torah actually stands in continuity with the orthodox tradition. His practice and his developed theological theory notwithstanding, he is quite capable of suggesting apologetically that the Torah is still in force, and it is the Christians and they alone who fulfil it. It is also they alone who grasp the true meaning of the Torah, namely, that it points to Christ. Thus it is really Paul, and not his opponents, who 'establishes' the law (Rom 3.31). That the content of 'law' is never defined is only natural; this vagueness is absolutely necessary for Paul's contention.

The starting point of Paul's thinking about the Torah is the Christ event, not the law. This structure of thought he fully shares with other early Christian writers. No other writer, however, is led to such radical and negative conclusions with respect to the law as Paul: the law incites man to sin and increases transgressions; the law ought to be fulfilled 100 per cent; Jews do not fulfil the law whereas the Christians do; the law was given through angels, not by God. All these negative statements are made problematic because other *Pauline* statements contradict them. *Paul's most radical conclusions about the law are thus strangely ambiguous.* There is something strained and artificial in his negativity — artificial from his *own* point of view.[1] He seems at times to argue further in the negative direction than he really intends. The same ambiguity adheres to his fundamental assertion about the Torah as the Jewish mediator of salvation.

It is tempting to see in all this the mechanism at work which is called *secondary rationalization* in depth psychological theory: 'the actual driving forces have been concealed under the pretext of some more or less plausible rational reasons'.[2] Paul has, for all practical purposes, broken with the law, and he is now concerned to put forward 'rationalizations': it is, against all appearance, *he* who really upholds the law; and insofar as this is not the case, the fault lies with the law itself. He seems to be constantly looking for arguments against the law: empirical observations,[3] legal analogies[4] etc. The very inadequacy of these arguments betrays their secondary origin. Paul's argument runs 'backwards', having the Christ event as its starting point.

These problems indicate that Paul vacillates in his theological attitude to the law. All his 'main' letters, Romans included, witness to a process of

---

1 See above, p. 107 f.

2 Cf. Niederwimmer, 'Tiefenpsychologie' 266 f. That there is 'a great deal of defense or rationalization' in Galatians was observed by Andrews, *Teaching* 37 (cf. 143).

3 See above, p. 97 ff., 110, 148 ff.

4 See above, p. 61 f., 129.

thought that has not come to an end[5]. Paul is still looking for arguments for a radical stance toward the law, while at the same time trying to maintain a more conservative outlook. The law is a *theological problem* for him, and that in a way that tends to make his handling of the issue a theological problem (and not the solution of problems!) for us. We will try to shed some more light on Paul's situation and the reasons that led to it in the final chapter. Before that, however, a brief comparison with other early Christian *overall* views of the law is carried through in order to find out what is really peculiar to Paul in this regard.

---

5 Cf. E.P. Sanders's excellent discussion of the dynamics of Paul's thought on the law in *Law* 65–86. The complexities of Paul's positions are partly to be explained as 'an organic development with a momentum towards more and more negative statements until there is a recoil in Romans 7, a recoil which produces other problems.' (76) We have approached the subject from different angles, but the findings seem to converge to a remarkable degree.

VII. Paul's view of the law compared with other early Christian conceptions

In the previous chapters of this work individual peculiarities in Paul's view of the law were compared with such analogous (or opposite) features as were found in other early Christian writers. In this chapter we will be concerned with other *overall* views of the law as far as they can be briefly outlined on the basis of the extant texts; to avoid repetitions, reference will frequently be made to the discussions included in the previous chapters. Only those conceptions which are directly accessible will be surveyed, however. Thus, no attempt will be made to compare Paul's view with that of Jesus, or with those found in the Jerusalem community around Peter or James, or with the Hellenist group around Stephen, or with that of Q. These conceptions are only accessible by way of reconstructions that are by necessity a good deal more hypothetical than for instance interpretations of the views of the Evangelists (which in themselves are hypothetical enough!). While some such hypotheses will be ventured in ch. VIII, the present chapter will only be concerned with more tangible conceptions of the law. My purpose here is to sketch these other conceptions and briefly discuss their respective consistency, clarity and possible problems, in order to discover how Paul's position comes out in such a comparison.

1. The Deuteropauline letters

It is difficult to decide to what extent *Colossians* should be discussed in this context. To be precise, it is not clear what part the Torah may have in the Colossian "philosophy" attacked by the author, nor to what extent the criticisms expressed by the author with regard to that philosophy would, in his mind, apply to the Torah as well.

> What is reasonably clear is that the author takes issue, above all in the section 2.6–23, with a syncretistic philosophy which has caused confusion among the Colossian Christians.[1] This philosophy, in which angelic 'elements of the world' seem to have played a large part, was characterized by various ceremonial and ascetic commandments and prohibitions (2.16, 22). The question of circumcision also played a part (2.11, 13). The 'traditions' on which such precepts were based are branded by the author not just as being κατὰ τὰ στοιχεῖα τοῦ κόσμου, but also as mere human inventions (2.8, 22).

---

1 See, e.g., Dibelius, *Kol* 38 ff.; Lähnemann, *Kolosserbrief* 63 ff.; Lohse, *Kol* 186 ff.; Gnilka, *Kol* 163–170.

The writer never mentions the OT *nomos* in this connection (or elsewhere, for that matter). The closest he comes to it is the mention of a promissory note (χειρόγραφον) with its precepts (τοῖς δόγμασιν; the syntactical connection is unclear), which was against 'us', but was removed and nailed to the cross by God (2.14). Perhaps this imagery, which undoubtedly comes from the Colossian mythology, should be kept apart from the question of Torah altogether.[2] Jewish ideas were in any case only *one* strand in the Colossian heresy. As the issue at Colossae was not the Torah, the writer never develops his view of the law.

On the other hand, the δόγματα criticized in Col 2 clearly overlap with Jewish purity commandments (touching certain things and eating certain foods, v. 21; eating and drinking v. 16) and Jewish calendar piety including the Sabbath observance (v. 16). Even more striking is the application of Pauline theologoumena which originally had a bearing on the Torah to the Colossian syncretism: Christ's death on the cross signals a triumph over the powers behind the χειρόγραφον with its demands (v. 15); the Christians have died to the 'elements of the world' (v. 20), which is the *reason* for their freedom from the δόγματα.

It is difficult, then, to exclude the idea of the Torah altogether from the picture. *If* the idea of freedom from the Torah through the death of Christ is implied in 2.14 f., then this liberation is seen as a paradigm for freedom from any bondage to stipulations and prohibitions – from legalism, one might say.[3] This could be seen as a prolongation of the line of thought set forth by Paul in Gal 4, where the situation of the Jews under the law and that of non-Jews under the στοιχεῖα τοῦ κόσμου(!) fuse together. We would have before us a parallel example of a vacillating use of the notion of the law.[4]

There remains some obscurity as to the origin of the δόγματα. Can they really be, in the mind of the author, mere human traditions (so 2.22)? How could this, in the mind of a Christian, apply to the Sabbath, or to all food laws (2.16)? If the stipulations are human inventions, how can they nevertheless be regarded as a 'shadow of coming things' (2.17)?[5] In fact, 2.8 says both that the Colossian philosophy is κατὰ τὴν παράδοσιν τῶν ἀνθρώπων and that it is κατὰ τὰ στοιχεῖα τοῦ κόσμου. But how

---

2 Bläser, *Gesetz* 214 f. and Lueken assume that Paul is speaking of the law; thus also Maurer, *Gesetzeslehre* 54; Percy, *Probleme* 89 f.; Hanson, *Studies* 1 ff.; cf. Burger, *Schöpfung* 109 ff. Lohmeyer, *Kol* 116 f. thought the IOU was given by man to the Devil in Paradise; against this interpretation see e.g. Lohse. The equation of the δόγματα with the Mosaic ordinances is opposed by H. Weiss, 'Law', esp. 310 f.

The question is further complicated by the likelihood that an older liturgical piece here receives comment by the author and perhaps, in addition, by a Paulinist 'glossator' (thus Burger, op.cit. 111 f., 151 f.). It is impossible to deal with these questions here.

3 Cf. Schweizer, ad loc.: the author chose the term δόγμα, 'weil die in Kolossae wichtig gewordenen Vorschriften (according to Schweizer Pythagoraean stipulations) für ihn grundsätzlich auf der gleichen Ebene liegen wie die alttestamentlichen Gebote, obwohl er beides nicht einfach gleichsetzt ... Er will alles umfassen, was an Geboten oder Vorschriften die Heilsgewissheit gefährden könnte.' Schweizer, to be sure, is more explicit than the author himself, who is rather more vague.

4 See above, p. 31 on the change of persons which parallels exactly that in Gal 3–4.

5 Percy, op.cit. 140 regards therefore 2.17a as a reference to the OT law; cf. ibid. 84. Gnilka ad loc. devalues the expression 'shadow' to mean something that has no significance, thus denying any typological value; cf. Philo, *Flacc.* 165.

can it be *both*? Stipulations coming from inimical powers are, to be sure, even harder to be regarded as a typological 'shadow' of the real thing. Finally, verses 2.14 f. seem to suggest that Christ's triumph over the principalities and powers was the reason for which the demands of the elements can safely be disregarded. But why was such a dramatic victory necessary to get rid of some human inventions? There is a contradiction here reminiscent of that between Gal 3.13 and 3.19.[6] For the author of Colossians, as for Paul, the liberation effected by God in Christ stands out as clear, whereas the plight of man tends to appear more obscure. If Colossians is not by Paul,[7] then it must be by someone very close to him and his way of thinking. In any case, Colossians shows the natural development of Pauline insights in a wider context where the Torah is no longer the central issue. The trend is toward a case against 'legalism' in general, that is, against bondage to any kind of stipulations. By contrast, there is no trace of a polemic against boasting or human merits. Before the reconciliation in Christ, the readers were enemies of God in their *evil* works (1.21).

Thus, the battle of Colossians against the local philosophy bears not a little resemblance to Paul's argument in the undisputed letters. Yet is remains an open question, whether we are entitled to speak of the author's view of the *law* at all. The Torah is not in focus in this letter,[8] which is, in addition, far too short for far-reaching conclusions. This last reservation of course applies to most of the documents surveyed in this chapter.

By contrast, the author of *Ephesians* makes an explicit reference to the νόμος τῶν ἐντολῶν ἐν δόγμασιν (2.14). This law had stood as a separating wall between Jews and Gentiles, bringing about enmity. The enemies were, however, reconciled through the death of Christ, by which the law was destroyed. The author here uses more outspoken language than Paul, in that he makes the law without reservation the object of καταργεῖν; Paul always speaks of men being 'destroyed' with respect to the law (Rom 7.6 etc.).

Otherwise, the role and function of the old law is not reflected upon. It is not possible to sketch the 'doctrine of the law' of the author. The Torah is for him no longer a live issue. The works declined are not works of the *law*, and the boasting improper to a Christian is that of the *Gentile* Christian who felt superior to the Jewish Christians.[9] Nothing is said of the law as a way to salvation, and questions of its origin or purpose are not discussed.

There is one 'Pauline' inconsistency in the letter. On the one hand the

---

6 See above, p. 59.

7 The present study aroused indeed in me the suspicion that the authenticity of Colossians may not be totally excluded after all. This possibility cannot, of course, be explored here. See the careful discussion in Lähnemann, op.cit. 177 ff. It is intriguing to speculate that Paul might have composed the letter together with one of his assistants (Epaphras? Timothy?); cf. Lähnemann, op.cit. 181 f. n. 82; Schweizer, *Kol* 20 ff.

8 Cf. H. Weiss, art.cit. 311: ' ... the Mosaic law is no longer functioning as a recognizable entity'.

9 See above, p. 197 f.

author regards the law 'of commandments and ordinances' as annulled; on the other hand, he singles out one commandment of the Decalogue as particularly important (6.2). As a whole, the letter leaves most of our questions about the law unanswered.

In the *Pastorals*, too, the material concerning the law is so scanty that anything like a systematic picture of the view of the author cannot be attempted. Nevertheless, in comparison with the authentic Paul, some significant changes appear.

The author no longer has the problem of Jews and Gentiles before his eyes. He only comes to mention the law at all for the reason that the heresy he is concerned to oppose has a Jewish flavour, even though the Jewish elements have been given a Gnosticizing interpretation.[10] Much as in Paul's genuine letters, the concept of 'law' oscillates between the Jewish Torah on one hand and a more general moral or civil law on the other.[11]

I Tim 1.8 clearly has Paul's statements in Rom 7.12 and 7.16 as its background. Yet the view of the character of the law is quite different. For the author of 1 Tim the 'law' simply guarantees the order of society by holding sinners and criminals in check; the loyal citizen, who lives in the proper way anyhow, does not really need this law. There are no signs in the Pastorals of Paul's view that the law convicts humanity of sin,[12] let alone of the views that it leads to sin or that it cannot be fulfilled.[13] Nor do we hear of any history-of-salvation role reserved for the law in God's plan.[14]

It is therefore not without some justification that scholars speak of 'a positive travesty' of Paul's teaching[15] or comment that 'a greater misunderstanding of Paul's thesis in Rom 7.12, 16 is hardly thinkable'[16]. And yet one hesitates before blaming the author very severely for his misunderstanding. On the one hand, he had before his eyes Paul's statement that the law was 'good'; on the other hand he knew that Paul elsewhere spoke critically of the same law. 1 Tim 1.8 f. may be seen as a modest attempt to strike a balance between these contradictory assertions: the law is good if used in the proper way; for the 'righteous one' there is no law (νόμος οὐ κεῖται).[17] Thus there is

---

10 On the Jewish elements in the opponents' teaching see 1 Tim 1.4 ff., Tit 1.10, 1.14 ff., 3.9.

11 See above, p. 31.

12 Against Maurer, *Gesetzeslehre* 57 who (following Schlatter) finds that 1 Tim 1 agrees with Paul's world of thought.

13 Cf. Holtzmann, *Theologie* II 296; Lindemann, *Paulus* 146.

14 Holtzmann, ibid. Holtzmann points out that, unlike Gal 3.23, it is grace that keeps us under discipline (παιδεύουσα) according to Tit 2.11 f.

15 Houlden ad loc.

16 Luz, 'Rechtfertigung' 376. Cf. also Scott, ad loc.; Lindemann, op.cit. 136, 145; Aleith, *Paulusverständnis* 16.

17 Cf. Lindemann, op.cit. 145.

no need to speak of an end of the law. Unlike Paul, the author does not say that the righteous man has died to the law or anything like that; obviously, the law was not designed to have any significance for him at all (whereby 'righteous', of course, has a different meaning from that found in Paul).

No doubt Paul's powerful assertions about the law have been drastically domesticated in the Pastorals. The dramatic theological dimension is gone. In whatever way one wishes to evaluate this, it should be noted that the author has let go precisely those aspects in Paul's view that were shown to be the most artificial ones. In being silent on, e.g., the sin-engendering character of the law, the author simply shows his common sense. No contrast is set up between God's grace and the works of the law.[18] The inclusion of Gentiles is no longer a problem, it is a well-established fact. Paul's slogan 'everything is pure' has been given a new anti-heretical interpretation: 'he who sets up requirements of purity is himself impure' (Tit 1.13–16).[19] The Christian's freedom from ritual (and ascetic) stipulations is a self-evident assumption of the author.

One would like to know more about the author's view of the law. How did he think of its origin and purpose? What function, if any, did he ascribe to the ritual commandments found in the OT? Were they to be understood allegorically (cf. 1 Tim 5.18)? What was included in the 'commandments of men' (Tit 1.14)? One suspects that he would not have had satisfactory answers to such questions. What he does say about the law is certainly lacking in theological intensity, most of all in comparison with Paul, but it is also free of the many Pauline *sic et nons*. Obviously, the authentic Pauline statements just could not be handed over without thorough modifications.

2. Other letters

In *Hebrews* the law is seen from the cultic point of view as the basis of priesthood and sacrifices. The high-priestly sacrifice of Christ has superseded the old covenant with its sacrifices; they have been rendered superfluous. When priesthood changes, a 'change of law' is also necessary (7.12). The priesthood of Christ has brought about the abolition ($\dot{a}\vartheta\acute{\epsilon}\tau\eta\sigma\iota\varsigma$) of the previous 'commandment' (7.18). The old law was 'weak' and 'useless' (7.18); it did not make anything perfect (7.19, cf. 9.9). The law was 'fleshly' ($\sigma\acute{a}\rho\kappa\iota\nu o\varsigma$), which means that it was concerned with external matters[20] (7.16; cf. 7.28, 8.2) and brought about 'purity of flesh' alone (9.13). Besides the sacrifices, 'foods, drinks and ablutions' are singled out as merely fleshly ordinances ($\delta\iota\kappa\alpha\iota\acute{\omega}\mu\alpha\tau\alpha\ \sigma\alpha\rho\kappa\acute{o}\varsigma$) which only belong to the period before the

---

18 See above, p. 198.
19 Lindemann, op.cit. 141; cf. Dibelius-Conzelmann.
20 On the use of the word $\sigma\acute{a}\rho\kappa\iota\nu o\varsigma$ in Hebrews see Michel ad loc.

'reformation' (9.10).[21] Such things amount to 'dead works' (9.14). The law is replaced by the 'word of oath' that came *after* the law' (7.28). Interestingly enough, the 'chronological' argument of Hebrews reverses that of Paul in Gal 3.17[22], being no doubt the more natural one in terms of legal practice[23].

The law was closely connected with the old *covenant*, which God declared antiquated by establishing the new one (8.13, cf. 10.9). This was not a merely arbitrary stipulation, for the old covenant had grown old and was senile, and its disappearance was thus impending (8.13). The new covenant was 'better' in nature (7.22, 8.6). The old covenant was not 'blameless' (8.7); had it been, or had it been able to bring about perfection (7.11), then no new covenant would have been needed. The argument here parallels Gal 3.21. The law was a mere 'shadow of coming good things', not containing the real substance of things (10.1, cf. 8.5, 9.9, 9.23 f.).

Thus the basic conception of law in Hebrews stands out as very clear. In the death of Christ God has abolished the OT law which was weak and useless anyhow. This is an even more radical stance than Paul's. 'The only positive value of the old covenant consists paradoxically in the fact that it is surpassed and assimilated by the new one and thus through its own inefficiency indirectly witnesses to the power of the new covenant.'[24] Nevertheless, the OT text is cited as God's word to the Christians by the writer; the abolition

---

21 Whether 13.9 also refers to the OT food laws is controversial.

22 Cf. Gyllenberg ad loc.

23 Cf. also the author's insistence on the necessity of the death of the testator for the validity of a διαθήκη (9.16 f.) in contrast to Paul's vague use of the testament analogy in Gal 3.15 ff. (see above, p. 129.)

24 Luz, 'Bund' 332; cf. Lindemann, *Paulus* 237: 'es gibt hier keine Analogie, sondern einen qualitativen Umschlag'. This seems to be the correct view over against the idea that the old covenant was a genuine if imperfect analogy of the new one, a 'Vorform' of it; thus v. Campenhausen, *Bibel* 83 f.; Aleith, *Paulusverständnis* 8; Dassmann, *Stachel* 62. Dassmann speaks of a 'verheissende(n) 'evangelische(n)' Sinn' of the OT, asserting that 'wo Paulus noch echte Gegensätze gesehen hatte, kann der Hebräer-brief auf Analogien hinweisen'. As for the 'promise', however, it is the *new* covenant that has the character of a promise, having indeed the 'better promises' (8.6, 9.15). In view of the talk of the 'fleshly' character of the OT law and of the 'dead works' it leads to, the idea of analogy must not be interpreted in too positive a way. With such statements in mind one can hardly concur with Spicq, Comm. I 150 f. when he maintains that a pious Jew could not have taken offence at the theology of law in Hebrews. Correctly also Stylianopoulos, *Justin* 87 f.: in comparison with Paul, Hebrews 'is more firm about the inefficacy, even the intrinsic weakness of the law'. Differently Zimmermann, *Bekenntnis* 41–43, who senses a tension between texts like 7.11–25, 8.8–12 on one hand, and 5.1–4, 9.1–10ab on the other. The former passages construe an antithesis between the priesthood of Christ and that of the OT; the latter ones assume more an analogy. Zimmermann proposes a redaction-critical interpretation: the more radical passages represent tradition, whereas the author himself moves on the analogical line.

of the old covenant does not mean that the OT ceases to be God's word or speech of the Holy Spirit (9.8, 10.15).[25] Like Paul, Hebrews combines the assertion of the end of the law with a belief in its predictive or prefigurative function.

What is the relation of the view of the law in Hebrews to that of Paul? Schulz maintains: 'The law is in a quite un-Pauline way related only to the weak and useless law of cultic sacrifices and of priesthood ... '[26] There is indeed a clear difference here. In Hebrews, just the cultic side of the law is criticized – which Paul consistently *avoids* doing.[27] Both characterize the law as 'weak' (Heb 7.18, Rom 8.3). Yet the statements cannot be harmonized. Hebrews presents a rational criticism of the cult law: it is (self-evidently – by nature, as it were!) impossible that the blood of bulls and goats could take away sins (10.4). Such a law is 'fleshly' (7.16). Paul, however, claims that the law is *spiritual* (Rom 7.14) – a statement which would be impossible in Hebrews – and suggests that the weakness results from the encounter of the spiritual law with the fleshly man. In Hebrews, the inferiority of the law has nothing to do with man's condition. The author of Hebrews mounts a direct attack on the cultic law. If my reading is correct, a similar critique of the cultic law is also the actual starting-point of Paul; Paul, however, never spells this out and is just therefore compelled to develop his idiosyncratic criticisms of the law.

These *Pauline* criticisms are conspicuously lacking in Hebrews. The law is not associated with sin and death.[28] It is not said to be given 'because of transgressions', but as a pale shadow of what was to come, nor is its origin with God put in doubt (the angels, mentioned in 2.2, enhance the significance of the law, unlike Gal 3.19). There is no talk of the law as a misconceived way of salvation.[29]

It can be added that Paul and Hebrews display a similar structure of argument in that both take their stance with Christ and assess the previous period from this point of view (cf. e.g. Heb 10.11 and Gal 2.21). Hebrews, however, is more consistent in its thought and also less extravagant in its criticisms than is Paul.[30]

---

25 Cf. Luz, art cit. 333 f.

26 Schulz, *Mitte* 262.

27 See above, p. 23 ff.

28 Correctly Loisy, 'Épitres attribuées.' 311; D'Angelo, *Moses* 204 f. Cf. Windisch on 7.19.

29 See above, p. 196.

30 Cf. Loisy, art.cit. 315: the lack of foundation in the view of law (the assumption of the intrinsic weakness of the law) notwithstanding, 'l'idée en sa construction logique et même en son élaboration exégétique a quelque chose de plus régulier que la théorie de Paul et elle ne défie pas le bon sens dans sa psychologie ni dans la place qu'elle attribue à la Loi'.

One minor and one major problem remain, however. The minor problem is the question of what has happened to the moral content of the OT law in the mind of the author of Hebrews. This we do not learn.[31]

The major problem is connected with the assumptions of the writer.[32] Why did God give a weak, useless and 'fleshly' law? Why was the old covenant in itself 'blameful'? The Christian apriori of the author leads him to an insoluble problem of theodicy. This, however, he shares with Paul.

The author of Hebrews, then, has produced a solution which is beset with much fewer difficulties than Paul's. One has, of course, to take into account that he apparently did not have to wrestle with any such existential and practical problems as Paul had as regards the Torah. The letter reflects no dispute with actual Jews. The opposition between Jewish and Gentile Christians is lacking; the reasoning is 'purely academic'.[33] As the Torah is no existential problem to the author, he can afford a cool and logical solution. This privilege was not available to Paul in his different situation.

The references to the law in the letter of *James* are far too scanty to allow us to draw anything like a full picture of his conception of the law.[34] Rough outlines can nevertheless be detected. There is no dispute over the Jewish Torah whatsoever in the letter; 'the battle of the significance of the law has long since become a matter of the past'.[35] There is absolutely no trace of the Jewish-Gentile problem.[36] Thus the framework of James is quite different from that of Paul.

Everything James says about the *nomos* is absolutely positive; there are no traces of a negative criticism of the law. James speaks of a 'perfect law of liberty' (1.25, cf. 2.12)[37] and of a 'royal' law (2.8). The law of liberty leads man to true freedom.[38] This royal law is 'in accordance with the Scripture';

---

31 See above, p. 30.

32 See above, p. 155.

33 Vielhauer, *Geschichte* 247 f.

34 James probably could have said a lot more about the law had he wished to do so. Although the letter has first and foremost a paraenetic character, the common view that the writer merely sets forth an 'ethos' and has hardly a 'theology' at all needs some revision. See the attempts of Luck, 'Jakobusbrief' und Hoppe, *Hintergrund* to locate James in the neighbourhood of Jewish Wisdom theology.

35 Vielhauer, *Geschichte* 575; cf. Seitz, 'James', esp. 484.

36 This is one of the many indications that James the brother of the Lord cannot be the author. Laws, *James* 37 f. makes a good case that the author is a former 'God-fearer'. She also notes (92, on 1.27) that 'James's language is neither Jewish nor anti-Jewish; that is not the issue'.

37 The expression has nothing to do with the phrase *ḥq ḥrwt* found in 1 QS 10.6, 8, 11, where one has to read *ḥoq ḥārūt*, 'engraved ordinance' rather than *ḥērūt*, 'liberty'. See the discussion in Fabris, *Legge* 103–113.

38 Cf. Lührmann, *Glaube* 80, who notes a contrast with Paul's view (the law brings about enslavement, not freedom!) ; Luz, 'Gesetz' 134.

the love command (Lev 19.18) and two commandments of the Decalogue are cited (2.8, 11) to lend force to the writer's paraenesis. God is referred to as the law-giver (4.12); therefore one is not to oppose the law (4.11). In all this, James suggests in the mind of the reader that the old law is being spoken of, and indeed it is. The OT law, however, tacitly fuses together with the norms of the Christian life.[39] The law can be summed up in the love commandment (2.8)[40] as in Paul and in the Gospels.[41] In his vague portayal of *nomos* James thus closely resembles Paul.

Undoubtedly, James assumes a continuity between the old law and the new one. His words suggest even an identity[42]; one would like to know whether he acknowledged the actual differences and how he would have explained them — what was his view of the purpose of the ritual law, for example? — but such issues are not under discussion in his letter, which is concerned with purely inner-Christian questions. It should be noted, too, that he does not consider the law as unfulfillable; on the contrary, he vigorously incites his readers to fulfil it.

The controversy with a misunderstood Paul (2.14—26) has nothing to do with the problem of the Torah.[43] It would seem that James was *bound* to misunderstand Paul's statement about the exclusion of works, if this statement resulted from a Pauline distortion of the authentic Jewish attitude. James is not 'legalistic' in any pejorative sense of the word. For all his emphasis on 'works', his 'imperative' is certainly grounded in the 'indicative' — in

---

39 See above, p. 31 f.
40 Cf. Luck, art.cit. 169 n. 29; Hoppe, op.cit. 89. It is, to be sure, commonly assumed that for James, curiously enough, the love commandment is just one commandment among others (the 'one' commandment transgressed, which is referred to in 2.10). As I read it, the 'one' commandment of 2.10 is the $\pi\rho o\sigma\omega\pi o\lambda\eta\mu\psi la$, expressly mentioned in 2.9, which refers back to 2.1. Whoever transgresses this one demand of the law is guilty of transgressing the 'whole' law, that is the whole 'royal' law characterized in 2.8 through the citation of the love command. To be sure, it would be hard to point out a specific commandment of the OT law which could be said to prohibit $\pi\rho o\sigma\omega\pi o\lambda\eta\mu\psi la$; yet James seems to assume as a matter of course that it is something contrary to the 'law'.
41 Whether James regards Jesus as the authoritative interpreter of the law who summarized it in the love command, or even gave a new law, is not clear. A new law of Christ is assumed by Dibelius (on 1.25); Mitton ad loc.; Fabris, op.cit. 55 ff. 133 etc. In any case James does not say that the Lord has 'changed, interpreted or even confirmed' the old law; correctly Burchard, 'Jakobus 2, 14—26' 29. Be this as it may, it is certainly far-fetched to look to Jer 31 as the background of James' talk of the 'law of liberty'; thus, e.g., Mitton, and Fabris, op.cit. 149.
42 Unless Mussner, *Jak* 107 is correct in the suggestion that the expression 'perfect law' (1.25) refers to the law fulfilled by Jesus (Mt 5.17), which implies that the old law was imperfect. It is, however, quite plausible to take the verse as a reference to the capacity of the law to help man to perfection and freedom.
43 See above, p. 196.

good Jewish fashion. James' view of the law shares some of Paul's ambiguity, but, ignoring precisely those aspects of Paul's view that have proved artificial, it stands out as relatively clear.

The striking absence of problems connected with the law in the rest of the NT letters deserves to be pointed out at this juncture. So, for all the indubitable 'Paulinism' of *1 Peter*[44] , questions of law never turn up in that letter (addressed, among others, to the congregations in Galatia!)[45] which represents a sober ethics of good works and mutual love. *2 Peter* and *Jude* attack a libertinist heresy, but do not resort to appeal to the authority of the law in that connection.[46] In the *Johannine* letters there is much talk about the 'commandments' of Christ, but the law is never mentioned. The commandments of Christ are comprised in the love command (1 Jn 3.23). *God's* commandments are mentioned in 1 Jn 5.2 f., but the writer does not have the old law in mind even here.

3. The Gospels, Acts, Revelation

Long ago, Martin Werner showed convincingly that *Mark's* is not a particularly 'Pauline' gospel.[47] The problem of justification in the Pauline sense is never touched,[48] and the word *nomos* is altogether lacking in Mark.[49] Instead, 'commandments' (ἐντολή) are mentioned and discussed a few times.

In the gospel an implicit distinction is made between ritual stipulations and God's ethical will.[50] Like Paul, Mark never points out that this actually means abandoning parts of God's written law. A passage like Mark 7.15 ff. runs, of course, counter to important sections of that law. Mark, however, never sets forth either his editorial comments on Jewish customs or Jesus' critical remarks as a critique of the *Torah*. In some sections, on the other hand, he places great emphasis on the *continuity* between the best Jewish tradition and the teaching of Jesus.

---

44 It is intriguing to speculate how many of the ideas of the letter actually go back to Silas-Silvanus (5.12).

45 The reference to the liberation of the (Gentile Christian) readers from their 'futile walk, inherited from the fathers' (1.18) refers to thraldom under idols, not the Jewish halakah. 2.5, 9 shows how the ideas of sacrifice and priesthood are spiritualized. Problems of Torah are simply ignored.

46 Only the words of the prophets and the command of the Lord mediated through the apostles are mentioned in 2 Pet 3.2; cf. the characterization of the word of the Lord as the 'holy commandment handed over to them' in 2.21.

47 Werner, *Einfluss*. Cf. now also Romaniuk, 'Problème'; Lindemann, *Paulus* 151 ff.

48 The words δικαιοῦν and δικαιοσύνη are lacking in Mark, as are ἐπαγγελία and χάρις. Cf. Werner, op.cit. 79, 207 f.

49 For a comparison as regards the law see Werner, op.cit. 79–98. By contrast, νόμος occurs 75 times in Romans alone. Mark does not use the word even in 12.28–34; in the respective parallel passages it is introduced by both Matthew and Luke.

50 See above, p. 29.

In all this, Mark shares a characteristic anomaly of Paul. On the one hand he suggests that Jesus brings the intentions of the old religion to completion; on the other hand he ignores the material conflict between some sayings of Jesus and the actual contents of the Torah.

In 10.2–9 the Marcan Jesus confronts a stipulation of Moses with the divine order of creation, but in 7.10 Moses is appealed to against the Pharisees.[51] The role of the Mosaic legislation remains unclarified. We get no clear picture of its origin or intention.

That certain commandments of the law are valid and fulfillable is presupposed.[52] Moreover, the good Jewish question 'what shall I *do* to inherit eternal life' is *accepted* by Jesus as a valid question.[53] Mark does not tear apart faith and works in the Pauline way.

The gospel of Mark is thus free from most of the Pauline anomalies though not from all. It would seem that it is above all the ceremonial law that has been abrogated and, in addition, the too lenient stipulation concerning divorce. Mark's Jesus advocates a human and rational interpretation of the law, rejecting expressly only the superstitious traditions of the Jews (invented by men) and at least devaluing the non-rational sacrifices. What exactly was God's original purpose with the law, and what were its actual contents, we are not told. But this unclarity Mark largely shares with Paul. As a whole, the picture presented by him contains fewer difficulties than that painted by Paul.

Unlike Mark, *Matthew* shows a vital interest in the question of the law.[54] Some of his traditions emphasize the permanent validity and immutability of the law. On the other hand, Matthew views the law critically in the light of its kernel, the dual commandment of love. The law and the prophets can be summarized in the Golden Rule. Through the antitheses of the Sermon on the Mount (5.21–48) certain commandments of the Torah are radicalized and internalized, but some of the antitheses run counter to the Torah itself. How Matthew himself understood these antitheses is difficult to make out. Matthew's intention is evident in 5.17. Jesus did not come to abrogate the law (and the prophets), but to fulfil them.

It is not clear whether Matthew shares Paul's dilemma when the apostle claims to establish the law (Rom 3.31) while actually doing away with most

---

51 See above, p. 84 f.
52 See above, p. 119.
53 See above, p. 191 f.
54 For Matthew's understanding of the law see especially G. Barth, *Gesetzesverständnis*; Hübner, *Tradition* 196 ff.; Meier, *Law*; Luz, 'Gesetz' 79 ff.; Simonsen, 'Auffassung'; Broer, *Freihet*. Sigal's informative and stimulating study (*Halakhah*) is vitiated by his (conscious) refusal to distinguish between the Matthaean and the historical Jesus (partly due to his subscription to Matthaean priority).

of its contents. It is, namely, controversial whether or not Matthew thought
the ritual law to have been abrogated by Jesus.

Like Mark, Matthew shows no acquaintance with the Pauline antithesis
between works of law and faith in Christ. It is not wrong to speak of Christianity according to Matthew as a 'law religion', but this is certainly not 'legalism' in any pejorative sense.[55] Matthew differs from Paul just on those
points where Paul's view turned out to be artificial: the law can be fulfilled
(as can the 'new' law); sin is transgression of the law; the law has nothing to
do with sin.[56]

All told, Matthew is not very much interested in the law in itself. For him,
Christ has taken the place of the law in the new system. The words, teachings
and commandments of *Jesus* are the most important thing (28.16–20),
and special emphasis is put on the demand that the followers of Jesus have to
realize these words in their life (5.20, 7.15 ff., 25.31 ff.).[57] The teaching of
Jesus is, however, in harmony and continuity with the old law.[58] Matthew's
view parallels that of Paul in that the Torah's actual loss of significance is a
consequence of Christology.[59]

Luke has a conservative view of the law.[60] He does not reduce the permanently valid law to a moral law.[61] On the contrary, he is most concerned

---

55 See above, p. 193 f.

56 It is pointless to blame Matthew for not characterizing the law as the power of sin in
the Pauline way – the problem lies with Paul! Against Schulz, op.cit. 183; Luz,
'Erfüllung' 435 (he wishes to grant to Paul 'greater consistency and depth'); cf. id.,
'Gesetz' 86.

57 It has been assumed that 7.15–23 (see esp. v. 22) reveals that Matthew is fighting
against antinomian libertinists; thus Barth, op.cit. 149 ff.; Bornkamm, 'Risen' 215 f.;
Hummel, *Auseinandersetzung* 64 ff. To infer this from the use of ἀνομία in 7.23,
24.12 (cf. Barth, op.cit. 58, 69) is, however, a semantic mistake. The semantic
antonym of ἀνομία is not νόμος, but δικαιοσύνη; ἀνομία is synonymous with ἀμαρτία
(cf. Mt 23.28, Rom 6.19, 4.7, 2 Cor 6.14, Heb 1.9, 10.17, 1 Jn 3.4). Matthew is criticizing some group of pneumatics whose life does not, in his mind, show a good fruit;
the problem of Torah is not in focus. Correctly in this regard Walker, op.cit. 134 f.,
137; Meier, op.cit. 66 n. 61; Strecker, Weg 137 f. n. 4.

58 Barth, op.cit. 148.

59 Meier, op.cit. 88 f.; Luz, 'Erfüllung' 433; Simonsen, art.cit. 67.

60 Jervell, *Luke* 141 claims, with reference to Harnack, Acts 284 ff., that Luke's view is
the most conservative in the whole NT. Jervell sees the reason for Luke's conservatism in his ecclesiology. He tries to refute the standard notion of the church as the
new Israel in Luke: 'Luke knows only one Israel, one people of God, one covenant.'
(Ibid.) Jervell's view of Luke's ecclesiology has met with criticism; see, e.g., Eltester,
'Israel' 122 ff.; Wilson, *Gentiles* 220 ff.; Conzelmann, 'Literaturbericht' 43 f.; a more
positive assessment is found in Dahl, *Jesus* 94 ff. But many of Jervell's observations
on the law can stand even if his interpretation of them is rejected; cf. the acknow-
ledgement by Dahl, op.cit. 94. Jervell is followed by Sloyan, *Christ* 56 ff.

61 See above, p. 30.

about its ritual aspects. The Lukan Jesus does not criticize the law at all.[62] The charges against Stephen were *false,* and Paul is a Torah-abiding Pharisee. The law was given through angels (Acts 7.53, cf. 7.38), but this merely enhances its value.[63] The law consists of 'living words' which will remain valid forever.

The law was replaced by the Apostolic Decree as regards *Gentile* Christians. This decision was made because of God's clear guidance, in accordance with the words of the prophets. For Jewish Christians the law remains fully in force. Luke considers the law of Moses as a way to salvation for Jews; Paul's way of presenting things is still reflected here. The path of law and the path of faith are no opposites, however: faith makes up what is lacking in one's 'righteousness' so far.[64] Moreover, Luke is concerned to connect charismatic life and observance of the law in his portrait of the early church, Stephen and Paul.

We do find some mildly critical remarks on the law, to be sure (Acts 13.38, 15.10).[65] Surely Jervell is correct in commenting that 'the idea is obviously not that it is in principle impossible to keep the law', for this idea 'would make all other Lukan statements inconceivable'.[66] Yet his own explanation 'that we, that is, Jews and Christian Jews, have so far not kept the law'[67] contradicts the 'other Lukan statements' just as bluntly. Consider e.g. those passages where a picture of blameless Torah piety is painted both of the Jerusalem congregation and of their predecessors (Lk 1.6!). An anomaly remains. Another problem is: how can God-given 'living words'(Acts 7.38) be such a burden?

Jervell glosses over Acts 13.38 and 15.10 as mere 'reminiscences and echoes from tradition'.[68] This seems too easy a way out.[69] In fact, Jervell himself gives in another connection a better explanation. Acts contains 'a few statements that may be interpreted as reflecting a critical attitude toward the law'; the point is, however, that such statements come from Peter and James, not from Paul! 'What Paul says is actually far less critical than what Peter

---

62 See above, p. 91 f.

63 It is wrong to speak of a 'low view of the law and its institutions' in Luke-Acts; thus D'Angelo, *Moses* 257.

64 See above, p. 195.

65 For a detailed treatment of Acts 15.10 see Nolland, 'Look'.

66 Jervell, *Luke* 151 n. 55.

67 Ibid. The conclusion of the sentence is misleading: 'something which the history of Israel demonstrates (Acts 7, 53)'. Certainly Peter does not think of himself and his fellow Christians as permanent opponents of the Holy Spirit (thus Stephen on the Jews in 7.53)! It is a question of the ceremonial law; the 'burden' of the Gentiles will not be lightened with regard to the moral law.

68 Jervell, op.cit. 146.

69 Cf. Hartman's review (191).

and James have said. Since the faithfulness of these two towards Israel can not be doubted, Luke expects the readers to make the same inference about Paul.'[70] Since Luke and his readers know the faithfulness to the law of the historical James, Luke 'can attribute to him certain daring viewpoints' in order to defend Paul.[71]

Thus Luke is aware of some criticisms of the law made by Christians. In a tactically skilful way he puts the criticisms which he cannot avoid recording into the mouth of the acknowledged pillars of orthodoxy, whereas Paul is portrayed as an ultra-conservative Christian Pharisee. As Acts 21.20 ff. shows, Luke knew full well that Paul had been (and was, still in Luke's days, in some circles) suspect of apostasy from the law. He is at pains to exonerate Paul by showing that whatever criticisms of law there were, they were of a mild nature and were set forth by those known to be fully orthodox. In Luke's presentation Paul (like Stephen!) is actually far more conservative than Peter or James.[72] Thus Luke is bound to report some remarks on the heaviness of the law in order to be able to suggest *some* reason for the undeniable questioning of the law that had taken place among the Christians.

For all his tendency towards harmonizing the actual conflict, even Luke is thus not able to present a synthesis which is free from all contradictions. The tension between 'living words' and a 'heavy yoke' remains, as does the difficulty that the law from which not a single dot will disappear is nevertheless, from the Gentile point of view, a preliminary and inferior form of revelation. This suggests that Luke did not reflect very much on the purpose and nature of the law. On the whole, however, his conception is relatively clear. He does not oscillate between different concepts of law, nor does he distinguish between ritual and moral aspects. Both sides of the law are permanently valid. Instead, a distinction is made between different classes of people. *Jewish* Christians continue to observe the whole law; *Gentile* Christians observe the minimum law defined by the apostolic decree. On this basis it might have been possible at least to attempt a dialogue with the Judaizers of Galatia. Even though there would have been no final agreement, it might have been possible to find a common language and to agree on what the real problems were.

Luke's theory is thus not without merits. It is a bold attempt to show what Paul and the others *ought* to have taught about the law! For all his distortion of the historical conflict over the law, Luke's account serves to underline that it is Paul who is the odd man out in early Christianity. It is

---

70 Jervell, op.cit. 198.

71 Op.cit. 199.

72 Cf. Maurer, *Gesetzeslehre* 59: 'In der Ag. ist Petrus paulinischer als Paulus. Paulus wird eher mit den Eigenschaften des Petrus, wie sich dieser nach Gal. 2 darstellt, geschildert.'

doubtful, however, whether a Jew could reasonably have been expected to admit that the substitution of the apostolic decree (that is, the Noachian commandments) for the Torah as regards proselytes was well-founded. Quite reasonably, he would have regarded the extreme trust in the guidance of the Spirit on the part of the apostles as misguided enthusiasm. But surely he would have found this Lukan suggestion preferable to Paul's negative assertions about the Torah.

John has taken his stance beyond the framework of the law.[73] He lets Jesus speak to the Jews of 'your' law (7.19, 8.17, 10.34, cf. 7.22) and himself comments on 'their' law (15.25), thus dissociating himself from the law. The law was given through Moses, but it was superseded by the revelation of grace and truth in Christ (1.17).[74] The Christians have outgrown the Jewish religion (4.20 ff.).[75] Nevertheless, John is not indifferent to the law[76], nor does he take a strictly negative attitude to it.[77]

Pancaro has argued that in the background of the gospel lurks an intensive dispute with Jews;[78] indeed this must be one of the formative factors in the process that led to the production of the fourth gospel[79], even though the process seems to be over by the time of the final composition. John's presentation has little to do with real-life disputes with empirical Jews; the 'Jews' have become a mere foil against which the community is edified through its consciousness of possessing the key to understanding – the faith.[80] Against this background John argues that the Christians are the true Jews[81] or, rather, he presupposes this as self-evident.

The question of the right interpretation of the law is an important thread that runs through the gospel. Jesus' Jewish opponents appeal to the law and wish to reject Jesus precisely as disciples of Moses (9.28). Only the ignorant *am-ha-ares* that does not know the law runs after Jesus (7.49). The Jews believe that their law requires Jesus to be put to death because of his Christological claim (19.7).[82] John tries to show that the testimony of the law is on the side of the Christians. Moses will accuse the Jews, for if they really

---

73 See the thorough work of Pancaro, *Law.*
74 See above, p. 196.
75 Cf. Becker, *Joh* 84, 174 ff.
76 Thus v. Campenhausen, *Bibel* 65.
77 Thus Dassmann, *Stachel* 37 f.
78 Pancaro, op.cit. passim; see the summary pp. 530 ff.
79 Cf. also Dodd, *Interpretation* 75 ff.; Schulz, *Joh* 127.
80 Luz, 'Gesetz' 125 f.
81 Pancaro, op.cit. 531 f.
82 Dassmann confuses the evangelist's view of the law with his portrayal of its misunderstanding on the part of the Jews, when he writes (op.cit. 38) on 19.7: 'Geradezu Absurdität offenbart das Gesetz, wenn es zur Legitimierung der Verurteilung Jesu herangezogen wird ... '

believed him, they would believe in Jesus, for Moses wrote about Jesus
(5.45—47 etc.). Jesus blames his opponents for not 'doing the law' themselves
(7.19). Jesus' breaking of the Sabbath (ch. 5) was not against the intentions
of the law (7.21—23).

John can take a relatively positive attitude to the law, since he stresses
exclusively its *predictive* function. This is its only purpose after the revelation of Jesus has taken place. John does not speak of Jesus as the fulfilment
of the law. From the point of view of the Christians, the law is definitely a
thing of the past. Only the words of Jesus have an imperishable value, first of
all the new commandment of (fraternal) love. Thus John shows an even
greater freedom with regard to the law than does Paul. While being free from
the law, John does not construe the law as the opposite of the gospel or of
grace.[83] In John, continuity prevails. The Jews are slaves of sin (8.30—36),
but this can in no way be ascribed to the law. The Jews err in clinging to the
Law as the sole revelation of God and his will and, therefore, refusing to
accept Jesus.

As a whole, John's conception of the law is much clearer and much more
consistent than Paul's. There is no oscillation in the concept of the law which
means the Torah[84]: it is not claimed that the Christians fulfil the law.[85] The
law has been superseded; there is no 'Yes and No'. On the other hand, the law
is not denigrated. The only problems inherent in his view John shares with
Paul and other early Christians. He is not interested in the question why
God gave through Moses such a law as he did;[86] but perhaps he thinks that
it had served quite well as a revelation of God's will in the period before
Christ. The fundamental assumption that the law predicts Christ and witnesses to him is, of course, quite arbitrary; but this arbitrariness John fully
shares with early Christianity as a whole. Given this premise, the Johannine
conception is probably the clearest within the New Testament.

In the book of *Revelation*, 'works' are emphatically demanded of the
Christian. It is repeatedly stressed that everybody will be judged according to
his deeds (2.23, 20.12 f., 22.12), and the shining clean robe of the bride of

---

83 See above, p. 195 f.

84 Except in some places (10.34, 15.25) where the meaning is 'Scripture'.

85 Pancaro, op.cit. 530 f. thinks that the Johannine community nevertheless observed
the Torah, differing from their non-Christian Jewish brethren in their faith in Jesus
and, consequently, in their attitude to the law: while following the law, they did not
'agree that their relationship to God is determined by their relationship to the law'
(530). This sounds abstract and modern. Does observance of the law really fit in with
the Johannine distance from it ('your' and 'their' law)? Luz, art.cit. 155 n. 200 is
justified in his sharp rejection of Pancaro's thesis. Moreover, unlike most NT writers,
John does *not* pay any lip service to the notion of the Christians' fulfilment of the
Torah. *His* theory is not undermined by actual non-observance!

86 Luz, art.cit. 128 points out that John's Revealer renews all values in so radical a way
that the whole OT history fades altogether.

the Lamb is identical with the righteous works of the saints (19.8). On the other hand, the 'indicative' is not forgotten either, as is shown by the frequent mention of the death of the Lamb who has thus 'purchased' the believers (1.5, 5.9, 7.14, 13.8, 14.3 f.). Thus the soteriology of Revelation corresponds to the normal Jewish pattern: entrance into the community of saints is through a divine act (in this case, the slaying of the Lamb), whereas 'staying in' and consequently the reward of eternal life is tied to proper works. There is no sign of the Pauline conflict between faith and works of law. The law is not spoken of at all; authority belongs to the words of Christ (3.8, 10; they can also be called his 'works', 2.26). There is a general reference to keeping God's commandments in 12.17, 14.12. The only reflection of the old conflict over the law is found in the letter to the congregation of Thyatira, in which the eating of meat offered to idols is regarded as a severe sin (2.20). Those in Thyatira who have not fallen into this sin are promised that no further 'burden' (βάρος) will be put upon them (2.24 f.). The wording recalls the Apostolic Decree, cf. especially Acts 15.28.[87] Revelation shares with Acts the notion that the Jewish law is a 'yoke' as well as the view that the Torah is not to be imposed on Gentile Christians.[88] Its insistence on a 'minimum of legal requirements'[89] implies, however, that the Torah is now as before valid for Jewish Christians.

4. Later writings

While *Ignatius* never discusses the topic 'law' in his letters, he reveals in his polemical utterances against some 'Judaizers' a complete lack of sympathy for Judaism, from which 'Christianity' is clearly distinguished (Magn 10.3, Phld 6.1). Conformity to 'Judaism' shows that one has not 'received grace' (Magn 8.1). Judaism consists of 'erroneous teachings and ancient fables which are useless' (ἀνωφελής Magn 8.1; cf. Heb 7.18) and of 'obsolete practices' including Sabbath observance (9.1). Judaism is a 'deteriorated leaven' (10.2). 'It is absurd to have Jesus Christ on the lips and at the same time live like a Jew' (10.3). Ignatius even suggests that the Prophets who were 'in conformity with Christ Jesus' did not observe the obsolete practices (8.2, cf. 9.2, Phld 5.2).

Ignatius thus presupposes a complete and ruthless break with Judaism. Unfortunately, we are not told what he thought of the origin and nature of the OT law. What of the moral law? Was there a time when the deteriorated leaven was fresh and useful, or was there not? The extant sources are not sufficient to give answers to such questions.

---

87 A reference to the Decree is recognized here, e.g., by Charles, Bousset, Weiss-Heit-müller; U. Müller, *Theologiegeschichte* 17 ff.
88 Cf. Conzelmann-Lindemann, *Arbeitsbuch* 320.
89 Müller, op.cit. 20.

The 'Letter of *Barnabas*' is an 'academic' treatise[90] about the right relationship of Christians to Judaism by a Gentile Christian teacher (14.5, 16.7, 4.9).[91] It hardly owes its existence to any concrete danger from Judaism in the life of Christian congregations;[92] the question is an inner-Christian one, the problem of the relationship between the two covenants and of the continuity of salvation history.[93] The author takes a radical stance: there is one covenant only, and the Christians alone have a claim on it (esp. chs. 4 and 14). To be sure, God offered the covenant to the Jews, but they lost it forever when they turned to idolatry; Moses' breaking the tablets of law demonstrates that their covenant was shattered 'in order that the covenant of dear Jesus be sealed in our hearts' (4.7 f.).

Thus the OT law is a possession of the *Christians* who understand its meaning correctly. Moses 'legislated the law well' (10.11). Barn interprets the ceremonial part of the law by way of fanciful allegorizing (see esp. ch. 10 on the food laws), squeezing moral lessons from the rituals. In this he of course leans on Hellenistic Jewish models. The writer declines a literal interpretation of sacrifices, fasting and of the temple cult altogether, always looking for arguments for his view in the OT itself (chs. 2—3, 15—16). Moses himself intended that the law be understood in this way (10.1 f., 9). 2.6 suggests that the precepts of animal sacrifices were 'man-made'. Barn also spiritualizes circumcision and explains the literal understanding of the rite as a misinterpretation caused by an evil angel (9.4) — the closest counterpart of Gal 3.19 in post-Pauline early Christian literature![94]

Barn thus consistently reduces the God-given law to a moral law. The moral law remains in force, as is shown by the detailed description of the 'way of light' in ch. 19. Barn follows in fact without reservations the moral teaching of the Diaspora Synagogue. The OT law fuses completely together with 'the new law of our Lord Jesus Christ' which is 'without the yoke of compulsion' (2.6) — that is, without ritual precepts.[95] Otherwise, the 'new' law is by no means new in content.[96]

In terms of logic, the thesis of Barn is clear enough. The Jewish law is divided in two parts; of these one is a Jewish misunderstanding, the other is

---

90 Vielhauer, *Geschichte* 606.

91 Wengst, *Tradition*, assumes a 'school' activity behind Barn; see esp. 55 ff. Bihlmeyer, *Väter* XXII and Wilde, *Treatment* 87 regard the writer as a Jewish Christian.

92 Vielhauer, op.cit. 605 f.;note, however, 3.6 ('in order that we may not suffer destruction if we come across their law without preparation'); cf. 4.6. Wilde, op.cit. 88 assumes a danger that Judaism was presenting to the Church.

93 Vielhauer, op.cit. 606.

94 On Barnabas' view of circumcision see above, p. 139.

95 See Wengst, op.cit. 83; Hasler, *Gesetz* 30; Klevinghaus, *Stellung* 30.

96 Wengst, op.cit. 73, 83.

divine and valid. Some confusion is caused by the statement that God has 'abolished' (κατήργησεν) the sacrificial legislation (2.6) which would seem to presuppose that this legislation was once in force.[97] A more probable interpretation is, however, that καταργεῖν here and elsewhere (9.4, 16.2) refers to a timeless divine judgment on the essence of the sacrifices rather than to an eschatological act; that is, God makes it clear in the texts of the OT itself that sacrifices are not valid.[98] Logically, then, the solution of Barnabas is well and good. Its weakness lies in its brutally question-begging nature, the author's 'naive Christian preunderstanding'[99]. The question of Christianity's relationship to Judaism is answered from the 'enlightened' rational viewpoint of a total outsider; the Gordian knot is cut with force.[100]

Admittedly the writer is no very profound thinker, but his ability is often unduly depreciated.[101] But of course his situation was different than Paul's. It was easy for him to apply ruthless logic to the question, as the problem was not an existential one for him himself.

Marcion's aim was *separatio legis et evangelii* (Tertullian, *Adv. Marc.* I, 19). He thought through his fundamental thoughts with 'intransigent consistency'[102]. The contents of the OT exposed the god of the OT as a cruel and brutal demiurge, far inferior to the 'unknown God', the God of love, revealed by Jesus. In principle Marcion rejects the OT altogether as the book of the creator which has no use in the Christian congregation. He consistently carries through the abrogation line found in Paul's thought. Paul's other idea, that his teaching establishes the law (Rom 3.31), was impossible to Marcion and

---

97 Windisch, *Barn* 311, 393.
98 Klevinghaus, op.cit. 20 n. 1, 23 f.; Wengst, op.cit. 73 ff. 'Nicht ein christliches Heilsdatum also hat die jüdischen Entwicklungen ... eschatologisch relativiert und abgeschafft, sondern die Schrift selbst sagt, dass diese Einrichtungen grundsätzlich und zu jeder Zeit falsch sind und waren' (Wengst, op.cit. 73 f.) The use of καταργεῖν in 9.4 (perfect tense) and 16.2 supports the timeless interpretation of 2.6; in 5.6 and 15.5 the same verb is, however, used in the sense of eschatological abolition (of death or of the 'period of the lawless one' respectively). Should Windisch (see previous note) therefore be right, after all, then a slight internal tension in Barn remains, pointing to the arbitrarily aprioristic nature of the writer's premises which make it difficult for him to deal with the concrete OT texts (which are his supreme, absolutely normative authority; see Wengst, op.cit. 78, 119 and passim).
99 Wengst, op.cit. 78.
100 To be sure, Barn comes rather close to liberal Jews like the Alexandrian allegorizers (Philo, *Migr. Abr.* 89 ff.), even though no dependence needs to be posited; cf. Windisch, *Barn* 395. Most probably, however, the 'allegorizers' did not combine any polemic against the ritual law with their spiritualization and personal non-observance of it. See above, p. 137.
101 Cf. e.g. Vielhauer, op.cit. 603 f. By contrast, Stylianopoulos, *Justin* 88 recognizes that, like Justin and Hebrews but unlike Paul, Barn is 'uncompromising' as regards the abolition of the ritual law.
102 von Campenhausen, *Bibel* 176.

the verse was cancelled by him as was the following chapter (Rom 4) with its Abraham typology.[103]

Thus the outline of Marcion's view of the law is free from the ambiguity inherent in Paul's position. Nevertheless, Marcion's conception contains several minor difficulties.[104] To be sure, the confusion may to a great extent be due to the lack of adequate sources as regards Marcion's thought.[105] Anyway, Marcion retained in his 'apostolos' several Pauline statements which we would have expected him to remove.[106] These include the statements that the law is good, just, holy and spiritual (Rom 7.12, 14) and that 'I serve God's law with my mind' (Rom 7.25), and that the law is summarized in the love command.

Thus the law of the creator is not wholly objectionable, after all. Marcion is simply not able, in view of the OT record and the use made of it in Christianity, to develop a consistently negative view of the law. He has to admit a good kernel in the OT law so that Christianity can be seen as the fulfilment of its deepest intention (the love command).[107]

Marcion, then, is (unlike Paul) quite consistent in his rejection of the law in the present situation. Of the nature and purpose of the law, however, he is not able to give a fully clear picture (if we are entitled to infer this much from the sparse evidence available).

A striking feature in Marcion's treatment of the OT is that he takes the book at face value. Besides rejecting the allegorical interpretation, he 'acknowledged the OT as a unitary whole, assumed no falsifications, interpolations etc. and did not regard the book as untrue either but rather as throughout credible'.[108] The OT was not subjected to such textual criticisms

---

103 Harnack, *Marcion* 48; 73*, 104*. Marcion also cancelled Gal 3.15−25 because of its 'promise' theology.

104 See Harnack, op.cit. 109 f. n. 2.

105 We know Marcion's thought only through excerpts in his opponents' works; moreover, we have to make inferences from his redaction of Luke and Paul and it is not self-evident that everything Marcion let stand in his text should be given full weight in the reconstruction of his own thought.

106 See above, p. 139 f.

107 Verweijs, *Gesetz* 259 f. contends (against Harnack) that the idea of fulfilment is 'scharf antithetisch ausgerichtet', for 'bei den Christen erfüllt ist, was beim Weltschöpfer niemals erfüllt werden konnte'. He refers to Marcion's rendering of Gal 5.14: 'in one word' is omitted and ἐν ὑμῖν added. This polemical orientation cannot be denied. Nevertheless, the fact remains that there *is* something in the creator's law that *deserves* to be fulfilled.

   A full rejection of the OT was carried out by some (not all!) Gnostics; see above all the 'Second Treatise of the great Seth' (NHC VII, 2, p. 62, 27−65, 1; NHL 335 f.) where 'Moses, a faithful servant' is called a 'laughingstock' (63, 26 ff.) − as is the OT god ('Archon', 64, 18 ff.). Cf. H-F. Weiss, 'Gesetz' 78 f.; Bethge, 'Ambivalenz' 104 ff.; see also Koschorke, 'Paulus' 180−183, 194−196.

108 Harnack, op.cit. 86.

as were the gospel and the 'apostolos'. Harnack sees in this difference of attitudes a psychological riddle and conjectures that Marcion had a Jewish (Proselyte) background.[109] Perhaps this is indeed the best hypothesis to account
for the striking combination of reverence for and a radical rejection of the
OT law, not quite unlike Paul's ambiguous attitude! It might also explain
Marcion's reluctance to make explicit distinctions within the law.

Given these tensions, Marcion's overall view of the law is still much clearer
than Paul's.[110] He has taken up Paul's radical line of thought and brought it
to its logical end. The price he had to pay was, of course, a complete elimination of salvation history and the assumption of two gods along with which
went a world-denying asceticism.

Justin breaks new ground in the Christian interpretation of the law.[111]
Apparently his conception was first formed in a battle with Marcionites; in
the *Dialogue* he later puts forward the same points of view in a confrontation
with Judaism.[112] The significant features are Justin's 'tripartite division of
the law'[113] and 'his historical concept of the purpose of the law'.[114]

From certain passages in the *Dialogue* (45.3, 67.4, 10, 44.2) it can be
inferred that Justin actually, if not explicitly, divides the law in three parts:
ethics, prophecy and historical dispensation.[115] This helps him to preserve
'the principle of the absolute authority and consistency of Scripture'.[116]
It is only the ritual part of the law that is a problem for Justin; God's moral
law is permanently valid. To solve the problem, Justin develops his view of
the ritual law as an historical dispensation.

The ritual law has been abolished through the new law (11.2; Justin often
calls Christ a νόμος.)[117] 'It is the death of Christ as the new criterion of salvation which renders the Mosaic Law obsolete.'[118] Justin formulates the teaching of the cessation of the law much more sharply than subsequent orthodox
writers, being even 'more thoroughgoing' than Paul in this regard.[119] He

---

109 Harnack, op.cit. 22, 67 n. 1. Cf. Conzelmann, *Heiden* 255 n. 217.
110 Cf. H-F. Weiss, art.cit. 76: 'Marcion's conception has, in comparison with Paul's,
     the advantage of being absolutely unequivocal'.
111 See the fine study of Stylianopoulos, *Justin*.
112 See Stylianopoulos, op.cit. 7—44, 153 ff.
113 Op.cit. 1, 51 ff.
114 Op.cit. 1, 131 ff.
115 Op.cit. 55.
116 Op.cit. 76.
117 Op.cit. 78 ff.
118 Op.cit. 86.
119 Op.cit. 87 and n. 24 (with reference to e.g. Rom 3.31). Stylianopoulos, op.cit. 90
     finds it possible that behind the sharp abrogation theology may lie the idea that 'a
     concept of fulfilment in the sense of bringing to perfection might well have suggested
     to Justin imperfection on the part of the Mosaic Law and thus, consequently, also
     of God ... ' This is indeed a dilemma of all 'fulfilment' theologies.

comes close to Marcion, the only important difference being that for Justin the law was given by the same God and Father of all. To be able to maintain this against the Marcionites, Justin had to find a purpose for the ritual law. This was given on the account of the sinfulness of the Jews.[120]

Thus Justin's view is much clearer and much more logical than Paul's. He divides the law into different parts and deals with them differently: some parts have been abolished, others not. The abolished parts, too, had a historical meaning in their time; Justin struggles to avoid the problem of theodicy, inherent in so many Christian views of the law. While his explanation is logical, its individual parts (the reasons given for the precepts of circumcision and Sabbath in the first place) are naive. Nevertheless, his was a bold attempt to combine a theology of the abolition of the law with the principle of the absolute divine authority of the OT scripture. Without a relativization of one of the two a much better solution was indeed hardly to be attained.

To be sure, Justin found himself in a favourable situation in comparison with Paul: the battle over the law was long since over. The law did not constitute a personal existential problem for Justin as it did for Paul.[121] Yet the fact that Justin *refrains* from making his tripartite division of the law *explicitly* deserves attention;[122] his high regard for the authority of Scripture may have unconsciously prevented him from working out a bolder and clearer breakdown of the unity of Scripture. The analogy with Paul's case lies at hand.

Probably the most lucid solution to the problems of the law in early Christianity in terms of rational thought was suggested by the Valentinian Gnostic *Ptolemy* in his letter to Flora.[123] In this short writing of 'unusually high intellectual and literary standards'[124] Ptolemy declines both the rejection of the OT by Marcion and the total acceptance of the book by the mainstream church and proceeds to make clear critical *distinctions within the OT law.*

The Mosaic law is not uniform nor of a single origin; it consists of different elements that are of different value. The law cannot have been given by the perfect God; he just could not have given an imperfect law which needed to be fulfilled by someone else and contained precepts incompatible with his own being and will (3.4). The law comes neither from this God nor from the devil (3.2)[125] Its proper assessment is made possible through the 'words of our Saviour' (3.8).[126]

---

120 See above, p. 155 f.

121 Nevertheless, the problem of the law was for Justin not just an academic problem either. In ch. 47 he refers to the law-abiding Jewish Christians of his time, to whom different Gentile Christians took a different attitude. Justin's tolerant viewpoint deserves attention.

122 See above, p. 32.

123 Text in Epiphanius, *Panarion* ch. 33.

124 Campenhausen, *Bibel* 98; cf. Aleith, *Paulusverständnis* 46.

125 The reference to the devil hints in a distorting way at Marcion's position; cf. v.

The words of Jesus concerning divorce and the traditions of the elders provide a clue for distinctions within the law (4.2–13). They expose additions both by Moses and by the elders. The contribution of Moses is revealed in the admission of divorce (4.2–10), that of the elders in Jesus' criticism of the Qorban institution (4.11–13). The rest is a law purified from human additions. Yet even this law turns out, in the light of the words of Jesus, to be non-uniform. Parts of it were accepted by Jesus and fulfilled through the interpretation given in the Sermon on the Mount. This is the pure legislation which is not mixed with evil (5.1). It is represented by the Decalogue. Nevertheless, even this part of the law was imperfect and had to be fulfilled by the Saviour (5.3) through his interpretation given in the Sermon on the Mount (6.11).

Other parts of the OT law, for example the laws of retaliation and killing, are in themselves righteous; nevertheless, they are not consonant with the goodness of the true God, but take man's weakness into account (5.4–5). Jesus, the Son of God, therefore abolished these ordinances, even though he admitted their origin with God (5.7, 6.2) – that is, with the demiurge. Still another part of the law is the ceremonial or 'typical' law of images and symbols; in interpreting this Ptolemy appropriates the established Jewish allegorical method (5.8–15, 6.4 f.). This part of the law has been transferred from the literal level to a spiritual one (6.4).

Ptolemy thinks that this distinction between different layers within the law (and it alone) solves all the problems connected with Paul's statements about the law (6.6). When the apostle now rejects the law and now accepts it, the explanation is that he has different parts of this complex entity in view.[127] The Gnostic thus anticipates the views of Cranfield, Käsemann and others.[128] In his view, Rom 7.12 is a statement on that law which is not mixed with evil, whereas Eph 2.15 is concerned with that mixed with unrighteousness (retaliation and the like). The fact that Ptolemy is forced to carry out these distinctions is another palpable piece of proof of the problematic nature of Paul's 'uniform' statements about the law. Where Paul strives after a global solution (on the conscious level of his reasoning), Ptolemy examines

---

Campenhausen, op.cit. 103 n. 33.

126 Quispel, *Lettre* 16 points out the similarity with Kerygmata Petrou (Hom 3.50). To what degree Hellenistic Judaism may have prepared the way for Ptolemy (cf. Fallon, 'Law' 51) is another matter. It is not clear that Ptolemy's distinctions regarding the origin of various parts of the law correspond to those made by Philo (see above, p. 135). The allegorizers rebuked by Philo (see above, p. 35) may have constituted a link, but then again they may not. A study of the gospel of Matthew would have sufficed to give Ptolemy his cue.

127 Campenhausen, op.cit. 101.

128 Cf. above, p. 42 ff., 65 f.

the *contents* of the law concretely on point after point; inescapably the result then must be a differentiated view about the law.

Unlike Paul (and even unlike Justin), Ptolemy is able to carry out these distinctions, since he feels free to criticize the OT from his own Valentinian frame of reference. It is the lack of existential commitment regarding the OT that helps him, unlike the mainstream Christians of his time, to provide 'a kind of scientifically critical account of the diversity of the Mosaic Law'. [129] The price he has to pay is, of course, that the unity of God is lost; not even the 'divine' part of the law comes from the perfect God, the Father of All (3.7), but from the demiurge. [130] Unlike more 'orthodox' writers, however, Ptolemy manages to avoid self-contradictions in God's revealed will. To be sure, he thus 'tends to deny history' [131]; yet it can be doubted whether it was at all possible to provide a much more convincing account (in intellectual terms) before the time of historical criticism. It is therefore justified to regard him as a kind of precursor of modern Biblical study. [132] In purely intellectual terms his account of the law is consistent and clear and far more impressive than Paul's.

Last but not least the *Kerygmata Petrou* are to be mentioned here. In these texts from about AD 200 [133] which have survived in the Pseudoclementine romance we at last find clear *distinctions* within the Mosaic law made *from within* and not from the standpoint of a detached outsider. Behind the KP stands a Christian community with a strictly Jewish identity which partly represents an intensified nomism. [134] According to KP, the OT contained some 'false pericopes'. [135] The original will of God which was revealed through Moses was partly forgotten because of false teaching etc. (Hom 1.18, Rec 1.15). As the revelation was written down only after Moses' death (Hom 3.47), the process of writing brought falsifications along with it (Hom 2.38). Jesus, the reformer of the Mosaic law, distinguished between right and false pericopes. He said that he did not come to annul the law; nevertheless it

---

129 Stylianopoulos, *Justin* 75.
130 Even this statement may be an oversimplification of Ptolemy's actual position. Campenhausen, op.cit. 103 f. notes that actually 'werden die drei verschiedenen Elemente des Gottesgesetzes nach valentinianischer Lehre vielmehr auf drei göttliche Potenzen zurückgeführt: den pneumatischen Samen, die Sophia und die Kräfte des Demiurgen. Ptolemaios schätzt den Wert des At also teils höher, teils noch niedriger ein, als seine Zusammenfassung erkennen lässt.' Cf. Quispel, op.cit. 23 ff. Quispel, op.cit. 9 refers to the exoteric and pedagogical nature of the letter to Flora.
131 Quispel, op.cit. 10, trying to play down the alleged 'modernity' of Ptolemy, who is in this respect 'even less "modern" than the works of the Fathers'.
132 Cf. C. Barth, *Interpretation* 103.
133 See Strecker, *Judenchristentum* 219.
134 Cf. Schoeps, *Theologie* 188 ff.; id., *Judenchristentum* 81 ff.
135 See on these Strecker, op.cit. 166 ff.; Schoeps, *Theologie* 148 ff.

seems as if he had abolished parts of it. From this it can be concluded that 'what he annulled (κατέλυεν) did not belong to the law' (Hom 3.51). The things that did disappear before heaven and earth (cf. Lk 16.17) could not be parts of the true law which is eternal. The false precepts included 'the sacrifices, the kingship and the female prophecy and other such things' (Hom 3.52).[136] The 'other things' included anthropomorphisms, the stories about the immorality of the patriarchs and Moses, etc.

This 'enlightened'[137] theory probably owes its existence to some acute crisis threatening the self-understanding of the Jewish-Christians responsible for it, whether the threat came from Marcionites[138] or just from contact with the non-Jewish environment in general.[139] The Jewish Christians in question tried to overcome the threat by conceding as much as they could to the opponents' position by way of 'Biblical criticism' while clinging all the more steadfastly to what was seen as the hard core of the Mosaic legislation. In a sense this attempt forms an analogy to the efforts of Philo and others to meet the criticisms of non-Jews through an allegorical interpretation of the offensive parts of Scripture.[140] The method chosen by KP is bolder and relatively more 'historical' and also more plausible. This differentiated view of the law also makes, in intellectual terms, more sense than Paul's vague suggestion of the angelic origin of the law in Gal 3.19. The law was not annulled; only illegitimate additions to it were removed. Noteworthy is the firm opposition to Paul, the 'enemy' par excellence, reflected in the KP.[141] In sum, the solution proposed by KP is one of the clearest in the period surveyed.

5. Conclusion

The above survey should have made clear that Paul shares some of his dilemmas with other early Christian writers, while others are peculiar to him. Thus, the concept of 'law' often oscillates in other writers, too (Pastorals, James, Mark, Matthew); it is by no means Paul alone who combines lip service to the idea of continuity with an actual break with the Torah-observance. The problem of the divine origin of an inferior revelation is also a common

---

136 On the prophecy see Strecker, op.cit. 175 ff.; Schoeps, *Judenchristentum* 72 ff.

137 Cf. Schoeps, op.cit. 77.

138 Thus Schoeps, op.cit. 78.

139 Strecker, op.cit. 171 regards the theory as a product of the 'Jewish-Christian Gnosis'; cf. id., 'Judenchristentum und Gnosis' 278 f. The analogy with Ptolemy's treatment of the question is indeed obvious; cf. above, n. 126.

140 Cf. Strecker, Judenchristentum 169.

141 Cf. Strecker, op.cit. 187 ff. It is not advisable to trace the theory of KP back to the primitive community in Jerusalem (thus Schoeps, *Theologie* 256 ff.; cf. Simon's attempt to connect Stephen with them: *Stephen* 113 ff.); see Strecker, op.cit. 180 etc.

one to most of the writers in question; it is indeed only solved by writers at the fringe of second century Christianity (Ptolemy, Kerygmata Petrou) who had the freedom and courage to introduce critical distinctions, refusing to regard the total OT legislation as God-given.

The Pauline tension between the annulment of the law and its continued validity still turns up in Ephesians. Other writers, however, are at pains to find a more consistent solution (in either direction). Indeed, the modern efforts to portray Paul as a consistent critic or else as a consistent upholder of the law (cf. the conflict between the views of Käsemann and Cranfield) can be seen as a continuation of this early hermeneutical necessity. Some ancient writers attempt to reconcile Paul's ideas by introducing new definitions (Pastorals) or distinctions (Ptolemy, explicitly interpreting Paul's apparent self-contradictions).

Several dilemmas in Paul's thought on the law are, however, peculiar to him alone. This applies, above all, to the many *negative* things said about the divine law (that Gnostics who denied the origin of the law with the supreme God said bad things about it is, of course, something different).

In sum, I am not able to find in the relevant literature *any* conception of the law which involves such inconsistencies or such arbitrariness as does Paul's. While most of the conceptions surveyed above are not free from problems either, all of them appear more consistent and less problematic than Paul's. The common view that Paul is *the* thinker in early Christianity is, I must conclude, misleading. On the contrary, the estimate of the philosopher von Hartmann at the beginning of this century has proved correct: 'Paul moves in more severe contradictions than any other New Testament writer.' [142] In part, however, this is due to the fact that Paul at least attempts to answer questions which were simply by-passed by others.

---

142 *Christentum* 176.

VIII. The origins of Paul's conception of the law

In this chapter I attempt to find a historical explanation for the rise of Paul's peculiar view of the law. How and why did Paul come to the ideas we now encounter in his letters? It is not, of course, difficult to account for the 'conservative', law-affirming elements in his view: obviously, they are part of Paul's Jewish heritage. A plausible theory about the origins of Paul's final view must, however, explain the perseverance of these elements among all those radical statements dictated by the apostle. Above all, a plausible theory ought to account for the distinctively Pauline features. While Paul was not alone in early Christianity in taking a liberal stance toward the Torah, it is he alone who put forward extremely negative statements about the connection between the law and sin, and the like. A plausible theory ought to suggest, at least, a reason why Paul speaks of the law in a way unlike any other early Christian.

I will engage in a search for such a theory by surveying the various possibilities. The enterprise is, of course, hypothetical to a rather high degree, and the *caveat* stated in the introduction should perhaps be repeated here: the analysis of part one in this work should *not* be deemed to depend on the plausibility of the solution developed here.

1. Paul's experience under the law?

It was earlier quite common to trace Paul's critical attitude to the law back to his Pharisaic experience: Paul broke down, it was held, under the distressing burden of the law. The demands were too high; Paul, as a very sincere man, was just incapable of fulfilling them. This interpretation was, of course, based on Romans 7, taken as an autobiography;[1] Acts 26.14 also played a part.[2] In recent times this explanation, while not wholly without its advocates[3], has generally been laid to rest,[4] and rightly so.

---

1 E.g. Deissmann, *Paul* 93 ff.; Weinel, *Paul* 68 ff. (p. 72 Paul is made to side with Luther); id., *Theologie* 416 ff.; Holtzmann, *Theologie* II 30; W.L. Knox, *Jerusalem* 28; Gulin, *Freude* 193 f.; Klausner, *Jesus* 463; Dodd, *Romans* 107 ff. (speaking of Paul's 'desperation', p. 115); Andrews, *Teaching* 148, 155 ff.; Grønbech, *Paulus* 9 ff.; cf. also Nock, *Paul* 67 ff.

2 Cf. still Caird, *Age* 119. On Acts 26.14 see Kümmel, *Römer* 7, 154 ff.

3 Cf. Dodd, *Studies* 74 ff.; Davies, *Paul* 23 ff.; Buber, *Zwei Glaubensweisen* 149 ff.; Sandmel, *Genius* 24 ff.; Hunt, *Portrait* 27 f.; Ben-Chorin, *Paulus* 60 ff. M. Grant,

In Phil 3.6 Paul unequivocally states that he was, in his past life, blameless according to Pharisaic standards. If the interpretation suggested above[5] is on the right track, Rom 7.14—25 represents a radicalization and generalization by Paul of a well-known psychological conflict. Man is not always able to realize what he knows to be right. Paul's 'apology of the law' in Rom 7 suggests that this is *always* the case within the dominion of the law. Despite the use of the first person pronoun as a stylistic device[6] Rom 7.14 ff. does not convey the impression of being the description of an intense personal experience.[7] As the preceding verses 7—13 obviously belong together with 14 ff.[8], there is no reason to understand the process there described in particularly personal terms either. In these verses, too, Paul speaks as if the events described were universally valid; he is speaking of the effects of the law always and everywhere (with overtones from the story of Adam, to be sure).[9] We do *not* have to do with his particular personal story.

Paul 23, 45 ff., 109; as one explanatory factor among several also Lindeskog, *Jesus* 163; Caird, op.cit. 119. Another version of this interpretation is that of Hunt, loc. cit.: Rom 7 describes an internal struggle rather than external actions; Paul had omitted to observe none of the commandments, and yet 'within him there were these inordinate desires'. Cf. Dodd, op.cit. 75. Yet the modern notion, stemming from Western Christian introspection, of an evil desire which spoils even good actions, was foreign to the men of antiquity before Augustine; cf. Stendahl, *Paul* 78 ff. According to the Jewish view, desire was the root of all evil because it led to evil *deeds*. Cf. Räisänen, 'Gebrauch' 91 with note 34. Moreover, there is no talk of 'desire' (mentioned in Rom 7.7 f.) any more in the section about the divided man in 7.14 ff. It is *not* said that the Ego performs externally good actions while tortured by evil desires. On the contrary, there is within that man the will for *good*, and yet he is unable to do 'external' good things (7.18b, cf. v. 15b. 16a).

4 To a great extent this is due to the careful study of Kümmel, *Römer 7.*

5 See above, III 4.

6 See Kümmel, op.cit. 119 ff.

7 Not even 7.24a. Dodd, op.cit. 107, comments on this verse: 'A man is not moved like that by an ideal construction'; cf. Buber, op.cit. 150; Nygren; Beker, *Paul* 240; Gundry, 'Frustration' 229. Yet such an exclamation seems to be a traditional topos in such a connection; cf. *infelix* in Ovid, *Metamorph.* 8, 18.

8 Verses 14 ff. state either the consequence of, or, more probably, the reason for the events described in vv. 7—13; see above, p. 142 f.

9 It is now fashionable to see the story of Adam reflected on in Rom 7.7—11 (thus Käsemann, Schlier, and many others). But why, then, did Paul not simply mention Adam (cf. Bornkamm, *Ende* 58 f.)? It is true that, according to some Jewish traditions, the law was proleptically given to Adam in the Paradise already (Targum Neofiti Gen 2.15 'to observe the law'; ibid. on Gen 3.24 the tree of life is identified with the law); cf. Lyonnet, *Histoire* 135 ff.; id., 'Tu ne convoiteras pas' 162 f. It does not automatically follow from the existence of such traditions, however, that Paul *must* have used them. If Paul was really speaking of Adam in Rom 7, a blunt contradiction arises between this chapter and Rom 5, where the law is explicitly dated in a much later time (cf. Luz, *Geschichtsverständnis* 166); cf. also Gal 3.15 ff. In Rom 7 Paul is concerned to develop an 'apology' for the *Mosaic* law (cf. the reference to the

If we are allowed to draw from Paul's Christian statements about sin and transgression conclusions about the degree of his pre-Christian scrupulousness, the picture converges with that suggested by Phil 3.6. Nothing indicates that Paul had an overly sensitive mind in the vein of Luther.[10] Paul the Christian seems on the contrary to possess a rather 'robust' conscience.[11] He can say that he has nothing on his conscience (1 Cor 4.4).[12] The only past sin (not classified as such in express words, to be sure!) of which he shows consciousness is his persecution of the church.[13] It is only natural to assume a mental continuity between the Jewish and the Christian Paul.

The nature of Paul's argument in Rom 2–3 points in the same direction.[14] In his effort to convict the Jew, along with the pagan, of sin, Paul does *not* try to show, say, that even the best actions of a man are spoiled by his evil desires; instead, he charges the Jew almost desperately with extremely gross transgressions. The way Paul the Christian talks about sin does not indicate a mind steeped in introspection. In sum, we can safely subscribe to the now common opinion that Paul's critique of the law was not born out of any personal moral difficulties. Paul was no Luther before Luther.

To say that Paul had no moral difficulties with the law is one thing. It is another to claim that Paul did not have and could not have *any* kind of difficulties, not even unconscious ones, amid his blameless fulfilment of the law. Conversions do have a psychological prehistory, even if the convert himself is the last one to see it. That Paul went through 'a volcanic internal crisis'[15] can hardly be denied. 'His conversion happened as a drastic psychological crisis, which he does not and could not explain, and which we cannot either';[16] nevertheless, some educated guesses on our part can hardly be out of place. Indeed 'analogies suggest that his conversion was not the sudden thing which it seemed to him'.[17]

Decalogue!). *If* Paul was speaking of Adam in Rom 7, then the confusion of his argument is worse than ever! But it is more natural to take the passage as an account of the fall of any Jew, described in the language of the Biblical story of the Fall (Barrett). For a critique of the 'Adam' interpretation see now Gundry, art.cit. 230–232.

10 M. Grant, *Paul* 109 postulates 'self-tortures' which 'continued throughout his life'! There is not a shred of evidence for this.

11 Stendahl, *Paul* 80; cf. Dahl, *Studies* 111; Gager, 'Notes' 698 f. See further the very interesting suggestions about the personality of first century Mediterranean people by Malina, 'Individual' 126 ff. Interestingly enough even Wenham, who holds that Paul speaks from personal experience in Rom 7.14–25 ('Life' 89) goes a long way toward Stendahl's position (art.cit. 82, 89, 94 n. 41).

12 On 1 Cor 4.4 see also Windisch, *Taufe* 125 f. One is reminded of the simple optimism of the pious psalm singers, see e.g. Ps 19.13 f.

13 Stendahl, op.cit. 89.

14 See above, III 2.

15 Nock, *Paul* 31.   16 Nock, op.cit. 67 f.

17 Nock, op.cit. 73; cf. M. Grant, op.cit. 46; Kuss, *Paulus* 345 n. 3.

In modern times it has become customary, most of all among German exegetes, to exclude categorically all psychological arguments from the interpretation of what Paul wrote.[18] All theories to the effect that encounter with Christians might have prepared Paul's mind can be put aside as 'pure phantasy'.[19] The reason is simply that Paul himself says nothing of the kind![20] This naïve trust on a man's testimony about himself is a curious fundamentalistic survival within critical scholarship. We have of course very little hope of being able to penetrate into the psychic life of a person of the ancient world 2000 years later.[21] Nevertheless, some psychological commonplaces are probably applicable. It is one such commonplace that the unconscious can break through in opposition to the conscious belief to which one clings. There is 'a polarity, a kind of opposition, between unconscious experience and consciousness' so that 'the more we are unconsciously smitten with doubts about an idea, the more dogmatically we fight for it in our conscious arguments.' 'A dynamic struggle goes on within a person between what he or she consciously thinks on the one hand and, on the other, some insight, some perspective that is struggling to be born.'[22]

---

18 Representatively Conzelmann, *Outline* 155.

19 Kümmel, *Römer* 7, 154.

20 Cf. Kümmel, op.cit. 160: 'Alle psychologisierenden Hypothesen und alle Behauptungen, die über das aus den Quellen zu Erhebende hinausgehen, führen nur an den Tatsachen vorbei und vergessen die Ehrfurcht vor der geschichtlichen Wirklichkeit.' As if the texts alone were the 'historical reality'! Bornkamm's inconsistent reasoning (*Paulus* 46) well reflects the problems inherent in this anti-psychological attitude: at first he admits that 'one has to assume with certainty' that the christological question, 'geweckt durch Glauben und Zeugnis seiner Jünger, an ihm (Paul) und in ihm gearbeitet hat'. Then he goes on, however: 'Freilich, er selbst schweigt darüber und bestätigt eindeutig (!), dass nicht ein langsamer Reifeprozess, sondern allein die souveräne und freie Tat Gottes die Wende heraufgeführt hat.' But one cannot have it both ways! Correctly Lowe, 'Examination' 130: 'Paul always thought of his conversion as a sheer bolt from the blue'; 'as a psychological description of the process, that may be all wrong; it probably is'.

21 Psychological study of the NT is still in its infancy. I cannot find much illumination in current psychoanalytical attempts to interpret Paul; cf. Vergote, 'Beitrag'; Rubenstein, *Paul*; Scroggs, *Paul*. Attempting to establish a parallel between Rom 7 and psychoanalytical insights into the Oedipus complex, Vergote interprets the 'law' of Rom 7 as 'the law of the father' (which prohibits desiring the mother) rather than the Torah; the pronoun ἐγώ, too, is interpreted in a framework totally foreign to Paul. Rubenstein's book is a curious combination of sound exegetical knowledge, profound theological insights and wild and hazardous psychoanalytical interpretations.

For some good comments see now Gager, 'Notes'. He sees Paul's notion of justification through faith 'as a theological commentary ... on Paul's own biography' (702). This presupposes, however, the old notion of the law as the path to righteousness in Paul's pre-conversion value system (700) which was simply turned upside down with the conversion.

22 May, *Courage* 59 (in a passage entitled 'Creativity and the Unconscious'). Beker, op.

But what insight, what perspective? What was Paul's unconscious struggle, if we may posit such a thing, all about? We have seen that a personal failure with respect to observance of the commandments does not come into question. There are other possibilities; it lies in the nature of the matter that they must remain highly conjectural.

With all caution, the question may be raised, why did Paul come later to speak of his (and other people's) non-Christian past repeatedly and strongly as *slavery*? Why is the contrast between past and present set forth so markedly as one between bondage and freedom? Given all secondary rationalizations and Paul's indubitable tendency to see things in black-and-white — are the strong contrasts of Gal 3–4, 2 Cor 3, Rom 5–6 etc. really explicable if Paul had *never* had any feelings of bondage, fear, and the like, in his pre-Christian past? For all the joy connected with the task of fulfilling God's commandments, the cheerful yoke of the law was, for the pious Jew, nevertheless *a yoke*; the image was not coined for nothing.[23] We may conclude that it is at least not impossible that Paul's great stress on the 'new situation in the Spirit' (Rom 7.6) and on the contrast between the freedom in the Spirit and the 'letter' of the law (2 Cor 3.6, Rom 7.6) had something to do with a personal experience of liberation. It is very one-sided to view Paul's conversion or call experience just as a theological reorientation. Early Christianity was a charismatic movement where ecstatic experiences were daily bread, and we have good reasons to assume that Paul was not an exception.

If the pneumatic experience of Christ had liberated Paul from the 'letter', what exactly was he liberated from? A full answer would presuppose an account of the attitude to the law of those Christians whom Paul had persecuted. What had *they* been liberated from? This might give a clue for the assessment of Paul's situation; we must, however, postpone a discussion of the views of the 'Hellenists' for a while (see below, VIII 6). Here we must content ourselves with a couple of clues from Paul's letters.

---

cit. 237 is quite justified in asking, 'How could the Christophany have been so traumatic and so radical in its consequences unless it lit up and answered a hidden quest in his (Paul's) soul?' Cf. also Gager, art.cit. 699 ff. Beker thinks that Paul's Christophany 'unmasked and resolved' 'a hidden conflict', making evident to Paul his actual transgression (cf. Rom 7), hypocrisy (cf. Rom 2.17 ff.), and boasting (cf. Rom 3.26); op.cit. 241. While agreeing with the notion of a hidden conflict I envisage the nature of that conflict quite differently (largely·because I read the texts from Romans mentioned above differently).

23 Cf. Rava's statement 'The precepts were not given for enjoyment, for their observance is the King's decree imposed upon them' (RSh 28a), cited by Urbach, *Sages* 389 who is discussing the concept of 'yoke'. In fairness to Paul, the possibility (indeed likelihood) of 'secondary rationalization' on the part of the Rabbis when speaking of the joy of the commandments must also be taken into account!'

It is unlikely that Paul's great experience of liberation had much to do with ordinances as such. He did not replace a bondage under 'rules' with a freedom with 'no rules';[24] on the contrary, he is not afraid of confronting his converts — the Thessalonians as well as the Corinthians — with pretty clear rules as to what is God's will.[25] Even the Christian Paul is quite contented with being a 'slave' of the Lord[26] which entails taking orders and behaving in a certain way.

In a revealing passage Paul writes to the Roman Christians that they are children of God, 'For you have not received a spirit of slavery to be again *in fear* (πάλιν εἰς φόβον), but you have received the Spirit of sonship ... ' (Rom 8.15). In the following relative clause which describes the effects of the Spirit bestowed on the believers Paul switches over to the first person: 'in which *we* cry, "Abba the father" '. It is thus unlikely that Paul thinks that only the recipients of the letter had lived in fear before becoming Christians (besides, part of them were Jewish Christians as he himself); he probably includes himself among those liberated from fear. May we conclude that, all his blamelessness notwithstanding, Paul was not free from fear in his pre-Christian life?[27] Was he one of those 'Pharisees of fear' who are criticized in Jewish sources for observing the law out of fear of punishment?[28] It is impossible to prove such a conjecture, but the possibility should not be rejected out of hand either.

Still another possibility which does not exclude the one just mentioned but may complement it arises more from a consideration of Paul's general background than directly from his letters, even though a few hints may be found there as well. Even if Paul had not spent his youth in the Dispersion but had received his parental upbringing and formal education in Jerusalem (a question which I would like to leave open)[29], he can hardly have escaped

---

24 See Schrage, *Einzelgebote*; cf. Hoheisel, *Judentum* 182.

25 See above, p. 115 n. 108.

26 Rom 1.1, Phil 1.1, Gal 1.10, cf. Rom 6.16 ff.

27 Attention was called to Rom 8.15 by Deissmann, *Paul* 83, who concluded that 'slavish terror' was 'the prevailing tone' in the mind of Paul the Pharisee. I am not suggesting anything so dramatic. I wish only to say that fear of punishment may not have to be excluded from Paul's motives for obeying the law.

28 See Moore, *Judaism* II, 193 f. Klausner, op.cit. 464 f. regarded Paul as just such a person.

29 van Unnik, *Sparsa* I 259 ff. has shown that Acts 22.3 reflects a current biographical pattern (cf. Acts 7.20) and indicates that, according to Luke, Paul had spent even his youth in Jerusalem, where he received a scribal education under Gamaliel I. van Unnik accepts this information as historical. His conclusion is shared by many scholars, e.g. Hengel, *Geschichtsschreibung* 71. Paul is, on the other hand, still seen as a Dispersion Jew e.g. by Sandmel, *Genius* 12 f.; Schoeps, *Paul*; Strecker, *Eschaton* 232 f. n. 10; Goodenough, 'Paul'. The most natural reading of Gal 1.22 is that Paul was unknown

the problem of the *motivation* of many apparently opaque stipulations (as the dietary laws) of the Torah. Hellenistic Judaism was hard put to discover 'grounds' for the ritual precepts; the problem was solved by way of allegorization. We have seen how tremendous a problem such stipulations posed for Philo; nevertheless, Philo was strict on the necessity of observing them to the point of recommending the lynching of apostates![30] But Palestinian and Hellenistic Judaism were not two watertight separate compartments.[31] The unmotivated precepts of the law were a problem for the Rabbis as well;[32] they were aware that both Gentile peoples and the evil inclination argued against the prohibition to eat pork and similar precepts.[33] The tendency of some circles to 'examine the grounds for the precepts' is attested in Rabbinic sources where it is criticized.[34]

Passages like LevR 13.3 or MidrPs 146.4 betray a certain amount of impatience with some of the more meticulous ritual stipulations, and a prospect of an eschatological compensation is held out for the efforts undertaken in this world to observe them: in the eschatological future God will declare permitted some things now forbidden and the righteous will then have the privilege of some enjoyments they have in this life abstained from.[35] In MidrPs

---

even to the congregation of Jerusalem (in view of the thrust of the context, where Paul is at pains to show his independence of Jerusalem, it is not very natural to exclude Jerusalem from the 'congregations of Judaea'). In a city of some 25,000 inhabitants (Jeremias, *Jerusalem* 98) this is curious, for Paul was, for the Christians, not just any Rabbinic pupil. It is moreover surprising that Paul did not go to Jerusalem after his conversion until three years later, if that city had been his residence until then (is fear a sufficient ground for this?). It is therefore likely that Paul did not *persecute* Christians in Jerusalem. Are we to suppose that he had recently moved from Jerusalem to the area of Damascus? Acts 22.3 does not easily combine with the data from Paul's letters. Furthermore, Paul's use of the LXX calls for attention.

30 See above, p. 36.

31 It is sufficient here to refer to the magisterial study of Hengel, *Judentum.*

32 See Urbach, *Sages* 311–314.

33 Sifra Ahare 13.10; cited by Urbach, op.cit. 320 f.

34 Schäfer, 'Torah' 38–42; cf. Jervell, 'Tora' 108.

35 In MidrPs 146.4 the words 'The Lord will loose the bonds' (Ps 146.7) are interpreted as follows. 'Some say that of every animal whose flesh it is forbidden to eat in this world, the Holy one, blessed be He, will declare in the time-to-come that the eating of the flesh is permitted ... Others say ... Though nothing is more strongly forbidden than intercourse with a menstruous woman ... in the time-to-come, God will permit such intercourse ... '

The idea of compensation is evident in LevR 13.3 (a description of the contest between the two beasts Behemoth and Leviathan in which both are killed; they provide the meat for the eschatological banquet, although they were not properly slaughtered, for God will give a new commandment): ' ... whoever has not been a spectator at the wild-beast contests of the heathen nations in this world will be accorded the boon of seeing one in the World to come ... whoever has not eaten *nebelah* in this world will have the privilege of enjoying it in the World to come.'

146.4 the only reason for some food laws is found in the statement that God wanted to 'see who would accept His commandments and who would not accept them'. Mainstream Rabbinic thought found this line of reasoning dangerous and the search for grounds for individual commandments was condemned, reference being made to Solomon who was revealed the grounds for two particular commandments which he then broke and was carried to calamity.[36] It is not unnatural to assume that Paul, too, was exposed to this kind of intellectual pressure, although he gloriously suppressed his doubts about the ritual law on the conscious level of his mind.

I tend to guess that part of Paul's liberation experience was freedom from the observance of *unmotivated* precepts. For him, 'everything is allowed' (1 Cor 10.23) in Christ; the Christian possesses freedom (v. 29). That nevertheless not everything is, in actual practice, admissible for a Christian, Paul must *argue* from the point of view that everything is not 'useful' (v. 23). Thus he brings in chs. 8 and 10 a motivated argument about what is the right attitude to meat offered to idols. In the same vein, he invites his fellow Christians to *test* (δοκιμάζειν) what God's will is (Rom 12.2, Phil 1.10). It is not impossible that Paul the Pharisee had (suppressed) doubts about some of the ritual stipulations; his fanatic persecution of those Christians who openly supported these doubts and drew practical conclusions would fit well with such a state of mind. The logical thing to do would have been a critique of the ritual part of the law or of the unmotivated precepts in it. Paul, however, in his extant letters shrinks back from making explicit distinctions within God's law and is therefore finally driven to criticize the law as a whole.

Some such uneasiness with the law (which, be it repeated, cannot be conclusively proved) could to some extent explain Paul's *conversion* to Christ along with which went the acceptance of a more or less lax attitude to Torah observance. The Christ experience liberated Paul from these possible suppressed misgivings about the law. Such problems with the law are hardly, however, a sufficient explanation for Paul's unique and radical critique of the law in his later epistles. Why did he apparently go much farther than the Hellenists he had persecuted? To find out, other possibilities must be explored.

2. Application of a current Jewish idea?

It has repeatedly been suggested that it was a common expectation in

---

Cf. the temptations of Jews in the Roman world reflected in the speech of Zambrias (Josephus, *Ant.* IV, 145–147; see above, p. 133). Zambrias charges Moses for 'having purposed to abolish things which all the world has unanimously admitted to be excellent and for having set up, over against universal opinion, thine own extravagances' (147).

36 Sanh 21b etc.; see Schäfer, art.cit. 41 f. (with n. 57).

Judaism that the law would cease in the Messianic age.[37] According to Schweitzer, Paul was only drawing the logical conclusion from the fact that the law ceases to be when the Messianic reign begins.[38] Schweitzer's only textual basis was, however, the silence of Jewish apocalypses about the law in the Messianic age. In addition, he speculated that, logically, the law is dispensable if evil no longer exists.[39] This kind of thinking totally ignores the fact that the law did not exist, according the Jewish view, merely to hold evil in check. It was the *order of creation*. From this point of view the idea of its abolition in the Messianic age becomes very difficult.[40]

In recent times the main representative of this interpretation has been Schoeps[41] who has also tried to adduce Rabbinic evidence.[42] He claims that it was a wide-spread opinion in Rabbinic literature that in the Messianic age the old law would be abolished along with the evil inclination and that God would give, through the Messiah, a new Torah.[43] Yet the Jewish material is sparse, marginal and partly late, and its interpretation is disputed; it is quite insufficient to support the notion of a well-known 'Messianic dogma' which

---

37 Earlier representatives of this view were Löwy, 'Lehre' (1904), 323 ff. and Bugge, 'Gesetz' 95 ff. (a rather fantastic version); cf. also Gottlob Klein, *Studien* 76 ff.

38 *Mystik* 186.

39 Ibid. 188 f.

40 See J. Maier, *Geschichte* 172 f.

41 *Paul* 171 ff.; Schoeps is followed by Ben-Chorin, *Paulus* 70 ff. Similarly Stendahl, *Paul* 84; cf. also Davies, *Setting* 184.

42 Sanh 97a (paralleled by AZ 9a, pMeg 70d) records a tradition from the midrash *Tanna debe Eliyahu*, according to which 2000 years of Tohuwabohu and 2000 years of the Torah will be followed by 2000 years of the days of the Messiah. The statement is embedded in a long section which focuses on the coming of the Messianic era (in AZ in a section about calendar matters) and it goes on (Sanh 97b): 'but through our many iniquities all these years (sc. the years of the Messianic era already passed by) have been lost'. Freedman (ET 657) is surely correct in commenting that the 2000 years of the Torah do 'not mean that the Torah should cease thereafter, but is mentioned merely to distinguish it from the next era'; cf. Schäfer, art.cit. 37: 'es geht um die Frage nach dem *Beginn* der messianischen Zeit ... ' Cf. also Davies, *Torah* 78 f.

The statement in Nid 61b that the commandments will cease in the Age to come is taken to refer to the state of the dead by Davies, *Torah* 80 ff.; id., *Setting* 181 f., which is plausible. The point is that it is therefore lawful to bury a person in a shroud with *kil'ayim*.

The statement that there will be neither merits nor guilt in the Messianic era (Shab 151b) is most naturally taken to mean that in the Messianic era Israel can perfectly understand the Torah and therefore *fulfil* it; perfect fulfilment is the point (Schäfer, art.cit. 37 f.).

Some passages, however, do contain the idea that individual commandments will be changed in the eschatological future, the most radical one being MidrPs 146.4. See above, p. 235 f. and below, p. 238.

43 Schoeps, op.cit. 172.

Paul could have taken up and developed.[44] Thus W.D. Davies rather more
cautiously concludes that the evidence 'cannot be regarded as very impressive'.[45] In the final analysis, the most important argument is that the Christians, according to Davies, found room for the concept of a 'Messianic
Torah'![46]

Thus, neither the idea of a new Torah nor the expectation of the abolition
of the old one are characteristic of Rabbinic Judaism. What *can* be verified is
a tendency in some circles to 'examine the grounds for the precepts'. In these
more radical groups even some purity and slaughter stipulations were expected to be changed in the eschatological future.[47] The most radical text in this
regard is the Midrash on Psalms 146.4, referred to above. This idea of a modification of the Torah is, however, limited to the periphery of Rabbinic
thought. It was by no means a well-known or accepted 'dogma' (it was
explicitly rejected by mainstream Rabbis) on which Paul or anyone else
could have built his theology without even mentioning the underlying
assumption.[48]

If the modification of the law is to take place in the Messianic age, it
follows that a new legislation by the Messiah is needed. Characteristically,
both Davies and Schoeps are led to assume that the idea of a 'law of the
Messiah' for the Christians played a part in Paul's thought. The phrase νόμος
τοῦ χριστοῦ (Gal 6.2) is taken as a reference to such a new law; Schoeps sees
even in the νόμος πίστεως of Rom 3.27 such a reference.[49] We have seen
before that such an interpretation of Gal 6.2 can hardly be upheld.[50]

Schoeps also refers to much later Jewish pseudomessianic movements (the
Sabbatians, the Frankists) who declared the Mosaic law to be superseded
because the end time had begun with their Messiah.[51] This is not a true
analogy, however, for unlike Paul Sabbatai Zwi and his followers were outspoken antinomists who ostentatiously broke the Torah. It is noteworthy
that the historian of the Sabbatian movement, G. Scholem, does *not* use this

---

44 Against Schoeps cf. Sandmel, *Genius* 40 f.; Bammel, 'Nomos' 121 ff.; Sanders, *Paul*
    479 f.
45 Davies, *Torah* 90.
46 Op.cit. 90 ff.
47 See above, p. 235 f.
48 Cf. also Urbach, *Sages* 297 ff.; Luz, 'Gesetz' 53 f. Contrast the view of Bugge, art.cit.
    107: Paul's latent presupposition was so self-evident and so well-known to his readers that it did not have to be set forth directly.
49 Schoeps, op.cit. 172 f.
50 See above, II 7.
51 Schoeps, op.cit. 173.

analogy to explain the rise of Paulinism which, in his view, 'did not arise out of any immanent logic'.[52]

The conclusive proof that Paul did not build his teaching on the law on a ready-made Rabbinic 'dogma' is the fact that he never makes a reference to such a 'generally accepted' (so the theory of Schoeps) premise. Such an accepted basis would have been more than welcome in Paul's argument with the Judaizers. Instead, Paul has to develop arguments of a different kind, arguments that are both more complicated and less persuasive. What a splendid opportunity to argue from that well-known dogma (had it existed) Paul would have had in Rom 7.1–6! Instead of appealing to the 'fact' that the law will come to an end when the Messiah has appeared Paul resorts to the argument that the law is not binding when a person has died[53] without, however, being able to keep his comparisons in order.[54] Likewise, 'the complicated argumentation of Gal 3, 17 ff. ... shows most clearly that he could not avail himself of the conception according to which the Law was either to be replaced in the Messianic age or supplemented by the Messiah'.[55]

At best we can thus say that Paul may have been (more or less unconsciously?) plagued by a similar questioning of the unmotivated commandments of the law as is implied in the quest of 'ground-searchers' – a questioning no doubt promptly suppressed by him on the conscious level of his mind. His theological argument is not constructed on such a basis.

Even less plausible is Hartmut Gese's and Peter Stuhlmacher's theory of an eschatological 'Zion Torah', allegedly expected by many Jews since the time of the Exile and, apparently, still by apocalyptic circles in Paul's times.[56] The picture of the 'Zion Torah' as portrayed by these scholars[57] is an artificial conglomerate from widely different contexts[58] and there is not a shred

---

52 Scholem, *Idea* 57. On Scholem's view see below, p. 262 n. 167.

53 Cf. Davies, *Setting* 183 n. 1; Sanders, op.cit. 479 f.

54 See above, p. 61 f.,   55 Bammel, art.cit. 124 f.

56 Gese, *Theologie* 73 ff.; Stuhlmacher, *Versöhnung* 142 ff. On p. 82 Gese clearly assumes that the expectation of the 'Zion Torah' was alive in apocalyptic circles, for he states: Paul 'geht vom letzten alttestamentlichen Gesetzesverständnis in der Apokalyptik aus, d.h. er setzt den Gegensatz alter und neuer Äon voraus und *dement-sprechend* den Gegensatz der Sinaitora und der Zionsoffenbarung' (my italics). On Stuhlmacher's view see below, n. 59.

57 The characteristics of the eschatological Torah according to Stuhlmacher, op.cit. 143, are as follows. It goes forth from Zion, not Sinai. Thanks to the gift of the Spirit and the annihilation of death this Torah will be in itself intelligible and practicable. In its centre will be the Todah, the thanksgiving offering after deliverance from danger of death. The Zion Torah is addressed to all nations. In all this it amounts to an eschatological fulfilment of the historically provisional Torah of Sinai. See the following note.

58 Gese and Stuhlmacher cite as evidence Jer 31.31 ff., Ezek 36.22 ff., Ezek 37, Ezek 20.25 f., Isa 2.2 ff., Mic 4.1 ff., Isa 25.7 ff., Ezek 40–48, and Ps 50. As for the

of evidence for the assumption that the apocalyptic contrast between the two aeons corresponded to a contrast between the Torah of Sinai and the revelation on Zion.[59] Paul did not take up a current Jewish expectation in his 'doctrine' of the law. The question still remains, however, whether he might not have seized on an expectation witnessed *in the OT* but neglected by subsequent generations. We therefore next turn to this question.

3. Taking up an Old Testament prophecy?

It is often suggested that Paul's theology of the law is due to his application of certain OT prophecies to the situation in which the Christians lived. The crucial prophecy is then, of course, the promise of the new covenant in Jer 31.31−34, in conjunction with Ezek 11.19 f., 36.25−27, 37, where a new spirit and a new heart are spoken of.[60] But did Paul perceive such a connection between his statements on the law and Jer 31?[61] If so, the estab-

---

characteristics of the Zion Torah mentioned in the preceding note it should be noted that there is no interest in Zion in Jer 31, Ezek 20.25 f. or Ezek 36 f.; no concern with Gentiles either in the just mentioned texts or in Ezek 40 ff. or in Ps 50; Ezek 36 f. are the only chapters to mention the Spirit, Isa 25 the only passage to mention annihilation of death, and Ps 50 to mention the Todah offering (Gese sees the meal described in Isa 25 as a Todah meal as well). No reference to an eschatological future is found in Ps 50. The individual text that contains most of the said characteristics (Zion, Gentiles, reference to the eschatological future, annihilation of death), namely Isa 25, is also the one which contains absolutely *no* reference to the law whatsoever! A conception which brings the eschatological face-to-face vision of God (Isa 25) and the everyday religion of Ps 50 together under the umbrella of a 'new revelation of the Torah from Zion' is surely a bit monstrous! The only text that can be said to contain any kind of critique of the Torah is Ezek 20.25 f.; in this text, however, there is no mention of Zion, the Gentiles, the Spirit, or eschatology. For a discussion of Jer 31 from this point of view see below, VIII 3.

59 Thus, Gese's reference to Paul's alleged apocalyptic background as regards his notion of the law is tacitly dropped by Stuhlmacher (cf. *Versöhnung* 144 ff.). It is not clear whether Stuhlmacher assumes that Paul was conscious of a 'Zion Torah' promised in the OT in the texts brought together by Gese (albeit ignored by the generation of the apostle) or whether he sees only a theological analogy between Paul and the 'Zion Torah' passages. If the latter alternative is true (and the former one would be well-nigh absurd), then Stuhlmacher's language is at least misleading: he produces, in his exegesis of *Paul*, statements like ' "the Torah of Christ" (sc. of Gal 6.2, HR) is the Zion Torah brought by Jesus' (op.cit. 158) etc.

60 Thus, e.g., Feuillet, 'Loi ancienne' 790 f., 803; Lyonnet, *Étapes* 160 ff. (trying to establish a correspondence between Rom 8.1−4 and the larger contexts of Jer 31 and Ezek 36, so that e.g. the condemnation of sin Rom 8.3 takes up the prophecy of Gog and Magog in Ezek 38 f.!); Michel on Rom 8.2; Cranfield on Rom 8.4; Bruce, 'Paul' 275 f.; Stuhlmacher, op.cit. 159, 161.

61 It is often not clear whether an interpreter assumes that Paul *consciously* took up a passage like Jer 31, or whether there is just a theological analogy between what he says and the OT passage (cf. above, n. 59); if the latter is the case this would not help

lishment of such a connection must have been a creative act of interpretation, for contemporary Judaism did not hold an expectation of a new law on the basis of these passages. Whether or not the idea of the new *covenant* which was so prominent in Qumran was based on Jer 31,[62] in Qumran that idea certainly did *not* have the notion of a *new* Torah as its corollary.

Curiously enough, Christian interpreters who see a connection between Jer 31 and Paul's teaching on the law are divided as to what kind of message Paul got from the prophetic passage. While some think that, just as Jer 31 anticipates, the old law is *replaced* with a quite new one in Paul[63], others claim that the similarity consists instead in the fact that the law *remains the same*; it is man, not the Torah, who changes.[64] What, then, is actually said about the law in Jer 31 and the related passages?

The point of Jer 31.31–34[65] is undoubtedly the miraculous change in man's *attitude* to God's law. This change is effected, in the eschatological future, by God himself. He will put his law in the inward parts of men, or write it in their hearts (v. 32). At that time it will be unnecessary to admonish anybody to 'know the Lord' for, as a result of the forgiveness of sins, all Israel will know him anyway. This great renewal in man's relation to Yahweh makes up the content of the new covenant which will supersede the old one that was broken by Israel. Men's hearts will be renewed. There is *no* reference to any changes in the *content* of the Torah,[66] let alone to the notion of a law of the Messiah. This is also clear from the fact that in parallel passages the same promise can be expressed without any Torah terminology at all. Thus, the promise of an 'eternal covenant' is paralleled in Jer 32.40 by the concomitant one that God will put the *fear* of him in the hearts of the Israelites,[67] and in Jer 24.7 the description of the restitution of Israel as Yahweh's people includes the statement that God will 'give them a heart so that they will know me' (without any mention of the law).[68]

Thus Jer 31.31 ff. appears to be wholly in keeping with the basic con-

---

to explain the rise of Paul's view although the analogy would be significant for a 'biblical theology'.

62 For the thesis that it was not see below, p. 242 f.

63 Thus Michel on Rom 8.2.

64 Thus Cranfield on Rom 8.4.

65 It is of course unnecessary to discuss here the authenticity of the passage; most probably it should be ascribed to a Deuteronomistic redaction. See for authenticity Rudolph ad loc.; against it Herrmann, *Heilserwartungen* 179–185; Perlitt, *Bundestheologie* 180; Böhmer, *Heimkehr* 74–78 (the passage is deuteronomistic).

66 Rudolph, ad loc.; von Rad, *Theology* II 270: 'The new thing lies in the human sphere, in a change in the hearts of men.'

67 This passage, too, appears to be Deuteronomistic and Exilic; cf. Böhmer, op.cit. 43.

68 Jer 24.7, too, seems to stem from Deuteronomistic redactors: Thiel, *Redaktion* 256; Böhmer, op.cit. 32.

ception of Deuteronomy, expressed classically in Deut 6.5: Israel is to *love* Yahweh with all its heart.[69] The passage in Jeremiah, however, displays no optimism as regards man's ability to do this. The reason is clear: between Deuteronomy and Jer 31 lay the catastrophe of the year 587. The Deuteronomic reform had failed to prevent the calamity. The hope of a better future could only be placed in Yahweh, in *his* ability to change man's obstinate heart. This expectation of a change in man's attitude, brought about by God himself, was one that stirred the minds in Exilic times to a remarkably great extent (in addition to the passages in Jeremiah see Ezek 11.19, 36.26, Deut 29.3 f., Deut 30.6).[70] It is not the *law* that is the problem for the circles in question; the problem lies with man. There is no basis for a theology of an abrogation of the law in Jer 31 or the related texts.[71] Judaism was quite justified in not expecting such an abrogation to take place on the basis of Jer 31.

Thus Paul could not seize on Jer 31 if he understood the passage in its original meaning or in consonance with contemporary Jewish understanding. At best, he could have gained support from Jeremiah or Ezekiel for his notion of the true fulfilment of the 'just requirement of the law' by Christians (Rom 8.4). No clear linguistic allusions to such prophecies, however, can be detected in Rom 8.4.

The possibility still remains, of course, that Paul understood Jer 31 differently. *He* might have thought that the passage referred to a transformation or even to an abrogation of the old law.[72] But what evidence is there that Paul actually has Jer 31 at the back of his mind?

The evidence is surprisingly slight. Paul does mention the new covenant, apart from the Lord's Supper tradition (1 Cor 11.25), in 2 Cor 3.6, 14 (cf. also Gal 4.21 ff.) but he does *not* cite Jer 31 in this connection. At least it is not clear that Jeremiah is in his mind at all. Paul did not have to turn to Jeremiah to get the key word 'new covenant'; it was already there in the tradition of the institution of the Eucharist (cf. 1 Cor 11.25). It is not clear, whether that tradition was influenced by Jer 31 either.[73] Chr. Wolff has argued that the idea of a new covenant in Judaism (Bar 2.35, Qumran) does

---

69 Herrmann, op.cit. 185, cf. 200.
70 Cf. Böhmer, op.cit. 76 f. Fiedler, *Jesus* 34 f. suggests that even the theocentric statements should be taken mainly as an appeal to the remaining rest of the people to repent (cf. Deut 30.1–10, Ezek 48, Ezek 33).
71 Ezek 36.27 (par 11.20) lets God say: 'My Spirit will I give within you and bring about that you will walk according to my commandments, obey my statutes and keep them'; there is no hint of any changes in these commandments. The one OT passage which might have lent itself to support the abrogation of the old law, Ezek 20.25 (see above, p. 158 ff.), is never alluded to by Paul.
72 The author of Hebrews seems to have deduced that from Jer 31.
73 Such an influence is denied by Wolff, *Jeremia* 131–134.

not go back to Jer 31[74], but rather to Deuteronomistic theology in general.[75]

Be that as it may, it is at any rate noteworthy that the distinguishing features of Jer 31.31 ff. were indeed taken up neither in Qumran nor among early Christians. We hear nothing of either the law being written in the hearts of the people or of the spontaneous knowledge of the Lord that renders all admonition superfluous.[76] There is none of this in 2 Cor 3.6 ff. either.

But what about 2 Cor 3.3? There a contrast is set up between what is written on 'stone tablets' on one hand and on 'the tablets of fleshly hearts' on the other. Some expositors read this as a reference to the law of Sinai and to the same law as written in the hearts of the Christians respectively.[77] Moreover, the verse is often taken as an indication of the influence of Jer 31 on Paul's thought,[78] although the mention of 'fleshly hearts' comes from Ezek 11.19, 36.26 (the hearts are not characterized as 'fleshly' in Jer 31.33; on the other hand, nothing is 'written' in the hearts in Ezek 11 or 36).

In 2 Cor 3.3, however, Paul does not speak of a *law* written in men's hearts (as he does, in a different context, in Rom 2.15[79]). He argues in 3.1–3 that, unlike his rivals, he does not need letters of recommendation. He has, namely, such a letter in the Corinthians themselves! This letter is written in Paul's heart where everybody can read it.[80] This somewhat odd image[81] is used by Paul in v. 2 without any OT reminiscences.

In v. 3 Paul tries to develop the comparison. The Corinthians, as a 'letter', are written by Christ and delivered by Paul. This living letter has been written, 'not with ink but with the Spirit of the living God'. This antithesis does not suggest any OT model.[82] The choice of 'Spirit' as a means used by Christ is a natural one, and Paul is still thinking of the image of letter-writing when mentioning 'ink' (he could not think of the Decalogue as being written with ink!).

It is only with the next phrase that the Decalogue enters the picture: Christ's letter of recommendation is not written on 'stone tablets' (cf. Ex

---

74 As against, e.g., F. Lang, 'Gesetz' 311.

75 Wolff, op.cit. 117–130, cf. 146.

76 Wolff, op.cit. 117 points out that a connection of a given passage with Jer 31 cannot be established with any certainty, if there is no reference to either of these specific features of Jer 31.

77 Thus Hughes ad loc.: 'It is most important to realize that it is the selfsame law which was graven on tablets of stone at Sinai that in this age of the new covenant is graven on the tablets of the human heart by the Holy Spirit.'

78 Thus, e.g., Cranfield, 'Paul' 57; id., *Romans* 854; Vos, *Untersuchungen* 137; van Unnik, *Sparsa I* 176, 185; Lang, art.cit. 315; Rissi, *Studien* 22.

79 For Rom 2.15 see above, p. 105.

80 Reading ἡμῶν. Barrett chooses the weakly attested reading ὑμῶν; similarly Rissi, op.cit. 20.

81 Cf. Robertson-Plummer, Lietzmann ad loc.; Georgi, *Gegner* 246 f.; Gale, *Use* 153 f.

82 Correctly Windisch ad loc.

31.18, 34.1). Paul's opponents had probably, along with their letters of recommendation, appealed to the revelation given to Moses. But why the 'tablets of fleshly hearts' as a counterpart? And *whose* heart is Paul now thinking of?

Starting from the picture used by Paul in v. 2 it would be logical to take the 'fleshly hearts' as a reference to Paul's own heart.[83] This, however, would render the contrast between stone and flesh inexplicable. Surely the impression is correct that 'as Paul wrote v. 3 the picture of the letters of recommendation gradually faded away as new thoughts crowded into the writer's mind'.[84] καρδίαι σαρκίναι is a reminiscence of Ezek 11.19, 36.26. Now it is a well-known Rabbinic association to establish a connection between the stone heart of the book of Ezekiel and the stone tablets of Exodus: it is proper that stone should watch over stone (the law over the stone heart, identified with the evil inclination).[85] This association may have been known to Paul; he, however, gives it a new turn. His thought flies from the stone heart to its opposite number, the heart of *flesh*; this he mentions as a contrast to the stone *tablets*, omitting to mention the heart of stone altogether. The reference is thus to the new life created by Christ with his Spirit in the hearts of the Corinthian believers − by Christ with his Spirit and not by the law for which the tablets of stone here stand.

It is noteworthy that the OT passage Paul undoubtedly alludes to is the promise of a new heart in *Ezekiel*.[86] It is quite clear that there is no mention of a change of the law in Ezekiel 11 or 36 f. It is uncertain, whether there is any allusion to Jer 31 in Paul's words here. There is at least no clear linguistic connection.[87] A dependence on Jer 31 is plausible on the assumption alone that Ezek 11.19 (36.26) and Jer 31.31 ff. belonged, in Paul's mind, inseparably together, so that the 'fleshly heart' (Ezek) without further ado brought to his mind the 'law written in the hearts' of Jeremiah as well. Such a connection is not a priori impossible.[88] It is difficult to establish it positively, either;

---

83 Cf. Kümmel ad loc.; Wolff, op.cit. 135.

84 Gale, op.cit. 155.

85 LevR 35.5; cf. Schechter, *Aspects* 274 f.

86 Wolff, op.cit. 135 is not justified in glossing over this reference.

87 The only link would be that between ἐπὶ καρδίας ... γράψω Jer 31.33 and ἐγγεγραμμένη ... ἐν καρδίαις 2 Cor 3.3. The link is tenuous. The alleged allusion to Jer 31 would be very colourless indeed. Even in Rom 2.15 there is a closer verbal similarity with Jer 31 (whether or not an allusion is intended; cf. above, p. 105). One could just as well see 2 Cor 3.3 as an allusion to Prov 7.3 ἐπίγραψον δὲ ἐπὶ τὸ πλάτος τῆς καρδίας σου (cf. Windisch, *2 Kor* 104; Wolff, op.cit. 135) − if there is any OT allusion at all. Nestle-Aland[26] takes 2 Cor 3.3 as an allusion to Prov 7.3 (*Novum Testamentum* p. 757), whereas no allusion to Jer 31 is found in 2 Cor 3 (see p. 763), unlike Rom 2.15. Ellis, *Use* 153. does not list a reference to Jer 31 in 2 Cor 3 either.

88 It seems that Ezek 36.26 was more often quoted in Rabbinic Judaism than was Jer

interestingly enough it has been argued that it is doubtful whether Paul ever used the book of Jeremiah at all![89]

But even on a 'maximalist' reading of 2 Cor 3.3 it is clear that Jer 31 is not of much help in our quest for the roots of Paul's theology of the law. At best we can detect in v. 3 a marginal theme which is not developed. The prediction of Jeremiah plays no part in v. 6 ff. where Paul elaborates the contrast between the Mosaic 'service' and his own apostleship. *If* Paul intended an allusion to Jer 31 in 2 Cor 3.3 or 3.6, it is all the more conspicuous that he *omits* what Jer 31 says about the *law*. For it is clear that it is *not* the *law* in any sense that has been written in the Corinthians' hearts according to verse 3.[90] The tablets of stone stand for the γράμμα which is the *opposite* of πνεῦμα (v. 6).[91]

As in the previous chapter, a quite simple observation may serve to produce the final confirmation that Paul did not make use of a pre-existent thesis in his theology of the law, in this case of the idea of a new covenant as expressed in Jer 31. Had Paul found in Jeremiah a confirmation of the notion that the law or parts of it were to be superseded (in whatever sense) at some point in the future, then why did he omit such a superb argument in his debates with more conservative Christians? Why did he never cite Jer 31 when arguing that Christ was the end of the law (contrast Heb 8.8–13, 10.16–18)? How much simpler would it have been to start from the new situation created by the new covenant than to develop the artificial analogy about the irrevocable human διαθήκη (Gal 3.15 ff.), or the marriage analogy in Rom 7.1 ff.! Paul did *not* derive his theology of the law from the promise of the new covenant in Jer 31.

4. *Taking up Jesus traditions?*

It has been said that instead of being 'an innovator', Paul was in his theology of the law 'an interpreter and exponent of the teachings of Jesus'.[92] Now what Jesus really 'taught' about the law is debated and it is not possible to discuss so complex a problem adequately in the framework of this study.[93] This is no great drawback, however, for Paul had no direct access to the

---

31.31 ff. In KohR I, 2, 4 Jer 31.33 and Ezek 36.26 do occur, however, in parallel trains of thought, ascribed to the Tannaites R. Judah and R. Nehemiah respectively.

89 Thus Wolff, op.cit. 141 f.

90 Lietzmann ad loc. is more correct in stating that what was written in the hearts of the Corinthians was 'the gospel'; similarly Barrett.

91 Lang, art.cit. 317 f. thinks that Paul *omitted* to cite Jer 31 precisely because of his view of the law, thus recognizing that Jer 31 would have been a poor support for a *contrast* between the law and the new covenant.

92 Branscomb, *Jesus* 279. Cf. Davies, *Paul* 136 ff.; Longenecker, *Paul* 128 ff.; Stuhl-macher, 'Rabbi' 68 f.

93 Cf. Hübner, *Tradition* 226 ff.; Banks, *Jesus* (a somewhat uncritical study); Braun, *Radikalismus* II, 3 ff.

teachings of Jesus. He was totally dependent on whatever traditions about the proclamation of Jesus were current in the congregations he had contact with, especially in Antioch; possibly Jerusalem traditions are relevant as well.[94] Our question, then, must take the following form: is Paul's teaching of the law explicable as an interpretation or a development of early Christian traditions about Jesus?

As is well-known, Paul has very few explicit quotations from the 'words of the Lord' in his letters. The actual quotations have no bearing on Paul's discussions about the law.[95] It is more difficult to decide whether Paul was consciously drawing on words of the Lord when chrystallizing the law into the commandment of loving one's neighbour (Rom 13.8–10, Gal 5.14).[96] The issue is complicated through the fact that the authenticity of the dual commandment of love (Paul, however, omits the love of God!) as part of Jesus' teaching is debated[97]; we cannot be sure that it was actually contained in any tradition of Jesus' sayings at the time Paul was writing. But even on the (to my mind, unlikely) assumption that Paul consciously took up a word of Jesus in this case, this state of affairs would hardly explain any of Paul's idiosyncracies as regards his view of the law. It would only account for *similarities* between Paul and, say, Matthew; their differences would stand out as a greater problem than ever.

The crucial statement of Paul to be discussed in this connection is, however, his assertion that 'nothing is unclean in itself' (οὐδὲν κοινὸν δι᾽ ἑαυτοῦ) in Rom 14.14, along with the statement that 'everything is clean' (πάντα μὲν καθαρά) in Rom 14.20. Both statements occur in a discussion of foods which posed a problem in a community like the Roman congregation, as the 'weak' (v. 1) refused to eat meat (v. 2, 21) or drink wine (v. 21). In v. 14 Paul introduces his statement with the affirmation 'I know and am convinced in Lord Jesus' (οἶδα καὶ πέπεισμαι ἐν κυρίῳ Ἰησοῦ). Is this clause intended by Paul as a citation formula which indicates that he is quoting a saying (Mk 7.15) from the traditions about Jesus?[98] This is often assumed but hardly any real arguments have been put forward to support the claim.[99]

---

94 Antiochian traditions, of course, went back to the Stephen circle in the first place. As Paul was relatively early in contact with Peter, he must have had a direct access to some Jerusalem traditions, too.

95 The saying on divorce (1 Cor 7.10) could have been relevant, but it is not used by Paul in any such way.

96 Cf. Barrett.

97 Cf. for different views Burchard, 'Liebesgebot' and R.H. Fuller, 'Doppelgebot'.

98 In favour of a quotation: i.a. Zahn, B. Weiss, Lagrange, Michel, H.W. Schmidt, Leenhardt, Käsemann; Jeremias, *Theology* 210 (with n. 1); Walter, 'Christusglaube' 428 (with n. 29). Against a quotation i.a. Lipsius, Sanday-Headlam, Kühl, Lietzmann, Barrett; Schlatter, *Gerechtigkeit* 374.

99 Some scholars suggest that the mention of the name 'Jesus' could contain a reference

To say the least, the οἶδα καὶ πέπεισμαι clause would be a very surprising formula to introduce a quotation from *verba domini*. In the indubitable quotations Paul refers to what the Lord has 'said' (1 Thess 4.15 ἐν λόγῳ κυρίου, cf. λέγει 1 Cor 7.12) or commanded (παραγγέλλω 1 Cor 7.10, διέταξεν 1 Cor 9.14; cf. ἐπιταγή 1 Cor 7.25).[100] These statements are surrounded by an air of objective authority; there is to be no discussion *pro et contra* about commandments of the Lord. In Rom 14 Paul's argument is quite different; no wonder, for his topic is an *adiaphoron*. The οἶδα καὶ πέπεισμαι statement gives expression to a deeply felt personal conviction which Paul has reached because of his communion with the Lord.[101] It is paralleled by a set of related statements in his letters: 'I trust (πέποιθα) in you in the Lord that' Gal 5.10; 'I am convinced (πέποιθα) in the Lord that ... ' Phil 2.24.[102] Paul can also express a similar trust without an 'in the Lord' formula: 'having this conviction I know that... '(πεποιθὼς οἶδα) Phil 1.25; 'I am convinced (πέπεισμαι) about you that ... ' (Rom 15.14); 'I am convinced (πέπεισμαι) that ... ' (Rom 8.38).[103] Interestingly enough it is only in Romans that Paul uses the form πέπεισμαι. It seems clear to me that Paul is in Rom 14.14 drawing on his Christian experience rather than on any saying of the Lord.[104]

Moreover, the similarity between Mk 7.15 and Rom 14.14 is limited to the words οὐδέν and κοινόν/κοινῶσαι.[105] Paul's usage in this passage has a closer affinity with the Markan commentary καθαρίζων πάντα τὰ βρώματα (Mk 7.19), for when Paul takes up in v. 20 the thought of v. 14 he uses the words πάντα (sc. βρώματα) μὲν καθαρά This indeed raises the possibility that Mark is influenced by Pauline traditions rather than vice versa.

---

to the historical Jesus; thus Zahn, B. Weiss, Lagrange (as a possibility), Cranfield (likewise), Leenhardt. This is a weak argument. For one thing, Paul mostly uses 'the Lord' instead of 'Jesus' in the indubitable cases when he refers to words of the historical Jesus (1 Cor 7.10, 12, 25; 9.14). And secondly, the formulation 'the Lord Jesus' occurs, to be sure, as a designation of the historical Jesus in 1 Cor 11.23 and 1 Thess 2.15 (cf. 2 Cor 4.14); however, the expression '(our) Lord Jesus' often enough also clearly refers to the exalted Kyrios. This is the case (without 'our') in 1 Cor 16.23, 2 Cor 11.31, Phil 2.19 and 1 Thess 4.2; with 'our' the formula refers to the earthly Jesus in 1 Cor 5.4 (twice), 2 Cor 1.14, 1 Thess 2.19, 3.11, 13.

100 Yet even the 'commandment of the Lord' in 1 Cor 14.37 is probably *not* a word of the Lord; neither are the 'orders' given 'through the Lord Jesus' 1 Thess 4.2. See above, p. 80, 82.

101 Cf. Lipsius, Lietzmann.   102 Cf. also 2 Thess 3.4.   103 Cf. also 2 Tim 1.12.

104 Dodd objects ('Ennomos' 106) that if Paul meant no more than 'I am convinced in virtue of my union with Christ as a member of his body', then 'it is not easy to see what reply Paul would have to one who should say "and *I* am convinced in the Lord Jesus that the reverse is true"'. I think that Paul actually had no reply; probably he would simply have denied the value of the other conviction.

105 Cf. Kühl.

Furthermore, Paul does *not* use the statement made in Rom 14.14 (20) in any of his extended discussions over the law. This silence must be deemed highly significant.[106] What an effective argument would a word from the Lord have been in the Galatians debate, for instance! It is even more difficult to conceive that Paul would have refrained from using such a weapon in the Antiochian conflict. There is no such hint in Gal 2.11 ff., however; instead, Paul develops his argument from theological insights gained after Easter. There would hardly have been a need to argue the case at all had a suitable word of the Lord been readily at hand. It is perhaps even more significant that there is no indication in Gal 2.1 ff. — and in this regard the account com-pletely agrees with Acts 15 — that decisions made by Jesus played any part in the discussions on the Apostolic Council; on the contrary, it was argued from what had been experienced in the missionary work (Gal 2.8, cf. Acts 15.8 f., 12). It must be concluded that if Paul knew a word of the Lord like Mk 7.15, in any case he did not argue from it; he did *not* base his theology of the law on it. And as Paul went to the council as a representative of the Antiochian congregation which no doubt cherished the traditions of the Hellenists who had founded it, it is clear that whatever the attitude of the Hellenists to the law, it was *not* argued on the basis of such sayings. The natural conclusion is that the saying was not known either to Paul or to his predecessors in Gentile mission. Whether we should also conclude that the historical Jesus never took so radical an attitude to the law as implied in Mk 7.15 is not to be debated here.[107]

Add to this that Paul speaks of Jesus both as one who 'came under the law' (Gal 4.4 f.) and as a 'servant of circumcision' (Rom 15.8), and it seems rather unlikely that he would have attributed a critical attitude to the law to the historical Jesus.[108]

It should still be added that even if, contrary to all likelihood, there existed a genetic connection between the saying in Mk 7.15 and Paul's view of the law, that could at best explain a feature shared by Paul with many of his Christian contemporaries (his neglect to observe the ritual law among Gentiles). It would not account for the radical features, e.g. the close connec-tion between law and sin; no saying pointing to such a connection can be found in the Jesus traditions.

---

106 Cf. Müller, 'Rezeption' 159.
107 Cf. Merkel, 'Markus 7, 15'; Carlston, 'Things'; Percy, *Botschaft* 118, for different answers to the question; and see my articles 'Herkunft' and 'Jesus'.
108 Cf. Wrede, *Paulus* 83, 92; Lütgert, *Freiheitspredigt* 10; Wernle, *Anfänge* 216; Bacon, *Matthew* 357. It should be recalled here that even Paul himself, who says he is (unlike Christ, according to Gal 4.4) *not* 'under the law', behaved toward 'those under the law' as being himself in the same position (1 Cor 9.20). How much more must this apply to the historical Jesus who was a servant of the *circumcised* (alone)!

5. Meditation on Deut 21.23?

It is not uncommon to trace Paul's attitude to the Torah back to a meditation on Deut 21.23 (cited in Gal 3.13) in the light of his Christophany.
Certainly Paul the Pharisee was offended by the Christians' proclamation
largely because they proclaimed a crucified Messiah, 'a scandal to the Jews'
(1 Cor 1.23). In Paul's time, the statement of the Torah concerning the curse
inflicted by God on a person hanged on a tree (Deut 21.23) was quite commonly applied to those who underwent the Roman penalty of crucifixion,
too.[109] It is likely, then, that Paul (and other opponents of the new sect)
had persecuted the Christians in the conviction that on the basis of the law
itself Jesus could not have been the real Messiah.

The Christian Paul, however, has an explanation for the dilemma of the
crucified Messiah: Jesus became 'a curse' on behalf of us, in order to redeem
us from the curse pronounced on us by the law (Gal 3.13). Many interpreters
see in this very verse an indication of what it was that changed Paul's mind as
regards the status of the Torah. The Christophany, it is held, proved to Paul
not only that God had vindicated Jesus as the Messiah by resurrecting him
from the dead, but also that the law which contained the curse over the crucified was wrong or no longer valid. Thus Schweitzer argued that at this point
the law was proved to be wrong at one particular; consequently it must be
totally invalid.[110] This interpretation is clearly wrong: Deut 21.23 is *not*
invalidated in Gal 3.13. It is the very point of that verse that Christ *was*
indeed under a curse while hanging on the cross.[111] Only, this is shown to
be explicable on account of the idea of a vicarious curse.

A more usual interpretation is as follows. Paul's encounter with the risen
Christ revealed to him that the law had come to an end, for God's vindication
of Jesus simultaneously signalled his judgment over the very law that had
condemned Jesus, put him under a curse and brought him to the cross.[112]
Paul was able to conclude from his Christophany, it is held, that God himself
had revoked the law. This interpretation, too, is based on incorrect premises.
Thus Paul never suggests that it was the *law* that condemned Jesus or brought
him to the cross.[113] He does not indicate that Jesus was killed, say, because

---

109 See above, p. 59.

110 *Mystik* 73. Cf. also Kim, *Origin* 274.

111 It is Justin (*Dial.* 111.2), not Paul, who denies that Christ was under the curse on the
cross.

112 Thus Maurer, *Gesetzeslehre* 62 f., 97; Stuhlmacher, *Gerechtigkeit* 95; id., *Versöhnung*
182, 185, 194–196; Beker, *Paul* 185 f., 261; Weder, *Kreuz* 190 ff.; cf. also Duncan;
Kim, *Origin* 274. Luz, 'Gesetz' 91 would apparently attribute a similar view to Christians before Paul.

113 Cf. Leivestad, *Christ* 105: 'The execution of Jesus can never be conceived as a lawful
act. He is not convicted according to the Mosaic law. His condemnation cannot be

of his critical attitude to the law;[114] on the contrary, he states that Jesus was a 'servant of circumcision' (Rom 15.8) and, therefore, himself 'under the law' (Gal 4.4).[115] The crucifixion is attributed to cosmic powers rather than to zealous legalists (1 Cor 2.8)[116] and, in the final analysis, to God's salvific purpose. Christ took the curse voluntarily upon him (cf. e.g. Phil 2.8) on behalf of others. It is by no means obvious that the idea of a person bearing the curse of others should logically lead to the idea that the law which entailed the curse must be abolished, just as the destiny of the OT scapegoat did not lead to the idea of an abolition of the Torah. It is indeed hardly to be doubted that Paul's Jewish Christian opponents shared with him the idea of Christ's death on behalf of us.[117] It did not occur to them, however, that the law had therefore come to an end. It is not clear that the logic ascribed to Paul by his interpreters at this point is compelling. If there was a connection between Paul's exegesis of Deut 21.23 and his critique of the law, he never spells it out.

It is indeed quite likely that Gal 3.13 should be taken in another sense. It shows that Paul had found an intellectual solution to the dilemma of a crucified Messiah by ascribing a vicarious value to the curse the reality of which, in the light of God's word in the Torah, could not be doubted. The idea of a vicarious curse, then, answers the question why the Messiah had died in such a scandalous way.

The Christophany, it would seem, convinced Paul that Jesus was *no longer* under the curse of the law. He *had been*, but for quite a specific purpose. The law was not wrong in pronouncing that curse; indeed the framework of the Torah is not surrendered in the course of this particular argument. God thus did not have to annul anything in the law. Jesus suffered the curse on behalf of others; the curse itself remains as valid as ever for transgressors (Gal 3.10!). What has changed is not the status of the law but the situation of the believers in Christ. For them there is no condemnation (Rom 8.1). It is very hard to see how antinomian consequences should follow from *these* considerations alone, i.e. from a meditation upon Deut 21.23 in the light of Paul's call vision alone. Something more was needed.

It should be noted, moreover, that there is no reference to the resurrection of Jesus in the context of Gal 3.13. Conversely, no reference to the theme of

---

justified through a legitimate reference to the law. Therefore the law cannot be directly responsible for his death.'

114 Thus Pannenberg, *Jesus* 254; Edwards, *Christ* 267 f., 316 f., 347; Weder, *Kreuz* 191 n. 262; Türcke, *Potential* 81–83.

115 Cf. above, p. 248.

116 Beker, op.cit. 262 would include the law among these powers in 1 Cor 2.8.

117 Cf. Mussner, *Gal* 185; Grafe, *Lehre* 20: 'Aber durch diese Tilgung der auf den Gesetzesübertretern lastenden κατάρα glaubten sie (Paul's adversaries) das Gesetz nun erst recht in seinem Bestande befestigt und den Menschen zu erneuter Erfüllung des Gesetzes befähigt.' See also Eckert, *Verkündigung* 111.

'curse' occurs in Paul's — admittedly brief — accounts of his call experience.

Some interpreters would read even more out of Gal 3.13. J.C. Beker writes: 'In his conversion experience, Paul discovers the strange truth that the power of sin does not collide with the Torah but allies itself with it. Otherwise, the Torah could not have condemned the Son of God, who was sent by God to redeem us.' Paul can thus conclude that ' "the power of sin" operates not only behind our individual "sins" ... but even more behind the poisonous function of the law. How otherwise could those who, like Paul, had been most faithful to the law have persecuted and crucified the Messiah of God on the very basis of the law?'[118] Such a construction, were it tenable, might indeed make Paul's allegations of the close connection between law and sin more intelligible. Yet it must be repeated that according to Paul, it was *not* the Torah that had *caused* the condemnation and crucifixion of Jesus. The alleged connection between law and sin cannot, therefore, be accounted for in this way. When Paul speaks of the sin-engendering capacity of the law, the context always shows that he has *transgressions* of the law in mind rather than legalistic hybris.[119]

6. Adopting a pattern set by the 'Hellenists'?

It is a real pity that we know so little about the 'Hellenist' group around Stephen.[120] Quite indubitably there was some point of contact at least between their thinking and Paul's. Paul had persecuted Christians before his conversion. Not all Christians, however, were persecuted at this point, but most probably just the 'Hellenists'.[121] The Hellenists must therefore have held views different from those of the 'Hebrews'. It is a natural conclusion that these differences had something to do with the law. Luke's account of the accusations against Stephen (Acts 6.11, 13 f.), whatever its historical value, points to the same direction. According to Luke, the accusation was that Stephen had blasphemed against Moses and God (v. 11) by claiming that Jesus would destroy the temple and change 'the customs' delivered by Moses (v. 14). Whether the speech in Acts 7 can cast any light on the views of the historical Stephen is not clear.[122] It would seem that the Hellenists displayed

---

118 Beker, op.cit. 261 f.

119 Cf. above, p. 141 f.

120 For reconstructions of their activity and teachings see Wilson, *Gentiles* 138 ff.; Dunn, *Unity* 268 ff.; Schneider, 'Stephanus'; and above all Hengel, 'Jesus'.

121 Acts 11.19 clearly indicates (against 8.1) that not *all* Christians of Jerusalem were dispersed by a persecution, as does the fact that the Apostles could remain in the city (8.1). That a conflict over the law was the reason for the persecution is doubted by Strecker, *Eschaton* 233 f. and by Hultgren, 'Persecutions' 97 ff.; cf. also Schade, *Christologie* 111. But why else should just the Hellenists have been persecuted while the Hebraist leaders were not?

122 Simon, *Stephen* and Scharlemann, *Stephen* still build on it; cf. Scroggs, 'Christianity';

some disregard if not hostility toward the Temple and its cult as well as some laxity as regards the ritual Torah in general. What exactly this entailed we cannot say; in any case, they must have taken a noticeably different attitude from that of the Hebrews.

To be sure, the attitude of the Hellenists to the law is often taken to have been a lot more radical. It is held that they repudiated the law altogether [123] or at least sat light to its cultic-ritual part.[124] There is no great difference between these two views, since a rejection of the law must have become visible to outsiders first and foremost as non-observance of the ritual Torah. The assumption that the Hellenists had expressly rejected the law 'as a way of righteousness'[125] is, in the absence of evidence, dubious; for, as we have seen, it is very much the question whether there existed in Judaism at all the idea of the law 'as a way of righteousness' which could be either accepted or rejected. This contrast is distinctively Pauline and should not be read back to the teaching of Stephen. As for the rejection of the ritual law as a whole, this thesis makes Paul, for all his radicalism, to appear somewhat reactionary. Whereas Stephen had, on this view, suggested in *Jerusalem*, faced with *Jews*, that 'the' ritual law was obsolete, Paul remained 'a Jew for the Jews' (1 Cor 9.19) wherever he was among them. Is this really plausible? I think not.

Dunn, op.cit. 270 f.; Schneider, art.cit. 236 f. Yet it is discarded even by Hengel, 'Jesus' 186 f.

123 W.L. Knox, *Jerusalem* 11; Schmithals, *James* 23, 25; Suhl, *Paulus* 31 f.; Hahn, *Gottesdienst* 50 f.; Kasting, *Anfänge* 55.

124 Hengel, 'Mission' 27; id., 'Jesus' 191 n. 137; Conzelmann, *Heiden* 236 f.; cf. Kim, *Origin* 45. For a more cautious view see Hultgren, art.cit. 98 n. 4: Stephen was only against the temple and its cult; Kraft, *Offenbarung* 73. Dunn, op.cit. speaks of Stephen's 'outspoken attack on the temple', but also notes thàt this does *not* mean attacking the *law* as well (272 f.): 'Stephen himself probably did not yet consider his position as constituting a breach with Judaism and the law; he may indeed have believed that Jesus' coming and exaltation as the prophet like Moses (Acts 7.37) constituted a call to return to the authentic religion of Moses, stripped of all its later idolatrous abuses and corruptions (sacrifices, ritual and temple).' Scroggs, art.cit. (esp. 201) argues that the Hellenists may have rejected just the temple (which is not mentioned in the Pentateuch!). Cf. also Stuhlmacher, *Versöhnung* 80 ff., 154, 216 (he attributes the tradition cited by Paul in Rom 3.25 f. to the Hellenists and evaluates this as a rejection of the old expiation system by them). Cf. also Luz, 'Gesetz' 91. Stuhlmacher also regards the Epistle to the Hebrews as representative of what the Hellenists taught (op.cit. 155). Even so, Paul's peculiarly negative statements on the law would not be accounted for; see on the differences between Hebrews and Paul in this regard above, p. 209.

125 Cf. S. Brown, 'Community' 198 f.: Paul was converted 'to a form of Christianity which repudiated the law as a way of righteousness' which 'can only be explained if his hostility was directed against and caused by this very form of belief'. Yet Brown (205), too, stresses the difference of view between the Hellenists and Paul in that for Paul the Torah takes on 'demonic overtones'.

It was these Hellenists who began the Gentile mission and founded the mixed congregation in Antioch (cf. Acts 11.19 ff.). It would be tempting to locate the events hinted at in Acts 11.19 ff., with Schmithals, in the time *before* the death of Stephen.[126] If it was known in Jerusalem that these people had admitted Gentiles as Proselytes[127] without circumcision and without imposing the Torah on them, their persecution would cause no surprise. This reconstruction, however, hangs pretty much in the air.[128] Yet the other possibility merits serious consideration: that the Christians *Paul* persecuted in the region of Damascus were Hellenists or their adherents who had *already* accepted Gentiles into the community.[129] This would presuppose that some time had elapsed since the death of Stephen. The advantage of this theory is that it explains why Paul's vision at once convinced him of being called an apostle *to the Gentiles*.[130] It would seem natural to infer that the status of the Gentiles, and thus the status of circumcision, was an important bone of contention between Paul the Pharisee and the Christians persecuted by him.

It is to be kept in mind that over long years Paul worked among Gentiles along with Barnabas who had close connections with the Hellenists. The evidence suggests that for quite a long time Paul worked as a *junior partner* of Barnabas.[131] The Antiochian conflict that took place later was hardly a success for Paul.[132] He apparently did not win over Peter and the people

---

126 Schmithals, op.cit. 32. He traces the liberalism of the Hellenists back to Galilaean influences, assuming that the new faith spread to Syria directly from Galilee; cf. Kasting, *Anfänge* 101 f.; Suhl, op.cit. 34. His underlying assumption that Galilaeans were generally quite lax in their Torah observance (22) is dubious, however; cf. Hengel, art.cit. 162–164.

127 There was, of course, no separate entity 'Christianity' at this stage, so that conversions to the new faith would have been regarded as admission of proselytes to Judaism.

128 Cf. Wilson, op.cit. 151. Had this really been the reason for the split between the Hebrews and the Hellenists, then the Hebrews would have taken sides against the admission of Gentiles without circumcision; had this been the case, then their later tolerance in this matter would be very difficult to account for.

129 Cf. Scroggs, 'Christianity' 199; Stuhlmacher, *Evangelium* I, 74; Schrage, 'Ekklesia' 197; Müller, 'Rezeption' 167 f.; and the cautious reflections of Luz, art.cit. 88 f. In any case, even Acts tells – prior to the conversion of Paul – that the Hellenist Philip proclaimed Christ to *Samaritans*.

130 This is so even if the conjecture were correct that Paul had been interested (if not engaged) in Jewish missionary work before his conversion. It was *circumcision* that stood between Jewish and Christian mission to Gentiles.

131 See Loisy, *Birth* 136 ff.; cf. Käsemann, *Versuche* II, 244; Ollrog, *Paulus* 10–12. In Acts 13.1 ff. Paul is one of the many prophets and teachers in Antioch, whereas Barnabas is singled out as the leading figure. In the account of the 'first missionary journey' Barnabas is often mentioned before Paul (still in 14.14), and *his* comparison with Zeus in 14.12 suggests that he is viewed as the leader.

132 Thus e.g. Gaechter, *Petrus* 251 ff.; Mussner, *Gal*; Haenchen, *Apg* 458 f.; Dunn, *Unity*

around him. He from now on had to part ways with Barnabas. This shows that Barnabas did not at all fully share Paul's theory of the law (or at least all its practical implications) as Paul set it forth then in Antioch; it may be assumed that Gal 2.15 ff. still reflects the thrust of that argument.[133] It follows, then, that Paul can hardly have set forth any thoroughgoing critique of the law long before that time.

It may well be that 1 Thess conveys a picture of what Paul's attitude to the law was before his conflict with the Judaizers. Even if the letter is not very early[134] but belongs to the time after the apostolic council, it serves to indicate what Paul's relation to the law was when he was not engaged in actual polemics — when the 'earlier mood' was still present. 1 Thess conveys the impression of a total disinterest in the law, positively as well as negatively. There is no critique of the law; the law is simply bypassed in the summary of the missionary proclamation (1.9 f.). There is no positive interest in the law either; the ethos of the letter is not Torah-oriented even though 'orders' concerning the right way of life are not lacking (cf. 4.1 ff.). The law seems to be a non-entity, an *adiaphoron.* When the circumstances allow it (i.e., when there is no 'Judaizing' agitation), Paul can simply ignore the law when communicating with a (predominantly) Gentile congregation, even though many of its members must have been recruited from those who were previously under the influence of the Synagogue.[135]

It would thus seem likely that Paul met with the Hellenists a *somewhat* relaxed attitude to the observance of the ritual Torah, perhaps even a neglect of circumcision as part of the missionary strategy. Certainly he found in Antioch a mixed congregation not scrupulous about the Torah. We might say that the (ritual) law was dealt with more or less as an *adiaphoron.*[136] This of course implied *some* criticisms of details of the law, but no hostility. We are reminded of those mysterious allegorizers of Alexandria, mildly rebuked by Philo in *Migr. Abr.* 89 ff.[137] Were they in some sense predecessors of the Hellenists? It is in any case difficult not to connect the 'liberalism' of the Hellenists in one way or another with their Dispersion background.[138] They

---

254. Paul would hardly have omitted to mention his success to the Galatians, had he had any. The separation from Barnabas points to the same direction.

133 Even though the speech begun in 2.15 flows smoothly into an address to the Galatians; see above, p. 47 n. 21.

134 Cf. above, p. 10.

135 Cf. Acts 17.1 ff. and the reflections on the circumstances of Paul's work in Haenchen, *Apg* 493.

136 Cf. Wrede, *Paulus* 84; Strecker, *Eschaton* 230 f.

137 See above, p. 35, 93.

138 Cf. Böhlig, *Geisteskultur* 165 f.; Lake, *Epistles* 23 ff. (yet I would reduce the evidence presented by Lake to the Alexandrian allegorizers only). Hengel, art.cit. 185 assumes, not without reason, that those Dispersion Jews who returned to Jerusalem

may have felt the pressure from their non-Jewish environment as a sore problem. The breakthrough of a new way of life, characterized by some neglect of the Torah, must have been connected with the experience of eschatological fulfilment found in the new community. One conjectures that ecstatic experiences of the Spirit played a part, even though the portrait of Stephen as a charismatic in Acts 6 is palpably Lukan style.[139] It is more difficult to determine to what extent their liberalism was due to what they heard of the life style of the historical Jesus.[140] It is not clear that Jesus ever attacked the Torah in so many words; if he did, it is by no means obvious that his followers in Jerusalem should have made much of it. But at least Jesus' not uncritical stance to the temple and his saying about its eschatological destruction must have established a link between Jesus and Stephen.[141]

Whatever the origin and nature of the liberalism of the Hellenists, both Acts and Paul suggest that the rise of the circumcision-free Gentile mission was 'haphazard'. 'There was no decisive theological step;'[142] 'action preceded theology'.[143] Surely the experience that uncircumcised Gentiles displayed the same kind of ecstatic gifts as circumcised Jewish Christians (cf. Acts 10.44 ff., 15.7–12, Gal 2.8) was important.[144]

It would seem that Paul at first, as a consequence of his Christophany, simply adopted this 'liberal' pattern. Had it been clear to him from the start that 'Christ is the end of the law' (or even that the Torah leads to sinning!),

---

had a strong religious motivation. But as little as in the case of Paul does a sincere religiosity necessarily exclude latent difficulties with the Torah due to an 'enlightened' environment in the minds of some of them. Hengel, 'Mission' 27 n. 44 suggests indeed a connection between the thought of the Hellenists and the preponderance of the ethical commandments as well as the common ethical or spiritual-allegorical interpretation of the ritual stipulations in Hellenistic Jewish writings. Differently S. Brown, art.cit. 202. The fact that the nature of the worship in the temple did not necessarily meet the high expectations of the pilgrims (cf. Hengel, 'Jesus' 203) could easily have made some of them receptive to the new faith.

139 Hengel, art.cit. 193 ff. infers from Acts 6 that the critique of law and temple on the part of the Hellenists was connected with their eschatological enthusiasm. Strecker, art.cit. 481 n. 8 correctly points out that the mention of the Spirit in Acts 6 goes back to Lucan redaction. Nevertheless, Luke may be right. Whatever the actual experience behind the confused account in Acts 2, there must have been some striking charismatic phenomena in the Jerusalem community, and nothing tells against the assumption that people like Stephen shared in them. Cf. the description of the Hellenist Philip as an ecstatic in Acts 8 and the mention that his daughters were prophetesses (Acts 21.9).

140 Hengel, art.cit. 199 ff. construes a close connection; cf. Kasting, op.cit. 101–103 (via the Galilaeans); S. Brown, art.cit. 202; Müller, 'Rezeption' 164–167.

141 Cf. Wilson, op.cit. 150.

142 Wilson, op.cit. 152.

143 Jervell, *Luke* 136; id., 'Minority' 19.

144 Cf. S. Brown, art.cit. 203 f.

then one would expect him to have expressed this conviction in his later letters in a much more consistent way. But in fact the perseverance of law-*affirming* elements in Paul's thought is as striking as is the extreme nature of some of his negative comments. Should my analysis of Paul's theological difficulties with the law be on the right track, then these very inconsistencies indicate that as late as in the fifties Paul was still *looking for arguments* for his peculiar view of the law; and in part, at least, the arguments are palpably tentative (let me once more refer to the marriage analogy Rom 7.1–6, the image of the will Gal 3.15–18 and the attribution of the legislation to angels in Gal 3.19–20). One would imagine that Paul would have found some firmer ground to stand on if he had reflected on the problem for twenty years! It is my contention that the theory of a theology of the law which was basically 'ready' with Paul's conversion cannot adequately explain the nature of the extant material. In his letters, Paul is trying to cope with recent events, among which his conflicts with 'Judaizing' opponents had played an eminent part. It may be that had it not been for these conflicts Paul's stated view of the law would have been a good deal different.[145]

7. The significance of the missionary experience and the conflict with the 'Judaizers'

Before Paul entered the stage, Christian mission to the Gentiles had begun:

---

145 Besides Wrede and Strecker (above, n. 136) cf. also Case, 'Bias' 26; Enslin, *Ethics* 12 f., 85 f.; Sloyan, *Christ* 96, 103; Baumbach, 'Dialog' 12 f. Stuhlmacher, *Versöhnung* 90 f., 156 objects to this theory by appealing to Paul's subjection to flogging by the Jews (a penalty 'typical of offenses against the law'). But Paul was not the only one to be persecuted in this way; the question is indeed, just how much laxity with regard to the law did one have to display to get punished in this way? Mt 23.34 (cf. 10.17) as compared with Lk 11.49 shows indeed that the flogging experience was not foreign to Matthew's (!) community, surely not suspect of radical antinomism. On the question of flogging see Hare, *Theme* 43–46. Hare concludes that disturbance of the public order and peace (through divisive missionary activity) may have been a sufficient reason for flogging. E.P. Sanders, *Law* 191 argues that, in the case of Paul, 'the issue was circumcision; that is, the admission of Gentiles to the people of God without requiring them to make full proselytization to Judaism' (195).

Kim's critique of Strecker (*Origin* 269 ff.) misses the point, confusing the law-free Gentile mission without circumcision with the full-blown theology of justification by faith alone. He asks: 'How is one to believe that Paul the Pharisee whose whole life had been oriented to achieving his salvation by keeping the law could perceive God's saving work in the crucified and risen Jesus Christ and yet fail to consider how this saving work of God in Christ was related to the law?' (270) This problem disappears, if Paul's life had been oriented to the law as an expression of God's revealed will which was not, in itself, a 'way to salvation'. Then it is quite conceivable that Paul did consider the relation between God's work in Christ and the law, but drew less radical conclusions than he was later to propose.

a mission that abstained from requiring circumcision of the converts. As we have seen, this giving up of important parts of the ritual law (besides circumcision, other ritual precepts as the food laws were also neglected) was apparently a spontaneous response to the new eschatological situation which was characterized by charismatic phenomena. The Gentile question had received a practical solution but hardly a theological foundation.

This state of affairs was tolerated, perhaps even welcomed, by Palestinian Jewish Christians for quite a long time.[146] It is only some fifteen years later that we see a reaction coming. Some time around 48 A.D. a serious theological debate about the situation arose. This is probably due to the growing number of former Pharisees joining the new faith (cf. Acts 15.5).[147] By that time some Jewish Christians produced weighty history-of-salvation arguments to the effect that the sign of God's covenant had to be taken seriously and the covenantal law had to be observed even in the new situation. If Gentile Christians wished to be part of the eschatological Israel, they had to be circumcised and take upon themselves the yoke of the law. As we have seen, this was a thoroughly Biblical position, probably stemming from a deep sense of responsibility and reverence for God's word revealed in Scripture. Ought not God's revealed word to be kept above decisions based on pneumatic experiences like glossolalia?[148] Perhaps the notion of the Pauline Christ as 'an agent of sin' (Gal 2.17) reflects the argument of these Christians: Paul's version of Christianity incited people to ignore (parts of) the law, thus leading them to sin.[149]

This attempt at a theological restoration did not remain ineffective. To be sure, the requirement of circumcising the Gentile converts did not prevail at the Jerusalem meeting, where the liberal policy of the Antiochian congregation was accepted.[150] The restorative pressure did not cease, however. Even

---

146 This is emphasized by Jervell, 'Volk' 91 f. Jervell, art.cit. 102 n. 38, remarks that not until about AD 48 did Jewish Christians awake to a theological consciousness. See further id., 'Minority' 17–21. A quite different picture is drawn by Holtz, 'Bedeutung' 130 ff.: at first, converted Gentiles were circumcised even in Antioch (133 f.); Paul, too, subscribed to this practice (137). On this theory, it was only after the Gentile converts were no longer willing to submit to the rite that Paul became aware of the true practical implications of his theology (138 f.) This is a quite unlikely account of the Hellenists' mission.

147 Jervell, 'Minority' 20 persuasively suggests that 'the Jewish Christians could tolerate Gentiles when they were few ... But they were confronted with a totally new situation when the Gentiles ... threatened to become the majority.'

148 See above, p. 183 f.

149 Cf. Betz, *Gal* ad loc.

150 It is notoriously difficult to find out what exactly was decided in the meeting; cf. Haenchen ad loc. and Wilson, op.cit. 185 ff. For the present purpose it is enough to note the 'minimum' result mentioned in the text (cf. Haenchen). Obviously, whatever the decision was, it was not capable of clearing up the situation for long.

if the admission of Gentiles remained an established fact, the relations between Jewish and Gentile Christians appeared all the more problematic. Some time after the meeting[151] the Apostolic Decree was laid down, which tried to impose on the Gentile Christians the stipulations which foreigners sojourning in Israel had to observe according to Lev 17–18.[152] The restoration trend is clearly reflected in the incident in Antioch, described by Paul in Gal 2.11 ff.[153] It seems that Peter, Barnabas and others recognized the force of the restorative arguments. One would think that they thereby displayed just that kind of flexibility that Paul proclaims when stating that he is 'all things to all men' (1 Cor 9.22).[154] Paul, however, saw the situation quite differently.

It is clear that over the years Paul had become internally alienated from the ritual aspects of the law.[155] In the course of his work among Gentiles he had fully internalized the Gentile point of view and identified himself with it. While agreeing with the moral content of the Torah, Paul seldom based his ethical instruction explicitly upon it. Often complying with the ritual precepts for strategic reasons, he felt free from the law and dead to it (Gal 2.19). He had rightfully torn down the law with its food regulations (Gal 2.18) and could say that all food was clean (Rom 14.14, 20). He was capable of pouring scorn on the sacred rite of circumcision (Gal 5.12, cf. Phil 3.2). That is no longer a genuinely Jewish stance.

Paul had had ample time to develop this attitude. For more than a decade the Gentiles had been allowed to flourish without paying attention to the ritual law. Then, all of a sudden, the demand was raised that they ought either to be circumcised or to form isolated separate congregations. The situation might have been different, had such a debate been raised right at the beginning of the Gentile mission. Now the restorers, however orthodox their theology, were definitely too late.

Paul could not contemplate Gentile Christians living separately from the community which stood for the continuity with old Israel. After all, it was

---

151 It is also difficult to date the decree with any certainty. Obviously, it was well-established in Luke's time. Most scholars would date it relatively shortly after the meeting; recently Strobel, 'Aposteldekret'; Pesch, 'Abkommen'. This is not the place for a discussion of the peculiar theses of these scholars in detail. Catchpole, 'Paul' argues that the decree was the immediate cause of the incident in Antioch (Gal 2.11 ff.). This must remain conjectural. The recent attempt of Borse, 'Paulus' 51 f., 61 to attribute the decree to the Jerusalem council after all is hardly persuasive.

152 Haenchen, Conzelmann.

153 Pace Lüdemann, *Paulus* 77 ff., 101 ff., who would date the incident *before* the apostolic meeting (thus reversing the chronological order between Gal 2.1–10 and 2.11–14). The assumption that Paul does not stick to the chronological order in Gal 2 is somewhat strange and it is hardly rendered likely through Lüdemann's rhetorical analysis.

154 Cf. Richardson, 'Inconsistency' 360 ff.

155 See above, p. 76 f.

Israel and Scripture which gave Christians, Gentiles as well as Jewish, their identity. The unity of all believers in Christ (Gal 3.28) was a very real thing to Paul, confirmed by his long experience. On the other hand, it was impossible for him to consider the possibility that any parts of the Torah could be imposed on Gentile Christians for reasons of practical unity.

It would seem that the Antiochian episode reveals us a great deal of how Paul's 'final' theology of the law took shape. It is a great pity that we have only his account of that incident and nothing at all from the other side. Whatever the circumstances were – whether Peter and others were persuaded by James' men because of theological considerations or, as Paul's wording suggests, because of fear of the Jews[156] – the behaviour which Paul so strongly condemns reminds a detached observer of his own maxim of being 'to those under law as being myself under the law', not to mention the demonstration of loyalty which Paul undertook according to Acts 21. Probably Peter did not in any way attempt to 'compel the Gentiles live in the Jewish way' as Paul insinuates (Gal 2.14).[157] *He* decided to behave, in the given circumstances, in the 'Jewish way', probably leaving it free to the Gentile Christians to continue *their* way of daily life. The issue must have seemed to him mainly a pastoral one. It is *Paul* who turns it into a question of soteriology, to a matter of life and death. 'To live in the Jewish way' takes on the meaning to try to attain 'righteousness through the law'. This *metabasis eis allo genos* is comparable to the distortion of the other side's motives in the statement that Peter, Barnabas and others acted as 'hypocrites' (v. 13).[158]

The context of Gal 2.15 ff. makes it abundantly clear that when Paul here speaks of the 'works of the law' (v. 16) he has the keeping of *ritual* requirements in mind. It is that part of the law which constituted a wall between Jews and Gentiles that had been 'torn down' (v. 18) by Paul and Peter, when they had admitted uncircumcised Gentiles to the congregation and mixed with them, at table as elsewhere. It was *this* construction that Peter was in fact building up again through his changed behaviour, thus indicating that his previous life style had been an error, a transgression.[159] Paul does not view

---

156 Cf. S. Brown, art.cit. 210 n. 74.
157 Eckert, *Verkündigung* 198 f. Differently Holtz, art.cit. 123 f.; Catchpole, art.cit. 441. For an interesting attempt to reconstruct the events in Antioch from a pro-Petrine point of view see Gaechter, *Petrus* 213 ff.
158 See on this Richardson, art.cit. 350, 360 f.
159 The most natural way to interpret Gal 2.18 is to take συνιστάνω as a reference to Paul's (and Peter's) *previous* behaviour: I *show* myself to *have been* a transgressor. The period of non-observance turns out, in retrospect, to have been a time of arbitrary laxity (if the food regulations need to be 'rebuilt'). Cf. Oepke, Mussner. Several scholars would, however, take συνιστάνω in a future sense: by subjecting myself to stipulations which I will not be able to observe I *make* myself a transgressor of the law *from now on* (Lietzmann, Schlier, Gyllenberg; Hahn, 'Gesetzesverständnis' 53).

the situation from the missionary's own point of view as he does in 1 Cor 9. His point of view is now completely that of the Gentile Christians. *They* are being hurt in this situation. Unlike the situation in Corinth or Rome, it is they who are in a 'weak' position: under pressure from that party which feels strong in its conviction.[160]

It is in such a situation that Paul sets up the contrast between faith in Christ and works of law; whether he really spoke in this way at that time in Antioch or whether he formulates the contrast in retrospect because of the analogy with the Galatian situation. It is in the course of such a conflict that the law 'becomes' the Jewish (or the heretical Jewish Christian) 'way of salvation' which it was *not* for genuine Jewish thought (if the reasoning set forth in ch. V is on the right track). If it was to these people *so* important to comply with the law, at the cost of the well-being of their Gentile brethren, was the law then not, for all practical purposes, made the cornerstone of salvation? If they wished to exclude uncircumcised Gentiles from established table-fellowship, did they not indeed (again for all practical purposes) exclude them from the salvation in Christ? Or, at least, was not their behaviour bound to suggest to the Gentile Christians that actually they, too, ought to get circumcised?[161] In some such way Paul may (unconsciously, to be sure) have reasoned. His understanding of the logic of his opponents' position was probably different from theirs. The same was probably true of the Galatian situation. It is quite possible that circumcision was not propagated in Galatia for *soteriological* reasons but rather as the proper response, in the light of Scripture, to what God had done.[162]

Bultmann, *Exegetica* 398 gives a similar interpretation with a different motivation: I make myself a transgressor, because to be under law is by definition to remain in sin (cf. Rom 4.15); cf. van Dülmen, *Theologie* 21 n. 28; Byrne, *'Sons'* 146 (in re-erecting the barrier between Jews and Gentiles I 'transgress' the command of the law: 'Die!', expressed in v. 19!); and already Mundle, 'Gal 2.17.18' 153. This seems far-fetched. In addition, συνιστάνω clearly means 'show, demonstrate' in Rom 3.5, 5.8, whereas no clear cases for the meaning 'to make oneself' have been adduced. To be sure, Schlier (ad loc.) refers to Num 27.23, P. Tebt. 317, 10 f., P. Oxy II 261. But these occurrences refer to cases when one is 'appointed to a charge' or 'appointed as a representative'; cf. Liddell-Scott, *Lexicon* s.v. IV 1 d, e (Schlier also refers to Liddell-Scott, but the lexicon does not support *his* interpretation).

Lambrecht, 'Line of Thought' 488 correctly opts for the meaning 'to show myself' for συνιστάνω; nevertheless, he would take the verb in a future sense. But it is not clear what value v. 18 would have as a 'proof' if the transgressions mentioned are not yet there. V. 18 makes perfectly good sense if it is taken to refer to the return to the ritual law of a previously liberal Jewish Christian.

160 Cf. Richardson, art.cit. 352, 362.
161 Ironically, Jews might probably have inferred from Paul's way of life analogously that he encouraged Jewish Christians to neglect the Torah; see above, p. 77 n. 181.
162 See above, p. 182 ff.

One could claim that in some sense Paul was justified in his diagnosis. It all depends on one's perspective. What seemed simple obedience to God's revealed word to a Jew, must have seemed rather different from the *Gentile* point of view. For most [163] of them, acceptance of circumcision and food regulations would have meant a much more strenuous effort than for the born Jew. Observance of the Torah would have exposed them to derision from friends and neighbours, and circumcision might have endangered even their lives.[164] Psychologically, such an achievement might have had the flavour of man's effort to make himself acceptable to God. Paul attacked the Jewish Christian position, because he came to assess it from a Gentile's point of view.

The conflict with Jewish Christian 'covenantal nomism' brought Paul, the. partly alienated Jew, face to face with the adamant demand that God's revealed law had to be taken seriously *as a whole*. Selectivity about God's law could not be tolerated. Acceptable forms for the intercourse between Jewish and Gentile Christians had to be created. In face of this challenge the old practical liberalism simply would not do. It had to give way either to a more conservative or else to a more radical position. Peter, Barnabas and others at least temporarily opted for the former course. Paul, not being able to retrace his steps, had to *develop a consciously radical position*. He had to argue *why* his attitude was different and why it *had* to be different. Through the pressure of events he was led to search for arguments for a global rejection of the law; for in his conscious thinking he, too, was against selectivity.[165] He thus came

---

163 The Galatians seem to be expectional in their apparent willingness to accept circumcision.

164 Cf. Smallwood, *Jews* 123f.

165 Linton, 'Paulus' 186 points out that Paul is not a rebel against the law. What he is really fighting for is the freedom of Gentile Christians from circumcision. 'We might think that Paul would have proceeded by turning first of all against circumcision. But this law cannot, according to Paul's basic conviction which he shares with the Rabbis, be torn asunder from the general framework (Gal 5.3). It is quite foreign to Paul to set himself above the law. Therefore he had to go the way he has gone and put the whole law in the light of his new faith. Paul could not envisage any revision of the law. That would have been sheer arbitrariness.' Only, Linton does not show awareness of the irony of a couple of his statements. Precisely because of his refusal to undertake a conscious revision of the law – a refusal probably due to inherited reverence for God's word, cf. above p. 28, 32, 223 – Paul was actually led to extremely arbitrary conclusions, much more so than those (like Ptolemy) who did put themselves in the position of passing judgment on different parts of the law.

Cf. also Cerfaux, *Christian* 409 f.: 'At the time which we are dealing with, it was impossible to dissociate "material" practices in the law from those which were purely moral ... It was thus necessary to abolish the law altogether, so that we might live according to the Spirit.' See also the view of Bousset, referred to above, p. 25.

upon several *ad hoc* arguments for the termination of the law (the analogies of marriage and will; the legislation through angels) and its allegedly sin-engendering and sin-enhancing nature etc. The numerous problems and self-contradictions in his statements expose the overall theory as more or less artificial.[166] It would seem that the difficulties can best be explained if the whole theory owes its origin to a polemical situation.[167] We have found indications that Paul went in his theorizing often a great deal further in a radical direction than his 'natural' reasoning would suggest. One may venture the statement that 'Paul the theologian' develops a radical theory which does not quite correspond to the thoughts of 'Paul the man'.

The above description of the emergence of Paul's radicalized stance as a result of his conflicts with fellow Christians may be oversimplified, since Paul did have conflicts with non-Christian Jews as well, possibly long before the battle with the Christian 'Judaizers'.[168] Unfortunately, we know little either about the exact reasons for or the chronology of Paul's persecution by the Jews, although 2 Cor 11.24 ff. gives some idea of its intensity. It is difficult to know to what extent these persecutions were due to fear of laxity in the observance of the law as a consequence of Paul's preaching. [169] Paul did not ostensibly disregard the Torah among his kinsmen (1 Cor 9.20). To be sure, he came to be regarded as an antinomistic apostate by the Jews (cf. Acts 21), but just how early did he get such a reputation (was it perhaps only after the apostles' meeting or after the Antiochian incident?)? No doubt the anger of the Jews was often aroused by the fact that Paul's preaching was suited to win over many of the 'God-fearers' from the fringes of the Synagogue to the Christian community, not least because they did not have to bother about circumcision.[170] In 1 Thess 2.16a Paul complains that the Jews

---

166 On the artificiality of Paul's radical line of thought see already Wrede, *Paulus* 78 f.

167 A casual observation by Scholem therefore seems to be close to the truth: Paulinism 'did not arise out of any immanent logic', but received 'its direct impulse from the outside'. Paul, that is, had 'in the interest of Christian propaganda ... to forgo demanding of Gentile Christians that they keep the law or accept its obligation'. Afterwards (as in Romans 7), however, 'the crisis of the tradition is explained out of the inner dynamic of the redemption itself in which the considerations that led to this theology have become unimportant and have receded completely into the background ...' *Idea* 57 f.

168 Luke lets the Jewish persecution begin as early as Acts 9.23 ff. Paul does not mention Jews in 2 Cor 11.32 f., where he refers to the same incident, and it seems that the role ascribed to the Jews is Lukan style; cf. Haenchen. Haenchen thinks it was Paul's proclamation of Lord Jesus and the imminent end of this world that made him suspect in the eyes of the ruling power. On the other hand, Windisch (on 2 Cor 11.32 f.) regards it as possible that Paul was made suspect by the Jews, who could then have been the ultimate case of the ambush.

169 Cf. Smith, 'Persecution'.

170 Cf. Schmithals, *Römerbrief* 78 and Theissen, *Untersuchungen* 265, who points out

are hindering him from speaking to Gentiles 'in order that they may be saved'.[171] This may well refer to Jewish attempts to protect the non-Jewish sympathizers from the new propaganda.

Should conflicts over the Torah with non-Christian Jews predate the battle with Jewish Christians, it is of course possible that the radical development of Paul's view of the law had begun already in that connection. But even if this were so, it would seem, as 1 Thess 2.16a indicates, that the question of what happens to the *Gentiles* was an important driving force in this process. And in any case, Paul's language got its biting sharpness in the battle with .fellow Christians. The decisive phase is tangible in Gal 2.11 ff. We there find Paul ascribing soteriological significance to something which the other side understood in a rather different way.[172]

---

the social and financial importance of the 'God-fearers' for the Jewish communities in the Dispersion.

171 There is no reason to doubt the authenticity of 1 Thess 2.14–16 on the score that it clashes with Rom 11.25 ff. Paul has here concrete hostile Jews in mind, whereas in writing Romans he – in a different mood, to be sure – considers the subject more calmly from a theological point of view. Cf. Davies, 'People' 8. Schade, *Christologie* 128 objects that Paul is speaking of the Jews generally in 1 Thess as well; but this would not be the only case that Paul expresses rather sweeping generalizations while starting from limited experiences!

As regards our problem, it is noteworthy that this polemical outburst does *not* lead Paul to any explicit comments on the *law*. Could this be taken as another indication that it was indeed the Jewish *Christian* rather than the Jewish opposition that made the question of law acute to Paul?

For the authenticity of the passage see recently Schade, op.cit. 126–128; Okeke, 'Fate'; Lüdemann, 'Judentum', section 3.2. Paul makes use here of traditional topoi, but v. 16a seems to be his own 'addition' (cf. Schade, op.cit. 127).

172 Let me try to construe an analogy. Suppose that a modern Christian missionary decided to give up baptising his converts, since they have displayed charismatic gifts in their unbaptised status. An average Christian theologian need hardly attribute saving value *ex opere operato* to baptism to be somewhat upset by such events. If our imaginary missionary now in the course of a debate ascribed to his critics the view that a mixture of hydrogen and oxygen is the basis of man's salvation (that they indeed teach 'salvation by water' or sacramental magic as *Heilsweg*), this would seem to be more or less analogous to the case of Paul. There are, of course, two basic differences. There is in baptism nothing inherently repulsive to the mind of a convert, as was often the case with circumcision. And, more importantly, Paul and others had ample time to establish the liberal practice before it came to be questioned.

Some concluding reflections

Paul's thought on the law is full of difficulties and inconsistencies. A short summary of these was set forth in ch. VI, to which the reader is referred.[1] The result of ch. VII was that while Paul shares some of the difficulties with other early Christian writers, no one else gets involved in so many and so drastic problems.[2] In ch. VIII the suggestion was developed that the historical reason for Paul's plight should be looked for in his conflict with the Jewish Christian 'restorers' and their program.

It may be pointed out in passing that it is not just in his treatment of the law that Paul gets involved in intellectual difficulties. He likewise contradicts himself when discussing the not unrelated problem of Israel's reluctance to accept the gospel. In Rom 9 he resorts to the extreme explanation of divine hardening which takes place regardless of any of man's doings (9.6–23), whereas he in the very next chapter puts all emphasis on Israel's own notorious disobedience. In chapter 11, at last, Paul definitely discards his predestinarian construction and replaces it with the statement that Israel's obduracy is of a temporary nature.[3] This runs counter to 1 Thess 2.14–16 as well. The observations made in the course of this study about Paul's self-contradictions suggest that one should hardly posit a theological development in Paul's thinking about Israel from 1 Thess to Romans.[4] It is sufficient to note that Paul finds himself in a different situation. No wonder that precisely in issues concerning his relationship to his Jewish heritage Paul gets caught in theological difficulties. He is torn into two directions, and he is incapable of resolving the tension in terms of theological thought.[5]

It remains to draw some theological conclusions. We find Paul struggling with the problem that a *divine* institution has been *abolished* through what

---

1 See above, p. 199 ff.

2 See above, p. 227 f.

3 On Paul's inconsistencies in Rom 9–11 see Räisänen, *Hardening* 79–87; cf. also Ruether, *Faith* 105f; Goodenough, 'Paul' 63f.; E.P. Sanders, *Law* 198: 'Paul's solution to the problem posed by Israel's unfaith (sc. in ch. 11) is to be seen as a somewhat desperate expedient ... How can the promise be irrevocable if it is conditional on a requirement which most Jews reject? He has a problem, a problem of conflicting convictions which can be better asserted than explained ...' Sanders also correctly points out the analogy with Paul's dilemma in Rom 7.

4 See, however, also Lüdemann, *Judentum* 41–43.

5 Cf. Lowe, 'Examination' 141 (cited above, p. 11 n. 72).

God has done in Christ. Most of Paul's troubles can be reduced to this simple formula. Paul tries to hush up the abolition; he never admits that he has actually rejected large parts of the law. Instead, he has recourse to the arbitrary assertion that it is *his* teaching that really fulfils or 'upholds' the law. A Christian who regards this assertion as convincing should by way of logic not object if a Muslim claims that the Koran is the fulfilment of the (Jewish and) Christian Scripture, or if a Hindu asserts that Christianity attains its fulfilment in Hinduism.[6] He is only tasting his own medicine. Paul Wernle's comments on Christian claims of fulfilling the law are to the point:[7] 'These claims were in reality untrue. No one in the world fulfils circumcision, Sabbath or food laws through neglecting them. Yet how often has theological ingenuity managed to make a yes of a no and a no of a yes!'[8]

The problem of an abolition of a divine institution is clearly reflected in Paul's inability to give a satisfactory answer to the question 'Why then did God give this weak and imperfect law in the first place?' In fact, Paul gives two incompatible answers, neither of which is satisfactory.[9] Either he must attribute to God an unsuccessful first attempt to carry through his will (as if it took God a long time to devise an adequate means for this), or else he gets involved in the cynicism that God explicitly provides men with a law 'unto life' while knowing from the start that this instrument will not work. This problem, like the preceding one, Paul to be sure shares with many other NT writers.

If something is truly divine, it is hardly capable of being abrogated! Of course, we may from our modern point of view deem Paul's view to display 'an historical realism': 'his views are determined by the new experience of God who gives life through the Spirit. Paul claimed that the Judaizers who wanted to combine this experience with the law, were dragging the past into the present!'[10] Only, it must be borne in mind that the 'past' was taken to represent God's absolutely authoritative word embodied in Scripture and this not by the Judaizers alone. From the point of view of Paul's opponents Paul's 'realism' must have seemed identical with misguided enthusiasm, an excessive and arbitrary reliance on feelings and charismatic experiences. Can we really blame them for this?[11] The course of history has shown the Utopian,

---

6 For Hinduism cf. Hick, *God* 131 f.

7 Wernle is commenting on Mt 5.17 ff., but his words are applicable to Paul as well.

8 *Anfänge* 313. On the hybris of the Christian 'fulfilment' position see also Ruether, op.cit. 94 f.

9 See above, p. 151 ff.   10 Moxnes, *Theology* 265.

11 Cf. Ruether, *Faith* 244 f. Radical as it may seem in its implications, Ruether's section on Christology (246–251) is helpful and very important (more so than her 'dualistic' interpretation of Paul in the same book); cf. Ruether, 'Discussion' 242–246. Cf. also von der Osten-Sacken, 'Notwendigkeit'. Mussner, *Traktat* 356–363 does not succeed in refuting Ruether.

character of the first Christians' expectation of the Parousia and thereby proved that the Jewish suspicion of the new charismatic movement was not groundless.[12]

The only reasonable way to cope with the Torah theologically (if you are not an orthodox Jew or a Fundamentalist Christian) is to admit that it was *not* a direct divine revelation to Moses. It consists of a long series of human attempts to respond appropriately to what God was believed to have done. Its commandments are therefore historically conditioned.[13] From such a critical point of view one is enabled to make distinctions within the Torah and give some parts more importance than others. But this was *not* the starting point of Paul (or of Jesus, or of any Christian of the first generations)[14]; only later was the idea that parts of the law are human intimated by people like Ptolemy or, above all, the Jewish Christians behind Kerygmata Petrou. Paul did (at times even passionately) cling to the traditional idea that the law was all divine; this is why he was caught up in so many inconsistencies in trying to relate the new experience to the authoritative tradition. While his life was totally oriented to the new powerful experience of Christ, he was bound to pay lip service (surely never realized as such by himself) to the tradition in order not to undercut the unity of the divine purpose and will.

It is a fundamental mistake of much Pauline exegesis in this century to have portrayed Paul as the 'prince of thinkers' and the Christian 'theologian

---

12 Cf. also Lapide, 'Rabbi' 55 ff.

13 Even the Decalogue was originally probably not transmitted as words of God. It was, according to Smend, 'Gesetz' 15 ff., originally connected with 'Belehrung im Rahmen der Grossfamilie' (16) rather than with the events on Sinai; the speaker was 'zunächst das Familienhaupt oder eine andere Autoritätsperson'. Deuteronomy and the Priestly Code represent obvious retrojections of more recent customs into a Mosaic setting; cf. ibid. 27, 31.

14 Cf. Montefiore, *Gospels* I 157 (commenting on Mk 7.15, but his point is applicable to Paul as well): Jesus is illogical, since he holds fast to the law on one hand and utters a principle which invalidates it on the other. ' ... Amos could have uttered the principle without inconsistency, because in his day there was no perfect, divine, immutable Mosaic Law in existence; and we, to-day, can consistently utter the principle because we no longer believe in such a Law – because we *do* separate the moral from the ritual – but Jesus could only utter the principle at the cost of an inconsistency, which does not, indeed, lessen the greatness of the principle or of him who spoke it, but which justifies, exonerates, and explains the opposition and disbelief of the Rabbis and Pharisees, who saw more clearly than Jesus whither the principle must tend and how much it implied.' Cf. the prudent reflections on the Sabbath pp. 157 f.; further p. 160: 'Yet I cannot see that the Rabbis were wrong in their opposition to (Mark) vii. 15. If the Law is throughout Mosaic, perfect and divine, then it must be obeyed throughout. But a saying like vii. 15 would imply that God made a mistake. In ordering Moses to bid the children of Israel observe *for ever* certain laws about food, etc., God apparently meant that there *was* such a thing as outward defilement.'

par excellence'.[15] Paul was indeed an original and imaginative thinker, and his letters are full of seminal insights and thought-provoking suggestions. He is, however, first and foremost a missionary, a man of practical religion who develops a line of thought to make a practical point, to influence the conduct of his readers;[16] in the next moment he is quite capable of putting forward a statement which logically contradicts the previous one when trying to make a different point[17] or, rather, struggling with a different problem. Paul will

---

15 See above, pp. 1 f. notes 10–14. My assessment of Paul's thought converges with that of Andrews in an undeservedly ignored study, in which she sought to approach Paul and his ethical teaching 'by way of his social experience'. 'The predominance of practical problems, which this approach reveals, shows that Paul has been greatly over-estimated as an intellectual, particularly as the important early Christian theologian. Practice was uppermost with Paul.' *Teaching* 169.

16 See the assessments of Paul's thought in the quotations adduced above, pp. 11 f. notes 71–75.

17 No doubt my assessment of Paul's thought also runs counter to attempts to interpret his letters as carefully planned *rhetorical* products which follow the set rules of the time (even though good rhetoric does not, of course, in itself guarantee good logic). See esp. Betz, 'Composition'; id., *Galatians*; cf. also Lüdemann, *Paulus* 63 ff.

Besides reversing Paul's own judgment of his rhetorical skill (1 Cor 2.1–5) Betz's analyses leave a rather strained impression. To mention just a few points: Betz tries to analyze Galatians as an 'apologetic letter' ('Composition' 354, *Galatians* 14), but in the end he shifts his ground and makes of it a 'magical letter' as well ('Composition' 379, *Gal* 25). Thus the addressees who are first identified with the *jury* in a fictitious law court situation ('Composition' 377, *Gal* 24) become all of a sudden *defendants,* who 'will either go free – be acquitted – or they will be sent back to the cosmic "prison" guarded by the "elements of the world" ...' (*Gal* 25; cf. 'Composition' 379). Furthermore, Betz admits that the central section of Galatians (chs. 3–4) is 'extremely difficult' to analyze in terms of rhetoric. Determined to demonstrate, however, that the section is indeed designed to make up the *probatio* of the rhetoricians, he makes a virtue out of a necessity and declares that 'Paul has been very successful – as a skilled rhetorician would be expected to be – in disguising his argumentative strategy' ('Composition' 369, *Gal* 129)! Finally, I fail to see why the use of an amanuensis should in itself 'rule out a haphazard writing of the letter' and 'presuppose the existence of Paul's first draft' ('Composition' 356, cf. *Gal* 312).

Add to this that 'the most famous example' (Betz, *Gal* 15, following Momigliano, *Biography* 60–62) of an apologetic letter, Plato's Epistle 7, does *not* at all display such a rhetorical organization as Betz (arguing from the nature of the *genre*!) postulates for Galatians (*Gal* 16–23). Plato's Epistle 7 (the authenticity of which is disputed) can be characterized as a 'lengthy, and somewhat confused, narrative' which includes a philosophical digression (Bury, *Plato* 9, p. 471, cf. 463). Edelstein (arguing for inauthenticity) characterizes it and other ancient letters as 'historical novels' (*Letter* 159); ' ... what the epistle tells about Plato's teaching is incidental to the historical narrative' (op.cit. 70). On the whole I suspect that Betz's cardinal mistake consists in comparing Galatians mainly to text-books of the rhetoricians rather than to actual 'apologetic letters' or the like. Cf. Meeks's review (esp. 306).

have to be carefully listened to in Christian theology and in interreligious discussions, but his contribution must be assimilated critically.[18]

It seems that Paul has by way of *intuition* (or because of his faith in Christ, if you like) arrived at important insights regarding for example the Christian's freedom.[19] Having my roots in 'Gentile' Lutheran Christianity I fully concur with his emphasis on the Gentile Christian's freedom from the Jewish Torah as well as from the 'elements of the world'. Christian theology will always remain in Paul's debt thanks to his consistent underlining of the priority of God's gracious initiative over human efforts to secure salvation (a contention fully in line with the best Jewish tradition). But I can find no fault with the Jew who says that, as a Jew, Paul should not have said much that he actually said. In his attempt to tell what the law is all about Paul gets involved in self-contradictions. What is worse, he conveys a distorted picture of the Jewish religion which has, contrary to Paul's intentions to be sure, had a share in the tragic history of the Jews at the mercy of Christians.[20]

Christian theology should have fastened on Paul's intuition. But to later Christianity for which the Torah was no longer an issue Paul's intuition about the ritual law (largely shared by him with the Hellenists) seemed simply a matter of course. Instead, especially in Protestantism, the rationalizations

---

18 Cf. the prudent counsel of von Rad, *Theology* II, 409: 'Such a bold interpretation' as Paul's (who was 'only one of many charismatic interpreters of the Old Testament') 'could scarcely be taken as normative'. 'Every age has the task of hearing what the old book has to say to it, in the light of its own insight and its own needs.'

19 Deissmann, *Paul* 104 f. correctly points out that 'too much has been made of' Paul's 'dialectic'. 'Logical proof ... and progress in a direct line of argument are not Paul's strong points. ... In controversy, for instance, Paul is much too impulsive a nature to be a great dialectician ... in dealing with religious problems he is more successful generally on the intuitive and contemplative side than on the purely speculative.' Cf. Sandmel, *Genius* 7.

20 Parkes, the historian of the Christian-Jewish relationships, concludes (*Judaism* 105): 'The bare fact is that nearly two thousand years of Jewish history owe their sufferings more to the writings of Paul than to any other individual outside the evangelists.' In both cases, 'it was not the effect which the author intended'. 'It is the Paulinists rather than Paul himself who bear the direct responsibility ... ' Nevertheless: ' ... Paul himself must be held primarily responsible for the fact that instead of a gradual and peaceful development, without schism, a violent break between the two faiths took place. Out of the mass of his teaching on the subject, the simple Gentile Christians of his day retained only two ideas about Judaism', namely that the law was a tutor to Christ, now superfluous, and that the law consists of a set of external rules (ibid. 107 f.). Cf. Flusser, 'Thesen' 182 (thesis 22).

After this I should perhaps add that this study was *not* conceived or carried out (for better or for worse) out of guilt feelings because of the maltreatment of Jews by Christians. Even if Christians had dealt with Jews throughout history as with angels, this would not free us from the duty to examine whether Paul is fair in his polemics.

Paul contrived in support of his intuition came to be seen as his actual inval-
uable accomplishment. I propose that we return to stress the intuition.[21]

One of the lessons to be learnt from Paul's dealing with the Torah is something like this. It is worth while taking new experiences in new situations very
seriously. If we take the risk of pursuing our theological quest in unorthodox
directions, we may have the right to look unto Paul as our 'patron saint'.
Imitation of the apostle is neither desirable nor possible. But if we stop
'dragging the past into the present'[22] despite the fact that pure doctrine and
Scripture are often enough on the opposite side of the controversy, we may
well find ourselves within the Pauline trajectory. Paul himself did not realize
that Scripture was not on his side. *We* may be expected to realize and to
admit that Scripture and tradition are *not* always on our side — and nevertheless continue our pilgrimage in the 'dangerous' direction. Certainly a person
trying to deal with sacred tradition with 'historical realism'[23] is not *bound* to
be able to appeal to Paul. And yet there simply *are* in Paul's work fascinating
elements which justify the claim that it is a blueprint for radical if responsible
Christian and theological freedom.

---

21 Having noted that Paul's treatment of circumcision in Galatians 'is marked by a great
deal of defense or rationalization', Andrews (*Teaching* 37) remarked critically: 'it
is with the rationalization that many writers on Paul expend most of their energy'.
    Brandt, *Rhetoric* 22 points out that 'argumentative thinking is probably always a
secondary process, a reduction from some sort of intuited understanding that takes
place first'.
22 Moxnes; see above, p. 265.
23 Again Moxnes; see preceding note.

Bibliography

Standard text editions, translations, concordances and synopses are not listed, unless special reference is made to them in the footnotes. Only works referred to are listed.

Aleith, E., *Paulusverständnis in der alten Kirche*. BZNW 18. Berlin 1937.

Althaus, P., *Der Brief an die Römer*. NTD 6[11]. Göttingen 1970.

Althaus, P., *Die christliche Wahrheit*. Lehrbuch der Dogmatik. Gütersloh 1966[7].

Althaus, P., *Paulus und Luther über den Menschen*. Ein Vergleich. Gütersloh 1963[4].

Aly, W., *Strabon von Amaseia*. Untersuchungen über Text, Aufbau und Quellen der Geographika. Antiquitas, Reihe 1, 5. Berlin 1957.

Andrews, M.E., *The Ethical Teaching of Paul*. A Study in Origin. Chapel Hill 1934.

Andrews, M.E., Paul, Philo and the Intellectuals. *JBL* 53, 1934, 150–166.

Aulén, G., *Christus Victor*. An Historical Study of the Three Main Types of the Idea of the Atonement. Transl. A.G. Hebert. London 1970 (repr.).

Bacon, B.W., Jesus and the Law. A Study of the First 'Book' of Matthew (Mt. 3–7). *JBL* 47, 1928, 203–231.

Bacon, B.W., *Studies in Matthew*. London 1930.

Bamberger, B.J., *Proselytism in the Talmudic Period*. New York 1968 (repr.).

Bammel, E., Gottes ΔΙΑΘΗΚΗ (Gal. III. 15–17) und das jüdische Rechtsdenken. *NTS* 6, 1959–60, 313–319.

Bammel, E., Νόμος Χριστοῦ. *StudEv* III, 1964, 120–128.

Bandas, R.G., *The Master-Idea of Saint Paul's Epistles, or the Redemption*. A Study of Biblical Theology. Bruges 1925.

Bandstra, A.J., *The Law and the Elements of the World*. An Exegetical Study in Aspects of Paul's Teaching. Kampen 1964.

Banks, R., *Jesus and the Law in the Synoptic Tradition*. MSSNTS 28. Cambridge 1975.

Baring-Gould, S., *A Study of St. Paul*. His character and opinions. London 1897.

Barr, J., *The Semantics of Biblical Language*. Oxford 1961.

Barrett, C.K., *A Commentary on the Epistle to the Romans*. BNTC. London 1957.

Barrett, C.K., *A Commentary on the First Epistle to the Corinthians*. BNTC. London 1968.

Barrett, C.K., *A Commentary on the Second Epistle to the Corinthians*. BNTC. London 1973.

Bartchy, S.S., ΜΑΛΛΟΝ ΧΡΗΣΑΙ: First-Century Slavery and the Interpretation of 1 Corinthians 7.21. SBL Diss 11. Missoula 1973.

Barth, C., *Die Interpretation des Neuen Testaments in der valentinianischen Gnosis*. TU 37/3. Leipzig 1911.

Barth, G., *Das Gesetzesverständnis des Evangelisten Matthäus*. G. Bornkamm – G. Barth – H.J. Held, Überlieferung und Auslegung im Matthäusevangelium, WMANT 1, Neukirchen 1961[2], 54–154.

Barth, K., *Die kirchliche Dogmatik* I:2. Die Lehre vom Wort Gottes. Zollikon 1938.

Barth, M., St. Paul – A Good Jew. *Horizons in Biblical Theology* 1, 1979, 7–37.

Barth, M., Die Stellung des Paulus zu Gesetz und Ordnung. *EvTh* 33, 1973, 496–526.

Bauer, W., *Griechisch-Deutsches Wörterbuch zu den Schriften des Neuen Testaments und der übrigen urchristlichen Literatur*. Berlin 1958[5].

Baulès, R., *L'Évangile, Puissance de Dieu*. Commentaire de l'Épitre aux Romains. LeDiv 53. Paris 1968.

Baumbach, G., Der christlich-jüdische Dialog – Herausforderung und neue Erkenntnisse. *Kairos* 23, 1981, 1–16.

Beck, I., Altes und Neues Gesetz. Eine Untersuchung über die Kompromisslosigkeit des paulinischen Denkens. *MThZ* 15, 1964, 127–142.

Becker, J., *Der Brief an die Galater*. NTD 8[14], Göttingen 1976, 1–85.

Becker, J., *Das Evangelium nach Johannes*. ÖTK 4. Gütersloh 1979–1981.

Beker, J.C., *Paul the Apostle*. The Triumph of God in Life and Thought. Philadelphia 1980.

Ben-Chorin, S., *Paulus*. Der Völkerapostel in jüdischer Sicht. München 1970.

Benoit, P., *Exégèse et théologie* II. La théologie de Saint Paul. Paris 1961.

Berger, K., Abraham in den paulinischen Hauptbriefen. *MThZ* 17, 1966, 47–89.

Berger, K., *Exegese des Neuen Testaments*. Neue Wege vom Text zur Auslegung. UTB 658. Heidelberg 1977.

Berger, K., *Die Gesetzesauslegung Jesu*. Ihr historischer Hintergrund im Judentum und im Alten Testament. 1. Markus und Parallelen. WMANT 40.1. Neukirchen 1972.

Berger, K., Hartherzigkeit und Gottes Gesetz. Die Vorgeschichte des antijüdischen Vorwurfs in Mc 10₅. *ZNW* 61, 1970, 1–47.

Bernays, J., *Gesammelte Abhandlungen* I. Berlin 1885.

Bertram, G., Hebräischer und griechischer Qohelet. Ein Beitrag zur Theologie der hellenistischen Bibel. *ZAW* 64, 1952, 26–49.

Bertram, G., Das Problem der Umschrift und die religionsgeschichtliche Erforschung der Septuaginta. *Werden und Wesen des Alten Testaments*, BZAW 66, Berlin 1936, 97–109.

Bertram, G., Die religiöse Umdeutung altorientalischer Lebens-Weisheit in der griechischen Übersetzung des Alten Testaments. *ZAW* 54, 1936, 153–167.

Bertram, G., Vom Wesen der Septuaginta-Frömmigkeit. *WO* II:3, 1956, 274–284.

Best, E., *The First and Second Epistles to the Thessalonians*. BNTC. London 1977.

Best, E., *The Letter of Paul to the Romans*. CBC. Cambridge 1967.

Bethge, H-G., Die Ambivalenz alttestamentlicher Geschichtstraditionen in der Gnosis. *AFG*, 1980, 89–109.

Betz, H.D., *Galatians*. A Commentary on Paul's Letter to the Churches of Galatia. Hermeneia. Philadelphia 1979.

Betz, H.D., The Literary Composition and Function of Paul's Letter to the Galatians. *NTS* 21, 1974–75, 353–379.

Betz, H.D., Spirit, Freedom, and Law. Paul's Message to the Galatian Churches. *SEA* 39, 1974, 145–160.

Betz, O., *Offenbarung und Schriftforschung in der Qumransekte*. WUNT 6. Tübingen 1960.

Bickermann, E., *Der Gott der Makkabäer*. Untersuchungen über Sinn und Ursprung der makkabäischen Erhebung. Berlin 1937.

Bihlmeyer, K., *Die apostolischen Väter*. Neubearbeitung der Funkschen Ausgabe. SQS, 2. Reihe 1. Tübingen 1956.

Blackman, E.C., *Marcion and His Influence*. London 1948.

Bläser, P., *Das Gesetz bei Paulus*. NTA 19, 1/2. Münster 1941.

Blank, J., *Paulus und Jesus*. Eine theologische Grundlegung. StANT 18. München 1968.

Blank, J., Warum sagt Paulus: 'Aus Werken des Gesetzes wird niemand gerecht'? *EKK. V*. 1, Neukirchen 1969, 79–95.

Blass, F. – Debrunner, A. – Rehkopf, F., *Grammatik des neutestamentlichen Griechisch*. Göttingen 1979[15].

Bligh, J., *Galatians*. A Discussion of St Paul's Epistle. HousCom 1. London 1969.

Böhlig, H., *Die Geisteskultur von Tarsos im augusteischen Zeitalter mit Berücksichtigung der paulinischen Schriften*. FRLANT, NF 2. Göttingen 1913.

Böhmer, S., *Heimkehr und neuer Bund*. Studien zu Jeremia 30–31. GTA 5. Göttingen 1976.

Bogaert, P-M., Introduction littéraire VI. La datation du livre. In: *Pseudo-Philon, Les Antiquités Bibliques* II, SC 230, Paris 1976, 66–74.

Bonnard, P., *L'Epitre de Saint Paul aux Galates*. CNT (N) 9. Neuchâtel 1953.

Borgen, P., Observations on the Theme "Paul and Philo". PLT, 1980, 85–102.

Bornkamm, G., *Das Ende des Gesetzes*. Paulusstudien. Gesammelte Aufsätze I. BEvTh 16. München 1963[4].

Bornkamm, G., *Geschichte und Glaube* II. Gesammelte Aufsätze IV. München 1971.

Bornkamm, G., *Paulus*. UB 119 D. Berlin 1969.

Bornkamm, G., The Risen Lord and the Earthly Jesus. Matthew 28.16–20. *The Future of Our Religious Past*, Essays in Honour of R. Bultmann, London 1971, 203–229.

Bornkamm, G., *Studien zu Antike und Urchristentum*. Gesammelte Aufsätze II. BEvTh 28. München 1963[2].

Borse, U., Paulus in Jerusalem. *KuE*, 1981, 43–64.

Borse, U., *Der Standort des Galaterbriefes*. BBB 41. Köln-Bonn 1972.

Bousset, W., Der Brief an die Galater. *SNT* 2, 31–74.

Bousset, W., *Die Offenbarung Johannis*. KEK 16. Göttingen 1966[6] (repr.).

Bousset, W. – Gressmann, H., *Die Religion des Judentums im späthellenistischen Zeitalter*. HNT 21. Tübingen 1966.

Brandenburger, E., *Adam und Christus*. Exegetisch-religionsgeschichtliche Untersuchung zu Röm. 5[12–21] (1. Kor. 15). WMANT 7. Neukirchen 1962.

Brandt, W.J., *The Rhetoric of Argumentation*. New York 1970.

Branscomb, B.H., *Jesus and the Law of Moses*. London 1930.

Branscomb, B.H., *The Gospel of Mark*. MNTC. London 1948[5].

Braun, H., Römer 7, 7–25 und das Selbstverständnis des Qumran-Frommen. *ZThK* 56, 1959, 1–18.

Braun, H., *Spätjüdisch-häretischer und frühchristlicher Radikalismus*. Jesus von Nazareth und die essenische Qumransekte. II. Die Synoptiker. BHTh 24. Tübingen 1957.

Braun, H., *Wie man über Gott nicht denken soll*. Dargelegt an Gedankengängen Philos von Alexandria. Tübingen 1971.

Breech, E., These Fragments I Have Shored Against My Ruins: The Form and Function of 4 Ezra. *JBL* 92, 1973, 267–274.

Bremer, P.L., *Paul's Understanding of the Death of Christ according to Romans 1–8*. Diss. Princeton 1974 (microfilm).

Bring, R., *Christus und das Gesetz*. Die Bedeutung des Gesetzes des Alten Testaments nach Paulus und sein Glauben an Christus. Leiden 1969.

Bring, R., *Commentary on Galatians*. Transl. E. Wahlstrom. Philadelphia 1961.

Bring, R., Paul and the Old Testament. A Study of the ideas of Election, Faith and Law in Paul, with special reference to Romans 9.30–10.30 (sic). StTh 25, 1971. 21–60.

Broer, I., *Freiheit vom Gesetz und Radikalisierung des Gesetzes*. Ein Beitrag zur Theologie des Evangelisten Matthäus. SBS 98. Stuttgart 1980.

Brooke, G., Review of E.P. Sanders, Paul and Palestinian Judaism. JJS 30, 1979, 247–250.

Brown, R.E., *The Gospel according to John* 1–2. AncB. New York 1966.

Brown, S., The Matthaean Community and the Gentile Mission. *NT* 22, 1980, 193–221.

Bruce, F.F., Paul and the Law of Moses. *BJRL* 57, 1975, 259–279.

Buber, M., *Zwei Glaubensweisen*. Zürich 1950.

Buck, Ch. – Taylor, G., *Saint Paul.* A Study of the Development of His Thought. New York 1969.

Büchler, A., *Studies in Sin and Atonement in the Rabbinic Literature of the First Century.* LBS. New York 1967 (Repr.).

Bugge, Chr. A., Das Gesetz und Christus nach der Anschauung der ältesten Christengemeinde. *ZNW* 4, 1903, 89–110.

Bultmann, R., *Exegetica.* Aufsätze zur Erforschung des Neuen Testaments. Tübingen 1967.

Bultmann, R., *Glauben und Verstehen* II. Gesammelte Aufsätze. Tübingen 1961[3].

Bultmann, R., Ein neues Paulus – Verständnis? *ThLZ* 84, 1959, 481–486.

Bultmann, R., *Theology of the New Testament.* Transl. K. Grobel. London 1978[9].

Bultmann, R., *Der zweite Brief an die Korinther.* KEK Sonderband 2. Göttingen 1976.

Burchard, C., Das doppelte Liebesgebot in der frühen christlichen Überlieferung. *Der Ruf Jesu und die Antwort der Gemeinde* (Festschrift J. Jeremias), Göttingen 1970, 39–62.

Burchard, C., Versuch, das Thema der Bergpredigt zu finden. *JCHT,* 1975, 409–432.

Burchard, C., Zu Jakobus 2_{14-26}. *ZNW* 71, 1980, 27–45.

Burger, C., *Schöpfung und Versöhnung.* Studien zum liturgischen Gut im Kolosser- und Epheserbrief. WMANT 46. Neukirchen-Vluyn 1975.

Burton, E.D., *A critical and exegetical commentary on the Epistle to the Galatians.* ICC. Edinburgh 1921.

Bury, R.B., *Plato,* Works 9. LCL. London 1952.

Bussmann, C., *Themen der paulinischen Missionspredigt auf dem Hintergrund der spätjüdisch-hellenistischen Missionsliteratur.* EHS.T 3. Bern-Frankfurt a.M. 1971.

Byrne, B., *'Sons of God' – 'Seed of Abraham'.* A Study of the Idea of Sonship of God of All Christians in Paul against the Jewish Background. AnBib 83. Rome 1979.

Caird, G.B., *The Apostolic Age.* Studies in Theology. London 1966 (= 1955).

Caird, G.B., *Principalities and Powers.* A Study in Pauline Theology. Oxford 1956.

Caird, G.B., Review of E.P. Sanders, Paul and Palestinian Judaism. *JThS* 29, 1978, 538–543.

Callan, T., Pauline Midrash: the Exegetical Background of Gal 3.19b. *JBL* 99, 1980, 549–567.

Cambier, J.-M., Le jugement de tous hommes par Dieu seul, selon la vérité, dans Rom 2_1-3_{20}. *ZNW* 67, 1976, 187–213.

Campbell, D.H., The Identity of ἐγώ in Romans 7.7–25. *StudBibl,* 1980, 57–64.

Campbell, W.S., Christ the End of the Law: Romans 10.4. *Stud Bibl,* 1980, 73–81.

Campenhausen, H. Fr. v., *Die Entstehung der christlichen Bibel.* BHTh 39. Tübingen 1968.

Carlston, C.E., The Things That Defile (Mark vii. 15) and the Law in Matthew and Mark. *NTS* 15 (1968–69), 75–96.

Case, S.J., The Jewish Bias of Paul. *JBL* 47, 1928, 20–31.

Catchpole, D.R., Paul, James and the Apostolic Decree. *NTS* 23 (1976–77), 428–449.

Cavallin, H.C., "The Righteous Shall Live by Faith". A Decisive Argument for the Traditional Interpretation. *StTh* 32, 1978, 33–43.

Cerfaux, L., *The Christian in the Theology of Saint Paul.* Transl. L. Soiron. London 1967.

Chadwick, H., 'All Things to All Men' (1 Cor ix. 22). *NTS* 1, 1954–55, 261–275.

Charles, R.H., *A critical and exegetical commentary on the Revelation of St. John* 1–2. ICC. Edinburgh 1920.

Charlesworth, J.H., *The Pseudepigrapha and Modern Research.* SCS 7. Missoula 1976.

Clements, R.E., *God's Chosen People.* A Theological Interpretation of the Book of

Deuteronomy. London 1968.

Collange, J-F., *Enigmes de la deuxième épître de Paul aux Corinthiens.* Étude exégetique de 2 Cor. 2.14–7.4. MS SNTS 18. Cambridge 1972.

Colson, F.H., *Philo* 7. LCL. London 1958.

Conzelmann, H., *Die Apostelgeschichte.* HNT 7. Tübingen 1972[2].

Conzelmann, H., *Der erste Brief an die Korinther.* KEK 5. Göttingen 1969.

Conzelmann, H., *Grundriss der Theologie des Neuen Testaments.* EETh 2. München 1968[2]. (ET: An Outline of the Theology of the New Testament, transl. J. Bowden, London 1969).

Conzelmann, H., *Heiden – Juden – Christen.* Auseinandersetzungen in der Literatur der hellenistisch-römischen Zeit. BHTh 62. Tübingen 1981.

Conzelmann, H., Literaturbericht zu den Synoptischen Evangelien. *ThR* 43, 1978, 3–51.

Conzelmann, H., *Die Mitte der Zeit.* Studien zur Theologie des Lukas. BHTh 17. Tübingen 1962[4].

Conzelmann, H. – Lindemann, A., *Arbeitsbuch zum Neuen Testament.* UTB 52. Tübingen 1980[5].

Cranfield, C.E.B., *A critical and exegetical commentary on the Epistle to the Romans* 1–2. ICC. Edinburgh 1975–1979.

Cranfield, C.E.B., *The Gospel according to Saint Mark.* CGTC. Cambridge 1963[2].

Cranfield, C.E.B., Some Notes on Romans 9.30–33. *Jesus und Paulus*, Festschr. W.G. Kümmel, Göttingen 1975, 35–43.

Cranfield, C.E.B., St. Paul and the Law. *SJTh* 17, 1964, 43–68.

Crouch, J.E., *The Origin and Intention of the Colossian Haustafel.* FRLANT 109. Göttingen 1972.

Cullmann, O., *Heil als Geschichte.* Heilsgeschichtliche Existenz im Neuen Testament. Tübingen 1965.

Dabelstein, R., *Die Beurteilung der 'Heiden' bei Paulus.* BET 14. Frankfurt a.M. – Bern – Cirencester 1981.

Dahl, N.A., *Jesus in the Memory of the Early Church.* Minneapolis 1976.

Dahl, N.A., Rev. E.P. Sanders, Paul and Palestinian Judaism. *RSRev* 4, 1978, 153–158.

Dahl, N.A., *Studies in Paul.* Theology for the Early Christian Mission. Minneapolis 1977.

Dalbert, P., *Die Theologie der hellenistisch-jüdischen Missionsliteratur unter Ausschluss von Philo und Josephus.* ThF 4. Hamburg 1954.

D'Angelo, M.R., *Moses in the Letter to the Hebrews.* SBL Diss 42. Ann Arbor 1979.

Danker, F.W., Romans v. 12: Sin under Law. *NTS* 14, 1967–68, 424–439.

Dassmann, E., *Der Stachel im Fleisch.* Paulus in der frühchristlichen Literatur bis Irenäus. Münster 1979.

Davies, W.D., From Schweitzer to Scholem. Reflections on Sabbatai Svi. *JBL* 95, 1976, 529–558.

Davies, W.D., Paul and the People of Israel. *NTS* 24, 1977–78, 4–39.

Davies, W.D., *Paul and Rabbinic Judaism.* Some Rabbinic Elements in Pauline Theology. HTB 146. New York 1967 (revised ed.)

Davies, W.D., Review of J. Munck, Paulus und die Heilsgeschichte. *NTS* 2, 1955–56, 60–72.

Davies, W.D., *The Setting of the Sermon on the Mount.* Cambridge 1964.

Davies, W.D., *Torah in the Messianic Age and/or the Age to Come.* JBL. MS 7. Philadelphia 1952.

Deissmann, A., *Paul.* A Study of Social and Religious History. New York 1957.

Delling, G., στοιχεῖον. *ThWNT* VI, 670–687.

Démann, P., Moses und das Gesetz bei Paulus. In: *Moses in Schrift und Überlieferung,* Düsseldorf 1963, 205–264.

Dequeker, L., Der jüdisch-christliche Dialog eine Herausforderung für die Theologie? Offene Fragen und Interpretationen. *FrRu* 28, 1976, 13–16.

Derrett, J.D.M., *Law in the New Testament*. London 1970.

Dibelius, M., *An die Kolosser, Epheser, an Philemon*. HNT 12. Tübingen 1927[2].

Dibelius, M., *Der Brief des Jakobus*. KEK 15[11]. Göttingen 1964.

Dibelius, M., *Die Geisterwelt im Glauben des Paulus*. Göttingen 1909.

Dibelius, M., *Studies in the Acts of the Apostles*. Ed. H. Greeven. Transl. M. Ling. London 1956.

Dibelius, M. – Conzelmann, H., *Die Pastoralbriefe*. HNT 13. Tübingen 1966[4].

Dietrich, W., *Prophetie und Geschichte*. Eine redaktionsgeschichtliche Untersuchung zum deuteronomistischen Geschichtswerk. FRLANT 108. Göttingen 1972.

Dietzfelbinger, Chr., Die Antithesen der Bergpredigt im Verständnis des Matthäus. *ZNW* 70, 1979, 1–15.

Dietzfelbinger, Chr., *Pseudo-Philo: Antiquitates Biblicae*. JüdSchrHell-röm Zeit II:2. Gütersloh 1975.

Dinkler, E., *Signum crucis*. Aufsätze zum Neuen Testament und zur Christlichen Archäologie. Tübingen 1967.

Dix, G., *Jew and Greek*. A Study in the Primitive Church. Glasgow 1953.

Dodd, C.H., ΕΝΝΟΜΟΣ ΧΡΙΣΤΟΥ. *Studia Paulina*, in honorem J. de Zwaan, Haarlem 1953, 96–110.

Dodd, C.H., *The Interpretation of the Fourth Gospel*. Cambridge 1968 (Repr.).

Dodd, C.H., *The Epistle of Paul to the Romans*. MNTC London 1947 (Repr.).

Dodd, C.H., *New Testament Studies*. Manchester 1967 (Repr.).

Doeve, J.W., Some Notes with Reference to ΤΑ ΛΟΓΙΑ ΤΟΥ ΘΕΟΥ in Romans III 2. *Studia Paulina* in honorem J. de Zwaan, Haarlem 1953, 111–123.

Donfried, K.P., Justification and Last Judgment in Paul. *ZNW* 67, 1976, 90–110.

Donfried, K.P. (ed.), *The Romans Debate*. Minneapolis 1977.

Drane, J.W., *Paul – Libertine or Legalist?* A Study in the Theology of the Major Pauline Epistles. London 1975.

Drane, J.W., Theological Diversity in the Letters of St. Paul. *TynB* 27, 1976, 3–26.

Drane, J.W., Tradition, Law and Ethics in Pauline Theology. *NT* 16, 1974, 167–178.

Drane, J.W., Why Did Paul Write Romans? *PSt* 208–227.

van Dülmen, A., *Die Theologie des Gesetzes bei Paulus*. SBM 5. Stuttgart 1968.

Dugandzic, I., *Das "Ja" Gottes in Christus*. Eine Studie zur Bedeutung des Alten Testaments für das Christusverständnis des Paulus. FzB 26. Würzburg 1977.

Duncan, G.S., *The Epistle of Paul to the Galatians*. MNTC. London 1944 (Repr.).

Dunn, J.D.G., Rom. 7, 14–25 in the Theology of Paul. *ThZ* 31, 1975, 257–273.

Dunn, J.D.G., *Unity and Diversity in the New Testament*. An Inquiry into the character of Earliest Christianity. London 1977.

Eckert, J., *Die urchristliche Verkündigung im Streit zwischen Paulus und seinen Gegnern nach dem Galaterbrief*. BH 6. Regensburg 1971.

Edelstein, L., *Plato's Seventh Letter*. Leiden 1966.

Edwards, E.G., *Christ, a Curse, and the Cross*. An Interpretative Study of Galatians 3.13. Diss. Princeton 1972 (microfilm).

Egger, W., *Nachfolge als Weg zum Leben*. Chancen neuerer exegetischer Methoden dargelegt an Mk 10, 17–31. Österreicher Biblische Studien 1. Klosterneuburg 1979.

Ehrlich, E., Über die Tora. *Wegweisung*, VIKJ 8, Berlin 1978, 66–71.

Eichholz, G., *Glaube und Werk bei Paulus und Jakobus*. TEH NF 88. München 1961.

Eichholz, G., *Die Theologie des Paulus im Umriss*. Neukirchen-Vluyn 1972.

Eichrodt, W., *Ezekiel*. A Commentary. Transl. C. Quin. OTL. London 1970.

Eissfeldt, O., *Einleitung in das Alte Testament* ... NTG. Tübingen 1964[3].

Ellis, E.E., *Paul's Use of the Old Testament*. Edinburgh-London 1957.

Ellis, E.E., *Prophecy and Hermeneutic in Early Christianity*. New Testament Essays. WUNT 18. Tübingen 1978.

Eltester, W., Israel im lukanischen Werk und die Nazarethperikope. W. Eltester (ed.), *Jesus in Nazareth*, BZNW 40, Berlin 1972, 76–147.

Enslin, M.S., *The Ethics of Paul*. New York-London 1930.

Fabris, R., *Legge della libertà in Giacomo*. Suppl. RivBib 8. Brescia 1977.

Fallon, F.T., The Law in Philo and Ptolemy: A Note on the Letter to Flora. *VigChr* 30, 1976, 45–51.

Feine, P., *Das gesetzesfreie Evangelium des Paulus nach seinem Werdegang dargestellt*. Leipzig 1899.

Feine, P. *Theologie des Neuen Testaments*. Berlin 1951[8].

Feld, H., 'Christus Diener der Sünde'. Zum Ausgang des Streites zwischen Petrus und Paulus. ThQ 153, 1973, 119–131.

Fenton, J., *Saint Matthew*. PNTC. London 1973 (repr.).

Feuillet, A., Loi ancienne et Morale chrétienne d'après l'Epître aux Romains. *NRTh* 92, 1970, 785–805.

Feuillet, A., Loi de Dieu, loi du Christ et loi de l'Esprit d'après les épîtres pauliniennes. Les rapports de ces trois lois avec la Loi Mosaique. *NT* 22, 1980, 29–65.

Fiedler, P., Jesus und die Sünder. Beiträge zur biblischen Exegese und Theologie 3. Frankfurt a.M. – Bern 1976.

Fischer, K.M., *Tendenz und Absicht des Epheserbriefes*. FRLANT 111. Göttingen 1973.

Fleischhauer, Die paulinische Lehre vom Gesetz. *ThSW* 4, 1883, 37–71.

Flückiger, F., Christus, des Gesetzes *telos*. *ThZ* 11, 1955, 153–157.

Flückiger, F., Die Werke des Gesetzes bei den Heiden (nach Röm 2, 14 ff.). *ThZ* 8, 1952, 17–42.

Flusser, D., Die Christenheit nach dem Apostelkonzil. *Antijudaismus im Neuen Testament?* München 1967, 60–81.

Flusser, D., Das Erlebnis, ein Jude zu sein. In: *Richte unsere Füsse auf den Weg des Friedens,* Festschrift H. Gollwitzer, München 1979, 15–25.

Flusser, D., Thesen zur Entstehung des Christentums aus dem Judentum. *FrRu* 27, 1975, 181–184.

Friedländer, M., *Geschichte der jüdischen Apologetik als Vorgeschichte des Christentums*. Eine historisch-kritische Darstellung der Propaganda und Apologie im Alten Testament und in der hellenistischen Diaspora. Amsterdam 1973 (repr.).

Friedländer, M., *Die religiösen Bewegungen innerhalb des Judentums im Zeitalter Jesu*. Berlin 1905.

Friedrich, G., *Der erste Brief an die Thessalonicher*. NTD 8[14]. Göttingen 1976.

Friedrich, G., Das Gesetz des Glaubens Röm. 3, 27. *ThZ* 10, 1954, 401–417.

Fuchs, E., *Die Freiheit des Glaubens*. Römer 5–8 ausgelegt. BEvTh 14. München 1949.

Fuller, D.P., *Gospel and Law: Contrast or Continuum? The Hermeneutics of Dispensationalism and Covenant Theology*. Grand Rapids 1980.

Fuller, D.P., Paul and the 'Works of the Law'. *WThJ* 38, 1975–76, 28–42.

Fuller, R.H., Das Doppelgebot der Liebe. Ein Testfall für die Echtheitskriterien der Worte Jesu. *JCHT*, 1975, 317–329.

Fung, R. Y-K., Justification by Faith in 1 & 2 Corinthians. *PSt* 246–261.

Furnish, V.P., Development in Paul's Thought. *JAAR* 38, 1970, 289–303.

Furnish, V.P., *The Love Command in the New Testament*. Nashville-New York 1972.

Furnish, V.P., *Theology and Ethics in Paul*. New York 1968.

Gaechter, P., *Petrus und seine Zeit*. Neutestamentliche Studien. Innsbruck 1958.

Gager, J.G., *Kingdom and Community*. The Social World of Early Christianity. Prentice-Hall Studies in Religion series. Englewood Cliffs, N.J., 1975.

Gager, J., *Moses in Greco-Roman Paganism*. SBL MS 16. Nashville 1972.

Gager, J.G., Some Notes on Paul's Conversion. *NTS* 27, 1981, 697–704.

Gale, H.M., *The Use of Analogy in the Letters of Paul*. Philadelphia 1964.

Gardner, P., *The Religious Experience of Saint Paul*. London-New York 1913[2].

Garnet, P., Qumran Light on Pauline Soteriology. *PSt* 19–32.

Garnet, P., *Salvation and Atonement in the Qumran Scrolls*. WUNT, 2. Reihe 3. Tübingen 1977.

Garscha, J., *Studien zum Ezechielbuch*. Eine redaktionskritische Untersuchung von Ez 1–39. EHS. T 23. Bern-Frankfurt a.M. 1974.

Gaston, L., Paul and the Torah. *Antisemitism and the Foundations of Christianity* (éd. A.T. Davies), New York-Ramsey-Toronto 1979, 48–71.

Gayer, R., *Die Stellung des Sklaven in den paulinischen Gemeinden und bei Paulus*. Zugleich ein sozialgeschichtlich vergleichender Beitrag zur Wertung des Sklaven in der Antike. EHS.T 78. Bern-Frankfurt 1976.

Georgi, D., *Die Gegner des Paulus im 2. Korintherbrief*. Studien zur religiösen Propaganda in der Spätantike. WMANT 11. Neukirchen-Vluyn 1964.

Georgi, D., *Die Geschichte der Kollekte des Paulus für Jerusalem*. ThF 38. Hamburg-Bergstedt 1965.

Gerhardsson, B., 1 Kor 13. Zur Frage von Paulus' rabbinischem Hintergrund. *Donum Gentilicium*, in honour of D. Daube, Oxford 1978, 185–209.

Gerhardsson, B., Bibelns ethos. *Etik och kristen tro*, Lund 1971, 13–92.

Gerhardsson, B., *Memory and Manuscript*. Oral Tradition and Written Transmission in Rabbinic Judaism and Early Christianity. ASNU 22, Uppsala 1961.

Gerleman, G., Religion och moral i Septuagintas Proverbiaöversättning. SvTK 26, 1950, 222–232.

Gese, H., Ezechiel 20, 25 f. und die Erstgeburtsopfer. *Beiträge zur Alttestamentlichen Theologie*, Festschr. W. Zimmerli, Göttingen 1977, 140–151.

Gese, H., Psalm 50 und das alttestamentliche Gesetzesverständnis. *RF*, 1976, 57–77.

Gese, H., *Vom Sinai zum Zion*. Alttestamentliche Beiträge zur biblischen Theologie. BEvTh 64, München 1974.

Gese, H., *Zur biblischen Theologie*. Alttestamentliche Vorträge. BEvTh 78. München 1977.

Gifford, E.H., *The Epistle of St. Paul to the Romans*. With notes and Introduction. London 1886.

Glock, J.Ph., *Die Gesetzesfrage im Leben Jesu und in der Lehre des Paulus*. Eine biblisch-kritische Untersuchung ... Karlsruhe & Leipzig 1885.

Gnilka, J., *Der Epheserbrief*. HThK 10.2. Freiburg-Basel-Wien 1971.

Gnilka, J., *Der Kolosserbrief*. HThK 10.1. Freiburg-Basel-Wien 1980.

Gnilka, J., *Der Philipperbrief*. HThK 10.3. Freiburg-Basel-Wien 1968.

Goodenough, E.R., *By Light, Light*. The Mystic Gospel of Hellenistic Judaism. New Haven 1935.

Goodenough, E.R., *An Introduction to Philo Judaeus*. Oxford 1962[2].

Goodenough, E.R., Paul and the Hellenization of Christianity. *RelAnt*, 1968, 23–68.

Goppelt, L., *Christentum und Judentum im ersten und zweiten Jahrhundert*. Ein Aufriss der Urgeschichte der Kirche. BFChTh 2. Reihe 55. Gütersloh 1954.

Goppelt, L., *Christologie und Ethik*. Aufsätze zum Neuen Testament. Göttingen 1968.

Grässer, E., *Albert Schweitzer als Theologe*. BHTh 60. Tübingen 1979.

Grässer, E., Die antijüdische Polemik im Johannesevangelium. *NTS* 10, 1964–65, 74–90.

Grafe, E., *Die paulinische Lehre vom Gesetz nach den vier Hauptbriefen*. Leipzig 1893[2].

Grant, F.C., *Ancient Judaism and the New Testament*. Edinburgh-London 1960.

Grant, F.C., *An Introduction to New Testament Thought*. New York-Nashville 1950.

Grant, F.C., Prolegomenon, in: A. Büchler, *Studies in Sin and Atonement*, New York 1967, xvii–xxxix.

Grant, F.C., *Romans – Revelation*. NBC 7. New York 1962.

Grant, M., *Saint Paul*. London 1976.

Grant, R.M., *The Letter and the Spirit*. London 1957.

Grant, R.M., The Wisdom of the Corinthians. *The Joy of Study* (Festschrift F.C. Grant), New York 1951, 51–55.

Grønbech, V., *Paulus*. Jesu Kristi apostel. København 1940.

Gronemeyer, R., *Zur Frage nach dem paulinischen Antinomismus*. Exegetisch-systematische Überlegungen mit besonderer Berücksichtigung der Forschungsgeschichte im 19. Jahrhundert. Diss. Hamburg 1970.

Grosheide, F.W., *Commentary on the First Epistle to the Corinthians*. NLC 6. London 1954[2].

Gross, H., Tora und Gnade im Alten Testament. *Kairos* 14, 1972, 220–231.

Grundmann, W., *Das Evangelium nach Markus*. ThHK 2. Berlin 1980[8].

Grundmann, W., Gesetz, Rechtfertigung und Mystik bei Paulus. Zum Problem der Einheitlichkeit der paulinischen Verkündigung. *ZNW* 32, 1933, 52–65.

Güttgemanns, E., *Der leidende Apostel und sein Herr*. Studien zur paulinischen Christologie. FRLANT 90. Göttingen 1966.

Güttgemanns, E., *Studia linguistica neotestamentica*. Gesammelte Aufsätze zur linguistischen Grundlage einer neutestamentlichen Theologie. BEvTh 60. München 1971.

Gulin, E.G., *Die Freude im Neuen Testament* I. AASF 26.2. Helsinki 1932.

Gundry, R.H., The Moral Frustration of Paul before his Conversion. *PSt* 228–245.

Gunther, J.J., *St. Paul's Opponents and their Background*. A Study of Apocalyptic and Jewish Sectarian Teachings. NT. S 25. Leiden 1973.

Gutbrod, W., νόμος B-D. ThWNT IV, 1029–1077.

Gutbrod, W., *Die paulinische Anthropologie*. BWANT 15. Stuttgart-Berlin 1934.

Guthrie, D., *Galatians*. CeB. London 1969.

Guttmann, A., The Significance of Miracles for Talmudic Judaism. *HUCA* 20, 1947, 363–406.

Guttmann, M., *Das Judentum und seine Umwelt* I. Eine Darstellung der religiösen und rechtlichen Beziehungen zwischen Juden und Nichtjuden mit besonderer Berücksichtigung der talmudisch-rabbinischen Quellen. Allgemeiner Teil. Berlin 1927.

Gyllenberg, R., *Hebrealaiskirje*. SUTS. Helsinki 1971[2].

Gyllenberg, R., *Korinttolaiskirjeet*. SUTS. Helsinki 1969[2].

Gyllenberg, R.G., *Rechtfertigung und Altes Testament*. FDV 1966. Stuttgart 1973.

Gyllenberg, R., *Viisi Paavalin kirjettä*. (Five Letters of Paul, incl. *Galatians*). SUTS. Helsinki 1975.

Haacker, K., *Die Stiftung des Heils*. Untersuchungen zur Struktur der johanneischen Theologie. AzTh I, 47. Stuttgart 1972.

Haenchen, E., *Die Apostelgeschichte*. KEK 3[16]. Göttingen 1977[7].

Haenchen, E., *Der Weg Jesu*. Eine Erklärung des Markus-Evangeliums und der kanonischen Parallelen. de Gruyter-Lehrbuch. Berlin 1968[2].

Hahn, F., Das Gesetzesverständnis im Römer- und Galaterbrief. *ZNW* 67, 1976, 29–63.

Hahn, F., *Der urchristliche Gottesdienst*. SBS 41. Stuttgart 1970.

Hanson, A.T., *Studies in Paul's Technique and Theology*. London 1974.

Hanson, S., *The Unity of the Church in the New Testament*. Colossians and Ephesians. ASNU 14. Uppsala 1946.

Hare, D.R.A., *The Theme of Jewish Persecution of Christians in the Gospel according to St. Matthew*. MS SNTS 6. Cambridge 1967.

Harnack, A., *Beiträge zur Einleitung in das Neue Testament*. III. Die Apostelgeschichte.

Leipzig 1908.

Harnack, A., *Kritik des Neuen Testaments von einem griechischen Philosophen des 3. Jahrhunderts.* Die in Apocriticus des Macarius Magnes enthaltene Streitschrift. TU 3.7/4, Leipzig 1911.

Harnack, A., *Marcion: Das Evangelium vom fremden Gott.* Eine Monographie zur Geschichte der Grundlegung der katholischen Kirche. TU 45. Leipzig 1924².

Harnisch, W., Die Berufung des Reichen. Zur Analyse von Markus 10, 17–27. *Festschrift E. Fuchs,* Tübingen 1973, 161–176.

Harnisch, W., *Verhängnis und Verheissung der Geschichte.* Untersuchungen zum Zeit- und Geschichtsverständnis im 4. Buch Esra und in der syrischen Baruchapokalypse. FRLANT 97. Göttingen 1969.

Harrington, D.J., *God's People in Christ.* New Testament Perspectives on the Church and Judaism. Overtures to Biblical Theology. Philadelphia 1980.

Hartman, L., Bundesideologie in und hinter einigen paulinischen Texten. *PLT,* 1980, 103–118.

von Hartmann, E., *Das Christentum des neuen Testaments.* Sachsen im Harz 1905.

Hasler, V.E., *Gesetz und Evangelium in der alten Kirche bis Origenes.* Eine auslegungsgeschichtliche Untersuchung. Zürich 1953.

Hasler, V., Glaube und Existenz. Hermeneutische Erwägungen zu Gal. 2, 15–21. *ThZ* 25, 1969, 241–251.

Haufe, Chr., *Die sittliche Rechtfertigungslehre des Paulus.* Halle (Saale) 1957.

Haufe, Chr., Die Stellung des Paulus zum Gesetz. *ThLZ* 91, 1966, 171–178.

Hays, R.B., Psalm 143 and the Logic of Romans 3. *JBL* 99, 1980, 107–115.

Hedenius, I., *Helvetesläran.* Stockholm 1972.

Heinemann, I., *La loi dans la pensée juive.* Adaptation française par C.Touati. Présences du judaisme. Paris 1962.

Heinemann, I., *Philons griechische und jüdische Bildung.* Kulturvergleichende Untersuchungen zu Philons Darstellung der jüdischen Gesetze. Breslau 1932.

Helfgott, B.W., *The Doctrine of Election in Tannaitic Literature.* New York 1954.

Hengel, M., Anonymität, Pseudepigraphie und "Literarische Fälschung" in der jüdisch-hellenistischen Literatur. *Pseudepigrapha I.* Pseudopythagorica – Lettres de Platon – Littérature pseudépigraphique juive. Entretiens sur l'antiquité classique 18. Genève 1972. P. 229–308.

Hengel, M., *Judentum und Hellenismus.* Studien zu ihrer Begegnung unter besonderer Berücksichtigung Palästinas bis zur Mitte des 2. Jh.s v.Chr. WUNT 10. Tübingen 1973².

Hengel, M., Die Ursprünge der christlichen Mission. *NTS* 18, 1971–72, 15–38.

Hengel, M., *Zur urchristlichen Geschichtsschreibung.* Calwer paperback. Stuttgart 1979.

Hengel, M., Zwischen Jesus und Paulus. Die "Hellenisten", die "Sieben" und Stephanus (Apg 6, 1–15; 7, 54–8, 3). *ZThK* 72, 1975, 151–206.

Héring, J., *La première épitre de Saint Paul aux Corinthiens.* CNT. Neuchâtel 1949.

Héring, J., *La seconde épitre de Saint Paul aux Corinthiens.* CNT 8. Neuchâtel 1958.

Herrmann, S., *Die prophetischen Heilserwartungen im Alten Testament.* Ursprung und Gestaltwandel. BWANT Fünfte Folge 5. Stuttgart 1965.

Hick, J., *God and the Universe of Faiths.* Fount Paperbacks. Glasgow 1977.

Hickling, C.J.A., Centre and Periphery in the Thought of Paul. *StudBibl,* 1980, 199–214.

Hickling, C.J.A., The Sequence of Thought in II Corinthians, Chapter Three. *NTS* 21, 1974–75, 380–395.

Hoheisel, K., *Das antike Judentum in christlicher Sicht.* Ein Beitrag zur neueren Forschungsgeschichte. Studies in Oriental Religions 2. Wiesbaden 1978.

Holsten, C., *Das Evangelium des Paulus* I. Die äussere Entwicklungsgeschichte des paulinischen Evangeliums. Abt. 1. Der Brief an die Gemeinden Galatiens und der erste Brief an die Gemeinde in Korinth. Berlin 1880.

Holsten, C., *Zum Evangelium des Paulus und Petrus.* Rostock 1868.

Holtz, T., Die Bedeutung des Apostelkonzils für Paulus. *NT* 16, 1974, 110–148.

Holtz, T., Zur Frage der inhaltlichen Weisungen bei Paulus. *ThLZ* 106, 1981, 385–400.

Holtzmann, H.J., *Lehrbuch der neutestamentlichen Theologie* II. Tübingen 1911².

Hommel, H., Das 7. Kapitel des Römerbriefs im Licht antiker Überlieferung. *ThViat* 8, 1961–62, 90–116.

Hooker, M.D., Beyond the Things that are Written? St. Paul's Use of Scripture. *NTS* 27, 1980–81, 295–309.

Hooker, M.D., *Pauline Pieces.* London 1979.

Hoppe, R., *Der theologische Hintergrund des Jakobusbriefes.* FzB 28. Würzburg 1977.

Horbury, W., Paul and Judaism. *ET* 89, 1977–78, 116–118.

Horsley, R.A., Wisdom of Word and Words of Wisdom in Corinth. *CBQ* 39, 1977, 224–239.

van der Horst, P., Pseudo-Phocylides and the New Testament. *ZNW* 69, 1978, 187–202.

van der Horst, P.W., *The Sentences of Pseudo-Phocylides.* With Introduction and Commentary. SVTP Leiden 1978.

Houlden, J.L., *The Pastoral Epistles.* PNTC. Harmondsworth 1976.

Howard, G.E., Christ the End of the Law. The Meaning of Romans 10_4 ff. *JBL* 88, 1969, 331–337.

Howard, G., The 'Faith of Christ'. *ET* 85, 1973–74, 212–215.

Howard, G.E., On the 'Faith of Christ'. *HThR* 60, 1967, 459–465.

Howard, G., *Paul: Crisis in Galatia.* A Study in Early Christian Theology. MSSNTS 35. Cambridge 1979.

Howard, G., Romans 3.21–31 and the Inclusion of the Gentiles. *HThR* 63, 1970, 223–233.

Howard, R.E., *Newness of Life.* A Study in the Thought of Paul. Kansas City 1975.

Hruby, K., Gesetz und Gnade in der rabbinischen Überlieferung. R. Brunner (ed.), *Gesetz und Gnade im Alten Testament und im jüdischen Denken,* Zürich 1969, 30–63.

Hübner, H., ἐπιθυμία etc. *EWNT* II, 68–71.

Hübner, H., Gal 3, 10 und die Herkunft des Paulus. *KuD* 19, 1973, 215–231.

Hübner, H., Das ganze und das eine Gesetz. *KuD* 21, 1975, 239–256.

Hübner, H., Das Gesetz als elementares Thema einer Biblischen Theologie? *KuD* 22, 1976, 250–276.

Hübner, H., *Das Gesetz bei Paulus.* Ein Beitrag zum Werden der paulinischen Theologie. FRLANT 119. Göttingen 1980². (Cited as *Gesetz*)

Hübner, H., *Das Gesetz in der synoptischen Tradition.* Studien zur These einer progressiven Qumranisierung und Judaisierung innerhalb der synoptischen Tradition. Witten 1973. (Cited as *Tradition*)

Hübner, H., Mark. 7.1–23 und das 'jüdisch-hellenistische' Gesetzesverständnis. *NTS* 22, 1975–76, 319–345.

Hübner, H., Pauli Theologiae Proprium. *NTS* 26, 1979–80, 445–473.

Hughes, P., *Paul's Second Epistle to the Corinthians.* London-Edinburgh 1962.

Hultgren, A., Paul's Pre-Christian Persecutions of the Church: Their Purpose, Locale, and Nature. *JBL* 95, 1976, 97–111.

Hultgren, A.J., The *Pistis Christou* Formulation in Paul. *NT* 22, 1980, 248–263.

Hummel, R., *Die Auseinandersetzung zwischen Kirche und Judentum im Matthäusevangelium.* BEvTh 33. München 1963.

Hunt, E.W., *Portrait of Paul.* London 1968.

Illman, K.-J., Die Tora – Mitte der jüdischen Bibel. *Der Herr ist einer, unser gemeinsames Erbe*, Abo 1979, 27–42.

Jackson, B.S., Legalism. *JJS* 30, 1979, 1–22.

Jacoby, F., *Die Fragmente der griechischen Historiker* II. Berlin 1926.

Jaubert, A., *La notion d'alliance dans le Judaïsme aux abords de l'ère chrétienne*. PatSor 6. Paris 1963.

Jeremias, J., *Jerusalem zur Zeit Jesu*. Eine kulturgeschichtliche Untersuchung zur neutestamentlichen Zeitgeschichte. Göttingen 1969[3].

Jeremias, J., *New Testament Theology* I. The Proclamation of Jesus. Transl. J. Bowden. NTL. London 1971.

Jeremias, J., Paulus als Hillelit. *Neotestamentica et Semitica* in honour of M. Black, Edinburgh 1969, 88–94.

Jeremias, J., *Der Schlüssel zur Theologie des Apostels Paulus*. CwH 115. Stuttgart 1971.

Jervell, J., Die Beschneidung des Messias. *Theologie aus dem Norden*, SNTU A 2, 1977, 68–78.

Jervell, J., *Gud og hans fiender*. Forsøk på å tolke Romerbrevet. Oslo-Bergen-Tromsø 1973.

Jervell, J., *Imago Dei*. Gen 1, 26 f. im Spätjudentum, in der Gnosis und in den paulinischen Briefen. FRLANT 76. Göttingen 1960.

Jervell, J., The Letter to Jerusalem. *RD*, 1977, 61–74.

Jervell, J., *Luke and the People of God*. A New Look at Luke-Acts. Minneapolis 1972.

Jervell, J., The Mighty Minority. *StTh* 34, 1980, 13–38.

Jervell, J., Die offenbarte und die verborgene Tora. Zur Vorstellung über die neue Tora im Rabbinismus. *StTh* 25, 1971, 90–108.

Jervell, J., Paul in the Acts of the Apostles. Tradition, History, Theology. In: *Les Actes des Apôtres*. Traditions, rédaction, théologie. BEThL 48. Leuven 1979, 297–306.

Jervell, J., Der unbekannte Paulus. *PLT*, 1980, 29–40.

Jervell, J., Das Volk des Geistes. *GCHP*, 1977, 87–106.

Jewett, R., *Dating Paul's Life*. London 1979.

Jewett, R., *Paul's Anthropological Terms*. A Study of their Use in Conflict Settings. AGJU 10. Leiden 1971.

Joest, W., *Gesetz und Freiheit*. Das Problem des tertius usus legis bei Luther und die neutestamentliche Parainese. Göttingen 1951.

Jülicher, A., Der Brief an die Römer. *SNT* 2, 223–335.

Jüngel, E., Das Gesetz zwischen Adam und Christus, Eine theologische Studie zu Röm. 5, 12–21. *ZThK* 60, 1963, 42–74.

Jüngel, E., *Paulus und Jesus*. Eine Untersuchung zur Präzisierung der Frage nach dem Ursprung der Christologie. HUTh 2. Tübingen 1962.

Käsemann, E., *Commentary on Romans*. Transl. G.W. Bromiley. Grand Rapids 1980.

Käsemann, E., *Exegetische Versuche und Besinnungen* I–II. Göttingen 1960.

Käsemann, E., *Paulinische Perspektiven*. Tübingen 1972[2].

Kasting, H., *Die Anfänge der urchristlichen Mission*. Eine historische Untersuchung. BEvTh 55. München 1969.

Kaye, B.N., *The Thought Structure of Romans with Special Reference to chapter 6*. Austin 1979.

Keck, L.E., The Function of Rom 3.10–18. Observations and Suggestions. *GCHP*, 1977, 141–157.

Keck, L.E., The Law and 'The Law of Sin and Death' (Rom 8.1–4): Reflections on the Spirit and Ethics in Paul. *The Divine Helmsman* (Studies on God's Control of Human Events, Presented to Lou H. Silberman), New York 1980, 41–57.

Kellermann, U., *Messias und Gesetz*. Grundlinien einer alttestamentlichen Heilserwartung.

Eine traditionsgeschichtliche Einführung. BSt 61. Neukirchen-Vluyn 1971.

Kertelge, K., *"Rechtfertigung" bei Paulus.* Studien zur Struktur und zum Bedeutungsgehalt des paulinischen Rechtfertigungsbegriffes. NTA 3. Münster 1967.

Kettunen, M., *Der Abfassungszweck des Römerbriefs.* AASF Diss. Hum.Litt. 18. Helsinki 1979.

Kim, S., *The Origin of Paul's Gospel.* WUNT, 2. Reihe 4. Tübingen 1981.

King, N., Review of E.P. Sanders, Paul and Palestinian Judaism. *Bib.* 61, 1980, 141–144.

Kirk, K.E., *The Epistle to the Romans.* ClBib. Oxford 1937.

Klausner, J., *Von Jesus zu Paulus.* Übers. von F. Thieberger. Jerusalem 1950.

Klein, Ch., *Theologie und Anti-Judaismus.* Eine Studie zur deutschen theologischen Literatur der Gegenwart. ACJD 6. München 1975.

Klein, Gottlob, *Studien über Paulus.* Stockholm 1918.

Klein, Günther, *Rekonstruktion und Interpretation.* Gesammelte Aufsätze zum Neuen Testament. BEvTh 50. München 1969.

Klevinghaus, J., *Die theologische Stellung der apostolischen Väter zur alttestamentlichen Offenbarung.* BFChTh 44.1. Gütersloh 1948.

Klinzing, G., *Die Umdeutung des Kultus in der Qumrangemeinde und im Neuen Testament.* StUNT 7. Göttingen 1971.

Knox, J., *Chapters in a Life of Paul.* Nashville 1950.

Knox, J., *The Ethic of Jesus in the Teaching of the Church.* Its Authority and Its Relevance. London 1961.

Knox, W.L., *St. Paul and the Church of the Gentiles.* Cambridge 1939.

Knox, W.L., *St. Paul and the Church of Jerusalem.* Cambridge 1925.

Koch, K., Review M. Noth, Gesammelte Studien zum Alten Testament. *ThLZ* 83, 1958, 831–833.

König, A., Gentiles or Gentile Christians? On the Meaning of Romans 2.12–16. *JTSA* 15, June 1976, 53–60.

Köster, H., φύσις. *ThW* IX, 246–271.

Koschorke, K., Paulus in den Nag-Hammadi-Texten. Ein Beitrag zur Geschichte der Paulusrezeption im frühen Christentum. *ZThK* 78, 1981, 177–205.

Kraabel, A.T., The Disappearance of the 'God-Fearers'. *Numen* 28, 1981, 113–126.

Kraft, H., *Die Offenbarung des Johannes.* HNT 16a. Tübingen 1974.

Kraus, H-J., *Biblisch-theologische Aufsätze.* Neukirchen 1972.

Kremer, J., "Denn der Buchstabe tötet, der Geist aber macht lebendig". Methodologische und hermeneutische Erwägungen zu 2 Kor 3, 6b. *Begegnung mit dem Wort* (Festschr. H. Zimmermann), BBB 53, Bonn 1980, 219–250.

Kühl, E., *Der Brief des Paulus an die Römer.* Leipzig 1913.

Kühl, E., Stellung und Bedeutung des alttestamentlichen Gesetzes im Zusammenhang der paulinischen Lehre. *ThStKr* 67, 1894, 120–146.

Kuhn, H-W., *Ältere Sammlungen im Markusevangelium.* StUNT 8. Göttingen 1971.

Kuhn, H-W., Jesus als Gekreuzigter in der frühchristlichen Verkündigung bis zur Mitte des 2. Jahrhunderts. *ZThK* 72, 1975, 1–46.

Kuhn, H-W., Zum Problem des Verhältnisses der markinischen Redaktion zur israelitisch-jüdischen Tradition. *Tradition und Glaube* (Festschr. K.G. Kuhn), Göttingen 1971, 299–309.

Kuhn, K.G., προσήλυτος. *ThWNT* VI, 727–745.

Kuhn, K.G. – Stegemann, H., Proselyten. *PRE* Suppl. 9 (1962), 1248–1283.

Kuhr, F., Römer 2_{14} f. und die Verheissung bei Jeremia 31_{31} ff. *ZNW* 55, 1964, 243–261.

Kümmel, W.G., Äussere und innere Reinheit des Menschen bei Jesus. *Das Wort und die Wörter* (Festschr. G. Friedrich), Stuttgart etc. 1973, 35–46.

Kümmel, W.G., *Das Bild des Menschen im Neuen Testament.* In: Römer 7 und das Bild des Menschen im Neuen Testament. Zwei Studien. TB 53. München 1974.

Kümmel, W.G., 'Individualgeschichte' und 'Weltgeschichte' in Gal. 2.15–21. *Christ and the Spirit in the New Testament* (in honour of C.F.D. Moule), Cambridge 1973, 157–173.

Kümmel, W.G., *Introduction to the New Testament*. Transl. H.C. Kee. Nashville-New York 1975.

Kümmel, W.G., *Römer 7 und die Bekehrung des Paulus*. UNT 17. Leipzig 1929.

Kümmel, W.G., *1 Kor.*: see Lietzmann, H.

Kurfess, A., *Sibyllinische Weissagungen*. Urtext und Übersetzung. Tusculum-Bücherei. Berlin 1951.

Kuss, O., Die Heiden und die Werke des Gesetzes (nach Röm 2, 14–16). *MThZ* 5, 1954, 77–98.

Kuss, O., Nomos bei Paulus. *MThZ* 17, 1966, 173–227.

Kuss, O., *Paulus*. Die Rolle des Apostels in der theologischen Entwicklung der Urkirche. Auslegung und Verkündigung III. Regensburg 1971.

Kuss, O., *Der Römerbrief*. I–III. Regensburg 1959, 1963, 1978.

Lackmann, M., *Vom Geheimnis der Schöpfung*. Die Geschichte der Exegese von Römer I, 18–23, II, 14–16 und Acta XIV, 15–17, XVII, 22–29 vom 2. Jahrhundert bis zum Beginn der Orthodoxie. Stuttgart 1952.

Ladd, G.E., Paul and the Law. *Soli Deo Gloria*, in honour of W.C. Robinson, Richmond 1968, 50–67.

Lähnemann, J., *Der Kolosserbrief*. Komposition, Situation und Argumentation. StNT 3. Gütersloh 1971.

Lagrange, M-J., *Saint Paul, Épitre aux Galates*. EtB. Paris 1942[4].

Lagrange, M-J., *Saint Paul, Épitre aux Romains*. EtB. Paris 1922.

Lake, K., *The Earlier Epistles of St. Paul*. Their Motive and Origin. London 1911.

Lambrecht, J., Jesus and the Law. An Investigation of Mk 7, 1–23. *EThL* 53, 1977, 24–82.

Lambrecht, J., The Line of Thought in Gal. 2.14*b*–21. *NTS* 24, 1977–78, 484–495.

Lang, F., Gesetz und Bund bei Paulus. *RF*, 1976, 305–320.

Lang, F.G., Sola gratia im Markusevangelium. Die Soteriologie des Markus nach 9, 14–29 und 10, 17–31. *RF*, 1976, 321–337.

Lapide, P., Der Rabbi von Tarsus. In: P. Lapide – P-Stuhlmacher, *Paulus – Rabbi und Apostel*, Ein jüdisch-christlicher Dialog, Stuttgart-München 1981, 35–61.

Laws, S., *A Commentary on the Epistle of James*. BNTC. London 1980.

Lebram, J.C.H., Der Idealstaat der Juden. *Josephus-Studien*. Untersuchungen zu Josephus, dem antiken Judentum und dem Neuen Testament. Festschrift O. Michel. Göttingen 1974. P. 233–253.

Leenhardt, F., *L'Épitre de Saint Paul aux Romains*. CNT 6. Neuchâtel 1957.

Leivestad, R., *Christ the Conqueror*. Ideas of Conflict and Victory in the New Testament. London 1954.

Liedke, G. – Petersen, C., *tōrā* Weisung, *THAT* II, 1032–1043.

Lietzmann, H., *An die Galater*. HNT 10. Tübingen 1971[4].

Lietzmann, H., *An die Korinther* 1.2. (Erg. von W.G. Kümmel.) HNT 9. Tübingen 1969[5].

Lietzmann, H., *An die Römer*. HNT 8. Tübingen 1971[5].

Lightfoot, J.B., *Saint Paul's Epistle to the Galatians*. London 1890[10].

Limbeck, M., *Von der Ohnmacht des Rechts*. Untersuchungen zur Gesetzeskritik des Neuen Testaments. Theologische Perspektiven, Zur gegenwärtigen Problemlage. Düsseldorf 1972.

Limbeck, M., *Die Ordnung des Heils*. Untersuchungen zum Gesetzesverständnis des Frühjudentums. KBANT. Düsseldorf 1971.

Lindemann, A., *Die Aufhebung der Zeit*. Geschichtsverständnis und Eschatologie im Epheserbrief. StNT 12. Gütersloh 1975.

Lindemann, A., *Paulus im ältesten Christentum*. Das Bild des Apostels und die Rezeption der paulinischen Theologie in der frühchristlichen Literatur bis Marcion. BHTh 58. Tübingen 1979.

Lindeskog, G., *Judarnas Jesus*. Stockholm 1972[2].

Linton, O., Den paulinska forskningens båda huvudproblem. *SvTK* 11, 1935, 115–141.

Linton, O., Paulus och juridiken. *SvTK* 21, 1945, 173–192.

Lipsius, R.A., *Briefe an die Galater, Römer, Philipper*. HC 2.2, Freiburg i.B. 1891.

Ljungman, H., *Das Gesetz erfüllen*. Matth. 5,17 ff. und 3.15 untersucht. LUA 50:6. Lund 1954.

Löning, K., *Die Saulustradition in der Apostelgeschichte*. NTA 9. Münster 1973.

Lohfink, N., *Das Siegeslied am Schilfmeer*. Christliche Auseinandersetzungen mit dem Alten Testament. Frankfurt a.M. 1966[2].

Lohmeyer, E , *Die Briefe an die Kolosser und an Philemon*. KEK 9.2[10]. Göttingen 1954.

Lohmeyer, E., *Das Evangelium des Markus*. KEK I/2[15]. Göttingen 1959.

Lohmeyer, E., *Probleme paulinischer Theologie*. Darmstadt 1954.

Lohse, E., *Die Briefe an die Kolosser und an Philemon*. KEK 15. Göttingen 1977[2].

Lohse, E., *Grundriss der neutestamentlichen Theologie*. ThW 5. Stuttgart 1974.

Lohse, E., ὁ νόμος τοῦ πνεύματος τῆς ζωῆς. Exegetische Anmerkungen zu Röm 8, 2. *Neues Testament und christliche Existenz*, Festschr. H. Braun, Tübingen 1973, 279–287.

Lohse, E., *Israel und die Christenheit*. Göttingen 1960.

Lohse, E., *Die Offenbarung des Johannes*. NTD 11. Göttingen 1976[11].

Loisy, A., *Les Actes des Apôtres*. Paris 1920.

Loisy, A., *The Birth of the Christian Religion*. Transl. L.P. Jacks. London 1948.

Loisy, A., *L'Épitre aux Galates*. Paris 1916.

Loisy, A., L'épîtres attribuées a Paul et les épîtres catholiques. *RHLR* 7, 1921, 289–348.

Loisy, A., Les épîtres de Paul. *RHLR* 7, 1921, 76–125, 213–250.

Loisy, A., *The Origins of the New Testament*. Transl. L.P. Jacks. London 1950.

Loisy, A., *Remarques sur la littérature épistolaire du Nouveau Testament*. Paris 1935.

Longenecker, R.N., *Paul, Apostle of Liberty*. New York 1964.

Lowe, J., An Examination of Attempts to Detect Developments in St. Paul's Theology. *JThS* 42, 1941, 129–142.

Löwy, M., Die Paulinische Lehre vom Gesetz. Nach ihren Quellen untersucht. *MGWJ* 47, 1903, 322–339, 417–433, 534–544; 48, 1904, 268–276, 321–327, 400–416.

Luck, U., Der Jakobusbrief und die Theologie des Paulus. *ThGl* 61, 1971, 161–179.

Lueken, W., Die Briefe an Philemon, an die Kolosser und an die Epheser. *SNT* 2, 335–383.

Lüdemann, G., *Paulus, der Heidenapostel*. I: Studien zur Chronologie. FRLANT 123. Göttingen 1980.

Lüdemann, G., *Paulus und das Judentum*. TEH 215. München 1983.

Lüdemann, G., Zum Antipaulinismus im frühen Christentum. *EvTh* 40, 1980, 437–455.

Lührmann, D., *Der Brief an die Galater*. ZBK NT 7. Zürich 1978.

Lührmann, D., *Glaube im frühen Christentum*. Gütersloh 1976.

Lührmann, D., *Das Offenbarungsverständnis bei Paulus und in paulinischen Gemeinden*. WMANT 16. Neukirchen 1965.

Lütgert, W., *Freiheitspredigt und Schwarmgeister in Korinth*. Ein Beitrag zur Charakteristik der Christuspartei. Gütersloh 1908.

Lütgert, W., *Gesetz und Geist*. Eine Untersuchung zur Vorgeschichte des Galaterbriefes. BFChTh 22.6. Gütersloh 1919.

Lull, D.J., *The Spirit in Galatia*. Paul's Interpretation of *Pneuma* as Divine Power. SBL Diss. 49. Chico 1980.

Lust, J., *Traditie, Redactie en Kerygma bij Ezechiel*. Een Analyse van Ez., XX, 1–26. VVAW.L 31, Nr. 65, Brussel 1969.

Luz, U., Der alte und neue Bund bei Paulus und im Hebräerbrief. *Evth* 27, 1967, 318–336.

Luz, U., Die Erfüllung des Gesetzes bei Matthäus (Mt 5, 17–20). *ZThK* 75, 1978, 398–435.

Luz, U., *Das Geschichtsverständnis des Paulus*. BEvTh 49. München 1968.

Luz, U., Das Gesetz im Frühjudentum; Das Neue Testament. In: R. Smend – U. Luz, *Gesetz*. Biblische Konfrontationen 1015, Stuttgart etc. 1981. Pp. 45–139, 148–156. (Cited as: Luz, 'Gesetz'.)

Luz, U., Rechtfertigung bei den Paulusschülern. *RF*, 1976, 365–383.

Luz, U., Review H. Hübner, Das Gesetz bei Paulus. *ThZ* 35, 1979, 121–123.

Lyonnet, S., *Les Étapes du mystère du Salut selon l'epître aux Romains*. Bibliothèque Oecuménique 8. Paris 1969.

Lyonnet, S., L'histoire du salut selon le chapître VII de l'épître aux Romains. *Bib* 43, 1962, 117–151.

Lyonnet, S., Le Nouveau Testament à la lumière de l'Ancien. À propos du Rom 8, 2–4. *NRTh* 87, 1965, 561–587.

Lyonnet, S., "Tu ne convoiteras pas" (Rom. vii 7). *Neotestamentica et Patristica*, Festschrift O. Cullmann, NT.S 6, Leiden 1962, 157–165.

Maher, M., 'Take my Yoke upon you' (Matt. XI. 29). *NTS* 22, 1975–76, 97–103.

Maier, J., Jüdische Faktoren bei der Entstehung der Gnosis? *AFG*, 1980, 239–258.

Maier, J., *Geschichte der jüdischen Religion*. Von der Zeit Alexander des Grossen bis zur Aufklärung mit einem Ausblick auf das 19./20. Jahrhundert. de Gruyter Lehrbuch. Berlin-New York 1972.

Maier, J., "Gesetz" und "Gnade" im Wandel des Gesetzesverständnisses der nachtalmudischen Zeit. R. Brunner (ed.), *Gesetz und Gnade im Alten Testament und im jüdischen Denken*, Zürich 1969, 64–176.

Maier, J. – Neusner, J., Die gesetzlichen Überlieferungen. *Literatur und Religion des Frühjudentums*. Eine Einführung (ed. J. Maier – J. Schreiner), Würzburg 1973, 57–72.

Malina, B.J., The Individual and the Community – Personality in the Social World of Early Christianity. *BTB* 9, 1979, 126–138.

van Manen, W.C., *Die Unechtheit des Römerbriefes*. Transl. G. Schläger. Leipzig 1906.

Manson, T.W., *The Sayings of Jesus*. As recorded in the Gospels according to St. Matthew and St. Luke. London 1950.

Manson, T.W., *The Teaching of Jesus*. Studies of its Form and Content. Cambridge 1955 (repr.).

Marcus, R., *Law in the Apocrypha*. OSCU 26. New York 1927.

Marshall, L.H., *The Challenge of New Testament Ethics*. London 1966 (Repr.).

Marxsen, W., Der ἕτερος νόμος Röm. 13, 8. *ThZ* 11, 1955, 230–237.

Mauerhofer, E., *Der Kampf zwischen Fleisch und Geist bei Paulus*. Ein Beitrag zur Klärung der Frage nach der Stellung der Gläubigen zur Sünde im paulinischen Heiligungs- und Vollkommenheitsverständnis. Frutigen 1980.

Maurer, Chr., *Die Gesetzeslehre des Paulus nach ihrem Ursprung und in ihrer Entfaltung* dargelegt. Zürich 1941.

Mauser, U., Galater iii. 20: die Universalität des Heils. NTS 13, 1966–67, 258–270.

Mauser, U., *Gottesbild und Menschwerdung*. Eine Untersuchung zur Einheit des Alten und Neuen Testaments. BHTh 43. Tübingen 1971.

May, R., *The Courage to Create*. New York 1975.

McEleney, N.J., Conversion, Circumcision and the Law. *NTS* 20, 1973–74, 319–341.

Meeks, W.A., Review of H.D. Betz, Galatians. *JBL* 100, 1981, 304–307.

Meier, J.P., *Law and History in Matthew's Gospel*. A Redactional Study of Mt. 5.17–48. AnBib 71. Rome 1976.

Merk, O., Der Beginn der Paränese im Galaterbrief. *ZNW* 60, 1969, 83–104.

Merk, O., *Handeln aus Glauben*. Die Motivierungen der paulinischen Ethik. MThSt 5. Marburg 1968.

Merkel, H., Markus 7, 15 – das Jesuswort über die innere Verunreinigung. *ZRGG* 20, 1968, 340–363.

Meyer, P.W., Romans 10.4 and the 'End' of the Law. *The Divine Helmsman* (Studies in God's Control of Human Events, Presented to Lou H. Silberman), New York 1980, 59–78.

Michel, O., *Der Brief an die Hebräer*. KEK 13^{12}. Göttingen 1966.

Michel, O., *Der Brief an die Römer*. KEK 4^{14}. Göttingen 1978.

Michels, F., *Paul and the Law of Love*. Milwaukee 1967.

van der Minde, H-J., *Schrift und Tradition bei Paulus*. Ihre Bedeutung und Funktion im Römerbrief. Paderborner Theol. Studien 3. München-Paderborn-Wien 1976.

Mitton, C.L., *The Epistle of James*. London-Edinburgh 1966.

Momigliano, A., *The Development of Greek Biography*. Four Lectures. Cambridge, Mass. 1971.

Montefiore, C.G., *Judaism and St. Paul*. Two Essays. London 1914.

Montefiore, C.G., *The Synoptic Gospels* 1-2. Library of Biblical Studies. New York 1968 (repr.).

Moore, G.F., Christian Writers on Judaism. *HThR* 14, 1921, 197–254.

Moore, G.F., *Judaism in the first centuries of the Christian era*. The age of Tannaim. 1–3. Cambridge, Mass. 1927–30.

Moule, C.F.D., Interpreting Paul by Paul. An Essay in the Comparative Study of Pauline Thought. *New Testament Christianity for Africa and the World*, Essays in honour of H. Sawyerr, London 1974, 78–90.

Moule, C.F.D., Obligation in the ethic of Paul. *Christian History and Interpretation*, Studies presented to J. Knox, Cambridge 1967, 389–406.

Moxnes, H., *Theology in Conflict*. Studies in Paul's Understanding of God in Romans. NT.S 53. Leiden 1980.

Müller, U.B., *Zur frühchristlichen Theologiegeschichte*. Judenchristentum und Paulinismus in Kleinasien an der Wende vom ersten zum zweiten Jahrhundert n. Chr. Gütersloh 1976.

Müller, U.B., Zur Rezeption gesetzeskritischer Jesusüberlieferung im frühen Christentum. *NTS* 27, 1980–81, 158–185.

Munck, J., *Paulus und die Heilsgeschichte*. AJut 26, 1. København 1954.

Mundle, W., *Der Glaubensbegriff des Paulus*. Eine Untersuchung zur Dogmengeschichte des ältesten Christentums. Darmstadt 1977 (=Leipzig 1932).

Mundle, W., Das religiöse Problem des IV. Esrabuches. *ZAW* 47, 1929, 222–249.

Mundle, W., Zur Auslegung von Gal 2$_{17.18}$. *ZNW* 23, 1924, 152–153.

Mundle, W., Zur Auslegung von Röm 2, 13 ff. *ThBl* 13, 1934, 249–256.

Murphy-O'Connor, J., Review of E.P. Sanders, Paul and Palestinian Judaism. *RB* 85, 1978, 122–126.

Murray, G., *Aeschylos, Oresteia*. London 1928.

Murray, J., *The Epistle to the Romans*. NLC 11. London-Edinburgh 1967.

Mussner, F., *Der Galaterbrief*. HThK 9. Freiburg-Basel-Wien 1974.

Mussner, F., *Der Jakobusbrief.* HThK 13.1. Freiburg-Basel-Wien 1967[2].

Mussner, F., Theologische 'Wiedergutmachung'. Am Beispiel der Auslegung des Galaterbriefes. *FrRu* 26, 1974, 7−11.

Mussner, F., Wer ist "der ganze Samen" in Röm 4, 16? *Begegnung mit dem Wort* (Festschr. H. Zimmermann), BBB 53, Bonn 1980, 213−217.

Mussner, F., *Traktat über die Juden.* München 1979.

Myers, J.M., *Grace and Torah.* Philadelphia 1975.

Myre, A., Les caractéristiques de la loi mosaïque selon Philon d'Alexandrie. *ScEs* 27, 1975, 35−69.

Myre, A., La loi de la nature et la loi mosaïque selon Philon d'Alexandrie. *ScEs* 28,1976, 163−181.

Neil, W., *The Acts of the Apostles.* NCeB. London 1973.

Neil, W., *The Letter of Paul to the Galatians.* CBC. Cambridge 1967.

Nestle, W., Die Haupteinwände des antiken Denkens gegen das Christentum. *ARW* 37, 1941/42, 51−100.

Neusner, J., Comparing Judaisms. *HR* 18,.1978, 177−191.

Neusner, J., The Idea of Purity in Ancient Judaism. Studies in Judaism in Late Antiquity 1. Leiden 1973.

Neusner, J., "Judaism" after Moore: A Programmatic Statement. *JJS* 31, 1980, 141− 156.

Neusner, J., *The Rabbinic Traditions about the Pharisees before 70* I. The Masters. Leiden 1971.

Neusner, J., The Use of Later Rabbinic Evidence for the Study of Paul. *Approaches to Ancient Judaism* II (ed. W.S. Green), Brown Judaic Studies 9, Chico 1980, 43−63.

Nickelsburg, G.W.E., Rev. Ch. Klein, Anti-Judaism in Christian Theology. *RSRev* 4, 1978, 161−168.

Niederwimmer, K., *Der Begriff der Freiheit im Neuen Testament.* TBT 11. Berlin 1966.

Niederwimmer, K., Johannes Markus und die Frage nach dem Verfasser des zweiten Evangeliums. *ZNW* 58, 1967, 172−188.

Niederwimmer, K., Tiefenpsychologie und Exegese. *WzM* 22, 1970, 257−272.

Nikiprowetzky, V., *Le commentaire de l'Écriture chez Philon d'Alexandrie.* Son caractère et sa portée. Observations philologiques. ALGHJ 11. Leiden 1977.

Nikiprowetzky, V., *La Troisième Sibylle.* EtJ 9. Paris 1970.

Nikolainen, A.T., *Roomalaiskirje.* SUTS. Hämeenlinna 1975.

Nineham, D.E., *Saint Mark.* PNTC. London 1969 (repr.).

Nissen, A., *Gott und der Nächste· im antiken Judentum.* Untersuchungen zum Doppelgebot der Liebe. WUNT 15. Tübingen 1974.

Noack, B., Are the Essenes Referred to in the Sibylline Oracles? *StTh* 16, 1962, 90−102.

Noack, B., Evangeliet om Loven. En side af Romerbrevet. *Festschrift N.H. Søe*, København, 131−150.

Nock, A.D., Posidonius. *JRS* 49, 1959, 1−15.

Nock, A.D., *St. Paul.* London 1960 (repr.).

Nolland, J.L., A Fresh Look at Acts 15.10. *NTS* 27, 1980−81, 105−115.

Nolland, J.L., Uncircumcised Proselytes? *JSJ* 12, 1981, 173−194.

Norden, E., Jahve und Moses in hellenistischer Theologie. *Festgabe A. v. Harnack*, Tübingen 1921, 292−201.

Noth, M., *Gesammelte Studien zum Alten Testament.* ThB 6. München 1957. (ET: *The Laws in the Pentateuch and Other Essays.* Transl. D.R. Ap-Thomas. Edinburgh-Philadelphia 1966.)

Nygren, A., *Der Römerbrief.* Transl. I. Nygren. Göttingen 1959[3].

Odeberg, H., *Pharisaism and Christianity.* Saint Louis 1964.

Oepke, A., *Der Brief des Paulus an die Galater* (bearb. J. Rohde). ThHk 9. Berlin 1973[3].

Okeke, G.E., I Thess. ii. 13–16: The Fate of the Unbelieving Jews. *NTS* 27, 1980–81, 127–136.

Ollrog, W-H., *Paulus und seine Mitarbeiter*. Untersuchungen zur Theorie und Praxis der paulinischen Mission. WMANT 50. Neunkirchen-Vluyn 1979.

O'Neill, J.C., *Paul's Letter to the Romans*. Penguin Books. London 1975.

O'Neill, J.C., *The Recovery of Paul's Letter to the Galatians*. London 1972.

Ortkemper, F-J., *Leben aus dem Glauben*. Christliche Grundhaltungen nach Römer 12– 13. NTA 14. Münster 1980.

von der Osten-Sacken, P., Befreiung durch das Gesetz. In: *Richte unsere Füsse auf den Weg des Friedens,* Festschrift H. Gollwitzer, München 1979, 349–360.

von der Osten-Sacken, P., Das paulinische Verständnis des Gesetzes im Spannungsfeld von Eschatologie und Geschichte. Erläuterungen zum Evangelium als Faktor von theologischem Antijudaismus. *EvTh* 37, 1977, 549–587.

von der Osten-Sacken, P., Paulus und das Gesetz. *Wegweisung,* VIKJ 8, Berlin, 59–66.

von der Osten-Sacken, P., *Römer 8 als Beispiel paulinischer Soteriologie*. FRLANT 112. Göttingen 1975.

von der Osten-Sacken, P., Von der Notwendigkeit theologischen Besitzverzichts. Nachwort in R. Ruether, *Nächstenliebe und Brudermord,* ACJD 7, München 1978, 244– 251.

Pallis, A., *To the Romans*. A Commentary. Liverpool 1920.

Pancaro, S., *The Law in the Fourth Gospel*. The Torah and the Gospel, Moses and Jesus, Judaism and Christianity according to John. NT.S 42. Leiden 1975.

Panimolle, S.A., *Il dono della legge e la grazia della verità* (Gv 1,17). Teologia oggi 21. Roma 1973.

Pannenberg, W., *Jesus – God and Man*. Transl. L.L. Williams and D. Priebe. Philadelphia 1968.

Parkes, J., *The Conflict of the Church and the Synagogue*. A Study in the Origins of Antisemitism. London 1934.

Parkes, J., *Jesus, Paul and the Jews*. London 1936.

Parkes, J., *The Foundations of Judaism and Christianity*. London 1960.

Parkes, J., *Judaism and Christianity*. London 1948.

Parkes, J., *Prelude to Dialogue*. Jewish-Christian Relationships. London 1969.

Paschen, W., *Rein und Unrein*. Untersuchung zur biblischen Wortgeschichte. StANT 24. München 1970.

Pasinya, L.M., *La Notion de NOMOS dans le Pentateuque Grec*. AnBib 52. Rome 1973.

Pearson, B.A., *The Pneumatikos-Psychikos Terminology in 1 Corinthians*. A Study in the Theology of the Corinthian Opponents of Paul and Its Relation to Gnosticism. SBL Diss. 12. Missoula 1973.

Percy, E., *Die Botschaft Jesu*. Eine traditionsgeschichtliche und exegetische Untersuchung. *LUA* 49. Lund 1953.

Percy, E., *Die Probleme der Kolosser- und Epheserbriefe*. SHVL 39. Lund 1946.

Perrot, C., Introduction littéraire, in: *Pseudo-Philon, Les Antiquités Bibliques* II, SC 230, Paris 1976, 10–65.

Perrot, C. - Bogaert, P-M., Commentaire. *Pseudo-Philon, Les Antiquités Bibliques* II, SC 230, Paris 1976, 79–245.

Pesch, R., Das Jerusalemer Abkommen und die Lösung des Antiochenischen Konflikts. Ein Versuch über Gal 2, Apg 10, 1–11, 18, Apg 11, 27–30; 12, 25 und Apg 15, 1–41. *KuE*, 1981, 105–122.

Pesch, R., *Das Markusevangelium* I–II. HThK 2.1–2. Freiburg-Basel-Wien 1976–77.

Petuchowski, J.J., *Heirs of the Pharisees*. New York 1970.

Pfleiderer, O., *Der Paulinismus.* Ein Beitrag zur Geschichte der urchristlichen Theologie. Leipzig 1890[2].

Pohlenz, M., Paulus und die Stoa. *ZNW* 42, 1949, 69–104.

Prat, F., *The Theology of Saint Paul* I. Transl. J.L. Stoddard. London-Dublin 1945.

Pregeant, R., Grace and Recompense: Reflections on a Pauline Paradox. *JAAR* 47, 1979, 73–96.

Przybylski, B., *Righteousness in Matthew and his World of Thought.* MSSNTS 41. Cambridge 1980.

Quispel, G., *Ptolémée, Lettre à Flora.* Texte, traduction et introduction. SC 24, Paris 1949.

von Rad, G., *Das fünfte Buch Mose.* Deuteronomium. ATD 8. Göttingen 1968[2].

von Rad, G., *Old Testament Theology* I–II. Transl. D.M.G. Stalker. London 1975 (repr.).

Räisänen, H., Das 'Gesetz des Glaubens' (Röm. 3.27) und das 'Gesetz des Geistes' (Röm. 8.2). *NTS* 26, 1979–80, 101–117.

Räisänen, H., *The Idea of Divine Hardening.* A Comparative Study of the Notion of Divine Hardening, Leading Astray and Inciting to Evil in the Bible and the Qur'an. PFES 25, Helsinki 1976[2].

Räisänen, H., Jesus and the Food Laws. Reflections on Mark 7.15. *JSNT* 16, 1982, 79–100.

Räisänen, H., Legalism and Salvation by the Law. Paul's Portrayal of the Jewish Religion as a Historical and Theological Problem. PLT, 1980, 63–83.

Räisänen, H., Paul's Theological Difficulties with the Law. *StudBibl,* 1980, 301–320.

Räisänen, H., Sprachliches zum Spiel des Paulus mit *nomos. Glaube und Gerechtigkeit,* In memoriam R. Gyllenberg, PFES 38, 1983, 131–154.

Räisänen, H., Zum Gebrauch von EPITHYMIA und EPITHYMEIN bei Paulus. *StTh* 33, 1979, 85–99.

Räisänen, H., Zur Herkunft von Mk 7, 15. *Logia.* Les paroles de Jésus, BEThL 59, Leuven 1982, 477–484.

Reicke, B., Der geschichtliche Hintergrund des Apostelkonzils und der Antiochia-Episode, Gal. 2, 1–14. *Studia Paulina* in honorem J. de Zwaan, Haarlem 1953, 172–187.

Reicke, B., The Law and this World according to Paul. Some Thoughts Concerning Gal 4[1–11]. *JBL* 70, 1951, 259–276.

Reicke, B., Syneidesis in Röm. 2, 15. *ThZ* 12, 1956, 157–161.

Reinhardt, K., *Poseidonios über Ursprung und Entartung.* Interpretation zweier kulturgeschichtlicher Fragmente. Orient und Antike 6. Heidelberg 1928.

Reploh, K-G., *Markus – Lehrer der Gemeinde.* Eine redaktionsgeschichtliche Studie zu den Jüngerperikopen des Markus-Evangeliums. SBM 9. Stuttgart 1969.

Reventlow, H., *Das Heiligkeitsgesetz formgeschichtlich untersucht.* WMANT 6. Neukirchen 1961.

Richardson, P., *Israel in the Apostolic Church.* MSSNTS 10. Cambridge 1969.

Richardson, P., Pauline Inconsistency: 1 Corinthians 9.19–23 and Galatians 2.11–14. *NTS* 26, 1979–80, 347–362.

Richter, G., *Studien zum Johannesevangelium* (ed. J. Hainz). BU 13. Regensburg 1977.

Ridderbos, H.N., *The Epistle of Paul to the Churches of Galatia.* NIC. Grand Rapids 1970[6].

Ridderbos, H., *Paulus.* Ein Entwurf seiner Theologie. Übers. E-W. Pollmann. Wuppertal 1970.

Riddle, D.W., The Jewishness of Paul. *JR* 23, 1943, 240–244.

Riedl, J., *Das Heil der Heiden nach R 2, 14–16.26.27.* StGSt 20. Wien 1965.

Rissi, M., *Studien zum zweiten Korintherbrief.* Der alte Bund – Der Prediger – Der Tod. AthANT 56. Zürich 1969.

Ritschl, A., *Die christliche Lehre von der Rechtfertigung und Versöhnung* II. Bonn 1882[2].

Ritschl, A., *Die Entstehung der altkatholischen Kirche*. Eine kirchen- und dogmengeschichtliche Monographie. Bonn 1857[2].

Robertson, A. – Plummer, A., *A Critical and Exegetical Commentary on the First Epistle of St. Paul to the Corinthians*. ICC. Edinburgh 1914[2].

Robinson, D.W.B., The Circumcision of Titus, and Paul's "Liberty". *ABR* 12, 1964, 24–42.

Robinson, D.W.B., The Distinction Between Jewish and Gentile Believers in Galatians. *ABR* 13, 1965, 29–48.

Robinson, J.A.T., *Redating the New Testament*. London 1976.

Roetzel, C.J., *Judgement in the Community*. A Study of the Relationship between Eschatology and Ecclesiology in Paul. Leiden 1972.

Roloff, J., *Das Neue Testament*. Neukirchener Arbeitsbücher. Neukirchen-Vluyn 1977.

Romaniuk, K., Le Problème des Paulinismes dans l'Évangile de Marc. *NTS* 23, 1976–77, 266–274.

Rordorf, W., *Der Sonntag*. Geschichte des Ruhe- und Gottesdiensttages im ältesten Christentum. AThANT 43. Zürich 1962.

Rose, M., *Der Ausschliesslichkeitsanspruch Jahwes*. Deuteronomistische Schultheologie und Volksfrömmigkeit in der späteren Königszeit. BWANT 6.6. Stuttgart 1975.

Rubenstein, R.L., *My Brother Paul*. HTB. New York 1972.

Rudolph, W., *Jeremia*. HAT 1, 12. Tübingen 1968[3].

Ruether, R.R., *Faith and Fratricide*. The Theological Roots of Anti-Semitism. London 1975.

Ruether, R.R., The *Faith and Fratricide* Discussion: Old Problems and New Dimension. *Antisemitism and the Foundations of Christianity* (ed. A.T. Davies), New York-Ramsey-Toronto 1979, 230–256.

Saldarini, A.J., Review of E.P. Sanders, Paul and Palestinian Judaism. *JBL* 98, 1979, 299–303.

Sánchez Bosch, J., *'Gloriarse' segun San Pablo*. Sentido y teología de *kaukhaomai*. AnBib 40. Rome 1970.

Sand, A., *Der Begriff "Fleisch" in den paulinischen Hauptbriefen*. BU 2. Regensburg 1967.

Sand, A., *Das Gesetz und die Propheten*. Untersuchungen zur Theologie des Evangeliums nach Matthäus. BU 11. Regensburg 1974.

Sanday, W. – Headlam, A., *A critical and exegetical Commentary on the Epistle to the Romans*. ICC. Edinburgh 1925 (repr.).

Sandelin, K-G., *Die Auseinandersetzung mit der Weisheit in 1. Korinther 15*. Publications of the Research Institute of the Åbo Akademi Foundation 12. Åbo 1976.

Sandelin, K-G., Vishetstradition såsom bakgrund till 1. Kor. 15. *TAik* 83, 1978, 148–155.

Sanders, E.P., The Covenant as a Soteriological Category and the Nature of Salvation in Palestinian and Hellenistic Judaism. *Jews, Greeks and Christians* (essays in honor of W.D. Davies), Studies in Judaism in Late Antiquity 21, Leiden 1976, 11–44.

Sanders, E.P., Literary Dependence in Colossians. *JBL* 85, 1966, 28–45.

Sanders, E.P., On the Question of Fulfilling the Law in Paul and Rabbinic Judaism. *Donum Gentilicium*, New Testament Studies in Honour of D. Daube, Oxford 1978, 103–126.

Sanders, E.P., *Paul, the Law, and the Jewish People*. Forthcoming. (Cited as *Law*).

Sanders, E.P., *Paul and Palestinian Judaism*. A Comparison of Patterns of Religion. London 1977. (Cited as *Paul*).

Sanders, E.P., Puzzling out Rabbinic Judaism. *Approaches to ancient Judaism* II (ed. W.S. Green), Brown Judaic Studies 9, Chico 1980, 65–79.

Sanders, J.A., Torah and Christ. *Interp.* 29, 1975, 372–380.

Sanders, J.A., Torah and Paul. *GCH* 1977, 132–140.

Sanders, J.T., *Ethics and the New Testament*. Change and Development. Philadelphia 1975.

Sandmel, S., *The Genius of Paul*. A Study in History. Philadelphia 1979.

van de Sandt, H.W.M., An Explanation of Rom. 8, 4a. *Bijdr.* 37, 1976, 361–378.

van de Sandt, H.W.M., Research into Rom. 8, 4a: The Legal Claim of the Law. *Bijdr.* 37, 1976, 252–269.

Schade, H-H., *Apokalyptische Christologie bei Paulus*. Studien zum Zusammenhang von Christologie und Eschatologie in den Paulusbriefen. GTA 18. Göttingen 1981.

Schäfer, P., Die Torah der messianischen Zeit. *ZNW* 65, 1974, 27–42.

Scharlemann, M.H., *Stephen: A Singular Saint*. AnBib 34. Rome 1968.

Schechter, S., *Some Aspects of Rabbinic Theology*. London 1909.

Schlatter, A., *Der Glaube im Neuen Testament*. Stuttgart 1963[5].

Schlatter, A., *Gottes Gerechtigkeit*. Ein Kommentar zum Römerbrief. Stuttgart 1935.

Schlier, H., *Der Brief an die Galater*. KEK 7[14]. Göttingen 1971[5].

Schlier, H., *Grundzüge einer paulinischen Theologie*. Freiburg-Basel-Wien 1978.

Schlier, H., *Der Römerbrief*. HThK 6. Freiburg-Basel-Wien 1977.

Schlier, H., Von den Juden in Römer 2, 1–29. *EvTh* 5, 1938, 263–275.

Schlink, E., Gesetz und Paraklese. *Antwort* (Festschrift K. Barth), Zollikon-Zürich 1956, 323–335.

Schmid, H., Gesetz und Gnade im Alten Testament. R. Brunner (ed.), *Gesetz und Gnade im Alten Testament und im jüdischen Denken*, Zürich 1969, 3–29.

Schmidt, H.W., *Der Brief des Paulus an die Römer*. ThHK 6. Berlin 1963.

Schmithals, W., *Paul and the Gnostics*. Transl. J.E. Steely. Nashville 1972.

Schmithals, W., *Paul and James*. Transl. D.M. Barton. SBT 46. London 1965.

Schmithals, W., *Der Römerbrief als historisches Problem*. StNT 9. Göttingen 1975.

Schmithals, W., *Die theologische Anthropologie des Paulus*. Auslegung von Röm 7, 17–8, 39. Kohlhammer Taschenbücher 1021. Stuttgart 1980.

Schnackenburg, R., Römer 7 im Zusammenhang des Römerbriefes. *Jesus und Paulus*, Festschr. W.G. Kümmel, Göttingen 1975, 283–300.

Schneider, G., Stephanus, die Hellenisten und Samaria. *Les Actes des Apôtres*. Traditions, rédaction, théologie. BEThL 48, Leuven 1979, 215–240.

Schneidermeyer, W., Galatians as Literature. *JRT* 28, 1971, 132–138.

Schniewind, J., *Zur Erneuerung des Christenstandes*. KVR 226/227. Göttingen 1966.

Schoeps, H-J., *Das Judenchristentum*. Untersuchungen über Gruppenbildungen und Parteikämpfe in der frühen Christenheit. DTb 376. Bern-München 1964.

Schoeps, H-J., *Paul*. The Theology of the Apostle in the Light of Jewish Religious History. London 1961.

Schoeps, H-J., *Studien zur unbekannten Religions- und Geistesgeschichte*. Veröffentlichungen der Gesellschaft für Geistesgeschichte. Göttingen 1963.

Schoeps, H-J., *Theologie und Geschichte des Judenchristentums*. Tübingen 1949.

Scholem, G., *The Messianic Idea in Judaism and Other Essays on Jewish Spirituality*. London 1971.

Schottroff, L., Die Erzählung vom Pharisäer und Zöllner als Beispiel für die theologische Kunst des Überredens. *Neues Testament und christliche Existenz*, Festschrift H. Braun, Tübingen 1973, 439–461.

Schottroff, L., Die Schreckensherrschaft der Sünde und die Befreiung durch Christus nach dem Römerbrief des Paulus. *EvTh* 39, 1979, 497–510.

Schrage, W., "Ekklesia" und "Synagoge". Zum Ursprung des urchristlichen Kirchenbegriffs. *ZThK* 60, 1963, 178–202.

Schrage, W., *Die konkreten Einzelgebote in der paulinischen Paränese*. Ein Beitrag zur neutestamentlichen Ethik. Gütersloh 1961.

Schrage, W., Das Verständnis des Todes Jesu Christi im Neuen Testament. *Das Kreuz Jesu Christi als Grund des Heils*, STAEKU, Gütersloh 1969[3], 49–90.

Schrenk, G., δίκη κτλ. *ThWNT* II, 180–229.

Schubert, K., Die jüdisch-christliche Oekumene. Reflexionen zu Grundfragen des christlich-jüdischen Dialogs. *Kairos* 22, 1980, 1–33.

Schürer, E., *Geschichte des jüdischen Volkes im Zeitalter Jesu Christi* 1–3. Leipzig 1907–11[4].

Schürmann, H., "Das Gesetz des Christus" (Gal 6, 2). Jesu Verhalten und Wort als letztgültige sittliche Norm nach Paulus. *NTK* 1974, 282–300.

Schulz, S., Die Decke des Moses. Untersuchungen zu einer vorpaulinischen Überlieferung in II Cor 3_{7-18}. *ZNW* 49, 1958, 1–30.

Schulz, S., *Die Mitte der Schrift*. Der Frühkatholizismus im Neuen Testament als Herausforderung an den Protestantismus. Stuttgart/Berlin 1976.

Schulz, S., Die neue Frage nach dem historischen Jesus. *Neues Testament und Geschichte*, Festschrift O. Cullmann, Zürich 1972, 33–42.

Schulz, S., *Das Evangelium nach Johannes*. NTD 4[12]. Göttingen 1972.

Schulz, S., *Q*. Die Spruchquelle der Evangelisten. Zürich 1972.

Schulz, S., *Die Stunde der Botschaft*. Einführung in die Theologie der vier Evangelisten. Hamburg 1967.

Schweitzer, A., *Die Mystik des Apostels Paulus*. UTB 1091. Tübingen 1981 (repr. 1930).

Schweizer, E., *Der Brief an die Kolosser*. EKK. Zürich 1976.

Schweizer, E., *Das Evangelium nach Markus*. NTD 1[13]. Göttingen 1973[3].

Schweizer, E., "Der Jude im Verborgenen ..., dessen Lob nicht von Menschen, sondern von Gott kommt". Zu Röm 2, 28 f und Mt 6, 1–18. *NTK*, 1974, 115–124.

Scott, E.F., *The Pastoral Epistles*. MNTC. London 1957[7].

Scroggs, R., The Earliest Hellenistic Christianity. *RelAnt*, 1968, 176–206.

Scroggs, R., *Paul for a New Day*. Philadelphia 1977.

Seitz, O.J.F., James and the Law. *StEv* I, 472–486.

Sieffert, F., Die Entwicklungslinie der paulinischen Gesetzeslehre nach den vier Hauptbriefen des Apostels. *Theologische Studien*, Festschrift B. Weiss, Göttingen 1897, 332–357.

Sieffert, F., *Des Paulus Brief an die Galater*. KEK 6. Göttingen 1880.

Siegert, F., Gottesfürchtige und Sympathisanten. *Journal for the Study of Judaism* 4, 1973, 109–164.

Siegwalt, G., *La Loi, chemin du Salut*. Etude sur la signification de la loi de l'Ancien Testament. BT(N), Neuchâtel 1971.

Sigal, P., *The Halakhah of Jesus of Nazareth according to the Gospel of Matthew*. Diss. Pittsburgh (microfilm) 1979.

Simon, M., *St Stephen and the Hellenists in the Primitive Church*. London 1958.

Simon, M., *Verus Israel*. Étude sur les relations entre chretiens et juifs dans l'empire Romain (135–425). Paris 1948.

Simonsen, H., Die Auffassung vom Gesetz im Mattäusevangelium. *Theologie aus dem Norden*, SNTU A 2, 1977, 44–67.

Sjöberg, E., *Gott und die Sünder im palästinischen Judentum nach dem Zeugnis der Tannaiten und der apokryphisch- pseudepigraphischen Literatur*. BWANT 79. Stuttgart 1938.

Sjöberg, E., Herrens bud 1 Kor. 14.37. *SEÅ* 22–23, 1957–58, 168–171.

Slaten, A.W., The Qualitative Use of νόμος: in the Pauline Epistles. *AJT* 23, 1919, 213–219.

Sloyan, G., *Is Christ the End of the Law?* Biblical Perspectives on Current Issues. Philadelphia 1978.

Smallwood, E.M., *The Jews under Roman Rule.* From Pompey to Diocletian. Studies in Judaism in Late Antiquity 20. Leiden 1976.

Smend, R., Das Alte Testament. In: *R. Smend – U. Luz, Gesetz.* Biblische Konfrontationen 1015. Stuttgart etc. 1981. Pp. 9–44, 145–148.

Smith, M., The Reason for the Persecution of Paul and the Obscurity of Acts. *Studies in Mysticism and Religion* presented to G.G. Scholem, Jerusalem 1967, 261–268.

Smith M., Pauline Problems. Apropos of J. Munck, 'Paulus und die Heilsgeschichte'. HThR 50, 1957, 107–131.

Souček, J.B., Zur Exegese von Röm. 2, 14 ff. *Antwort,* Festschrift K. Barth, Zollikon-Zürich 1956, 99–113.

Spicq, C., *L'Épitre aux Hébreux.* EtB. Paris 1952–53.

Stacey, W.D., *The Pauline View of Man In Relation to its Judaic and Hellenistic Background.* London 1956.

Stamm, R.T., The Epistle to the Galatians. *IntB* 9. New York 1953.

Stanton, G., Stephen in Lucan Perspective. *Stud Bibl,* 1980, 345–360.

Steck, R., *Der Galaterbrief nach seiner Echtheit untersucht* nebst kritischen Bemerkungen zu den paulinischen Hauptbriefen. Berlin 1888.

Stegemann, E., Der Jude Paulus und seine antijüdische Auslegung. In: R. Rendtorff-E. Stegemann (ed.), *Auschwitz-Krise der christlichen Theologie,* ACJD 10, München 1980, 117–139.

Stemberger, G., *Das klassische Judentum.* Kultur und Geschichte (70 v. Chr. bis 1040 n. Chr.). Beck'sche Elementarbücher. München 1979.

van Stempvoort, P., Gal. 6.2. *NedThT* 7, 1952–53, 362–363.

Stendahl, K., *Paul Among Jews and Gentiles and other Essays.* Philadelphia 1976.

Stern, M., *Greek and Latin Authors on Jews and Judaism* I. From Herodotus to Plutarch. Publications of the Israel Academy of Sciences and Humanities. Jerusalem 1974.

Stevens, G.B., *The Pauline Theology.* A Study of the Origin and Correlation of the Doctrinal Teachings of the Apostle Paul. Rev. ed. New York 1900.

Stoike, D.A., *"The Law of Christ":* A Study of Paul's Use of the Expression in Galatians 6.2. Diss. Claremont 1971 (microfilm).

Strachan, R.H., *The Second Epistle of Paul to the Corinthians.* MNTC. London 1946 (Repr.).

Strack, H. – Billerbeck, P., *Kommentar zum Neuen Testament aus Talmud und Midrasch* 1–6. München 1954–56[2].

Strecker, G., Die Antithesen der Bergpredigt (Mt 5$_{21-48}$ par). *ZNW* 69, 1978, 36–72.

Strecker, G., *Eschaton und Historie.* Aufsätze. Göttingen 1979.

Strecker, G., *Das Judenchristentum in den Pseudoklementinen.* TU 70. Berlin 1958.

Strecker, G., Judenchristentum und Gnosis. *AFG,* 1980, 261–282.

Strecker, G., *Der Weg der Gerechtigkeit.* Untersuchung zur Theologie des Matthäus. FRLANT 82. Göttingen 1962.

Strelan, J.G., Burden-bearing and the Law of Christ: A Re-examination of Galatians 6.2. *JBL* 94, 1975, 266–276.

Strobel, A., Das Aposteldekret als Folge des antiochenischen Streites. Überlegungen zum Verhältnis von Wahrheit und Einheit im Gespräch der Kirchen. *KuE,* 1981, 81–104.

Stuhlmacher, P., *Gerechtigkeit Gottes bei Paulus.* FRLANT 87. Göttingen 1966[2].

Stuhlmacher, P., *Das paulinische Evangelium* I. Vorgeschichte. FRLANT 95. Göttingen 1968.

Stuhlmacher, P., Paulus, ein Rabbi, der Apostel wurde. Zur Diskussion. In: P. Lapide – P. Stuhlmacher, *Paulus – Rabbi und Apostel*, Ein jüdisch-christlicher Dialog, Stuttgart-München 1981, 62–69.

Stuhlmacher, P., *Versöhnung, Gesetz und Gerechtigkeit.* Aufsätze zur biblischen Theologie. Göttingen 1981.

Stylianopoulos, T., *Justin Martyr and the Mosaic Law.* SBL Diss. 20. Missoula 1975.

Suggs, M.J., The Antitheses as Redactional Products. *JCHT*, 1975, 433–444.

Suhl, A., *Paulus und seine Briefe.* Ein Beitrag zur paulinischen Chronologie. StNT 11. Gütersloh 1975.

Synofzik, E., *Die Gerichts- und Vergeltungsaussagen bei Paulus.* Eine traditionsgeschichtliche Untersuchung. GTA 8. Göttingen 1977.

Tannehill, R.C., *Dying and Rising with Christ.* A Study in Pauline Theology. BZNW 32. Berlin 1967.

Taylor, V., *The Gospel according to Mark.* London 1952.

Tcherikover, V., The Ideology of the Letter of Aristeas. *HThR* 51, 1958, 59–85.

Theissen, G., *Studien zur Soziologie des Urchristentums.* WUNT 19. Tübingen 1979.

Therrien, G., *Le discernement dans les écrits pauliniens.* EB. Paris 1973.

Thiel, W., *Die deuteronomistische Redaktion von Jeremia 1–25.* WMANT 41. Neukirchen 1973.

Thiselton, A.C., Realized Eschatology at Corinth. *NTS* 24, 1977–78, 510–526.

Thompson, A.L., *Responsibility for Evil in the Theodicy of IV Ezra.* A Study Illustrating the Significance of Form and Structure for the Meaning of the Book. SBL Diss. 29. Missoula 1977.

Thüsing, W., *Per Christum in Deum.* Studien zum Verhältnis von Christozentrik und Theozentrik in den paulinischen Hauptbriefen. NTA 1. Münster 1969[2].

Thyen, H., Exegese des Neuen Testaments nach dem Holocaust. In: R. Rendtorff-E. Stegemann (ed.), *Auschwitz – Krise der christlichen Theologie*, ACJD 10, München 1980, 140–158.

Trilling, W., *Das wahre Israel.* Studien zur Theologie des Matthäusevangeliums. EThSt 7. Leipzig 1959.

Trocmé, E., Paul-la-colère: éloge d'un Schismatique. *RHPR* 61, 1981, 341–350.

Türcke, C., *Zum ideologiekritischen Potential der Theologie.* Konsequenzen einer materialistischen Paulus-Interpretation. Pahl-Rugenstein Hochschulschriften 8. Köln 1979.

Tyson, J.B., "Works of Law" in Galatians. *JBL* 92, 1973, 423–431.

Ulonska, H., *Paulus und das Alte Testament.* Diss. Münster 1964.

van Unnik, W.C., Josephus' account of the story of Israels sin with alien women in the country of Midian (Num. 25.1 ff.). *Travels in the World of the Old Testament* (Festschr. M.A. Beek), Assen 1974, 241–261.

van Unnik, W.C., *Sparsa Collecta* I. NTS 29. Leiden 1973.

Urbach, E.E., *The Sages* – Their Concepts and Beliefs I–II. Transl. I. Abrahams. Publications of the Perry Foundations in the Hebrew University of Jerusalem. Jerusalem 1975.

Vanhoye, A., Un médiateur des anges en Ga 3, 19–20. *Bib.* 59, 1978, 403–411.

da Vaux, R., *Studies in Old Testament Sacrifice.* Cardiff 1964.

Vergote, A., Der Beitrag der Psychoanalyse zur Exegese. Leben, Gesetz und Ich-Spaltung im 7. Kapitel des Römerbriefs. *Exegese im Methodenkonflikt* (ed. X. Léon-Dufour), München 1973, 73–116.

Vermes, G., The Decalogue and the Minim. *In memoriam P. Kahle*, BZAW 103, Berlin 1968, 232–240.

Verweijs, P.G., *Evangelium und neues Gesetz in der ältesten Christenheit bis auf Marcion.* STRT 5. Utrecht 1960.

Viard, A., *Saint Paul. Épitre aux Romains.* SBi. Paris 1975.

Vielhauer, P., *Geschichte der urchristlichen Literatur.* Einleitung in das Neue Testament, die Apokryphen und Apostolischen Väter. GLB. Berlin-New York 1975.

Vielhauer, P., Gesetzesdienst und Stoicheiadienst im Galaterbrief. *RF,* 1976, 543–555.

Vielhauer, P., On the 'Paulinism' of Acts. *Studies in Luke-Acts* (Festschrift P. Schubert), Nashville-New York 1966, 33–50.

Vielhauer, P., Paulus und das Alte Testament. *Studien zur Geschichte und Theologie der Reformation,* Festschrift E. Bizer, Neukirchen 1969, 33–62.

Volkmar, G., *Paulus Römerbrief.* Der älteste Text deutsch und im Zusammenhang erklärt. Zürich 1875.

Vos, J.S., *Traditionsgeschichtliche Untersuchungen zur paulinischen Pneumatologie.* GTB 47. Assen 1973.

von Wahlde, U.C., Faith and Works in Jn VI 28–29. Exegesis or Eisegesis? *NT* 22, 1980, 304–315.

Walker, R., Allein aus Werken. Zur Auslegung von Jakobus 2, 14–26. *ZThK* 61, 1964, 155–192.

Walker, R., Die Heiden und das Gericht. Zur Auslegung von Römer 2, 12–16. *EvTh* 20, 1960, 302–314.

Walker, R., *Die Heilsgeschichte im ersten Evangelium.* FRLANT 91. Göttingen 1967.

Wallis, G., Torah und Nomos. Zur Frage nach Gesetz und Heil. *ThLZ* 105, 1980, 321–332.

Walter, J., *Der religiöse Gehalt des Galaterbriefes.* Göttingen 1904.

Walter, N., Christusglaube und heidnische Religiosität in paulinischen Gemeinden. *NTS* 25, 1978–79, 422–442.

Weber, F., *Jüdische Theologie auf Grund des Talmud und verwandter Schriften.* Leipzig 1897[2].

Wedderburn, A.J.M., Adam in Paul's Letter to the Romans. *StudBibl,* 1980, 413–430.

Wedderburn, A.J.M., Keeping up with Recent Studies. VIII. Some Recent Pauline Chronologies. *ET* 92, 1980–81, 103–107.

Weder, H., *Das Kreuz Jesu bei Paulus.* Ein Versuch, über den Geschichtsbezug des christlichen Glaubens nachzudenken. FRLANT 125. Göttingen 1981.

Weinel, H., *St Paul.* The Man and His Work. Transl. G.A. Bieneman, ed. W.D. Morrison. London 1906.

Weiss, B., *Der Brief an die Römer.* KEK 4[9]. Göttingen 1899.

Weiss, H., The Law in the Epistle to the Colossians. *CBQ* 34, 1972, 294–314.

Weiss, H-F., Das Gesetz in der Gnosis. *AFG,* Berlin 1980, 71–88.

Weiss, J., *Der erste Korintherbrief.* KEK 5[9]. Göttingen 1910.

Weiss, J., *Das Urchristentum* (ed. R. Knopf). Göttingen 1917. (ET: History of Early Christianity. ed. F.C. Grant, New York 1959 repr.)

Weiss, J. – Heitmüller, W., *Die Offenbarung des Johannes.* SNT 4. Göttingen 1918[3].

Wellhausen, J., *Israelitische und jüdische Geschichte.* Berlin 1904[5].

Wells, G.A., *The Jesus of the Early Christians.* A Study of Christian Origins. London 1971.

Wendland, H-D., Gesetz und Geist. Zum Problem des Schwärmertums bei Paulus. *SThKAB* 6, 1952, 38–64.

Wengst, K., *Tradition und Theologie des Barnabasbriefes.* AKG 42. Berlin 1971.

Wenham, D., The Christian Life: A Life of Tension? A Consideration of the Nature of Christian Experience in Paul. *PSt* 80–94.

Werblowsky, R.J.Z., Paulus in jüdischer Sicht. *Paulus – Apostat oder Apostel* (ed. M. Barth etc.), Regensburg 1977, 135–146.

Werblowsky, R.J.Z., Tora als Gnade. *Kairos* 14, 1972, 156–163.

Werner, M., *Der Einfluss paulinischer Theologie im Markusevangelium.* Eine Studie zur neutestamentlichen Theologie. BZNW 1. Giessen 1923.

Wernle, P., *Die Anfänge unserer Religion.* Tübingen-Leipzig 1904[2]. (ET: The Beginnings of Christianity I, transl. G.A. Bienemann. New York 1903.)

Wernle, P., *Der Christ und die Sünde bei Paulus.* Freiburg i.B. – Leipzig 1897.

Westerholm, S., Review of H. Hübner, Das Gesetz bei Paulus. *SEÅ* 44, 1979, 194–199.

Westerholm, S., *Jesus and Scribal Authority.* CB.NT 10. Lund 1978.

Wevers, J.W., *Ezekiel.* CenB. London 1969.

Wevers, J.W., Septuaginta-Forschungen. *ThR* 22, 1954, 85–138, 171–190.

Whiteley, D.E.H., *The Theology of St. Paul.* Oxford 1964.

Wilckens, U., *Der Brief an die Römer* 1–2. EKK 6/1–2. Zürich 1978–80.

Wilckens, U., Zur Entwicklung des paulinischen Gesetzesverständnisses. NTS 28, 1982, 154–190.

Wilckens, U., Jesusüberlieferung und Christuskerygma – zwei Wege urchristlicher Überlieferungsgeschichte. *ThViat* 10, 1965–66, 310–339.

Wilckens, U., *Rechtfertigung als Freiheit.* Paulusstudien. Neukirchen-Vluyn 1974.

Wilde, R., *The Treatment of the Jews in the Greek Christian Writers of the First Three Centuries.* Washington 1949.

Wiles, M.F., *The Divine Apostle.* The Interpretation of St. Paul's Epistles in the Early Church. Cambridge 1967.

Wiles, M.F., St. Paul's Conception of Law. *ChM* 69, 1955–56, 144–152, 228–234.

Williams, S.K., *Jesus' Death as Saving Event.* The Background and Origin of a Concept. Harvard Dissertations in Religion 2. Missoula 1975.

Williams, S.K., The "Righteousness of God" in Romans. *JBL* 99, 1980, 241–290.

Wilson, S.G., *The Gentiles and the Gentile Mission in Luke-Acts.* MSSNTS 23. Cambridge 1973.

Windisch, H., *Die apostolischen Väter.* III. Der Barnabasbrief. HNT Erg. Tübingen 1920.

Windisch, H., *Der Hebräerbrief.* HNT 14. Tübingen 1931[2].

Windisch, H., Das Problem des paulinischen Imperativs. *ZNW* 23, 1924, 265–281.

Windisch, H., *Taufe und Sünde im ältesten Christentum bis auf Origenes.* Ein Beitrag zur altchristlichen Dogmengeschichte. Tübingen 1908.

Windisch, H., *Der zweite Korintherbrief.* KEK 6[9]. Göttingen 1970 (repr.).

Wolff, Chr., *Jeremia im Frühjudentum und Urchristentum.* TU 118. Berlin 1976.

Wolff, H-W., Das Kerygma des deuteronomistischen Geschichtswerks. *ZAW* 32, 1961, 171–186.

Wolfson, H.A., *Philo* I. Foundations of Religious Philosophy in Judaism, Christianity, and Islam. Cambridge, Mass. 1947.

Worgul, G.S., Romans 9–11 and Ecclesiology. *BTB* 7, 1977, 98–109.

Wrede, W., *Paulus.* RV 1.516. Halle 1907[2]. (ET: *Paul.* Transl. E. Lummis. London 1907.)

Wuellner, W., Paul's Rhetoric of Argumentation in Romans: An Alternative to the Donfried-Karris Debate over Romans. *RD*, 1977, 152–174.

Wuellner, W., Toposforschung und Torahinterpretation bei Paulus und Jesus. *NTS* 24, 1977–78, 463–483.

Würthwein, E., Gesetz II. Im AT. *RGG* II, 1513–1515.

Zahn, A., *Das Gesetz Gottes nach der Lehre und Erfahrung des Apostel Paulus.* Halle 1876.

Zahn, T., *Der Brief des Paulus an die Römer.* KNT 6. Leipzig 1925.

Zehnpfund, R., Das Gesetz in den paulinischen Briefen. *NKZ* 8, 1897, 384–419.

Zeller, D., *Juden und Heiden in der Mission des Paulus.* Studien zum Römerbrief. FzB 1. Stuttgart 1973.

Zenger, E., Die späte Weisheit und das Gesetz. *Literatur und Religion des Frühjudentums* (ed. J. Maier-J. Schreiner), Würzburg 1973, 43–56.

Ziener, G., *Die theologische Begriffssprache im Buche der Weisheit.* BBB 11, Bonn 1956.

Zimmerli, W., *Ezechiel.* BK AT 13. Neukirchen-Vluyn 1969.

Zimmerli, W., *The Law and the Prophets.* A Study of the Meaning of the Old Testament. Transl. R.E. Clements. Oxford 1965.

Zimmerli, W., *Gottes Offenbarung.* Gesammelte Aufsätze zum Alten Testament. TB. München 1963.

Zimmermann, H., *Das Bekenntnis der Hoffnung.* Tradition und Redaktion im Hebräerbrief. BBB 47. Köln 1977.

Index of Passages

THE OLD TESTAMENT

THE NEW TESTAMENT

DEAD SEA SCROLLS

JOSEPHUS AND PHILO

RABBINIC LITERATURE

EARLY CHRISTIAN LITERATURE

OTHER ANCIENT LITERATURE

Index of Authors